COUNTRY	CURRENCY	SYMBOL
Malaysia	ringgit	M$
Malta	lira	Lm
Mexico	peso	Ps
Morocco	dirham	DH
Netherlands	guilder	f/
Netherlands Antilles	guilder	NAf
New Zealand	dollar	NZ$
Nicaragua	cordoba	C$
Niger	CFA franc	CFAF
Nigeria	naira	₦
Norway	krone	NOK
Oman	rial	RO
Pakistan	rupee	PRs
Panama	balboa	B/.
Papua New Guinea	kina	K
Paraguay	guarani	₡
Philippines	peso	₱
Portugal	escudo	Esc
Qatar	riyal	QR
Saudi Arabia	riyal	SR
Senegal	CFA franc	CFAF
Singapore	dollar	S$
Solomon Islands	dollar	SBD
South Africa	rand	R
Spain	peseta	Ptas.
Sudan	pound	£S
Sweden	krona	SEK
Switzerland	franc	SFr
Thailand	baht	Bht
Turkey	lira	TL
United Arab Emirates	dirham	UD
United Kingdom	pound sterling	£
United States	dollar	$
Uruguay	new peso	N$U
Vanuatu	vatu	VT
Venezuela	bolivar	Bs.
Western Samoa	tala	WST
Zaire	zaire	Z
Zambia	kwacha	K
Zimbabwe	dollar	Z

International Dimensions of Financial Management

International Dimensions of Financial Management

Dennis J. O'Connor
Alberto T. Bueso

California State University, Fullerton

Macmillan Publishing Company

New York

Collier Macmillan Publishers

London

Editor: Caroline Carney
Production Supervisor: John Travis
Production Manager: Nick Sklitsis
Text and cover designed by Jane Edelstein
Cover illustration: Slide Graphics

This book was set in Palatino by Science Typographers, Inc.
and printed and bound by R. R. Donnelley & Sons.

Macmillan Publishing Company
866 Third Avenue, New York, New York 10022

Collier Macmillan Canada, Inc.

Library of Congress Cataloging in Publication Data

O'Connor, Dennis J.
       International dimensions of financial management/Dennis
O'Connor, Alberto Bueso.
           p.   cm.
       Includes bibliographical references.
       ISBN 0-02-388881-4
       1. International business enterprises—Finance.   2. Foreign
exchange problem.   3. International finance.   I. Bueso, Alberto T.
II. Title.
HG4027.5.O28 1990   89-13028
658.15′99—dc20   CIP

Printing: 1 2 3 4 5 6 7 8   Year: 0 1 2 3 4 5 6 7

To Peggy Y. O'Connor
To Manola and Guillermo Bueso

Preface

Today there is an explosion of interest in international finance and economics. International finance news stories are no longer relegated to the business section but are presented on the front pages of major newspapers in the United States. Political candidates focus their campaign platforms on such issues as the impact of trade on domestic employment, the acquisition of American assets by foreigners, the financing of U.S. Government deficits by foreigners, the trade deficit, etc. There is no doubt that international finance and economics have become important issues in our society.

The importance of international finance is also reflected in the business and academic fields. American firms are no longer ignoring the impact of the international environment on their revenues, costs, profits, or market prices. The actions of foreign competitors are closely monitored. American firms are fighting to gain access to foreign markets. Foreign firms are investing heavily in the United States and American firms are also investing heavily abroad. American firms have come to the realization that managers must adopt a global outlook.

The academic community has responded to the needs of American firms. The American Association of Collegiate Schools of Business (AACSB) has mandated that international aspects be incorporated into every undergraduate business administration program. In response, most colleges and universities have incorporated the international dimension of business decisions into their programs. Incorporating the international dimension within the Finance discipline has been accomplished in two ways: (1) the inclusion of one or two weeks' coverage of international topics in the basic finance course, and (2) the development of a specialized International Financial Management course. The specialized course is usually offered as an elective to finance majors or as a required course in an undergraduate international business program. This book is especially designed to meet the needs of undergraduates enrolled in an international financial management course.

For the Instructor

This book is divided into five parts. Part I focuses on foreign exchange rates. We begin by looking at the market for foreign exchange and answer a number of important questions. How is foreign currency bought and sold in financial markets? How is the price of such transactions reported? What makes the value of the dollar, as well as other currencies, go up and down? Can the firm forecast the future value of foreign currencies?

Part II evaluates the impact of foreign exchange fluctuations on the value of the firm. The risk to the firm is divided into economic, transaction, and translation exposure. For each of these areas, we attempt to answer the following questions: Why and how do fluctuating exchange rates place the American firm at risk? What can the firm do to minimize the risk associated with fluctuating exchange rates?

Part III focuses on issues relating to the way a firm raises capital. We look at foreign capital markets and euromarkets. And we examine the impact of the internationalization of the world's capital markets on the way firms raise capital and on the cost of capital of the firm. A number of important questions will be answered. Should the firm borrow abroad? Should the firm borrow foreign currency? How does foreign borrowing affect the riskiness of the American firm? What is the impact of international transactions on the optimal capital structure of the firm? What is the impact of the international environment on the cost of capital of the firm?

Part IV deals with short-term financial management issues. We examine the different ways in which multinational firms shift funds from foreign subsidiaries to their parents. We show how the desire to minimize taxes and to avoid currency restrictions can lead to unusual actions with respect to the transfer of funds. Also discussed in this part of the book is the management of international accounts receivable. We evaluate the use of letters of credit, accounts receivable insurance, and factoring.

Part V begins with a discussion of taxation as it relates to the American firm engaged in international commerce. Particular attention is paid to how income earned in foreign countries is taxed in the United States. In addition, the alternatives open to United States firms to minimize corporate tax bills will be evaluated. The book concludes with an important discussion of long-term asset acquisition. How does the firm evaluate foreign investment alternatives that involve large outlays and promise benefits over a long period of time? What factors make foreign investing attractive or unattractive?

The sequence of Parts can be altered without encountering significant difficulties. However, Parts I and II should always be covered first. One of the authors successfully covered Part V before Part IV. We recommend, however, that the sequence of chapters within each Part remain as written. Where appropriate, we have included footnotes directing the student to specific previous or future chapters.

The numerical problems at the end of selected chapters have been designed for the purpose of illustration. We have found these numerical problems more responsive to class lectures. Students should not have significant difficulties in solving most of the numerical problems prior to class discussion.

In addition to end-of-chapter problems, this book contains end-of-chapter: (1) review questions, (2) questions for discussion, and (3) research activities. Students should be able to answer any of the review questions using the information included in the text. Discussion questions, however, often require integration of textbook information and general knowledge. Discussion questions are designed to provide for open "give and take" classroom sessions. Research activities require a significant search of outside materials and should be assigned selectively. The information presented in *International Dimensions of Financial Management* is sufficient to allow students to solve most currently available casebooks, such as Gunter Dufey and Ian H. Giddy's *50 Cases in International Finance*, Reading, MA: Addison-Wesley Publishing Company, 1987.

To the Student

This book is titled *International Dimensions of Financial Management*. Its goal is to integrate international aspects into the traditional financial management framework. We have assumed that students have completed one basic finance course prior to the use of this book. Those readers with a weak background in financial management are advised to review the basic finance material before proceeding with specific chapters in this book. We have provided references to a basic finance textbook where appropriate.

Some Final Comments

Writing a textbook is a long and arduous undertaking and requires many revisions and iteration. In this respect *International Dimensions of Financial Management* is no different from other books. Our students, colleagues and reviewers have all made suggestions that have been incorporated in this, our latest version. While comments and suggestions have significantly improved this manuscript, there are still errors and shortcomings for which the authors must assume full responsibility.

Those colleagues who have reviewed the manuscript are acknowledged below in alphabetical order:

Professors Alan Cook, Baylor University; Kee S. Kim, Southwest Missouri State University; Susan C. LeBlanc, University of Central Florida; Boyden Lee, New Mexico State University; Sammy O. McCord, Auburn University; M. Rahman, Ball State University; Henry Rennie, University of Toledo; Gary D. Tallman, Northern Arizona University; Jot K. Yau, George Mason University; and M. Raquib Zaman, Ithaca College.

No book is solely the result of the authors' efforts. Publishers play a significant role in bringing the project to fruition. Macmillan Publishing Company has provided invaluable assistance to the authors in this undertaking. Ken MacLeod, Senior Editor, Business and Economics, has guided us through the publishing thicket from the beginning to the end of this project. We would also like to express our thanks to Bob Horan, former Acquisitions Editor for SRA, Inc. whose early encouragement was very important to us. While all authors have a certain degree of pride in their writing style, we must acknowledge the efforts of Helen Greenberg, whose comments resulted in a significant improvement in the writing style of this book.

One group of reviewers needs to be especially recognized: our students at California State University, Fullerton (CSUF). First, their questions and comments encouraged us to undertake this project. Second, three different drafts of the book were class tested at CSUF. Student suggestions towards the improvement of the manuscript were invaluable. They reminded us at every step that our goal was to prepare a textbook for student use. It is no exaggeration to say that this book could not have been finished without the assistance of our students.

Dennis J. O'Connor
Alberto T. Bueso

CONTENTS

3

The International Monetary System   46

4

Factors Affecting Exchange Rates   68

8

Estimating and Managing Translation Exposure   196

PART **III**

International Sources of Funds

9

International Financial Markets   231

10

International Dimensions of Capital Structure   260

11

International Risks and the Cost of Capital   285

PART **IV**

International Working Capital Management

12

International Dimensions of American Banking   **317**

13

Managing the Multinational's Internal Funds Flow   **343**

14

Managing International Accounts Receivable   373

PART V

International Capital Budgeting

15

International Dimensions of Business Taxation   399

16

International Dimensions of Long-Term Asset Acquisitions 428

1

Introduction to International Financial Management

This book is designed to change the way most students look at the financial management problem facing the American firm. While the typical introductory financial management textbook assumes that the firm acquires and manages assets and financing solely within the United States, this book treats the same topics within a richer and more realistic international context. The same concepts and approaches used in basic domestic financial management are applied to the international situation. The principles of financial management are the same for all firms, domestic and international.

International Dimensions of Financial Management also includes a number of important new concepts, some of which are quite challenging to the student. The impact of fluctuating exchange rates on the management strategy of the firm is complicated but must be understood. International taxation is much more complicated than U.S. taxation when studied in isolation. The flow of funds within the units of a multinational firm are much more complicated than the flows within a purely domestic corporation. Managing international accounts receivable and long-term assets presents a real challenge to management. Thus, while the principles of international financial management are the same as those for domestic firms, the context in which these principles are applied is much more dynamic and complicated.

The amount of material that can be included in a book dealing with the international aspects of financial management is enormous. Separate books have been written about the financial and tax systems of almost every country in the world. Hundreds of books have been written about exchange rates and hundreds more about most of the other topics included in this book. Individually, the topics included in *International Dimensions of Financial Management* have a great and rich literature, but a literature that is beyond the interest and time constraints of the student of business and the professional business manager. Our objective is to abstract from that literature and to present a concise and comprehensive view of international financial management.

Since this book is concerned with financial management of the firm, we have minimized the discussion of the national economic policy aspects of foreign trade and exchange rates. Instead, we have tried to focus on the managerial implications of balance of payments "imbalances" and exchange rate movements. In addition, *International Dimensions of Financial Management* has as its primary focus the manager of the American firm. While the principles of financial management for firms of other nations are not very different from those of American firms, in some cases they are different. These differences, however, are beyond the scope of this book.

The Objective of the American Firm

The goal of financial management (as discussed in the introductory financial management course) is generally accepted to be the maximization of stockholder wealth, subject to legal and social constraints. Translated into more popular terms, managers are supposed to keep the price of the firm's common stock as high as possible. The price is determined by the amount, timing, and riskiness of the cash flows associated with the stock. As shown in Figure 1-1, the stock market performs an impersonal evaluation of these factors and assigns a "grade" to the performance of financial managers. The grade is the market price of the common stock. Other things being equal, policies that lead to an increase in the expected cash flows to stockholders (dividends), a speeding up of the timing of the cash flows, or a reduction in the riskiness of the cash flows result in an increase in the market price of the common stock. If the market is efficient, the market price is the correct price based on all the known information concerning cash flows. The objective of financial management is to make decisions that will result in a combination of the amount, timing, and riskiness of cash flows that will maximize the market price of the common stock.

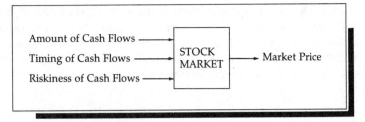

FIGURE 1-1 Maximization of Stockholder Wealth

The Gordon model is a useful way of looking at stock price determination. This model assumes that dividends grow at a constant annual rate and indicates the relationship between dividends, the growth in dividends, and the riskiness (uncertainty) of those dividends:

$$\text{Price} = \frac{D1}{Ks - g} \tag{1-1}$$

Where $D1$ = expected dividend next year
Ks = required rate of return of stockholders (a function of risk)
g = constant annual growth rate in dividends for the foreseeable future

This equation should not be viewed as a means of predicting the correct market price, but rather as a device that facilitates the understanding of the factors affecting the market price of common stock. If management is able to increase the expected dividends or their rate of growth without affecting the risk, the market price should increase. If management is able to reduce the risk without affecting expected cash flows, the market price should also increase. In actual practice, managers face a more complicated situation, since policies that increase expected dividends often are accompanied by an increase in risk, and vice versa. The manager must somehow weigh the relative merits of each factor.

It is helpful to look at international financial management decisions in the context of Equation 1-1. Whenever possible, we will come back to the idea that expected changes in risk and cash flows must be analyzed simultaneously. For example, borrowing foreign currencies may result in an increase in expected cash flows, but it may also increase the risk so much that stockholder wealth will be reduced. Firms may use costly letters of credit because they reduce risk and may lead to increases in stockholder wealth. American firms investing in foreign countries must balance the expectation of high profits against the possibility of high political and foreign exchange rate risks. The approach used in this book is consistent with Equation 1-1 and the objective of stockholder wealth maximization.

This book builds on the introductory business finance course, but it cannot duplicate it. We recommend that students interested in international financial management review basic financial management concepts before attempting to master these materials. This will be of particular importance in the last three sections of the book.[1]

Involvement in the World Economy

American firms are becoming more and more involved in the world economy. They are beginning to face up to the fact that they no longer operate in a purely domestic environment. Table 1-1 shows the merchandise exports and imports of the United States from 1968 to 1988. The reader should note that exports have grown from $34 to $320 billion during this period. Although some American firms ignored this market in the past, its sheer size, growth potential, and competitive implications will make it unwise to do so in the future. Failure to tap this market will result in lower sales, lower cash flows, and greater risk, which in turn will reduce stockholder wealth. Imports have also increased from $33 to $446 billion during the same period. American producers, distributors, and retailers can no longer ignore the possibility that low-cost, high-quality products may be available from abroad. Retailers will not be competitive unless they obtain access to foreign products.

Even a purely domestic firm can be affected by international commerce, and the managers of such a firm must also be familiar with the international aspects of financial management. For example, consider the case of the Donegal Corporation, an American manufacturer of personal computers. Since all inputs are produced in the United States and the entire output is sold in the United States, management does not perceive itself as being involved in international commerce. The Donegal Corporation will get a rude awakening if foreign competitors enter the U.S. market. Foreign firms may produce similar products, export them to the United States, and sell them at prices below Donegal's production cost. This foreign competition may result in a decline of Donegal's market share and/or a reduction in profitability. As it turns out, the Donegal Corporation is very much involved in foreign commerce, even though it may not realize this until it is too late. Recent history provides many examples of similar situations. The steel, automobile, and computer chip

---

[1]A widely used textbook is Eugene F. Brigham, *Fundamentals of Financial Management*, 4th ed., Chicago, Dryden Press, 1986. Most other basic finance textbooks, however, can be used to accomplish the same objective.

TABLE 1-1 Exports and Imports of the United States (Billions of Dollars)

Year	GNP*	Merchandise Exports	% of GNP	Merchandise Imports	% of GNP	Trade[†] Balance
1988	$4,864	$320	6.58	$446	9.17	($126)
1987	$4,489	$251	5.59	$410	9.13	($159)
1986	$4,235	$224	5.29	$369	8.71	($145)
1985	$4,010	$216	5.39	$338	8.43	($122)
1984	$3,772	$220	5.83	$332	8.80	($112)
1983	$3,305	$201	6.08	$263	7.96	($62)
1982	$3,069	$211	6.88	$248	8.08	($37)
1981	$2,938	$236	8.03	$264	8.99	($28)
1980	$2,633	$224	8.51	$250	9.49	($26)
1979	$2,418	$184	7.61	$219	9.06	($35)
1978	$2,128	$142	6.67	$176	8.27	($34)
1977	$1,900	$121	6.37	$152	8.00	($31)
1976	$1,702	$115	6.76	$124	7.29	($9)
1975	$1,516	$107	7.06	$98	6.46	$9
1974	$1,413	$98	6.94	$104	7.36	($6)
1973	$1,307	$71	5.43	$70	5.36	$1
1972	$1,171	$49	4.18	$56	4.78	($7)
1971	$1,056	$43	4.07	$45	4.26	($2)
1970	$977	$42	4.30	$40	4.09	$2
1969	$930	$36	3.87	$36	3.87	$0
1968	$864	$34	3.94	$33	3.82	$1

*GNP = gross national product.
[†]Trade balance = merchandise exports − merchandise imports.
Source: Board of Governors of the Federal Reserve System, *Federal Reserve Bulletin*, various issues.

industries are just a few of a long list of industries for which this scenario has been a reality.

Even firms in industries that, by their nature, do not face foreign competition, are affected by international trade developments. For example, a large public utility company that supplies electricity to local customers does not have to worry about price competition from foreign suppliers. However, even this type of firm frequently uses factors of production whose price and availability may be affected by the international environment. Many electrical utilities, for example, use oil to power their generators, and the price of oil is very much determined in international markets. While some American firms are more involved in international commerce than others, very few firms today are completely isolated from international economic developments. Even those firms that appear to be insulated from the international environment can experience a significant change in stockholder wealth as a result of changes in international markets. Although such an impact appears immediate and obvious to importers and exporters, purely domestic firms can also be affected.

TABLE 1-2 Direct Investment (DI) in International Markets Affecting the
United States (Billions of Dollars)

Year	Americans' DI Abroad (1)	Foreigners' DI in the U.S. (2)	GPDI*	Col. 2 as % of GPDI	Net Direct (1) − (2)
1988	$20	$42	$767	5.48	($22)
1987	$38	$41	$718	5.71	($3)
1986	$28	$25	$684	3.65	$3
1985	$17	$19	$661	2.87	($2)
1984	$3	$25	$662	3.78	($22)
1983	$5	$12	$472	2.54	($7)
1982	($4)	$14	$415	3.37	($18)
1981	$9	$21	$484	4.34	($12)
1980	$19	$14	$395	3.54	$5
1979	$25	$12	$416	2.88	$13
1978	$17	$6	$375	1.60	$11
1977	$13	$4	$303	1.32	$9
1976	$12	$4	$243	1.65	$8
1975	$6	$2	$184	1.09	$4
1974	$8	$3	$215	1.40	$5
1973	$5	$3	$220	1.36	$2

*GPDI = gross private domestic investment in the United States.

Source: Board of Governors of the Federal Reserve System. *Federal Reserve Bulletin*, various issues.

International Direct Investment

The internationalization of world commerce is not limited to merchandise
trade. International capital flows may also have an important impact on
American firms. Table 1-2 shows the extent to which Americans made
direct investments in foreign countries, as well as direct investments in
the United States made by foreigners. Direct investments are characterized by the fact that the investor maintains direct managerial control over
the asset acquired (for example, a factory).[2] While American firms have
always been heavy investors in plant and equipment abroad, recently
foreigners have become heavy direct investors in the U.S. economy.
Today it is more likely than ever that American firms will find themselves
competing against foreign firms with manufacturing plants in the United
States.

International Financial Investments

American financial markets have also been significantly affected by international capital flows. Table 1-3 compares the international financial

---

[2] Depending on how widely the stock of a corporation is held, a 10 percent ownership of
the common stock of a firm is usually considered enough to give control to the owner.

TABLE 1-3 International Private Financial Investments (FI) Affecting
the United States (Annual Changes in Billions of Dollars)

Year	Americans' Foreign FI (1)	Foreigners' American FI (2)	Total U.S. Financial Assets (3)	Col. 2 as a % of Col. 3	Balance (1) − (2)
1988	$71	$129	$713	18.09	($58)
1987	$37	$154	$685	22.48	($117)
1986	$66	$154	$828	18.60	($88)
1985	$7	$112	$869	12.89	($105)
1984	$11	$74	$756	9.79	($63)
1983	$43	$67	$549	12.20	($24)
1982	$116	$77	$387	19.90	$39
1981	$90	$52	$376	13.83	$38
1980	$54	$25	$357	7.00	$29
1979	$34	$40	$394	10.15	($6)
1978	$40	$24	$396	6.06	$16
1977	$19	$10	$334	2.99	$9
1976	$33	$14	$263	5.32	$19
1975	$21	$6	$202	2.97	$15
1974	$25	$19	$187	10.16	$6
1973	$9	$10	$195	5.13	($1)

Note: Total net borrowings by domestic nonfinancial sectors in the United States is used as a proxy for total change in U.S. financial assets.

Source: Board of Governors of the Federal Reserve System. *Federal Reserve Bulletin,* various issues.

investments of Americans with those of foreigners, including bank deposits, stocks, and bonds. Financial investments differ from direct investments in that financial investments are in portfolio assets and do not give management control to the holder of the assets. The reader should also note that Americans acquire large amounts of financial assets abroad. The acquisition by foreigners of American financial assets, however, has taken a quantum leap in recent years. In fact, as of 1987, America is a net debtor nation. This means that total financial assets held by foreigners in the United States exceed those held by Americans in foreign economies. Increasingly, foreigners are becoming involved in financing American business.

Are Foreigners Buying the United States?

The materials presented in the previous sections may give rise to irrational fears on the part of some Americans. There is no need to run into the street, shouting "The Japanese are coming" or "The Germans are coming." The data presented in Tables 1-1, 1-2, and 1-3 must be viewed

TABLE 1-4   Exports as a Percentage of GNP

Year	Canada (%)	West Germany (%)	Japan (%)
1987	27	31	13
1986	28	33	11
1985	29	35	16
1984	29	33	17
1983	26	31	15
1982	27	32	16
1981	28	31	16

Source: International Monetary Fund, *International Financial Statistics*, August 1988, pp. 156, 243, 312.

in their proper perspective. Yes, the dollar value of imports appears to be a huge $446 billion in 1988. This figure, however, must be compared to the total size of the U.S. economy. As shown in Table 1-1, merchandise imports as a percentage of the U.S. GNP have fluctuated from a low of 3.82 percent in 1968 to a high of 9.49 percent in 1980 and was 9.17 percent in 1988. Although somewhat lower, a similar relationship exists for exports as a percentage of GNP. While there is no question that international trade has a significant impact on American firms, firms in other countries have a much greater dependence on international trade. Table 1-4 reveals that exports as a percentage of GNP are approximately 30 percent for Canada and West Germany and about 15 percent for Japan. The economies of these countries are more dependent on international trade than is the U.S. economy. All of the Western industrialized countries are heavily involved in international commerce, and most firms are either directly or indirectly affected by international trade factors. This is a global, not a national, reality.

The direct investment data presented in Table 1-2 must also be interpreted with caution. Although the absolute amount of direct investments by foreigners in the U.S. economy has been increasing in recent years, it is less than 6 percent of the total GPDI of the United States.[3] Fears of foreigners buying America are somewhat exaggerated.[4] In fact, during 1986, Americans made more direct investments abroad than foreigners made in the United States.

Financial investments by foreigners in the American market are increasing in both absolute and percentage terms (Table 1-3). However, annual foreign financial investments in the United States constitute less

---

[3]The GPDI measures the total investment in the U.S. economy. This includes plant and equipment, buildings, and so on, constructed by both individuals and business. The comparison of foreign direct investments in the United States to GPDI is made for illustrative purposes.

[4]Foreigners may have a disproportionate impact on a particular industry and/or geographical area. For example, the Japanese have acquired a significant percentage ownership of the hotel industry in Waikiki, Hawaii.

than 23 percent of the total change in the financial assets of the United States as of 1987.[5] This may be a more significant development than the actual ownership and control of American enterprises by foreigners, since changes in the willingness of foreigners to hold American financial assets could force a significant disruption in the American economy.

Summary and Conclusions

The goal of financial management is to maximize stockholder wealth. The ability of the firm to participate in international markets affects the amount, timing, and riskiness of expected cash flows. Management can no longer ignore the impact of the international environment on the wealth of stockholders.

Review Questions

1. What should be the goal of the management of a firm?
2. What are the factors that influence the market price of common stock?
3. How does increased involvement by the United States in international trade affect management decisions with respect to shareholder wealth maximization?
4. "The importance of international trade is the same for the United States and Germany." Evaluate the validity of this statement.
5. "Foreigners are buying up the United States." Evaluate the validity of this statement.

Questions for Discussion

1. Assume that you are a member of the management team of a large American manufacturer of automobiles. What would be the likely effect of the following events on shareholder wealth? (Make additional assumptions if necessary.)
   a. U.S. relations with Japan deteriorate, and the likelihood of the United States increasing its tariffs on automobile imports increases. However, the issue is not yet decided, and there is some likelihood that the rift will be patched up and all restrictions on automobile imports and exports will be completely eliminated.
   b. Political conditions in Japan deteriorate, and the Japanese economy experiences disruptions in production. In anticipation of a decline in the output of the Japanese automobile industry, your firm plans to expand production capacity.
2. Assume that you are the general manager of a small American manufacturer of specialized measuring devices that are used to determine whether or not agricultural products are ready for harvesting. All of your work is done in Chicago, and

---

[5]Total net borrowings by domestic nonfinancial sectors in the United States are used to estimate the total growth in financial assets in the American economy during the period.

all of your inputs are purchased from local vendors. All of your sales are made to American farmers, but farmers in Europe use similar devices produced by European firms. What would be the effect of the following events on shareholder wealth? (Make additional assumptions if necessary.)

a. You find that a firm in Singapore is now producing devices that are comparable to yours.

b. There are indications that the Soviet Union is interested in purchasing many of these devices from Western firms.

Research Activities

1. Look at all or part of your city and/or state, and try to determine the percentage of businesses owned by foreigners. It may be wise to proceed on an industry-by-industry basis. Do foreigners own the businesses in your area?

2. Go to a local department store and try to determine the percentage of items that are made in foreign countries. Look at (a) housewares, (b) ladies' clothing, (c) furniture, and (d) appliances.

3. Go to a local supermarket and try to determine the percentage of items that are made in foreign countries.

4. Look at the things that you own and use every day, and try to determine the percentage that are imported from foreign countries.

Bibliography

Sources of Information

Board of Governors of the Federal Reserve System. *Federal Reserve Bulletin*. Washington, DC: monthly.

Dow Jones & Company, Inc. *The Wall Street Journal*. New York: daily.

International Monetary Fund. *International Monetary Statistics*. Washington, DC: monthly.

U.S. Department of Commerce. *Survey of Current Business*. Washington, DC: monthly.

Corporate Finance

Bierman, Harold, Jr., and Smidt, Seymour. *Financial Management for Decision Making*. New York: Macmillan Publishing Company, 1986.

Brigham, Eugene F. *Financial Management: Theory and Practice*, 5th ed. Chicago: Dryden Press, 1988.

_____ *Fundamentals of Financial Management*, 4th ed. Chicago: Dryden Press, 1986.

Gitman, Lawrence J. *Principles of Managerial Finance*, 4th ed. New York: Harper & Row, Publishers, 1985.

Gitman, Lawrence J., Joehnk, Michael D., and Pinches, George E. *Managerial Finance*. New York: Harper & Row, Publishers, 1985.

Kolb, Robert W. *Principles of Finance*. Glenview, IL: Scott, Foresman and Company, 1988.

Levy, Haim, and Sarnat, Marshall. *Principles of Financial Management*. Englewood Cliffs, NJ: Prentice-Hall, Inc., 1988.

Viscione, Jerry A., and Roberts, Gordon S. *Contemporary Financial Management*. Columbus, OH: Merrill Publishing Company, 1987.

Van Horne, James C. *Financial Management and Policy*, 7th ed. Englewood Cliffs, NJ: Prentice-Hall, Inc., 1986.

International Finance

Abdullah, Fuad A. *Financial Management for the Multinational Firm*. Englewood Cliffs, NJ: Prentice-Hall, Inc., 1987.

Eiteman, David K., and Stonehill, Arthur I. *Multinational Business Finance*, 4th ed. Reading, MA: Addison-Wesley Publishing Company, 1986.

Henning, Charles N., Pigott, William, and Scott, Robert Haney. *International Financial Management*. New York: McGraw-Hill Book Company, 1978.

Madura, Jeff. *International Financial Management*. St. Paul, MN: West Publishing Company, 1986.

Pippenger, John E. *Fundamentals of International Finance*. Englewood Cliffs, NJ: Prentice-Hall, Inc., 1984.

Rivera-Batiz, Francisco L., and Rivera-Batiz, Luis. *International Finance and Open Economy Macroeconomics*. New York: Macmillan Publishing Company, 1985.

Rodriguez, Rita M., and Carter, E. Eugene. *International Financial Management*, 3rd ed. Englewood Cliffs, NJ: Prentice-Hall, Inc., 1984.

Shapiro, Alan C. *Multinational Financial Management*, 2nd ed. Boston, MA: Allyn and Bacon, Inc., 1986.

PART I

The Mechanics of Foreign Exchange

2

The Market
for Foreign Currencies

In order to conduct international transactions, firms must have the ability
to convert one currency into another. For example, an American firm may
wish to buy a quantity of shoes from a British firm and would be required
to make payment in pounds sterling (£). In such a case, the buyer may
have to convert dollars to pounds. Consider another situation in which
an American firm sells a quantity of wheat to a Spanish firm and agrees
to accept payment in pesetas. In this case, the seller may have to convert
pesetas to dollars. Other types of transactions, such as those involving
loans, investments, and their related payments, are also ordinary and
regular features of international business. By some estimates, hundreds of
billions of dollars of transactions involving the exchange of currencies
take place every day. The foreign exchange market is the most active
financial market in the world.

The buying and selling of the various national currencies takes place
in what is called the *foreign exchange market*.[1] This chapter explains how
the foreign exchange market is organized, the mechanics of currency

---

[1]In this context, foreign exchange is the foreign currency available to be exchanged for
domestic currency.

exchange transactions, and the way currency prices are reported. This is the first of seven chapters dealing with foreign exchange issues. Chapter 3 discusses international monetary systems. Chapters 4 and 5 describes the factors that affect the value of a currency. Chapters 6 through 8 consider how a firm measures and manages the risks associated with conducting business in foreign currencies, as well as the alternative ways of dealing with such risks.

The Role of Commercial Banks

Let us begin by looking at situations in which an American firm acquires foreign currency (in order to make a payment abroad) or receives a foreign currency (from a foreign source). In the first case, the American firm wants to convert dollars to a foreign currency. In the second, it wishes to convert a foreign currency to dollars. The institutional arrangements that facilitate such a trade are outlined in Figure 2-1.

The key participants in the institutional arrangement depicted in Figure 2-1 are the large money center banks. Included in this classification are such giants as Citibank, Chase Manhattan, BankAmerica, and a handful of other large American banks. In addition, large British and Japanese banks, as well as other large foreign banks, play a very important role in the operation of the foreign exchange market. While there are hundreds of banks that could be classified as being in the crucial large money center bank segment, it is worth noting that 20 banks handle 50 percent of all foreign exchange transactions.

The money center banks regularly buy, sell, and maintain inventories of a wide range of foreign currencies. During any given day, a money center bank will receive hundreds of requests to convert a foreign currency to dollars. At the same time, other customers request that dollars be converted to a foreign currency. The large bank basically takes the foreign currency it has received from one group of customers and passes it along to the other group of customers. While it is probably necessary

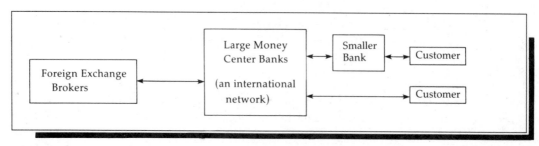

FIGURE 2-1

TABLE 2-1 Hypothetical Day of Foreign Exchange Transactions at a Large Money Center Bank

Receives DM Customer Requests $	Receives $ Customer Requests DM
1. DM10,000,000	6. $1,000,000
2. DM 1,000,000	7. $18,000,000
3. DM40,000,000	8. $4,000,000
4. DM 500,000	9. $2,000,000
5. DM 3,000,000	10. $5,000,000
DM54,500,000 received	$30,000,000 received
DM53,571,429 sold (for $)	$30,520,000 sold (for DM)
+DM928,571 inventory change	−$520,000 inventory change

for the bank to maintain an inventory of the foreign currency, purchases and sales generally offset each other and large inventories of foreign currencies are not required.

A simplified picture of the situation is presented in Table 2-1. Here the hundreds of transactions are compressed into 10 and the currencies are restricted to two: the dollar and the deutsche mark (DM). On this particular day, the bank accepts DM54,500,000 from firms wishing to convert marks to dollars and $30,000,000 from firms wishing to convert dollars to marks. Obviously, the bank can use one inflow to offset the other. Naturally, the amount of each currency received on any day will vary, and the bank may need to maintain an inventory of each currency in order to even out swings in the supply of and demand for each currency. These inventories need not be large, since money center banks always have the option of acquiring currencies (buying or borrowing) from other money center banks (in the United States or abroad) or from foreign exchange brokers. Note that in the illustration, the currency inventories of the bank do not remain the same. The bank received DM54,500,000 and sold only DM53,571,429. Thus, its DM holdings increased by 928,571.[2] The bank received $30,000,000 and sold $30,520,000. Therefore, its dollar inventories declined by $520,000. The bank must decide whether or not these changes in inventories are desirable.

Actually, the interbank foreign exchange market in the United States makes extensive use of foreign exchange brokers, of which there are approximately 10. These brokers are specialized financial services firms that buy and sell foreign currency to banks (in the United States and abroad). If, for example, a bank has more requests for deutsche marks than it has marks available, it can acquire the marks through a broker. On

---

[2] The actual exchange rate between the dollar and the German mark will be discussed in a later section of this chapter.

the other hand, if the bank has received a large number of marks, and is unable to sell them to customers and unwilling to hold them in inventory, it can sell the marks through a foreign exchange broker. The broker will sell the marks to another bank. The advantage of the foreign exchange broker arrangement is that it permits banks to deal with each other on an anonymous basis.

Customers may deal with large money center banks either directly or through a smaller bank that has a correspondent relationship with one of the large banks. Larger customers are likely to maintain banking arrangements with one or more of the large money center banks in the United States and abroad. Smaller customers are likely to conduct foreign exchange transactions through a smaller bank. In a typical situation, a smaller firm requiring foreign currency requests a smaller bank to acquire the currency. The smaller bank typically maintains a regular relationship with one or more of the large money center banks and executes the transaction on behalf of its customer. In fact, the customer may never realize that the smaller bank is acting only as a middleman, since the transactions can be conducted almost instantly through electronic communications systems.

The market for foreign exchange is best viewed as a network of geographically dispersed individuals and institutions that interact with each other through an elaborate electronic network. The participants in this market tend to be well known to each other. For example, the small bank tends to conduct transactions only for those customers with whom a satisfactory banking relationship has been established. In a similar sense, large banks know the small banks with which they do business. This is not a market that an outsider can just enter and buy or sell currency. It is not a market to which speculators have easy access. The participants are typically firms and financial institutions involved in international commerce.

Mechanics of Making a Foreign Payment

A typical transaction in the foreign exchange market involves a series of telephonic or computer computations accompanied by the altering of bank balances. For example, assume that a moderate-sized American firm receives a request for payment from a foreign supplier and that the payment is to be made in a foreign currency. It is likely that the request will be accompanied by an instruction that the foreign currency be deposited directly in a foreign account whose number is provided.

1. The American firm initiates the payment process by calling its regular (smaller) bank and requesting that the payment be made as directed.

The bank then computes the number of dollars required to purchase the foreign currency and deducts that amount from the American firm's bank account.

2. The smaller bank then contacts the large money center bank with which it has regular dealings of this type and instructs the large bank to make the required transfer to the designated foreign account. Since the small bank typically maintains a bank balance in the larger bank, the dollar equivalent of the transaction is simply deducted from the small bank's account. Note that the small bank received its money from the customer by debiting a bank account and that the large bank pursues the same course. No currency is really changing hands.

3. The large bank then contacts its branch or correspondent in the foreign country and instructs it to complete the transaction. Once again, bank accounts are debited and credited. While no currency has yet changed hands, the foreign supplier has been paid and has access to the funds.[3]

This illustration is only one of many types of transactions that are conducted through the foreign exchange market. In a similar fashion, foreign currency can be converted into dollars and paid into an American account. More complicated arrangements involving loans can also be facilitated. The amazing thing about such transactions is that they can be executed in minutes and their cost is relatively low. The efficiency can be attributed to the fact that the participants are known to each other and that bank accounts are available for debiting and crediting. A cash transaction would be much more time-consuming and expensive.

Costs Associated with International Payments

Two types of costs are involved in conducting a transaction such as the one just outlined. One cost is best described as a *transfer fee*. This fee compensates the banks for the time and expense involved in actually transferring the money from one location to another. Note that transfer fees are paid whether or not a foreign currency is involved. For example, an American firm wishing to pay a foreign supplier in dollars would be expected to pay a fee for such a service. The size of this fee, of course, is negotiable and depends on the size of the customer, balances maintained

---

[3]In the typical situation, the settlement date is usually 2 working days after the transaction is completed. In actual practice, this is when accounts are credited and debited.

at the bank, and similar considerations. None of these factors has much to do with foreign exchange.

The typical foreign transaction involves not only the movement of funds from one location to another but also the conversion of one currency into another. In other words, there is a cost associated with transferring funds from New York to London that is different from the cost of converting dollars to British pounds. It is easiest to understand the nature of this *foreign exchange cost* (the cost of converting currencies) if the explanation is organized around an example. In this example, we will look at one currency, the French franc (FF), and one bank. We will assume that the bank is heavily involved in converting French francs to dollars (so that French firms can pay American suppliers) and dollars into French francs (so that American firms can pay French suppliers).

1. On a given day, French firms take FF10,000,000 to the bank and request their conversion to dollars. The bank establishes a price at which it will buy the francs (called the *bid price*) at $0.1564 per French franc. Accordingly, the bank must deliver $1,564,000 (FF10,000,000 × 0.1564) to the French firms or their designees.
2. In order to make our illustration simple, we will assume that on exactly the same day, American firms need F10,000,000 to pay French suppliers. The bank agrees to sell the francs it has accumulated and establishes a sale price (called the *ask price*) of $0.1664 per French franc. Accordingly, the American firms pay $1,664,000 for the FF10,000,000.
3. Note that the bank charged more (ask of $0.1664) than it paid (bid of $0.1564) for each franc involved in the transactions. Therefore, the bank made a profit of $100,000.

Since the bid (buy) price is always less than the ask (sell) price, a firm always pays more for a foreign currency than it would receive if it wished to dispose of the foreign currency. Assume, for example, that on Monday morning an American firm believes it is going to acquire an investment in France and purchases FF1,000,000 at the ask price of $0.1664 (paying a total of $166,400). Further assume that on Monday afternoon it becomes obvious that the French acquisition will not be completed. The American firm now has FF1,000,000 that it does not need. Accordingly, the francs are sold back to the bank at the bid price of $0.1564 and the firm receives a total of $156,400. As can be easily computed, this movement into and out of francs cost the firm $10,000. It is important to note that there is a cost associated with a foreign exchange transaction even though no specific commission is charged.

The magnitude of the cost of converting one currency to another is reflected in the size of the spread between the bid and the ask prices for a currency. The cost measure most frequently used is called the *percentage spread*, which is computed as follows:

$$\% \text{ spread} = \frac{\text{ask price} - \text{bid price}}{\text{ask price}} \times 100 \qquad (2\text{-}1)$$

For our French franc example, the percentage bid–ask spread is 6.01 percent.

$$\% \text{ spread} = \frac{0.1664 - 0.1564}{0.1664} \times 100 = 6.01\%$$

The results obtained in the French franc example are quite unrealistic, since the spread is greater than one would encounter in real foreign exchange markets. The size of the spread on a foreign currency depends on the volume of trading in that particular currency and the risks perceived by the dealers. In the real world, the most heavily traded currencies have spreads of one-tenth of 1 percent or even less. The spreads can be appreciably higher for currencies that are traded less frequently. For example, if the bid price on the German mark is $0.5600 and the ask price $0.5610, then the spread is 0.2 percent. This is a more realistic spread for a heavily traded currency.

The size of the spread is determined by competitive market forces. Dealers expect to earn a rate of return that reflects the risk of their investment. Therefore, the lower the risk, the lower the required rate of return. Currencies that are actively traded have a lower risk to dealers and thus have a smaller spread. Currencies with small price fluctuations have a lower risk to dealers and thus have a smaller spread. Currencies that are freely convertible also have lower risks and thus smaller spreads. The reader should be aware that dealers prefer much higher spreads. This market, however, is very competitive. Therefore, dealers are unable to charge very high transaction costs.

Direct and Indirect Price Quotations

Two methods of quoting foreign currency prices are used in foreign exchange markets. An *indirect quote* expresses the value of a single unit of home country currency in terms of the number of units of foreign currency units needed to purchase it. For example, in the United States (the home country in this illustration), the indirect quote on the deutsche mark would be expressed as DM1.8136 per U.S. dollar (written here as $1 = DM1.8136). This quote can be interpreted in two ways. On the one hand, a dollar can be viewed as being able to purchase DM1.8136. On the other, a dollar can be viewed as costing DM1.8136.

Foreign currency prices can also be expressed using direct quotes. When *direct quotes* are used, the price of a single unit of foreign currency

TABLE 2-2 Foreign Exchange Quotations (October 19, 1988)

The New York foreign exchange selling rates below apply to trading among banks in amounts of $1 million and more, as quoted at 3 p.m. Eastern time by Bankers Trust Co. Retail transactions provide fewer units of foreign currency per dollar.

Country	U.S. $ equiv. Wed.	U.S. $ equiv. Tues.	Currency per U.S. $ Wed.	Currency per U.S. $ Tues.
Argentina (Austral) ...	.06680	.06680	14.97	14.97
Australia (Dollar)	.8195	.8103	1.2202	1.2341
Austria (Schilling)	.07848	.07882	12.74	12.68
Bahrain (Dinar)	2.6518	2.6518	.37710	.37710
Belgium (Franc)				
Commercial rate	.026322	.026427	37.99	37.84
Financial rate	.026082	.026184	38.34	38.19
Brazil (Cruzado)	.002422	.002422	412.81	412.81
Britain (Pound)	1.7501	1.7520	.5713	.5707
30-Day Forward	1.7477	1.7465	.5721	.5725
90-Day Forward	1.7354	1.7376	.5762	.5755
180-Day Forward ...	1.7239	1.7258	.5800	.5794
Canada (Dollar)	.8337	.8329	1.1994	1.2005
30-Day Forward	.8323	.8316	1.2014	1.2024
90-Day Forward	.8302	.8296	1.2044	1.2054
180-Day Forward ...	.8271	.8264	1.2089	1.2100
Chile (Official rate) ...	.004054	.004054	246.64	246.64
China (Yuan)	.2686	.2686	3.7220	3.7220
Colombia (Peso)	.0031847	.0031847	314.00	314.00
Denmark (Krone)	.1431	.1437	6.9865	6.9585
Ecuador (Sucre)				
Official rate	.004008	.004008	249.50	249.50
Floating rate	.0019569	.0019569	511.00	511.00
Finland (Markka)	.2335	.2339	4.2820	4.2745
France (Franc)	.1615	.1622	6.1895	6.1625
30-Day Forward	.1616	.1623	6.1877	6.1608
90-Day Forward	.1617	.1624	6.1835	6.1575
180-Day Forward ...	.1618	.1625	6.1795	6.1535
Greece (Drachma)	.006736	.006775	148.45	147.60
Hong Kong (Dollar) ..	.1279	.1279	7.8130	7.8135
India (Rupee)	.067934	.067934	14.72	14.72
Indonesia (Rupiah)	.0005861	.0005861	1706.00	1706.00
Ireland (Punt)	1.4772	1.4772	.67695	.67695
Israel (Shekel)	.6123	.6123	1.6330	1.6330
Italy (Lira)	.0007423	.0007437	1347.00	1344.50
Japan (Yen)	.007852	.007885	127.35	126.82
30-Day Forward	.007878	.007912	126.93	126.39
90-Day Forward	.007933	.007963	126.04	125.57
180-Day Forward ...	.008008	.008040	124.87	124.37
Jordan (Dinar)	2.2701	2.2701	.4405	.4405
Kuwait (Dinar)	3.54886	3.54886	.28178	.28178

Country	U.S. $ equiv. Wed.	U.S. $ equiv. Tues.	Currency per U.S. $ Wed.	Currency per U.S. $ Tues.
Lebanon (Pound)	.002136	.002136	468.00	468.00
Malaysia (Ringgit)	.373176	.373203	2.6797	2.6795
Malta (Lira)	2.9629	2.96296	.3375	.3375
Mexico (Peso)				
Floating rate	.0004378	.0004378	2284.00	2284.00
Netherland (Guilder) .	.4893	.4915	2.0435	2.0345
New Zealand (Dollar)	.6195	.6185	1.6142	1.6168
Norway (Krone)	.1493	.1497	6.6950	6.6780
Pakistan (Rupee)	.054794	.054794	18.25	18.25
Peru (Inti)	.002123	.002123	471.00	471.00
Philippines (Peso)	.048309	.048309	20.70	20.70
Portugal (Escudo)	.0066934	.0066934	149.40	149.40
Saudi Arabia (Riyal) ..	.26663	.26663	3.7505	3.7505
Singapore (Dollar)	.4957	.4956	2.0172	2.0175
South Africa (Rand)				
Commercial rate	.409500	.409500	2.4420	2.4420
Financial rate	.2437	.2463	4.1025	4.0600
South Korea (Won)	.0014084	.0014084	710.00	710.00
Spain (Peseta)	.008385	.008417	119.25	118.80
Sweden (Krona)	.1603	.1607	6.2350	6.2190
Switzerland (Franc) ..	.6525	.6544	1.5325	1.5280
30-Day Forward	.6551	.6570	1.5263	1.5219
90-Day Forward	.6605	.6622	1.5139	1.5100
180-Day Forward ...	.6680	.6696	1.4969	1.4934
Taiwan (Dollar)	.034602	.034602	28.90	28.90
Thailand (Baht)	.039603	.039603	25.25	25.25
Turkey (Lira)	.0005945	.0005945	1682.00	1682.00
United Arab (Dirham) .	.27229	.27229	3.6725	3.6725
Uruguay (New Peso)				
Financial	.002463	.002463	406.00	406.00
Venezuela (Bolivar)				
Official rate	.1333	.1333	7.50	7.50
Floating rate	.02688	.02688	37.20	37.20
W. Germany (Mark) ..	.5515	.5537	1.8130	1.8058
30-Day Forward	.5532	.5546	1.8076	1.8003
90-Day Forward	.5566	.5587	1.7964	1.7896
180-Day Forward ...	.5613	.5636	1.7814	1.7743
— — —				
SDR	1.32751	1.32537	0.753211	0.754507
ECU	1.14668	1.14579	....	....

Special Drawing Rights (SDR) are based on exchange rates for the U.S., West German, British, French and Japanese currencies. Source: International Monetary Fund.

European Currency Unit (ECU) is based on a basket of community currencies. Source: European Community Commission.

z-Not quoted.

is expressed in terms of American dollars. For example, the direct quote on the deutsche mark might be $0.5514 per mark (written here as DM1 = $0.5514). The quotations actually used among traders in foreign exchange markets are discussed in Appendix 2A.

Direct and indirect foreign currency quotes include exactly the same information. In fact, they are nothing more than reciprocals of each other. Mathematically, their relationship can be expressed as follows:

$$\text{Direct quote} = \frac{1}{\text{indirect quote}} \qquad (2\text{-}2)$$

$$\text{Indirect quote} = \frac{1}{\text{direct quote}} \qquad (2\text{-}3)$$

Obviously, if one has a direct quote, it is a simple and unambiguous procedure to convert it to an indirect quote. This is also true for converting indirect to direct quotes.

Both direct and indirect quotes are reported in the financial press. The usual information included in a typical financial section of a good newspaper is presented in Table 2-2. The first thing to note is that the newspaper is likely to include both spot and forward rates. The *spot rate* is the rate that applies to trades currently taking place. In other words, if a customer called a bank and asked to exchange currencies immediately (on the spot), the spot rate is the rate that would apply. In newspapers, the spot rate appears directly opposite the name of the country. We will discuss the forward rate in a later section of this chapter.

As previously mentioned, direct quotes show the number of dollars necessary to purchase one unit of foreign currency. From Table 2-2, we can see that you would need $1.7501 in order to purchase one British pound on October 19, 1988. Expressed in another fashion, you would receive $1.7501 for every British pound that you sold to the financial institution. Other examples of direct quotes are as follows:

Britain	£1	= $1.7501
Canada	C$1	= $0.8337
Germany	DM1	= $0.5515
France	FF1	= $0.1615
Japan	Y1	= $0.007852
Mexico	Ps1	= $0.0004378

Indirect quotes, on the other hand, measure the units of foreign currency necessary to purchase one dollar. Table 2-2 also shows the indirect quotes. You can see from the table that you would need 2,284 Mexican pesos in order to buy one dollar on October 19, 1988. Expressed in another fashion, you could sell one dollar for 2,284 pesos. Other examples of indirect quotes are as follows:

Britain	$1 = £0.5713
Canada	$1 = C$1.1994
Germany	$1 = DM1.8130
France	$1 = FF6.1895
Japan	$1 = Y127.35
Mexico	$1 = Ps2,284

Note once again that the information contained in the two types of quotes is exactly the same. Using the British pound as an example, we see that the reciprocal of the direct quote is exactly equal to the indirect quote.

$$\text{Indirect quote} = \frac{1}{\text{direct quote}} = \frac{1}{1.7501} = 0.5713$$

Unfortunately (for the student), both types of quotes are widely used. Interbank and foreign exchange broker dealings are usually conducted on a direct quote basis. Banks in the United States tend to use indirect quotes when dealing with commercial customers. The financial press seems to use both kinds of quotes. Most Americans find it easier to understand direct quotes for currencies like the British pound or the German mark. However, currencies such as the Mexican peso, the Japanese yen, or the Italian lira are easier to express in indirect quotes. If you say that a Mexican peso is worth $0.0004378, somehow the idea does not take hold. It is simply easier to grasp the relative value of the peso by using the indirect quote of $1 = Ps2,284. In order to simplify the presentation in the sections that follow, we will use direct quotes whenever possible. We suggest that any indirect quotes encountered in the future be converted to direct quotes before proceeding with computations.

The second feature of Table 2-2 that deserves notice is that both the direct and indirect quotes are reported and that quotes are provided for two days. For example, the Wednesday direct quote for the Australian dollar (A$) was A$1 = $0.8195. The previous day, the Australian dollar was A$1 = $0.8103. The amount of U.S. dollars needed to purchase one Australian dollar increased by $0.0092. By comparing the daily rates provided, the changes in the value of a currency can be noted.

It is also important to recognize that the quotes reported in newspapers are not the rates at which a small firm or individual can conduct transactions. These are interbank rates for transactions of $1 million or more. There is no mention of bid or ask prices in the newspaper reports, since the information provided constitutes neither an offer to buy nor to sell currencies at the prices listed. The price listed corresponds most closely to the ask price, but should be viewed as a general indicator rather than a specific price. The rates published in the *The Wall Street Journal* are those that were reported by a specific bank (Bankers Trust Company) and at a specific time (3 P.M. Eastern Standard Time, October 19, 1988). Rates vary over time and also among banks. For example, the table of rates published by the *Los Angeles Times* for October 19, 1988, differs slightly because the information reported was based on the rates being charged by a different institution at 3:30 P.M. Eastern Standard Time.

Exchange Rate Uniformity

The prices charged by different American banks for foreign exchange cannot vary greatly. In other words, the exchange rate available from one bank must be fairly close to the exchange rate available from other banks. Prices are kept more or less in line with each other through a process called *locational arbitrage*.[4] If the price of foreign exchange varies from

---

[4]*Arbitrage* is defined as the simultaneous purchase and sale of an item (in this case, foreign currency) in different markets in order to profit from unequal prices. An arbitrageur is a person who conducts arbitrage transactions.

TABLE 2-3　Hypothetical Locational Arbitrage Opportunity

	Bank 1	Bank 2
Bid price for DM	$0.50	$0.52
Ask price for DM	$0.51	$0.53

bank to bank, the arbitrageur will be able to buy cheaply at one bank and sell at a higher price to another bank. This arbitrage activity should lead to an increase in the foreign exchange rate at the low-priced bank and a reduction in the exchange rate at the high-priced bank. The arbitrage activity will continue as long as the difference in prices is large enough to generate a profit. Eventually, prices will come into equilibrium and profitable arbitrage opportunities will cease to exist.

The nature and implications of locational arbitrage can be better understood by working through a numerical example. Table 2-3 provides price information at two banks for the deutsche mark. Note that for both banks the bid (buy) price is lower than the ask (sell) price. The prices, however, are different, and in this illustration a profitable arbitrage opportunity exists. An arbitrageur could buy deutsche marks from Bank 1 at a price of $0.51 and simultaneously sell them to Bank 2 at $0.52. If $1,000,000 were available, the arbitrageur could purchase DM1,960,784 at Bank 1 ($1,000,000/$0.51) and simultaneously sell them to Bank 2 for $1,019,608 (DM1,960,784 × $0.52). Without taking any risk, the arbitrageur would make a profit of $19,608. The lure of profits would generate a high demand for deutsche marks at Bank 1, which in turn would lead to a price increase at that location. On the other hand, Bank 2 would experience an increased inflow of deutsche marks, which should result in a lowering of the price at that location. As soon as the difference between the bid price at Bank 2 and the ask price at Bank 1 is eliminated, the arbitrage opportunity ceases to exist.

An opportunity such as that presented in Table 2-3 rarely exists, and when it does, foreign exchange market dealers immediately act to take advantage of the price differential. Such a situation usually disappears before most firms even become aware of it. In almost every case, the bid and ask prices at various banks are very close to each other. The reader should note, however, that prices can vary slightly from place to place.

What is true in the United States is also true in unregulated world currency markets. For example, the price of the deutsche mark should be more or less the same in Frankfurt, London, and New York. Any temporary disequilibrium would be rectified by the activities of arbitrageurs. There is no reason to expect prices to be better in one free-market location than in another.

Of course, not all currency markets are free. In some countries (usually less developed countries with balance of payments difficulties), governments establish the official rate at which currencies can be exchanged. Naturally, all banks within that country buy and sell currencies at the same rate. For example, for many years the Egyptian government established an official rate for the exchange of its pound (E£) in terms of dollars. All exchange transactions within Egypt took place at that rate. In addition, the Egyptian government prohibited the importation or exportation of its own currency. This policy was designed to force all exchange transactions involving the Egyptian pound to take place in Egypt at the official rate. In practice, some Egyptian pounds did enter and leave Egypt, and a "gray" market for Egyptian pounds did exist in other countries. A buyer of Egyptian pounds in a foreign market, however, faced the problem of getting them back into Egypt. The point is that for currencies like the Egyptian pound, different prices existed at different locations. The prohibition on importation and exportation of the currency makes locational arbitrage impossible (or at least illegal), and price differences can exist for a long period of time. There are no legal ways to capitalize on these differences in locational exchange rates.

Even though a firm involved in international commerce is faced with relatively uniform foreign exchange prices, it may still be profitable to shop for the best deal. Small differences in the prices asked by banks do exist, and when a large number of currency units are involved, shopping can be profitable. Savings are not likely to be significant when transactions are smaller.

The Forward Exchange Market

At this point, our discussion shifts from the spot market to the forward market for foreign exchange. A spot transaction involves the immediate exchange of currencies. A *forward market* transaction involves entering into a legally binding contract to exchange currencies at a future time, with the exchange rate agreed upon at the time the contract is established. For example, assume that an American importer anticipates that it will need DM2,000,000 in 90 days. The firm would contact its bank and enter into an agreement to deliver a specified number of dollars and receive a specified number of deutsche marks in 90 days. Note that no currencies are exchanged at the time the agreement is made.

Let us assume that the current spot rate is DM1 = $0.49, but the bank is unwilling to agree to the future exchange of currencies at that rate. Instead, the bank has a special rate for this future exchange, called the *90-day forward rate*. If we assume that this rate is DM1 = $0.50, the firm is agreeing to deliver $1,000,000 in 90 days and, in return, the bank is committed to deliver DM2,000,000. It does not matter what the spot rate is in 90 days, the terms of the exchange have been established by contract and must be honored. In other words, the bank has one rate if the

TABLE 2-4 Spot and Forward Rates for Canadian Dollars and Deutsche Marks October 19, 1988 (Direct Quotes—in U.S. Dollars)

	Canadian Dollars	Deutsche Marks
Spot rate	$0.8337	$0.5515
30-day forward rate	$0.8323	$0.5532
90-day forward rate	$0.8302	$0.5566
180-day forward rate	$0.8271	$0.5613

Source: See Table 2-2.

currencies are exchanged on the spot, but other rates may apply if the exchange is to be postponed until a future time.

A look back at the *The Wall Street Journal* data presented in Table 2-2 shows that forward exchange rate data are available for the most widely traded currencies. Table 2-4 extracts information for two of these currencies, the Canadian dollar and the deutsche mark. Note that the 180-day forward rate for the Canadian dollar is lower than the spot rate. In other words, the 180-day price of the Canadian dollar is lower than the current spot price. This means that a firm can get more Canadian dollars for a given number of U.S. dollars if the date at which the transaction is to be completed is postponed for 180 days. The situation of the deutsche mark is precisely the reverse. A firm would have to pay more for a mark if it wants to wait 180 days before completing the contractual exchange.

Discounts and Premiums on Foreign Currencies

The difference between the spot rate and the forward rate is called either a *forward discount* or a *forward premium*. In the previous illustration, the Canadian dollar is said to be selling at a forward discount, since the price for future delivery is lower than the price for spot delivery. On the other hand, the deutsche mark is said to be selling at a forward premium, since its forward price is higher than its spot price. It is possible to compute the annualized percentage forward discount or premium using the following formula:

$$\% \frac{\text{discount}}{\text{premium}} = \frac{\text{forward rate} - \text{spot rate}}{\text{spot rate}} \times \frac{360}{N} \times 100 \qquad (2\text{-}4)$$

where N is the number of days in the forward contract. If the forward rate is higher than the spot rate (deutsche mark), the result of the equation will be positive, which indicates that the currency is selling at a forward premium. If the forward rate is lower than the spot rate (Canadian dollar), the result will be negative, indicating a forward discount. The percentage discount/premium for both currencies can be computed as follows:

$$\frac{\text{C\$ \% discount/premium}}{(180 \text{ days})} = \frac{0.8271 - 0.8337}{0.8337} \times \frac{360}{180} \times 100 = -1.58\%$$

$$\frac{\text{DM \% discount/premium}}{(180 \text{ days})} = \frac{0.5613 - 0.5515}{0.5515} \times \frac{360}{180} \times 100 = +3.55\%$$

Percentage discounts or premiums for periods other than 180 days are computed by inserting the appropriate exchange rates and substituting the appropriate number of days for 180 in the preceding computations. The actual size of the forward discount or premium depends on a variety of factors. The two most important factors are relative interest rates between countries (discussed in the next section of this chapter) and market forecasts about the movement of the exchange rate (discussed in Chapter 5).

Characteristics of the Forward Market

Looking back at the *The Wall Street Journal* exchange rate information presented in Table 2-2, you will notice that forward rates are available for a limited number of currencies. These are the currencies that are most heavily and frequently traded, since the countries involved are major participants in international trade. Forward contracts may be available for a few other currencies, but not for all. Banks are only willing to make a forward market for currencies with significant trading activity. For such currencies, there will be large numbers of buy and sell orders for future delivery.

Traditionally, most forward contracts had maturities of 180 days or less. In recent years, however, forward contracts for longer periods have become available. One-year contracts are available for all of the major currencies and even for some that are less frequently traded. In recent years, contracts for 5 and even 10 years have been infrequently used for major currencies. The actual maturities and amounts involved in a forward contract can be tailored to meet the needs of the customer. For example, it would be possible to have a forward contract that obligates the firm to deliver FF18,375,221 in 47 days. The bank and the firm would have to negotiate the rate applicable to this particular transaction.

Two other characteristics of forward exchange contracts are worth noting. First, firms that utilize forward contracts must be "qualified" in the sense that they must possess the highest credit rating. In order for the system to work, the bank must be confident that the firm will be able and willing to deliver the contractually agreed-upon currency at the agreed date. For example, if the bank enters into a forward contract that obligates it to accept DM2,000,000 in 90 days, it will simultaneously make a commitment to use the deutsche mark inflow when it is received. Failure to receive the deutsche mark inflow as promised would place the bank in the awkward position of being unable to fulfill its other obligations. For this reason, only financially strong firms have easy access to the forward market. The second point worth noting is that the amount of an individual contract tends to be very large. In other words, the forward market for foreign exchange is dominated by large banks, large firms, and large amounts. Smaller firms, with local reputations and transactions of moderate size, do not have easy access to the forward market for foreign exchange.

There are many different types of participants in the forward exchange market. First, there are the hedgers, who use a forward exchange contract to reduce the risk associated with fulfilling a commitment to receive or accept a foreign currency. For example, an American firm selling a product to a British buyer, may agree to accept a payment of £10,000,000 in 73 days. The firm may be able to hedge the risk of unexpected changes in the value of the pound by selling the pounds forward. This *locks in* an exchange rate at the time the sale is made and eliminates the exchange risk from this particular transaction. Similarly, a firm that has a commitment to deliver a foreign currency at a future date could hedge the risk of an exchange rate movement by buying the foreign currency in the forward exchange market. For example, assume that an American firm purchases something from a French seller and agrees to make a payment of FF50,000,000 in 35 days. The firm can eliminate the exchange rate risk associated with this transaction by buying the required amount of francs in the forward market.

Firms with future foreign currency commitments are major participants in the foreign exchange market. In fact, the forward market for foreign exchange originated in the desire of banks to meet such business needs. At the same time, it is necessary to recognize that some of the participants in the forward market are motivated by other considerations. Speculators have a different motive than firms involved in hedging an expected foreign currency inflow or outflow. A speculator enters into a forward exchange contract with the expressed desire to "beat" the forward exchange market. Assume, for example, that the 60-day forward rate on the British pound is £1 = $1.52. A speculator who believes that the spot price of the pound will be higher than the forward rate (e.g., $1.70) will be tempted to buy pounds in the forward market. If the speculator enters into a contract to deliver $1,520,000 in 60 days (£1 = $1.52), the bank will be required to deliver £1,000,000 to the speculator on that date. If the spot exchange rate of £1 = $1.70 materializes as expected by the speculator, the £1,000,000 could be immediately sold for $1,700,000. In other words, the speculator delivers $1,520,000 to get the pounds and immediately sells them for $1,700,000. This is a nice profit of $180,000 in 60 days. Note that no funds were tied up by the speculator in the investment. Of course, the speculator would have lost money if the price of the pound had dropped below $1.52. The ability of the speculator to make a profit depends on the ability to make accurate forecasts of future spot exchange rates. As we will see in a later chapter, forecasting exchange rates is not something that can be done consistently well.

The term *speculator* defines a role played by the regular foreign exchange market participants. This role may be played by a firm, a bank, or a foreign exchange broker. That is, the same individuals and firms that are involved in hedging are also occasionally involved in speculating. While some organizations and individuals are more involved in this activity than others, one has to fight against the negative image created by the word *speculator*. There is no sizable, separate group of "gamblers" as such operating in the forward exchange market. Speculators play an interesting and positive role in the foreign currencies market. If the price of a currency is higher or lower than the "correct" price, the speculator either sells or buys this currency in order to make a profit. These actions by the speculator move the price of the currency toward an equilibrium or correct price.

Another role assumed by forward exchange market participants is that of arbitrageur. We have already seen how a worldwide uniformity of spot exchange rates is created by the actions of locational arbitrageurs. Just as in spot foreign exchange, banks establish a bid and an ask price for forward foreign exchange. Look back at Table 2-3 and assume that the quotes listed there are for 30-day forward transactions. The locational arbitrageur could make a profit on forward transactions in exactly the same way as a profit is made on spot transactions. Specifically, the arbitrageur would buy 30-day forward deutsche marks from Bank 1 and enter into a contract to deliver them in 30 days to Bank 2. If the conditions exhibited in Table 2-3 hold, a risk-free profit could be earned. Just as in the spot market, such opportunities are fleeting and are usually available only to those who participate continuously in the foreign exchange market. It is important to note, however, that the existence of locational arbitrage means that forward exchange rates are basically the same throughout the free foreign exchange market. All banks generally offer the same forward exchange rate. On large forward market transactions, however, even small differences rates could mean a substantial saving. It still pays to shop for the best deal when the amount involved is large.[5]

Interest Rate Parity

The arbitrage activities of foreign exchange market participants are also important in establishing a well-defined relationship between spot and

---

[5]Some alternatives to the forward market are discussed in Chapters 7 and 9.

forward exchange rates. This relationship, called *interest rate parity*, asserts that the discount or premium on a currency (the percentage difference between the spot and forward rates) is equal to the difference in the interest rates between the two countries. Algebraically, the relationship can be expressed as follows (where i is the interest rate)[6]:

$$\% \ \frac{discount}{premium} = i(home) - i(foreign) \qquad (2\text{-}5)$$

For example, assume that the annual 90-day interest rate in the United States (home) stands at 10 percent and the annual rate in France is 15 percent. This means that the French franc should be selling at a 5 percent discount. That is, if the spot rate on the French franc is FF1 = $0.1600, then the 90-day forward rate on the franc would be 5 percent lower, or $0.1580.[7]

There have been many investigations of interest rate parity, and the evidence overwhelmingly supports its existence. Only when national governments restrict capital movements and/or impose a tax on interest income is interest rate parity violated. Transactions costs could also result in small departures from interest rate parity. After recognizing exceptions, however, it is best to assume that differences between the spot and forward exchange rates for the currencies of the major industrialized nations are explained by differences in national interest rates. The behavior of forward exchange rates is very predictable in this way.

Covered Interest Arbitrage

The process called *covered interest arbitrage* is what brings about interest rate parity. When there is a disequilibrium between interest rate differentials and the forward discount or premium on a currency, the covered interest arbitrageur can make a profit by borrowing in one country, investing in high-quality government securities in the other country, and simultaneously entering into a forward contract. For example, consider a situation in which the direct spot quote on the British pound is £1 = $1.00, while the 1-year forward rate is £1 = $1.10. This means that the pound is selling at a forward premium of 10 percent. We will assume that the annual interest rate is 25 percent in the United States and 10 percent in

---

[6]The preceding equation is a convenient and easy-to-understand approximation. A more precise expression of the relationship between interest rates and the discount/premium is

$$\% \ \frac{discount}{premium} = \left(\frac{1 + i(home)}{1 + i(foreign)} - 1 \right) \times 100$$

[7]On an annualized basis, the forward discount will be

$$\% \ discount = \frac{0.1580 - 0.1600}{0.1600} \times \frac{360}{90} \times 100 = -5\%$$

the United Kingdom. Thus, the difference in annual interest rates is 15 percent. In addition, we will make three assumptions: (1) the borrowing rate is equal to the lending rate, (2) the investment risk in both countries is zero, and (3) there is no difference between the bid and ask prices. In other words, an arbitrageur can borrow at 10 percent in the United Kingdom and invest the funds at the same rate. For the United States, the investor can borrow and invest at 25 percent. Interest rate parity does not exist, since the forward premium (10 percent) is not equal to the difference in interest rates (15 percent).

In this situation, the covered interest arbitrageur would make a profit by borrowing pounds at the lower interest rate and investing the funds in dollars at the higher interest rate. In effect, the arbitrageur can earn 15 percent more interest than would have to be paid (25 percent − 10 percent). At this point in the interest arbitrage transaction, the person executing the deal is at risk (speculating), since he or she has a liability in pounds (a loan repayment) and an asset in dollars (an interest and principal receipt). Fluctuations in the value of the British pound could result in the speculator incurring a substantial loss. The risk associated with the interest rate arbitrage activity can be eliminated if the transaction is "covered" with a forward contract. Specifically, the future dollar receipts could be sold forward, locking in an exchange rate and, in this case, a sure profit. Covered interest arbitrage involves borrowing in one country, investing in another, and covering the foreign exchange risk with a forward contact.

Let us work through the illustration and see exactly how the profit is earned and how the risk is avoided. We will assume that the arbitrageur borrows £1,000,000.

Step 1. The arbitrageur borrows £1,000,000 at an interest rate of 10 percent. This means that at the end of 1 year, a principal and interest payment of £1,100,000 is due.

Step 2. The pounds are immediately converted to dollars and invested at 25 percent. The £1,000,000 is converted to dollars at the spot rate of £1 = $1.00. Thus, there is $1,000,000 to invest at 25 percent. At the end of 1 year, the arbitrageur has $1,250,000.

Step 3. At exactly the same time that the arbitrageur borrows and invests, she or he enters into a forward contract that commits a bank to deliver pounds for the dollar inflow expected by the arbitrageur. The arbitrageur agrees to deliver $1,250,000. The bank agrees to a 1-year forward rate of £1 = $1.10, which means that the bank is obligated to deliver £1,136,364 ($1,250,000/$1.10).

Step 4. At the end of the year, the arbitrageur liquidates the dollar investment and delivers the $1,250,000 to the bank. The bank pays the arbitrageur £1,136,364. The £1,100,000 loan repayment is then made. The arbitrageur makes a profit of £36,364.

The profitability of this transaction can also be determined using internal rates of return. The investor invests £1,000,000 and will receive £1,136,364 in 1 year. This is a rate of return of 13.64 percent. The investment offers a higher rate of return than its 10 percent cost. Thus, the investment is profitable. It is important to note that the covered interest arbitrage transaction is riskless. The exchange rate, the amount to be received, and the amount to be paid are all known. Unfortunately for arbitrageurs, situations similar to the one just described cannot persist for any length of time in free currency markets. The conditions of interest rate parity are the rule.

If interest rate parity did not exist, arbitrageurs would quickly bring it about. In the preceding illustration, for example, there would be a tremendous demand for British pound borrowings, since everyone would want to get into the act. This would drive up British interest rates. At the same time, interest rates in the United States would fall, since investment funds would rush into the country. The difference between the interest rates in the two countries [i(home) − i(foreign)] would narrow.

The rush to covered interest arbitrage investments would also alter both the spot and the forward exchange rates for the pound. The spot rate on the pound would fall as more and more people requested that their pound borrowings be converted to dollars. The forward rate on the pound would rise because many investors would be requesting that dollars be converted to pounds at the future date. A falling spot rate and a rising forward rate mean that the premium on the pound would increase.

The simultaneous increase in the premium on the pound and the reduction in the difference in interest rates would eventually result in a situation in which the premium would be equal to the differences in interest rates. In other words, interest rate parity would be established. Once interest rate parity existed, covered interest arbitrage opportunities would cease to exist. In effect, the feasibility of conducting covered interest arbitrage more or less ensures that interest rate parity does exist.[8]

Whenever interest rate differentials among countries differ from the forward discount or premium on the currencies involved, an opportunity for covered interest arbitrage exists. Figure 2-2 can be used to determine the nature of the arbitrage activity that will capitalize on a disequilibrium

---

[8]In actual practice, there may be slight discrepancies between interest rate differentials and the forward discount or premium. A more precise estimate of the relationship would require that the more accurate equation be used (see footnote 6). In addition, the existence of transaction costs, government restrictions on capital flows, and taxes may result in situations in which profits are unobtainable even though the principle of interest rate parity appears to be violated. For this illustration, the interest rate differential is not 15 percent but

$$\% \frac{\text{discount}}{\text{premium}} = \left(\frac{1 + 0.25}{1 + 0.10} - 1 \right) \times 100 = 13.64\%$$

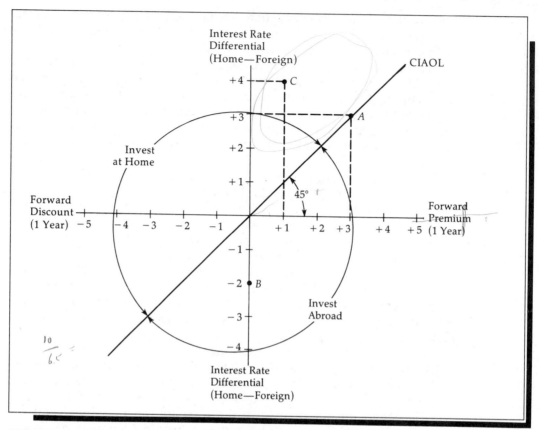

FIGURE 2-2 The Covered Interest Arbitrage Opportunities Line (CIAOL).

situation. The horizontal axis records the size of the discount or premium on the direct quote of the foreign currency. The vertical axis records the interest rate differential between the home and foreign countries. The 45-degree line, called the *covered interest arbitrage opportunities line* (*CIAOL*), represents the equilibrium situations, since the discounts or premiums will be exactly equal to the interest rate differentials along the line. A quick look at three cases will help clarify the meaning of Figure 2-2.

Case A (*indicated by point A on Figure 2-2*). Assume that the 1-year interest rate in the United States is 10 percent, while the comparable rate in the United Kingdom is 7 percent. Thus, the interest rate differential, $i(h) - i(f)$, is equal to a positive three percentage points (+3 percent). Assume also that the British pound is selling at a 3 percent premium. Under these conditions, covered interest arbitrage profits are unobtainable. Profits that could be earned by borrowing at lower U.S. rates and investing at higher British interest rates would be offset by the fact that the pound is selling at a forward premium. In other words, interest rate parity exists. Graphically, this is confirmed by the fact that the ordered pair (+3 percent interest differential and +3 percent forward premium) falls on the CIAOL in Figure 2-2.

Case B (*indicated by point B on Figure 2-2*). In this case, we will assume that the forward rate and the spot rate on the British pound are exactly the same (£1 = $1.50). In other words, the discount/premium is equal to 0 percent. By assuming that the interest rate in the United States is 8 percent and the interest rate in the United Kingdom is 10 percent, we are assuming that interest rate parity does not exist. An interest rate differential $i(h) - i(f)$ of two percentage points (−2 percent) with a discount/premium of 0 percent means that a covered interest arbitrage opportunity exists. Figure 2-2 becomes very useful at this point in the discussion because we know that whenever the point (point *B* in this case) falls below the CIAOL, the investment should be made abroad. The funds should be borrowed in the United States; pounds would be purchased in the spot market and sold in the forward market.[9]

Case C (*indicated by point C on Figure 2-2*). In this case, it is assumed that the British pound is selling at a 1 percent premium and that interest rates in the United States are four percentage points higher than in the United Kingdom. Interest rate parity does not exist, since the interest rate differential (+4 percent) is greater than the premium on the pound (+1 percent). Since point *C* falls above the CIAOL, the covered interest arbitrageur could make a riskless profit by investing in the United States, borrowing in the United Kingdom, and simultaneously buying the pounds forward.[10]

---

[9]For example, $1,500,000 could be borrowed in the United States at an 8 percent interest rate. At the end of 1 year, the borrower must repay $1,620,000. The $1,500,000 can be immediately converted into £1,000,000 at the spot rat of £1 = $1.50. This amount, invested at 10 percent for one year, will yield £1,100,000 at the end of the year. A forward contract can be used to ensure that the £1,100,000 could be converted to dollars at the forward rate of £1 = $1.50. Thus, $1,650,000 (£1,100,000 × $1.50) would be available to meet the required loan repayment in the United States. The covered interest arbitrageur would be assured a riskless profit of $30,000 ($1,650,000 − $1,620,000).

[10]For example, £1,000,000 could be borrowed in the United Kingdom at an assumed 10 percent interest rate. At the end of 1 year, the borrower must repay £1,100,000. The £1,000,000 can be immediately converted to $1,500,000 at the spot rate of £1 = $1.50. This amount, invested at 14 percent (4 percent higher) for 1 year, will yield $1,710,000 at the end of the year. A forward contract can be used to ensure that the $1,710,000 could be converted to pounds at the forward rate of £1 = $1.5150 (1 percent forward premium). Thus, £1,128,713 ($1,710,000/£1.5150) would be available. to meet the required loan repayment in the United Kingdom. The covered interest arbitrageur would be assured a riskless profit of £28,713 (£1,128,713 − £1,100,000).

As discussed earlier, situations such as those described in Cases *B* and *C* cannot persist for any length of time. Foreign exchange market participants will enter the market quickly and reestablish the conditions of interest rate parity. The intersection of forward market differentials and interest differentials will usually be very close to or exactly on the CIAOL.

A couple of very practical conclusions can be drawn from the discussion of interest rate parity and covered interest arbitrage. First, the size of the discount or premium on a foreign currency will depend on relative interest rates. If the U.S. interest rate is higher than the foreign interest rate, the foreign currency will always be at a premium (the forward rate is higher than the spot rate, using direct quotes). In cases where the U.S. interest rate is lower than that in the foreign country, the foreign currency will be at a discount (the forward rate is lower than the spot rate, using direct quotes). This must be true or the rule of interest rate parity will be violated (which is not often the case). Thus, if you look back at the *Wall Street Journal* exchange rate data presented in Table 2-2, there is no real mystery about why some currencies are selling at a forward discount and others at a premium.

The second conclusion worth noting is that any changes in relative interest rates will lead to a change in the forward discount or premium on a currency. We can see this most clearly by taking another look at the covered interest arbitrage example presented a few paragraphs ago. If the U.S. interest rate increased while the British interest rate remained the same, more covered interest arbitrage would take place and the premium on the pound would increase. Of course, the opposite would be true if the interest rate differential narrowed. The point is that interest rate changes are likely to have an impact on spot rates, forward rates, and the discount/premium on a currency.

Computing Cross Rates for Foreign Currencies

Both the direct and indirect quotes published in the financial press and provided by banks in the United States are usually expressed in terms of the U.S. dollar. On occasion, it is useful to know the price of one foreign currency in terms of another (called the *cross rate*); this information can be computed from the regularly available dollar-based data. For example, suppose that we are interested in finding the direct quote of one foreign currency in terms of another. The following formula (used for direct quotes only) is appropriate:

$$\text{Units of currency } A \text{ per unit of currency } B = \frac{\text{direct quote of } B}{\text{direct quote of } A} \quad (2\text{-}6)$$

For example, assume that one wishes to know the number of French francs (FF) needed to buy a deutsche mark (DM). This can be computed using the direct dollar quote of the mark (DM1 = $0.50) and the franc (FF1 = $0.14).

$$\frac{FF}{DM} = \frac{\text{direct quote of DM}}{\text{direct quote of FF}} = \frac{0.50}{0.14} = 3.57$$

$$DM1 = FF\ 3.57$$

As is now obvious, the dollar quotations appearing in the American financial press can be used to compute the exchange rates between any two foreign countries for which data are included. For example, if one wishes to know the number of Canadian dollars (C$) that would be received for £100,000, the number of Canadian dollars per pound would be computed, with the resulting quote being multiplied by 100,000. Using the information presented in Table 2-2, it can be computed as follows:

$$\frac{C\$}{£} = \frac{\text{direct quote of } £}{\text{direct quote of C\$}} = \frac{1.7501}{0.8337} = 2.0992$$

$$£1 = C\$2.0992$$

Since each pound is worth C$2.0992, £100,000 is worth C$209,920. Note that all of the information required to complete this computation is retrieved from dollar-denominated quotes appearing in the American financial press.

Summary and Conclusions

This chapter has described the foreign exchange market. The discussion highlighted the role played by banks, foreign exchange brokers, business firms, and arbitrageurs. The costs of buying and selling, as well as hedging foreign exchange exposure, are very important to the firm. In addition, the role of the arbitrageur in foreign exchange markets was discussed in two areas: (1) to equalize prices throughout the world and (2) to ensure the relationship between interest rates and the forward discount/premium on foreign currencies.

This chapter constitutes an introduction to the foreign exchange problem faced by firms involved in international business. Later chapters will expand these discussions and examine various approaches used to manage the foreign exchange exposure problem. You have taken one small step in a long journey.

Review Questions

1. Discuss the function of the large money center banks in the foreign exchange market.

2. Explain why the bid–ask spread on foreign exchange transactions is important to the banks involved in such transactions.

3. Explain how a firm pays for the foreign exchange services provided by commercial banks.

4. Describe the costs of an American firm associated with converting dollars to British pounds and using the pounds to make a payment in London.

5. Give a definition of (a) the direct quote on a foreign currency and (b) the indirect quote on a foreign currency. Explain the relationship between the two types of quotes.

6. What is the significance of locational arbitrage?

7. Assume that the spot rate on the British pound in New York is £1 = $1.56, while the price in London is £1 = $1.50. (Assume that the bid price equals the ask price.) Explain why such a situation could not persist for more than a very short period of time.

8. Explain why the forward discount/premium on a foreign currency must be equal to the difference in interest rates between the two countries involved.

Questions for Discussion

1. Assume that your firm purchases something from a foreign buyer and you are instructed to arrange an immediate payment of DM4,000,000. How would you go about doing this? Where will you get the best price on the foreign currency (Germany, the United States, a large bank, a small bank)?

2. Assume that your firm purchases something from a foreign buyer and you are instructed to arrange for a £1,000,000 payment in 90 days. What are your alternative courses of action? Where will you get the best price on the British pound?

3. Assume that your firm purchases something from a foreign buyer and you are instructed to arrange for a payment of Ps20,000,000 (Mexican pesos) in 90 days. What are your alternative courses of action?

4. Assume that you receive inflation and interest rate forecasts for both the United States and the United Kingdom. These forecasts show that inflation in the United Kingdom is expected to be higher than in the United States, and thus British interest rates are expected to increase more than U.S. interest rates. What would you expect to happen to the forward discount/premium on the British pound?

5. Assume that you are employed in the currency trading department of a large money center bank. How would you identify covered interest arbitrage opportunities? What conditions must be present in order for you to take advantage of such opportunities? Would you be able to pursue an arbitrage scheme on your own without the resources of the bank?

Research Activities

1. Look at a recent issue of *The Wall Street Journal* and copy the direct quote for 10 currencies. Compute the indirect quote for these currencies. Compare the indirect quotes so computed to those published in *The Wall Street Journal*.

2. Go to the library and collect information about inflation and interest rate forecasts for Japan, the United Kingdom, Canada, and France. Compare these forecasts to forecasts for the United States and use these comparisons to predict whether the

foreign currencies will be selling at discounts or premiums. Compare your predictions to the forward rates published in *The Wall Street Journal*.

Problems

1. Calculate the bid–ask spread of the following foreign exchange quotations:

	Bid	Ask
British pound	$1.5600	$1.5650
Canadian dollar	$0.7500	$0.7547
Japanese yen	$0.0075	$0.0078

2. Compute the indirect quotes of the following direct quotes:

   1 British pound   = $1.5000
   1 Canadian dollar = $0.8000
   1 Mexican peso   = $0.0010

3. Your firm has to buy and sell British pounds at different time periods. Your bank provides the following quotes on the pound:

	Bid	Ask
Spot rate	$1.5000	$1.5050
30-day forward	$1.5100	$1.5180
90-day forward	$1.5200	$1.5290
180-day forward	$1.5300	$1.5400

   a. How many dollars would you receive if you sell £1,000,000 for delivery today?
   b. How many dollars would you have to pay in order to buy £2,000,000 for delivery today?
   c. How many dollars would you receive if you sell £3,000,000 for delivery in 90 days?
   d. How many dollars would you have to pay in order to buy £2,500,000 for delivery in 180 days?
   e. How many pounds could you purchase today with $5,000,000?
   f. How many pounds could you purchase for delivery in 90 days with $3,000,000?
   g. What is the forward discount/premium (use bid price) of the pound for
      i. 30 days?
      ii. 90 days?
   h. Should interest rates on securities with a similar risk with 180-day maturity be higher in the United States or the United Kingdom?

4. You are an arbitrageur and can borrow up to £10 million in London OR $16 million in New York. The interest rate for borrowing and/or investing in the United States is 20 percent. The rate in London is 10 percent. Your bank offers the following exchange rates (assume that bid = ask):

   Spot rate $1.6000
   1-year forward $1.7000

Are there any arbitrage opportunities in this situation? If so, what are the profits that can be derived from arbitrage? (Note: See Figure 2-2.)

5. Using all the information presented in Problem 4, are there any arbitrage opportunities, given the following change in our interest rate assumptions?

Country	Borrowing Rate	Investing Rate
United States	20%	18%
United Kingdom	12%	10%

6. Using the same interest rate and exchange rate information shown in Problem 4, and assuming that a firm has $5,000,000 in idle cash for 1 year:
   a. How many dollars would it have at the end of 1 year if the funds are invested in the United States?
   b. How many dollars would it have at the end of 1 year if the funds are invested in the United Kingdom and the firm does not want to assume any risks due to foreign exchange fluctuations? (Note: Footnotes 9 and 10 may help you answer this problem.)
   c. What would you recommend?

7. The direct quotes for the deutsche mark and the Canadian dollar are as follows:

DM1 = $0.30
C$1 = $0.75

Calculate the number of deutsche marks that will be needed to purchase one Canadian dollar.

8. American Manufacturing wants to take advantage of covered interest arbitrage. The firm's credit rating is so high that it can borrow either $10 million in the United States or DM20 million in Germany for 90 days. Are there any arbitrage opportunities, given the following information?

	Borrowing	Investing
90-day interest rate in the U.S.	3.4%	3.4%
90-day interest rate in Germany	2.5%	2.5%

	Bid	Ask
DM spot	$0.50	$0.50
90-day forward	$0.51	$0.51

9. Williams Manufacturing wants to take advantage of covered interest arbitrage. The firm's credit rating is so high that it can borrow either $1 million in the United States or DM2 million in Germany for 90 days. Given the following information:

	Borrowing	Investing
90-day interest rate in the U.S.	3.4%	3.3%
90-day interest rate in Germany	2.5%	2.4%

	Bid	Ask
DM spot	$0.495	$0.500
90-day forward	$0.505	$0.510

Furthermore, any time funds move from the United States to Germany (and vice versa), there is a $200 wire transfer fee. In addition, investing in either the United States or Germany will cost a brokerage fee of $800 or DM1,600.

a. Are there any arbitrage opportunities?

b. Compare the results with those of Problem 8. What are the reasons for any differences?

10. The Donegal Corporation has $5,000,000 in idle cash. These funds will not be needed for 90 days. The firm wants to be absolutely certain about the number of dollars available in 90 days. Given the following information:

	Borrowing	Investing
90-day interest rate in the U.S.	3.4%	3.3%
90-day interest rate in Germany	2.5%	2.4%

	Bid	Ask
DM spot	$0.495	$0.500
90-day forward	$0.505	$0.510

a. Where should the firm invest these idle funds?

b. Would you change your answer if there is a $200 wire transfer fee any time funds move between the two countries?

11. The Donegal Germany is a foreign subsidiary of the Donegal Corporation. The subsidiary has DM20,000,000 in idle cash. These funds will not be needed for 90 days. The firm wants to be absolutely certain about the number of deutsche marks available in 90 days. Given the following information:

	Borrowing	Investing
90-day interest rate in the U.S.	3.4%	3.3%
90-day interest rate in Germany	2.5%	2.4%

	Bid	Ask
DM spot	$0.495	$0.500
90-day forward	$0.505	$0.510

a. Where should the firm invest these idle funds?

b. Would you change your answer if there is a $200 wire transfer fee any time funds move between the two countries?

Bibliography

Aliber, Robert Z. "The Interest Rate Parity Theorem: A Reinterpretation." *Journal of Political Economy*, December 1973, pp. 1451–1459.

Chrystal, Alec K. "A Guide to Foreign Exchange Markets." *Federal Reserve Bank of St. Louis Review*, March 1984, pp. 5–18.

Cornell, Bradford W. "Spot Rates, Forward Rates, and Exchange Market Efficiency." *Journal of Financial Economics*, August 1977, pp. 55–66.

_____ "Determinants of the Bid–Ask Spread on Forward Exchange Contracts Under Floating Exchange Rates." *Journal of International Business Studies*, Fall 1978, pp. 33–41.

Dufey, Gunter. "Corporate Finance and Exchange Rate Variations." *Financial Management*, Summer 1978, pp. 51–57.

Frenkel, Jacob A., and Levich, Richard M. "Covered Interest Arbitrage: Unexploited Profits?" *Journal of Political Economy*, April 1975, pp. 325–338.

_____ "Transaction Costs and Interest Arbitrage: Tranquil versus Turbulent Periods." *Journal of Political Economy*, November–December 1977, pp. 1209–1228.

Giddy, Ian H. "Measuring the World Foreign Exchange Market." *Columbia Journal of World Business*, Winter 1979, pp. 36–48.

_____ "Research on the Foreign Exchange Market." *Columbia Journal of World Business*, Winter 1979, pp. 4–6.

Hilley, John L., Beidleman, Carl R., and Greenleaf, James A. "Does Covered Interest Arbitrage Dominate in Foreign Exchange Markets?" *Columbia Journal of World Business*, Winter 1979, pp. 99–107.

Kohlhagen, Steven W. "Evidence on the Cost of Forward Cover in a Floating System." *Euromoney*, September 1975, pp. 138–141.

Logue, Dennis E., and Oldfield, George S. "What's So Special About Foreign Exchange Markets?" *Journal of Portfolio Management*, Spring 1977, pp. 19–24.

Riehl, Heinz, and Rodriguez, Rita. *Foreign Exchange and Money Markets*, New York: McGraw-Hill Book Company, 1983.

Ruck, Adam. "Understanding Foreign Exchange Trading." *Euromoney*, April 1981, pp. 117–124.

Stokes, Houston H., and Neuburger, Hugh. "Interest Arbitrage, Forward Speclation and the Determination of the Forward Exchange Rate." *Columbia Journal of World Business*, Winter 1979, pp. 86–98.

Walmsley, Julian. "The New York Foreign Exchange Market." *Banker's Magazine*, January–February 1984, pp. 64–69.

Weisweiller, Rudy. *Introduction to Foreign Exchange*. Cambridge: Woodhead-Faulkner, Ltd., 1983.

Appendix 2A

Trader Quotations of Exchange Rates

When dealing with each other, foreign exchange traders quote exchange rates differently than they do for commercial customers. First of all, they use indirect quotes for all foreign currencies except the British pound. For example, a commercial customer would receive a direct quote on the deutsche mark (DM1 = $0.50), while a foreign exchange trader would get an indirect quote ($1 = DM2.00). The pound is always quoted as a direct quote (which is sometimes referred to as being quoted on a *sterling basis*).

Foreign exchange trades have also adopted another important convention that specifies the number of decimal places to be included in each quote. The quote on most currencies tends to be carried to a fourth decimal place. For example, the deutsche mark may be quoted at DM1.7870 and the French franc at FF5.9755. Those currencies for which a relatively large number of currency units are required for a single dollar are carried to only two decimal places. For example, the Turkish lire would tend to be quoted as TL810.55.

While a commercial customer may simply want to know the price at which currency can be bought or sold, foreign exchange traders are interested in the spread between the bid and ask prices for particular currencies. For foreign exchange traders who deal in large volumes of foreign currency on a daily basis, even small differences in the spread can have significant implications for profitability. Thus, quotes among traders include both a bid and an ask price. Since by tradition the bid price precedes the ask price, the dollar spot quote on the deutsche mark would be given as 1.7870/12. This means that the bid price (the price at which the trader is willing to buy dollars—sell marks) is DM1.7870 and the ask price (the price at which the trader is willing to sell dollars—buy marks) is 12 points higher (DM1.7882). Note that the spot quote is written with a #/#. On the telephone, the spot quote on the deutsche mark is likely to be stated as "1.7870 to 12." When the full quote is given for a currency, the quote is said to be on an *outright basis*. When the quote is expressed as a spread, it is said to be on a *points basis*.

The situation becomes even more complicated for those currencies that are bought and sold in the forward market. There is, of course, a bid price and an ask price for spot transactions and for each period for which a forward contract is available. Since the number of digits that would have to be quoted in order to give a complete description of the total price structure for a particular currency is very large, traders have simplified the way in which they make quotes to each other. The method used by traders has fewer digits, which saves time and reduces errors. The quotation method used by traders assumes that the individuals involved have some knowledge of the quotation system. To the uninitiated, however, the system is difficult to understand.

Tables 2A-1 and 2A-2 illustrate the relationship between the quote on an outright basis and a points basis. Table 2A-1 gives the deutsche mark quotes on the dollar. Looking at the outright quotes, we can see immediately that the dollar is selling at a discount. That is, fewer deutsche marks will have to be given up for a dollar if the trader is willing to accept an exchange at a future date. The dollar is less expensive if one is willing to wait, the dollar is at a discount.

How much less expensive is the forward dollar? The outright quotes give the answer directly. The points basis gives the discount on the

TABLE 2A-1 Deutsche Mark Quotations on the U.S. Dollar (Hypothetical Prices)

	Outright Basis		Points Basis
	Bid	**Ask**	
Spot	1.7870	1.7882	1.7870/12
30-day forward	1.7841	1.7855	29/27
90-day forward	1.7778	1.7795	92/87
180-day forward	1.7692	1.7714	178/168

TABLE 2A-2 Canadian Dollar Quotations on the U.S. Dollar (Hypothetical Prices)

	Outright Basis		Points Basis
	Bid	**Ask**	
Spot	1.3411	1.3426	1.3411/15
30-day forward	1.3426	1.3442	15/16
90-day forward	1.3453	1.3473	42/47
180-day forward	1.3499	1.3525	88/99

dollar. Specifically, the 30-day forward bid rate on the dollar is at a discount of 29 points. The discount is computed by subtracting the spot bid outright quote from the forward bid outright quote (1.7841 − 1.7870 = −0.0029). The point discount on the dollar for any forward contract period can be computed in a similar fashion. For example, the 180-day forward ask price is 168 points lower (−168) than the spot ask price. Again, this is computed by subtracting the outright spot ask rate from the outright forward ask rate. Note that the negative signs are not included when the quote is reported on a points basis. For the inexperienced, the points basis is difficult to interpret. However, to foreign exchange traders, the meaning is clear and understandable immediately.

The situation can get a little more complicated. Consider Table 2A-2, which gives the Canadian dollar quotes. Note that the American dollar is selling at a premium relative to the Canadian dollar. Specifically, the forward American dollar is more expensive (in terms of Canadian dollars) than the spot American dollar. How much more expensive is the forward American dollar (what is its premium)? The answer can be found in the points basis quotation. For example, the 30-day forward bid price is 15 points higher than the spot bid price. This is computed by subtracting the spot bid price from the 30-day forward bid price (1.3426 − 1.3411 = +0.0015). All of the other points can be computed by subtracting the spot rate from the forward rate. For example, the 99-point premium for the ask price on the 180-day forward dollar is computed by subtracting the spot ask price from the 180-day ask price (1.3525 − 1.3426 = +0.0099).

To those who are not familiar with the points basis quotation system, it is difficult to tell if the American dollar is selling at a discount or a premium relative to the other currency. We know that if the dollar is at a discount, the points must be subtracted from the spot rate. We also know that if the dollar is at a premium, the points must be added to the spot rate. The forward points themselves tell us whether the American dollar is at a discount or a premium. Looking back at Table 2A-1, we can see that the American dollar is at a discount. In every case, the number of bid points is greater than the number of ask points (29 > 27, 92 > 87, 178 > 168). Whenever the bid points are higher than the ask points, the American dollar is at a discount and the points must be subtracted from the outright spot quote. Looking at Table 2A-2 (the American dollar at a premium), we see that the bid points are always lower than the ask points (15 < 16, 42 < 47, 88 < 89). Whenever the bid points are lower than the ask points, the American dollar is at a premium and the points must be added to the outright spot quote.

3

The International Monetary System

Since nations have different currencies and trade with each other, it is necessary to have a system that facilitates the exchange of one country's currency for that of another. This chapter describes the different international monetary systems that have been used in the world economy. The basic nature of both gold standard and fluctuating exchange rate systems will be analyzed. The emphasis will be on the role assigned to exchange rates in bringing about a balance between imports and exports. The chapter then examines the exchange rate systems that have existed since World War II. We will show how exchange rate fluctuations have been assigned an ever-increasing role in the battle to bring about stability in the import–export relations among countries. The conclusion drawn from this chapter is that exchange rate systems are in a state of flux. The businessperson affected by international trade must recognize that the system is likely to change in the future. Such changes may have important implications for the management of the firm.

TABLE 3-1   Comparative Advantage and International Trade

No Trade		
	Cars	**Wheat**
American production and consumption	100	300
Japanese production and consumption	120	300
Specialization and Trade		
	Cars	**Wheat**
American production	0	600
Japanese production	240	0
Terms of Trade: 110 Cars = 300 Bushels of Wheat		
	Cars	**Wheat**
American consumption	110	300
Japanese consumption	130	300

The Rationale
for International Commerce

Trade among nations has economic and political benefits. However, it also creates some problems. The primary economic benefit is related to the efficiencies associated with specialization. The general idea incorporated in David Ricardo's *law of comparative advantage* is widely held. According to this view, each nation should specialize in the production of those goods for which it is relatively efficient. If each nation focuses on what it does best, total world output will be increased. Presumably, the terms of trade among nations will be such that everyone will get a share of the larger pie. Therefore the world's welfare would be maximized. This view of the world provides the underlying economic rationale for the free trade argument so popular in the post–World War II period.

The law of comparative advantage can best be illustrated by an example.[1] Table 3-1 shows the consumption and production possibilities

---

[1] For a more complete discussion of the law of comparative advantage, see Beth V. Yarbrough and Robert M. Yarbrough, *The World Economy: Trade and Finance*, Chicago: Dryden Press, 1988, pp. 33–36, 62–64, and 67–70.

of the United States and Japan under two different assumptions: (1) no trade and (2) international trade. Under the no-trade assumption, the United States produces and consumes 100 cars and 300 bushels of wheat. At the same time, Japan produces and consumes 120 cars and 300 bushels of wheat. The law of comparative advantage suggests that each country should specialize in the production of those goods in which it is *relatively* more efficient. In our illustration, the United States is relatively more efficient at growing wheat, since it would have to forgo only 100 cars in order to increase wheat production from 300 to 600 bushels. Japan, on the other hand, would have to give up 120 cars in order to increase wheat output by 300 bushels. Since the United States has to give up less to produce wheat, it should specialize in wheat production. The Japanese should specialize in building cars.[2]

We now turn to the benefits from international trade. Let us assume that only 600 bushels of wheat are needed for consumption and that the Japanese and Americans agree on the following terms of trade: 300 bushels of wheat exchanged for 110 cars. Thus the U.S. consumption of wheat will be 300 bushels (600 produced minus 300 sold to Japan) and 110 cars (imported from Japan). The Japanese consumption will be 130 cars (240 produced minus 110 sold to the United States) and 300 bushels of wheat (imported from the United States). As you can see from Table 3-1, the United States has increased its consumption of cars from 100 to 110 due to trade. Japan has also increased its consumption of cars from 120 to 130 due to trade. Automobile production in the world has been increased without reducing the production of wheat. The level of satisfaction is increased in both countries through specialization and trade.

This illustration is designed only to show the central thoughts behind the law of comparative advantage. Specifically, specialization of production and international trade will increase the goods available for worldwide consumption. This proposition has become almost an article of faith for political and economic leaders. It is the powerful economic logic that supports free trade.[3]

This Ricardian view of the world has important political implications. As nations specialize, interdependence grows. Countries come to depend on each other for such things as food, automobiles, airplanes, oil, and computers. Many people hope that this mutual interdependence of nations will lead to greater political cooperation. Clearly, this was one of the most important motivations behind the formation of the European

---

[2]In the real world, the factors of production cannot be shifted entirely from car to wheat production, and vice versa.

[3]The law of comparative advantage is much more complicated than is suggested by this discussion. Economists are particularly concerned with the possible advantages of protecting infant industries and the manner in which the terms of trade are determined. It is possible that world output is increased through specialization without every country benefiting from such an increase.

Economic Community (EEC) in the aftermath of World War II.[4] The idea that future Western European wars could be eliminated by uniting the interests of France and Germany had widespread appeal. France was the initiator. Germany, exhausted and ashamed, was very happy to go along. The postwar reconciliation between Japan and the World War II allies also reflected political realities as perceived at the end of the War. While integrating Japan into the West was always recognized as having important economic implications, the necessity of having a powerful capitalist Asian ally was viewed as being an essential component of the struggle against world communism. It is clear that the call for free trade among nations reflects political as well as economic realities. Today, any move away from expanded international trade would be resisted on both political and economic grounds.

Problems Created by International Trade

Unfortunately, increased international trade and economic integration have created important economic and political problems. The solutions to these problems are still being sought. The major economic problem relates to long-term imbalances between the imports and exports of some countries. A number of countries regularly import more than they export. There are many reasons for this phenomenon. Countries like Brazil view imports as an important component of national economic development plans. Countries such as Israel need imports in order to meet what are perceived to be important defense needs. The governments of other countries use imports in order to maintain a military apparatus that can sustain the existing political order. While the reasons are many, the results are the same: Some countries regularly import more than they export.

Basically, when a country imports more than it exports, the difference is financed by international borrowing. But in order for net importers to borrow, there must be willing lenders, and international lenders are not an altruistic lot. Lenders want to be repaid *with interest*. As interest and principal accumulate, chronic net importers find themselves with huge foreign debts. Continued importing will be possible only if lenders continue to relend (in effect, not asking for repayment).

---

[4]The Common Market is composed of the following European countries: Belgium, Denmark, France, Germany, Greece, Ireland, Italy, Luxembourg, the Netherlands, Portugal, Spain, and the United Kingdom. The goal of this organization is eventual economic integration between member nations. By 1992, they would have common tariffs, free movement of capital and labor, and so on between member nations.

The foreign debt crisis of the 1980s reflected the fact that accumulated lending to some countries has reached the point where the ability of some borrowers to repay is in doubt. It appears that some debtor nations will no longer be able to finance net imports. This, of course, has important implications for the continued expansion of international trade. With no more loans there are no more imports for debtor nations and no more exports for creditor nations. Additionally, bank losses due to defaults on previous loans to chronic importers may jeopardize the ability of these same banks to provide loans to even the most creditworthy foreign customers. The international debt crisis is in reality a crisis of international trade with important economic and political implications.[5]

Of course, this is not the scenario that was envisioned by those who advocated more international trade and economic integration. In this context, international borrowing was viewed as a temporary phenomenon. A few years of net importing were expected to be followed by a period during which exports would exceed imports. In the ideal case, the net exports would be used to repay previous loans. It was anticipated that in the long run, imports would be equal to exports and financial crises would thus be avoided.

What has gone wrong? There are a number of contributing factors. Some countries have come to view the ability to import more than is exported as a "free lunch." Many governments have adopted the politically popular position of embarking on ambitious economic development or military adventures without reducing domestic consumption. Citizens have been led to believe, and often have come to expect, that ambitious programs can be achieved without domestic sacrifice. While such a scenario is theoretically possible, it rarely exists in the real world.

Interestingly, some governments have been extremely willing to export more than they import. Both Germany and Japan have pursued policies that have led to tremendous trade surpluses. Their willingness to pursue such policies reflects a desire to maintain high domestic employment and to avoid the political problems associated with fluctuations in economic activity. In effect, the high export levels in Germany and Japan have resulted in low unemployment rates. Workers are employed to meet the consumption needs of foreigners. If countries like Germany and Japan suddenly exported less, there is a substantial probability that domestic unemployment would increase and that the governments of these countries would face political problems. It should also be noted that these countries have maintained greater economic stability during the postwar period.

The American political climate of the 1980s was such that a substantial portion of the population and its representatives no longer want to

---

[5]See Chapter 12 for a more detailed discussion of the impact of the debt crisis on the American banking system.

serve as the market of last resort. Some Americans argue that the United States has been exporting jobs and assuming a huge foreign debt that will have to be repaid by future generations. The United States has been particularly critical of the Japanese. From the American perspective, Japanese policies that generate high employment in the Japanese automobile industry are viewed as causing unemployment (and political problems) in the United States and other industrial countries. The situation has reached the point where even though the Japanese may be willing to remain net exporters, the United States is no longer willing to be a net importer. Americans are recognizing that the price of the free lunch has been industry dislocation, relatively high unemployment, increased debts to foreigners, and depressed agriculture. These costs are being weighed against the fact that the Japanese policy has greatly benefited the American consumer by providing high-quality goods at relatively low prices.

The economic and political benefits associated with international trade and economic integration are being threatened by the pursuit of national self-interest. The capitalist nations are searching for a solution to this dilemma. Is it possible to solve the long-term import–export problem and at the same time avoid economic and political isolation? Is it possible to avoid another trade war in which tariffs and other trade barriers are used as retaliatory devices?[6] To many economists and government officials, the only viable solution lies in opening all national markets to all competitors. In this view, fluctuating exchange rates would play a major role in bringing imports and exports into long-term equilibrium. As such, fluctuating exchange rates are perceived as contributing to the attainment of important economic and political objectives. Before looking at how fluctuating exchange rates are supposed to work the wonders attributed to them, it is necessary to consider alternative solutions. Keep in mind that each of the systems under discussion is designed to solve the import–export problem.

A Simplified Barter System

One extreme solution to the import–export problem involves reverting to some type of international barter system. Imagine, for example, a situation in which American computers are exchanged for Brazilian coffee, with the amount of each being established through negotiations. With this arrangement, exports equal imports by definition. There is no need to finance differences in value, and there is no exchange rate problem.

---

[6]At the time of this writing, the U.S. Congress has passed a trade bill considered by some highly protectionist. President Reagan signed this legislation.

Actually, barter arrangements such as this one are being used today. They are particularly common in communist Eastern Europe. The Soviet Union, for example, agrees to ship a specific quantity of oil to Hungary in return for a specified quantity of television sets. Barter arrangements such as this exist throughout the Soviet bloc. A type of barter, often called *countertrade*, also exists in the West. In a typical countertrade arrangement, a firm in an industrialized country agrees to accept payment in terms of a product produced in a developing country. Presumably, the product accepted as payment is then sold by the firm in the industrialized country. In addition to this type of transaction, there are some government-to-government barter arrangements even in the noncommunist world. Note that these barter-type arrangements do not involve the use of currencies. Imports always equal exports.

The primary problem associated with the barter system is that it depresses the level of international trade. Except at the government level in planned economies, it is difficult to find buyers and sellers with reciprocal needs. The specialization in production that characterizes the modern world means that the typical pattern of exchange is very complicated. Imagine a situation in which the United States buys automobiles from Japan and sells computers to Italy. Italy, in turn, sells television sets to Egypt, which exports cotton to Japan. While it is conceivable that such an arrangement could be worked out through barter, it is highly unlikely. If barter were the rule of the day, international trade would be greatly reduced and the economic benefits of specialization would be significantly diminished. The political benefits associated with free trade would also be foregone. Reverting to barter is a little like throwing out the baby with the bath water. A better solution must be found.

A Simplified Gold Standard

One sometimes hears that a return to the gold standard will solve the import–export problem. In the paragraphs that follow, we will show how a simplified gold standard would indeed foster the desired solution. However, note the strong assumptions about the characteristics of the gold standard, and imagine the political implications associated with these assumptions. Such a simplified gold standard has never existed in the modern world and is not likely to exist in the foreseeable future. The only reason for examining this standard is that such a study provides insight into how fluctuating exchange rate systems can bring about a balance between imports and exports.

In our simplified gold standard, we will assume that gold (or a currency fully backed by gold and freely convertible into gold) is the only form of money in use throughout the world. In addition, we will make the usual perfect-market assumptions such as flexible factor prices, no restrictions on imports or exports, no transportation costs, and no product differentiation. The reader must also keep in mind the important relationship between money (gold) and price levels. Generally, increasing the supply of gold would increase the money supply, which would lead to increases in the general price level and vice versa.

Let us see how a net importing nation would be forced into a position in which imports equal exports. In order to make our illustration easier to understand, we will assume that there are only two countries in the world. The United States is the net importer, and Japan is the net exporter.

1. As the United States imports more than is exported and payment is made in gold, gold is shipped from the United States to Japan.
2. The shipment of gold to Japan reduces the money supply in the United States and leads to a general price decline (deflation). Japan has an increase in its money supply, and its prices increase (inflation).
3. To the American buyer, prices are now lower in the United States and higher in Japan. This will discourage Americans from importing.
4. To the Japanese buyer, prices are now higher in Japan and lower in United States. This will encourage the Japanese to import.
5. A new equilibrium position will be established when imports equal exports for both countries. This is a self-correcting system.

Prices play the crucial role in bringing about equality between imports and exports in our simplified gold standard. Japan experiences a rise in the prices of all goods and services (inflation caused by the increase in its money supply), and prices fall in the United States (deflation caused by the decrease in its money supply).

Most governments are unwilling to allow the general price level to be dictated by international trade considerations. The general feeling is that the money supply should be managed in such a way that domestic economic goals become achievable. In the United States, for example, the Federal Reserve System seeks high economic growth, low unemployment, and price stability. The Federal Reserve is expected to accomplish these objectives by managing the money supply. International trade (more specifically, balance of payments problems) are considered to be of secondary importance.

To put it succinctly, since almost no government is willing to let the domestic price level be dictated by international trade considerations, our simplified gold standard cannot work. Any of the actual gold standards that were used over the centuries ultimately faced the same problem. The reluctance of nations to relinquish control over their money supply makes it impossible for the gold standard to solve the important import–export problem. Another solution is needed.[7]

A Simplified Fluctuating Exchange Rate System

Fluctuating exchange rates offer an alternative mechanism for solving the import–export problem. The attractiveness of such a system reflects the facts that it neither restricts the level of international trade (as does the barter system) nor requires nations to give up control over monetary policy (as does the gold standard).

The simplified fluctuating exchange rate system outlined here assumes that currencies are freely traded, with no government or central bank interference. The relative supply of and demand for various currencies determine the rate at which these currencies are exchanged. For simplicity, we will assume that there is no planned international lending. Let us see how a chronic net importing nation would be forced into a position in which imports equal exports. We will continue to assume that the United States is the net importing country and Japan is the net exporting country.

1. When the United States imports more than it exports, Japan winds up holding additional dollars. By definition, these dollars are not used to purchase products from the United States. By assumption, they will not be lent back to the United States.
2. The only thing that the Japanese can do with the dollars is to convert them to yen. Presumably, this allows the Japanese to purchase goods and services in Japan. Alternatively, the yen could be deposited in Japanese bank accounts or otherwise invested in Japan.
3. As the excess dollars are converted to yen, they eventually make their way from the commercial banking system to the central bank. Since, by definition, the central bank will not buy from or lend to the United States, it will try to unload the excess dollars. This will increase the supply of dollars in the foreign exchange market.
4. There is now an oversupply of dollars, and the rate of exchange between the dollar and the yen will decline. More dollars will be needed to purchase a given amount of yen. Looked at from the other

---

[7]There are some political considerations that make the return to a gold standard even less likely. The Soviet Union and South Africa are the most important gold producers in the world. The United States and other major industrialized countries may not want to give these two countries such control over the international monetary system.

point of view, fewer yen are needed to purchase a dollar. The dollar weakens, and the yen strengthens.

5. Since the dollar can be purchased for fewer yen, products produced in the United States are less expensive for Japanese buyers and should lead to an increase in exports from the United States to Japan.

6. At the same time, United States buyers must give up more dollars to acquire a given amount of yen.[8] This makes Japanese goods more expensive and discourages American imports from Japan.

7. The forces of supply and demand will force the exchange rates to fluctuate until imports and exports are in equilibrium.

This simplified fluctuating exchange rate system uses a price mechanism to bring about import–export equilibrium. However, the price mechanism works quite differently than under the gold standard. Unlike the gold standard, domestic prices do not necessarily change. Prices are higher (or lower) only for buyers who wish to pay in foreign currency. There is no reason for a country to force itself into inflation or deflation in order to bring about a new equilibrium between imports and exports. International trade considerations do not dictate national monetary policies. A fluctuating exchange rate system leads to the same result as the gold standard, and it causes fewer complications.

Thus far, we have assumed that no international investing takes place. It should be clear, however, that international investing can offset the disequilibria between exports and imports. For example, a net importing nation may be able to borrow the "overhang" of its currency. In our illustration, for example, Americans could have borrowed the extra dollars from the Japanese. This would have removed the pressure on the dollar and may have prevented its fall in price. Under this scenario, Japan would be investing in the United States, presumably in anticipation of receiving interest and principal at a later date. International investing of this type has been a very important factor with respect to exchange rate fluctuations. For example, America's huge current account deficits in the early and middle 1980s were largely offset by foreign investments in the United States. International investing does not solve the import–export problem; it just postpones the ultimate solution. As long as the initial exchange rate is maintained, the net importing nation continues to import more than is exported. It will only be a question of time before the repayment of the debt becomes a problem. Eventually, the exchange rate must change, and imports and exports must adjust to economic reality.

Why do exchange rates fluctuate? Why does the value of the dollar go up and down? Because the international arrangement for resolving

---

[8]It is simplistic to assume that a 30 percent increase in the value of the yen will result in a 30 percent increase in the cost of Japanese products to American consumers. Japanese firms will also experience a reduction of their raw material costs if they are imported. In addition, Japanese firms may be willing to reduce their profit margin in order to maintain market share.

the disequilibria between imports and exports has features that resemble the simplified fluctuating exchange rate system previously described. As noted earlier, some nations are chronic importers and others are chronic exporters. The solutions suggested by barter arrangements and gold standards have been rejected by the international political community. During the post–World War II period, reliance has been placed on a combination of exchange rate movements and domestic economic policy. Over time, the recognition that few nations were capable of instituting the politically unpopular domestic policies that would be needed to solve payments disequilibria has resulted in an increased reliance on fluctuating exchange rates. By the late 1980s, however, a backlash against fluctuating exchange rates had become apparent. At present, the international community is seeking a better way to solve the export–import problem. The prospects for the future can be better evaluated by an increased understanding of the recent past.

Fixed Exchange Rates:
Bretton Woods — 1944 to 1971

In 1944, near the end of World War II, the Western Allies met at Bretton Woods, New Hampshire, to plan the postwar international financial system. The task facing the planners was substantial. The physical and human resources of most of the countries at the meeting had been severely diminished. World recovery was perceived as requiring a coordinated effort and a stable international financial system. If recovery was to be achieved within a reasonable time frame, some countries would need extensive and continuing net imports. Of course, this required that other countries assume the role of continuous net exporter. The consensus at the time was that this increased level of international trade could better be accommodated by minimizing fluctuations in exchange rates (reducing exchange rate risk). Accordingly, the system that emerged from the Bretton Woods Conference has come to be known as the *fixed exchange rate system*. Under the Bretton Woods formula, fluctuating exchange rates were assigned a backup role. Other methods of bringing export and imports into equilibrium were to be tried first.

The view that prevailed at the Bretton Woods Conference seems to have been that the disequilibria between imports and exports during the postwar period would be at least partially offset by long-term financial flows. International investing, loans from foreign governments, and international aid would permit some countries to import more than they exported. In addition, the participants at Bretton Woods agreed to contribute to a fund that would be used to lend foreign currency to those nations experiencing short-term difficulties in meeting foreign currency bills. In simple terms, a country that imported more than it exported would be able to pay for the difference by borrowing from a fund created by contributions from all of the nations involved.

It is necessary to keep in mind that the situation in 1944 was very unusual. World War II was coming to an end, and the victors were planning for a prosperous postwar world. The participants at Bretton Woods were concerned about the difficulty of rebuilding the economies of Europe and avoiding another Great Depression. Most particularly, the trade wars that appeared during the 1930s were to be avoided. Tariffs, quotas, and other barriers to free trade were to be minimized. Balance of payments disequilibria that could not be offset by borrowing from the International Monetary Fund and/or foreign investments were to be addressed directly by the nations with the balance of payments problems. Specifically, national governments were expected to act forcefully to control the domestic inflation and budget deficits that are often associated with excessive imports. While such policies would be politically unpopular today, the wartime perspective was quite different. The establishment of a world financial system that required national discipline seemed to be a much nicer alternative than the possibility of another war. Free trade and stable exchange rates were part of the international peace plan. Somehow, over the years, this relationship has been forgotten.

The fixed exchange rate system was organized around the American dollar. The United States government set the price of gold at $35 per ounce and guaranteed that foreign governments could convert dollars to gold at that rate. Official exchange rates were set when other countries established a price of gold in terms of their currencies. The price of an ounce of gold in Germany, for example, could be set at 140 marks. Thus, 140 marks would be equal to $35. The exchange rate would then be four marks per dollar. Note that only the United States was required to redeem its currency in gold. Thus, the American dollar (as the equivalent of gold) became the key currency.

While gold played an important role under the Bretton Woods system, what emerged was a far cry from the simplified gold standard discussed earlier. Most importantly, national governments retained authority over monetary policy. There was no automatic inflating and deflating of national economies as a result of disequilibria in international payments. Nor did the Bretton Woods system resemble the simplified fluctuating exchange rate system presented earlier. In fact, the participants in the system committed themselves to the pursuit of policies that would prevent exchange rates from varying by more than plus or minus 1 percent. In unusual circumstances, a country could devalue or revalue its currency by up to 10 percent without the approval of other nations. Such a change would be executed by an official action changing the price of gold in terms of the particular currency in question. However, it was assumed that changes of such magnitude would be infrequent. Changes in exchange rates exceeding 10 percent required prior international approval. Thus, under the Bretton Woods system, exchange rates could fluctuate but such changes tended to be infrequent. When a change did take place, it was usually a last resort and was often of considerable magnitude. For example, one day a foreign currency might be worth as much as 50 percent less than it was on the previous day. The devaluation would have been the result of a government action (the possibility of which would have been denied up to the last minute). This was quite different from the daily fluctuations in the dollar exchange rates that we see today. The important thing to remember is that exchange rates did change under the so-called fixed exchange rate system.

The Bretton Woods Conference laid the groundwork for the formation of the International Monetary Fund (IMF), which played a central role during the period prior to 1971 and still continues to be an important component of the international financial system. The IMF collected contributions from its members, with each member contributing in proportion to its expected involvement in postwar international trade. Nations contributed their own currency to the fund but could withdraw an equivalent amount in any currency (including the dollar) if such currency was needed to meet temporary payments problems (caused by seasonal, cyclical, and random movements, but not structural problems). Interestingly, countries were given access to these hard currencies in amounts greater than their contribution. In the early days of the IMF, a nation could borrow up to 125 percent of its initial contribution. The idea was that these funds could be used to offset short-term payment imbalances. It was recognized from the outset that the IMF solution to the problem of exchange rate volatility was temporary. Fundamental payment problems would require more drastic (and less popular) action at the national level.

Looking back at the international financial system in place during the immediate postwar period, one is struck by the fact that it was quite successful. Europe was rebuilt, former enemies became economic partners, and major depressions and trade wars were avoided. As the horror of the war and the urgent need for reconstruction faded from memory, the cooperative atmosphere of the 1940s began to diminish. Nations became less willing to alter domestic programs in order to make the "fixed rate" system function. While defections of smaller countries from the "proper" domestic economic policy could be tolerated, the failure of larger countries such as France, the United Kingdom, and the United States to maintain domestic policies under which exchange rates could be stabilized doomed the system. The U.S. involvement in Vietnam during the 1960s, which was financed by government deficits and inflation, led to soaring imports and great downward pressure on the dollar.[9] This pressure, coupled with the Johnson and Nixon administrations' unwill-

---

[9]The impact of balance of payments on the value of a currency will be discussed in Chapter 4.

ingness to alter domestic policies, finished off what was an already ailing system.

A Mixed Exchange
Rate System — 1971 to the Present

The formal demise of the fixed rate system came during the 1971–1972 period. In August 1971, President Richard Nixon suspended official purchases of gold by the U.S. Treasury. The worth of a dollar was no longer measured in terms of a specific amount of gold, but rather in terms of how much a dollar would likely buy in the marketplace. Many foreign currencies were allowed to float against the dollar, and by the end of 1971 the dollar was de facto devalued.

In the period from 1971 to 1976, governments searched for a way to salvage some of the features of the system that had prevailed under the Bretton Woods Agreement. The fluctuating exchange rates that characterized this period were viewed as necessary until a new fixed rate system could be implemented. At that point, most governments still believed that a revitalized fixed rate system coupled with better international cooperation would be more conducive to the maintenance of world economic and political harmony. It was not until the IMF conference held in January 1976 that fluctuating exchange rates were accepted as a more or less permanent method of solving international payments problems.

It is important for the manager involved in international commerce to appreciate that the floating rate is a relatively new system. Businesses have limited experience with this system. It is also obvious that floating rates were accepted as a last resort and with reservations. As you will see, there is still considerable willingness for a return to the fixed rate system.

Unlike the Bretton Woods period, when almost every nation was part of a system featuring fixed exchange rates, the situation today is more diverse. As illustrated in Table 3-2, different countries are committed to different exchange rate management policies.

Most currencies are still fixed, or *pegged*. That is, the governments of these countries pursue essentially the same policies they would have pursued under the Bretton Woods arrangements. The big difference between then and now is that the currencies are no longer pegged to gold. The U.S. dollar, the French franc, and the SDR are frequently used as the peg to which the currency is tied.[10] Most of the countries using

---

[10]The special drawing right (SDR) is a unit of account developed by the IMF. Its value is based on a portfolio of widely held currencies. At the present time, the SDR is composed of U.S. dollars (42 percent), the German deutsche mark (19 percent), the Japanese yen (15 percent), the French franc (12 percent), and the British pound (12 percent). Currencies pegged to the SDR are essentially fixed relative to a group of currencies rather than to a single currency.

TABLE 3-2 Exchange Rate Arrangements (As of June 30, 1988)*

Currency Pegged to					Flexibility Limited in Terms of a Single Currency or Group of Currencies		More Flexible		
U.S. Dollar	French Franc	Other Currency	SDR	Other Composite†	Single Currency‡	Cooperative Arrangements§	Adjusted According to a Set of Indicators#	Other Managed Floating	Independently Floating
Afghanistan	Benin	Bhutan (Indian rupee)	Burma	Algeria	Bahrain	Belgium	Brazil	Argentina	Australia
Antigua and Barbuda	Burkina Faso		Burundi	Austria	Qatar	Denmark	Chile	China, P.R.	Bolivia
Bahamas, The	Cameroon	Kiribati (Australian dollar)	Iran, I.R. of	Bangladesh	Saudi Arabia	France	Colombia	Costa Rica	Canada
Barbados	C. African Rep.		Jordan	Botswana	United Arab Emirates	Germany	Madagascar	Dominican Rep.	Gambia, The
Belize	Chad		Libya	Cape Verde		Ireland	Portugal	Egypt	Ghana
Djibouti	Comoros	Lesotho (South African rand)	Rwanda	Cyprus		Italy		Greece	Guinea
Dominica	Congo		Seychelles	Fiji		Luxembourg		Guinea-Bissau	Japan
Ecuador	Côte d'Ivoire			Finland		Netherlands		India	Lebanon
El Salvador	Equatorial Guinea	Swaziland (South African rand)		Hungary				Indonesia	Maldives
Ethiopia	Gabon			Iceland				Jamaica	New Zealand
Grenada	Mali			Israel				Korea	Nigeria
Guatemala	Niger	Tonga (Australian dollar)		Kenya				Mauritania	Philippines
Guyana	Senegal			Kuwait				Mexico	South Africa
Haiti	Togo			Malawi				Morocco	Spain
Honduras				Malaysia				Pakistan	United Kingdom
Iraq				Malta				Singapore	United States
Lao P.D. Rep.				Mauritius				Sri Lanka	Uruguay
Liberia				Nepal				Tunisia	Zaire
Mozambique				Norway				Turkey	
Nicaragua				Papua New Guinea				Yugoslavia	

Oman
Panama
Paraguay
Peru
St. Kitts and Nevis

St. Lucia
St. Vincent
Sierra Leone
Sudan
Suriname

Syrian Arab Rep.
Trinidad and
  Tobago
Uganda
Venezuela
Vietnam

Yemen Arab Rep.
Yemen, P.D. Rep.
Zambia

Poland
Romania
Sao Tome and Principe

Solomon Islands
Somalia

Sweden
Tanzania
Thailand
Vanuatu
Western Samoa

Zimbabwe

*Excluding the currency of Democratic Kampuchea, for which no current information is available for members with dual or multiple exchange markets. The arrangement shown is that in the major market.

†Comprises currencies which are pegged to various "baskets" of currencies of the members own choice, as distinct from the SDR basket.

‡Exchange rates of all currencies have shown limited flexibility in terms of the U.S. dollar.

§Refers to the cooperative arrangement maintained under the European Monetary System.

#Includes exchange arrangements under which the exchange rate is adjusted at relatively frequent intervals, on the basis of indicators determined by the respective member countries.

Source: International Monetary Fund, *International Financial Statistics,* September, 1988, p. 20.

this approach are categorized as developing or Third World countries; however, several Eastern European countries are also listed. These countries are not powerful economically, although several have great potential. These countries, both individually and as a group, are relatively small participants in international trade. Apparently, they perceive it to be in their best interest to encourage buyers, sellers, lenders, and investors to view a specific amount of their currency in terms of a number of units of a better-known currency. As shown in Table 3-2, the currencies of El Salvador, Venezuela, and other nations are pegged to the U.S. dollar. On the other hand, Jordan's currency is pegged to the SDR.

The "limited flexibility" countries in Table 3-2 are divided into two groups, both of which are very important. The first group encompasses some of the most important oil-producing countries, including Saudi Arabia, the most important oil supplier in the world. The currencies of this group, while not officially pegged to the U.S. dollar, tend to change in the same way as the dollar. This partly reflects conscious national policies, as well as the fact that the world price of oil tends to be expressed in terms of dollars.

Also included in the "limited flexibility" group are those countries that belong to the European Monetary System (EMS). The EMS is a subgroup of the European Economic Community (EEC or Common Market), with some Common Market countries (Greece, Portugal, Spain, and the United Kingdom) unwilling or unable to participate at the present time. The members of the EMS believe that economic integration and political cooperation can best be maintained by reducing the fluctuations in exchange rates among member countries. The essence of the EMS is that exchange rates among the EMS countries are fixed. However, as a group, the currencies fluctuate against outside currencies.

Exchange rates for EMS currencies are permitted to fluctuate against each other, but the range of fluctuation is strictly limited. At present, exchange rates are permitted to fluctuate by no more than $2\frac{1}{4}$ percent (6 percent for the Italian lire). When exchange rates vary by more than this percentage amount, both of the countries involved are required to take action in the foreign exchange markets (affecting the supply of and the demand for the currencies) in order to bring the currencies back to the exchange rate fixed by agreement.[11] For example, if the French franc were to depreciate by more than $2\frac{1}{4}$ percent against the deutsche mark, action by both the French and German governments would be required. The initial response would most likely be at the central bank level. The central banks in both countries would buy francs (increasing the demand for francs) in an attempt to keep the value of the franc high. If disequilibria continue to exist within the EMS, member countries are required to take domestic actions (reduce budget deficits, stimulate employment,

---

[11]The impact of supply and demand on the value of a currency is discussed in Chapter 4.

reduce inflation, etc.) that will solve the problem. The official target exchange rates are changed only through official EMS actions and are a last-resort solution to a payments problem.

The EMS has had some of the same problems that existed under the Bretton Woods Agreement. National governments are often unwilling or unable to take the domestic actions necessary to solve a payments problem. For example, Germany has been unwilling to inflate its economy, while other countries have been unwilling or unable to limit inflation. Thus, exchange rate adjustments have been necessary, although such adjustments have been relatively small. Compared to the Bretton Woods arrangement, the countries in the EMS have greater cultural, political, and economic homogeneity, as well as a shared political vision. This suggests that the EMS may succeed where the Bretton Woods system failed.

As noted earlier, the EMS currencies fluctuate against currencies not included in the system. Thus, for example, all the EMS currencies fluctuate against the dollar in the foreign exchange markets. If the deutsche mark weakens against the dollar, so does the French franc (although the size of the fluctuation may vary slightly). From an American perspective, it is convenient to look at the EMS currencies as fluctuating as a group against the dollar.

The "more flexible" category in Table 3-2 includes those currencies that more or less float against all other currencies. The so-called independently floating currencies include those of many of the most important trading countries, including Canada, Japan, the United Kingdom, and the United States. It is important to recognize that *independently* floating does not mean *freely* floating. What exists is something called a *dirty float*, which implies that central banks intervene in the foreign exchange market and attempt to affect exchange rates by influencing the supply of and the demand for currencies. Such exchange rate market intervention is sometimes undertaken by a single central bank, but quite frequently the central banks of a number of countries coordinate an effort to alter exchange rates. For example, in 1984, treasury and central bank officials from the major trading nations met a number of times and agreed to drive down the value of what was perceived to be an overvalued dollar. This is one of the factors that contributed to a remarkable decline in the value of the dollar over the 1985–1987 period.

The dramatic fall in the dollar (and those currencies pegged to the dollar) substantially changed import–export prices and caused great concerns in many countries, including Japan and Germany. The steady rise in the value of the dollar in the early 1980s and its subsequent rapid fall led many economic and political leaders once again to question the desirability of a fluctuating exchange rate system that permitted such large fluctuations in currency values. Businessmen, bankers, and governments began to call for a new international financial system under which exchange rates would be more fixed than freely fluctuating. By and large, the current system was perceived as the cause of major political and economic problems. For some, the costs associated with fluctuating exchange rates seemed to outweigh their benefits.

What followed were a number of monetary "summit meetings" at which those responsible for executing policy in the various countries agreed to try to stabilize the exchange rates. Target zones were mentioned and coordinated efforts pledged. At the time of this writing (1988), it seems doubtful that such policies will succeed in stabilizing exchange rates because no international political consensus exists. Governments do not seem willing to commit themselves to international cooperation when such cooperation may have unfavorable domestic political consequences. Whether or not currencies will continue to fluctuate independently in the future remains to be seen. It is important for the reader to keep in mind that the current exchange rate system is on trial and that the exchange rate system of the future may be quite different from the one existing at the present time.

Summary of the Present International Monetary System

As is now obvious, the fluctuation in the value of the dollar in the foreign exchange markets is much more complicated than is suggested by the label *floating exchange rate*. The following list summarizes the relationships between the dollar and other currencies.

1. The dollar is fixed relative to some currencies. This means that official government action is required to alter the exchange rate. Changes in the exchange rates for this group of countries against the key currency are likely to be infrequent. However, when changes do take place, they are likely to be of considerable magnitude. Included in this category are those currencies pegged to the U.S. dollar, as well as to the French franc and the SDR.
2. The important oil-exporting countries, such as Saudi Arabia, have currencies that have exhibited relatively little variation against the dollar. They behave almost as if they were pegged to the dollar.
3. The currencies of the EMS countries fluctuate more or less as a bloc against the dollar. The dollar does not float independently against individual currencies in this group.
4. The dollar indeed floats against most of the other currencies in the world. It would be a mistake, however, to conclude that all movements in dollar exchange rates reflect changes in the underlying international payments situation in the United States compared to

other countries. The float is not clean. Individual countries or groups of countries get together and try to affect the dollar exchange rate.

It is also important for the student and businessperson to keep in mind that the publication of official or even market exchange rates does not say anything about the convertibility of a currency. While the dollar can be converted to almost all currencies, it is not uncommon to find that foreign currencies cannot be converted to dollars. For example, for many years the Egyptian pound was pegged to the U.S. dollar, but conversion of pounds to dollars was possible in only a limited set of circumstances. The fact that a currency is pegged to another currency does not mean that it can be converted to that currency. Many of the currencies in the "more flexible" category also have limited convertibility. In addition, the pegged rate is often unrealistic in terms of market forces. For example, the black market price of an Egyptian pound was often one-half of the official price that was established by pegging the pound to the U.S. dollar.

Summary and Conclusions

This chapter has focused on the historical development of foreign exchange systems. We have shown that the international monetary system has experienced remarkable changes in the last 50 years and that these changes represent attempts to solve the import–export equality dilemma *without* incurring unacceptable political costs. All systems, whether barter, gold standard, fixed rates, or fluctuating rate, attempt to devise a mechanism to eventually establish a rough equality between exports and imports. The problem is that all such systems have costs such as lower employment, price fluctuations, interest rates changes, or high volatility in exchange rates.

Projecting the future is fraught with dangers. Dissatisfaction with the current exchange rate system is high, and we can be certain that the international monetary system will be changed in order to accommodate changes in the political environment. The current desire is to provide greater stability in exchange rates. The problem is that countries are not willing to subordinate national goals in order to achieve this objective.

Review Questions

1. Explain how a balance between imports and exports would be restored under an international barter system.
2. Explain how a balance between imports and exports would be restored under a gold standard.
3. Explain how a balance between imports and exports would be restored under a fluctuating exchange rate system.

4. Discuss the basic political difficulties associated with the use of a gold standard.
5. Why did the Bretton Woods exchange rate arrangement collapse?
6. Describe the current exchange rate system.
7. Explain how exchange rates are determined within the European monetary system (EMS).

Questions for Discussion

1. Assume that you are a member of the management team of a large American corporation that exports 25 percent of its output. Also assume that the U.S. government is unable to reduce its balance of payments deficit, and a bill is introduced in Congress that would require all future foreign trade transactions to be conducted on a barter basis. What position would you take on this bill? How would you support that position?
2. Assume that you are employed by a firm that is just getting involved in international trade. Top management is afraid to commit the firm too strongly to an international strategy because it has observed that exchange rates fluctuate widely. In its attempt to understand the magnitude of the risks involved in international trade, top management has looked at exchange rates and found some surprising things. For example, the dollar hardly fluctuates against some currencies, and it appears to have a uniform rate of fluctuation against many others. These findings seem inconsistent with the generally held belief that the dollar fluctuates freely. In order to resolve this misunderstanding, top management asks you to make a presentation that will explain these phenomena.

Research Activities

1. Under a fluctuating exchange rate system, trade deficits should be associated with declining currency values. (Assume that other factors are held constant. These other factors will be discussed more fully in the next chapter.) Look at the trade deficit of the United States in recent years and match it with exchange rate movements over the period of time investigated.

Bibliography

Abrams, Richard K. "International Trade Flows Under Flexible Exchange Rates." *Economic Review*, March 1980, pp. 3–10.

Agmon, Tamir, Hawkins, Robert G., and Levich, Richard M., eds. *The Future of the International Monetary System*. Lexington, MA: Lexington Books. 1984.

Batten, Dallas S., and Ott, Mack. "What Can Central Banks Do About the Value of the Dollar?" *Federal Reserve Bank of St. Louis Review*, May 1984, pp. 16–26.

Bordo, Michael D. "The Classical Gold Standard: Some Lessons for Today." *Federal Reserve Bank of St. Louis Review*. May 1981, pp. 2–17.

Brenner, M. J. *The Politics of International Monetary Reform*. Cambridge, MA: Ballinger, 1976.

Coes, Donald V. "The Crawling Peg and Exchange Rate Uncertainty." In John Williamson, ed., *Exchange Rate Rules*. New York: St. Martin's Press, 1981.

Deppler, Michael C., and Ripley, Duncan M. "The World Trade Model: Merchandise Trade." *IMF Staff Papers*, March 1978, pp. 147–206.

Fleming, J. Marcus. "Floating Exchange Rates, Asymmetrical Intervention, and the Management of International Liquidity." *IMF Staff Papers*, July 1975, pp. 263–283.

Frenkel, Jacob A., and Johnson, Harry G., eds. *The Economics of Exchange Rates*. Reading, MA: Addison-Wesley Publishing Company, 1978.

Friedman, Milton, and Roosa, Robert V. "Free versus Fixed Exchange Rates: A Debate." *Journal of Portfolio Management*, Spring 1977, pp. 68–73.

Lindert, Peter H. *International Economics*, 8th ed. Homewood, IL: Irwin Publications, 1986.

Lomax, David F. "Prospects for the European Monetary System." *National Westminster Bank Quarterly Review*, May 1983, pp. 33–50.

Machlup, Fritz. *International Monetary Systems*. Morristown, NJ: General Learning Press, 1975.

Makin, John H. "Fixed versus Floating: A Red Herring." *Columbia Journal of World Business*, Winter 1979, pp. 7–14.

Pringle, R. "Shape of Currency Crisis in the 1980's." *Banker*, February 1981, pp. 29–33.

Scammel, W. M. *International Monetary Policy: Bretton Woods and After*. New York: John Wiley & Sons, 1975.

Shafer, Jeffrey R., and Loopesko, Bonnie E. "Floating Exchange Rates After Ten Years." *Brookings Papers on Economic Activity*. Washington, DC: The Brookings Institution, 1983.

Taylor, Dean. "Official Intervention in the Foreign Exchange Market, or Bet Against the Central Bank." *Journal of Political Economy*, April 1982, pp. 356–368.

Ungerer, Horst, Evans, Owen, Meyer, Thomas, and Young, Philip. *The European Monetary System: Recent Developments*. Washington, DC: The International Monetary Fund, 1986.

Yarbrough, Beth V., and Yarbrough, Robert M. *The World Economy: Trade and Finance*. Chicago: Dryden Press, 1988.

Zis, George. "Exchange Rate Fluctuations: 1973–82." *National Westminster Bank Quarterly Review*, August 1983, pp. 2–13.

4

Factors Affecting Exchange Rates

Why do foreign exchange rates fluctuate? Can the risk and uncertainty associated with exchange rate movements be eliminated by permanently fixing the rate of exchange between two currencies? If exchange rates cannot be fixed, is it possible to forecast future rates, thus eliminating uncertainty? Are there any indicators of the direction of change in exchange rates? These are the issues addressed in this and the next chapter. This chapter is designed to help managers engaged in international commerce develop answers to these important questions. The next chapter will discuss forecasting foreign exchange rates.

The Supply of and Demand for Currencies

It would be very useful for those involved in international commerce to be able to predict exchange rate movements. For example, an American firm selling to a British buyer and agreeing to accept a future payment in

British pounds is at risk. If the pound declines in value between the date of agreement and the date on which it is delivered, the American firm will receive fewer dollars than had been anticipated. A firm with the ability to forecast such an exchange rate movement would be able to either avoid the risk by refusing to sell or, more likely, charge a higher price in British pounds for the item being sold. Indeed, the ability to forecast exchange rates accurately would eliminate one of the great risks involved in international commerce. Is it possible to forecast floating exchange rates? It turns out that there is no simple answer to this question.

Ultimately, the value of every currency must reflect economic reality. The concepts of supply and demand help us to better understand the nature of this economic reality. The supply of a currency reflects the extent to which the currency is used to make foreign purchases or investments. For example, Americans contribute to the supply of dollars in foreign exchange markets by purchasing foreign goods or investing in foreign countries. The demand for the dollar reflects the extent to which foreigners purchase American goods or invest in the United States. By and large, it is the interaction of these supply and demand factors that determines the exchange rate for the dollar.

Figure 4-1 shows the supply–demand schedule of the British pound compared to the dollar. The price of the pound in terms of dollars (the

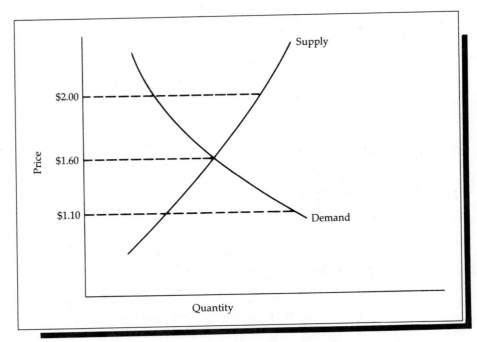

FIGURE 4-1 Supply-Demand Schedule of the British Pound

exchange rate expressed as a direct quote) is on the vertical axis. The number of pounds that will be offered for exchange at various prices (exchange rates) is on the horizontal axis. Notice that when the price of the pound (exchange rate) is high (e.g., £1 = $2.00), the quantity of pounds offered for sale (supply) exceeds the quantity that buyers are willing to buy (demand). Stated in supply–demand terminology, the amount supplied exceeds the amount demanded. Stated in commonsense terms, when holders of pounds can receive $2 for each pound, many pounds will be offered for exchange. The strong pound means that holders of pounds can purchase American goods and services at relatively low pound prices. In addition, the relatively large number of dollars that can be received for pounds means that investments in the United States appear to be inexpensive. Thus, at high prices for the pound, a relatively large number of pounds will be offered for exchange.

At a low price–exchange rate (e.g., £1 = $1.10), the quantity that buyers are willing to buy exceeds the quantity offered for sale. This indicates that the amount demanded exceeds the amount supplied at that price. Holders of pounds receive relatively few dollars for each pound. This makes American goods, services, and investment opportunities seem relatively expensive to holders of British pounds.

Neither the price of £1 = $1.10 nor the price of £1 = $2.00 is an equilibrium price. This means that the price–exchange rate of the pound will tend to move from those levels. At the lower price ($1.10), there will be a great demand for the few pounds offered for sale, which will tend to drive up the price of the pound. At the higher price ($2.00), there are not enough buyers for all of the pounds being offered for exchange, and the price of the pound will fall. Equilibrium will exist only if the quantity demanded exactly equals the quantity supplied. In our hypothetical example, this takes place only when the price–exchange rate of the British pound is $1.60. This is the price that will persist until outside forces generate changes in the supply and/or demand schedules for the pound.

Impact of Changes
in Supply or Demand

Changes in the supply and demand curves (schedules) for a currency will lead to changes in the price–exchange rate for that currency. The left-hand portion of Figure 4-2 shows what happens to the exchange rate if there is less demand for the pound at each price level. As can be seen, the demand curve shifts downward and the new equilibrium price declines from $1.60 to $1.20. On the other hand, an increase in the demand for pounds shifts the demand curve to the right and leads to a new, higher

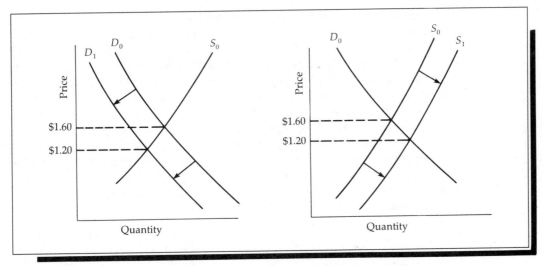

FIGURE 4-2   Changes in the Supply-Demand Schedule of the British Pound

equilibrium price. The tentative conclusion that must be drawn from this analysis is that shifts in demand will lead to changes in the equilibrium price–exchange rate of a currency.

A change in the supply curve will have a corresponding effect on the equilibrium exchange rate. As shown in the right-hand portion of Figure 4-2, the supply curve for the pound has shifted to the right. This means that more pounds are now being offered for exchange at each price–exchange rate. As can be seen, the supply curve's shift to the right leads to a fall in the equilibrium price from $1.60 to $1.20. That is, the price of the pound should fall. On the other hand, if there had been a reduction in the number of pounds offered for exchange at each price–exchange rate (a shift to the left in the supply curve), the equilibrium price would have been at a higher level.

We are now in a position to recognize that shifts in either the supply or demand schedule of the pound will lead to changes in the equilibrium exchange rate. In addition, changes in equilibrium exchange rates must be related to either a change in demand or a change in supply. In order to understand why exchange rates fluctuate, we must understand the economic and political factors that lead to changes in supply and demand. In order to forecast exchange rates, we must be able to forecast the factors that lead to changes in the supply of and demand for currencies.

In the sections that follow, we will describe and evaluate four factors that affect exchange rates: (1) balance of payments, (2) relative inflation rates, (3) relative interest rates, and (4) political stability. Keep in mind that these approaches represent different ways of explaining why supply and demand change. They represent attempts to implement the supply and demand analysis presented in this section.

Figures 4-1 and 4-2 also highlight an important point that is very easy to overlook. Exchange rate movements depend on developments in both countries. We cannot explain fluctuations in the dollar price of the pound in terms of developments in the United States alone. The supply of pounds is largely in the hands of British policy makers and reflects economic conditions in Britain. As such, the dollar exchange rate could fluctuate markedly, regardless of American conditions. We must avoid the temptation to look to the United States for all explanations of dollar exchange rate movements. The ability to explain and forecast exchange rate movements requires a high degree of international economic and political understanding.

Balance of Payments and Exchange Rate Movements

National governments have maintained records of international transactions for many centuries. Over time, the accuracy and completeness of these records have improved to the point where it is now possible to get a good measure of such things as purchases from foreign countries, sales to foreign countries, investment flows, and other payments to and from foreign countries. While the records are not complete, an analyst can get a good indication of how much a country is spending abroad and how much foreigners are spending at home. This relative spending information is compiled and published as what is called the *balance of payments*. The balance of payments data provide the basis for estimating the supply of and demand for particular currencies. As noted earlier, changes in either supply or demand should be reflected in exchange rate movements.

Balance of payments (relative spending) data for many nations are compiled by the IMF and published monthly in *International Financial Statistics*.[1] A sample of the IMF balance of payments data for the United States, Mexico, and West Germany is presented in the appendixes to this chapter.

---

[1]The IMF obtains these data from many sources. A more complete analysis would require going to the original sources. For example, the Department of Commerce or the Federal Reserve System provides more complete information for the United States.

In a technical sense, the U.S. balance of payments is a set of accounts that records transactions between U.S. residents and foreigners.[2] Any time an American resident buys a foreign product, travels abroad, or purchases a foreign asset, the balance of payments changes. Similarly, when an American resident sells products, provides services, or sells assets to foreigners, the balance of payments is affected. In other words, any transaction between an American and a foreigner should give rise to an entry in the U.S. balance of payments accounts.[3]

Balance of payments entries may be divided into two major categories: (1) autonomous and (2) accommodating. The autonomous category includes those transactions that are undertaken for a valid business or consumption purpose. Examples include purchases of foreign-made automobiles, the purchase of U.S. government bonds by individual foreigners, an American corporation increasing its checking account balances in a London bank, or foreign travel.

Accommodating transactions have two characteristics: (1) they must be undertaken by a government, and (2) their purpose must be to finance a deficit or surplus in the balance of payments. Note that not all international financial transactions conducted by governments are classified as accommodating. For example, American foreign aid is given for humanitarian or political reasons, not to help finance balance of payments deficits or surpluses. Some government transactions are difficult to classify. For example, it is difficult to determine whether an increase in the American bank deposits held by the Japanese government is an autonomous transaction or an accommodating transaction. In order to classify such government transactions properly, it is necessary to know the precise reasons for depositing the funds. If a deposit is designed to increase dollar liquidity in anticipation of purchases from U.S. suppliers, the transaction is autonomous. However, if the deposit is intended to maintain the value of the dollar artificially, it is an accommodating transaction.

Autonomous transactions are generally divided into three major categories: (1) the current account, (2) the capital account, and (3) short-term flows. The current account includes payments for all goods and services exchanged between one country and the rest of the world. This includes exports and imports of goods (e.g., autos, wheat) and services (e.g., insurance, travel), unilateral transfers (e.g., private gifts, foreign aid),

---

[2]In the context of balance of payments, the term *residents* includes individuals or firms domiciled in the United States. Thus, any business operating in the United States, regardless of the nationality of its owners, is viewed as a resident. For balance of payments purchases, American-owned businesses operating abroad are considered foreigners, since they are not domiciled in the United States.

[3]See Appendix 4A for a further discussion of balance of payments accounting.

and interest and dividend payments. The capital account shows transfers of capital. One major type of capital transfer is labeled *portfolio investment*. Portfolio investment includes financial assets such as stocks and bonds. Under portfolio investment, the owner of the assets does not control the assets. In other words, when Americans buy foreign stocks or lend to foreign firms, the portfolio investment account is affected. The other important type of long-term investment is called *direct investment*. Direct investment takes place when real assets such as land, factories, and equipment are acquired in a foreign country. It also includes the acquisition of stock if control can be exercised by the buyer. In other words, direct investments require control over the assets. Short-term capital flows are more difficult to evaluate. The data provided by the IMF do not differentiate between short-term flows of private organizations and those of governments.

Using IMF Balance of Payments Data

The balance of payments data presented in the appendixes include a substantial amount of detail. To the non-expert, the detail makes interpretation of the data more difficult than it should be. In fact, significant insight into what is happening to the balance of payments can be gained by focusing on only three lines in the published data. As illustrated in

TABLE 4-1   Simplified International Payments Data for the United States, 1982 to 1988 (Billions of Dollars)

	1982	1983	1984	1985	1986	1987	1988
A. Current account (77 a.d)	−9	−46	−107	−115	−139	−154	−135

B.   Capital accounts
  + Long-term investment
    (direct, portfolio, and other)							

= The basic balance (77 c.d)
  (preliminary balance on
   autonomous transactions)
	−16	−48	−69	−42	−66	−125	−60

+ Short-term investment
   (short-term capital and
   errors and omissions)							

= The performance balance (77 f.d)	2	−4	1	6	−34	−57	−36

	1982	1983	1984	1985	1986	1987	1988
Exchange rate: SDR1* = $	1.10	1.05	0.98	1.10	1.22	1.42	1.35

*The SDR is the weighted average of the values of five major international currencies.

Source: Based on *International Financial Statistics*, Appendix 4B.

Table 4-1, these three lines can be used to summarize what is happening to the autonomous accounts in the balance of payments.

1. The balance on the *current account* (line 77a.d) indicates the balance on current spending.[4] It tells us whether we are spending more abroad than foreigners are spending in our country (ignoring investment flows and accommodating transactions). The most important types of transactions included in the current account are imports and exports of goods and services. Also included are net transfer payments and payments of interest and dividends. In 1988, for example, the United States spent $135 billion more in foreign countries than foreigners spent in the United States. When this number is expected to remain negative for the foreseeable future, one would expect that the dollar would decline relative to other currencies. If the number is expected to remain positive, the dollar should strengthen.

2. The *basic balance* (line 77c.d) is the sum of the balance on the current account and the long-term investment accounts. It gives us some idea of the extent to which autonomous long-term investments are affecting the balance of payments. When a country is the net recipient of long-term investment funds, this number should be more positive than the number reported in the current account. In Table 4-1, for example, the 1988 figure of −$60 billion is more positive than −$135 billion. This means that foreigners invested (long-term) $75 billion more in the United States than Americans invested abroad. Thus net foreign long-term investment alleviated some of the pressure on the dollar. Nevertheless, the basic balance was still substantially negative, indicating that long-term investments were not sufficient to offset the large current account deficit. Generally speaking, a positive basic balance indicates that a currency should strengthen. A negative basic balance indicates that a currency should weaken. We have used the term *preliminary balance on autonomous transactions* as equivalent to the basic balance. We assume that *all* long-term capital flows are autonomous. In other words, if a foreign government invests in long-term financial assets within the United States, it does so for a valid business reason.

3. The *performance balance* (line 77 f.d) provides a summary of all autonomous flows *plus* some accommodating transactions. It is computed by adding the short-term capital accounts to the basic balance. The performance balance provides insight into the extent to which

---

[4]The balance of trade, which is used frequently by the media, only measures total exports of goods less total imports of goods. The balance of the current account is a broader measurement.

short-term investments are affecting the pressure on a currency. When the performance balance is more positive than the basic balance, this means that the country is the net recipient of short-term investments (plus errors and omissions).[5] In the U.S. situation for 1988, this net inflow amounts to $24 billion $[-60 - (-36)]$. The problem is that the IMF data do not differentiate between private and government short-term capital flows. If the entire $24 billion were from private sources, the performance balance would be the same as the balance of autonomous transactions. If some of the $24 billion were from government sources, they should be considered accommodating transactions.

A negative performance balance means that additional accommodating transactions will be required to meet payment requirements. Of course, a country's ability to execute accommodating transactions is limited by the availability of reserves. Countries that are unable to offset negative performance balances have no choice but to restrict current and capital account activities.

The U.S. Balance of Payments — An Illustration

Looking at the 1982–1988 data for the United States and using the three-line approach allows a simple story to unfold. Over the period 1982–1984, the dollar strengthened (the dollar price of an SDR went down). In 1985, the dollar began to weaken (the dollar price of an SDR increased). These developments can be explained in terms of balance of payments developments.

The current account balances show that at the beginning of 1983, U.S. residents were spending much more abroad than foreigners were spending in the United States (downward pressure on the dollar). The huge negative current account balances after 1984 were partly offset by a substantial improvement in the long-term investment situation. The basic balance was highly negative, which suggests that even after the long-term capital flows provided some relief, the dollar had to weaken.

---

[5]Errors and omissions are cash flows known to have taken place but more difficult to classify. Monetary authorities have data that indicate that in 1985, a net amount of +$23 billion flowed into the United States. The information available, however, does not permit these funds to be allocated to one of the other categories.

Note, however, that the performance balance was positive for the 1984–1985 period. This was due to the fact that short-term capital flowed into the United States at a rate high enough to offset the basic balance shortfall. The neutralization process was, however, only temporary and was due to unusually high real interest rates in the United States. In effect, high interest rates in the United States attracted huge amounts of short-term capital. Short-term U.S. government securities became a particularly attractive investment for foreigners. These developments reduced the pressure on the dollar, so that the value of the dollar remained high throughout 1985 despite huge deficits in the current account and basic balances.

Of course, the huge negative current account balances were compatible with a strong dollar only so long as the United States could continue to attract a large volume of foreign investment. Autonomous short-term investments are particularly vulnerable to change because they are closely related to interest rate levels. Foreign investors, particularly the Japanese and Germans, found high U.S. interest rates very attractive, since real interest rates in their home countries were relatively low. In some cases, the expected rates of return on marketable securities and bank accounts in the United States were double those that were expected in foreign countries. It is no wonder that foreign investors flocked to purchase American securities. In order for the performance balance of the U.S. balance of payments to have remained positive (given the negative basic balance), interest rates in the United States would have had to remain high enough to continue to attract huge amounts of foreign short-term capital. As shown in Table 4-1, that was not the case.

In the particular case of the United States, there is another factor to be considered. Let us assume that autonomous short-term flows were insufficient to offset deficits in the basic balance. Foreign governments, however, can take up the slack. If Germany and Japan did not want a decline in the value of the dollar in order to protect their export industries, they could purchase short-term securities in the United States. This would show as an improvement in the performance balance for the United States. As previously mentioned, the IMF statistics do not differentiate between the short-term flows of private individuals and foreign governments.

In the United States, high interest rates were viewed by many as detrimental to economic growth. High interest rates were accused of discouraging investment and employment at home. In addition, the strong dollar contributed to high levels of imports, since foreign-produced goods appeared to be inexpensive in terms of dollars. This *competition with imports* caused massive reorganization of American industry as American producers struggled to find ways to compete with low-priced imports. Manufacturers and farmers lost long-held market share both in the United States and abroad. To political leaders, lowering interest rates was seen as the solution to these problems. As interest rates came down, the flood of short-term investment by foreigners began to subside and the value of the dollar fell.[6]

The analytic strategy suggested by the simplified payments approach (Table 4-1) is relatively easy to follow. Large and/or continuous negative current accounts is the real "red flag" that suggests a downward pressure on a currency. The basic balance and the performance balance indicate the extent to which solutions are to be found in opposite investment flows. The investment flows, especially the short-term flows, cannot be counted on to solve a continuous current account deficit.

Limitations of the
Balance of Payments Approach

The view presented in the previous paragraphs is oversimplified but works most of the time. There can be other scenarios. For example, during the period 1983–1985, the United Kingdom had a positive current account balance but a negative basic balance.[7] This has been attributed to the fact that the investment climate in Britain was perceived to be unpromising. In this case, the downward pressure on the pound was the result of negative long-term investment flows. Focusing on the simplified payments format isolates these types of situations, as well as most of the other situations that can arise.

Viewed from the perspective of 1988, the data presented in Table 4-1 suggest that, in general, the dollar should decline in value. This general statement, however, may not be particularly useful to a businessperson. A firm involved in international commerce often wants to know what will happen to the dollar versus a particular currency rather than against all currencies. For example, during the period 1984–1987, the dollar weakened against the deutsche mark but strengthened dramatically against the Mexican peso (see Appendix C). In order to understand situations like these, the analyst must analyze and compare the simplified payments data for the two countries (i.e., construct a Table 4-1 for each country).

Table 4-2 presents a summary of the balance of payments data for two countries: the United States and West Germany. Data for only 1985

---

[6]The analyst must be careful not to overestimate the importance of any single factor in explaining exchange rate movements. The situation that existed in 1985 was unusual, and U.S. interest rates were exceptionally important in explaining the movement of exchange rates. In many cases, however, other factors are more important.

[7]*International Monetary Statistics*, International Monetary Fund, February 1987.

TABLE 4-2 1985 Balance of Payments: West Germany and the United States (Billions of Dollars)

	United States	West Germany
Current account balance (77 a.d)	−$115	+$17
Basic balance (77 c.d)	−$42	+$12
Performance balance (77 f.d)	+$6	−$1

Source: International Financial Statistics. See Appendixes B and D.

are included. If we look only at the performance balance, it would appear that the dollar should have become stronger against the deutsche mark. This, however, was not the case. Compare the basic balance for the two countries. Germany had a positive balance, while the United States had a negative one. The United States relied on very heavy inflows of short-term capital. Germany, on the other hand, was increasing its short-term investments abroad. Therefore, the deutsche mark was in a stronger position than the dollar. The current account and the basic balances gave a truer picture of the nature of exchange rate pressures.

The balance of payments data prepared by the IMF are very useful in understanding the general pressures on exchange rates and the possible direction of change. Unfortunately, they are not particularly useful in predicting what the exchange rate will be next year or next month. It is possible for imbalances to exist for very long periods of time. For example, U.S. deficits in the current accounts increased dramatically over the period 1981–1985. At the same time, the dollar increased in value. Most analysts predicted that the dollar would weaken long before it actually did (1985), because they were not prepared to forecast net investment inflows of the amounts that actually materialized over the period in question. This suggests that the balance of payments should be used as a method of estimating general trends rather than a way of making point estimates of exchange rates.

Relative Inflation Rate Approach (Purchasing Power Parity)

Economists and businesspersons frequently look at relative inflation rates and attempt to predict the future level of floating exchange rates. The frame of reference used in such forecasts is called the *Purchasing power parity* theory. This theory asserts that the percentage change in the direct quote of a foreign currency will be equal to the difference between the inflation rate at home and the inflation rate in the foreign country. Mathematically, it can be expressed as follows[8]:

$$\%E(f) = I(h) - I(f) \tag{4-1}$$

where $E(f)$ = direct quote of the foreign currency
$\quad\quad\ I(h)$ = inflation rate at home (percent)
$\quad\quad\ I(f)$ = inflation rate in foreign country (percent)

For example, assume that the direct quote on sterling is £1 = $1.5000, the inflation rate in the United Kingdom is 10 percent and the inflation rate in the United States is 6 percent. Under these assumptions, the exchange rate of the pound compared to the dollar should decline by 4 percent.[9]

$$\%E(f) = 6\% - 10\% = -4\%$$

The new direct quote would be forecasted at £1 = $1.4400 ($1.500 × 0.96).

The logic behind the theory of purchasing power parity is straight-forward. If prices in one country increase more than prices in another, consumers in both countries are discouraged from buying in the higher-priced country. Thus, the country with higher inflation should experience an increase in imports and a reduction in exports. Using the balance-of-payments terminology, the current account of the higher-inflation country should be reduced (move in a negative direction). The demand for its currency will decline and/or the supply of its currency will increase. Other things being equal, this should lead to a decrease in the value of the currency of the higher-inflation country.

Continuing our previous example, the higher United Kingdom inflation rate should encourage the British to make purchases at lower prices in the United States. This will be reflected in an increase of imports into the United Kingdom. At the same time, American buyers should now see

---

[8]Equation 4-1 represents a simplified version of the purchasing power parity theory. The more exact version of the theory is

$$\%E(f) = \frac{I(h) - I(f)}{1 + I(f)} \times 100$$

[9]Using the exact equation shown in footnote 8, the decline should be

$$\%E(f) = \frac{0.06 - 0.10}{1 + 0.10} \times 100 = -3.64\%$$

British goods as being relatively more expensive, and American imports from the United Kingdom (United Kingdom exports to the United States) should go down. The impact on Britain's current account will be negative, and the pound should lose value relative to the dollar.

The empirical relationship between relative inflation rates and exchange rates has been studied extensively, sometimes with conflicting conclusions.[10] The implications of this total body of knowledge are as follows:

1. Over short periods of time, inflation rates and exchange rates do not behave as suggested by the purchasing power parity theory. This reflects the fact that many factors (other than inflation) affect exchange rates. Of particular importance in this regard is the interference of governments in determining exchange rates. Governments may "defend" the value of their currencies until a crisis occurs.

2. Over longer periods of time, however, there appears to be a strong relationship between relative rates of inflation and exchange rates. Countries with high rates of inflation will almost always experience a decrease in currency value at some time. This is true not only for currencies that float but also for pegged and fixed currencies. In this context, the real question is not whether currencies of relatively high-inflation countries will be devalued, but when and by how much. When there is a great disparity in inflation rates, the purchasing power parity theory successfully predicts the direction of change but not the amount or the timing of change.

The purchasing power parity theory does provide a useful frame of reference for managers engaged in international commerce. Most importantly, any major increase or decrease in the expected inflation rate of a foreign country (relative to the U.S. inflation rate) should be taken to indicate that eventually exchange rates will change. For example, in 1987 the inflation rate in Brazil resumed its rapid rise. Should such a rise continue for even a short time, the cruzado will have to be devalued. Used in this fashion, the purchasing power parity theory provides a convenient forecasting device that is most useful when there are substantial differences in national rates of inflation. When differences in inflation rates are small, purchasing power parity is less potent as an indicator of exchange rate movements.

---

[10]See Alan C. Shapiro, *Multinational Financial Management*, 2nd. ed., Boston, Allyn & Bacon, 1986, pp. 105–108.

Relative Interest Rate Approach (International Fisher Effect)

Interest rate comparisons are another frequently used method of predicting exchange rate movements. This approach is known as the *international fisher effect* and asserts that the percentage change in the direct quote of a foreign currency will be equal to the differences in the nominal interest rates between the home country and the foreign country. This relationship can be expressed as follows:[11]

$$\%E(f) = i(h) - i(f) \tag{4-2}$$

where $E(f)$ = direct quote of the foreign currency
$i(h)$ = interest at home (percent)
$i(f)$ = interest rate in the foreign country (percent)

For example, assume that the direct quote on the German mark is DM1 = $0.50 and that the interest rate in the United States is 6 percent, while the interest rate in Germany is 3 percent. Under these conditions, the mark should increase by 3 percent.[12]

$$\%E(f) = 6\% - 3\% = +3\%$$

The new value of the mark should be DM1 = $0.515. In other words, since Germany has a lower interest rate, the value of the mark should increase.

The economic logic used to support the international fisher effect is based on the relationship between interest rates and inflation. High interest rates are expected to be associated with high inflation and a declining value of a currency. Low interest rates are associated with low inflation rates and a strong currency. In a sense, the international fisher effect is an alternate version of the purchasing power parity theory.

The international fisher effect theory, while still popular in some circles, has lost favor in recent years. This partly reflects the fact that the

---

[11]Equation 4-2 represents a simplified version of the international fisher effect. The more exact version is

$$\%E(f) = \frac{i(h) - i(f)}{1 + i(f)} \times 100$$

[12]Using the exact equation shown in footnote 11, the DM should increase by

$$\%E(F) = \frac{0.06 - 0.03}{1 + 0.03} \times 100 = +2.913\%$$

U.S. experience in 1985–1986 directly conflicts with the developments predicted by the international fisher effect. As noted earlier, the fall in interest rates was followed by a fall in the value of the dollar.

The relationship between interest rate differentials has been studied extensively and has been found to be very complex. While in the past analysts used interest rate differentials as a predictor of exchange rate movements, the evidence today suggests that such a policy may be unwise. While the relationship may hold true in the long run, a substantial deviation from the hypothesized behavior is exhibited in the short run.[13]

Political Stability and Exchange Rates

Noneconomic factors may also affect the value of currencies. The political stability of a country may have a significant impact on the value of its currency. Fears of future negative political changes may reduce the value of a currency and, in some instances, make it worthless. The expectation of drastic changes in such systems can create tremendous volatility in the value of currencies.

History is full of such examples. Germany after World War I, China after World War II, and South Vietnam in the mid-1970s all illustrate situations in which political developments caused currencies to become virtually worthless. It is important to note that potential political changes do not have to be as dramatic as those just mentioned to affect the value of a currency. The election of socialist President Mitterrand of France in 1981, for example, created uncertainty about the future course of French economic policy. The reaction to such fears, founded or unfounded, created a significant decrease in the value of the French franc. Fears of what is perceived as an undesirable change may increase the supply of a currency in international markets as individuals, businesses, and governments become less willing to hold the currency as an asset. Such developments lead to shifts in the supply schedule of the currency and a reduction in the currency's value (other things held constant).

Political stability, on the other hand, contributes to an increase in the value of a currency. The existence of political stability in a country encourages economic units to accept its currency as a means of payment and hold that currency as an asset. In effect, political stability creates a high demand for a currency, which in turn leads to a high exchange rate. For example, many observers believe that political stability in the United States has maintained the dollar at a value higher than would be justified

---

[13]Shapiro, op cit., pp. 114–115.

by purely economic considerations. While political stability by itself cannot maintain or increase the value of a currency, it is often an important contributing factor to exchange rate movements.

Summary and Conclusions

This chapter focused on two issues: (1) the factors affecting foreign exchange rate fluctuations and (2) the usefulness of various techniques in suggesting future changes in exchange rates. Fluctuations in currency values create significant difficulties for business firms. Since today's manager lives in a world of fluctuating exchange rates, managers must understand the factors that affect the value of currencies. While there is no foolproof method for forecasting future exchange rates, clues to the direction of change can be found in the balance of payments data published by the IMF. In addition, relative inflation and interest rates both suggest the expected direction of exchange rate movements. While there is no complete answer to the exchange rate forecasting problem, indicators of change are available and should be incorporated into business decision making. More formal forecasting techniques will be discussed in Chapter 5.

Review Questions

1. What is the major difference between autonomous and accommodating transactions in the balance of payments?
2. What is the meaning and significance of the following balance of payments concepts?
   a. The current account balance.
   b. The basic balance.
   c. The performance balance.
3. Define the theory of purchasing power parity and explain how it can be used as an indicator of future exchange rate movements.
4. Why should the political stability of a country affect the value of its currency?
5. Is it true that a negative current account balance will always lead to a decline in the value of a currency?
6. Assume that we are trying to predict the movement of the Japanese yen against the American dollar. What kind of pressure are the following events likely to place on the dollar? Defend your answer using the concept of supply and demand for the dollar.
   a. Japan reduces restrictions on imports of farm products from the United States.
   b. Interest rates in the United States increase (other things being equal).
   c. Political instability in Japan increases.
   d. U.S. consumers lose confidence in the quality of Japanese products.
   e. Japan increases public works expenditures.

7. When using balance of payments data to predict the exchange rate for a particular currency, it is necessary to look at the balance of payments for both of the countries involved. True or false? Explain.

Questions for Discussion

1. Your employer listens to the radio and frequently hears references to the balance of payments deficits in the trade balance and exchange rates. She knows that there is some connection but does not understand the precise relationship. Knowing that you have taken a course in international finance, she asks you to make a presentation describing the relationship between balance of payments and exchange rates.

Research Activities

1. Look at the IMF data for the United States and Japan for the last 10 or 15 years. Plot the current account balances, basic balances, and performance balances for each country. Compare these relative balances to exchange rate movements. How well does the balance of payments explain past exchange rate movements?
2. Using *International Financial Statistics*, gather information about interest rates in the United States and Canada for the past 15 years (note that more than one interest rate indicator is available). How well have differences in interest rate explained exchange rate movements?
3. Using *International Financial Statistics*, gather information about inflation rates in the United States and Mexico for the past 15 years (note that more than one inflation indicator is available). How well have differences in inflation rates explained exchange rate movements?

Bibliography

Bame, Jack J. "Analyzing U.S. International Transactions." *Columbia Journal of World Business*, Fall 1976, pp. 72–84.

Bell, Geoffrey. "The New World of Floating Exchange Rates." *The Journal of Portfolio Management*, Spring 1977, pp. 25–28.

Brittain, Bruce. "Tests of Theories of Exchange Rate Determination." *Journal of Finance*, May 1977, pp. 519–529.

Calderon-Rossell, Jorge R., and Ben-Horim, Moshe. "The Behavior of Foreign Exchange Rates." *Journal of International Business Studies*, Fall 1982, pp. 99–111.

Cornell, Bradford W. "Relative Price Changes and Deviations from Purchasing Power Parity." *Journal of Banking and Finance*, September 1979, pp. 263–279.

Cosset, Jean-Claude, and Doutriaux de la Rianderie, Bruno. "Political Risk and Foreign Exchange Risk: An Efficient Market Approach." *Journal of International Business Studies*, Fall 1985, pp. 21–56.

Crockett, Andrew. "Determinants of Exchange Rate Movements: A Review." *Finance and Development*, March 1981, pp. 33–37.

Dornbush, Rudiger. "Expectations and Exchange Rate Dynamics." *Journal of Political Economy*, December 1976, pp. 1161–1176.

Gailliot, Henry. "Purchasing Power Parity as an Explanation of Long Term Changes in Exchange Rates." *Journal of Money, Credit and Banking*, August 1970, pp. 348–357.

Giddy, Ian H. "An Integrated Theory of Exchange Rate Equilibrium." *Journal of Financial and Quantitative Analysis*, December 1976, pp. 863–892.

Gray, Peter H., and Makinen, Gail E. "Balance Payments Contributions of Multinational Corporations." *Journal of Business*, July 1967, pp. 339–343.

Hall, Thomas W. "Inflation and Rates of Exchange: Support for SFAS No. 52." *Journal of Accounting, Auditing and Finance*, Summer 1983, pp. 299–312.

Hung, Tran Quoc. "Capital Inflows Should Keep the Dollar Strong." *Euromoney*, February 1983, pp. 83–85.

Isard, Peter. "How Far Can We Push the Law of One Price?" *American Economic Review*, December 1977, pp. 942–948.

Johnson, Harry G. "The Monetary Approach to the Balance of Payments: A Non-Technical Guide." *Journal of International Economics*, August 1977, pp. 251–268.

Koveos, Peter, and Seifert, Bruce. "Purchasing Power Parity and Black Markets." *Financial Management*, Autumn 1985, pp. 40–46.

Kravis, Irving B., and Lipsey, Robert E. "Price Behavior in the Light of Balance of Payments Theories." *Journal of International Economics*, May 1978, pp. 193–246.

Mishkin, Frederick S. "Are Real Interest Rates Equal Across Countries? An Empirical Investigation of International Parity Conditions." *Journal of Finance*, December 1984, pp. 1345–1357.

Rogalski, Richard J., and Vinso, Joseph D. "Price Level Variations as Predictors of Flexible Exchange Rates." *Journal of International Business Studies*, Spring–Summer 1977, pp. 71–81.

Taylor, Dean. "Official Intervention in the Foreign Exchange Market, or Bet Against the Central Bank." *Journal of Political Economy*, April 1982, pp. 356–368.

Wihlborg, Clas. "Interest Rates, Exchange Rate Adjustments, and Currency Risks: An Empirical Study, 1967–1975." *Journal of Money, Credit and Banking*, February 1982, pp. 58–75.

Appendix 4A

Balance of Payments Accounting: An Illustration

This appendix provides a simplified view of a complicated process: balance of payments accounting. The objective is to illustrate how a number of the most common types of transactions affect the current account, the basic balance (preliminary balance on autonomous transactions), and the performance balance. The illustration analyzes the United

TABLE 4A-1 U.S. Balance of Payments (Hypothetical)

	Credit (+)	Debit (−)
A. Current account		
Exports and imports	+$4,000(4)	−$9,000(1)
Services		−$500(6)
Unilateral transfers		−$300(7)
Interest and dividends		−$400(9)
	+ $4,000	− $10,200
B. Capital accounts		
B.1. Long-term capital		
Portfolio investment		−$1,000(3)
Direct investment	+$5,000(8)	−$2,000(5)
	+ $5,000	− $3,000
B.2. Short-term capital	+$3,000(2)	

Changes in Key Balances

Change in current account balance	− $6,200
Change in basic balance (current account + change in long-term capital)	− $4,200
Change in performance balance (basic balance + short-term capital)	− $1,200

States and assumes that only the following transactions took place during the time period under consideration.

1. Americans bought $9,000 in Japanese cars.
2. Japanese firms increased their checking account balances in American banks by $3,000.
3. An American bought a $1,000 German bond.
4. British citizens bought $4,000 in American wheat.
5. An American bought a $2,000 home on the French Riviera.
6. An American paid $500 to Air France for a trip to Paris.
7. The U.S. government gave $300 in foreign aid to Egypt.
8. Nissan of Japan bought a factory in California for $5,000.
9. An American bank paid $400 in interest to a French firm.

Table 4A-1 shows the impact of these transactions on the various balance of payments accounts. Note that we have divided the entries into the two major categories: current and capital accounts. In addition, the current account has four subcategories: exports and imports (goods), services, unilateral transfers (gifts), and interest payments. The capital account is subdivided into short-term investments, long-term portfolio investments, and direct investments.

Note that entries that give rise to an inflow of dollars into the United States are positive. For example, when the Japanese bought the California plant (8), they gave $5,000 to the American owner. When Japanese firms increased their checking accounts in American banks (2), they gave $3,000 to those banks. Entries that give rise to an outflow of dollars from the United States are negative. When an American bank paid interest to a French firm (9), it gave $400. When the American government gave foreign aid to Egypt (7), it gave $300. When an American bought the German bond (3), $1,000 left the United States. Note in Table 4A-1 that the United States has a deficit in the current account of $6,200. However, it has a surplus in the capital account (including autonomous short-term flows) of $5,000. The performance balance has a deficit of $1,200.

This simple illustration shows how the balance of payments can affect the demand and supply schedule for dollars. Foreigners need a total of $12,000 ($4,000 + $5,000 + $3,000) to pay for their transactions. This represents the demand for dollars. Foreigners have received $13,200 ($10,200 + $3,000) from Americans. This represents the supply of dollars. In other words, foreigners have an excess of $1,200 above and beyond their dollar needs. The negative $1,200 shows up as the performance balance, which is the sum of all the autonomous transactions in the balance of payments accounts.

In order for the dollar to retain its value, this excess $1,200 must be absorbed by some means. Since it has been assumed that there are no other autonomous transactions, accommodating transactions are needed to relieve the pressure on the dollar. The U.S. government could artificially increase the demand for dollars by offering to exchange $1,200 for gold or foreign currencies. A foreign government could artificially increase the demand for dollars by offering to buy $1,200 in exchange for its own currency. Either of these actions would be considered an accommodating transaction undertaken to finance the $1,200 deficit in autonomous transactions.[14]

If neither the United States nor foreign governments are willing to do this, the result should be a decline in the value of the dollar in international markets. Private foreigners have more dollars than they desire and would try to sell them in international markets. This would result in an increase in the supply of dollars and thus a reduction in the value of the dollar.

This illustration is very simple. Only nine transactions out of several million were used. However, the detail is sufficient to illustrate the nature

---

[14]The foreign government could have purchased $1,200 in short-term securities in the United States in order to maintain the value of the dollar (an accommodating transaction). This would show as an increase of $1,200 in short-term capital flows. Thus, the performance balance would be equal to *zero*. As indicated in the chapter, this is a major shortcoming of the data published by the IMF.

of the balance of payments systems and the meaning of the current, basic, and performance balances. The balance of payments indicates the direction and magnitude of the pressures exerted on exchange rates.

 Problem

A1. During 1988, these were the only autonomous transactions that took place between the United States and foreigners:

  1. Americans bought $20,000 in French wines.
  2. Germans bought $12,000 in American beef.
  3. Americans invested $4,000 in French common stocks.
  4. An American bought land for $2,000 in Japan.
  5. The United States gave Israel $800 in foreign aid.
  6. Americans paid $200 in interest to German banks.
  7. A Japanese firm bought a hotel in Hawaii for $10,000.
  8. A French firm bought $2,000 in U.S. Treasury bills.

Calculate the current, basic, and performance balances for the United States during 1988.

Appendix 4B

International Monetary Fund Data for the United States

United States
111

	1982	1983	1984	1985	1986	1987	1988	1986 I	1986 II	1986 III	1986 IV	1987 I	1987 II	1987 III	1987 IV
Exchange Rates												*End of Period (sa and sc) Period Averages (sb and sd)*			
US Dollar/SDR Rate...........aa= ..... **sa**	1.10311	1.04695	.98021	1.09842	1.22319	1.41866	1.34570	1.13827	1.17757	1.21342	1.23319	1.28563	1.27802	1.27964	1.41866
US Dollar/SDR Rate....................... **sb**	1.10401	1.06900	1.02501	1.01534	1.17317	1.29307	1.34392	1.12489	1.16106	1.20275	1.20586	1.26085	1.29415	1.27661	1.34210
SDR/US Dollar Rate ....ac= ... **sc**	.90653	.95515	1.02019	.91040	.81753	.70489	.74311	.87853	.84921	.82412	.81753	.77783	.78246	.78147	.70489
SDR/US Dollar Rate .... **sd**	.90579	.93545	.97560	.98489	.85239	.77335	.74409	.88898	.86128	.83143	.82929	.79312	.77271	.78332	.74510
												Dollars per ECU:			
ECU Rate .... **ea**	.96770	.82740	.70890	.88790	1.07040	1.30340	1.17260	.93670	.97820	1.02960	1.07040	1.14800	1.13280	1.12970	1.30340
ECU Rate .... **eb**	.98121	.89128	.78899	.76219	.98119	1.15432	1.18388	.91450	.95897	1.01323	1.03807	1.12453	1.15013	1.12830	1.21430
												Index Numbers (1985=100):			
MERM Effective Exchange Rate ...... **amx**	84.2	89.1	96.1	100.0	81.9	72.2	68.0	86.5	82.9	79.5	78.9	74.4	72.1	73.2	69.2
Nominal Effective Exchange Rate.... **neu**	85.5	89.7	96.8	100.0	80.2	70.3	65.9	85.2	81.1	77.2	77.2	72.6	70.1	71.3	67.0
Real Effective Exchange Rate.......... **reu**	86.4	89.2	96.2	100.0	*80.5*	*70.2*	*66.3*	*85.3*	*81.5*	*77.7*	77.5	*72.7*	*70.1*	*71.1*	*66.7*
Fund Position												*Billions of SDRs:*			
Quota **2f.s**	12.61	17.92	17.92	17.92	17.92	17.92	17.92	17.92	17.92	17.92	17.92	17.92	17.92	17.92	17.92
SDRs...................................... **1b.s**	4.76	4.80	5.75	6.64	6.86	7.25	7.16	6.89	6.97	6.84	6.86	6.80	6.93	7.09	7.25
Reserve Position in the Fund **1c.s**	6.66	10.81	11.77	10.88	9.59	8.00	7.24	10.56	10.25	9.83	9.59	9.11	8.85	8.53	8.00
incl.: Fund Borrowing: SFF.......... **1cts**	1.14	1.43	1.32	1.10	.77	.42	.19	1.05	.96	.87	.77	.69	.60	.51	.42
International Liquidity												*Billions of US Dollars Unless Otherwise Indicated:*			
Total Reserves minus Gold.............. **1l.d**	22.81	22.63	23.84	32.10	37.45	34.72	36.74	33.83	35.51	37.00	37.45	37.74	34.07	34.00	34.72
SDRs...................................... **1b.d**	5.25	5.03	5.64	7.29	8.39	10.28	9.64	7.84	8.21	8.29	8.39	8.74	8.86	9.08	10.28
Reserve Position in the Fund....... **1c.d**	7.35	11.31	11.54	11.95	11.73	11.35	9.75	12.02	12.07	11.92	11.73	11.71	11.31	10.92	11.35
Foreign Exchange **1d.d**	10.21	6.29	6.66	12.86	17.33	13.09	17.36	13.97	15.23	16.79	17.33	17.29	13.90	14.00	13.09
Gold (Million Fine Troy Ounces).... **1ad**	264.03	263.39	262.79	262.65	262.04	262.38	261.87	262.66	262.51	262.52	262.04	262.44	262.15	262.29	262.38
Gold (National Valuation).............. **1and**	11.15	11.12	11.10	11.09	11.06	11.08	11.06	11.09	11.08	11.08	11.06	11.08	11.07	11.08	11.08
External Liabilities .... **5..d**	419.98	485.17	543.91	605.05	736.80	869.77	1,001.04	623.71	649.92	707.65	736.80	739.58	765.65	816.71	869.77
Central Banks & Governments **5a.d**	163.89	170.08	174.58	172.49	205.16	253.49	296.06	174.58	189.20	203.58	205.16	220.85	232.58	233.85	253.49
Industrial Countries **5agd**	86.73	96.75	97.48	98.46	126.08	175.56	*206.55*	98.05	109.30	122.30	126.08	143.14	160.61	159.19	175.56
OPEC Countries **5ahd**	58.38	51.94	48.52	41.64	32.76	24.86	*24.06*	43.20	40.92	37.77	32.76	30.48	28.58	27.84	24.86
Other Countries **5aid**	18.79	21.38	28.58	32.39	46.32	53.07	*65.45*	33.34	38.98	43.51	46.32	47.23	43.39	46.82	53.07
Other Banks & Other Foreigners. **5b.d**	246.91	303.98	355.12	416.45	517.34	607.03	696.83	429.01	444.18	491.36	517.34	505.14	521.35	572.19	607.03
International Agencies **5c.d**	9.19	11.11	14.21	16.11	14.31	9.26	8.15	20.11	16.54	12.71	14.31	13.59	11.72	10.67	9.26
By Type: Long-Term Marketable ... **5e.d**	83.58	89.01	110.45	139.66	159.05	184.64	233.17	147.38	156.29	162.07	159.05	166.47	175.52	176.98	184.64
Nonmarketable **5f.d**	10.48	7.25	5.80	3.55	1.30	.30	.52	2.75	1.80	1.30	1.30	1.30	.70	.30	.30
Fund Gold Dep. & Invest. **5g.d**	—	—	—	—											
Other Readily Marketable. **5h.d**	15.76	14.46	13.70	11.80	8.97	10.09	11.30	11.72	10.39	9.58	8.97	8.88	8.90	9.36	10.09
External Claims .... **6..d**	401.53	433.13	443.37	446.78	506.70	549.56	603.83	441.04	455.22	474.61	506.70	482.45	500.40	523.45	549.56
Deposit Money Banks: Assets **7a.d**	360.54	397.17	409.88	417.32	470.29	*511.25*	*556.27*	414.57	425.02	441.10	470.29	448.86	466.42	488.57	*511.25*
of which: Claims on Nonbanks **7add**	107.04	121.08	119.01	110.69	110.27	*107.54*	*103.67*	110.43	109.00	106.41	110.27	108.48	107.79	110.05	*107.54*
Deposit Money Banks: Liabilities ... **7b.d**	254.55	305.78	338.12	381.26	477.22	*572.95*	*641.07*	389.14	398.74	444.23	477.22	469.89	486.84	540.32	*572.95*
of which: Liabilities to Nonbanks **7bdd**	45.55	58.83	67.45	73.84	80.59	81.16	*86.28*	73.23	74.56	77.54	80.59	76.00	77.85	83.33	81.16
Monetary Authorities												*Billions of US Dollars: Average of*			
Foreign Assets................................ **11**	34.0	33.7	34.8	43.2	48.4	45.8	47.8	44.9	46.6	48.1	48.4	48.8	45.1	45.1	45.8
Claims on Central Government...... **12a**	149.3	160.4	167.4	191.1	222.1	20.6	23.1	186.5	193.8	201.2	222.1	18.7	20.2	19.7	20.6
Federal Reserve Float................. **13a**	3.0	2.1	1.5	1.4	1.4	1.2	1.0	.6	.7	.6	1.4	.4	.8	.7	1.2
Reserve Money **14**	180.8	191.7	203.8	224.0	257.4	269.1	283.9	223.2	230.6	238.2	257.4	249.2	250.5	256.7	269.1
of which: Currency Outside DMBs **14a**	136.5	150.6	160.8	173.1	186.2	199.3	214.9	172.2	177.4	179.5	186.2	182.9	188.6	190.9	199.3
Foreign Liabilities **16c**	.4	.6	.4	.5	.4	.3	.4	.4	.4	.4	.4	.5	.3	.5	.3
Central Government Deposits **16d**	9.3	6.8	8.6	17.7	18.2	14.4	20.3	12.5	13.2	18.0	18.2	14.4	23.0	18.3	14.4
Other Items (Net) **17r**	-4.2	-2.9	-9.1	-6.5	-4.1	-216.2	-232.7	-4.0	-3.0	-6.7	-4.1	-196.1	-207.7	-210.2	-216.2
Deposit Money Banks															
Commercial Banks												*Billions of US Dollars: Average of*			
Reserves................................... **20**	42.5	39.0	40.3	47.6	67.8	65.9	64.7	47.7	49.9	55.2	67.8	62.7	58.2	61.9	65.9
Foreign Assets............................ **21**	264.3	258.1	189.3	189.6	198.6	229.0	245.1	186.0	188.6	196.2	198.6	214.8	228.3	221.5	229.0
Claims on Central Government..... **22a**	136.3	184.2	186.0	198.2	203.5	201.2	197.0	201.7	200.6	200.9	203.5	199.9	199.3	205.0	201.2
Claims on State and Local Govts. ... **22b**	158.5	163.2	174.2	231.3	202.8	173.7	152.6	213.7	208.4	217.1	202.8	192.0	185.0	179.5	173.7
Claims on Private Sector................ **22d**	1,146.0	1,234.1	1,396.1	1,539.2	1,752.7	1,920.2	2,115.3	1,561.4	1,605.7	1,655.8	1,752.7	1,768.1	1,824.0	1,859.5	1,920.2
Checkable Deposits **24**	327.3	349.0	363.1	408.2	482.2	479.2	493.9	397.2	423.1	438.3	482.2	457.7	467.8	465.9	479.2
Time and Savings Deposits **25**	586.0	743.7	820.1	900.8	970.0	1,004.4	1,080.7	917.8	940.0	957.2	970.0	982.0	985.5	993.3	1,004.4
Money Market Instruments **26aa**	431.7	415.7	458.6	477.2	486.9	522.1	552.7	479.0	470.3	481.3	486.9	488.7	507.4	519.6	522.1
Bonds **26ab**	31.2	39.6	52.5	69.4	75.0	77.0	64.1	70.6	71.9	75.1	75.0	77.4	75.8	77.4	77.0
Foreign Liabilities **26c**	163.5	176.7	155.0	179.5	208.7	261.5	294.1	180.6	179.9	193.6	208.7	239.4	250.7	255.7	261.5
Central Government Deposits **26d**	21.9	21.1	24.9	28.7	38.1	44.6	45.2	30.3	32.0	32.5	38.1	34.1	50.3	46.9	44.6
Other Items (Net) **27r**	186.1	138.2	111.7	142.1	164.3	201.3	244.0	134.9	135.9	147.2	164.3	158.3	157.4	168.5	201.3
Other Monetary Institutions												*Billions of US Dollars: Average of*			
Cash.. **20..t**	42.7	48.6	42.8	55.0	70.6	59.6	55.5	57.0	58.3	58.4	70.6	61.5	63.0	57.2	59.6
Claims on Central Government **22a.t**	18.1	33.7	38.0	26.1	28.8	41.6	38.5	24.2	28.3	31.5	28.8	35.4	41.3	43.4	41.6
Claims on State and Local Govts. **22b.t**	3.3	3.1	2.8	3.4	3.1	3.3	3.3	3.2	3.1	3.3	3.1	2.9	2.9	3.0	3.1
Claims on Private Sector............. **22d.t**	814.1	933.7	1,074.1	1,160.7	1,257.6	1,379.1	1,460.0	1,183.3	1,215.8	1,240.3	1,257.6	1,288.1	1,318.3	1,345.0	1,379.1
Checkable Deposits .... **24..t**	23.0	34.1	41.5	54.3	72.2	81.4	88.7	56.1	62.8	66.6	72.2	76.8	81.1	81.2	81.4
Time and Savings Deposits........ **25..t**	710.2	796.3	876.3	941.6	990.2	1,040.2	1,090.9	953.3	969.4	981.1	990.2	1,007.3	1,019.0	1,028.4	1,040.2
Money Market Instruments........ **26aat**	63.3	96.3	147.3	151.9	154.9	163.0	174.0	155.9	157.6	159.1	154.9	147.5	146.7	153.7	163.0
Other Items (Net)....................... **27r.t**	80.0	92.5	92.0	97.4	142.8	198.8	203.7	102.7	116.0	127.4	142.8	156.2	178.8	185.4	198.8
Travelers Checks: Nonbanks .... **24..j**	4.1	4.6	4.9	5.5	6.0	6.5	6.9	5.8	6.5	6.9	6.0	6.4	7.1	7.6	6.5

United States — 111

End of Period (sa and sc) Period Averages (sb and sd)

	1988			1989		1988						1989			
	I	II	III	IV	I	July	Aug	Sept	Oct	Nov	Dec	Jan	Feb	Mar	Apr	**Exchange Rates**
1.38729	1.31061	1.29039	1.34570	1.29271	1.29648	1.28818	1.29039	1.34592	1.36637	1.34570	1.31093	1.32150	1.29271	1.29566	US Dollar/SDR Rate……aa= …… sa
1.36804	1.36807	1.29695	1.34387	1.31552	1.30514	1.29206	1.29368	1.31949	1.35659	1.35588	1.32525	1.31652	1.30486	1.29975	US Dollar/SDR Rate …… sb
.72083	.76300	.77496	.74311	.77357	.77132	.77629	.77496	.74299	.73187	.74311	.76282	.75672	.77357	.77181	SDR/US Dollar Rate……ac= …… sc
.73098	.73096	.77104	.74412	.76016	.76620	.77396	.77299	.75787	.73714	.73753	.75458	.75958	.76637	.76938	SDR/US Dollar Rate …… sd

End of Period (ea) Period Average (eb)

I	II	III	IV	I	July	Aug	Sept	Oct	Nov	Dec	Jan	Feb	Mar	Apr	Series
1.25170	1.14100	1.10420	1.17260	1.10033	1.11190	1.10570	1.10420	1.17100	1.19520	1.17260	1.12000	1.13580	1.10033	1.10720	ECU Rate …… ea
1.23377	1.21773	1.11400	1.17003	1.12630	1.12740	1.10390	1.11070	1.14030	1.18540	1.18440	1.13820	1.12490	1.11580	1.11240	ECU Rate …… eb

Period Averages

I	II	III	IV	I	July	Aug	Sept	Oct	Nov	Dec	Jan	Feb	Mar	Apr	Series
67.2	66.7	70.7	67.6	69.0	70.0	71.1	71.0	69.1	67.0	66.7	68.4	68.9	69.8	70.0	MERM Effective Exchange Rate …… amx
64.9	64.5	68.7	65.6	67.2	68.1	69.1	69.0	67.1	65.0	64.8	66.6	67.0	67.9	….	Nominal Effective Exchange Rate…. neu
65.0	64.7	69.4	65.9	67.2	68.6	69.8	69.7	67.7	65.3	64.9	66.5	67.1	68.0	….	Real Effective Exchange Rate…. reu

Fund Position — *End of Period*

I	II	III	IV	I	July	Aug	Sept	Oct	Nov	Dec	Jan	Feb	Mar	Apr	Series
17.92	17.92	17.92	17.92	17.92	17.92	17.92	17.92	17.92	17.92	17.92	17.92	17.92	17.92	17.92	Quota …… 2f.s
7.14	7.00	7.03	7.16	7.30	6.93	7.03	7.03	7.03	7.16	7.16	7.16	7.30	7.30	7.24	SDRs …… 1b.s
7.67	7.62	7.47	7.24	7.00	7.54	7.49	7.47	7.49	7.39	7.24	7.19	7.08	7.00	7.05	Reserve Position in the Fund …… 1c.s
.35	.29	.22	.19	.13	.27	.25	.22	.22	.20	.19	.18	.16	.13	.13	incl.: Fund Borrowing: SFF …… 1cts

International Liquidity — *End of Period*

I	II	III	IV	I	July	Aug	Sept	Oct	Nov	Dec	Jan	Feb	Mar	Apr	Series
32.12	29.96	36.73	36.74	38.79	32.81	36.72	36.73	39.14	37.88	36.74	37.13	38.31	38.79	39.24	Total Reserves minus Gold …… 1l.d
9.90	9.18	9.07	9.64	9.44	8.98	9.06	9.07	9.46	9.78	9.64	9.39	9.65	9.44	9.38	SDRs …… 1b.d
10.64	9.99	9.64	9.75	9.05	9.77	9.64	9.64	10.08	10.10	9.75	9.42	9.35	9.05	9.13	Reserve Position in the Fund …… 1c.d
11.58	10.79	18.02	17.36	20.30	14.06	18.02	18.02	19.60	18.00	17.36	18.32	19.31	20.30	20.73	Foreign Exchange …… 1d.d
262.01	262.03	262.01	261.87	261.96	262.01	261.98	262.00	261.93	261.87	261.86	….	….	261.96	261.96	Gold (Million Fine Troy Ounces)…. 1ad
11.06	11.06	11.06	11.06	11.06	11.06	11.06	11.06	11.06	11.06	11.06	….	….	11.06	11.06	Gold (National Valuation) …… 1and
884.87	926.57	951.99	1,001.04	….	935.21	947.73	951.99	946.68	972.90	1,001.04	….	….	….	….	External Liabilities …… 5..d
279.21	256.00	284.17	296.06	….	286.30	285.62	284.17	291.41	297.22	296.06	297.89	299.76	….	….	Central Banks & Governments …… 5a.d
197.30	204.11	200.95	206.55	….	203.52	200.58	200.95	206.24	209.31	206.55	207.67	206.63	….	….	Industrial Countries …… 5agd
24.16	22.90	22.61	24.06	….	23.02	22.59	22.61	22.11	23.28	24.06	24.56	28.16	….	….	OPEC Countries …… 5ahd
57.75	28.98	60.61	65.45	….	59.76	61.46	60.61	63.06	64.63	65.45	65.66	64.97	….	….	Other Countries …… 5aid
596.29	657.27	655.89	696.83	….	636.50	652.05	655.89	645.23	666.76	696.83	….	….	….	….	Other Banks & Other Foreigners …… 5b.d
9.37	13.31	11.92	8.15	….	12.42	10.06	11.92	10.04	8.91	8.15	7.63	8.18	….	….	International Agencies …… 5c.d
211.34	223.68	222.26	233.17	….	223.68	223.68	222.26	222.26	222.26	233.17	233.17	233.17	….	….	By Type: Long-Term Marketable …… 5e.d
.79	.50	.51	.52	….	.51	.51	.51	.52	.52	.52	.52	.53	….	….	Nonmarketable …… 5f.d
….	….	….	….	….	….	….	….	….	….	….	….	….	….	….	Fund Gold Dep. & Invest. …… 5g.d
9.89	10.09	10.57	11.30	….	10.02	10.09	10.57	10.89	11.01	11.30	….	….	….	….	Other Readily Marketable …… 5h.d
533.76	546.95	574.30	603.83	….	559.96	557.84	574.30	563.07	582.90	603.83	594.53	603.77	….	….	External Claims …… 6..d
495.94	510.63	538.11	556.27	….	523.64	521.52	538.11	526.87	546.70	556.27	546.97	556.21	….	….	Deposit Money Banks: Assets …… 7a.d
103.25	105.50	106.90	103.67	….	103.83	103.79	106.90	106.55	107.24	103.67	….	….	….	….	of which: Claims on Nonbanks…. 7add
553.61	583.69	608.88	641.07	….	591.06	604.37	608.88	600.75	622.25	641.07	621.15	635.72	….	….	Deposit Money Banks: Liabilities …… 7b.d
82.04	83.84	88.07	86.28	….	85.93	86.07	88.07	87.65	86.78	86.28	84.47	87.01	….	….	of which: Liabilities to Nonbanks 7bdd

Monetary Authorities — *Figures for Last Month in Period*

I	II	III	IV	I	July	Aug	Sept	Oct	Nov	Dec	Jan	Feb	Mar	Apr	Series
43.2	41.0	47.8	47.8	….	47.8	47.8	50.2	48.9	47.8	48.2	….	49.4	….	….	Foreign Assets …… 11
20.0	23.0	25.0	23.1	….	20.9	21.1	25.0	22.3	22.0	23.1	21.2	21.3	….	….	Claims on Central Government …… 12a
.7	.6	1.0	1.0	1.1	.7	.6	1.0	1.2	1.0	1.0	1.0	1.3	1.1	….	Federal Reserve Float …… 13a
264.2	269.2	275.4	283.9	….	276.0	273.8	275.4	276.9	280.4	283.9	279.2	277.5	….	….	Reserve Money …… 14
199.1	205.7	208.0	214.9	213.9	208.0	207.9	208.0	209.0	211.3	214.9	211.8	211.9	213.9	….	of which: Currency Outside DMBs 14a
.6	.4	.4	.4	….	.3	.3	.4	.3	.3	.4	.3	.3	….	….	Foreign Liabilities …… 16c
10.9	17.5	24.7	20.3	….	13.4	15.8	24.7	18.6	17.1	20.3	23.6	19.1	….	….	Central Government Deposits …… 16d
-211.9	-222.5	-226.6	-232.7	….	-224.2	-220.4	-226.6	-222.1	-225.8	-232.7	-232.7	-224.9	….	….	Other Items (Net) …… 17r

Deposit Money Banks / Commercial Banks — *Figures for Last Month in Period*

I	II	III	IV	I	July	Aug	Sept	Oct	Nov	Dec	Jan	Feb	Mar	Apr	Series
61.1	59.3	63.0	64.7	….	63.7	61.7	63.0	63.5	64.6	64.7	62.4	61.0	….	….	Reserves …… 20
228.0	232.5	235.0	245.1	252.6	234.3	231.4	235.0	236.4	237.8	245.1	246.8	249.8	252.6	….	Foreign Assets …… 21
201.1	196.1	196.7	197.0	213.6	195.7	196.3	196.7	196.2	195.1	197.0	200.9	208.0	213.6	….	Claims on Central Government …… 22a
166.5	161.1	158.2	152.6	149.9	160.0	159.4	158.2	156.5	154.2	152.6	151.4	150.8	149.9	….	Claims on State and Local Govts…. 22b
1,966.7	2,028.7	2,064.7	2,115.3	….	2,041.9	2,055.3	2,064.7	2,080.2	2,096.7	2,115.3	….	….	….	….	Claims on Private Sector …… 22d
464.1	478.9	477.1	493.9	468.4	481.8	477.9	477.1	477.7	481.3	493.9	486.8	467.9	468.4	….	Checkable Deposits …… 24
1,028.3	1,047.3	1,060.2	1,080.7	1,098.3	1,054.5	1,057.1	1,060.2	1,067.0	1,077.3	1,080.7	1,085.7	1,089.7	1,098.3	….	Time and Savings Deposits …… 25
526.7	541.4	548.4	552.7	….	541.8	552.0	548.4	549.0	553.4	552.7	….	….	….	….	Money Market Instruments …… 26aa
62.0	62.9	64.5	64.1	70.5	63.4	64.1	64.5	63.6	63.6	64.1	65.6	68.4	70.5	….	Bonds …… 26ab
258.7	273.3	281.3	294.1	296.1	278.0	284.1	281.3	280.7	287.0	294.1	295.6	296.5	296.1	….	Foreign Liabilities …… 26c
45.5	45.4	45.2	45.2	36.3	41.5	27.5	45.4	53.1	37.4	45.2	43.0	44.1	36.3	….	Central Government Deposits …… 26d
238.2	233.6	240.8	244.0	….	234.7	241.6	240.8	240.8	248.6	244.0	….	….	….	….	Other Items (Net) …… 27r

Other Monetary Institutions — *Figures for Last Month in Period*

I	II	III	IV	I	July	Aug	Sept	Oct	Nov	Dec	Jan	Feb	Mar	Apr	Series
60.8	59.3	57.4	55.5	56.8	58.7	58.0	57.4	56.6	55.7	55.5	55.7	56.8	56.8	….	Cash …… 20..t
37.1	38.0	37.5	38.5	41.0	37.9	37.6	37.5	37.7	38.0	38.5	38.8	39.0	41.0	….	Claims on Central Government …. 22a.t
3.1	3.0	3.2	3.3	3.5	3.5	3.1	3.2	3.2	3.3	3.3	3.3	3.4	3.5	….	Claims on State and Local Govts. 22b.t
1,386.1	1,407.3	1,435.1	1,460.0	1,484.5	1,417.0	1,427.3	1,435.1	1,443.0	1,451.2	1,460.0	1,468.5	1,477.4	1,484.5	….	Claims on Private Sector …… 22d.t
82.5	87.6	88.1	88.7	85.8	88.9	88.4	88.1	88.0	88.6	88.7	87.5	85.4	85.8	….	Checkable Deposits …… 24..t
1,070.9	1,085.8	1,091.3	1,090.9	1,088.2	1,091.9	1,091.1	1,091.3	1,096.1	1,094.4	1,090.9	1,092.7	1,089.2	1,088.2	….	Time and Savings Deposits …… 25..t
165.2	166.6	172.2	174.0	173.2	166.5	167.9	172.2	174.7	174.9	174.0	174.9	174.3	173.2	….	Money Market Instruments …… 26aat
168.6	167.7	181.7	203.7	238.6	169.3	178.8	181.7	181.9	190.3	203.7	211.4	227.7	238.6	….	Other Items (Net) …… 27r.t
6.9	7.6	7.9	6.9	7.0	8.2	8.2	7.9	7.5	7.1	6.9	7.0	7.1	7.0	….	Travelers Checks: Nonbanks …… 24..j

United States

111

		1982	1983	1984	1985	1986	1987	1988	1986 I	1986 II	1986 III	1986 IV	1987 I	1987 II	1987 III	1987 IV
Monetary Survey																
																Billions of US Dollars: Average of
Foreign Assets (Net)	**31n**	134.4	114.6	68.7	52.8	37.8	13.0	-1.6	49.9	55.0	50.3	37.8	23.8	22.4	10.4	13.0
Domestic Credit	**32**	2,408.6	2,697.9	3,018.4	3,319.0	3,630.3	3,909.6	4,169.6	3,345.1	3,425.2	3,516.3	3,630.3	3,659.5	3,737.2	3,809.3	3,909.6
Claims on Central Govt. (Net)	**32an**	272.7	350.3	357.9	369.0	398.1	204.4	193.1	369.6	377.5	383.1	398.1	205.5	187.6	202.8	204.4
Claims on State and Local Govts.	**32b**	161.8	166.3	176.9	234.7	205.9	176.8	155.9	216.9	211.5	220.4	205.9	194.9	187.9	182.5	176.8
Claims on Private Sector	**32d**	1,974.1	2,181.4	2,483.6	2,715.3	3,026.4	3,528.4	3,820.6	2,758.6	2,836.2	2,912.9	3,026.4	3,259.0	3,361.7	3,424.0	3,528.4
Businesses	**32dy**	910.5	1,008.1	1,150.6	1,247.5	1,474.3	1,625.4	1,753.3	1,285.2	1,338.4	1,385.1	1,474.3	1,506.0	1,550.1	1,574.7	1,625.4
Consumers	**32dz**	1,063.7	1,173.3	1,333.0	1,467.7	1,552.1	1,689.3	1,838.0	1,473.3	1,497.7	1,527.8	1,552.1	1,564.4	1,608.0	1,645.0	1,689.3
Money (M1)	**34**	490.9	538.3	570.3	641.0	746.5	766.4	804.4	631.3	669.8	691.2	746.5	723.7	744.6	745.5	766.4
Quasi-Money	**35**	1,296.2	1,540.0	1,696.4	1,842.4	1,960.2	2,044.6	2,171.6	1,871.1	1,909.4	1,938.3	1,960.2	1,989.3	2,004.5	2,021.7	2,044.6
Money Market Instruments	**36aa**	464.8	478.9	580.9	597.2	598.9	650.2	696.6	600.3	592.5	604.0	598.9	597.6	613.7	636.6	650.2
Bonds	**36ab**	34.6	43.3	57.3	77.9	87.0	93.1	82.1	79.9	81.9	86.9	87.0	92.3	90.0	92.5	93.1
Other Items (Net)	**37r**	254.9	212.2	181.7	213.4	275.7	368.3	413.4	212.8	226.8	246.8	275.7	280.5	306.9	323.4	368.3
Money(M1),Seasonally Adjusted.	**34..b**	481.3	526.9	557.5	627.0	730.5	752.3	790.3	640.5	667.5	693.1	730.5	734.8	741.3	747.9	752.3
Other Banking Institutions																
																Billions of US Dollars: Average of
Balances Outstanding	**45..*m***	236.3	181.4	230.2	241.6	291.6	310.6	326.9	256.4	272.3	286.6	291.6	297.9	292.3	297.7	310.6
Nonbank Financial Institutions																
																Billions of US Dollars:
Foreign Assets	**41..*s***	20.70	21.80	22.39	23.91	24.22	30.68	33.00	24.40	24.25	24.43	24.22	25.31	26.64	29.39	30.68
Claims on Central Government	**42a.*s***	16.53	28.64	41.20	51.70	59.03	57.08	62.00	53.79	53.95	54.20	59.03	61.25	57.64	57.25	57.08
Claims on State and Local Govts	**42b.*s***	9.05	9.99	8.71	9.71	11.66	11.76	....	9.97	10.71	11.11	11.66	10.86	11.49	11.09	11.76
Claims on Private Sector	**42d.*s***	466.04	513.49	554.14	631.40	707.92	814.01	912.83	654.73	677.38	685.52	707.92	762.90	789.67	823.05	814.01
Real Estate	**42h.*s***	20.62	22.23	25.77	28.82	32.08	34.17	37.50	29.80	30.35	31.79	32.08	31.86	32.44	33.18	34.17
Incr.in Total Assets(Within Per.).	**49z.*s***	61.27	68.67	61.52	84.38	108.99	-895.05	1.15	29.90	30.00	14.56	34.54	-895.62	.27	.36	-.05
Money (National Definitions)																
																Billions of US Dollars: Average of
M2	**59mb**	1,958.1	2,191.6	2,378.3	2,580.5	2,814.7	2,918.7	3,077.0	2,594.4	2,668.7	2,729.3	2,814.7	2,826.5	2,850.0	2,878.9	2,918.7
M2, Seasonally Adjusted	**59mbc**	1,953.8	2,184.6	2,369.1	2,569.5	2,801.2	2,909.9	3,069.3	2,598.9	2,667.6	2,736.8	2,801.2	2,833.3	2,848.0	2,885.3	2,909.9
M3	**59mc**	2,450.3	2,702.4	2,997.2	3,218.4	3,507.5	3,688.5	3,927.6	3,262.0	3,335.0	3,417.1	3,507.5	3,527.2	3,578.8	3,628.4	3,688.5
M3, Seasonally Adjusted	**59mcc**	2,443.1	2,692.8	2,985.4	3,205.2	3,492.3	3,677.6	3,917.8	3,263.8	3,336.9	3,422.7	3,492.3	3,532.7	3,579.0	3,630.9	3,677.6
Interest Rates																
																Percent Per Annum
Discount Rate *(End of Period)*	**60**	8.50	8.50	8.00	7.50	5.50	6.00	6.50	7.10	6.50	5.50	5.50	5.50	5.50	6.00	6.00
Federal Funds Rate	**60b**	12.26	9.09	10.23	8.10	6.81	6.66	7.61	7.83	6.92	6.21	6.27	6.22	6.65	6.84	6.92
Commercial Paper Rate	**60bc**	11.89	8.87	10.10	7.95	6.50	6.81	7.66	7.51	6.64	5.98	5.85	6.02	6.77	6.91	7.56
Treasury Bill Rate	**60c**	10.72	8.62	9.57	7.49	5.97	5.83	6.67	6.89	6.13	5.53	5.34	5.53	5.73	6.03	6.00
Treas. Bill Rate(Bond Equivalent).	**60cs**	11.07	8.95	9.89	7.73	6.13	6.01	6.89	7.12	6.32	5.58	5.48	5.69	5.91	6.23	6.20
Certificates of Deposit Rate	**60lc**	12.35	9.09	10.37	8.05	6.52	6.86	7.73	7.58	6.66	6.00	5.83	6.05	6.82	6.94	7.64
Lending Rate (Prime Rate)	**60p**	14.86	10.79	12.04	9.93	8.35	8.21	9.32	9.33	8.50	8.07	7.50	7.50	8.08	8.40	8.87
Govt. Bond Yield: Med.-Term	**61a**	12.92	10.45	11.89	9.64	7.06	7.67	8.24	7.94	7.18	6.66	6.48	6.52	7.72	8.15	8.29
Long-Term	**61**	13.00	11.11	12.52	10.62	7.68	8.38	8.85	8.56	7.60	7.31	7.26	7.19	8.34	8.88	9.12
Prices, Production, Employment																
																Index Numbers (1985=100):
Industrial Share Prices	**62**	64.3	86.9	87.2	100.0	126.2	159.2	147.6	116.9	129.1	128.3	130.4	152.2	163.8	179.6	141.3
Producer Prices	**63**	96.9	98.1	100.5	100.0	97.1	Ɨ99.6	103.6	98.6	96.8	96.3	96.7	97.8	99.4	100.5	100.9
Industrial Goods	**63a**	Ɨ96.4	97.5	99.6	100.0	96.4	98.9	102.5	98.5	96.2	95.2	95.6	97.2	98.4	99.8	100.4
Finished Goods	**63b**	Ɨ95.6	97.1	99.1	100.0	98.7	100.8	***103.2***	99.5	98.2	98.0	99.0	99.5	100.8	101.3	101.4
Consumer Goods	**63ba**	Ɨ96.3	97.6	99.5	100.0	97.7	99.8	***102.3***	98.9	97.2	96.9	97.7	98.4	99.9	100.5	100.5
Capital Equipment	**63bb**	Ɨ92.9	95.5	97.8	100.0	102.0	103.8	***106.2***	101.2	101.7	101.6	103.2	103.4	103.7	103.7	104.6
Consumer Prices	**64**	89.7	92.6	96.6	100.0	102.0	105.7	109.9	101.6	101.3	102.1	102.6	103.8	105.1	106.3	107.2
Wages: Hourly Earnings(Mfg)	**65ey**	89.2	92.6	96.4	100.0	102.1	104.0	106.7	101.7	101.9	102.0	102.7	103.3	103.6	104.0	105.0
Industrial Production, Seas. Adj.	**66..*c***	82.8	87.7	97.8	100.0	99.4	104.3	***110.2***	100.4	99.9	100.4	101.2	102.0	103.1	105.0	107.0
Crude Petroleum Production	**66aa**	96.4	96.8	99.2	100.0	96.8	93.1	90.9	100.1	98.6	95.0	94.3	92.9	93.0	92.4	94.0
Nonagr.Employment, Seas.Adj.	**67..*c***	91.8	92.4	96.8	100.0	102.6	***104.6***	***108.6***	101.3	101.7	102.2	102.9	103.6	104.2	104.8	105.8
International Transactions																
																Billions of US Dollars
Exports	**70**	216.44	205.64	223.98	218.82	227.31	254.48	321.60	55.08	58.98	53.94	59.13	58.04	63.08	62.64	70.37
Imports, cif	**71**	254.88	269.88	346.36	352.46	382.30	424.44	459.57	90.14	95.68	96.76	99.72	97.22	105.38	108.00	113.84
Petroleum	**71a**	62.66	55.27	59.21	52.36	37.64	44.71	41.81	12.32	8.19	8.70	8.42	9.08	10.44	13.28	11.91
Crude Petroleum	**71aa**	47.45	39.51	37.95	34.12	24.18	30.84	27.75	7.94	5.00	5.64	5.60	5.90	7.30	9.48	8.16
Imports, fob	**71.v**	243.95	258.05	325.73	345.28	369.96	406.31	441.49	92.87	90.80	92.29	94.00	92.97	100.56	103.74	109.05
																1985=100
Volume of Exports	**72**	101.9	95.4	101.9	100.0	99.0	111.9	132.0	100.3	97.2	94.9	103.7	103.6	111.4	109.6	122.9
Volume of Imports	**73**	67.2	74.2	92.0	100.0	110.5	113.4	117.7	109.0	110.0	112.0	111.2	108.3	113.7	113.1	118.5
Unit Value of Exports	**74**	98.4	99.4	100.8	100.0	101.0	102.7	109.9	100.4	100.7	101.3	101.3	101.2	102.2	104.0	103.4
Unit Value of Imports	**75**	105.1	100.8	102.6	100.0	96.6	103.6	108.6	98.7	95.7	95.5	98.0	99.4	102.5	106.3	106.2
Balance of Payments																
																Billions of US Dollars:
Current Account, nie	**77a.*d***	-8.64	-46.29	-107.14	-115.16	-138.84	-153.95	-135.13	-28.71	-34.92	-39.42	-35.79	-33.05	-41.79	-47.31	-31.80
Merchandise: Exports fob	**77aad**	211.20	201.81	219.90	215.94	223.98	249.57	320.14	54.27	58.17	53.82	57.72	57.17	61.43	61.70	69.27
Merchandise: Imports fob	**77abd**	-247.65	-268.89	-332.41	-338.09	-368.52	-409.85	-446.43	-87.11	-92.67	-92.53	-96.21	-93.73	-101.32	-104.44	-110.36
Trade Bal.,*77aad+77abd*	**77acd**	-36.45	-67.08	-112.51	-122.15	-144.54	-160.28	-126.29	-32.84	-34.50	-38.71	-38.49	-36.56	-39.89	-42.74	-41.09
Other Goods,Serv.&Income:Cre .	**77add**	138.35	132.73	140.85	144.65	151.11	175.27	187.97	38.57	37.53	37.00	38.01	41.67	40.98	41.01	51.61
Other Goods,Serv.&Income:Deb.	**77aed**	-101.65	-102.46	-123.37	-122.65	-130.09	-155.53	-183.20	-31.54	-33.87	-33.54	-31.14	-35.26	-39.87	-42.66	-37.74
Private Unrequited Transfers	**77afd**	-1.19	-.99	-1.41	-1.65	-1.38	-1.22	-1.04	-.35	-.32	-.30	-.41	-.31	-.32	-.29	-.30
Official Unrequited Trans.,nie	**77agd**	-7.70	-8.49	-10.70	-13.36	-13.94	-12.19	-12.57	-2.55	-3.76	-3.87	-3.76	-2.59	-2.69	-2.63	-4.28
Direct Investment	**77bad**	16.16	11.58	22.57	.96	6.28	-2.47	21.81	-8.17	-3.10	1.78	15.77	-2.97	-.71	7.82	-6.61
Portfolio Investment, nie	**77bbd**	-.88	4.73	28.76	64.43	71.59	31.99	41.11	17.34	25.70	17.00	11.55	15.13	13.96	8.00	-5.10
Other Long-Term Capital, nie	**77bcd**	-22.68	-17.97	-12.79	7.91	-5.22	-.93	12.65	-2.70	-.37	.13	-2.28	-1.48	.52	-.86	.89
Total,*77a.d+77bad—77bcd*	**77c.*d***	-16.04	-47.95	-68.60	-41.86	-66.19	-125.36	-59.56	-22.24	-12.69	-20.51	-10.75	-22.37	-28.02	-32.35	-42.62
Other Short-Term Capital,nie	**77d.*d***	-18.05	32.71	42.58	29.86	16.85	49.94	6.60	14.02	-13.05	9.88	6.00	15.77	-2.73	31.15	5.75
Net Errors and Omissions	**77e.*d***	36.12	11.19	26.74	17.80	15.56	18.48	16.60	6.06	10.86	-4.29	2.93	-10.67	15.70	.26	13.20
Total,*lines 77c.d—77e.d*	**77f.*d***	2.03	-4.05	.72	5.80	-33.78	-56.94	-36.36	-2.16	-14.88	-14.92	-1.82	-17.27	-15.05	-.94	-23.67
C'part to Mon./Demon. of Gold	**78a.*d***	-.03	-.28	-.24	-.04	-.24	.15	-.19	—	-.04	—	-.20	.17	-.13	.07	.04
Counterpart to SDR Allocation	**78b.*d***	—	—	—	—	—	—	—	—	—	—	—	—	—	—	—
C'part to Valuation Changes	**78c.*d***	-1.09	-1.37	-1.91	4.41	5.67	6.41	-1.90	1.61	1.70	1.77	.58	2.26	-.26	-.05	4.46
Total,*lines 77f.d—78c.d*	**78d.*d***	.91	-5.70	-1.44	10.17	-28.35	-50.38	-38.45	-.55	-13.22	-13.15	-1.44	-14.85	-15.44	-.91	-19.18
Exceptional Financing	**79a.*d***	—	—	—	—	—	—	—	—	—	—	—	—	—	—	—
Liab.Const.Fgn Author. Reserves	**79b.*d***	2.95	5.25	2.41	-1.96	33.46	47.80	40.28	2.28	14.85	14.64	1.69	15.31	11.64	.90	19.95
Total Change in Reserves	**79c.*d***	-3.86	.45	-.97	-8.21	-5.11	2.58	-1.83	-1.73	-1.63	-1.49	-.25	-.46	3.80	.01	-.77

United States

111

		1988				1989	1988						1989			
		I	II	III	IV	I	July	Aug	Sept	Oct	Nov	Dec	Jan	Feb	Mar	Apr
Monetary Survey		*Figures for Last Month in Period*														
Foreign Assets (Net)	31n	11.8	-.3	1.1	-1.6	....	-.1	-5.3	1.1	5.5	-.5	-1.6	-.9	***2.4***	....	....
Domestic Credit	32	3,948.7	4,034.6	4,087.5	4,169.6	....	4,054.2	4,087.8	4,087.5	4,100.6	4,145.8	4,169.6	....	....	....	....
Claims on Central Govt. (Net)	32an	201.9	199.2	189.2	193.1	....	199.6	211.7	189.2	184.5	200.6	193.1	194.3	***205.1***	....	....
Claims on State and Local Govts.	32b	169.6	164.1	161.4	155.9	153.4	163.0	162.5	161.4	159.8	157.5	155.9	154.8	154.3	153.4	....
Claims on Private Sector	32d	3,577.2	3,671.3	3,736.9	3,820.6	....	3,691.5	3,713.6	3,736.9	3,756.3	3,787.7	3,820.6	....	....	....	....
Businesses	32dy	1,659.9	1,697.5	1,717.0	1,753.3	....	1,703.3	1,707.0	1,717.0	1,724.2	1,738.6	1,753.3	....	....	....	....
Consumers	32dz	1,707.2	1,755.7	1,801.8	1,838.0	....	1,771.0	1,791.0	1,801.8	1,815.2	1,824.8	1,838.0	1,840.5	***1,849.2***	....	....
Money (M1)	34	752.6	779.9	781.0	804.4	***775.1***	786.9	782.3	781.0	782.1	788.3	804.4	793.0	772.3	***775.1***	....
Quasi-Money	35	2,099.2	2,133.1	2,151.5	2,171.6	***2,186.5***	2,146.4	2,148.2	2,151.5	2,163.1	2,171.7	2,171.6	2,178.4	2,178.9	***2,186.5***	....
Money Market Instruments	36aa	654.1	671.9	688.5	696.6	....	673.5	686.6	688.5	692.5	697.7	696.6	....	....	....	....
Bonds	36ab	77.9	80.2	82.1	82.1	86.2	80.9	81.7	82.1	82.1	81.7	82.1	83.1	84.9	86.2	....
Other Items (Net)	37r	376.7	369.3	385.6	413.4	....	366.4	384.2	385.6	386.3	405.9	413.4	....	....	....	....
Money(M1),Seasonally Adjusted.	34..b	763.8	776.5	783.7	790.3	***786.3***	782.5	782.4	783.7	785.4	786.6	790.3	786.3	787.4	***786.3***	....
Other Banking Institutions		*Figures for Last Month in Period*														
Balances Outstanding	45..m	332.1	315.2	314.7	326.9	***344.0***	314.5	314.8	314.7	315.9	324.8	326.9	331.0	337.0	***344.0***	....
Nonbank Financial Institutions		*End of Period*														
Foreign Assets	41..s	30.94	31.35	31.95	33.00	34.19	31.51	31.69	31.95	32.24	32.62	33.00	33.37	33.75	34.19	....
Claims on Central Government	42a.s	57.60	59.35	59.87	62.00	60.34	59.60	59.57	59.87	60.55	61.65	62.00	61.95	61.28	60.34	....
Claims on State and Local Govts	42b.s	12.00	12.99	....	....	....	....	....	....	....	....	....	....	....	....	....
Claims on Private Sector	42d.s	843.41	871.76	892.55	912.83	***928.80***	878.64	885.89	892.55	901.48	907.25	912.83	918.43	923.81	***928.80***	....
Real Estate	42h.s	35.06	35.55	36.50	37.50	38.70	35.81	36.16	36.50	36.82	37.14	37.50	37.87	38.27	38.70	....
Incr.in Total Assets(Within Per.).	49z.s	.33	.33	.23	.27	***.14***	.08	.08	.08	.11	.09	.07	.06	.04	***.04***	....
Money (National Definitions)		*Figures for Last Month in Period*														
M2	59mb	2,962.4	3,015.5	3,028.5	3,077.0	***1,064.6***	3,031.4	3,030.5	3,028.5	3,038.4	3,057.8	3,077.0	3,076.0	3,057.0	***1,064.6***	....
M2, Seasonally Adjusted	59mbc	2,969.3	3,013.1	3,035.0	3,069.3	***3,079.1***	3,023.9	3,029.7	3,035.0	3,042.2	3,059.3	3,069.3	3,065.7	3,069.5	***3,079.1***	....
M3	59mc	3,750.3	3,815.9	3,861.5	3,927.6	***3,949.1***	3,839.7	3,853.6	3,861.5	3,877.5	3,905.7	3,927.6	3,930.3	3,920.2	***3,949.1***	....
M3, Seasonally Adjusted	59mcc	3,755.9	3,815.6	3,863.4	3,917.8	***3,954.4***	3,838.2	3,852.6	3,863.4	3,879.8	3,900.6	3,917.8	3,922.8	3,932.3	***3,954.4***	....
Interest Rates		*Percent Per Annum*														
Discount Rate *(End of Period)*	60	6.00	6.00	6.50	6.50	7.00	6.00	6.50	6.50	6.50	6.50	6.50	6.50	7.00	7.00	***7.00***
Federal Funds Rate	60b	6.66	7.16	7.98	8.62	9.44	7.75	8.01	8.19	8.36	8.75	8.76	9.12	9.36	9.85	***9.82***
Commercial Paper Rate	60bc	6.69	7.18	8.08	8.67	9.45	7.82	8.26	8.17	8.24	8.66	9.11	9.04	9.37	9.95	***9.65***
Treasury Bill Rate	60c	5.76	6.23	6.99	7.70	8.53	6.73	7.02	7.23	7.34	7.68	8.09	8.29	8.48	8.83	***8.70***
Treas. Bill Rate(Bond Equivalent).	60cs	5.93	6.41	7.21	7.99	8.62	6.94	7.24	7.46	7.59	8.02	8.37	8.58	8.59	8.69	***8.75***
Certificates of Deposit Rate	60lc	6.72	7.22	8.17	8.80	9.60	7.94	8.35	8.23	8.36	8.78	9.25	9.20	9.51	10.09	***9.94***
Lending Rate (Prime Rate)	60p	8.59	8.78	9.71	10.18	11.17	9.29	9.84	10.00	10.00	10.05	10.50	10.50	11.50	11.50	***11.50***
Govt. Bond Yield: Med.-Term	61a	7.58	8.10	8.51	8.75	***9.39***	8.44	8.63	8.46	8.43	8.72	9.11	9.20	9.32	***9.66***	***9.15***
Long-Term	61	8.42	8.91	9.10	8.96	***9.19***	9.06	9.26	8.98	8.80	8.96	9.11	9.09	9.17	***9.30***	***9.02***
Prices, Production, Employment		*Period Averages*														
Industrial Share Prices	62	143.2	146.9	147.8	152.4	161.6	149.6	145.9	147.9	153.5	150.1	153.6	158.9	163.5	162.5	***167.7***
Producer Prices	63	I101.5	103.3	104.7	105.2	107.5	104.5	104.7	104.8	104.9	105.0	105.7	106.9	107.4	108.1	***108.9***
Industrial Goods	63a	I100.7	102.3	103.1	103.7	106.1	102.9	103.3	103.1	103.3	103.6	104.2	105.5	106.1	106.7	***107.7***
Finished Goods	63b	I101.4	102.7	103.9	***104.9***	106.7	103.7	104.0	103.8	***104.6***	105.0	105.2	106.1	106.8	107.3	***108.0***
Consumer Goods	63ba	I100.4	101.8	103.1	***104.0***	106.0	103.1	103.3	103.1	***103.7***	104.0	104.2	105.3	106.2	106.6	***107.7***
Capital Equipment	63bb	I104.7	105.7	106.3	***107.9***	109.0	106.1	106.4	106.2	***107.8***	107.9	108.1	108.7	109.1	109.2	***109.3***
Consumer Prices	64	I107.9	109.2	110.7	111.8	113.1	110.1	110.6	111.3	111.7	111.8	112.0	112.5	113.0	113.7	***114.4***
Wages: Hourly Earnings(Mfg)	65ey	105.6	106.4	106.8	108.1	***108.9***	106.6	106.2	107.6	107.5	108.1	108.8	108.8	108.8	***109.0***	***109.1***
Industrial Production, Seas. Adj.	66..c	108.0	109.2	111.1	***112.4***	***112.9***	110.8	111.2	111.3	***112.0***	112.4	***112.8***	***113.1***	***112.8***	***112.9***	***113.3***
Crude Petroleum Production	66aa	92.5	91.3	90.0	89.9	***85.7***	91.5	91.6	86.9	90.6	87.8	***90.6***	***89.9***	***80.3***	***86.9***	....
Nonagr.Employment, Seas.Adj.	67..c	107.2	108.2	109.1	110.0	111.0	108.9	109.0	109.3	109.6	110.0	110.3	110.7	***111.0***	***111.2***	***111.3***
International Transactions		*Billions of US Dollars*														
Exports	70	74.86	81.86	79.08	85.80	***88.87***	25.10	26.54	27.24	28.63	27.85	28.91	27.30	***27.96***	***33.61***	....
Imports, cif	71	110.29	114.34	114.39	120.55	***117.29***	37.08	39.37	37.94	40.29	39.90	41.00	37.56	***38.13***	***41.60***	....
Petroleum	71a	10.69	10.87	10.42	9.84	***11.39***	3.42	3.70	3.30	3.14	3.13	3.58	3.85	3.54	***4.00***	....
Crude Petroleum	71aa	7.06	7.54	6.85	6.29	***7.41***	2.29	2.34	2.22	2.12	1.91	2.27	2.51	2.25	***2.65***	....
Imports, fob	71.v	106.15	109.76	109.78	115.80	***112.63***	35.58	37.74	36.46	38.73	38.34	39.36	36.03	***36.69***	***39.91***	....
		1985=100														
Volume of Exports	72	131.6	135.4	127.2	133.9	....	121.0	129.1	131.5	132.6	128.4	140.7	....	....	....	....
Volume of Imports	73	115.2	115.7	116.2	123.7	....	111.3	120.1	117.1	124.8	123.1	123.1	....	....	....	....
Unit Value of Exports	74	104.8	108.5	112.9	113.5	....	112.1	112.6	114.1	113.4	113.4	113.7	....	....	....	....
Unit Value of Imports	75	106.8	109.9	109.5	108.4	....	111.1	109.2	108.2	107.8	108.1	109.4	....	....	....	....
Balance of Payments		*Minus Sign Indicates Debit*														
Current Account, nie	77a.d	-31.98	-34.62	-38.53	-30.00	....	....	....	....	....	....	....	....	....	....	....
Merchandise: Exports fob	77aad	75.90	81.14	77.97	85.13	....	....	....	....	....	....	....	....	....	....	....
Merchandise: Imports fob	77abd	-107.47	-111.68	-110.46	-116.82	....	....	....	....	....	....	....	....	....	....	....
Trade Bal.,*77aad+77abd*	77acd	-31.57	-30.54	-32.49	-31.69	....	....	....	....	....	....	....	....	....	....	....
Other Goods,Serv.&Income:Cre	77add	45.17	44.19	45.61	53.00	....	....	....	....	....	....	....	....	....	....	....
Other Goods,Serv.&Income:Deb.	77aed	-42.58	-45.52	-48.53	-46.57	....	....	....	....	....	....	....	....	....	....	....
Private Unrequited Transfers	77afd	-.27	-.20	-.23	-.34	....	....	....	....	....	....	....	....	....	....	....
Official Unrequited Trans.,nie	77agd	-2.73	-2.55	-2.89	-4.40	....	....	....	....	....	....	....	....	....	....	....
Direct Investment	77bad	.11	10.89	3.99	6.82	....	....	....	....	....	....	....	....	....	....	....
Portfolio Investment, nie	77bbd	4.18	17.09	10.16	9.68	....	....	....	....	....	....	....	....	....	....	....
Other Long-Term Capital, nie	77bcd	2.27	.96	4.07	5.35	....	....	....	....	....	....	....	....	....	....	....
Total,*77a.d+77bad—77bcd*	77c.d	-25.42	-5.68	-20.31	-8.15	....	....	....	....	....	....	....	....	....	....	....
Other Short-Term Capital,nie	77d.d	-1.09	8.34	1.10	-1.75	....	....	....	....	....	....	....	....	....	....	....
Net Errors and Omissions	77e.d	.22	-9.21	28.84	-3.25	....	....	....	....	....	....	....	....	....	....	....
Total,*lines 77c.d—77e.d*	77f.d	-26.29	-6.55	9.63	-13.15	....	....	....	....	....	....	....	....	....	....	....
C'part to Mon./Demon. of Gold	78a.d	-.18	.01	-.01	-.01	....	....	....	....	....	....	....	....	....	....	....
Counterpart to SDR Allocation	78b.d	—	—	—	—	—	—	—	—	—	—	—	—	—	—	—
C'part to Valuation Changes	78c.d	-1.10	-2.12	-.62	1.94	....	....	....	....	....	....	....	....	....	....	....
Total,*lines 77f.d—78c.d*	78d.d	-27.57	-8.66	9.00	-11.22	....	....	....	....	....	....	....	....	....	....	....
Exceptional Financing	79a.d	—	—	—	—	....	....	....	....	....	....	....	....	....	....	....
Liab.Const.Fgn Author. Reserves	79b.d	24.79	6.51	-2.25	11.23	....	....	....	....	....	....	....	....	....	....	....
Total Change in Reserves	79c.d	2.78	2.15	-6.75	-.01	....	....	....	....	....	....	....	....	....	....	....

United States
111

		1982	1983	1984	1985	1986	1987	1988	1986 I	1986 II	1986 III	1986 IV	1987 I	1987 II	1987 III	1987 IV
Government Finance																*Billions of US Dollars:*
Deficit (-) or Surplus	80	-125.7	-202.5	-178.3	-212.1	-212.6	-147.5	-149.6p	....	....	....	....	....	....	....	....
Revenue	81	659.9	653.4	718.5	791.7	823.2	910.0	966.3p	....	....	....	....	....	....	....	....
Grants Received	81z	—	—	—	—	—	—	—p								
Exp. & Lending Minus Repay.	82z	785.6	856.0	896.8	1,003.8	1,035.8	1,057.5	1,115.9p	....	....	....	....	....	....	....	....
Expenditure	82	764.9	842.6	881.9	977.3	1,032.5	1,054.1	1,109.5p	....	....	....	....	....	....	....	....
Lending Minus Repayments	83	20.7	13.4	14.9	26.5	3.3	3.4	6.4p	....	....	....	....	....	....	....	....
Financing																
Net Borrowing	84	138.8	215.6	174.1	200.5	233.1	148.6		....	....	....	....	....	....	....	....
Domestic	84a	129.3	200.1	158.5	167.9	191.4	132.0		....	....	....	....	....	....	....	....
Foreign	85a	9.5	15.5	15.6	32.6	41.6	16.5		....	....	....	....	....	....	....	....
Use of Cash Balances	87	-13.1	-13.1	4.2	11.6	-20.4	-1.0	17.2p	....	....	....	....	....	....	....	....
																Billions of US Dollars:
Debt	88	987.7	1,174.5	1,373.4	1,598.5	1,813.3	1,967.7	2,091.2	1,657.9	1,686.5	1,744.1	1,813.3	1,837.8	1,870.0	1,894.5	1,967.7
Held by: Monetary Authorities	88aa	139.3	151.9	160.9	181.3	211.3	222.5	238.4	184.8	183.8	190.8	211.3	196.4	212.3	211.9	222.5
Commercial Banks	88ab	131.4	188.8	186.0	198.2	203.5	201.2	195.0	201.7	200.6	200.9	203.5	199.9	199.3	205.0	201.2
Other Financial Inst.	88ac	44.1	65.3	64.5	78.5	105.6	120.6	....	84.0	88.6	96.4	105.6	112.2	112.2	118.4	120.6
State & Local Govts	88ad	115.0	149.0	173.0	226.7	262.8	282.6	....	225.6	227.1	251.2	262.8	264.6	268.7	273.0	282.6
Corporations	88ae	24.5	39.7	50.1	59.0	68.8	84.6	86.1	59.6	61.2	65.7	68.8	73.5	79.7	81.8	84.6
Individuals	88af	116.5	133.4	143.8	154.8	162.8	173.4	187.4	157.8	159.5	158.0	162.8	163.0	165.4	168.9	173.4
Money Market Funds	88ag	42.6	22.8	25.9	25.1	28.0	14.3	18.8	29.9	22.8	24.9	28.0	18.5	20.6	15.2	14.3
Foreign & International	88ca	149.5	166.3	192.9	212.5	251.6	287.3	349.3	217.9	237.1	253.1	251.6	260.3	268.6	267.0	287.3
Others	88d	224.8	257.3	376.3	462.4	518.9	581.2	....	496.6	505.8	502.8	518.9	549.4	543.2	553.3	581.2
Intragovernmental Debt	88s	210.7	237.5	290.8	350.1	404.3	478.6	589.5	353.8	375.6	384.1	404.3	408.7	439.2	458.3	478.6
National Accounts																*Billions of US Dollars: Quarterly Data*
Exports	90c	270.3	263.8	282.8	281.3	291.0	332.0	407.9	285.1	286.4	291.6	300.7	307.2	323.0	343.1	354.6
Gov't Consumption & Investment	91ff	641.7	675.0	735.9	820.8	871.2	924.8	964.9	847.8	868.8	881.8	886.5	903.8	915.7	932.2	947.3
of which: Gross Capital Form	93gf	77.2	64.1	73.0	99.3	101.7	98.4	93.1	100.4	103.6	99.2	103.5	101.3	93.6	96.3	102.3
Private Gross Fixed Capital Form	93ee	471.8	509.4	601.9	631.8	650.4	673.7	718.1	642.6	648.3	652.3	658.4	647.8	665.8	688.3	692.9
Increase in Stocks	93i	-24.5	-7.1	68.6	11.3	15.6	39.2	48.4	44.0	19.5	.7	-2.0	37.7	32.7	14.5	72.0
Private Consumption	96f	2,050.7	2,234.5	2,426.4	2,629.0	2,807.5	3,012.1	3,227.6	2,739.0	2,772.1	2,842.8	2,876.0	2,921.7	2,992.2	3,058.2	3,076.3
Less: Imports	98c	-295.2	-319.8	-388.6	-399.9	-430.2	-484.5	-527.4	-418.9	-419.9	-436.6	-445.4	-458.2	-473.4	-495.1	-511.3
Gross Domestic Product	99b	3,114.8	3,355.9	3,724.8	3,974.2	4,205.4	4,497.2	4,839.4	4,139.6	4,175.2	4,232.5	4,274.1	4,359.9	4,455.9	4,541.2	4,631.8
Net Factor Income from Abroad	90e	51.2	49.8	49.7	40.7	34.9	29.5	24.9	40.8	32.4	35.9	30.5	31.9	28.3	26.8	31.0
Gross Nat'l Expenditure = GNP	99a	3,166.0	3,405.7	3,774.5	4,014.9	4,240.3	4,526.7	4,864.3	4,180.4	4,207.6	4,268.4	4,304.6	4,391.8	4,484.2	4,568.0	4,662.8
Nat'l Income, Market Prices	99e	2,782.9	3,009.1	3,356.6	3,577.7	3,784.4	4,046.8	4,357.9	3,732.6	3,754.1	3,810.5	3,840.2	3,923.1	4,007.2	4,083.4	4,173.3
Gross Nat'l Prod. 1985 Prices	99a.r	3,512.6	3,638.1	3,879.7	4,014.9	4,129.2	4,268.1	4,433.5	4,126.5	4,117.9	4,128.7	4,143.5	4,190.1	4,241.5	4,288.4	4,352.5
								Millions: Mid-Year Estimates								
Population	99z	232.52	234.80	237.00	239.28	241.60	243.77	....	....	....	....	**Population** 99z				

Date of Fund membership: December 27, 1945

Standard Sources:
B: Board of Governors of the Federal Reserve System, *Federal Reserve Bulletin*
S: U.S. Department of Commerce, *Survey of Current Business, Highlights of U.S. Export and Import Trade*
N: U.S. Treasury Department, *Treasury Bulletin*

Exchange Rates: Data of lines *sb* and *sd* relate to geometric averages. Data relate to the par value through June 1974 or to the rate determined through a method known as the standard 'basket' valuation thereafter.

International Liquidity: *Gold (National Valuation) (line 1and)* is the U.S. dollar value of official holdings of gold as reported in the country's standard sources. *Line 5a.d* reports on the financial obligations of residents of the United States to the central banks and the governments of foreign countries, i.e., to the holders of international reserves in the rest of the world. However, *line 5a.d* includes some official placements in the United States that are not classified as official foreign exchange reserves in the reports that countries submit to the Fund for purposes of measuring each country's international reserves in *IFS* lines 1d.d. The breakdown of *line 5a.d,* identifying obligations to official holders in the industrial countries *(line 5agd),* OPEC countries *(line 5ahd),* and other countries *(line 5aid),* is not strictly in accordance with the usual *IFS* classification of countries. For example, Bahrain and Ecuador are classified as OPEC countries *(line 5ahd)* and South Africa is classified among the industrial countries *(line 5agd),* whereas these are included in the *IFS* category of non-oil developing countries.

Lines 6 and *7* are derived from the U.S. Treasury International Capital (TIC) reports. *Line 6* includes the claims of commercial banks' domestic customers in addition to the commercial banks' own claims shown in *line 7. Line 7* differs from the commercial banks' foreign assets *(line 21)* and liabilities *(line 26c),* reported in section 20, mainly because they include the accounts of international banking facilities (IBFs). See notes on commercial banks in section on deposit money banks.

Monetary Authorities: Consolidates the Federal Reserve Banks, the Exchange Stabilization Fund, and monetary functions undertaken by the central government. The contra-entry to Treasury IMF accounts, Treasury issues of coin, and Treasury gold account is included in *line 12a.* Data are derived from source B.

Currency Outside Deposit Money Banks (line 14a) is currency outside the U.S. Treasury, Federal Reserve banks, and commercial banks. It also excludes currency held by other monetary institutions to service checkable deposits. It is an average of daily figures while other data on monetary authorities are averages of beginning and end-of-month data.

Deposit Money Banks: Comprises commercial banks and other monetary institutions. The following institutions are included: domestically chartered commercial banks, their domestic affiliates, Edge Act corporations (affiliates of banks engaged in international activities), branches and agencies of foreign banks in the U.S., and banks in the U.S. possessions. International banking facilities (IBFs), which commenced operations in December 1981, are excluded from this sector. Data for other monetary institutions cover mutual savings banks, savings and loan associations, and credit unions. In addition, *line 24..j* is the outstanding amount of U.S. dollar denominated travelers' checks of nonbank issuers.

Lines 24, 24..j, 24..t, 25, 25..t, 26aa, and *26aat* are averages of daily figures and are derived from source B. Other data for deposit money banks are largely based on averages of beginning and end-of-month data, although some series have been interpolated from quarterly data. These data are as reported for *IFS* purposes by the national authorities and are largely based on estimates of stocks from the 'Flow of Funds Accounts' of the Board of Governors of the Federal Reserve System. Because of timing and compilation differences, *lines 27r* and *27r.t* contain a balancing item.

Data for commercial banks distinguish where possible between domestic and foreign claims on the basis of residency; such a separation is not available for other monetary institutions. Positions of commercial banks vis-à-vis IBFs are included in *Foreign Assets* and *Foreign Liabilities (lines 21* and *26c)* respectively. Commercial banks' *Foreign Assets* include acceptances issued by nonresident banks and foreign customers' liabilities under acceptances. *Foreign Liabilities* include acceptances issued by commercial banks held by nonresidents but do not include repurchase agreements with nonresidents other than foreign official institutions and banks. From January 1984 certain foreign assets and liabilities of commercial banks, which were previously reported on a gross basis, are now reported on a net basis.

Claims on Central Government (lines 22a and *22a.t)* exclude, and *Claims on Private Sector (lines 22d* and *22d.t)* include, claims on government-sponsored credit agencies and government enterprises. *Checkable Deposits (lines 24* and *24..t)* include negotiable order of withdrawal (NOW) and automatic transfer service (ATS) accounts. *Line 24* excludes checkable deposits of other monetary institutions at commercial banks. *Time and Savings Deposits (lines 25* and *25..t)* include money market deposit accounts and exclude time deposits of $100,000 and over (which are largely negotiable certificates of deposit). The latter and repurchase agreements are included in *Money Market Instruments (lines 26aa* and *26aat). Line 26aa* also includes bankers' acceptances held by residents other than the issuing bank. Acceptances of resident banks held by other resident

Appendix 4B International Monetary Fund Data for the United States

United States

111

1988 I	1988 II	1988 III	1988 IV	1989 I	1988 July	Aug	Sept	Oct	Nov	Dec	1989 Jan	Feb	Mar	Apr		
Year Ending September 30															**Government Finance**	
....	....	....	....	....	....	....	....	....	....	....	....	....	....	....	Deficit (-) or Surplus	80
....	....	....	....	....	....	....	....	....	....	....	....	....	....	....	Revenue	81
....	....	....	....	....	....	....	....	....	....	....	....	....	....	....	Grants Received	81z
....	....	....	....	....	....	....	....	....	....	....	....	....	....	....	Exp. & Lending Minus Repay	82z
....	....	....	....	....	....	....	....	....	....	....	....	....	....	....	Expenditure	82
....	....	....	....	....	....	....	....	....	....	....	....	....	....	....	Lending Minus Repayments	83
															Financing	
....	....	....	....	....	....	....	....	....	....	....	....	....	....	....	Net Borrowing	84
....	....	....	....	....	....	....	....	....	....	....	....	....	....	....	Domestic	84a
....	....	....	....	....	....	....	....	....	....	....	....	....	....	....	Foreign	85a
....	....	....	....	....	....	....	....	....	....	....	....	....	....	....	Use of Cash Balances	87
Year Ending December 31																
1,998.6	2,014.7	2,052.9	2,091.2	....	....	....	2,052.9	....	....	2,091.2	....	....	....	....	Debt	88
217.5	227.6	229.2	238.4	....	224.5	222.8	229.2	225.6	....	238.4	....	....	....	....	Held by: Monetary Authorities	88aa
201.0	202.5	203.0	195.0	....	....	....	203.0	....	....	195.0	....	....	....	....	Commercial Banks	88ab
125.5	132.2	135.0	....	....	....	....	135.0	....	....	....	....	....	....	....	Other Financial Inst.	88ac
285.8	286.3	287.0	....	....	....	....	287.0	....	....	....	....	....	....	....	State & Local Govts	88ad
83.0	86.5	86.0	86.1	....	....	....	86.0	....	....	86.1	....	....	....	....	Corporations	88ae
176.7	180.1	184.5	187.4	....	....	....	184.5	....	....	187.4	....	....	....	....	Individuals	88af
14.9	13.1	10.8	18.8	....	....	....	10.8	....	....	18.8	....	....	....	....	Money Market Funds	88ag
321.0	333.8	334.3	349.3	....	....	....	334.3	....	....	349.3	....	....	....	....	Foreign & International	88ca
573.2	552.6	583.1	....	....	....	....	583.1	....	....	....	....	....	....	....	Others	88d
491.4	534.7	550.7	589.5	....	534.9	536.9	550.7	562.5	566.4	589.5	....	....	....	....	Intragovernmental Debt	88s
Seasonally Adjusted at Annual Rates															**National Accounts**	
383.1	402.9	420.0	425.5	***441.7***	....	....	....	....	....	....	....	....	....	....	Exports	90c
945.2	961.6	955.3	997.5	***1,010.9***	....	....	....	....	....	....	....	....	....	....	Gov't Consumption & Investment	91ff
88.2	91.5	85.2	107.3	***109.1***	....	....	....	....	....	....	....	....	....	....	*of which:* Gross Capital Form	93gf
698.1	714.4	722.8	737.2	***754.2***	....	....	....	....	....	....	....	....	....	....	Private Gross Fixed Capital Form	93ee
65.3	43.7	49.7	34.7	***61.8***	....	....	....	....	....	....	....	....	....	....	Increase in Stocks	93i
3,128.1	3,194.6	3,261.2	3,326.4	***3,380.4***	....	....	....	....	....	....	....	....	....	....	Private Consumption	96f
−517.6	−514.6	−526.7	−550.5	***−559.1***	....	....	....	....	....	....	....	....	....	....	Less: Imports	98c
4,702.1	4,802.5	4,882.2	4,970.7	***5,090.0***	....	....	....	....	....	....	....	....	....	....	Gross Domestic Product	99b
22.4	21.3	26.8	29.0	***26.8***	....	....	....	....	....	....	....	....	....	....	Net Factor Income from Abroad	90e
4,724.5	4,823.8	4,909.0	4,999.7	***5,116.8***	....	....	....	....	....	....	....	....	....	....	Gross Nat'l Expenditure = GNP	99a
4,226.2	4,320.6	4,401.3	4,483.5	***4,592.2***	....	....	....	....	....	....	....	....	....	....	Nat'l Income, Market Prices	99e
4,389.2	4,421.5	4,448.3	4,474.9	***4,535.7***	....	....	....	....	....	....	....	....	....	....	Gross Nat'l Prod. 1985 Prices	99a.r

banks (which should be netted as interbank accounts) are included in *lines 22d* and *26aa*, as they are not separately identifiable.

Monetary Survey: In the monetary survey (see Introduction for the standard method of calculation), *lines 20* through *24..j* are consolidated. The contra-entry for *line 24..j* is included in *line 32dy*.

Money (line 34) is equivalent to M_1 in source B. *Money* plus *Quasi-Money (line 34* plus *line 35)* differs from M_2 in source B by the latter's inclusion of overnight repurchase agreements at commercial banks, some overnight Eurodollar deposits held by U.S. residents, balances of general purpose and broker/dealer money market mutual funds, and the exclusion of IRA/Keogh (tax-deferred) accounts.

Other Banking Institutions: Comprises money market mutual funds. Data are derived from source B. *Line 45..m* comprises balances of general purpose and broker/dealer money market mutual funds as well as institution-only money market mutual funds.

Nonbank Financial Institutions: Comprises life insurance offices. Data are derived from source B.

Interest Rates: All interest rate data are from source B. *Discount Rate (End of Period):* Rate at which the Federal Reserve Bank of New York discounts eligible paper and makes advances to member banks. Establishment of the discount rate is at the discretion of each Federal Reserve bank but is subject to review and determination by the Board of Governors in Washington every fourteen days; these rates are publicly announced. Borrowing from a Federal Reserve bank is a privilege of being a member of the Federal Reserve system. Borrowing may take the form either of discounts of short-term commercial, industrial, and other financial paper or of advances against government securities and other eligible collateral; most transactions are in the form of advances. Federal Reserve advances to or discounts for member banks are usually of short maturity up to fifteen days. Federal Reserve banks do not discount eligible paper or make advances to member banks automatically. Ordinarily, the continuous use of Federal Reserve credit by a member bank over a considerable period of time is not regarded as appropriate. The volume of discounts is consequently very small.

Federal Funds Rate: Rates at which banks purchase (or borrow) funds in this interbank market to meet their reserve requirements in the short run or finance loans and investments in the longer run. Monthly figures are averages of all calendar days, where the rate for a weekend or holiday is taken to be the rate prevailing on the preceding day. The daily rate is the average of the rates on a given day weighted by the volume of transactions at these rates.

Commercial Paper Rate: Three-month rates for commercial paper placed for firms whose bond rating is AA or the equivalent. Yields are quoted on a bank discount basis rather than an investment yield basis. Monthly figures are averages of business day data.

Treasury Bill Rate: Discount on new issues of three-month bills and annual averages of these. Source B annual data are averages of weekly data.

Treasury Bill Rate (Bond Equivalent): Monthly data refer to the simple arithmetic average of daily yields on a coupon equivalent basis on three-month bills. This rate is used in calculating the SDR interest rate.

Certificates of Deposit Rate: Unweighted averages of offered rates quoted by at least five dealers early in the day for three-month certificates of deposit in the secondary market. Monthly figures are averages of business day data.

Lending Rate (Prime Rate): Rate that the largest banks charge their most creditworthy business customers on short-term loans. It is the base from which rates charged on loans to other business customers are scaled upward. Generally speaking, the prime rate has not been considered a sensitive rate that fluctuates daily in response to short-term changes in demand and supply as measured by a national market. Monthly figures are averages of daily rates.

Government Bond Yield: Medium-term series refer to three-year constant maturities. Long-term series refer to 10-year constant maturities.

Prices, Production, Employment: *Industrial Share Prices:* Data are from source S and are produced as a Laspeyres-type index of the Standard and Poors Corporation for 400 industrials on the New York Exchange, based on daily closing quotations, base 1941–43. *Producer Prices:* The index for producer prices is a composite of wholesale and producer prices, but is primarily a producer price index. The index covers prices received by producers of commodities at all stages of production. It is compiled by the Bureau of Labor Statistics (U.S. Department of Labor) and published in source S. The index has implicit quantity weights representing the net selling value of commodities in 1972. *Consumer Prices:* The index of consumer prices covers all urban consumers representing about 80 percent of the non-institutional population. The index is compiled by the Bureau of Labor Statistics (U.S. Department of Labor) and published in source S. Beginning January 1983, the cost of shelter to the homeowner is measured by a rental equivalence; from January 1987, an enhanced housing survey represents more adequately both owners and renters in the estimation of shelter costs. The weights are compiled from the Consumer Expenditure Survey carried out from 1982 through 1984. Beginning January 1983, the cost of shelter to the homeowner is measured by a rental equivalence, and since January 1987 an enhanced housing survey represents optimally both owners and renters in the estimation of shelter costs. Reference base 1982-84=100. *Wages: Hourly Earnings (Mfg):* This series is from source S and represents earnings in U.S. dollars per hour, including overtime, for production and nonsupervisory workers in manufacturing.

Industrial Production, Seasonally Adjusted: Data are from source B and are produced as an index with value added weights. The index is seasonally adjusted according to the X-11 version of Method II of the Bureau of Census, base 1977. *Crude Petroleum Production:* Data are from the *Monthly Energy Review* of the U.S. Department of Energy and refer to total daily domestic production, including Alaska, multiplied by the number of days in the period. *Nonagricultural Employment, Seasonally Adjusted:* Data are from source B and represent an establishment survey that covers all full- and part-time employees who worked during or received pay for the pay period that includes the 12th of the month. The survey excludes proprietors, self-employed persons, domestic servants, unpaid family workers, and members of the Armed Forces.

International Transactions: All trade value data are from the *Highlights of U.S. Export and Import Trade.* Total trade data include trade of the U.S. Virgin Islands. Beginning January 1975, data include exports and imports, respectively, of nonmonetary gold, which prior to January 1975 are excluded. The volume and unit value data are Fisher indexes and are from source S, base 1977. ‡ Beginning in 1987, all trade data are reported on the revised statistical month based on import entry and export declaration transaction dates, whereas previous data reflect import entries and export declarations transmitted to the U.S. Bureau of the Census during a fixed monthly processing period.

Government Finance: Annual data are as reported in the *Government Finance Statistics Yearbook* (with the exception of outstanding debt data) and relate to the consolidated central government. Data agree with the revised data in sources B

(Continued in the back of the book.)

Appendix 4C

International Monetary Fund Data for Mexico

Mexico
273

Units (as noted at right of each section): Exchange Rates — *Pesos per SDR* (wa) / *Pesos per US Dollar* (we, wf, xe, xf); Fund Position — *Millions of SDRs*; International Liquidity — *Millions of US Dollars Unless Otherwise Indicated*; Monetary Authorities / Deposit Money Banks / Monetary Survey / Other Banking Institutions — *Billions of Pesos*.

	1982	1983	1984	1985	1986	1987	1988	1986 I	1986 II	1986 III	1986 IV	1987 I	1987 II	1987 III	1987 IV
Exchange Rates															
Principal Rate ...aa= wa	106.4	150.7	188.7	408.3	1,129.6	3,134.8	3,069.5	539.1	677.6	912.5	1,129.6	1,447.6	1,730.1	2,010.1	3,134.8
Principal Rate ...ae= we	96.5	143.9	192.6	371.7	923.5	2,209.7	2,281.0	473.6	575.4	752.0	923.5	1,126.0	1,353.7	1,570.8	2,209.7
Principal Rate ...rf= wf	56.4	120.1	167.8	256.9	611.8	1,378.2	2,273.1	423.6	522.2	665.7	835.6	1,025.7	1,241.7	1,460.8	1,784.6
Secondary Rate xe	149.3	161.4	210.0	450.8	914.5	2,245.0	2,295.0	485.8	641.5	770.5	914.5	1,120.0	1,347.0	1,564.0	2,245.0
Secondary Rate xf	....	150.3	185.2	310.2	637.4	1,405.8	2,288.3	462.8	553.5	686.6	846.5	1,018.5	1,229.5	1,452.3	1,922.8
Fund Position															
Quota 2f.s	803	1,166	1,166	1,166	1,166	1,166	1,166	1,166	1,166	1,166	1,166	1,166	1,166	1,166	1,166
SDRs 1b.s	5	22	3		7	498	293	1	7	—	7	—	463	308	498
Reserve Position in the Fund 1c.s	—	91													
Use of Fund Credit: Gen. Dept. 2e.s	201	1,204	2,408	2,703	3,319	3,639	3,570	2,970	2,945	2,913	3,319	3,269	3,606	3,733	3,639
incl.: Credit Tranche: Ordinary 2ees	201	201	201	201	617	674	674	467	442	417	617	592	700	699	674
Credit Tranche: EAR 2dhs					225	667	1,017				225	225	492	667	667
Extended Facility: Ordinary 2kxs	—	502	1,103	1,124	1,124	1,107	998	1,124	1,124	1,124	1,124	1,124	1,124	1,119	1,107
Extended Facility: EAR 2djs	—	502	1,103	1,379	1,354	1,191	881	1,379	1,379	1,373	1,354	1,354	1,329	1,248	1,191
International Liquidity															
Total Reserves minus Gold 1l.d	834	3,913	7,272	4,906	5,670	12,464	5,279	5,003	3,461	3,334	5,670	7,740	12,552	13,314	12,464
SDRs 1b.d	6	23	3		9	706	394	1	8	—	9	—	592	394	706
Reserve Position in the Fund 1c.d	—	95													
Foreign Exchange 1d.d	828	3,795	7,269	4,906	5,661	11,758	4,885	5,002	3,453	3,334	5,661	7,740	11,960	12,920	11,758
Gold (Million Fine Troy Ounces) 1ad	2.065	2.308	2.422	2.362	2.568	2.536	2.555	2.534	2.537	2.535	2.568	2.575	2.514	2.531	2.536
Gold (National Valuation) 1and	826	831	709												
Deposit Money Banks: Assets 7a.d	1,433	2,179	1,912	2,121	2,003	2,824	2,638	2,128	1,822	1,958	2,003	2,016	1,875	1,877	2,824
Liabilities 7b.d	9,221	10,751	10,284	9,446	8,672	7,020	8,477	9,135	8,987	8,849	8,672	6,530	6,741	6,799	7,020
Other Banking Insts.: Assets 7e.d	152	338	386	383	484	377	468	389	380	425	484	465	463	355	377
Liabilities 7f.d	22,991	23,137	23,715	25,342	27,310	29,635	28,310	25,434	25,844	26,242	27,310	27,682	27,984	28,162	29,635
Monetary Authorities															
Foreign Assets 11	176	708	1,561	2,168	6,214	30,306	14,969	2,820	2,540	3,371	6,214	10,048	18,609	22,850	30,306
Claims on Central Government 12a	2,126	3,321	4,335	6,607	10,697	12,151	34,440	7,364	8,831	10,212	10,697	10,289	6,303	6,489	12,151
Claims on Deposit Money Banks 12e	235	53	54	45	51	52	171	48	37	47	51	50	53	59	52
Claims on Other Banking Insts. 12f	73	73	129	79	111	126	853	95	98	106	111	96	102	108	126
Reserve Money 14	2,068	3,225	4,879	5,706	8,444	14,402	20,457	6,053	6,304	6,484	8,444	8,970	9,612	10,965	14,402
of which: Currency Outside DMBs 14a	505	681	1,122	1,738	3,067	7,339	13,201	1,735	1,857	1,903	3,067	3,064	3,711	4,263	7,339
Time & Foreign Currency Deposits 15	48	198	376	565	373	1,350	1,193	501	358	341	373	743	885	1,345	1,350
Foreign Liabilities 16c	25	181	453	1,094	3,716	11,411	10,851	1,591	1,982	2,640	3,716	4,715	6,217	7,482	11,411
Other Items (Net) 17r	467	551	373	1,534	4,540	15,472	17,932	2,183	2,859	4,271	4,540	6,055	8,352	9,714	15,472
Deposit Money Banks															
Reserves 20	1,480	2,514	3,801	3,927	5,310	7,075	8,503	4,330	4,530	4,580	5,310	6,001	5,996	6,264	7,075
Foreign Assets 21	138	313	367	781	1,833	6,241	5,953	1,001	1,041	1,462	1,833	2,260	2,529	2,939	6,241
Claims on Central Government 22a	487	717	986	3,488	10,959	26,579	30,422	4,351	5,701	7,671	10,959	13,640	18,226	20,879	26,579
Claims on Local Government 22b	23	19	72	71	89	250	181	73	76	72	89	63	120	155	250
Claims on Nonfin.Pub.Enterprises 22c	228	578	1,011	1,355	2,838	5,789	6,527	1,633	1,892	2,432	2,838	2,828	3,595	4,465	5,789
Claims on Private Sector 22d	1,269	1,822	3,376	5,167	8,742	22,571	41,499	5,600	6,422	7,405	8,742	9,992	12,363	16,145	22,571
Claims on Other Banking Insts. 22f	71	162	213	340	974	2,759	2,300	455	575	670	974	1,160	1,455	1,902	2,759
Demand Deposits 24	455	676	1,075	1,610	2,468	4,928	7,130	1,587	1,690	1,766	2,468	2,642	3,124	3,630	4,928
Time, Savings,& Fgn.Currency Dep. 25	1,976	3,300	5,641	7,909	15,136	38,679	20,956	8,912	10,200	12,048	15,136	19,676	24,663	28,885	38,679
Foreign Liabilities 26c	78	114	142	211	478	1,752	3,457	260	420	461	478	586	905	962	1,752
Long-Term Foreign Liabilities 26cl	810	1,430	1,832	3,267	7,458	13,760	15,676	4,037	4,715	6,146	7,458	6,735	8,185	9,682	13,760
Central Government Deposits 26d	8	15	24	20	63	82	178	49	32	36	63	159	68	69	82
Credit from Monetary Authorities 26g	22	38	83	128	159	385	528	102	93	99	159	198	285	284	385
Capital Accounts 27a	68	96	169	281	633	2,105	4,085	330	393	475	633	831	1,157	1,549	2,105
Other Items (Net) 27r	279	456	856	1,703	4,350	9,573	43,375	2,166	2,694	3,261	4,350	5,117	5,897	7,688	9,573
Monetary Survey															
Foreign Assets (Net) 31n	211	726	1,333	1,644	3,853	23,384	6,614	1,970	1,179	1,732	3,853	7,007	14,016	17,345	23,384
Domestic Credit 32	4,271	6,681	10,104	17,097	34,363	70,180	116,115	19,533	23,575	28,546	34,363	37,929	42,119	50,102	70,180
Claims on Central Govt. (Net) 32an	2,605	4,023	5,297	10,075	21,593	38,648	64,684	11,666	14,500	17,847	21,593	23,770	24,460	27,299	38,648
Claims on Nonfin.Pub.Enterprises 32c	228	578	1,011	1,355	2,838	5,789	6,527	1,633	1,892	2,432	2,838	2,828	3,595	4,465	5,789
Claims on Private Sector 32d	1,271	1,826	3,382	5,177	8,758	22,608	41,570	5,611	6,434	7,419	8,758	10,012	12,387	16,173	22,608
Claims on Other Banking Insts. 32f	144	235	342	419	1,085	2,885	3,533	550	673	776	1,085	1,256	1,557	2,010	2,885
Money 34	1,031	1,447	2,315	3,462	5,790	12,627	20,774	3,406	3,646	3,795	5,790	6,059	7,075	8,468	12,627
Quasi-Money 35	2,024	3,300	6,017	8,474	15,509	40,029	22,149	9,413	10,558	12,389	15,509	20,419	25,548	30,230	40,029
Long-Term Foreign Liabilities 36cl	810	1,430	1,832	3,267	7,458	13,760	15,676	4,037	4,715	6,146	7,458	6,735	8,185	9,682	13,760
Other Items (Net) 37r	615	1,032	1,271	3,538	9,459	27,148	64,130	4,648	5,832	7,948	9,459	11,723	15,327	19,067	27,148
Money, Seasonally Adjusted 34..b	893	1,254	2,006	3,010	5,048	11,047	18,207	3,329	3,694	4,085	5,048	5,900	7,146	9,105	11,047
Other Banking Institutions															
Cash 40	77	92	111	142	264	632	748	152	162	200	264	396	354	793	632
Foreign Assets 41	15	49	74	141	443	834	1,057	183	217	317	443	521	556		834
Claims on Central Government 42a	1,132	1,697	2,381	5,139	14,098	42,933	48,983	6,402	8,085	10,871	14,098	17,631	23,007	27,785	42,933
Claims on Local Government 42b	128	133	240	280	155	239	490	292	310	195	155	173	185	171	239
Claims on Nonfin.Pub.Enterprises 42c	1,016	1,394	1,922	3,226	7,208	13,282	11,702	4,229	4,987	5,791	7,208	8,770	9,061	9,830	13,282
Claims on Deposit Money Banks 42e	1,248	448	839	1,577	2,939	7,192	13,384	1,757	2,027	2,463	2,939	3,413	4,356	5,795	7,192
Time, Savings,& Fgn.Currency Dep. 45	41	96	130	183	418	1,017	2,275	210	272	339	418	484	529	798	1,017
Foreign Liabilities 46c	1,254	470	793	1,241	2,226	5,732	9,024	1,431	1,619	1,958	2,226	2,788	3,645	4,175	5,732
Long-Term Foreign Liabilities 46cl	5	1	5	5	46	19	107	8	7	9	46	56	13	16	19
Central Government Deposits 46d	2,209	3,322	4,547	9,326	24,945	65,465	63,788	11,956	14,760	19,583	24,945	30,978	37,723	44,071	65,465
Credit from Monetary Authorities 46g	180	266	384	674	430	1,932	6,154	827	761	349	430	619	681	996	1,932
Credit from Deposit Money Banks 46h	106	102	154	228	483	1,429	312	249	287	366	483	607	737	914	1,429
Capital Accounts 47a	86	127	234	329	541	932	2,346	351	566	550	541	599	704	991	932
Other Items (Net) 47r	-363	-546	-666	-1,482	-3,772	-10,426	-5,166	-1,920	-2,330	-3,140	-3,772	-4,897	-6,195	-6,282	-10,426

Mexico — 273

	1988 I	II	III	IV	1989 I	1988 July	Aug	Sept	Oct	Nov	Dec	1989 Jan	Feb	Mar	Apr	Item	Code
Exchange Rates																	
End of Period																	
	3,164.4	2,989.5	2,943.4	3,069.5	3,062.4	2,957.3	2,938.3	2,943.4	3,070.0	3,116.7	3,069.5	3,028.2	3,089.7	3,062.4	*3,105.7*	Principal Rate....aa=	wa
End of Period (we and xe) Period Average (wf and xf)																	
	2,281.0	2,281.0	2,281.0	2,281.0	2,369.0	2,281.0	2,281.0	2,281.0	2,281.0	2,281.0	2,281.0	2,310.0	2,338.0	2,369.0	*2,397.0*	Principal Rate....ae=	we
	2,249.4	2,281.0	2,281.0	2,281.0	2,324.2	2,281.0	2,281.0	2,281.0	2,281.0	2,281.0		2,294.8	2,324.3	2,353.4	*2,384.4*	Principal Rate....rf=	wf
	2,295.0	2,295.0	2,295.0	2,295.0	....	2,295.0	2,295.0	2,295.0	2,295.0	2,295.0	2,295.0	2,327.0	....	....		Secondary Rate	xe
	2,268.2	2,295.0	2,295.0	2,295.0	....	2,295.0	2,295.0	2,295.0	2,295.0	2,295.0	2,295.0	2,307.8	....	....		Secondary Rate	xf
Fund Position																	
End of Period																	
	1,166	1,166	1,166	1,166	1,166	1,166	1,166	1,166	1,166	1,166	1,166	1,166	1,166	1,166	*1,166*	Quota	2f.s
	420	299	302	293	276	411	352	302	352	268	293	206	297	276	405	SDRs	1b.s
	—	—	—	—	—	—	—	—	—	—	—	—	—	—	—	Reserve Position in the Fund	1c.s
	3,910	3,810	3,718	3,570	3,466	3,799	3,768	3,718	3,718	3,661	3,570	3,560	3,516	3,466	*3,429*	Use of Fund Credit: Gen. Dept.	2e.s
	674	674	674	674	674	674	674	674	674	674	674	674	674	674	*638*	incl.: Credit Tranche: Ordinary	2ees
	1,017	1,017	1,017	1,017	1,017	1,017	1,017	1,017	1,017	1,017	1,017	1,017	1,017	1,017	*1,017*	Credit Tranche: EAR	2dhs
	1,090	1,065	1,036	998	956	1,061	1,048	1,036	1,036	998	998	994	969	956	*956*	Extended Facility: Ordinary	2kxs
	1,128	1,053	990	881	818	1,047	1,028	990	990	972	881	847	856	818	*818*	Extended Facility: EAR	2djs
International Liquidity																	
End of Period																	
	14,524	12,855	8,591	5,279	....	10,474	10,914	8,591	7,646	5,485	5,279	*5,472*	....	....	525	Total Reserves minus Gold	1l.d
	583	392	390	394	357	532	454	390	474	367	394	270	392	357	—	SDRs	1b.d
	—	—	—	—	—	—	—	—	—	—	—	—	....	....	—	Reserve Position in the Fund	1c.d
	13,941	12,463	8,201	4,885	....	9,942	10,460	8,201	7,172	5,118	4,885	*5,202*	....	....	525	Foreign Exchange	1d.d
	2.544	2.627	2.674	2.555	....	2.668	2.670	2.674	2.673	2.631	2.555	*2.435*	....	....		Gold (Million Fine Troy Ounces)	1ad
	....	....	....	....	....	....	....	....	....	....	....	....	....	....		Gold (National Valuation)	1and
	2,262	1,943	2,291	2,638	....	2,212	2,420	2,291	2,191	2,510	2,638	....	....	....		Deposit Money Banks: Assets	7a.d
	7,296	7,728	8,040	8,477	....	7,826	8,071	8,040	8,166	7,983	8,477	....	....	....		Liabilities	7b.d
	397	382	414	468	....	391	410	414	412	494	468	....	....	....		Other Banking Insts.: Assets	7e.d
	28,397	27,652	27,607	28,310	....	27,323	27,448	27,607	28,058	28,596	28,310	....	....	....		Liabilities	7f.d
Monetary Authorities																	
End of Period																	
	36,029	32,293	22,593	14,969	....		26,916	22,593	20,554	15,628	14,969	....	....	....		Foreign Assets	11
	9,870	14,804	21,630	34,440	....	18,917	20,699	21,630	24,605	29,457	34,440	....	....	....		Claims on Central Government	12a
	48	66	181	171	....	109	171	181	167	186	171	....	....	....		Claims on Deposit Money Banks	12e
	125	121	117	853	....	150	119	117	116	473	853	....	....	....		Claims on Other Banking Insts.	12f
	15,675	19,535	16,721	20,457	....	18,866	18,252	16,721	17,158	17,799	20,457	....	....	....		Reserve Money	14
	8,518	9,856	10,010	13,201	....	10,370	9,757	10,010	10,051	11,541	13,201	....	....	....		of which: Currency Outside DMBs	14a
	998	931	620	1,193	....	710	709	620	596	951	1,193	....	....	....		Time & Foreign Currency Deposits	15
	12,247	11,275	10,841	10,851	....	11,128	10,966	10,841	11,305	11,298	10,851	....	....	....		Foreign Liabilities	16c
	17,151	15,543	16,339	17,932	....	15,388	19,161	16,339	16,383	15,696	17,932	....	....	....		Other Items (Net)	17r
Deposit Money Banks																	
End of Period																	
	7,511	9,767	6,209	8,503	....	8,791	8,599	6,209	7,354	7,690	8,503	....	....	....		Reserves	20
	5,106	4,385	5,171	5,953	....	4,993	5,462	5,171	4,944	5,666	5,953	....	....	....		Foreign Assets	21
	33,717	33,288	35,916	30,422	....	34,431	32,344	35,916	33,396	27,804	30,422	....	....	....		Claims on Central Government	22a
	180	188	165	181	....	144	151	165	153	218	181	....	....	....		Claims on Local Government	22b
	5,885	6,287	6,582	6,527	....	6,228	6,342	6,582	6,416	6,475	6,527	....	....	....		Claims on Nonfin.Pub.Enterprises	22c
	22,755	27,889	30,312	41,499	....	28,082	29,140	30,312	35,627	37,219	41,499	....	....	....		Claims on Private Sector	22d
	3,095	3,689	4,082	2,300	....	3,749	3,799	4,082	3,867	3,349	2,300	....	....	....		Claims on Other Banking Insts.	22f
	5,053	6,336	5,868	7,130	....	5,887	5,994	5,868	6,925	6,959	7,130	....	....	....		Demand Deposits	24
	46,053	49,716	51,168	20,956	....	50,348	48,629	51,168	47,965	35,398	20,956	....	....	....		Time, Savings,& Fgn.Currency Dep.	25
	2,037	2,229	2,382	3,457	....	2,118	2,198	2,382	2,566	2,632	3,457	....	....	....		Foreign Liabilities	26c
	14,431	15,212	15,765	15,676	....	15,545	16,019	15,765	15,865	15,385	15,676	....	....	....		Long-Term Foreign Liabilities	26cl
	194	170	199	178	....	168	166	199	230	205	178	....	....	....		Central Government Deposits	26d
	176	520	506	528	....	536	638	506	489	499	528	....	....	....		Credit from Monetary Authorities	26g
	2,542	3,141	3,645	4,085	....	3,326	3,484	3,645	3,879	3,965	4,085	....	....	....		Capital Accounts	27a
	7,763	8,169	8,904	43,375	....	8,490	8,709	8,904	13,838	23,378	43,375	....	....	....		Other Items (Net)	27r
Monetary Survey																	
End of Period																	
	26,851	23,174	14,541	6,614	....	18,663	20,398	14,541	11,627	7,364	6,614	....	....	....		Foreign Assets (Net)	31n
	75,481	86,153	98,669	116,115	....	91,593	92,489	98,669	104,016	104,860	116,115	....	....	....		Domestic Credit	32
	43,392	47,922	57,347	64,684	....	53,180	52,876	57,347	57,771	57,056	64,684	....	....	....		Claims on Central Govt. (Net)	32an
	5,885	6,287	6,582	6,527	....	6,228	6,342	6,582	6,416	6,475	6,527	....	....	....		Claims on Nonfin.Pub.Enterprises	32c
	22,804	27,946	30,376	41,570	....	28,142	29,202	30,376	35,693	37,289	41,570	....	....	....		Claims on Private Sector	32d
	3,220	3,810	4,082	3,153	....	3,899	3,618	4,082	4,199	3,983	3,153	....	....	....		Claims on Other Banking Insts.	32f
	14,055	16,975	16,667	20,774	....	16,541	16,440	16,667	17,385	19,024	20,774	....	....	....		Money	34
	47,051	50,647	51,788	22,149	....	51,058	49,338	51,788	48,561	36,349	22,149	....	....	....		Quasi-Money	35
	14,431	15,212	15,765	15,676	....	15,545	16,019	15,765	15,865	15,385	15,676	....	....	....		Long-Term Foreign Liabilities	36cl
	26,795	26,493	28,990	64,130	....	27,112	31,090	28,990	33,832	41,466	64,130	....	....	....		Other Items (Net)	37r
	13,659	*17,129*	17,922	*18,207*	....	17,105	*17,508*	17,922	18,358	*18,817*	*18,207*	....	....	....		*Money, Seasonally Adjusted*	34..b
Other Banking Institutions																	
End of Period																	
	870	985	1,087	748	....	565	984	1,087	643	757	748	....	....	....		Cash	40
	897	862	934	1,057	....	883	926	934	931	1,114	1,057	....	....	....		Foreign Assets	41
	41,921	40,682	42,768	48,983	....	40,284	42,082	42,768	43,756	45,802	48,983	....	....	....		Claims on Central Government	42a
	272	380	380	490	....	276	360	380	404	461	490	....	....	....		Claims on Local Government	42b
	14,104	14,480	13,707	11,702	....	14,316	13,871	13,707	13,481	13,283	11,702	....	....	....		Claims on Nonfin.Pub.Enterprises	42c
	7,917	9,382	10,763	13,384	....	10,028	10,524	10,763	11,941	12,412	13,384	....	....	....		Claims on Private Sector	42d
	975	1,946	2,258	2,275	....	1,945	1,855	2,258	1,832	2,188	2,275	....	....	....		Claims on Deposit Money Banks	42e
	7,158	7,754	8,567	9,024	....	7,713	8,310	8,567	8,086	8,645	9,024	....	....	....		Time, Savings,& Fgn.Currency Dep.	45
	19	24	36	107	....	26	32	36	33	109	107	....	....	....		Foreign Liabilities	46c
	64,074	62,386	62,273	63,788	....	61,643	61,919	62,273	63,293	64,433	63,788	....	....	....		Long-Term Foreign Liabilities	46cl
	1,642	2,134	3,504	6,154	....	2,358	3,345	3,504	4,089	4,571	6,154	....	....	....		Central Government Deposits	46d
	1,889	2,442	2,795	312	....	2,539	2,487	2,795	2,567	2,344	312	....	....	....		Credit from Monetary Authorities	46g
	1,065	1,192	1,073	2,074	....	1,171	1,125	1,073	1,073	1,134	2,074	....	....	....		Credit from Deposit Money Banks	46h
	1,920	2,559	2,796	2,346	....	2,708	2,744	2,796	2,920	2,056	2,346	....	....	....		Capital Accounts	47a
	-10,811	-9,878	-9,147	-5,166	....	-9,861	-9,360	-9,147	-9,073	-7,277	-5,166	....	....	....		Other Items (Net)	47r

Mexico
273

	1982	1983	1984	1985	1986	1987	1988	1986 I	II	III	IV	1987 I	II	III	IV
Banking Survey														*Billions of Pesos:*	
Foreign Assets (Net) 51n	1220	774	1,402	1,780	4,250	24,199	7,564	2,145	1,389	2,040	4,250	7,472	14,628	17,885	24,199
Domestic Credit 52	16,471	9,852	14,760	26,226	57,248	129,009	181,367	30,836	37,550	46,741	57,248	66,041	76,490	90,677	129,009
Claims on Central Govt. (Net)... 52an	13,557	5,454	7,294	14,540	35,261	79,649	107,513	17,241	21,824	28,369	35,261	35,261	40,782	46,786	54,088	79,649
Claims on Nonfin.Pub.Enterprises 52c	1,244	1,972	2,933	4,581	10,046	19,071	18,229	5,862	6,879	8,223	10,046	11,598	12,656	14,295	19,071
Claims on Private Sector 52d	11,519	2,274	4,221	6,754	11,697	29,800	54,954	7,368	8,461	9,882	11,697	13,425	16,743	21,968	29,800
Liquid Liabilities 55l	3,330	5,443	9,185	13,255	23,612	58,555	52,201	14,306	15,881	18,206	23,612	29,343	36,384	42,996	58,555
Long-Term Foreign Liabilities 56cl	3,019	4,752	6,379	12,593	32,403	79,225	79,464	15,993	19,475	25,729	32,403	37,713	45,908	53,753	79,225
Other Items (Net) 57r	1342	427	597	2,158	5,483	15,428	57,266	2,681	3,580	4,846	5,483	6,457	8,826	11,813	15,428
Interest Rates														*Percent Per Annum*	
Money Market Rate................ 60b	....	....	49.9	62.4	88.4	95.6	....	75.9	83.4	96.1	98.3	96.7	93.6	90.2	102.8
Treasury Bill Rate 60c	45.75	59.19	49.47	63.36	88.57	103.07	61.95	75.99	81.66	91.11	105.52	103.85	98.80	96.25	113.38
Deposit Rate....................... 60l	43.62	54.70	48.36	59.48	84.68	97.24	....	75.18	80.94	88.30	94.30	94.30	94.30	94.25	106.10
Average Cost of Funds........... 60n	40.40	56.65	51.08	56.07	80.88	94.64	....	70.21	75.16	84.49	93.67	96.11	94.78	92.03	95.65
Lending Rate....................... 60p	46.02	63.03	54.73	....	....	....	....	....	....	....	....	....	....	....	....
Prices and Production													*Index Numbers (1985=100):*		
Wholesale Prices 63	18.4	38.2	65.1	100.0	188.4	443.9	922.5	142.3	164.9	201.6	244.7	295.6	381.7	488.5	609.8
Consumer Prices 64	19.0	38.3	63.4	100.0	186.2	431.7	924.6	142.1	165.6	198.0	239.3	297.5	371.4	463.8	594.3
Wages, Monthly (1980=100)...... 65	207.2	311.3	494.2	....	....	....	....	....	....	....	....	....	....	....	....
Industrial Production 66	99.9	91.6	95.1	100.0	94.7	97.9	....	96.2	97.5	92.8	92.2	93.8	97.8	98.7	101.1
Manufacturing Production 66ey	96.5	89.3	93.8	100.0	95.2	97.7	....	97.9	98.8	92.6	91.5	94.8	98.4	98.0	99.7
Mining Production 66zx	102.0	97.8	99.1	100.0	95.8	101.6	....	91.7	96.9	97.9	96.6	98.0	100.1	102.9	105.3
Crude Petroleum 66aa	98.7	96.6	100.4	100.0	96.2	....	....	91.8	96.4	102.0	94.5	98.1	99.3	104.1	....
International Transactions														*Billions of Pesos*	
Exports.......................... 70	1,231.8	2,632.0	4,082.4	5,705.1	10,083.5	28,939.9	247,208.0	1,769.3	1,975.7	2,480.3	3,858.2	4,992.8	6,760.4	7,728.6	9,457.3
Petroleum 70a	941.9	1,822.0	2,754.3	3,799.9	3,896.2	11,788.7	15,075.0	718.7	737.5	969.2	1,470.8	2,068.7	2,751.1	3,398.3	3,570.6
Crude Petroleum 70aa	912.5	1,780.5	2,507.7	3,438.2	3,426.2	10,751.3	13,215.0	619.2	651.2	861.7	1,294.1	1,890.3	2,537.5	3,076.3	3,247.2
Coffee 70e	19.0	61.6	79.5	139.6	519.0	680.6	1,082.4	96.5	116.3	168.4	137.8	172.8	206.1	204.5	97.2
Shrimp 70bl	27.4	46.8	68.1	92.0	98.5	658.6	....	34.7	19.0	30.4	14.5	86.8	76.2	94.8	400.8
Imports, cif 71	774.7	972.4	2,010.8	3,597.5	7,229.7	17,951.0	44,577.5	1,317.5	1,677.7	1,859.4	2,375.1	2,718.6	3,761.4	5,029.0	6,441.9
Imports, fob.................... 71.v	742.8	923.4	1,920.2	3,456.0	6,905.2	17,145.1	42,573.0	1,258.4	1,602.4	1,775.9	2,268.5	2,596.6	3,592.6	4,803.3	6,152.8
Balance of Payments														*Millions of US Dollars:*	
Current Account, nie 77a.d	-6,307	5,403	4,194	1,130	-1,673	3,883	....	-470	-922	-722	441	1,429	1,380	479	595
Merchandise: Exports fob 77aad	21,230	22,312	24,196	21,663	16,031	20,655	....	4,009	3,768	3,666	4,588	4,827	5,360	5,211	5,257
Merchandise: Imports fob 77abd	-14,435	-8,550	-11,255	-13,212	-11,432	-12,222	....	-2,967	-3,063	-2,693	-2,709	-2,512	-2,915	-3,308	-3,487
Trade Bal.,77aad+77abd 77acd	6,795	13,762	12,941	8,451	4,599	8,433	....	1,042	705	973	1,879	2,315	2,445	1,903	1,770
Other Goods,Serv.&Income:Cre . 77add	6,290	6,266	8,182	7,881	7,653	9,105	....	2,034	1,896	1,798	1,925	2,176	2,235	2,242	2,452
Other Goods,Serv.&Income:Deb. 77aed	-19,695	-14,927	-17,339	-16,202	-14,389	-14,323	....	-3,665	-3,641	-3,610	-3,473	-3,191	-3,591	-3,790	-3,751
Private Unrequited Transfers ... 77afd	232	255	325	327	345	384	....	79	91	90	85	82	102	102	98
Official Unrequited Trans.,nie... 77agd	71	47	85	673	119	284	....	40	27	27	25	47	189	22	26
Direct Investment................. 77bad	1,655	461	390	491	1,523	3,248	....	201	461	272	589	497	824	800	1,127
Portfolio Investment, nie 77bbd	921	-653	-756	-984	-816	-29	....	-165	-184	-170	-297	-124	—	4	91
Other Long-Term Capital, nie ... 77bcd	5,773	-67	42	-796	-274	708	....	-287	-290	87	216	-500	3,043	-938	-897
Total,77a.d+77bad—77bcd... 77c.d	2,042	5,144	3,870	-159	-1,240	7,810	....	-721	-935	-533	949	1,302	5,247	345	916
Other Short-Term Capital,nie 77d.d	-6,886	-8,527	-3,574	-1,782	694	-3,158	....	740	57	340	-443	246	-1,178	-257	-1,969
Net Errors and Omissions........ 77e.d	-6,791	-925	-973	-1,765	458	918	....	-171	-769	180	1,217	496	343	524	-446
Total,lines 77c.d—77e.d 77f.d	-11,635	-4,308	-677	-3,706	-88	5,570	....	-152	-1,647	-13	1,723	2,044	4,412	612	-1,499
C'part to Mon./Demon. of Gold.. 78a.d	42	120	65	72	46	74	....	9	11	14	12	15	19	20	20
Counterpart to SDR Allocation .. 78b.d	—	—	—	—	—	—	....	—	—	—	—	—	—	—	—
C'part to Valuation Changes 78c.d	-12	30	139	-313	-190	39	....	-118	7	-104	24	-125	-50	-31	245
Total,lines 77f.d—78c.d 78d.d	-11,605	-4,158	-472	-3,947	-232	5,684	....	-260	-1,628	-103	1,759	1,935	4,381	601	-1,233
Exceptional Financing 79a.d	6,846	7,558	2,827	975	—	—	....	—	—	—	—	—	—	—	—
Liab.Const.Fgn Author. Reserves 79b.d	1,217	-1,217	—	—	—	—	....	—	—	—	—	—	—	—	—
Total Change in Reserves........ 79c.d	3,542	-2,183	-2,355	2,972	232	-5,684	....	260	1,628	103	-1,759	-1,935	-4,381	-601	1,233
Government Finance				*Billions of Pesos: Year Ending December 31*											
Deficit (-) or Surplus............. 80	-1,454	-1,363	-2,094	-3,978	-10,407	-18,160P	-38,232P	....	....	....					
Revenue............................ 81	1,520	3,222	4,774	7,820	12,643	25,597P	68,607P	....	....	....					
Grants Received................... 81z	—	—	—	—	—	—P	—P	....	....	....					
Expenditure....................... 82	2,829	4,468	6,747	11,784	22,800	43,589P	106,045P	....	....	....					
Lending Minus Repayments....... 83	144	117	121	15	250	168P	794P	....	....	....					
Financing															
Net Borrowing: Domestic...... 84a	1,228	807	1,526	3,692	9,391	....	....	....	....	....					
Foreign............. 85a	228	561	586	309	1,024	....	....	....	....	....					
Use of Cash Balances 87	-2	-5	-18	-23	-8	....	....	....	....	....					
Total Debt........................ 88	14,485	7,437	11,092	21,694	61,179	....	....	....	....	....					
National Accounts				See page for Nicaragua											
				Millions: Mid-Year Estimates											
Population 99z	73.12	74.98e	76.79e	78.52e	79.56e	81.16e	....	....	....	....					

Government Finance
Deficit (-) or Surplus........................ 80
Revenue...................................... 81
Grants Received............................. 81z
Expenditure.................................. 82
Lending Minus Repayments............. 83
Financing
  Net Borrowing: Domestic.............. 84a
               Foreign............... 85a
Use of Cash Balances 87
Total Debt.................................... 88

National Accounts

Population 99z

Date of Fund membership: December 31, 1945
Standard Sources:
A: Bank of Mexico, *Annual Report*
B: Bank of Mexico, *Economic Indicators*
S: Statistical Office,
    Monthly Bulletin of Economic Information,
    Statistical Review

Exchange Rates: A dual exchange rate system is in effect, consisting of a controlled market, which is adjusted daily, and a free parallel market. The controlled market rate applies to: (i) receipts on most merchandise export; (ii) payments by in-bond industries for wages, salaries, leasing or rents, and the purchase of Mexican goods and services, other than fixed assets; (iii) payments of principal, interest, and related expenses resulting from financial and suppliers' credits by the public and private sector; (iv) payments for virtually all imports; (v) payments for the Mexican foreign service and contributions to international

organizations; and (vi) other authorized transactions. The free market rate, which is determined by market forces, applies to all other transactions, except the repayment of certain specified obligations which are transacted at varying rates.

    Principal Rate relates to the middle rate between average buying and selling rates reported by main commercial banks to the Bank of Mexico through July 1982, the preferential rate for essential imports from August through November 1982, and the midpoint between the buying and selling rates in the controlled market thereafter.

    Secondary Rate relates to the floating rate under the two-tier system for August 1982, the ordinary rate under the two-tier system from September through November 1982, and the free market rate thereafter.

    International Liquidity: Line 1and is equal to line 1ad, converted into U.S. dollars at the dollar price of gold used by national sources, as reported to *IFS*.

Mexico

273

		1988 I	1988 II	1988 III	1988 IV	1989 I	1988 July	Aug	Sept	Oct	Nov	Dec	1989 Jan	Feb	Mar	Apr
Banking Survey		*End of Period*														
Foreign Assets (Net)	**51n**	27,729	24,012	15,439	7,564	....	19,520	21,292	15,439	12,525	8,369	7,564	....	....	....	....
Domestic Credit	**52**	134,833	145,029	158,584	181,367	....	150,240	152,063	158,584	165,526	168,425	181,367	....	....	....	....
Claims on Central Govt. (Net)	**52an**	83,671	86,470	96,611	107,513	....	91,106	91,613	96,611	97,438	98,287	107,513	....	....	....	....
Claims on Nonfin.Pub.Enterprises	**52c**	19,989	20,767	20,289	18,229	....	20,544	20,213	20,289	19,897	19,758	18,229	....	....	....	....
Claims on Private Sector	**52d**	30,721	37,328	41,139	54,954	....	38,170	39,726	41,139	47,634	49,701	54,954	....	....	....	....
Liquid Liabilities	**55l**	68,416	75,612	77,241	52,201	....	75,540	74,308	77,241	74,297	64,309	52,201	....	....	....	....
Long-Term Foreign Liabilities	**56cl**	78,505	77,598	78,038	79,464	....	77,188	77,938	78,038	79,158	79,818	79,464	....	....	....	....
Other Items (Net)	**57r**	15,641	15,831	18,744	57,266	....	17,032	21,109	18,744	24,596	32,667	57,266	....	....	....	....
Interest Rates		*Percent Per Annum*														
Money Market Rate	**60b**	130.8	50.2	43.6	....	....	42.6	43.7	44.5	31.0	*47.0*	....	....	....	....	....
Treasury Bill Rate	**60c**	129.29	44.11	32.46	41.96	....	32.48	32.45	32.45	32.45	....	51.47	50.62	*49.39*	....	....
Deposit Rate	**60l**	104.59	43.62	....	....	....	....	....	....	....	....	....	....	....	....	....
Average Cost of Funds	**60n**	125.19	62.79	40.17	....	....	40.72	39.90	39.90	39.00	*40.03*	....	....	....	....	....
Lending Rate	**60p**	....	....	....	....	....	....	....	....	....	....	....	....	....	....	....
Prices and Production		*Period Averages*														
Wholesale Prices	**63**	850.7	917.6	951.9	970.0	*1,023.0*	944.8	955.2	955.7	968.7	966.9	974.3	1,012.0	*1,024.7*	*1,032.3*	....
Consumer Prices	**64**	825.4	920.0	961.7	991.3	*1,047.3*	954.1	962.8	968.3	975.7	988.7	1,009.4	1,034.1	1,048.1	*1,059.5*	....
Wages, Monthly (1980=100)	**65**	....	....	....	....	....	....	....	....	....	....	....	....	....	....	....
Industrial Production	**66**	....	....	....	....	....	....	....	....	....	....	....	....	....	....	....
Manufacturing Production	**66ey**	....	....	....	....	....	....	....	....	....	....	....	....	....	....	....
Mining Production	**66zx**	....	....	....	....	....	....	....	....	....	....	....	....	....	....	....
Crude Petroleum	**66aa**	....	....	....	....	....	....	....	....	....	....	....	....	....	....	....
International Transactions		*Billions of Pesos*														
Exports	**70**	12,012.5	12,430.9	11,409.9	***11,354.8***	....	3,811.4	4,196.4	3,402.1	3,498.8	3,951.4	***3,904.5***	....	....	....	....
Petroleum	**70a**	4,017.0	4,132.0	3,536.0	***3,390.0***	....	1,266.0	1,339.0	931.0	1,050.0	1,080.0	***1,260.0***	....	....	....	....
Crude Petroleum	**70aa**	3,540.0	3,615.0	3,070.0	***2,990.0***	....	1,149.0	1,155.0	766.0	910.0	930.0	***1,150.0***	....	....	....	....
Coffee	**70e**	257.0	406.6	215.2	***203.6***	....	81.2	90.8	43.3	22.2	123.7	***57.7***	....	....	....	....
Shrimp	**70bl**	214.9	101.5	91.8	....	....	13.8	14.0	64.0	86.4	167.0	....	....	....	....	....
Imports, cif	**71**	8,737.8	10,834.1	12,201.9	***12,803.8***	....	3,770.3	4,315.8	4,115.9	4,110.3	4,607.0	***4,086.5***	....	....	....	....
Imports, fob	**71.v**	8,342.1	10,347.7	11,654.2	***12,229.0***	....	3,601.0	4,122.1	3,931.1	3,925.8	4,400.1	***3,903.1***	....	....	....	....
Balance of Payments		*Minus Sign Indicates Debit*														
Current Account, nie	**77a.d**	502	-334	....	....	....	....	....	....	....	....	....	....	....	....	....
Merchandise: Exports fob	**77aad**	5,274	5,439	....	....	....	....	....	....	....	....	....	....	....	....	....
Merchandise: Imports fob	**77abd**	-3,738	-4,585	....	....	....	....	....	....	....	....	....	....	....	....	....
Trade Bal.,*77aad+77abd*	**77acd**	1,536	854	....	....	....	....	....	....	....	....	....	....	....	....	....
Other Goods,Serv.&Income:Cre	**77add**	2,784	2,615	....	....	....	....	....	....	....	....	....	....	....	....	....
Other Goods,Serv.&Income:Deb.	**77aed**	-3,952	-3,960	....	....	....	....	....	....	....	....	....	....	....	....	....
Private Unrequited Transfers	**77afd**	96	116	....	....	....	....	....	....	....	....	....	....	....	....	....
Official Unrequited Trans.,nie	**77agd**	38	41	....	....	....	....	....	....	....	....	....	....	....	....	....
Direct Investment	**77bad**	566	962	....	....	....	....	....	....	....	....	....	....	....	....	....
Portfolio Investment, nie	**77bbd**	158	—	....	....	....	....	....	....	....	....	....	....	....	....	....
Other Long-Term Capital, nie	**77bcd**	597	-619	....	....	....	....	....	....	....	....	....	....	....	....	....
Total,*77a.d+77bad—77bcd*	**77c.d**	1,823	9	....	....	....	....	....	....	....	....	....	....	....	....	....
Other Short-Term Capital,nie	**77d.d**	-270	-1,306	....	....	....	....	....	....	....	....	....	....	....	....	....
Net Errors and Omissions	**77e.d**	287	161	....	....	....	....	....	....	....	....	....	....	....	....	....
Total,*lines 77c.d—77e.d*	**77f.d**	1,840	-1,136	....	....	....	....	....	....	....	....	....	....	....	....	....
C'part to Mon./Demon. of Gold	**78a.d**	—	—	....	....	....	....	....	....	....	....	....	....	....	....	—
Counterpart to SDR Allocation	**78b.d**	—	—	—	—	—	—	—	—	—	—	—	—	—	—	—
C'part to Valuation Changes	**78c.d**	-38	-68	....	....	....	....	....	....	....	....	....	....	....	....	....
Total,*lines 77f.d—78c.d*	**78d.d**	1,801	-1,204	....	....	....	....	....	....	....	....	....	....	....	....	....
Exceptional Financing	**79a.d**	—	—	....	....	....	....	....	....	....	....	....	....	....	....	....
Liab.Const.Fgn Author. Reserves	**79b.d**	—	—	....	....	....	....	....	....	....	....	....	....	....	....	....
Total Change in Reserves	**79c.d**	-1,801	1,204	....	....	....	....	....	....	....	....	....	....	....	....	....

Beginning April 1976, gold is revalued daily on the basis of the London market quotations, less a 5 percent discount.

Monetary Authorities: Comprises the Bank of Mexico only.

Deposit Money Banks: Consolidates the commercial banks and national credit corporations. Comprises development banks. Beginning 1982, data reflect the introduction of a new plan of accounts which provides an improved sector classification of domestic and foreign accounts. In particular, *Foreign Assets* (*line 21*) and *Foreign Liabilities* (*line 26c*) are available on a gross basis, and *Time, Savings, and Foreign Currency Deposits* (*line 25*) exclude liabilities to official trust funds.

Other Banking Institutions: Comprises development banks. Beginning 1982, data reflect the introduction of a new plan of accounts which provides an improved sector classification of domestic and foreign accounts. In particular, *Claims on Local Government* (*line 42b*) include, and *Claims on Central Government* exclude, claims on the Federal District; *Foreign Assets* (*line 41*) and *Foreign Liabilities* are available on a gross basis, and *Time, Savings, and Foreign Currency Deposits* (*line 45*) exclude liabilities to Official Trust Funds.

Interest Rates: All interest rate data are from source B.

Money Market Rate: Weighted average of daily discount rates among dealers on the Mexican Securities Exchange for one- to three-month bankers acceptances.

Treasury Bill Rate: Average yield on bills with a maturity of approximately three months, calculated from the weighted average rate of discount on daily transactions among dealers on the Mexican Securities Exchange.

Deposit Rate: Net return offered by commercial banks on three-month fixed term deposits expressed as a simple rate per annum.

Average Cost of Funds: For September 1977 through November 1979, the weighted average cost of funds for financial and mortgage institutions and prior to that the average cost of funds for finance companies.

Lending Rate: Weighted average nominal rate charged by commercial banks on new loans during the month. Rates are based on a sample of businesses in the metropolitan area of Mexico City and exclude credit subject to preferential rates.

Prices and Production: *Wholesale Prices:* Source S index of wholesale prices, 210 home and imported goods in Mexico City, base 1978. *Consumer Prices:* Source B index of consumer prices, covering 172 commodities and services in the entire country, base 1978. The weights and selected items are based on a national income and expenditure survey conducted in 1963. In 1979 the weights were modified on the basis of national accounts data, and the coverage of the index was increased from 7 to 16 towns. *Wages, Monthly:* Source B index on average nominal wage rate in manufacturing, base 1978.

Industrial Production: Source B indexes on total industrial production, manufacturing production, mining production, and petroleum production (crude and derivatives), base 1970. From 1975 onwards, annual data have been adjusted to include production of petroleum and gas and petroleum refining. Monthly data have been adjusted from January 1979 onwards.

International Transactions: All trade data are from source S. Beginning 1970, trade data exclude exports and imports of in-bond industries. *Exports:* Total exports are adjusted by the Bank of Mexico to reflect transaction values of certain commodities which are valued by Customs at administrative prices. Silver exports, which are not published in source S, are directly reported by the national authorities and included in total exports by *IFS*. *Imports, f.o.b.* are calculated from *Imports, c.i.f.* by applying a freight and insurance factor estimated by *IFS*.

Government Finance: Data are as reported in the *Government Finance Statistics Yearbook* and relate to the consolidated central government.

National Accounts: Prior to 1968, data relate to the 1958 SNA. Data are derived from source A. *Line 93i* data are included in *line 96f* when they are not separately shown. Beginning in 1960, *line 99b.p* is based on national data at 1970 prices.

Appendix 4D

International Monetary Fund Data for West Germany

Germany 134		1982	1983	1984	1985	1986	1987	1988	1986 I	1986 II	1986 III	1986 IV	1987 I	1987 II	1987 III	1987 IV
Exchange Rates																*Deutsche Mark per SDR:*
Market Rate	aa	2.6215	2.8517	3.0857	2.7035	2.3740	2.2436	2.3957	2.6379	2.5890	2.4520	2.3740	2.3207	2.3386	2.3524	2.2436
																Deutsche Mark per US Dollar:
Market Rate	ae	2.3765	2.7238	3.1480	2.4613	1.9408	1.5815	1.7803	2.3175	2.1986	2.0207	1.9408	1.8051	1.8299	1.8383	1.5815
Market Rate	rf	2.4266	2.5533	2.8459	2.9440	2.1715	1.7974	1.7562	2.3463	2.2464	2.0856	2.0076	1.8395	1.8052	1.8393	1.7055
																Deutsche Mark per ECU:
ECU Rate	ea	2.3001	2.2575	2.2318	2.1839	2.0761	2.0603	2.0778	2.1714	2.1479	2.0906	2.0761	2.0722	2.0729	2.0780	2.0603
ECU Rate	eb	2.3770	2.2705	2.2380	2.2263	2.1287	2.0715	2.0744	2.1675	2.1522	2.1119	2.0831	2.0678	2.0763	2.0748	2.0671
																Index Numbers (1985=100):
Market Rate	ahx	***120.5***	***114.6***	***102.9***	100.0	135.1	***162.7***	***166.6***	124.6	130.1	***140.1***	***145.5***	***158.8***	***161.8***	***158.8***	***171.5***
MERM Effective Exchange Rate	amx	100.6	102.9	100.1	100.0	110.8	119.2	118.4	107.5	108.7	112.0	115.1	119.2	118.6	118.2	120.9
Nominal Effective Exchange Rate	neu	97.4	101.1	100.0	100.0	108.8	115.4	114.6	106.0	106.9	109.7	112.7	115.7	114.9	114.6	116.4
Real Effective Exchange Rate	reu	***101.5***	***103.0***	***100.6***	100.0	***108.7***	***115.3***	***114.1***	***106.6***	***106.6***	***109.2***	***112.5***	***115.2***	***115.0***	***114.8***	***116.2***
Fund Position																*Millions of SDRs:*
Quota	2f.s	3,234	5,404	5,404	5,404	5,404	5,404	5,404	5,404	5,404	5,404	5,404	5,404	5,404	5,404	5,404
SDRs	1b.s	1,862	1,541	1,390	1,408	1,651	1,384	1,380	1,553	1,526	1,577	1,651	1,815	1,566	1,410	1,384
Reserve Position in the Fund	1c.s	2,799	3,580	3,826	3,467	3,146	2,749	2,487	3,384	3,295	3,132	3,146	3,174	3,106	3,035	2,749
incl.: Fund Borrowing: GAB	1cas	583	—	—	—	—	—	—	—	—	—	—	—	—	—	—
Fund Borrowing: SFF	1cts	622	878	853	723	424	173	—	657	598	518	424	391	276	232	173
International Liquidity																*Millions of US Dollars Unless Otherwise Indicated:*
Total Reserves minus Gold	1l.d	44,762	42,674	40,141	44,380	51,734	78,756	58,528	45,485	44,632	48,973	51,734	60,437	62,290	63,549	78,756
SDRs	1b.d	2,054	1,613	1,362	1,547	2,020	1,964	1,857	1,768	1,797	1,913	2,020	2,334	2,001	1,804	1,964
Reserve Position in the Fund	1c.d	3,088	3,748	3,750	3,808	3,848	3,900	3,346	3,852	3,880	3,800	3,848	4,081	3,969	3,883	3,900
Foreign Exchange	1d.d	39,620	37,313	35,028	39,025	45,866	72,893	53,324	39,865	38,955	43,260	45,866	54,022	56,320	57,862	72,893
Gold (Million Fine Troy Ounces)	1ad	95.18	95.18	95.18	95.18	95.18	95.18	95.18	95.18	95.18	95.18	95.18	95.18	95.18	95.18	95.18
Gold (National Valuation)	1and	5,761	5,026	4,349	5,562	7,054	8,656	7,690	5,907	6,227	6,775	7,054	7,584	7,481	7,447	8,656
Monetary Authorities:Other Assets	3..d	1,042	913	794	1,003	1,263	1,542	....	1,064	1,120	1,214	1,263	1,356	1,338	1,330	1,542
Other Liab.	4..d	6,475	5,177	4,813	7,451	12,137	12,794	15,306	8,071	10,238	11,203	12,137	12,616	11,696	13,493	12,794
Deposit Money Banks: Assets	7a.d	81,729	74,756	75,232	112,932	178,478	232,608	229,765	122,006	136,241	159,222	178,478	196,344	205,268	203,846	232,608
of which: Claims on Nonbanks	7add	38,292	35,495	32,357	45,313	57,997	74,404	70,471	48,181	50,414	57,549	57,997	62,983	62,659	63,983	74,404
Deposit Money Banks: Liabilities	7b.d	64,692	57,923	58,224	75,773	101,288	131,375	130,995	79,707	83,831	96,783	101,288	107,645	111,263	113,692	131,375
of which: Liab. to Nonbanks	7bdd	15,342	15,952	17,465	21,919	29,467	41,467	36,432	21,532	24,047	26,788	29,467	33,018	34,439	35,854	41,467
Monetary Authorities																*Billions of Deutsche Mark:*
Foreign Assets	11	108.0	111.0	111.8	108.7	110.5	140.7	113.6	107.0	103.5	108.9	110.5	123.1	126.7	129.4	140.7
Claims on Central Government	12a	22.0	24.0	23.0	20.9	25.1	22.9	24.2	24.6	22.8	22.9	25.1	22.9	22.8	22.7	22.9
Claims on Deposit Money Banks	12e	74.9	85.5	96.3	105.3	96.4	82.4	144.7	105.8	106.2	95.4	96.4	97.7	85.4	92.4	82.4
Reserve Money	14	152.1	160.6	166.7	172.2	182.9	199.7	221.1	180.7	181.4	175.4	182.9	193.3	196.0	196.9	199.7
of which: Currency Outside DMBs	14a	88.6	96.4	99.8	103.9	112.2	124.1	142.6	104.2	105.4	107.1	112.2	111.4	115.4	117.5	124.1
Foreign Liabilities	16c	15.4	14.1	15.2	18.3	23.6	20.2	27.3	22.4	22.5	22.6	23.6	21.9	21.4	24.8	20.2
Central Government Deposits	16d	1.2	2.1	.9	2.2	1.1	4.6	3.5	4.3	6.2	3.9	1.1	7.5	4.3	5.0	4.6
Other Items (Net)	17r	36.2	43.7	48.3	42.3	24.3	21.5	30.7	30.0	22.4	25.0	24.3	21.0	13.0	17.8	21.5
Deposit Money Banks																*Billions of Deutsche Mark:*
Reserves	20	69.0	69.5	75.6	I78.3	80.2	83.6	89.0	76.1	73.8	65.6	80.2	77.5	76.2	72.1	83.6
Foreign Assets	21	194.2	203.6	236.8	I278.0	346.4	367.9	409.1	282.8	299.5	321.7	346.4	354.4	375.6	374.7	367.9
Claims on Central Government	22a	290.5	306.7	322.0	I338.0	337.3	361.3	397.7	330.0	329.2	330.6	337.3	332.5	333.9	343.8	361.3
Claims on Official Entities	22bx	118.2	121.2	124.8	129.1	134.4	139.2	143.7	130.9	131.5	132.7	134.4	135.6	136.7	137.4	139.2
Claims on Private Sector	22d	1,306.3	1,399.4	1,489.0	I1,594.6	1,665.5	1,726.1	1,818.6	1,599.4	1,626.5	1,639.8	1,665.5	1,663.6	1,677.6	1,703.6	1,726.1
Demand Deposits	24	167.4	181.1	194.2	I209.7	227.2	240.8	264.9	194.4	207.1	208.1	227.2	212.4	228.5	226.3	240.8
Time Deposits	25	634.1	663.5	699.7	I759.9	804.1	847.1	874.3	756.5	755.7	766.7	804.1	809.0	802.7	807.4	847.1
Bonds	26ab	634.1	687.8	739.6	I796.2	843.3	894.7	917.1	817.2	819.5	831.6	843.3	864.7	874.2	882.5	894.7
Foreign Liabilities	26c	153.7	157.8	183.3	I186.5	196.6	207.8	233.2	184.7	184.3	195.6	196.6	194.3	203.6	209.0	207.8
Central Government Deposits	26d	34.6	34.2	32.7	I35.9	42.0	41.2	41.0	32.5	36.1	35.7	42.0	35.6	37.3	36.8	41.2
Central Govt. Lending Funds	26f	129.8	136.8	144.2	I152.2	157.5	162.8	168.1	153.2	154.0	155.0	157.5	158.7	159.9	161.1	162.8
Credit from Monetary Authorities	26g	74.9	85.5	96.3	I105.3	96.4	82.4	144.7	105.8	106.2	95.4	96.4	97.7	85.4	92.4	82.4
Capital Accounts	27a	115.8	126.1	137.4	I153.9	169.2	183.0	190.0	163.2	166.7	167.1	169.2	177.2	180.2	181.2	183.0
Other Items (Net)	27r	34.0	27.7	20.9	I18.3	27.5	18.3	24.7	11.9	31.0	35.4	27.5	13.9	28.3	34.8	18.3
Monetary Survey																*Billions of Deutsche Mark:*
Foreign Assets (Net)	31n	133.1	142.7	150.2	I181.8	236.7	280.6	262.2	182.7	196.2	212.4	236.7	261.3	277.3	270.3	280.6
Domestic Credit	32	1,702.7	1,817.0	1,926.5	I2,045.7	2,120.5	2,205.0	2,341.0	2,049.8	2,069.4	2,088.1	2,120.5	2,112.8	2,130.6	2,166.9	2,205.0
Claims on Central Govt. (Net)	32an	276.6	294.4	311.4	I320.8	319.2	338.4	377.4	317.8	309.6	314.0	319.2	312.3	315.0	324.7	338.4
incl:Net Clms.on Laender Gov	32anx	135.0	150.2	163.0	I174.9	183.0	200.9	219.0	170.0	172.2	171.0	183.0	180.6	183.1	184.7	200.9
Claims on Official Entities	32bx	118.2	121.2	124.8	I129.1	134.4	139.2	143.7	130.9	131.5	132.7	134.4	135.6	136.7	137.4	139.2
Claims on Private Sector	32d	1,307.8	1,401.3	1,490.3	I1,595.9	1,666.9	1,727.4	1,819.9	1,601.1	1,628.3	1,641.4	1,666.9	1,665.0	1,679.0	1,704.8	1,727.4
Money	34	256.7	278.2	294.8	I314.5	340.2	365.7	408.3	299.2	313.4	315.7	340.2	324.4	344.7	344.5	365.7
Quasi-Money	35	634.1	663.5	699.7	I759.9	804.1	847.1	874.3	756.5	755.7	766.7	804.1	809.0	802.7	807.4	847.1
Bonds	36ab	634.1	687.8	739.6	I796.2	843.3	894.7	917.1	817.2	819.5	831.6	843.3	864.7	874.2	882.5	894.7
Central Govt. Lending Funds	36f	129.8	136.8	144.2	I152.2	157.5	162.8	168.1	153.2	154.0	155.0	157.5	158.7	159.9	161.1	162.8
Other Items (Net)	37r	181.3	193.4	198.4	I204.8	212.0	215.3	235.4	206.6	223.1	231.2	212.0	217.3	226.5	241.8	215.3
Money, Seasonally Adjusted	34..b	247.8	268.0	283.7	I302.7	327.5	352.0	393.0	306.2	312.1	319.9	327.5	332.0	343.3	349.1	352.0
Nonbank Financial Institutions																
Building Societies																*Billions of Deutsche Mark:*
Claims on Central Government	42a.i	.39	.55	.63	.54	.62	.77	2.15	.58	.56	.56	.62	.55	.55	.52	.77
Claims on Private Sector	42d.i	133.18	139.23	145.09	145.88	143.12	139.40	131.64	144.73	144.79	144.20	143.12	141.26	140.62	140.11	139.40
Time and Savings Deposits	45..i	121.49	126.01	126.35	125.37	123.59	120.25	121.49	123.21	121.85	119.66	123.59	120.57	118.87	116.75	120.25
Other Items (Net)	47r.i	12.08	13.77	19.37	21.05	20.15	19.92	12.30	22.10	23.50	25.10	20.15	21.24	22.30	23.88	19.92
Life Insurance and Pension Funds																*Billions of Deutsche Mark:*
Claims on Central Government	42a.l	3.05	2.79	2.70	2.38	2.18	2.03	***2.83***	2.32	2.29	2.26	2.18	2.18	2.07	2.01	2.03
Claims on Private Sector	42d.l	232.69	258.75	285.39	316.51	350.48	381.46	***419.78***	327.44	335.41	343.83	350.48	358.29	363.16	375.90	381.46
of which: Policy Loans	42dxl	5.11	5.64	6.20	6.74	7.04	7.26	***7.39***	6.81	6.99	7.07	7.04	7.10	6.84	7.23	7.26
Real Estate	42h.l	23.31	24.81	26.43	27.87	28.78	28.98	***28.58***	27.77	28.20	28.58	28.78	28.35	28.54	28.97	28.98
Incr.in Total Assets(Within Per.)	49z.l	30.27	27.35	28.79	32.00	35.79	31.46	***38.05***	9.75	8.38	9.14	8.52	5.45	5.75	12.64	7.62

Germany — 134

Column groups: **1988** = I, II, III, IV; **1989** = I; monthly **1988** = July, Aug, Sept, Oct, Nov, Dec; **1989** = Jan, Feb, Mar, Apr.

Description	Code	88 I	88 II	88 III	88 IV	89 I	July	Aug	Sept	Oct	Nov	Dec	Jan	Feb	Mar	Apr
Exchange Rates																
End of Period Market Rate	aa	2.3019	2.3868	2.4257	2.3957	2.4467	2.4387	2.4151	2.4257	2.3801	2.3712	2.3957	2.4444	2.4178	2.4467	2.4336
End of Period (ae) Market Rate	ae	1.6593	1.8211	1.8798	1.7803	1.8927	1.8810	1.8748	1.8798	1.7684	1.7354	1.7803	1.8646	1.8296	1.8927	1.8783
Period Average (rf) Market Rate	rf	1.6758	1.7075	1.8661	1.7756	1.8493	1.8440	1.8874	1.8669	1.8215	1.7497	1.7555	1.8304	1.8521	1.8653	1.8704
End of Period (ea) ECU Rate	ea	2.0748	2.0752	2.0755	2.0778	2.0826	2.0849	2.0756	2.0755	2.0721	2.0783	2.0778	2.0885	2.0765	2.0826	2.0804
Period Average (eb) ECU Rate	eb	2.0673	2.0775	2.0779	2.0748	2.0830	2.0789	2.0819	2.0729	2.0732	2.0732	2.0780	2.0841	2.0839	2.0809	2.0805
Period Averages Market Rate	ahx	174.3	171.1	156.5	164.5	157.9	158.4	154.7	156.4	160.3	166.9	166.3	159.6	157.7	156.5	156.1
MERM Effective Exchange Rate	amx	120.8	119.2	116.2	117.5	115.6	116.5	115.6	116.5	116.9	117.9	117.6	115.9	115.4	115.5	115.5
Nominal Effective Exchange Rate	neu	116.2	114.9	113.2	114.0	112.7	113.3	112.7	112.6	113.4	114.3	113.9	112.8	112.4	112.7	....
Real Effective Exchange Rate	reu	115.1	114.6	113.1	113.7	112.2	113.3	112.6	113.3	113.4	114.0	113.7	112.6	112.0	112.0	....
Fund Position																
End of Period Quota	2f.s	5,404	5,404	5,404	5,404	5,404	5,404	5,404	5,404	5,404	5,404	5,404	5,404	5,404	5,404	5,404
SDRs	1b.s	1,451	1,408	1,443	1,380	1,329	1,412	1,443	1,443	1,467	1,380	1,380	1,341	1,329	1,329	1,326
Reserve Position in the Fund	1c.s	2,682	2,679	2,657	2,487	2,395	2,675	2,654	2,657	2,610	2,519	2,487	2,478	2,443	2,395	2,498
incl.: Fund Borrowing: GAB	1cas															
Fund Borrowing: SFF	1cts	111	66	66	—	—	66	66	66	36	—	—	—	—	—	—
International Liquidity																
End of Period Total Reserves minus Gold	1l.d	72,944	64,795	57,995	58,528	54,971	61,359	59,039	57,995	60,027	61,660	58,528	54,940	55,645	54,971	56,325
SDRs	1b.d	2,013	1,846	1,862	1,857	1,718	1,831	1,859	1,862	1,974	1,886	1,857	1,758	1,756	1,718	1,719
Reserve Position in the Fund	1c.d	3,720	3,511	3,428	3,346	3,095	3,468	3,419	3,428	3,513	3,442	3,346	3,248	3,228	3,095	3,237
Foreign Exchange	1d.d	67,211	59,439	52,705	53,324	50,157	56,060	53,762	52,705	54,540	56,332	53,324	49,934	50,660	50,157	51,370
Gold (Million Fine Troy Ounces)	1ad	95.18	95.18	95.18	95.18	95.18	95.18	95.18	95.18	95.18	95.18	95.18	95.18	95.18	95.18	95.18
Gold (National Valuation)	1and	8,250	7,517	7,283	7,690	7,233	7,278	7,302	7,283	7,741	7,889	7,690	7,342	7,483	7,233	7,289
Monetary Authorities:Other Assets	3..d															
Other Liab.	4..d	11,418	10,522	15,140	15,306	17,789	12,377	14,795	15,140	14,142	15,780	15,306	15,040	16,141	17,789	18,972
Deposit Money Banks: Assets	7a.d	219,123	207,929	215,395	229,765	....	206,247	211,783	215,395	226,646	233,560	229,765	213,402	215,364	....	....
of which: Claims on Nonbanks	7add	71,590	67,871	66,321	70,471	....	66,454	66,503	66,321	71,262	71,949	70,471	68,487	69,682	....	....
Deposit Money Banks: Liabilities	7b.d	128,783	121,778	124,987	130,995	....	123,020	125,741	124,987	132,634	134,741	130,995	127,963	132,149	....	....
of which: Liab. to Nonbanks	7bdd	39,643	38,092	39,196	36,432	....	38,506	38,628	39,196	40,675	40,751	36,432	33,165	33,521	....	....
Monetary Authorities																
End of Period Foreign Assets	11	133.7	125.4	116.0	113.6	110.3	121.1	117.6	116.0	116.2	117.8	113.6	109.7	110.2	110.3	112.3
Claims on Central Government	12a	22.8	23.1	23.5	24.2	27.6	25.2	24.9	23.5	24.1	29.7	24.2	29.9	29.0	27.6	24.9
Claims on Deposit Money Banks	12e	86.7	101.3	131.4	144.7	144.3	106.6	117.3	131.4	126.9	129.2	144.7	138.6	140.5	144.3	141.3
Reserve Money	14	194.9	212.6	200.8	221.1	205.0	210.5	209.6	200.8	209.4	228.1	221.1	224.3	228.0	205.0	215.0
of which: Currency Outside DMBs	14a	127.2	129.1	133.2	142.6	....	131.9	130.7	133.2	132.8	136.3	142.6	139.0	139.4	....	....
Foreign Liabilities	16c	19.0	19.2	28.5	27.3	33.7	23.3	27.7	28.5	28.6	27.4	27.3	28.0	29.5	33.7	36.8
Central Government Deposits	16d	8.1	3.5	7.9	3.5	1.3	.8	.7	7.9	1.1	.3	3.5	.7	9.9	1.3	1.2
Other Items (Net)	17r	21.3	14.5	33.7	30.7	42.3	18.3	21.9	33.7	28.6	20.9	30.7	25.3	21.3	42.3	25.5
Deposit Money Banks																
End of Period Reserves	20	68.2	77.5	69.6	89.0	....	75.9	77.2	69.6	80.9	87.8	89.0	82.0	84.6	....	....
Foreign Assets	21	363.6	378.7	404.9	409.1	....	388.0	397.1	404.9	400.8	405.3	409.1	397.9	394.0	....	....
Claims on Central Government	22a	367.1	376.2	388.7	397.7	....	380.5	386.2	388.7	391.9	397.9	397.7	400.8	401.2	....	....
Claims on Official Entities	22bx	140.5	140.6	141.5	143.7	....	141.1	141.0	141.5	142.6	142.9	143.7	144.3	144.2	....	....
Claims on Private Sector	22d	1,732.5	1,758.2	1,778.9	1,818.6	....	1,760.3	1,765.3	1,778.9	1,782.6	1,791.2	1,818.6	1,813.4	1,824.2	....	....
Demand Deposits	24	229.0	249.5	242.9	264.9	....	248.0	248.0	242.9	250.6	271.8	264.9	255.9	257.3	....	....
Time Deposits	25	839.8	835.4	844.7	874.3	....	836.3	843.4	844.7	849.4	852.1	874.3	872.7	874.4	....	....
Bonds	26ab	899.8	906.3	911.2	917.1	....	905.5	910.3	911.2	912.8	914.8	917.1	919.9	923.3	....	....
Foreign Liabilities	26c	213.7	221.8	235.0	233.2	....	231.4	235.7	235.0	234.6	233.8	233.2	238.6	241.8	....	....
Central Government Deposits	26d	34.7	37.4	34.1	41.0	....	33.1	32.7	34.1	32.7	33.6	41.0	35.6	35.3	....	....
Central Govt. Lending Funds	26f	163.5	164.3	165.9	168.1	....	164.7	165.9	165.9	167.0	167.9	168.1	168.1	168.8	....	....
Credit from Monetary Authorities	26g	86.7	101.3	131.4	144.7	....	106.6	117.3	131.4	126.9	129.2	144.7	138.6	140.5	144.3	141.3
Capital Accounts	27a	188.6	190.1	190.8	190.0	....	190.6	190.8	190.8	191.8	191.7	190.0	191.4	193.9	....	....
Other Items (Net)	27r	16.1	25.1	27.6	24.7	....	29.5	22.6	27.6	33.1	30.1	24.7	17.7	12.9	....	....
Monetary Survey																
End of Period Foreign Assets (Net)	31n	264.7	263.1	257.5	262.2	....	254.4	251.2	257.5	253.9	261.9	262.2	241.0	232.9	....	....
Domestic Credit	32	2,221.3	2,258.4	2,291.8	2,341.0	....	2,274.4	2,285.2	2,291.8	2,308.6	2,328.9	2,341.0	2,353.4	2,363.6	....	....
Claims on Central Govt. (Net)	32an	347.1	358.4	370.1	377.4	....	371.7	377.7	370.1	382.2	393.6	377.4	394.5	394.0	....	....
incl:Net Clms.on Laender Gov	32anx	200.6	203.8	206.6	219.0	....	208.7	209.6	206.6	213.4	219.6	219.0	220.2	218.2	....	....
Claims on Official Entities	32bx	140.5	140.6	141.5	143.7	....	141.1	141.0	141.5	142.6	142.9	143.7	144.3	144.2	....	....
Claims on Private Sector	32d	1,733.7	1,759.4	1,780.1	1,819.9	....	1,761.5	1,766.5	1,780.1	1,783.8	1,792.4	1,819.9	1,814.7	1,825.4	....	....
Money	34	356.9	379.5	376.9	408.3	....	380.6	379.3	376.9	384.2	408.8	408.3	395.5	397.3	....	....
Quasi-Money	35	839.8	835.4	844.7	874.3	....	836.3	843.4	844.7	849.4	852.1	874.3	872.7	874.4	....	....
Bonds	36ab	899.8	906.3	911.2	917.1	....	905.5	910.3	911.2	912.8	914.8	917.1	919.9	923.3	....	....
Central Govt. Lending Funds	36f	163.5	164.3	165.9	168.1	....	164.7	165.9	165.9	167.0	167.9	168.1	168.1	168.8	....	....
Other Items (Net)	37r	225.9	236.1	250.7	235.4	....	241.6	237.6	250.7	249.7	247.3	235.4	238.3	232.7	....	....
Money, Seasonally Adjusted	34..b	365.3	377.9	381.8	393.0	....	379.9	383.2	381.8	390.0	387.4	393.0	399.5	402.1	....	....
Nonbank Financial Institutions — Building Societies																
End of Period Claims on Central Government	42a.i	1.28	1.50	1.71	2.15	....	1.43	1.53	1.71	1.77	2.24	2.15	2.39	2.47	....	....
Claims on Private Sector	42d.i	137.83	136.92	135.91	131.64	....	136.49	136.38	135.91	135.46	134.47	131.64	131.68	129.64	....	....
Time and Savings Deposits	45..i	118.60	117.89	116.75	121.49	....	117.32	116.89	116.75	116.48	116.40	121.49	121.02	120.66	....	....
Other Items (Net)	47r.i	20.51	20.53	20.87	12.30	....	20.60	21.02	20.87	20.75	20.31	12.30	13.05	11.45	....	....
Life Insurance and Pension Funds																
End of Period Claims on Central Government	42a.l	2.34	2.47	2.57	2.83	....	....	....	....	....	....	....	....	....	....	....
Claims on Private Sector	42d.l	392.91	401.80	410.78	419.78	....	....	....	....	....	....	....	....	....	....	....
of which: Policy Loans	42dxl	7.32	7.31	7.35	7.39	....	....	....	....	....	....	....	....	....	....	....
Real Estate	42z.l	28.90	29.18	29.55	28.58	....	....	....	....	....	....	....	....	....	....	....
Incr.in Total Assets(Within Per.)	49z.l	10.19	9.18	9.39	9.29	....	....	....	....	....	....	....	....	....	....	....

Germany

134

		1982	1983	1984	1985	1986	1987	1988	1986 I	1986 II	1986 III	1986 IV	1987 I	1987 II	1987 III	1987 IV
Interest Rates																*Percent Per Annum*
Discount Rate *(End of Period)*	**60**	5.0	4.0	4.5	4.0	3.5	2.5	3.5	3.5	3.5	3.5	3.5	3.0	3.0	3.0	2.5
Money Market Rate	**60b**	8.7	5.4	5.5	5.2	4.6	3.7	4.0	4.7	4.5	4.5	4.6	4.0	3.7	3.7	3.5
Interbank Deposit Rate	**60bs**	8.9	5.8	6.0	5.4	4.6	4.0	4.2	4.6	4.6	4.6	4.7	4.2	3.8	3.9	4.1
Treasury Bill Rate	**60c**	8.31	5.63	5.66	5.04	3.86	3.28	3.62	4.07	3.66	3.84	3.87	3.57	2.99	3.18	3.40
Deposit Rate	**60l**	7.54	4.56	4.86	4.44	3.71	3.20	3.29	3.73	3.57	3.73	3.79	3.45	3.11	3.08	3.18
Lending Rate	**60p**	13.50	10.05	9.82	9.53	8.75	8.36	8.33	9.01	8.70	8.65	8.64	8.54	8.33	8.28	8.29
Government Bond Yield	**61**	9.0	7.9	7.8	6.9	5.9	5.8	6.1	6.1	5.7	5.8	6.0	5.7	5.5	6.0	6.2
Mortgage Bond Yield	**61a**	9.1	8.0	7.8	7.0	6.1	5.9	6.1	6.4	6.0	6.0	6.2	5.9	5.6	6.1	6.2
Prices and Production																*Index Numbers (1985=100):*
Industrial Share Prices	**62**	49.5	66.8	75.2	100.0	135.2	124.5	104.0	136.6	136.7	130.9	136.8	123.3	128.6	139.5	106.8
Prices: Industrial Products	**63**	93.5	94.9	97.6	100.0	97.5	95.1	96.3	99.3	98.0	97.2	95.5	95.0	94.7	95.1	95.4
Consumer Prices	**64**	92.5	95.6	97.9	100.0	99.8	100.1	101.2	100.3	100.0	99.5	99.2	99.8	100.1	100.1	100.2
Wages: Hourly Earnings	**65**	91.1	94.1	96.3	100.0	103.5	107.6	112.0	101.5	102.4	104.9	105.3	105.7	107.2	108.5	109.0
Industrial Production, Seas. Adj.	**66..c**	93	93	96	100	102	102	106	102	102	103	102	100	103	103	104
Investment Goods, Seas. Adj.	**66iyc**	90	89	91	100	104	105	108	104	104	105	104	103	105	105	106
Other Prod. Goods, Seas. Adj.	**66jyc**	93	95	99	100	99	99	105	99	100	99	98	96	99	100	101
Consumer Goods, Seas. Adj.	**66hyc**	95	97	99	100	102	103	106	101	101	103	103	102	103	104	104
Industrial Employment	**67**	104.1	99.8	98.7	100.0	101.7	101.6	***101.4***	100.8	101.2	102.6	102.3	101.4	101.3	102.1	101.6
International Transactions																*Billions of Deutsche Mark*
Exports	**70**	427.75	432.27	488.22	537.17	526.36	527.37	567.74	130.30	135.01	125.93	135.12	127.19	129.82	127.40	142.96
Imports, cif	**71**	376.47	390.20	434.26	463.81	413.73	409.64	439.76	107.75	106.86	96.50	102.62	99.48	101.78	99.51	108.87
Petroleum	**71a**	69.00	64.30	69.39	70.96	34.22	30.40	25.74	12.26	9.26	6.58	6.12	7.24	7.61	8.30	7.25
Crude Petroleum	**71aa**	44.71	37.77	41.66	39.92	16.95	16.02	14.83	6.49	3.79	3.35	3.32	3.82	3.97	4.32	3.91
Imports, fob	**71.v**	365.19	378.51	421.42	451.14	402.91	....	....	105.10	104.04	93.83	99.94	96.97	99.18	96.96	....
																1985=100
Volume of Exports	**72**	86.8	86.5	94.4	100.0	101.3	104.3	112.0	98.7	103.9	97.3	105.4	100.0	103.2	100.6	113.2
Volume of Imports	**73**	87.8	91.2	96.0	100.0	106.1	111.9	119.3	102.4	109.7	102.6	109.9	107.6	111.8	108.7	119.2
Unit Value of Exports	**74**	91.8	93.0	96.3	100.0	96.7	94.2	94.5	98.3	96.9	96.4	95.4	94.7	93.7	94.4	94.0
Export Prices	**76**	92.4	94.1	97.3	100.0	97.8	96.7	99.1	98.9	98.3	97.4	96.7	96.3	96.6	96.9	97.1
Unit Value of Imports	**75**	92.4	92.1	97.5	100.0	84.0	78.9	79.4	90.7	84.0	81.1	80.5	79.7	78.5	78.9	78.7
Import Prices	**76.x**	93.3	93.0	98.5	100.0	81.1	75.8	76.4	89.0	82.0	77.4	75.9	75.5	75.9	76.4	75.5
Balance of Payments																*Billions of US Dollars:*
Current Account, nie	**77a.d**	4.98	5.40	9.75	16.98	39.85	45.63	***48.57***	7.57	8.47	9.59	14.22	11.48	10.95	7.92	15.27
Merchandise: Exports fob	**77aad**	165.82	159.90	161.38	173.66	231.03	278.09	308.85	52.97	56.23	58.01	63.82	65.83	67.42	65.80	79.04
Merchandise: Imports fob	**77abd**	-141.08	-138.48	-139.09	-145.15	-175.30	-208.22	***-230.21***	-42.15	-44.14	-42.64	-46.36	-49.38	-51.10	-49.79	-57.95
Trade Bal.,*77aad+77abd*	**77acd**	24.73	21.42	22.29	28.51	55.74	69.88	***78.64***	10.82	12.09	15.37	17.46	16.45	16.32	16.01	21.09
Other Goods,Serv.&Income:Cre	**77add**	49.82	48.04	48.16	50.18	67.02	81.84	***86.46***	14.60	16.21	17.56	18.66	18.38	20.13	20.56	22.77
Other Goods,Serv.&Income:Deb.	**77aed**	-58.88	-54.19	-50.31	-51.73	-70.36	-89.81	***-98.37***	-14.95	-16.86	-20.24	-18.31	-19.85	-21.83	-24.80	-23.34
Private Unrequited Transfers	**77afd**	-4.46	-4.32	-3.99	-3.58	-4.73	-5.55	***-6.35***	-1.10	-1.08	-1.39	-1.16	-1.34	-1.38	-1.45	-1.37
Official Unrequited Trans.,nie	**77agd**	-6.23	-5.54	-6.40	-6.40	-7.82	-10.73	***-11.82***	-1.80	-1.89	-1.71	-2.42	-2.16	-2.29	-2.40	-3.88
Direct Investment	**77bad**	-1.66	-1.60	-3.75	-4.44	-9.09	-7.16	-8.71	.42	-2.13	-2.18	-5.20	-1.57	-2.07	-1.19	-2.32
Portfolio Investment, nie	**77bbd**	-.46	3.48	1.25	1.77	23.56	-2.69	-43.78	9.14	1.44	6.05	6.93	9.36	2.26	-6.61	-7.69
Other Long-Term Capital, nie	**77bcd**	-3.86	-5.11	-4.30	-1.95	.39	-3.60	3.89	-.15	.09	.41	.04	1.35	.63	-2.40	-3.18
Total,*77a.d+77bad—77bcd*	**77c.d**	-1.01	2.18	2.95	12.36	54.71	32.18	***-.04***	16.98	7.87	13.87	15.99	20.61	11.77	-2.28	2.08
Other Short-Term Capital,nie	**77d.d**	6.36	-3.91	-6.11	-14.58	-53.57	-12.76	***-19.29***	-15.38	-13.46	-10.44	-14.29	-11.04	-11.03	-1.10	10.40
Net Errors and Omissions	**77e.d**	-2.42	.51	2.03	3.11	.40	.93	***.90***	-.76	1.71	-.15	-.40	-2.22	.84	1.15	1.17
Total,*lines 77c.d—77e.d*	**77f.d**	2.92	-1.23	-1.13	.89	1.54	20.35	***-18.43***	.84	-3.88	3.28	1.30	7.35	1.58	-2.23	13.65
C'part to Mon./Demon. of Gold	**78a.d**	—	—	—	—	—	—	—	—	—	—	—	—	—	—	—
Counterpart to SDR Allocation	**78b.d**	—	—	—	—	—	—	—	—	—	—	—	—	—	—	—
C'part to Valuation Changes	**78c.d**	-.59	-2.23	-1.79	3.41	3.91	5.71	-3.97	.66	1.28	.72	1.25	1.78	-.72	-.02	4.68
Total,*lines 77f.d—78c.d*	**78d.d**	2.33	-3.46	-2.92	4.30	5.45	26.07	***-22.39***	1.50	-2.60	4.00	2.56	9.13	.86	-2.26	18.33
Exceptional Financing	**79a.d**	—	—	—	—	—	—	—	—	—	—	—	—	—	—	—
Liab.Const.Fgn Author. Reserves	**79b.d**	-.09	-.71	.79	1.34	3.89	1.15	***3.01***	.17	1.99	1.06	.67	-.15	.89	3.30	-2.89
Total Change in Reserves	**79c.d**	-2.25	4.17	2.12	-5.64	-9.34	-27.22	19.39	-1.67	.61	-5.05	-3.23	-8.98	-1.75	-1.05	-15.44
Government Finance																*Billions of Deutsche Mark:*
Deficit (-) or Surplus	**80**	-32.02	-32.95	-32.31	-20.00	-16.44[P]	-21.23[P]	....	-11.09	4.59	-7.09	-9.91	-7.46	-5.51	-5.64	-6.83
Revenue	**81**	478.05	490.83	514.61	551.33	572.55[P]	589.69[P]	....	58.56	73.53	62.61	71.32	63.63	67.77	64.86	74.42
Grants Received	**81z**	2.68	3.16	3.00	3.10	2.46[P]	2.22[P]	....	....	....	....	....	....	....	....	....
Adj. to Cash-Revenue & Grants	**81x**	—	—	—	—	—[P]	—[P]	....	....	....	....	....	....	....	....	....
Expenditure	**82**	506.03	520.05	549.04	564.55	582.70[P]	608.74[P]	....	69.65	68.94	69.70	81.23	71.09	73.28	70.50	81.25
Lending Minus Repayments	**83**	5.56	7.04	8.09	7.44	5.83[P]	4.55[P]	....	....	....	....	....	....	....	....	....
Overall Cash Adjustment	**80x**	-1.16	.15	7.21	-2.44	-2.92[P]	.15[P]	....	....	....	....	....	....	....	....	....
Financing																
Net Borrowing	**84**	36.63	31.82	28.03	23.49	22.21[P]	27.97[P]	....	8.97	-3.74	5.87	11.94	8.76	1.63	7.57	7.12
Domestic	**84a**	29.15	18.32	18.56	7.21	-5.54[P]	12.27[P]	....	....	....	....	....	....	....	....	....
Foreign	**85a**	7.48	13.50	9.47	16.28	27.75[P]	15.70[P]	....	....	....	....	....	....	....	....	....
Seigniorage	**86d**	....	....	....	....	....	....	....	.03	.11	.06	.13	.01	.06	.14	.19
Pending Redemptions	**87c**	....	....	....	....	....	....	....	1.12	1.52	-1.21	-2.04	3.40	.01	.01	—
Use of Cash Balances	**87**	-4.61	1.14	4.28	-3.49	-5.77[P]	-6.74[P]	....	.97	-2.48	2.37	-.12	-4.71	3.81	-2.08	-.48
Debt	**88**	314.44	347.27	373.91	399.15	422.00[P]	446.57[P]	....	401.32	397.59	403.46	415.39	424.15	425.78	433.35	440.48
Domestic	**88a**	247.73	267.08	284.25	293.21	288.30[P]	297.18[P]	....	....	....	....	....	....	....	....	....
Foreign	**89a**	66.71	80.19	89.66	105.94	133.70[P]	149.39[P]	....	....	....	....	....	....	....	....	....
Intragovernmental Debt	**88s**	2.80	2.86	2.57	2.25	....	....	....	....	....	....	....	....	....	....	....
National Accounts																*Billions of Deutsche Mark: Quarterly Data*
Exports	**90c.c**	517.6	524.9	590.7	647.5	638.1	638.4	***685.1***	634.0	651.2	638.4	628.8	621.2	631.2	642.4	658.8
Government Consumption	**91f.c**	326.2	336.2	350.2	365.6	382.5	397.2	409.7	374.0	383.6	387.2	385.2	387.6	399.2	400.0	402.0
Gross Fixed Capital Formation	**93e.c**	326.9	343.9	354.5	360.7	377.4	391.1	420.3	360.8	383.2	378.4	387.2	370.8	393.2	399.2	401.2
Increase in Stocks	**93i.c**	-11.7	-2.0	6.9	-.7	2.3	6.8	14.6	-2.4	-3.6	-1.2	16.4	30.4	-10.4	.4	6.8
Private Consumption	**96f.c**	918.1	964.2	1,003.6	1,038.5	1,068.6	1,113.9	1,157.2	1,049.6	1,074.0	1,074.8	1,076.0	1,078.8	1,116.8	1,121.6	1,138.4
Less: Imports	**98c.c**	-480.0	-486.9	-536.0	-567.3	-523.7	-527.2	***-565.5***	-532.4	-545.6	-507.2	-509.6	-504.8	-524.4	-532.0	-547.6
Gross Nat'l Expenditure = GNP	**99a.c**	1,597.1	1,680.3	1,769.9	1,844.3	1,945.2	2,020.2	2,121.4	1,883.6	1,942.8	1,970.4	1,984.0	1,984.0	2,005.6	2,031.6	2,059.6
Less:Net Factor Inc.from Abroad	**90e**	.8	-5.6	-14.1	-13.8	-14.0	-11.0	-10.6	....	....	....	....	....	....	....	....
Gross Domestic Product	**99b**	1,597.9	1,674.8	1,755.8	1,830.5	1,931.2	2,009.1	2,110.9	....	....	....	....	....	....	....	....
Nat'l Income, Market Prices	**99e**	1,396.0	1,469.0	1,547.9	1,612.5	1,704.5	1,770.6	1,860.7	....	....	....	....	....	....	....	....
Gross Nat'l Prod. 1985 Prices	**99a.r**	1,719.1	1,751.7	1,809.2	1,844.3	1,887.1	1,920.4	1,986.4	1,848.4	1,893.3	1,902.6	1,904.0	1,890.9	1,908.7	1,932.1	1,949.8
						Millions: Mid-Year Estimates										
Population	**99z**	61.64	61.42	61.18	61.02	61.05	61.17	....	....	....	....	**Population**				**99z**

Germany 134

Indicator	1988 I	II	III	IV	1989 I	July	Aug	Sept	Oct	Nov	Dec	Jan	Feb	Mar	Apr	Code
Interest Rates *(Percent Per Annum)*																
Discount Rate (End of Period)	2.5	2.5	3.5	3.5	4.0	3.0	3.5	3.5	3.5	3.5	3.5	4.0	4.0	4.0	4.5	60
Money Market Rate	3.2	3.4	4.6	4.8	5.6	4.4	4.7	4.7	4.7	4.6	4.9	5.2	5.9	5.6	5.9	60b
Interbank Deposit Rate	3.4	3.4	4.9	5.1	6.2	4.9	4.7	5.0	5.1	4.9	5.3	5.7	6.4	6.6	6.4	60bs
Treasury Bill Rate	3.15	3.15	3.96	4.20	5.30	3.15	4.33	4.40	4.20	4.20	4.20	4.42	5.49	6.00	....	60c
Deposit Rate	2.78	2.78	3.62	3.97	4.61	3.31	3.72	3.82	3.88	3.89	4.14	4.25	4.61	4.96	....	60l
Lending Rate	8.07	8.04	8.51	8.69	9.06	8.33	8.50	8.70	8.69	8.69	8.69	8.75	9.16	9.26	....	60p
Government Bond Yield	5.8	6.0	6.4	6.2	6.8	6.4	6.5	6.3	6.2	6.1	6.3	6.5	6.9	6.9	6.9	61
Mortgage Bond Yield	5.7	5.9	6.4	6.2	6.8	6.3	6.5	6.4	6.2	6.1	6.2	6.5	6.9	7.0	....	61a
Prices and Production *(Period Averages)*																
Industrial Share Prices	94.2	99.5	107.2	115.2	122.2	106.1	106.3	109.2	114.1	114.2	117.3	121.8	121.8	123.1	....	62
Prices: Industrial Products	95.4	96.0	96.5	97.0	98.4	96.4	96.5	96.7	96.8	97.0	97.2	98.2	98.4	98.7	....	63
Consumer Prices	100.6	101.2	101.3	101.7	103.3	101.3	101.4	101.4	101.4	101.7	101.9	103.0	103.3	103.5	104.1	64
Wages: Hourly Earnings	109.5	112.0	113.1	113.5	....	....	....	....	....	....	....	....	....	....	....	65
Industrial Production, Seas. Adj.	105	105	107	108	110	104	109	108	107	107	109	110	110	109	....	66..c
Investment Goods, Seas. Adj.	105	107	110	110	113	105	112	111	110	110	111	114	113	113	....	66iyc
Other Prod. Goods, Seas. Adj.	103	103	107	108	107	105	108	108	107	107	110	109	107	107	....	66iyc
Consumer Goods, Seas. Adj.	106	106	106	107	108	103	109	106	106	106	109	108	109	107	....	66hyc
Industrial Employment	100.7	100.9	102.0	101.8	101.6	101.6	102.1	102.4	102.0	102.0	101.4	101.3	101.6	101.9	....	67
International Transactions *(Billions of Deutsche Mark)*																
Exports	128.21	141.21	138.86	159.46	156.19	47.10	44.24	47.52	53.18	51.18	55.10	50.43	50.61	55.15	....	70
Imports, cif	103.02	107.19	107.21	122.34	120.17	36.04	34.94	36.23	42.62	38.12	41.62	38.61	39.25	42.31	....	71
Petroleum	6.17	6.34	6.95	6.27	....	2.55	2.30	2.11	2.17	1.81	2.28	....	....	....	....	71a
Crude Petroleum	3.67	3.61	4.02	3.52	....	1.39	1.34	1.30	1.25	1.01	1.26	....	....	....	....	71aa
Imports, fob	....	....	....	....	....	....	....	....	....	....	....	....	....	....	....	71.v
1985 = 100																
Volume of Exports	104.1	113.2	108.5	122.0	....	110.9	103.3	111.4	124.4	117.8	123.8	115.9	115.4	....	....	72
Volume of Imports	114.6	117.1	115.5	130.3	....	118.7	111.4	116.2	136.5	122.3	132.0	119.3	120.3	....	....	73
Unit Value of Exports	91.7	92.9	95.3	97.4	....	95.0	95.7	95.3	95.5	97.0	99.4	97.3	98.0	....	....	74
Export Prices	97.6	98.7	99.8	100.3	101.6	99.6	99.7	100.0	100.2	100.2	100.5	101.3	101.6	101.9	....	76
Unit Value of Imports	77.5	78.9	80.1	81.0	....	78.5	81.1	80.6	80.8	80.6	81.6	83.7	84.3	....	....	75
Import Prices	75.2	76.0	77.3	77.1	79.9	77.2	77.6	77.1	76.9	76.7	77.8	79.5	79.7	80.5	....	76.x
Balance of Payments *(Minus Sign Indicates Debit)*																
Current Account, nie	9.62	14.32	8.72	15.90	....	....	....	....	....	....	....	....	....	....	....	77a.d
Merchandise: Exports fob	73.15	78.28	71.60	85.82	....	24.53	22.58	24.48	27.76	27.95	30.10	....	....	....	....	77aad
Merchandise: Imports fob	-56.01	-57.66	-53.18	-63.36	....	....	....	....	....	....	....	....	....	....	....	77abd
Trade Bal.,77aa+77abd	17.14	20.62	18.42	22.46	....	....	....	....	....	....	....	....	....	....	....	77acd
Other Goods,Serv.&Income:Cre	20.45	22.36	20.79	22.86	....	....	....	....	....	....	....	....	....	....	....	77add
Other Goods,Serv.&Income:Deb	-23.81	-24.68	-26.01	-23.86	....	....	....	....	....	....	....	....	....	....	....	77aed
Private Unrequited Transfers	-1.62	-1.60	-1.64	-1.49	....	-.59	-.55	-.50	-.49	-.45	-.54	-.45	....	....	....	77afd
Official Unrequited Trans.,nie	-2.54	-2.37	-2.83	-4.07	....	-.64	-1.21	-.99	-1.37	-1.71	-.99	-.16	....	....	....	77agd
Direct Investment	-1.75	-3.84	-1.86	-1.26	....	-.85	-.51	-.50	-1.15	-.79	.68	-.37	-.38	....	....	77bad
Portfolio Investment, nie	-11.52	-12.54	-9.56	-10.15	....	-4.77	-2.90	-1.90	-3.33	-5.53	-6.28	-5.27	....	....	....	77bbd
Other Long-Term Capital, nie	-1.01	1.22	2.89	.79	....	1.97	.42	.50	.59	1.37	-1.17	1.28	1.07	....	....	77bcd
Total,77a.d+77bad—77bcd	-4.66	-.84	.19	5.28	....	....	....	....	....	....	....	....	....	....	....	77c.d
Other Short-Term Capital,nie	.84	-4.60	-10.90	-4.63	....	-1.92	-3.30	-5.68	.99	-3.28	-2.34	....	....	....	....	77d.d
Net Errors and Omissions	2.98	-.53	-1.38	-.17	....	....	....	....	....	....	....	....	....	....	....	77e.d
Total,lines 77c.d—77e.d	-.85	-5.97	-12.09	.48	....	....	....	....	....	....	....	....	....	....	....	77f.d
C'part to Mon./Demon. of Gold	—	—	—	—	—	—	—	—	—	—	—	—	—	—	—	78a.d
Counterpart to SDR Allocation	—	—	—	—	—	—	—	—	—	—	—	—	—	—	—	78b.d
C'part to Valuation Changes	-2.77	-2.47	.07	1.20	....	.25	-.15	-.02	1.78	.56	-1.14	-1.67	.38	....	....	78c.d
Total,lines 77f.d—78c.d	-3.62	-8.44	-12.01	1.68	....	....	....	....	....	....	....	....	....	....	....	78d.d
Exceptional Financing	—	—	—	—	—	—	—	—	—	—	—	—	—	—	—	79a.d
Liab.Const.Fgn Author. Reserves	-1.62	.42	5.07	-.86	....	1.84	3.02	.21	-.04	-.68	-.14	....	....	....	....	79b.d
Total Change in Reserves	5.24	8.03	6.95	-.82	....	3.58	2.32	1.05	-2.33	-1.66	3.17	3.54	-.73	....	....	79c.d
Government Finance *(Year Ending December 31)*																
Deficit (-) or Surplus	-11.36	-9.78	-8.45	-6.85	....	-4.74	-6.59	2.88	-5.99	-7.16	6.30	-10.10	-1.29	....	....	80
Revenue	64.31	65.42	67.81	76.74	....	20.47	20.20	27.14	19.34	20.70	36.70	17.45	22.74	....	....	81
Grants Received	....	....	....	....	....	....	....	....	....	....	....	....	....	....	....	81z
Adj. to Cash-Revenue & Grants	....	....	....	....	....	....	....	....	....	....	....	....	....	....	....	81x
Expenditure	75.67	75.20	76.26	83.59	....	25.21	26.79	24.26	25.33	27.86	30.40	27.55	24.03	....	....	82
Lending Minus Repayments	....	....	....	....	....	....	....	....	....	....	....	....	....	....	....	83
Overall Cash Adjustment	....	....	....	....	....	....	....	....	....	....	....	....	....	....	....	80x
Financing																
Net Borrowing	13.79	5.00	12.64	3.26	....	3.10	6.60	2.94	.12	6.88	-3.74	7.58	1.35	....	....	84
Domestic	....	....	....	....	....	....	....	....	....	....	....	....	....	....	....	84a
Foreign	....	....	....	....	....	....	....	....	....	....	....	....	....	....	....	85a
Seigniorage	.03	.11	.23	.19	....	.05	.05	.13	.03	.11	.05	.03	.02	....	....	86d
Pending Redemptions	-.01	.02	.01	.01	....	.01	—	—	-.01	.01	.01	—	—	....	....	87c
Use of Cash Balances	-2.45	4.65	-4.43	3.39	....	1.58	-.06	-5.95	5.85	.16	-2.62	2.49	-.08	....	....	87
Debt	454.27	459.27	471.91	475.17	....	462.37	468.97	471.91	472.03	478.91	475.17	482.75	484.10	....	....	88
Domestic	....	....	....	....	....	....	....	....	....	....	....	....	....	....	....	88a
Foreign	....	....	....	....	....	....	....	....	....	....	....	....	....	....	....	89a
Intragovernmental Debt	....	....	....	....	....	....	....	....	....	....	....	....	....	....	....	88s
National Accounts *(Seasonally Adjusted at Annual Rates)*																
Exports	662.8	676.8	690.0	710.8	....	....	....	....	....	....	....	....	....	....	....	90c.c
Government Consumption	403.2	408.4	414.0	413.2	....	....	....	....	....	....	....	....	....	....	....	91f.c
Gross Fixed Capital Formation	422.4	416.4	418.0	424.4	....	....	....	....	....	....	....	....	....	....	....	93e.c
Increase in Stocks	3.2	13.6	13.2	28.4	....	....	....	....	....	....	....	....	....	....	....	93i.c
Private Consumption	1,146.4	1,146.4	1,166.0	1,170.0	....	....	....	....	....	....	....	....	....	....	....	96f.c
Less: Imports	-543.2	-557.2	-570.0	-591.6	....	....	....	....	....	....	....	....	....	....	....	98c.c
Gross Nat'l Expenditure = GNP	2,094.8	2,104.4	2,131.2	2,155.2	....	....	....	....	....	....	....	....	....	....	....	99a.c
Less:Net Factor Inc.from Abroad	....	....	....	....	....	....	....	....	....	....	....	....	....	....	....	90e
Gross Domestic Product	....	....	....	....	....	....	....	....	....	....	....	....	....	....	....	99b
Nat'l Income, Market Prices	....	....	....	....	....	....	....	....	....	....	....	....	....	....	....	99e
Gross Nat'l Prod. 1985 Prices	1,975.1	1,973.7	1,995.6	2,001.3	....	....	....	....	....	....	....	....	....	....	....	99a.r

5

Formal Approaches to Forecasting Foreign Exchange Rates

Chapter 4 explained how and why exchange rates fluctuate. The relationships developed in that chapter can be and are used to make forecasts of future exchange rates. Some forecasts are simply judgmental. This means that the forecaster looks at the factors affecting exchange rates and makes an informal forecast of future rates. Judgmental forecasters are usually content to forecast the direction and general magnitude of changes in exchange rates. They do not provide precise estimates of an exchange rate at a particular point in time.

This chapter examines attempts to make more formal, precise forecasts of future exchange rates. We look at a number of forecasting approaches (models), examining the rationale behind them and evaluating their ability to forecast future exchange rates. We focus primarily on the attempts that have been made to forecast fluctuating exchange rates. The chapter concludes with a short section on the procedures used to forecast fixed or pegged exchange rates of currencies that are freely convertible.

This chapter may surprise you, since one of its conclusions is that there is no accurate and consistent method for forecasting exchange rates. However, learning what cannot be done is sometimes as important as learning what can be done. Understanding why it is so difficult to develop accurate formal forecasts is helpful to the manager, since it bolsters resistance to the idea that accurate forecasting is feasible. Understanding the limitations of exchange rate forecasting encourages managers to seek other alternatives to manage exchange rate risk.

Why Firms Attempt to Forecast Exchange Rates

We should not be surprised that firms have expended a good deal of time and money attempting to forecast exchange rates, since almost all business decisions are based on many different forecasts. This means that before a decision is made, managers look to the future and make assumptions about selected factors that are relevant to the decision. For example, a firm makes a sales forecast before marketing a new product, an interest rate forecast before borrowing, and a GNP forecast before deciding on expansion plans. Sometimes the forecasting technique is quite informal, but it is clear that forecasting is a natural and regular aspect of business decision making.

Forecasts represent an attempt to deal with the uncertainty associated with decision making. Managements believe that a better understanding of the future will reduce the likelihood of unfavorable consequences. In the context of exchange rate forecasting, knowledge of future exchange rates may reduce the uncertainty associated with three classes of problems:

1. Firms are concerned about the uncertainty related to the value of short-term commitments to accept or make payments in foreign currencies. For example, if an American firm purchases something from a foreign supplier and agrees to make a foreign currency payment in 60 days, the firm is at risk because it does not know the number of dollars that will be necessary to purchase the foreign currency. On the other hand, if a firm makes a sale to a foreign buyer and agrees to receive payment in a foreign currency at a future date, it is at risk because it does not know how many dollars can be obtained for the foreign currency. Having an accurate forecast of the future exchange rate would be helpful to a firm in these situations.

2. Firms are concerned about the uncertainty related to both short- and long-term investment decisions. When a firm invests money in foreign currency-denominated securities, it is at risk, since income is being earned in foreign currency but the future dollar value of the earnings is uncertain. When a firm builds a production facility in a foreign country, it is at risk, since it usually expects to earn foreign currency

income and the dollar value of that future income is unknown. Having an accurate forecast of the future exchange rate would be helpful to a firm in these situations.

3. Firms are concerned about the uncertainty related to financing decisions. They sometimes have the opportunity to borrow foreign currencies, and the attractiveness of such borrowing often depends on the exchange rate in effect at the time the borrowings must be repaid. For example, if a foreign currency strengthens after borrowing, more dollars will be needed to repay the foreign currency interest and principal. Having an accurate forecast of the future exchange rate would be helpful to a firm in these situations.

In each of the preceding situations, firms would like to know what the future exchange rate will be. Armed with an accurate forecast of exchange rates, the firm could protect itself against adverse movements in exchange rates. By adjusting prices, firms could buy and sell in foreign currencies without worrying about suffering unexpected losses. Firms could also make foreign currency investments and have a definite estimate of their dollar consequences. Firms could borrow foreign currency and know exactly how many dollars would be needed to repay the borrowings. Managerial decision making would be easier. Life would be wonderful. Of course, the task of the manager engaged in international commerce is neither easy nor wonderful. There are no accurate, readily available forecasts of future exchange rates. Managers face an uncertain world and are constantly attempting to make that world less uncertain.

To Forecast or Not to Forecast?

Managers involved in foreign currency–related decisions have no choice. They must incorporate future exchange rates into their analysis. Decision makers, unsure about future exchange rates, often throw up their hands, seemingly refuse to make a forecast, and assume that the future exchange rate will be the same as the present one. What they do not realize is that they are making a forecast—that there will be no change in the exchange rate. It is a forecast of "no change".

The nature of the no-change forecast can best be illustrated by an example. Assume that you are planning a 1-month vacation in the United Kingdom, and you would like to know how many dollars the trip will cost. You must have a forecast in order to determine whether or not you can afford the trip and how many dollars you will need. For example, assume that the spot rate is £1 = $2.00 and you have forecasted the rate during your future vacation at £1 = $2.10. If you estimate that the trip will involve an outlay of £1,000, then your forecasted dollar outlay would be $2,100. The other alternative is to forget about making a separate forecast of exchange rates and incorporate the present exchange rate into your analysis. In making your cost estimate, you use the present exchange rate of £1 = $2.00, which gives a total forecasted dollar cost of $2,000. When you use the current spot rate (£1 = $2.00) in the preceding computation, you have made a forecast (whether you realize it or not). Your forecast is that the future exchange rate will be equal to the present one.

Managers are often dissatisfied with this no-change approach to exchange rate forecasting. They believe that if exchange rates are studied closely, estimates that are better than those based on the no-change approach will emerge. Managers tend to believe that logic and/or detailed analysis of exchange rate–related data will improve forecast accuracy and make decisions a little less risky. In their struggle to make better estimates about future exchange rates, they have employed a variety of more formal forecasting approaches.

How Accurate a Forecast is Needed?

The ideal forecast would be one that provides the decision maker with the exact exchange rate at every future point in time. A forecast of the British pound made on March 11 would be able to indicate the precise exchange rate prevailing on the afternoon of May 31, the morning of December 12, and at every other time period in the future. In the ideal case, there are no forecast errors: That is, the forecasted exchange rate is always exactly equal to the future spot rate. Obviously, no available forecast meets the conditions outlined in the ideal case. Any forecast used by management is less than ideal. There is no approach for which forecasted exchange rate values will always equal future spot values. To some extent, every forecasting approach is inaccurate.

How accurate must an exchange rate forecast be in order to be useful? How large can forecast errors be before the forecast becomes useless? The answers to these questions depend on the situation confronting the decision maker. In long-term investment situations, for example, funds are being committed for long periods of time, and the decision maker is usually more concerned with long-term trends in currency values than with the value of the currency on any particular day, week, or even year. On the other hand, a firm that agrees to accept a single large foreign currency payment in exactly 90 days would want a highly precise forecast of the exchange rate on that day. Generally speaking, the forecasting approaches available are accurate enough for us to answer most of the longer-term questions. They are usually accurate enough to suggest the direction of change in currency values. Their accuracy with respect to forecasting the magnitude of change in exchange rates is usually tolerable. However, their ability to predict the precise timing of change has not been established. Thus, we may know that present conditions justify a forecast that the dollar will strengthen relative to the Mexican peso. We may accurately anticipate that the dollar's value relative to the peso would increase by approximately 100 percent. But we have no accurate way of forecasting the precise value of the peso next week, next month, or next year. Forecasts can do some things, but they cannot do everything we would like.[1]

Forecasts, while not capable of providing accurate point estimates of future exchange rates, are of help to business. They help to plan investments in foreign countries. They are useful in analyzing the attractiveness of borrowing foreign currencies. They help firms make decisions about adopting a long-term exporting strategy. Most managers involved in making decisions affected by foreign exchange rates believe forecasting to be a worthwhile activity.

The Forward Rate
as a Short-Term Forecaster

The forward rate of a foreign currency is sometimes used to forecast its future spot rate. For example, if the 90-day forward rate on the French franc is FF1 = $0.16, the forecasted spot rate in 90 days would also be $0.16. But why should the forward rate on a currency serve as a forecast of the future spot rate? One can approach the answer to this question from both the logical and the empirical point of view. The logical explanation requires an understanding of the institutions and motivations that support the forward exchange market. Remember that banks act as the clearing house for both spot and forward exchange transactions. Firms entering into forward exchange contracts must feel that the rates offered are more or less what would be received if the exchange positions were left uncovered and future cash inflows were converted at future spot rates. Let us examine how this works.

On any given day, some firms want to buy forward deutsche marks, while others want to sell them. Of course, the market participants will buy or sell only if they believe that the price quoted is reasonable. For example, assume that an American exporter is expecting a DM4,000,000 payment in 60 days. The current spot rate on the deutsche mark is DM1 = $0.48, and the 60-day forward rate is DM1 = $0.50. If the exporter enters into a forward contract, it would receive $2,000,000 in 60 days. Of course, the exporter would not enter into such a contract if he or she was

---

[1]Richard M. Levich, "Currency Forecasters Lose Their Way," *Euromoney*, August 1983, pp. 140–148.

convinced that the spot rate in 60 days is likely to be higher than DM1 = $0.50. If the exporter is convinced that the future spot rate will be DM1 = $0.60, she or he would wait for 60 days and then convert at the spot rate and receive $2,400,000 (DM4,000,000 × 0.60). Thus, if the quote offered by the bank is too low, there will be no forward sellers for the deutsche marks. If there are no sellers of forward deutsche marks, the bank's ability to enter into contracts with other customers will be limited.[2] Firms wishing to convert dollars to marks would also encounter difficulties. A situation like this cannot persist. The forward price will have to change.

If the forward exchange market is to provide a service to businesses, the forward price established must be acceptable to both the buyers and sellers of the foreign currency. In this sense, the forward price is viewed as an equilibrium price that clears the market for a particular currency. The price represents a consensus as to what constitutes a reasonable price for a currency in the future. Sellers of the currency believe that the forward price is high enough. Buyers believe that the price is low enough. Everyone goes away happy.

A firm's decision on whether to accept the price associated with a forward contract is often based on considerable amounts of information. Firms involved in international commerce regularly monitor international financial conditions and make at least an informal forecast about what spot rates are likely to be in the future. When a firm participates in a forward exchange contract, it is, in effect, saying that its own forecast of the future spot rate is not significantly different from the forward rate being offered. The forward rate being offered at any time indicates that the informal future spot rate forecasts of a large number of firms are consistent with the rate being offered. In a sense, the forward rate represents the consensus forecast about the level of future spot rates. The forward rate is what most firms believe the future spot rate will be.

Evaluation of the Forward Rate Forecasts

But how good is this informal forecast of the future spot rate that is inherent in the consensus forward rate? The answer to this question depends on the way *good* is defined. In situations such as this, it is defined by two criteria: accuracy and unbiasedness. The forward rate is a good forecasting device in the sense that it is an unbiased estimator of

---

[2] The level of risk that banks are willing to take in the forward market is discussed in Chapter 12.

TABLE 5-1 An Illustration: Unbiasedness and Accuracy of a Forward Rate Forecast—the 30-Day Forward Rate on the Deutsche Mark

	Forecasted Values: 30-Day Forward Rates	Actual Spot on Forward Contract Maturity Date	(Forward − Spot) Error
Case 1	$0.50	$0.40	+0.10
Case 2	0.70	0.45	+0.25
Case 3	0.35	0.60	−0.25
Case 4	0.45	0.65	−0.20
Case 5	0.40	0.50	−0.10
Case 6	0.60	0.35	+0.25
Case 7	0.40	0.45	−0.05
Average	0.4857	0.4857	0

the future spot rate. On the other hand, the forward rate is not a good forecasting device because it is not very accurate.

An unbiased estimator is one that is just as likely to overestimate as to underestimate a value. Negative errors are just as probable as positive errors. Positive errors tend to be offset by negative errors. The simple illustration presented in Table 5-1 will help clarify the meaning of unbiasedness. The data in the table represent hypothetical research on the relationship between the forward rate on the deutsche mark and the future spot rate. Assume that the investigator goes back to the past and selects a number of observations of the 30-day forward rate at different dates.[3] The investigator next looks at the actual spot rate 30 days later. The forward rate (forecast value) is then compared with the actual spot value 30 days later, and the errors are evaluated.

Note that the average of the forward rate forecasts (DM1 = $0.4857) is equal to the average of the actual spot rates that materialized 30 days later. Thus, on the average, the forward rate is a good forecaster of the future spot rate. Note, however, that huge individual forecast errors exist. In this illustration, the forward rate on any particular day was not necessarily a good forecaster of the spot rate 30 days later. In Case 2, the forward rate forecasted the price of the deutsche mark at $0.70, which was $0.25 higher than the actual spot price 30 days later. In other cases, the forward rate underestimated the future spot rate. With this simple

---

[3]An actual study would involve many more observations and would have to account for other phenomena. The errors included in the illustration are also much larger than those likely to be encountered in the actual data.

illustration in mind, it is now possible to develop an intuitive understanding of the difference between accuracy and unbiasedness.

Accuracy: An accurate forecast indicator is one that forecasts the future value accurately every time. Stated another way, in an accurate forecast, the forecast errors are small. In actual fact, the forward rate is not an accurate forecast indicator for the future spot rate.

Unbiasedness: An unbiased forecast indicator is one that forecasts accurately on the average, even though there may be large individual forecast errors. The forward rate is an unbiased estimator of the future spot rate.

The idea that the forward rate is an unbiased predictor is not only intuitively appealing, it is also supported by a number of empirical studies.[4] The various studies show that the market for foreign exchange rapidly assimilates new information regarding exchange rates, and both forward and spot rates adjust quickly to this new information. The forward rate neither consistently overestimates or underestimates the future spot rate. On the average, the forward rate will be equal to the future spot rate.

It would be wonderful if the forward rate were both an accurate and an unbiased estimator of the future spot rate, but it is not. However, the fact that the forward rate is an unbiased estimator of the future spot rate has important managerial implications, which will be discussed in later chapters. Also note that because the forward rate is an unbiased estimator, it can be viewed as the best-guess forecast of the future spot rate. Be sure to remember, however, that while it is probably the best single guess, the chance of error is relatively high.

The forward rate will be an unbiased estimator of the future spot rate only so long as the foreign exchange market remains competitive. That is, forward rates must reflect the actions and expectations of a large number of buyers and sellers of the forward currency. To the extent that governments interfere with the forward market or other market imperfections intrude, the unbiasedness of the estimator will be affected. Thus, the forward rate is likely to be an unbiased estimator of the future spot rate only for the heavily traded currencies that float freely against each other. Since at present there is a forward market for only a limited number of currencies, the forecasting usefulness of the forward rate is

---

[4]Ian H. Giddy and Gunter Dufey, "The Random Behavior of Flexible Exchange Rates," *Journal of International Business Studies*, Spring 1975, pp. 1–32. Bradford W. Cornell, "Spot Rates, Forward Rates and Market Efficiency," *Journal of Financial Economics*, August 1977, pp. 55–65. Steven W. Kohlhagen, "The Forward Rate as an Unbiased Predictor of the Future Spot Rate," *Columbia Journal of World Business*, Winter 1979, pp. 77–85.

limited. Also note that the time horizon associated with the forward rate forecast is very limited, since most forward contracts are for 180 days or less. For example, the forward market provides no readily available forecast for an exchange rate 2 years in the future.

Technical Forecasts of Future Exchange Rates

Technical forecasting is both popular and controversial. The individuals who engage in this type of forecasting are known as *technicians*, and they forecast future exchange rates by carefully examining past exchange rate movements. There are many different types of technicians. For example, a technician may have noted that, in the past, 20 consecutive daily increases in a currency value were almost always followed by another sharp rise in the value of that currency, and that rise always lasted for at least 10 days. A technician who has noted this pattern would constantly monitor exchange rates in order to identify when that currency has 20 consecutive daily increases in value. When such a situation is identified, the technician would recommend that the currency be purchased. Understand that what we have been discussing is only an example; there is no single technical theory applied by all technicians. Each technician studies the past and develops a personal sense about its meaning. To some extent, each technician develops an individual forecast about future currency values.

The actual techniques used by technicians vary. Some have developed sophisticated statistical models; others use elaborate charts of past exchange rate movements; and still others pore over past exchange rates and make simple, informal judgments and recommendations about the movement of future exchange rates. The one thing that all *pure* technicians have in common is that they focus solely on past exchange rates. In other words, a pure technician would argue that the clues to the future are to be found in the past. History does repeat itself. Thus, a purely technical position would ignore factors such as relative inflation rates, relative interest rates, disequilibria in balance of payments, political stability, and other factors that are believed by economists to affect the movement of exchange rates. In a sense, the technician views exchange rate movements as mechanistic rather than caused by economic and political factors.

Of course, technicians are not fools. There are few pure technicians in the sense that all outside factors affecting exchange rates are ignored. An oil embargo, a war, a drought, and many other factors are likely to be incorporated into the recommendation of the technician, usually in an informal fashion. In actual practice, however, most technical forecasters use past exchange rate movements (history) as their primary basis for forecasting. Recommendations are then modified on the basis of other relevant information.

Evaluation of Technical Forecasting

Most economists do not like either the idea or the practice of technical forecasting. In a sense, technicians are usually viewed as the astrologers of the marketplace. Just as science scorns the use of the stars as the basis for decision making, the science of economics scorns the use of exchange rate history to forecast future price movements. And as we will see, economists have mounted an impressive intellectual attack on technical forecasting. But the logic of economics has done no more to dissuade technicians and their clients than attacks on astrology have discouraged believers in the stars. Both technicians and astrologers remain very popular and are widely read, and their advice is sometimes followed.

Logic is on the side of the economists. First, there is the research, which supports the assertion that the prices in the foreign exchange market reflect all currently available public information.[5] If the foreign exchange market is efficient, all past information (as well as expectations about the future) is already incorporated in the existing price of foreign exchange. It does no good to go back and look for patterns of past behavior. Research has also indicated that exchange rates generally follow a *random walk*.[6] While this concept has a precise statistical definition, it generally refers to a situation in which a specific price change is unrelated to past changes. Price changes are, in effect, random and therefore unforecastable. The idea is that the future exchange rate will differ from the current exchange rate only to the extent to which unforeseen events intervene in the market (since foreseeable events are already reflected in the current exchange rate). Since the unforeseen events occur in a random fashion, changes in exchange rates are random. Knowledge of past exchange rate behavior is not helpful in predicting unforeseen events. Once again, the logic and indirect evidence against the technical forecasting approach are impressive.[7]

Technical forecasters ignore the logic of efficient markets and focus on results. They usually assert that their approach works (or would have worked if something had not gone wrong). In practice, it is very difficult to disprove these assertions. First, we must recognize that there are many

---

[5] This test of the efficient market hypothesis is called the *semistrong form*. For a more complete discussion of efficient markets, see James C. Van Horne, *Financial Management and Policy*, 7th ed., Englewood Cliffs, NJ: Prentice-Hall, Inc., 1986, pp. 55–56.

[6] This test of the efficient market hypothesis is called the *weak form*.

[7] Economists also attack the statistical assumptions that lie behind many technical forecasts.

(probably thousands) different technical forecasting systems, and these systems are changing all the time. For those economists who are willing to take aim at technical forecasts, they present a diverse and moving target. Second, an acceptable definition of forecast accuracy is not easy to state. The most frequently mentioned standard of accuracy is that *the forecast errors associated with a particular forecasting technique should be smaller than the forecast errors associated with the free forward market forecasts.* Not everyone accepts this standard.

The biggest problem associated with evaluating technical forecasts is that they sometimes work. This is not surprising or inconsistent with the efficient market hypothesis. The laws of chance applied to random events suggest that forecasters are sometimes right and sometimes wrong. The idea of the randomness of exchange rate movements is also perfectly consistent with the idea that a technical forecast could be correct for a number of periods in a row. We can illustrate this second proposition by taking a quick look at the probabilities associated with coin tossing. The consecutive "fair" tossing of an unbiased coin is a random process. The probability of getting a head or a tail on any single toss of an unbiased coin is always the same ($P = 0.5$). The fact that a head was thrown on a previous toss does not affect the probability of throwing a head on the next toss. The past does not predict the future. Coins do not have memories. In the case of coin tossing, this has been so well documented that there is no controversy. No one advocates making charts of past tosses with the realistic expectation that such charts will be useful aids in predicting future coin tosses. While it is possible to get five heads in a row, the probability of doing so is quite low (approximately 3 times out of 100). If we have thousands of tosses, occasionally we will get five heads in a row, but this does not mean that the coin is biased or that the tosser has a special knack for throwing heads. Tossing five heads in a row is consistent with the laws of probability.

Similarly, having five accurate technical forecasts in succession is consistent with the idea that exchange rates move in a random fashion. It is consistent with the idea that past exchange rate movements are not helpful in predicting future exchange rates. Surely some forecasters will have a streak of correct forecasts (just as there can be a number of heads in a row). However, to prove the efficacy of a technical system, it is necessary to show that the system yields forecasts that are consistently more accurate than the forward market forecast. Unfortunately, no known technical forecast measures up to this standard. Some technical forecasting systems are accurate some of the time, but none are accurate most of the time.

Technical forecasts are very popular. Some businesses subscribe to them. Often technical forecasts are used by business decision makers in conjunction with economic model–based forecasts. It is also true, however, that such models are particularly popular with speculators in the foreign exchange markets. The emphasis of the technicians seems to be on forecasting short-term exchange rates so that large, quick profits can be made. The efficacy of such forecasts for business decision-making purposes has yet to be proven.

Forecasting Exchange Rates with Economic Models

A variety of economic models are being used to forecast future exchange rates. Economic model forecasting differs from technical forecasting in that it is (or should be) based on established and verified economic relationships. For example, economic models designed to forecast exchange rates often incorporate information about the balance of payments, inflation and interest rates, and a number of other variables. Economic models adopt a *cause-and-effect* approach to forecasting. If, for example, we have established that a country's inflation rate affects its future exchange rate, it may be possible to forecast its future exchange rate by forecasting its future inflation rate.[8] Economic models are, at least to some extent, logical. We know why they should work.

Statistically Based Economic Forecasting Models

Economic models designed to forecast exchange rates are often statistical. The usual statistical model attempts to establish a quantitative relationship between future exchange rates (the dependent variable) and variables that can explain changes in exchange rates (independent variables). Frequently, the forecast is based on multiple regression. A hypothetical multiple regression model for forecasting exchange rates is as follows:

$$Y(t) = a + b1 \times X1(t) + b2 \times X2(t) + \mu(t) \qquad (5\text{-}1)$$

[handwritten annotation: *disturbance*]

$Y(t)$: This is the exchange rate that is being forecasted. The t is the time point or period for which the forecast is being made. It may be a forecast of an exchange rate at a particular point in time, or it may be an average exchange rate over a period of time. For example, some models are designed to forecast the average exchange rate on a quarterly basis (e.g., the average exchange rate for the first

---

[8]Strictly speaking, cause-and-effect relationships are not necessary. Forecasters look for variables that are related to each other, whether or not one is caused by the other.

quarter of 1991). A forecast of the dependent variable is the purpose of the exercise.

Xi: In the model described in Equation 5-1, there are two independent variables, each indicated by an X ($X1$ and $X2$). These are the variables that can explain (cause?) movements in exchange rates. In practice, the number and nature of the variables vary from model to model. Among the variables frequently found in exchange rate forecasts are

> Growth rates in GNP
> Interest rates
> Inflation rates
> Balance of payments data

μ: This variable in Equation 5-1 is the so-called disturbance factor. It is there because economists know that many other factors affect exchange rates and that not everything can be included in the model. These other factors are lumped together in the term μ. In order for an economic model to be usable for forecasting exchange rates, the disturbance factor (μ) must have several statistical characteristics and must not be too large.

A statistical economic model for forecasting exchange rates is constructed by looking at past data. Historical data on exchange rates and the independent variables used in the model are collected. They are then processed so as to arrive at the statistics needed to make a forecast. These statistics are the a and the b's. The problems associated with statistical forecasts can best be described by fleshing out the example. Let us assume the following:

$Y(t)$ = the direct quote on the deutsche mark at time t (in dollars)

$X1(t)$ = U.S. inflation rate − German inflation rate (in decimal form at time t)

$X2(t)$ = U.S. growth rate in GNP − German growth rate in GNP (in decimal form at time t)

Further, assume that historical data have been collected and processed using a multiple regression computer package. The computation yielded the following statistics: $a = +0.50$, $b1 = +1.0$, and $b2 = -1.2$. Note that the disturbance factor (μ) is not part of the computation process. It is incorporated into the forecasting process by making assumptions about how disturbances affect the computed values. A popular (often erroneous) assumption associated with forecasting is that the various disturbances tend to cancel each other. Therefore, their impact on the forecast is negligible and can be ignored. In other models, more specific assumptions are made. For example, it may be assumed that the disturbances are such that the computed values are likely to be higher than the true values. Once again, the forecasters must be both talented economists and competent statisticians. Forecasting is difficult.

With this new information, we are in a position to forecast exchange rates. The forecasting equation is

$$Y(t) = 0.50 + 1 \times X1(t) - 1.2 \times X2(t)$$

If the forecasted inflation rate (at some future time t) in the United States is 0.05 and the forecasted inflation rate in Germany is 0.03, then the difference will be +0.02. If the forecasted GNP growth in the United States is 0.04 and the forecasted GNP growth in Germany is 0.01, then the differences will be +0.03. These forecasted values would then be inserted into the statistical model in order to get an estimate of the future value of the deutsche mark:

$$Y(t) = 0.50 + 1(0.02) - 1.2(0.03) = \$0.484 \qquad \text{direct quote on DM}$$

In this hypothetical forecasting model, the forecast indicates that the direct quote will be DM1 = \$0.484 at time t. The higher forecasted U.S. inflation rate is more than offset by the fact that the forecast expects higher U.S. growth in GNP.

Advantages of a
Statistical Forecasting Model

We are now in a position to examine the advantages of a statistical economic model used to forecast foreign exchange rates. First, we can see that the forecast is specific and numerical. Note that different forecasters using the same model would arrive at exactly the same forecast. In addition, if the statistical model is constructed properly, it may be possible to establish a confidence interval around the forecasted exchange rate. For example, it may be possible to make a statement such as "There is a 90 percent chance that the direct quote on the deutsche mark will be between \$0.47 and \$0.51."

The advantages of statistical forecasting models have encouraged many operating and consulting firms to develop them. Ultimately, however, the development and use of a statistical model for forecasting exchange rates must be based on cost/benefit comparisons. Firms must ask whether the high cost of such a model is justified in terms of its accuracy and usefulness to the firm. These questions are addressed in the following sections.

Conceptual and Design Problems Associated with Economic Models

The economic assumptions that underlie statistical forecasting models are often criticized on the grounds that they are neither well conceived nor well designed. In order to be well designed, a forecasting model must (1) be consistent with economic theory, (2) include a sufficient number of explanatory (independent) variables to justify any forecasting efficacy and be able to justify the exclusion of certain variables from the model, and (3) have relationships among the variables that are consistent with the statistical model to be employed. Most (if not all) of the forecasting models currently in use can be criticized on one or more of these grounds, particularly in regard to factors (2) and (3).

Which variables should be included in the model (and excluded from it) is often a controversial issue. For example, a model that relies solely on differences in inflation rates and excludes other economic factors, such as interest rates and growth in GNP, may be criticized as being too simplistic. Other models are criticized because they exclude political factors such as the probability of war, labor unrest, and other factors that are known to have a substantial economic impact. Obviously, not every variable can be included in each model. How well the economic logic incorporated into the model must conform to reality is a subject of continuing debate.

The assumed mathematical relationships among the variables in statistical economic forecasting models are also debated. Economists are criticized for adopting a statistical technique and then forcing the observed data into the statistical framework. The problem is that the statistical technique employed may be inconsistent with actual economic relationships. This problem can be illustrated by taking a closer look at the forecasting model we employed in our example. In constructing the model, we assumed that independent variables (interest rate differentials and growth in GNP differentials) are *linearly* related to the dependent variable (the direct quote on the deutsche mark). This means that any given change in the independent variables will lead to precisely the same change in the dependent variable. For example, for every one-unit change in the difference in growth rates, the direct quote on the deutsche mark will go down by 1.2 times that amount. That is, the regression coefficient ($b2$) is constant (1.2) and is applied in every situation. Such an assumption may be unreasonable. It may be that the relationship between GNP growth differentials and exchange rates is quite different when the differentials are of different sizes. For example, the 1.2 regression coefficient may not apply when the difference in growth rates is greater than five percentage points. In more formal terms, it may be argued that the relationship is nonlinear and that the use of linear regression is inappropriate. In other words, the assumed mathematical relationship may not hold over the relevant range of observations.

Economists and statisticians are strongly aware of these and many other related difficulties, and try hard to overcome them. Unfortunately, not all forecasters are equally competent, and even the most competent ones have difficulty overcoming the tremendous statistical problems associated with forecasting exchange rates. The business decision maker must keep this in mind when adopting models or forecasts provided by consulting firms. An elaborate forecasting model that generates detailed forecasts of future exchange rates is no better than its assumptions. If such models are to be of any use at all, the people who construct them must be first rate.

Measurement Problems
Associated with Statistical Forecasts

In addition to the conceptual and design problems associated with developing statistical forecasting models for foreign exchange rates, there are a group of related problems that can be called *measurement problems*. In some cases, it is impossible to measure the independent variables in the model accurately and consistently. In other cases, the variables needed to make the desired forecast are unavailable in a timely fashion. When one or more of these conditions exist, it is difficult to imagine how a forecasting model can be useful.

Accurate, consistent measurements of the independent variables included in the model are necessary if a statistical model is to be useful for forecasting purposes.[9] For example, assume that we are trying to use our model to forecast the direct quote on the Mexican peso. In order to construct the model, it is necessary to gather historical data on inflation and the GNP in Mexico. The problem is that developing countries such as Mexico experience great difficulties in trying to formulate accurate and consistent measurements of this variable.[10] It is difficult to use GNP in a forecasting model when we do not have a good measure of GNP. Preliminary estimates of U.S. employment, exports, inflation, and many

---

[9]This is true when trying to make estimates of independent variables. Such a condition is not necessary when the purpose of the model is to determine the nature of the relationship among variables.

[10]Even the statistical series published for the United States are characterized by large measurement errors. For example, look back at the balance of payments data for the United States, and you will find a very large "errors and omissions" account.

other values are often subject to substantial revision at a later date. Again, we must recognize that these problems are addressed by competent and diligent economists. Even with these impressive efforts, however, there are still problems in measurement and the accuracy of the estimates may not be adequate for all purposes, especially forecasting.

Timeliness of Data Inputs

The second measurement problem associated with statistical models relates to the timeliness of the data used in the model. In order to forecast, it is necessary to have information concerning the independent variables prior to the time period being forecasted. For example, if the goal is to forecast the exchange rate for the first quarter of 1991, we need information about the independent variables before that date. The sooner we have this information, the greater the value of the forecast. If the data for the independent variables are not available until the first quarter of 1991 or later, the forecasting model is of no use, since we already know the exchange rate. Note that in the forecasting model described in Equation 5-1, it was assumed that the exchange rate was related to inflation and growth differentials in the same period. Thus, such a forecasting model would not be very useful because the independent variables are unavailable in a timely fashion.

An ideal forecasting model would relate independent variables at an earlier date than the forecasted exchange rate. Such a situation is illustrated in Equation 5-2:

$$Y(t + 2) = a + b1 \times X1(t0) + b2 \times X2(t - 1) + \mu(t) \qquad (5\text{-}2)$$

In this model, the exchange rate (Y) two periods in the future $(t + 2)$ is related to differences in national inflation rates $(X1)$ during the current period $(t0)$ and to differences in GNP growth rates $(X2)$ during the period prior to the present one $(t - 1)$. This model is acceptable for forecasting, since we are using current or historical data to predict future events. The independent variables in this model are available in a timely fashion. Unfortunately, relationships such as those described in Equation 5-2 are hard to find. That is, such relationships usually do not describe economic reality and are therefore useless for forecasting purposes. But this is the forecaster's dream. What the forecaster would like to have are accurate and consistent independent variables that "lead" the dependent variable. Unfortunately, such economic relationships rarely exist.

The unavailability of accurate, consistently leading independent variables has forced forecasters to develop alternative strategies. One such strategy calls for forecasting the independent variables and then using them to forecast exchange rates. For example, a forecaster of exchange rates may forecast interest rate or inflation rate differentials and then incorporate these forecasts into the forecast of exchange rates. The problem with this approach is that it is no easier to forecast variables such as inflation, interest rates, and GNP than it is to forecast exchange rates. It seems logical to conclude that a forecast of exchange rates based on an inaccurate forecast of independent variables is an unacceptable strategy.

Sample Design Problems

One general property of statistical models is that it is sometimes possible to establish confidence intervals around their estimates. For example, if a statistician is attempting to estimate the average size of company sales to foreign buyers, it may be able to arrive at an estimate (e.g., $17,500) and establish a confidence interval (e.g., a 95 percent chance that the average sale is between $16,700 and $18,300). In order to make probability statements about the accuracy of an estimate, however, the procedure used to take sample observations must be selected in a precise manner. Generally speaking, the sampling procedure must incorporate elements of randomness in order for the probability statements about the confidence intervals to have statistical validity.

It is virtually impossible to design exchange rate forecasting models that incorporate random sampling techniques. Data about most variables are historical in nature and limited in availability. Forecasters must work with the data that are available to them, and the nature of the economic data does not usually permit probability statements to be attached to forecasts of exchange rates. The user of statistical forecasts of foreign exchange rates is advised that probability statements are unreliable.

Evaluation of Forecasts
of Fluctuating Exchange Rates

It would be surprising if a particular forecasting approach could consistently outguess the forward exchange market. After all, the price established in the forward exchange market is a price that is agreed upon by many buyers and sellers, each of whom presumably has made a forecast or assumption about the fairness of the market price. In a sense, the market price represents an average forecast. To forecast a foreign exchange rate that is different from the market price of a currency is to assert that the particular forecasting model being employed is superior to the market forecast.

What conditions are necessary in order to have a forecast model that is consistently better than the market as a whole?[11]

1. A superior economic and statistical model is needed. That is, the individual forecast must be able to better define the economic relationships that underlie the movement of exchange rates and must be able to overcome the substantial statistical design problems associated with forecasting models.
2. The superior forecaster must have earlier access to information than other market participants.
3. The forecaster must also be able to forecast the probable direction and extent of government intervention, as well as other disturbances (oil embargos, etc.) that have an impact on exchange rates.

A forecaster who has all of these advantages must be able to act quickly and secretly in order to capitalize on his or her superior position. Waiting too long will allow others in the market to gain the same knowledge, which in turn would result in a change in the currency value. In other words, if a superior forecast suggests that the value of the French franc will decline and the forecaster waits before acting on the information, the value of the franc will drop as other market participants come to the same conclusion. If a forecaster makes his or her superior forecast known to others (publishes or sells it), the market will have an opportunity to absorb the new information contained in the forecast. The publication of the forecast and its evaluation by other foreign exchange market participants should lead to a currency price adjustment. In an efficient market, the advantage of a superior forecast is quickly eliminated.

The conditions needed for a consistently accurate foreign exchange rate forecasting model are such that it is unreasonable to expect any single forecaster to be consistently more accurate than others. In addition, the results of superior forecasts are likely to be quickly reflected in current exchange rates. It is not surprising, therefore, to find that the record of exchange rate forecasts is inconsistent and questionable. Richard M. Levich, for example, studied exchange rate forecasts at two different points in time.[12] His earlier study showed that 14 percent of forecasters seemed to perform better than the market. His later studies of commercial forecasting services showed that only 5 percent of the forecasters in the

---

[11]This presentation is a modification of the Giddy-Dufey conditions. See Ian H. Giddy and Gunter Dufey, "The Random Behavior of Flexible Exchange Rates," *Journal of International Business Studies*, Spring 1975, pp. 1–32.

[12]Richard M. Levich, "The Use and Analysis of Foreign Exchange Forecasts: Current Issues and Evidence," (paper presented at the Euromoney Treasury Consultancy Program, New York, September 4–5, 1980). Richard M. Levich, "Currency Forecasters Lose Their Way," *Euromoney*, August 1983, pp. 140–148.

study were able to outperform the 30-day forward rate as a forecasting device. Only 14 percent of the forecasters were more accurate than the 90-day forward rate.[13] The record highlights the inconsistency and inaccuracy of the exchange rate forecast. The only sure thing about exchange rate forecasts seems to be that they are not very reliable.

Implications for Management

What should the decision maker do? Remember that the firm must forecast exchange rates in order to develop strategies with respect to foreign currency sales and purchases, foreign currency investment decisions, and foreign currency financing decisions. Some assumption about the level of the future exchange rate is needed. Should the firm attempt to develop its own forecasting model and make its own forecast? Should the firm spend thousands of dollars for a commercial forecast? Or should the firm proceed as if future foreign exchange rates are basically unforecastable? These are the questions that management must answer.

It is probably unwise for firms to spend too much time and money attempting to develop a unique forecast of future exchange rates. The expertise and cost required to develop a superior forecast are substantial. Even if a superior model is developed, the ability of a firm to capitalize on it is doubtful. In addition, the likelihood of developing a superior model is quite small. Management should probably follow the forward rate developments and monitor general factors that affect exchange rates (balance of payments, inflation rates, etc.) in an informal fashion. There is little evidence to suggest that more formal techniques will yield superior forecasts.

Purchasing commercial exchange rate forecasts is not necessarily unwise. These forecasts can provide additional insights into the general factors affecting exchange rates and make the decision maker more aware of the risks and rewards associated with international commerce. However, it would be unwise for the manager to base detailed corporate decisions on commercial forecasts. These forecasts should be viewed as indicators of future possibilities rather than an accurate and consistent forecasts of future exchange rate developments.

Surprising as it may seem, and after spending an entire chapter discussing exchange rate forecasting, we recommend that the manager proceed as if future exchange rates are basically unforecastable. As this book develops, you will see that there are ways that the firm can structure its operations and engage in a number of activities that can

---

[13] Ibid.

minimize the impact of unfavorable movements in exchange rates. To a large extent, the success of the manager engaged in international commerce will depend on his or her ability to make decisions in the face of uncertain exchange rates. That is what this book is about.

Forecasting Fixed Exchange Rates for Convertible Currencies

Not all exchange rates fluctuate freely. Many convertible currencies are fixed relative to the dollar, the French franc, and the SDR. The currencies in the European Monetary System (EMS) are fixed relative to each other. This means that the governments of the various countries are committed to taking action that will maintain the value of their currencies against the designated target. In many cases, a government stands ready to intervene in world currency markets, either to buy or sell its own currency. For example, if the supply of French francs relative to other EMS currencies is too large (putting pressure on the franc to devalue), the governments of France and of other EMS countries may intervene in the market and buy francs. This would remove the pressure on the French franc and maintain the established exchange rate.

Of course, governments have limited willingness and ability to buy surplus currency in order to maintain a fixed exchange rate. At some point in time, the underlying economic realities will affect the exchange rate. At this point, when most other options have been exhausted, the government may announce a change in the value of its currency. Governments usually attempt to fool currency market participants right up to the last minute. Officials are likely to deny that any change in currency value is forthcoming and attempt to mislead the market in every way. Then, suddenly, the value of the currency is changed. The currency may be revalued upward or downward by a few percentage points, but often the changes are much more dramatic. In an instant, the value of the currency changes by 10 percent or even 100 percent. Managers of firms engaged in international commerce have great anxiety about such developments. A firm committed to accept large amounts of a foreign currency that is devalued would suffer a great loss. On the other hand, managers would like to possess foreign currencies that are suddenly revalued upward.

The approach used to forecast fixed exchange rates is quite different from the one used to forecast fluctuating exchange rates. While the forecast of fluctuating exchange rates focuses primarily on identifying economic factors that are likely to affect exchange rates, the forecast of fixed exchange rates places equal emphasis on both political and economic factors. Political analysis is important because governments act

TABLE 5-2   Steps in Forecasting Fixed Exchange Rates

Step one: Evaluate Economic Pressures on the Currency Value
   a. Study the balance of payments behavior and compare it to balance of payments developments in other countries.
   b. Compare past and expected inflation rates to developments in other countries.
   c. Compare past and expected GNP growth rates to developments in other countries.
   d. Compare past and expected interest rates to developments in other countries.
   e. Study other economic factors that are known to place pressure on exchange rates.

Step Two: Evaluate the Possible Impact of Economic Policy Alternatives
   a. Evaluate the political and economic consequences of changing the value of the currency.
   b. Evaluate the political and economic consequences of foreign exchange controls.
   c. Evaluate the political and economic consequences of placing limits on the movement of capital into and out of the country.
   d. Evaluate the political and economic consequences of policies designed to affect domestic growth, inflation, and interest rates.

Step Three: Evaluate Political Pressures on Decision Makers
   a. Examine the political philosophy and platform of the government in power. Opposition parties that have a likelihood of gaining power must also be studied.
   b. Study the personality and personal objectives of the powerful political figures who would have to approve a decision to devalue or revalue a currency.
   c. Study the pressures being exerted by political allies and important economic partners.
   d. Evaluate the election day phenomenon as it applies to the country in question.

Step Four: Make an Educated Judgmental Forecast

continuously over long periods of time to offset economic pressures exerted on currency values. A procedure for forecasting fixed exchange rates is outlined in Table 5-2.

Note that the recommended forecast procedure begins with an analysis of the economic factors affecting exchange rates. These are the same factors that would be considered in forecasting fluctuating exchange rates. Forecasters of fixed exchange rates, however, are not likely to place heavy emphasis on statistical models and tests. The forecaster is usually content with a general understanding of the magnitude and duration of disequilibrium conditions. There is no need to develop a specific numerical estimate of future exchange rates.

In some cases, the economic data suggest that the fixed value of the currency is approximately equal to its true economic value. The balance of payments, inflation rate, interest rates, and general economic conditions are such that there is no pressure on the government to change the fixed value of the currency. In the absence of substantial economic pressure on a currency, it is unlikely that a government will change the fixed exchange rates.

In other cases, downward economic pressure on the currency is substantial.[14] A country's balance of payments may indicate a large, continuous disequilibrium. Relative inflation rates, interest rates, and GNP growth rates may also suggest a strong pressure for devaluation. But, however strong these economic forces, the value of the currency involved may be maintained for a long time, since the government may pursue other strategies designed to relieve the pressure on its currency. An examination of these economic policy alternatives to devaluation is the second step in the forecasting process.

The intent of Step Two is to attempt to identify the factors that government decision makers will look at when making a decision with respect to altering fixed exchange rates. How will a devaluation affect domestic inflation, interest rates, and economic growth? Are these developments politically acceptable? Is it politically and economically feasible to limit the exchange of foreign currencies and/or to restrict investment flows?

Step three attempts to systematize the way the analyst looks at the political pressures on the government. In some countries, devaluation may be viewed as a disgrace and a blow to national pride. Politicians may fear that opposition parties will exploit any devaluation of a currency. For this reason, devaluations rarely occur within a year prior to an election, and then frequently occur immediately after an election. This is called the *election day effect*. It is also necessary to study the political pressures that are being exerted by foreign allies or economic powers. In the EMS, for example, foreign political pressure is often placed on Germany to revalue its currency upward (and Germany has reluctantly done so). At the same time, other countries (France, for example) have been pressured by other members of the community to devalue. These political pressures are important and powerful.

As you probably now realize, forecasting changes in fixed exchange rates is a complicated process. Successful forecasting requires both political and economic wisdom. It demands continuous monitoring of both economic and political conditions and a sensitivity to the political pressures that exist in foreign countries. A successful forecaster is likely to be an individual with maturity and experience. Forecasts of fixed exchange rates are not statistical or mechanical. The forecast is a judgment that is certainly based on observation and fact. However, the intuition of the forecaster may be the most important ingredient of a successful forecast.

---

[14] Our discussion will focus on currency devaluations, since upward revaluations are relatively infrequent events.

Another way of looking at the process of forecasting fixed exchange rates is to use economic analysis to determine whether or not a country will devalue, and political analysis to determine when a devaluation will take place, and how large it will be. This approach is based on the reality that no country can maintain its fixed exchange rate in the face of continuing negative economic conditions. In addition, foreign exchange controls and restrictions on investments are unlikely to stem the major forces generating the pressure to devalue.

Governments often fight hard to maintain currency values, but they usually must capitulate to economic reality. Governments have spent billions of dollars to defend a currency, only to eventually devalue. In effect, governments attempt to go against economic reality. This is possible because governments are not profit-making operations. In other words, governments are willing to lose large amounts in order to maintain the value of their currency at a desired level. In the past (and probably again in the future), speculators have realized large profits by "betting" against the ability of the government to go against economic reality for long periods of time. In effect, speculators profit from such government actions.

Summary and Conclusions

Accurate forecasts of foreign exchange rates would be invaluable to a firm operating in the international environment. The problem facing the firm is not in making forecasts but in making accurate and unbiased forecasts. This chapter discussed three different forecasting alternatives: (1) technical models, (2) economic models, and (3) the forward market.

Empirical evidence suggests that the forward market provides a better forecast than either the technical or the economic model alternatives. This does not mean that the forward market is a perfect forecaster of the future value of a foreign currency. The forward market is an unbiased indicator of the future value of foreign exchange. In other words, in the long run, the overestimates will balance the underestimates. The forward market, however, can have significant errors on individual forecasts. Thus, the forward market does not provide accurate forecasts. Technical or economic model forecasts, however, have not been able consistently to beat the forward market.

Should the firm ignore the more formal forecasting techniques and use the forward market as the only estimator of the future value of a foreign currency? The answer is probably no. More formal techniques (especially economic models) may give management better insights into the economic variables affecting international decisions. Although they would not be able to provide a better forecast, they would improve management's understanding of the international environment.

Review Questions

1. Why would a firm want to make a forecast of future exchange rates? Why not just ignore the problem?
2. "Since forecasting the future value of a foreign currency is so difficult, I will not make a forecast. Instead, I will assume that the exchange rate will remain constant." Is this a good strategy? Explain your answer.
3. How accurate must a forecast be in order for it to be useful to the firm?
4. "The forward rate is an accurate and unbiased estimator of the future spot rate." True or false? Explain your answer.
5. What is a technical forecast of foreign exchange rates? Why are such forecasts criticized by economists?
6. What are the conceptual problems associated with constructing an economic model useful for forecasting exchange rates?
7. How do the measurement problems associated with statistical economic models for forecasting foreign exchange rates influence the reliability of forecasts?
8. Why would it be unreasonable for you to place great reliance on a confidence interval forecast of a foreign exchange rate?
9. "Economic models have consistently provided the best forecasts of the future value of foreign currencies." True or false? Explain your answer.
10. How do forecasts of fixed or pegged exchange rates differ from forecasts of fluctuating exchange rates?
11. Explain the logic behind the statement "The forward rate provides a free forecast of the future spot exchange rate."
12. Why do the formal techniques used to forecast exchange rates have difficulty generating accurate predictions?

Questions for Discussion

1. Assume that you are the manager of the foreign exchange department of a large multinational firm that is regularly involved in many foreign currency transactions. In the past, fluctuations in currency values have resulted in large losses to the firm. Top management declares that this situation is intolerable. It is decided that your department will be given the resources necessary to make accurate forecasts of future exchange rates. You are instructed to go to the best graduate schools in the United States and hire two individuals with a strong background in economics and statistics. In addition, you will be given all the computer support required. Top management expects you to develop an economic model within one year and expects the model to begin reducing foreign exchange losses beginning in the second year. How would you respond to this request?
2. Assume that you are employed by a firm that is regularly engaged in international commerce and is concerned about the exchange rate of the dollar versus the deutsche mark and the Mexican peso. You are asked to determine whether the amount and timing of exchange rate movements can be accurately forecasted. You

are also asked to determine whether there are any general predictors of exchange rate movements for these two currencies.

Research Activities

1. Get copies of *The Wall Street Journal* for (a) today, (b) 30 days ago, (c) 90 days ago, and (d) 180 days ago. Copy the forward rates (for the currencies available) shown in these papers and see how well they predicted today's spot rate for those currencies. Why were the forward rate predictors inaccurate?

2. Conduct a test of the forward market's ability to forecast the future spot rate. Use the information provided in the financial section of any newspaper (e.g., *The Wall Street Journal*). Use the 30-day forward value of the British pound and include at least 24 observations.

3. Conduct a test of the forward market's ability to forecast the future spot rate. Use the information provided in the financial section of any newspaper (e.g., *The Wall Street Journal*). Use the 180-day forward value of the Japanese yen and include at least 24 observations.

4. Conduct a test of the forward market's ability to forecast the future spot rate. Use the information provided in the financial section of any newspaper (e.g., *The Wall Street Journal*). Use the 90-day forward value of the Mexican peso and include at least 24 observations.

Bibliography

Bilson, John F. O. "Leading Indicators of Currency Devaluation." *Columbia Journal of World Business*, Winter 1979, pp. 62–76.

Bowe, Kenneth D. "Break Even in the Long Run? You May Be Ruined Meanwhile." *Euromoney*, January 1978, pp. 97–100.

Bowe, Kenneth D. "'Chartists': The New Currency Gurus." *Business Week*, October 12, 1981, pp. 93–96.

Cornell, Bradford W. "Spot Rates, Forward Rates and Exchange Market Efficiency." *Journal of Financial Economics*, August 1977, pp. 55–65.

Cosset, Jean-Claude. "Forward Rates as Predictors of Future Interest Rates in the Eurocurrency Market." *Journal of International Business Studies*, Winter 1982, pp. 71–83.

Dufey, Gunter, and Giddy, Ian H. "Forecasting Exchange Rates in a Floating World." *Euromoney*, November 1975, pp. 28–35.

_____ "International Financial Planning: The Use of Market-Based Forecasts." *California Management Review*, Fall 1978, pp. 69–81.

_____ *The International Money Market*. Englewood Cliffs, NJ: Prentice-Hall, Inc., 1978.

Fama, Eugene F. "Forward Rates as Predictors of Future Spot Rates." *Journal of Financial Economics*, October 1976, pp. 361–377.

Folks, William R., Jr., and Stansell, Stanley, R. "The Use of Discriminant Analysis in Forecasting Exchange Rate Movements." *Journal of International Business Studies*, Spring 1975, pp. 35–40.

Frankel, Jeffrey. "Tests of Rational Expectations in the Forward Exchange Market." *Southern Economic Journal*, April 1980, pp. 1083–1101.

Giddy, Ian H., and Dufey, Gunter. "The Random Behavior of Flexible Exchange Rates: Implications for Forecasting." *Journal of International Business Studies*, Spring 1975, pp. 1–32.

Goodman, Stephen H. "No Better Than the Toss of a Coin." *Euromoney*, December 1978, pp. 75–85.

Goodman, Stephen H. "Two Technical Analysts Are Even Better Than One." *Euromoney*, August 1982, pp. 85–97.

Kohlhagen, Steven W. "The Forward Rate as an Unbiased Predictor of the Future Spot Rate." *Columbia Journal of World Business*, Winter 1979, pp. 77–85.

Levich, Richard M. "Are Forward Exchange Rates Unbiased Predictors of Future Spot Rates?" *Columbia Journal of World Business*, Winter 1979, pp. 49–61.

_____ *The International Monetary Market: An Assessment of Forecasting Techniques and Market Efficiency*. Greenwich, CT: JAI Press, 1979.

_____ "Currency Forecasters Lose Their Way." *Euromoney*, August 1983, pp. 140–148.

Madura, Jeff. "Detecting Bias in Forward Exchange Rates." *Journal of Business Forecasting*, Fall 1983, pp. 19–20.

Maldonado, Rita, and Saunders, Anthony. "Foreign Exchange Restrictions and the Law of One Price." *Financial Management*, Spring 1983, pp. 19–23.

Pitman, Joanna. "Unsettled Outlook for Forecasters." *Euromoney*, August 1988, pp. 99–104.

Poole, William. "Speculative Prices as Random Walks: An Analysis of Ten Time Series of Flexible Exchange Rates." *Southern Economic Journal*, April 1967, pp. 468–478.

Ricks, David A. "International Monetary Reserves and Devaluations: Is There a Forecastable Relationship?" *The Journal of Business of Seton Hall University*, December 1972, pp. 12–18.

Rosemberg, Michael R. "Is Technical Analysis Right for Currency Forecasting?" *Euromoney*, June 1981, pp. 125–131.

Van Horne, James C. *Financial Management and Policy*, 7th ed. Englewood Cliffs, NJ: Prentice-Hall, Inc., 1986.

PART II

Management of Foreign Exchange Risk

6

Estimating and Managing Economic Exposure

The fluctuating value of currencies creates a major problem for the business manager responsible for conducting business in foreign currencies, since the firm is never quite sure about the dollar value of costs, revenues, and profits. Occasional unexpected windfall profits due to exchange rate changes may or may not be offset by unexpected catastrophic losses. Whole markets can be gained or lost merely by a fluctuation in exchange rates. Management, while not causing exchange rate fluctuations, is often the beneficiary or victim of currency price movements. Almost all firms are, to some extent, exposed to this exchange rate risk, and dealing with the phenomenon of fluctuating exchange rates is one of the major challenges facing business today.

What does a manager do when faced with the possibility of fluctuating exchange rates? While there are no short, simple answers to this question, there is a general managerial approach that is recommended. First, managers should develop a better understanding of the precise nature of the firm's exposure; then they should attempt to define the extent to which the firm is vulnerable (exposed) to fluctuations in exchange rates. Once the manager understands the nature and amount of the exchange rate risk to which the firm is exposed, he or she can implement a number of strategies to minimize the risk. As we will show in the chapters that follow, these strategies are not perfect. Often the risk simply cannot be eliminated, and sometimes there are high costs associated with some strategies. Make no mistake about it, the management of exchange rate risk is a difficult task.

Types of Exchange Rate Risk Exposure

The extent to which the firm is exposed (vulnerable) to fluctuations in exchange rates can be perceived from a number of different vantage points. In this book, the focus will be on three types of exchange rate risk exposure.

1. *Transaction exposure* defines foreign exchange rate risk in terms of the impact of exchange rate movements on the firm's future contractual cash flows. This type of exposure arises from an obligation to either accept or deliver a foreign currency at a future time. While there are many different types of transactions that lead to transaction exposure, the most important ones are accounts payable and receivable that are denominated in a foreign currency. How much could the firm lose on a deutsche mark account payable if the dollar declines in value? How will exchange rate fluctuations affect the dollar value of foreign currency receivables? Is it possible for the firm to insulate itself against the effects of exchange rate fluctuations on the value of these and other foreign currency commitments? Answers to these questions will be sought in the next chapter.

2. *Translation exposure* defines foreign exchange rate risk in terms of the impact of exchange rate movements on the financial statements of the firm. How vulnerable are the income statement and balance sheet to an exchange rate movement? Will a strengthening of the dollar make it appear that the firm is losing money on its foreign operations? How will earnings per share be affected by a movement in exchange rates? As you will see, many managers want to develop answers to these questions. In some cases, managers enter into transactions designed to insulate financial statements from unexpected exchange rate movements. In Chapter 8, we will describe the procedures used to estimate the extent of the firm's translation exposure. In addition, we will evaluate the costs and benefits of the procedures used to manage translation (financial statement) exposure.

3. *Economic exposure* defines the foreign exchange rate risk in terms of its total impact on the cash flows of the firm. This type of exposure has a broader focus than the others. The value of all contractual and non-contractual cash flows is viewed as being exposed to exchange rate

fluctuations. Here the focus is on the impact of an exchange rate movement on sales, costs, and the cash flows from foreign investments. How will the firm's share of the domestic market be affected by an exchange rate movement? How will foreign market share be affected? How will an exchange rate movement affect the value of the cash flows that a multinational parent receives from a foreign subsidiary? Is there any way to insulate these types of cash flows from exchange rate variability? This is the broadest measure of exposure to exchange rate risk and will be the topic of this chapter.

Compensation for Taking Risks

Before proceeding with our discussion of exchange rate risk estimation and management, it is worthwhile, once again, to place the whole problem of risk in a reasonable perspective. The nature of business is such that every firm takes some risk (business risk, financial risk, etc.). If firms insisted on a zero level of risk, they would not be in business at all and funds would simply be invested in short-term government securities. The key thing to understand about risk and business is that firms are willing to assume risk, but only if they receive compensation. In other words, a firm should avoid a relatively risky alternative unless the excess returns that can be earned on that alternative provide compensation for the additional risk. In the context of international business, this means that firms may be willing to accept some exchange rate risk, provided that the profits are sufficiently high. It is not necessary to have zero exchange rate risk in order for international commerce to be attractive.

On the other hand, managers do have an obligation to ensure that the firm is not exposed to unnecessary risk. It may be possible to organize international business operations in such a way as to minimize risk without affecting profits. Less risk with the same returns means that stockholder wealth will be higher. A second point worth noting is that some techniques for minimizing or eliminating risk may simply be too expensive. Every strategy suggested for dealing with foreign exchange rate risk must be evaluated in terms of both risk and cost. As we will see, it is often possible to overemphasize the risk reduction aspects of exchange rate risk management policy and ignore the costs associated with the policy. We will try to avoid this trap.

Economic exposure may be visualized as the overall impact of foreign exchange fluctuations on stockholder wealth. As the theory of finance indicates, the maximization of stockholder wealth should be the goal of financial management. Stockholder wealth is maximized when the market value of the firm's common stock is maximized. The market value of the common stock is the present value of future dividends discounted at the rate of return that reflects the risk to the stockholders. This relationship is expressed as follows:

$$\text{Price} = \sum_{t=0}^{\infty} \frac{D(t)}{(1 + ks)^t} \qquad (6\text{-}1)$$

where $D(t)$ = expected dividend in year t
         ks = required rate of return of the
                    stockholders

Internationalization of a firm's operations will affect both expected dividends and the required rate of return of the stockholders. Future cash flows will change as new opportunities are exploited. However, the risk of the firm will also be affected by the added volatility of cash flows caused by economic exposure.

Before proceeding with our discussion of economic exposure, it is worthwhile to consider which exposure measure is best. Briefly stated, each of the exposure concepts outlined in the previous section is important in its own right. If managers are concerned with the long-term profitability and survival of the firm, the issue of economic exposure must be addressed. Since managers are also concerned with the impact of exchange rate movements on short-term cash flows (and the ability to pay bills), transaction exposure is important. To the extent that managers desire to make the firm's financial statements look as attractive and/or accurate as possible, translation exposure is important. However, while all of these exposures are important, they are not of equal importance. The relative importance of each type of exposure will become clearer in the next two chapters.

Economic Exposure
of a Purely Domestic Firm

Many firms that appear to be uninvolved in international commerce are strongly affected by exchange rate movements. For example, a manufacturer of ladies' garments, using only domestic inputs and selling only to domestic customers, may have economic exposure. A manufacturer of machine tools who purchases everything at home and sells only to customers in the United States may have economic exposure. In the past, most of these firms would have hardly realized the nature of their exposure. However, the lesson of the rising dollar during the early 1980s has made their vulnerability clear to all such firms.

A purely domestic firm is affected by changes in the value of the dollar because such changes affect domestic market share. As the dollar strengthens, importers who compete with the domestic manufacturer gain a price advantage. For example, assume that in 1980 an American manufacturer of machine tools had a German competitor. At that time, American buyers could purchase a machine tool from the German firm for DM500,000, which at the 1980 exchange rate (DM1 = $0.5501) was equal to $275,050. Assume that the American firm could maintain its market share as long as the effective dollar price charged by its competitor remained at $275,050.

By 1985, the dollar had strengthened dramatically against the deutsche mark and stood at DM1 = $0.3397. If the German machine tool supplier continued to sell his product at a price of DM500,000, the dollar price to the American buyer would have fallen to $169,850 (DM500,000 × $0.3397). Since the German competitor has a product that now costs the American buyer 38 percent less than it did in the past, the competing American seller will have a difficult time maintaining his market share. Note that the price reduction of the German competitor has nothing to do with cutting costs in Germany. The price in deutsche marks remains exactly the same as it was in the past. The new price advantage enjoyed by the German firm is entirely due to the exchange rate movement. The loss of market share by the American producer is attributable to the same factor: exchange rate movements.

This example also illustrates the fact that the purely domestic firm's economic exposure to exchange rate risk is a two-way street. As shown, a strengthening dollar can lead to a serious erosion of home market share. On the other hand, a weakening dollar can create a price advantage for the American firm. For example, by January 1987, the exchange rate for the deutsche mark stood at DM1 = $0.5529. At this new rate, the machine tool produced in Germany (still being sold for DM500,000) cost $276,450 in the United States. Of course, the American manufacturer was delighted by the effective price increase of $106,600 (almost 63 percent) and found himself in a position to regain lost market share.[1]

It is clear that even firms that perceive themselves to be purely domestic can be affected by exchange rate movements. The economic exposure of such an American firm is reflected by the fact that its long-term cash inflows can vary considerably in response to exchange rate movements. How should the firm respond to these huge swings in effective dollar prices charged by foreign competitors? Should new capacity be installed in order to accommodate the increased market share gained when the dollar weakens? What will happen when the dollar once again strengthens? There are no easy answers to these questions. To the extent to which solutions are available, they must be sought in a new

---

[1]The exchange rate movements included in this example reflect the actual movements that took place during the 1980–1987 period. The example is somewhat unrealistic in that the deutsche mark price of the product was assumed to be constant during the entire period.

approach to managing a firm in a world in which exchange rates fluctuate wildly. The domestic firm can no longer ignore the fact that it may have economic exposure to exchange rate risk.

Economic Exposure of an Importer or Exporter

The economic exposure of a firm engaged directly in international commerce is more complicated than the exposure of a purely domestic firm. Depending on the circumstances of a particular importer or exporter, fluctuations in exchange rates will affect not only domestic market share but also foreign sales. To the extent that a firm uses imported inputs, it is exposed to another aspect of exchange rate risk. In addition, the dollar value of receivables, payables, and other contractual commitments in foreign currency will be affected by exchange rate movements.

Let us begin our discussion of the economic exposure of importers and exporters by extending our example of the American machine tool manufacturer by assuming that this firm has sales in both the American and German markets. At this time, we will assume that all of the inputs used by the American machine tool manufacturer are domestic and therefore are not affected by exchange rate movements.

To the extent that an exporter is also involved in its home market, it is as exposed to exchange rate risk as if it were a purely domestic firm. A strengthening dollar will most likely result in a lost share of the domestic market. In addition, however, a strengthening dollar will also weaken the American firm's position in foreign markets. Continuing our previous example, in 1980 a German buyer paid DM499,909 for a $275,000 machine tool produced in America ($275,000/$0.5501). At the higher 1985 exchange rate, however, the same $275,000 machine required an outlay of DM809,538 ($275,000/$0.3397). The German buyer experienced a 62 percent price increase for the American product. It is hard to imagine how an American exporter would be able to maintain market share in the face of such a high foreign currency price increase. Thus, the American exporter is vulnerable to exchange rate movements in both the domestic and foreign markets. Of course, should the dollar weaken rather than strengthen, the American firm will gain market share both at home and abroad.

The economic exposure to exchange rate risk of an American importer is the opposite of the exposure of the exporter. A firm that imports final goods for sale in the United States will have to raise its prices as the dollar weakens. For example, U.S. importers of videocassette recorders from Japan were hurt by the 25 percent fall in the dollar that took place over the period 1985–1986. In 1985, when the exchange rate stood at $1 = Y200 (indirect quote of the yen), a videocassette recorder costing the importer Y50,000 had an effective dollar price of $250 (Y50,000/Y200). As the value of the dollar fell to $1 = Y150, the effective price increased to $333 (assuming no change in the yen price). Presumably, the increased price of imports resulted in a higher price in the American marketplace and made it difficult to maintain sales levels. Conversely, the importer would have faced lower dollar prices and improved sales prospects if the dollar had strengthened rather than weakened. It is clear that the dollar values of the cash outflows of the importer of final products for sale in the United States are strongly affected by exchange rates.

Some American firms import products and raw materials that are used in the production of goods within the United States. An American manufacturer of aluminum may import bauxite, or an American computer manufacturer may import computer chips. For such firms, changes in the value of the dollar relative to other currencies have a major impact on costs and profits. As the dollar weakens, the cost of imported inputs is increased. As the dollar strengthens, input costs go down. Over the period 1972–1987, the huge fluctuations in the value of the dollar meant that the costs of such firms oscillated wildly. Needless to say, it is very hard to manage a firm under these conditions.

As firms become more involved in international trade through importing and/or exporting, they also begin to have foreign currency–denominated accounts payable and accounts receivable. As noted in Chapter 2, if an American firm sells something to a foreign buyer and agrees to accept a future foreign currency payment (e.g., FF100,000 in 60 days), it is at risk. A commitment to make a payment in a foreign currency also involves an exchange rate risk. Both types of transactions (as well as many others that involve a commitment to deliver or accept a foreign currency) should be viewed as part of the economic exposure of the importer/exporter.

Summing up, importers and exporters face a greater variety of exchange rate risks than do purely domestic firms. Exporters are vulnerable in both foreign and domestic markets. Importers face loss of domestic markets because of price increases of imports and the possibility of increases in the cost of inputs. In addition, firms involved in international trade have other types of foreign currency–denominated commitments, such as accounts payable and receivable, the dollar value of which will be affected by exchange rate fluctuations.

Economic Exposure of the Multinational Corporation

The economic exposure of a multinational corporation is more complicated than that of an importer or exporter, since the multinational firm is involved in international commerce at various levels. A highly simplified

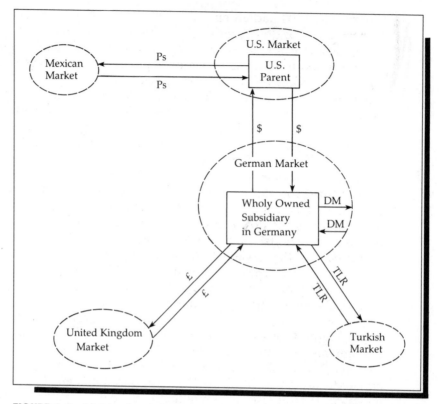

FIGURE 6-1 Multinational Cash Flows: A Hypothetical Multinational Corporation

depiction of a multinational corporation is presented in Figure 6-1. Fluctuations in the value of the dollar against any and all currencies threaten the multinational's U.S. market share, just as they would that of a purely domestic firm. The multinational corporation also has exposure similar to that of an importer or exporter, since it is buying and selling in Mexico. In this capacity, the multinational corporation is particularly vulnerable to changes in the value of the peso relative to the dollar. Our hypothetical multinational firm, then, has all of the exposure that typifies both purely domestic and import/export firms. As depicted in Figure 6-1, however, the firm also has another dimension of exchange rate risk.

The American parent corporation has invested in its German subsidiary (a dollar cash outflow). The investment was made, of course, in anticipation of future cash flows from the subsidiary. The attractiveness of the investment, from the parent's perspective, depends on how much it will get back from the subsidiary. The American parent makes its investment in dollars and is interested in the dollar (not the deutsche mark) return on its investment. Looked at from another perspective, since the parent's stockholders want dollar dividends, the parent is

TABLE 6-1   Projected and Actual Cash Flows Received
by a U.S. Parent from a German Subsidiary

Year	Projected Cash Flows		
	DM Cash Flows	**Exchange Rate**	**Dollar Cash Flows**
1	DM10,000,000	DM1 = $0.50	$5,000,000
2	DM10,000,000	DM1 = $0.50	$5,000,000
3	DM10,000,000	DM1 = $0.50	$5,000,000
4	DM10,000,000	DM1 = $0.50	$5,000,000
5	DM10,000,000	DM1 = $0.50	$5,000,000
Year	Actual Cash Flows		
	DM Cash Flows	**Exchange Rate**	**Dollar Cash Flows**
1	DM10,000,000	DM1 = $0.50	$5,000,000
2	DM10,000,000	DM1 = $0.50	$5,000,000
3	DM10,000,000	DM1 = $0.40	$4,000,000
4	DM10,000,000	DM1 = $0.40	$4,000,000
5	DM10,000,000	DM1 = $0.25	$2,500,000

interested in the dollar value of the cash payments received from the subsidiary.[2]

The vulnerability of the parent corporation is illustrated in Table 6-1. In this example, it is assumed that the American multinational invested in the German subsidiary anticipating both that the subsidiary would be able to pay DM10,000,000 per year to the parent and that these deutsche marks could be converted to dollars at a rate of DM1 = $0.50. Thus, the projected dollar receipts of the parent were $5,000,000 per year. In our example, things did not work out exactly the way the American parent had expected. It is true that the German subsidiary was able to operate profitably and make the projected DM10,000,000 cash payment to the parent. However, the declining value of the deutsche mark led to a shortfall in the dollar value of the receipts of the parent. The illustration highlights the fact that the cash flows between a subsidiary and its multinational parent are exposed to exchange rate risk. Such flows may be greater or less than anticipated, depending on the direction of change in the exchange rate. The multinational firm could experience windfall gains or major shortfalls in expected receipts.

The exposure of the multinational corporation increases in complexity as the analysis of Figure 6-1 is extended. Note that the German subsidiary also plays the role of importer/exporter. Just as the Mexican transactions of the American parent are exposed to fluctuations in the dollar/peso exchange rate, the German subsidiary is exposed to fluctuations in both the deutsche mark/British pound and the deutsche

---

[2] The evaluation of investments in foreign countries will be discussed in Chapter 16.

mark/Turkish lire exchange rates. As the value of the deutsche mark changes relative to these currencies, the subsidiary's domestic and foreign market shares may change. For example, if the deutsche mark declines in value against these other currencies (as well as against the dollar), the products of the German subsidiary gain a price advantage in the British, Turkish, and German markets. If all of these changes work out in the best possible way, the German subsidiary may actually be able to increase the deutsche mark payment to its American parent, thus offsetting the decline in the value of the mark relative to the dollar. On the other hand, exchange rate movements may be such that the deutsche mark profits are reduced beyond expectations, and the subsidiary may be unable to make its projected DM10,000,000 payment to the parent.

There are so many possibilities that only broad generalizations can be made about the impact of exchange rate movements on the cash flows between a foreign subsidiary and its American parent.

1. A weakening of the subsidiary's home currency is not necessarily bad for the parent. If the weakening of the currency generates higher subsidiary profits by increasing the subsidiary's domestic or foreign market share, the subsidiary's profits may be improved by the devaluation of its home currency. This may increase the ability of the subsidiary to make cash payments to the parent. Under some conditions, a multinational's subsidiaries in countries with devaluing currencies may perform better than expected. It is not necessarily true that multinational firms should avoid investing in countries that have currencies with devaluation potential.

2. The reverse of this situation is also true. It is not always attractive for a multinational to have subsidiaries in countries whose currency value strengthens. It is true that the dollar value of foreign currency payments will be increased by a strengthening of the foreign currency. The strengthening of the foreign currency may, however, impede the ability of the subsidiary to make profits. The domestic and foreign market shares are also affected when currencies strengthen.

When we think about what is going on in Figure 6-1, an interesting perspective on the economic exposure of the multinational firm begins to emerge. First, a multinational corporation may have exposure in many different currencies. Some of this exposure directly involves the parent (Mexican pesos and deutsche marks), while other exposure is indirect in the sense that it occurs through the operations of a subsidiary (British pounds and Turkish lire). The second (and very important) idea is that it may be less risky to be exposed in many currencies rather than just one. For example, the declining deutsche mark in our example may have helped the German firm gain an increased share of its domestic and foreign markets. This idea will be discussed more fully in the sections that follow.

Purchasing Power Parity and Economic Exposure

The purchasing power parity theory explained in Chapter 4 has important implications for the management of economic exposure to exchange rate risk. If purchasing power parity existed at all times (which it doesn't), firms would not have to worry about economic exposure. Under purchasing power parity equilibrium conditions, a change in the exchange rate would be offset by a domestic price change. Thus, the relative prices of domestic and foreign items would remain the same regardless of the exchange rate.

In order to illuminate this concept, let us review the idea and then apply some numbers. The purchasing power parity theory asserts that the percentage change in the direct quote for a foreign currency is equal to the difference between the rate of inflation in the United States and the rate of inflation in the foreign country:

$$\%E(f) = I(h) - I(f) \tag{6-2}$$

where $E(f)$ = direct quote of a foreign currency
$I(h)$ = inflation rate at home (percent)
$I(f)$ = inflation rate in the foreign country (percent)

In this illustration, we will assume that the initial conditions are such that the direct quote on the British pound is £1 = $1.50 and that a British firm is selling a product in the American market at a price of $150,000 (£100,000). Next, we will assume that the British pound devalues by 10 percent and that the new direct quote on it is £1 = $1.35. The initial result (assuming that other things remain as they were) of the devaluation of the pound is to reduce the price of the British product in the American market. Specifically, the American buyer now pays only $135,000 to acquire the £100,000 needed to purchase the product. Note that the British firm is selling its product at a lower price in the United States even though there has been no reduction in the pound price of the product.

The theory of purchasing power parity says that the advantage gained by the British firm will not last long. This is due to the fact that the advantage will be offset by relatively high price increases in Britain. In our illustration, prices in Britain would rise by 10 percent more than in the United States. Thus, if there is a 0 percent inflation rate in the United States, the inflation rate in Britain would be 10 percent. Under these

TABLE 6-2   Purchasing Power Parity: United States and Germany (1980–1986)

A. 1980–1986: Exchange Rate Movements Consistent with Purchasing Power Parity
    1. Difference in inflation rates   +14%
    2. Expected change in direct quote of DM   +14%
    3. Actual change in direct quote of DM   +16%

B. 1980–1984: Exchange Rate Movements Inconsistent with Purchasing Power Parity
    1. Difference in inflation rates   +8%
    2. Expected change in direct quote of DM   +8%
    3. Actual change in direct quote of DM   −46%

C. 1985–1986: Exchange Rate Movements Inconsistent with Purchasing Power Parity
    1. Difference in inflation rates   +5%
    2. Expected change in direct quote of DM   +5%
    3. Actual change in direct quote of DM   +52%

Notes: Exchange rate changes are computed from the beginning of the earlier year to the beginning of the later year. Price changes are based on differences in the average index numbers for the respective countries.

Source: International Financial Statistics, February 1987.

conditions, the pound price of the product increases to £110,000, which at the new exchange rate of £1 = $1.35 results in a dollar price of $148,500.[3] In other words, the exchange rate advantage gained by the British firm is offset by the relatively high rate of inflation in the United Kingdom. Looked at from the view of American firms competing with the British firm in the American market, the devaluation of the pound did not pose a significant threat to domestic market share.

Remember that the relationship between exchange rates and relative inflation rates is well researched. There is overwhelming evidence that, in the long run, no price advantage is gained by firms producing in countries that have devaluing currencies. The implication of this conclusion is that, in the long run, firms do not have economic exposure to exchange rate risk. In the long run, exchange rate movements will have no impact on domestic market share, foreign market share, or a multinational's cash flows from a subsidiary. The evidence is clear that, in the long run, there is no economic exposure.

The short-run situation may pose a much greater problem for firms engaged in international commerce. Consider the information presented in Part A of Table 6-2, which summarizes the purchasing power parity relationship between the United States and Germany during the early 1980s. Note that over the period 1980–1986, the difference in inflation rates (14 percent) was approximately equal to the actual change in the exchange rate. It seems safe to conclude that over the entire 1980–1986

---

[3]If the more precise formula for the purchasing power parity theory had been used (see footnote 8 in Chapter 4), the new dollar price would have been $150,000. In addition, as discussed in Chapter 4, other factors can affect the exchange rate of a currency.

period, the relationship postulated by the purchasing power parity theory was consistent with what happened. At the end of the period, American buyers had to pay 16 percent more for deutsche marks, thus increasing the price of German products in the United States. German producers did not lose their share of the American market, however, because the prices charged by their American competitors increased by 14 percent more than the prices in Germany. These two factors tended to cancel each other out, and in 1986 German and American firms competed on more or less the same price basis as before the strengthening of the deutsche mark against the dollar. In the long run (7 years in this case), fluctuating exchange rates placed neither German nor American firms at a competitive disadvantage.

Of course, firms live in the short as well as the long run. Indeed, it seems that sometimes the short run can last for a very long time. Looking once again at Table 6-2, we see that the long run (7 years) is composed of two very different short runs. During the period 1980–1984, the United States had 8 percent more inflation than Germany. The theory of purchasing power parity would have predicted an 8 percent appreciation in the direct quote on the mark. This would have balanced the effects of inflation and exchange rates and left relative prices unchanged. As you can see, this is not what actually took place. Instead of the deutsche mark appreciating by 8 percent as expected, it devalued by an astounding 46 percent. During this period, German products gained a worldwide price advantage, both because prices in the United States were increasing faster than in Germany (relative inflation) and because the mark was declining relative to the dollar. It is not surprising that many American firms lost their ability to compete during this period.

The situation was dramatically reversed during the 1985–1986 period. The actual appreciation in the value of the deutsche mark far exceeded the differences in national inflation rates. The 52 percent increase in the direct quote on the mark meant that suddenly the relative prices of German and American goods shifted in favor of U.S. producers. While the final report on this period is unavailable at the time of this writing, the indications are that American producers are gaining market share both at home and abroad.

As we can see, even though purchasing power parity may exist over the long run, firms should not ignore economic exposure to exchange rate risk. While Table 6-2 deals only with Germany and the United States, the pattern of exchange rate movements was more or less the same in many other currencies. That is, between 1980 and 1984, the dollar had a greater than expected appreciation against many of the world's currencies. Between 1985 and 1986, the decline in the value of the dollar against most of the currencies of the industrialized world was greater than would have been forecasted by purchasing power parity. During the first short-run period, many American firms lost markets permanently. Facing 5 years of unfavorable exchange rate movements was more than could be

TABLE 6-3 Dimensions of Economic Exposure for American Firms

Nature of Exposure	Types of Firms Exposed	Impact if the Dollar Strengthens*
U.S. market share	1. Purely domestic firm 2. Importers 3. Multinationals	1. Foreign firms gain a price advantage 2. U.S. firms using imported inputs gain an advantage
Foreign market share	1. Exporters 2. Multinationals	1. U.S. firms have more difficulty selling abroad 2. U.S. firms using foreign inputs gain an advantage
Value of subsidiary cash flows	1. Multinationals	1. Value of the *same* amount of foreign currency cash flows decreases

*The impact will be the opposite if the dollar weakens against foreign currencies.

borne by some American firms. In some cases, they were not in a position to reenter the market when the value of the dollar began to decline. The lesson to be learned from this period of wild fluctuations in exchange rates is that firms should be unwilling to trust their fortunes to the automatic adjustments associated with the purchasing power parity doctrine. A more positive management strategy is needed.

Measuring Economic Exposure

The general nature of economic exposure for different types of firms is summarized in Table 6-3. The exposure of any particular firm depends not only on its type but also on the nature of both the products and the markets in which the firm operates. Service firms (restaurants, department stores, etc.) are not usually faced with competitors that can charge lower prices because of an appreciation of the dollar. In addition, the ability of some foreign firms to compete in the American market is limited by the nature of the product involved. For example, while it is possible that some fresh milk can be shipped to the United States from Mexico and Canada, the nature of the product is such that most of it has, thus far, been produced in the United States. Similarly, the opportunity for American firms to export fresh milk is limited. It should be noted, however, that more and more products are becoming part of the international economy. For example, advances in technology now make it possible to ship fresh fruits and vegetables from Latin America to the United States. American producers who must compete with such imports may have substantial amounts of economic exposure.

Firms possessing significant monopoly power are likely to have relatively low economic exposure. For example, a firm with monopoly power resulting from patents and technological expertise (e.g., IBM before 1980) may be able to use this advantage to prevent foreign firms from gaining a foothold in the U.S. market. American consumers may ignore the price advantage gained by a foreign competitor through a strengthening of the dollar if they perceive the foreign product to be of lower quality. Similarly, a firm with monopoly power gained through technological superiority and patents could maintain foreign market share even with a strengthening dollar.

It is clear that firms are able to achieve monopoly power in ways other than achieving technological advantage. Some firms, for example, have used advertising to differentiate products sufficiently to develop a weak monopoly. While the Coca-Cola Corporation does not have a monopoly in the soft drink market, it does have a monopoly on Coke. A substantial number of consumers are convinced that Coke is very different from other drinks and would be unwilling to shift to other colas, even at a lower price. The brand-name type of monopoly power may be just as effective as technological superiority in helping to maintain domestic and foreign market shares.

Monopoly power may also be created by governments. Trade barriers implemented by foreign governments may effectively bar American firms from foreign markets or vice versa. For example, the huge decline in the value of the dollar relative to the yen over the period 1985–1987 was not great enough to permit American producers to enter the Japanese telecommunications or heavy construction markets. Thus, monopoly-type powers granted by some governments may deny American firms access to markets even when American firms have a price advantage. The failure, in some instances, of the U.S. government to grant monopoly-type protection from foreign competitors means that foreigners are able to enter the U.S. market when the dollar is strong. Firms that operate in this situation are very vulnerable to exchange rate movements. A strengthening of the dollar hurts them in the home market, while a weakening of the dollar does not help them in the foreign market. The vulnerability of a firm to this type of economic exposure depends on the nature of the product, the extent to which foreigners have access to American markets, and the extent to which the American firm has access to foreign markets.[4] This varies from firm to firm.

---

[4]The reader should be aware that the U.S. government has often helped domestic manufacturers by imposing tariffs and/or quotas on foreign products.

The size of foreign competitors may also be important. Throughout history, large firms have often pursued aggressive pricing policies designed to eliminate competition and/or to ensure that competitors are unable to gain a foothold in a market. This battle takes place in the international as well as the domestic economic environment, and it is tilted in favor of large firms. Large firms are better able to deal with challenges posed by competitors both at home and abroad. At one time, it appeared that large American firms were able to use their size to inhibit foreign sales in the U.S. market. At least on the surface, the power of large American firms today seems to be matched by that of large foreign competitors. Today even the largest firms in the United States must deal with the challenge of international competition. However, it still seems reasonable to assume that small and moderate-sized firms have a higher degree of risk (other things being equal) in this area.

The central point of this discussion is that while many firms have economic exposure to exchange rate risk, the extent of that exposure varies. Large firms and firms with some monopoly power may be less vulnerable to fluctuations in exchange rates. American firms of small or moderate size and American firms facing large, powerful foreign competitors have the most risk exposure. An American firm with a standard product that is not highly differentiated may be very vulnerable to foreign exchange rate movements.

Managing Economic Exposure

The uncertainty created by economic exposure to exchange rate risk is not easily managed. There is no simple financial transaction or trick that solves the problem. Those firms that are fortunate enough and wise enough to approach the problem from a long-term strategic perspective may have a significant advantage in managing this important risk. As we will see, however, some firms are simply not in a position to do much about economic exposure. The key to the management of economic

TABLE 6-4   Strategy for Managing Economic Exposure to Exchange Rate Risk

1. Diversify the operations of the firm.
   a. Make sales in as many currencies as possible.
   b. Purchase inputs from suppliers located in many
      different countries.
   c. Locate production facilities in many different countries.

2. Diversify the financing of the firm.

exposure is diversification. The recommended diversification strategy is outlined in Table 6-4.

Reducing Economic Exposure Through Diversification of Sales

With respect to the diversification of operations, it is desirable to operate in as many currencies as possible. If sales are concentrated in one foreign country, a change in the value in the currency of that country could have a profound effect on the firm. For example, assume that an American firm concentrates its foreign sales in the United Kingdom and that the value of the dollar relative to the British pound increases. With the stronger dollar, each pound received for a sale converts into fewer dollars. The American firm is faced with the choice of accepting fewer dollars (but the same number of pounds) or raising the pound price of the product. A price increase could, of course, lead to a loss of both British market share and revenue to the American firm. The American firm may be able to reduce the impact of a strengthening dollar by selling in other countries as well as the United Kingdom. Hopefully, a strengthening of the dollar against the British pound would be offset by a weakening of the dollar against other currencies. If this occurs, what is lost in one country may be gained in another.

While the concept of diversifying sales over many nations to minimize exchange rate risk is interesting, there are practical problems associated with its implementation. First, and perhaps most importantly, such diversification may be difficult and costly. There may not be a market for every product in every country. For example, the major market for large computers is restricted to a relatively few countries. In other cases, products sold in particular countries must be tailored to meet local consumer tastes and needs. For example, large American automobiles and appliances must be modified to meet local requirements if foreign sales are to be successful. The costs associated with making such modifications must be weighed against the benefits associated with the reduction of economic exposure to exchange rate risk. For example, the benefits associated with increasing sales efforts in Mexico may be great enough to justify the cost associated with such an effort. On the other hand, conditions in Argentina may be such that the costs of diversification may outweigh the benefits. Each situation must be evaluated separately. The American firm should not be willing to pursue diversification at all costs.

There is another important limitation associated with using sales diversification to manage economic exposure. Consider the trade information presented in Table 6-5.

TABLE 6-5 Relative Sizes of Foreign Markets for U.S. Merchandise Exports (in Millions of Dollars)

Country	Exports	Percentage
Canada	$70,862	23
Japan	$37,732	11
Mexico	$20,643	7
United Kingdom	$18,404	6
West Germany	$14,331	5
France	$10,086	3
All other countries	$137,383	44
Total	$309,441	100

Source: U.S. Department of Commerce, *Survey of Current Business*, May 1989, pp. S-16 and S-17.

As can be seen, a large proportion of all exports from the United States are concentrated in just a few countries. This creates a problem, since the dollar often moves in the same direction against many of these currencies. For example, during the period 1981–1984, the dollar became stronger against the currencies of most of the countries listed in Table 6-5. Under these conditions, an American firm that had diversified its sales into Germany, France, and Japan would still have encountered problems, since the dollar strengthened dramatically against all of these currencies. The ideal strategy with respect to diversification of sales would involve developing sales in countries with currencies that move independently of each other—for example, Germany and Mexico. Thus, as one currency is weakening against the dollar, others may be strengthening. This is easier said than done, since the most attractive markets are located in countries with currencies that may move in the same direction against the dollar. As a result, some sales diversification programs may have little impact on the firm's economic exposure. The big exception to this rule is Canada. Since the Canadian dollar is relatively stable against the U.S. dollar, sales to that country have relatively little exchange rate risk.[5]

Diversification of sales as a means of managing economic exposure to exchange rate risk is viable only for large exporters or multinational firms. Domestic firms, by definition, are not able to diversify sales on an international basis. Smaller exporters also have limited diversification opportunities.

The multinational firm has an additional advantage. The host country sales associated with foreign production (e.g., sales made by a German subsidiary in Germany) provide an additional dimension to sales diversification. In addition, many multinationals can export to third

---

[5]See Table 3-2 for a more complete description of the relationship between different currencies.

countries from their foreign facilities. For example, the subsidiary of an American multinational located in Brazil may be able to export to Argentina. In some cases, having production facilities located throughout the world increases the possibility of sales diversification.

Reducing Economic Exposure Through Diversification of Inputs

Economic exposure to exchange rate risk can also be controlled by diversifying the sources of inputs used in the production process. For example, as the dollar strengthened during the early 1980s, foreign firms gained an edge in both the United States and foreign markets, since foreign products carried lower dollar prices. An American manufacturer using foreign inputs in its production process experienced a cost reduction as the dollar strengthened. A producer that purchased all inputs in the United States had no comparable cost reduction and was at a competitive disadvantage. Of course, as the dollar weakened over the 1985–1987 period, this situation was reversed.

A diversification strategy designed to reduce economic exposure involves buying inputs from many different countries. In the ideal situation, a firm would be able to shift sourcing from one country to another as exchange rates varied. For example, as the dollar weakened, the firm could buy a higher percentage of inputs in the United States. As the dollar strengthened, more inputs could be purchased in foreign countries. However, it may be difficult to implement such a policy, since the relationship between buyers and sellers is often a long-term one and is not subject to starts and stops.

Even if this strategy is not feasible, diversification in a passive sense may be desirable. As exchange rates drive up the cost of one input, the cost of another may decline. The balancing aspect of diversified sourcing is the heart of economic exposure management. If sources are diversified, the firm is less vulnerable to movements in particular exchange rates. Of course, if all currencies move against the dollar in the same direction, the vulnerability of the firm remains. Also note that, just as in the diversification of sales, small firms are at a disadvantage. Large firms, especially multinational corporations, have more possibilities for diversification. Some multinationals may be in a particularly good position if they are able to produce the inputs in foreign countries and shift production from one location to another as exchange rates vary.

It is necessary to conclude every discussion of this type by reminding the reader that we are talking about possibilities, not absolute decision rules. Each firm must look at the particular features of its own business. If diversification of inputs is possible, this strategy should be investigated. As always, benefits must be weighed against costs.

Reducing Economic Exposure Through Diversification of Production

An alternative open only to the multinational corporation involves the diversification of production facilities. This implies that the firm will have production facilities in different countries. For example, an American automobile manufacturer may produce automobile parts in both the United States and Germany. If the dollar strengthens (making imports into the United States less expensive), the corporation may be able to meet foreign competition in both the home and foreign markets by substituting foreign for domestic production. In effect, one subsidiary of the multinational firm loses market share to another subsidiary rather than to an outside competitor. If the dollar weakens, the domestic (American) unit is in a good position to meet foreign competition in the home market and may be able to increase its penetration into the foreign market. By having facilities in different countries, the multinational is able to tolerate cash flow fluctuations in individual subsidiaries while at the same time minimizing the impact of exchange rate fluctuations on the cash flows to the corporation as a whole.

Even a passive diversification strategy, in which there is no shifting of production from one country to another as exchange rates vary, can minimize the firm's risk. As exchange rates vary, some subsidiaries should do better than others. This *canceling effect* results in more stable cash flows for the multinational corporation as a whole. Of course, the more diversified the production, the lower the exchange rate risk. That is, having production facilities located in 10 countries is less risky than having such facilities in only 2 countries.

The costs associated with diversification of production may be greater than the costs associated with other types of diversification. For one thing, the ability of the multinational corporation to manage a worldwide network of production facilities may be limited. The multinational firm must continually strive to ensure that the benefits of diversification are not offset by increased managerial inefficiency. The multinational firm may also have to consider the opportunity cost of forgoing the economies of scale that are often associated with large, integrated facilities. Scattering a number of small production facilities throughout the world may reduce exchange rate risk, but it may also be less efficient from a technological point of view. Once again, this is a problem for which there is no general solution. The multinational must evaluate every case on its own merits.

Reducing Economic Exposure
Through Diversification of Financing

Exchange rate risk can also be reduced by diversifying the currencies in which a firm raises capital. Today American corporations of moderate size are able to borrow funds denominated in a variety of currencies. While the major discussion of this activity will be postponed to a later chapter, it should be noted at this point that some firms are able to denominate their borrowings in most of the major currencies (deutsche mark, British pound, etc.) and repay those loans in the foreign currencies. In addition, multinational firms are sometimes able to raise capital in less developed countries. The ability to borrow in currencies other than the American dollar is a reality, not a dream.

For some firms, borrowing in foreign currencies could have a material impact on economic exposure to exchange rate risk. The advantage can be best understood by presenting an example. Assume that we are looking at the situation faced by a large American exporting or multinational firm with substantial sales abroad. If the firm borrows dollars to finance its business activities in foreign countries and agrees to make interest and principal payments in dollars, it is at risk. The risk comes from the fact that the inflows of the firm will be in foreign currency but the outflows will be in dollars. If the foreign currency declines in value, it will buy fewer dollars and the American firm may be hard pressed to pay its debt. This risk can be reduced by having the firm borrow in foreign currencies. One strategy calls for borrowing in the currencies that match the cash inflow currencies. That is, if the firm expects a large amount of French francs, it would borrow French francs. A second strategy simply calls for borrowing in a number of different currencies. The idea is that some currencies would weaken while others would strengthen. Hopefully, these exchange rate movements would cancel each other out, thus reducing the firm's exposure to exchange rate risk. Certainly, financing all operations in one currency is riskier than using a diversification strategy.[6]

Diversification and
Stockholder Wealth

Traditional financial theory, as presented in the United States, is usually confined to domestic firms and domestic capital markets. In this context,

---

[6]This discussion ignore differences in interest rates between the various countries. This topic will be discussed in greater detail in chapter 9.

financial theory suggests that diversification within the firm does not increase stockholder wealth. The rationale for this statement is based on the fact that stockholders already hold a well-diversified portfolio of common stocks and that further diversification at the firm level is unnecessary. In other words, in a purely domestic context, portfolio holders already have zero diversifiable risk. Additional domestic diversification by the firm will bring no risk reduction benefit to the stockholder.[7]

However, the firm's decision to provide internal diversification through internationalization may increase stockholder wealth. In other words, the firm that internationalizes may be able to reduce the correlation between its cash flows and the cash flows of purely domestic firms. This international diversification may reduce or even eliminate the international diversifiable risk borne by American portfolio holders. If the benefits of this reduction in risk are not offset by lower returns, stockholder wealth would be increased.

Some financial scholars contend that investors can achieve the same objective by building a diversified portfolio of securities that includes both domestic and foreign stocks. If this were a realistic alternative for American investors, the scholars would be correct and, from the stockholders' point of view, there would be no risk reduction benefit associated with internationalization at the firm level. At the present time, however, most American investors do not diversify internationally. This avoidance of foreign securities reflects the facts that foreign capital markets are less well developed than those in the United States and that American investors know little about foreign firms. Thus, diversification at the firm level offers a risk reduction possibility that the individual stockholder is unable or unwilling to pursue.

Summary and Conclusions

The financial condition of a firm can be affected by transaction, translation, or economic exposure to foreign exchange rate fluctuations. This chapter concentrated on the evaluation and management of economic exposure. Most firms, regardless of their involvement in international operations, can be affected by economic exposure.

Management must first estimate the firm's economic exposure and be aware of the alternative means of reducing such exposure. The primary risk management methodology discussed in this chapter involved diversification. It may be possible to ameliorate the risks of economic exposure

---

[7]Some introductory finance textbooks discuss this issue. Almost all intermediate finance textbooks address this problem in greater detail. For example, see James C. Van Horne, *Financial Management and Policy*, 7th ed., Englewood Cliffs, NJ, Prentice-Hall, Inc., 1986, chapter 7.

through the diversification of sales, sources of inputs, production facilities, and financing sources. The possible risk reduction benefits associated with diversification must be weighed against the costs of this strategy.

Review Questions

1. Define (a) economic exposure, (b) transaction exposure, and (c) translation exposure.
2. "A firm that has absolutely no dealings in international commerce has no economic exposure." True or false? Explain your answer.
3. Discuss the extent to which the following firms face economic exposure: (a) an American importer, (b) an American exporter.
4. Discuss the nature of the economic exposure faced by an American multinational firm.
5. How does the theory of purchasing power parity relate to the economic exposure of the firm to exchange rate risk?
6. Explain how sales diversification may reduce the economic exposure of the firm.
7. Explain how the diversification of inputs may affect the economic exposure of the firm.
8. Explain how diversification of production may affect the economic exposure of the firm.
9. Explain how diversifying sources of financing may affect the economic exposure of the firm.
10. "The firm should attempt to eliminate economic exposure to exchange rate risk by implementing a diversification strategy." True or false? Explain your answer.

Questions for Discussion

1. Assume that you are employed by an American manufacturer of farm equipment that produces only in the United States but is increasing its sales to foreign countries. In order to meet the growing foreign demand, your firm plans to increase production capacity in the United States by building an expensive new factory. Management is worried about exchange rate risk. Specifically, it is concerned that the dollar will strengthen to the extent that foreign sales at present local currency prices will no longer be profitable and the firm will have to raise local currency prices. The fear is that such price increases will result in loss of foreign market share and the company will be stuck with an underutilized factory in the United States. Top management asks you to evaluate this situation. They want to know if such fears are reasonable and consistent with historical experience. You are also asked to develop preliminary strategies that could be used to minimize any risks that might exist. Since top management recognizes that you will not be able to develop a definitive plan for managing risks without additional information, they ask you to list the types of information that will be needed to evaluate each of the general strategies you have outlined.
2. Assume that you are employed by a large American clothing manufacturer. Your firm is purely domestic, has a single production facility in the United States, uses domestic inputs, and sells only to American department stores. During the 1980–1984 period, your firm experienced a large loss in American market share,

and a consultant told management that this loss was attributable to the rise in the value of the dollar. Part of the lost market share was regained during the 1985–1989 period. Management is now worried that the situation of the early 1980s could be repeated and asks you to study the problem. Specifically, management wants to know if a domestic firm such as this one is vulnerable to fluctuations in exchange rates. If so, management wants to know if it is possible to forecast exchange rate movements. Management also wants your recommendations about strategies for dealing with this problem and wants to know what additional information you need to evaluate your recommendations.

Research Activities

1. Using *International Financial Statistics*, determine the extent to which purchasing power parity offset the economic exposure of American firms. Japan, Mexico, and the United Kingdom are interesting countries to study.
2. Read about the former International Harvester Corporation (currently Navistar) and relate its experience to economic exposure to exchange rate risk.

Bibliography

Adler, Michael, and Dumas, Bernard. "Exposure to Currency Risk: Definition and Management." *Financial Management*, Spring 1984, pp. 41–50.

Babbel, David F. "Determining the Optimum Strategy for Hedging Currency Exposure." *Journal of International Business Studies*, Spring–Summer, 1983, pp. 133–139.

Batra, Raveendra N., Donnenfeld, Shabtai, and Hadar, Josef. "Hedging Behavior by Multinational Firms." *Journal of International Business Studies*, Winter 1982, pp. 59–70.

Discepolo, Alfred J., and Burchett, Shannon B. "The Long Hedge Is Here to Stay." *Euromoney*, March 1984, pp. 195–196.

Eaker, Mark R., and Grant, Dwight. "Optimal Hedging of Uncertain and Long-Term Foreign Exchange Exposure." *Journal of Banking and Finance*, June 1985, pp. 222–231.

Eun, Cheol S., and Resnick, Brice G. "Currency Factor in International Portfolio Diversification." *Columbia Journal of World Business*, Summer 1985, pp. 45–54.

Fitzsimons, Robert B. "Exposure Management Is Too Important to Be Left to the Treasurer." *Euromoney*, March 1979, pp. 103–112.

Garner, C. Kent, and Shapiro, Alan C. "A Practical Method of Assessing Foreign Exchange Risk." *Midland Corporate Finance Journal*, Fall 1984, pp. 6–17.

Giddy, Ian H. "Exchange Risk: Whose View?" *Financial Management*, Summer 1977, pp. 23–33.

Heckermann, Donald. "The Exchange Risk of Foreign Operations." *Journal of Business*, January 1972, pp. 42–48.

Hekman, Christine R. "A Financial Model of Foreign Exchange Exposure." *Journal of International Business Studies*, Summer 1985, pp. 83–100.

Jacque, Laurent L. "Management of Foreign Exchange Risk: A Review Article." *Journal of International Business Studies*, Spring–Summer 1981, pp. 81–101.

Kohlhagen, Steven W. "A Model of Optimal Foreign Exchange Hedging Without Exchange Rate Projections." *Journal of International Business Studies*, Fall 1978, pp. 9–19.

Levich, Richard M., and Wihlborg, Clas G., eds. *Exchange Risk and Exposure*. Lexington, MA: Lexington Books, 1980.

Makin, John H. "The Portfolio Method of Managing Foreign Exchange Risk." *Euromoney*, August 1976, pp. 58–64.

_____ "Portfolio Theory and the Problem of Foreign Exchange Risk." *The Journal of Finance*, May 1978, pp. 517–534.

Rodriguez, Rita M. "Management of Foreign Exchange Risk in U.S. Multinationals." *Sloan Management Review*, Spring 1978, pp. 31–49.

_____ *Foreign Exchange Management in U.S. Multinationals*. Lexington, MA: Lexington Books, 1980.

_____ "Corporate Exchange Risk Management: Theme and Aberrations." *Journal of Finance*, May 1981, pp. 427–439.

Shapiro, Alan C. "Exchange Rate Changes, Inflation and the Value of the Multinational Corporation." *Journal of Finance*, May 1975, pp. 485–502.

Shapiro, Alan C., and Rutenberg, David P. "Managing Exchange Risk in a Floating World." *Financial Management*, Summer 1976, pp. 48–58.

Srinivasulu, S. L. "Classifying Foreign Exchange Exposure." *Financial Executive*, February 1983, pp. 36–44.

Van Horne, James C. *Financial Management and Policy*, 7th ed. Englewood Cliffs, NJ: Prentice-Hall, Inc., 1986.

Westerfield, Janice M. "How U.S. Multinationals Manage Currency Risk." *Business Review*, March–April 1980, pp. 19–27.

Wheelwright, Steven. "Applying Decision Theory to Improve Corporate Management of Currency-Exchange Risks." *California Management Review*, Summer 1975, pp. 41–49.

7

Estimating and Managing Transaction Exposure

The extent to which a firm is vulnerable (exposed) to exchange rate movements can be analyzed in many different ways. Chapter 6 examined economic exposure and showed that the appropriate defensive strategies for its management were long term (strategic) in nature. Long-term management of economic exposure involves diversification of sales, production, inputs, and financing. However, all firms, even those that are fortunate enough to be diversified, sometimes suffer the short-term ill effects of exchange rate movements. In this chapter, another measure of exposure, with a shorter-term focus, will be examined: transaction exposure. We will begin by defining and examining methods for measuring such exposure and then discuss how it can be managed. We will conclude with a discussion of the desirability of leaving the firm's transaction exposure position open (rather than managing it).

Definition of Transaction Exposure

Transaction exposure defines foreign exchange rate risk in terms of the impact of exchange rate movements on the firm's future contractually committed cash flows. This type of exposure arises from the firm's obligation to accept or deliver a specified amount of foreign currency at a future point in time. The nature of the contractual commitment is such that no written legal documents need be involved. Remember, however, that binding contracts need not be written. The most important types of transactions that contribute to transaction exposure are as follows:

1. *Accounts payable in foreign currencies.* When a firm increases its accounts payables denominated in foreign currencies, its transaction exposure is increased. The risk lies in the fact that the home currency may have to be converted to a foreign currency at an unknown future exchange rate. For example, an American firm purchasing electronics equipment from a Japanese supplier may agree to pay for its imports in yen at a future point in time. Since the future spot exchange rate is unknown, the number of dollars needed to make the yen payment is also unknown. It is this uncertainty about how many dollars will be needed to make the yen payment that constitutes the transaction exposure.

2. *Accounts receivable in foreign currencies.* A firm that sells on open account and agrees to accept payment at a future point in time in a foreign currency has a foreign currency account receivable and transaction exposure. For example, an American firm selling to a Canadian buyer and agreeing to accept payment in Canadian dollars at a future point in time has a foreign currency account receivable and transaction exposure.

3. *Nonrecorded commitments to pay in a foreign currency.* Conceptually, this exposure is identical to that incurred in a foreign currency account payable. Assume, for example, that an American firm agrees to buy something from a British supplier and pay in British pounds. While accounting statements will not be affected until the goods are shipped/received, the American firm does have transaction exposure, since it has an obligation to deliver a foreign currency and the future exchange rate is unknown.

4. *Nonrecorded commitments to accept payment in a foreign currency.* Conceptually, this exposure is identical to that incurred in a foreign currency account receivable. If, for example, an American firm agrees to ship goods to a French buyer and accept payment in French francs, the accounting statements are not affected until the shipment is made. However, since the firm has an obligation to fulfill its contract and

accept payment in a foreign currency at a future point in time, the firm has transaction exposure.

5. *Debt payments to be made in a foreign currency.* Today it is possible for American firms to borrow in foreign currencies and repay loans using foreign currencies. The commitment to repay a debt in a foreign currency is a form of transaction exposure, since the borrowing firm is unsure about the number of dollars that will be needed to acquire the specified amount of foreign currency at the future repayment date. For example, an American firm may borrow £1,000,000 at 10 percent for 1 year from a London bank. At the end of 1 year, £1,100,000 will be needed to make the required debt payment. Since the number of dollars that will be needed to acquire £1,100,000 in 1 year is unknown, the firm has transaction exposure.

6. *Commitments to accept loan repayments in a foreign currency.* On occasion, a firm may lend money to a foreign borrower and agree to accept repayment in the foreign currency. Transactions of this type may be purely financial and involve the purchase of foreign bonds or foreign currency deposits in banks. In other cases, firms may lend to foreign subsidiaries, suppliers, or customers. The willingness of the firm to accept repayment of principal and interest in a foreign currency generates transaction exposure.

7. *Anticipated payments from foreign subsidiaries.* A multinational corporation makes investments in foreign subsidiaries. In return, cash flows from the subsidiaries to the parent are expected in the future. Cash flows that are expected at some distant and unspecified future point in time are not considered part of transaction exposure. However, short-term, planned, or budgeted payments to the parent are exposed to fluctuations in exchange rate risk. Budgeted items such as dividend payments, royalty payments, payments for use of technology, payments for managerial assistance provided by the parent, and payments for centralized services provided by the parent are all included in the transaction exposure of the firm.

8. *Unperformed forward exchange contracts.* As noted in Chapter 2, there is a forward market for foreign exchange. In this market, a firm is able to enter into a contract that commits it to either accept or deliver a specified amount of a foreign currency at a future point in time. For example, an American firm may enter into a forward market contract that requires it to receive DM2,000,000 in 90 days. This contract involves transaction exposure because it constitutes an obligation to accept a foreign currency at a future point in time.

Each of these eight types of transactions (plus several others that have not been specified) requires that the firm either accept or deliver a certain amount of foreign currency at a future point in time. In the typical situation, the precise amount of foreign currency involved is specified. The firm has no choice but to fulfill its obligations, and therein lies the transaction exposure.

A closer look at the eight types of transactions should also indicate how transaction exposure can be managed (this is discussed more fully later in the chapter). It is clear that the exposure generated by one type of transaction can be offset by other types of transactions. For example, assume that an American firm purchases something from a German supplier and agrees to pay DM100,000 at a future date (an account payable). The resulting exposure can be offset by a sale to a German buyer for DM100,000 on the same date (an account receivable). If these were the only two transactions, the net transaction exposure in deutsche marks would be zero. Any of the eight types of transactions discussed can be used to offset exposure. In fact, forward contracts are designed specifically to offset exposure generated by other types of transactions.

Cash Budgets (by Currency)

Most firms engaged in international commerce are anxious to develop a procedure that will provide a numerical estimate of their transaction exposure. A cash budget (by currency) report provides this information. It tells management the expected magnitude of foreign currency inflows and outflows by period. An example of a cash budget (by currency) is presented in Table 7-1. In this illustration, it is assumed that the Interam Corporation has production facilities only in the United States. However,

TABLE 7-1 Interam Corporation: Projected Cash Budget (by Currency), 1988*
(in Millions)

	1st Q	2nd Q	3rd Q	4th Q	Annual
Receipts					
U.S. $ receipts	$300	$280	$320	$400	$1,300
U.K. £ receipts	£20	£25	£18	£40	£103
Canada $ receipts	C$40	C$20	C$45	C$50	C$155
Disbursements					
U.S. $ disbursements	$200	$160	$240	$300	$900
U.K. £ disbursements	£40	£15	£20	£40	£115
Canada $ disbursements	C$20	C$40	C$75	C$20	C$155
Net Exposure (Receipts − Disbursements)					
U.S. $	+$100	+$120	+$80	+$100	+$400
U.K. £	−£20	+£10	−£2	0	−£12
Canada $	+C$20	−C$20	−C$30	+C$30	0

*Assumes that all cash flows take place at the end of the quarter.

the firm makes sales and purchases in American dollars, Canadian dollars, and British pounds.

The cash budget (by currency) report is usually prepared by the accounting department of the firm; the procedures used are essentially those used to construct any cash budget. Detailed analysis is required in order to determine the estimated amount and timing of cash inflows and outflows.[1] The fact that several currencies are involved does not alter the basic conceptual nature of the statement. While the cash budget (by currency) report presented in Table 7-1 was prepared on a quarterly basis, in practice firms may use other periods (just as they do for domestic cash budgets). For example, a firm may choose to have a cash budget on a daily basis for the coming week, weekly cash budgets for the remainder of the month, and monthly cash budgets for 1 year. In fact, cash budget (by currency) reports may extend beyond 1 year. The precise dimensions of the cash budget (by currency) report depend on the extent to which the firm is involved in international commerce, the extent to which management is concerned about transaction exposure, and the cost of constructing the cash budget (by currency).

As shown in Table 7-1, the Interam Corporation expects to receive and disburse foreign currencies in each of the four quarters. The net exposure in each currency is reported in the lower section of the table. Looking at the first-quarter entry for the British pound, for example, we see −£20.[2] This entry reflects the fact that Interam expects to disburse £40 during the first quarter and receive only £20. Thus, a negative in the net exposure section of the table indicates that the firm expects to disburse more than it receives. This situation is referred to as being *short* in the foreign currency. In a similar sense, the net exposure of +£10, as forecasted for the second quarter, is referred to as being *long* in the foreign currency. This simply means that the firm expects to receive more of the foreign currency than it will disburse. Note that in the fourth quarter the firm has no exposure in the British pound. This absence of exposure is indicated by a zero entry in the net exposure portion of the cash budget (by currency) report.

Net Transaction Exposure

Both positive and negative net exposure numbers indicate that the firm is vulnerable to movements in foreign exchange rates. If a firm is short in a foreign currency, a strengthening of the foreign currency against the dollar will cause a loss. For example, Interam has a short position in

---

[1]For a more detailed description of cash budgets, see Eugene F. Brigham, *Fundamentals of Financial Management*, 4th ed., Chicago, Dryden Press, 1986, pp. 614–619.

[2]All the figures in this section of the chapter are expressed in millions.

TABLE 7-2   Consequences of Exchange Rate Movements

	Long Position	Short Position
Foreign currency weakens (dollar strengthens)	Firm loses	Firm gains
Foreign currency strengthens (dollar weakens)	Firm gains	Firm loses

British pounds for the first quarter (−£20). If the current spot rate on the pound (assumed to be £1 = $1.00) is maintained over the next 90 days, Interam will need $20 in order to acquire the £20. If, on the other hand, the pound strengthens (assume that the new exchange rate is £1 = $1.25), Interam will need $25 in order to purchase the required £20. A strengthening of the foreign currency (a weakening of the dollar) hurts the firm when the firm is short in that currency. This is the nature of transaction exposure.

When a firm is long in a foreign currency, it is hurt by a weakening of that currency (a strengthening of the dollar). For example, Interam is long in British pounds during the second quarter (+£10). If the spot exchange rate stayed at its present level (£1 = $1.00), Interam would receive $10 for these excess pounds. If the British pound weakens (assume that £1 = $0.75), the £10 would convert to only $7.5. Weakening foreign currencies hurt firms that are long in those currencies. The situation is summarized in Table 7-2.

Notice that Interam's transaction exposure is a function of time. If, for example, the firm chose to focus on the year as a whole, it would have no exposure to the Canadian dollar. On the other hand, there is substantial exposure, sometimes long and sometimes short, in each quarter. Conceivably, the firm could choose to ignore the transaction exposure, since it all "works itself out" over the year as a whole. This strategy could, however, be very risky. As exchange rates fluctuate, the firm may have to pay more dollars to discharge short positions and may receive fewer dollars from its long positions. In other words, taking too long a perspective can result in losses.

One of the conceptual problems associated with the cash budget (by currency) report is that it looks at each currency individually and independently. In a sense, it views total transaction exposure as a summation of the exposures in the individual currencies. Actually, the total exposure of the firm will be affected by the relationships among the currencies involved. For example, the Canadian dollar is fairly stable against the American dollar. For a firm operating in the Canadian dollar environment, the American dollar value of short and long positions is not likely to vary greatly. On the other hand, the British pound displays substantial volatility against the dollar. The conclusion that must be drawn is that net exposure in some currencies is less risky than net exposure in others.

The relationship among currencies affects the extent of exposure in another way. If an American firm has exposure in many different currencies, and if changes in exchange rates between the dollar and these currencies are not identical, the various exchange rate movements may cancel each other out. For example, assume that a firm is long in both the deutsche mark and the Hong Kong dollar. If the mark weakens, the firm would be hurt. However, the firm would gain if the Hong Kong dollar strengthens. By having exposure in both currencies, the firm may have less risk than if it were exposed in only one. The protection provided by diversification over many currencies may be less important for transaction exposure, since most of the important trading currencies for the United States (with the exception of the Canadian dollar and perhaps the Japanese yen) tend to move in the same direction against the dollar.

Consolidated Cash Budgets for the Multinational Firm

The construction of a cash budget (by currency) report for the multinational firm is a little more complicated than for the domestic firm. Conceptually, the recommended procedure involves constructing a cash budget (by currency) for every subsidiary of the company that has transaction exposure. The separate subsidiary cash budgets (by currency) are then consolidated into a firmwide cash budget (by currency). For example, assume that the Interam Corporation has a wholly owned foreign subsidiary in the United Kingdom called the Interam U.K. Corporation. This subsidiary has transactions in the United Kingdom, the United States, Germany, and Canada. Its expected cash flows are shown in Table 7-3. The methodology employed by the subsidiary in constructing the cash budget (by currency) is the same as that used by the parent.

The next step involved in constructing a corporatewide cash budget (by currency) requires that the budgets of all the subsidiaries be consolidated. An example of a consolidated cash budget is presented in Table 7-4. The amounts reported in Interam Corporation's consolidated report are nothing more than the summation of the two separate cash budgets. Notice that there is a canceling-out effect in this process. For example, at the end of the first quarter, the American operation is short pounds (−£20), while the British subsidiary is long in that currency (+£20). On a consolidated basis, however, the firm has zero exposure in pounds. In effect, the American operation will need £20 at the end of the first quarter and will have the funds available from the British subsidiary. The firm does not have to go outside to get the funds and therefore has no exposure in pounds for the first quarter. It is the consolidated cash

TABLE 7-3 Interam U.K. Corporation: Projected Cash Budget (by Currency), 1988*
(in Millions)

	1st Q	2nd Q	3rd Q	4th Q	Annual
Receipts					
U.S. $ receipts	$20	$50	$30	$40	$140
U.K. £ receipts	£100	£130	£180	£100	£510
Canada $ receipts	C$20	C$10	C$30	C$40	C$100
German DM receipts	DM80	DM70	DM90	DM60	DM300
Disbursements					
U.S. $ disbursements	$10	$30	$40	$60	$140
U.K. £ disbursements	£80	£100	£170	£120	£470
Canada $ disbursements	C$50	C$20	C$20	C$20	C$110
German DM disbursements	DM40	DM80	DM50	DM60	DM230
Net Exposure (*Receipts − Disbursements*)					
U.S. $	+$10	+$20	−$10	−$20	0
U.K. £	+£20	+£30	+£10	−£20	+£40
Canada $	−C$30	−C$10	+C$10	+C$20	−C$10
German DM	+DM40	−DM10	+DM40	0	+DM70

*Assumes that all cash flows take place at the end of the quarter.

budget (by currency) that gives the true picture of the multinational's transaction exposure. Note that although the parent corporation did not have an exposure in deutsche marks, the consolidated cash budget does show such exposure. This is caused by the fact that Interam U.K. did have an exposure in German marks.

Unlike economic exposure, transaction exposure is rather concrete. Its definition is unambiguous, and its origins are understandable. It is also possible, with some effort, to get a reasonably precise measurement of the amount and timing of foreign currency transaction risk. As we will see later in the chapter, it is also possible to develop effective strategies for minimizing this type of risk.

TABLE 7-4 Interam Corporation: Consolidated Projected Cash Budget
(by Currency), 1988* (in Millions)

	1st Q	2nd Q	3rd Q	4th Q	Annual
Net Exposure					
U.S. $	+$110	+$140	+$70	+$80	+$400
U.K. £	0	+£40	+£8	−£20	+£28
Canada $	−C$10	−C$30	−C$20	+C$50	−C$10
German DM	+DM40	−DM10	+DM40	0	+DM70

*Assumes that all cash flows take place at the end of the quarter.

An Introduction to Hedging Transaction Exposure

Before beginning our discussion of the methods employed by firms to manage transaction exposure, let us review certain principles of managerial finance that are often overlooked when making decisions relating to the management of foreign exchange rate risk. First and most importantly, remember that the objective of the firm is to maximize stockholder wealth, not to eliminate foreign exchange rate risk. Firms, by their very nature, are risk takers, and they take risks when adequate compensation is expected. Firms regularly engage in such risky endeavors as developing new products and technologies, entering new markets, and using large amounts of debt financing. Taking risks is nothing new to firms. It is not necessary for the foreign exchange rate risk to be zero in order to make international business attractive to firms. The only requirement for stockholder wealth maximization is that the manager weigh the risks of an alternative against its cash flow implications. The additional returns must compensate for the additional risks.

International diversification, an important strategy for managing economic exposure to exchange rate risk, can also be used to manage transaction exposure. If a firm has contractual future cash outflows and inflows in many different currencies, it is less vulnerable to a fluctuation in the price of any single currency. The strengthening of one currency could be offset by the weakening of another. Of course, the extent to which diversification reduces transaction exposure depends on the degree to which the foreign currencies involved are correlated with each other. If the foreign currencies held by the firm have a high positive correlation with each other, the benefits of diversification are less than if the currencies tend to move independently against the dollar. We must also keep in mind that, for some firms, diversification is not feasible. Potential markets, sources of materials, legal requirements, and many other factors may make diversification impractical.

The managers of firms engaged in international commerce also have other ways of reducing transaction exposure. Specifically, there is a financial transaction called a *hedge*, which may permit a firm to eliminate transaction exposure entirely. While we will focus primarily on hedges involving the forward exchange and money markets, it is also possible to use the currency futures and options markets to reduce risk.[3] Of course,

---

[3]The use of currency futures and options as a hedging device is discussed in Appendix 7A.

the various hedges available to the firm have an attached cost that must be weighed against the benefits associated with risk reduction. While this cost/benefit focus is difficult to maintain as we proceed through the technical discussion of hedging techniques, it will be reintroduced near the end of the chapter. At that point, we will show that despite the beauty of the techniques themselves and their extreme usefulness to some firms, it appears that many firms can increase stockholder wealth by leaving the risk position open. For this reason, certain types of firms are moving away from the use of hedges. While it is important to understand the details of the risk management techniques and the conditions under which they are useful, it is equally important to understand their limitations.

All of the hedging techniques that will be discussed in the following sections attempt to achieve exactly the same goal, and in more or less the same fashion. They differ only in the financial arrangements or instruments that are utilized. The general rules for hedging foreign exchange rate exposure are as follows:

1. If the firm is contractually obligated to accept a foreign currency at a future point in time (long exposure), it enters into another transaction that requires or permits it to deliver the same amount of the foreign currency at the same point in time in return for a specified number of dollars. For example, assume that an American firm is contractually obligated to accept FF10,000,000 in 90 days. The firm would enter into an immediate agreement (such as a forward contract) that would require (or permit) it to deliver the francs to another party in return for a specified number of dollars. The hedging techniques to be discussed differ in terms of the type of arrangement used to lock in the price at which the future exchange will take place.

2. If the firm is contractually obligated to deliver a foreign currency at a future point in time (short exposure), it enters into a transaction that requires or permits it to acquire the same amount of foreign currency at the same point in time for a specified number of dollars. For example, if an American firm has an obligation to pay DM5,000,000 in 60 days, it could enter into an immediate agreement that would require or permit it to acquire the marks in return for a specified number of dollars. Once again, there are many different types of financial transactions that can be used to establish contractually the dollar value of the future foreign currency payment.

In general, we can say that hedging involves entering into a financial "countertransaction" in order to offset the risk associated with a long or short exposure in a foreign currency at a future point in time. We will now introduce the various hedging techniques and show how they can be used to reduce transaction exposure.

Hedging with Forward Contracts

A forward market hedge involves the use of a financial arrangement known as the *forward contract* in order to reduce transaction exposure. Simply stated, a firm that is contractually obligated to accept a foreign currency at a future point in time may be able to enter into a forward contract with a bank. The forward contract requires the bank to accept the foreign currency in return for a specified number of dollars. A firm that is obligated to deliver a foreign currency at a future point in time may be able to enter into a forward contract that will require the bank to deliver to the firm the foreign currency at that time in return for a specified number of dollars.

Properly used, these forward market hedges should be used within a consolidated cash budget similar to the one presented in Table 7-4. Specifically, the firm should hedge expected net exposure positions rather than individual transactions. In Table 7-4, for example, the Interam Corporation expects to be short C$10,000,000 at the end of the first quarter. This means that expected Canadian dollar-denominated payments exceed expected Canadian dollar receipts. Presumably, the Interam Corporation will be required to convert American dollars to Canadian dollars in order to meet these obligations. Interam is at risk, since it is uncertain about the spot exchange rate that will prevail in the future and may be required to exchange an unexpectedly large number of dollars in order to meet the Canadian dollar-denominated obligations. Interam is faced with the opposite situation in regard to the German mark. The firm expects to receive deutsche marks at the end of the first quarter. In this situation, Interam anticipates a net inflow of DM40,000,000, and the rate at which they will be converted to dollars is uncertain. If the value of the deutsche mark decreases below the forecasted level, Interam may wind up with fewer dollars than anticipated. Note that at the end of the first quarter, the expected net inflow in British pounds is zero. Thus, Interam does not have any exposure in pounds at that time.

The firm may expect to engage in many different transactions during the period. Some will lead to foreign currency inflows and others to outflows. The expected net flow estimates for the Canadian dollar, the deutsche mark, and the British pound reflect the fact that inflows and outflows for each currency are netted out. The firm does not hedge individual transactions; it hedges the expected net short or long positions in the various currencies. This strategy reduces the transaction costs associated with exchanging one currency for another (reflected in the spread on a currency) and can result in substantial savings for the firm. For example, assume that an American firm had two expected British pound inflows, one for £50 and the other for £150, and two expected British pound outflows, one for £125 and the other for £75, in 90 days. The firm could use forward contracts to hedge every transaction. In effect, this would involve the firm in four currency conversions, resulting in the payment of the spread on a total of £400 worth of transactions. Of course, the firm paid these costs for nothing, since at the very beginning, anticipated foreign currency inflows (£200) were exactly equal to anticipated foreign currency outflows (£200) and the firm had no transaction exposure. Firms may be able to reduce substantially the costs of converting currencies by restricting the amounts hedged to the net currency flows for each currency.

To illustrate the appropriate hedging strategy, let us continue with the Interam Corporation's situation as presented in Table 7-4. As you will remember, Interam is short on Canadian dollars during the first quarter. That is, Interam expects to pay more Canadian dollars than it has available, and we assume that the firm will want to convert American dollars to Canadian dollars in order to meet these obligations. Note that the firm is at risk, since it is unsure of the future spot rate and does not know how many dollars will be needed in order to meet its foreign currency obligation. The uncertainty about the American dollar value of the Canadian dollar outflow can be eliminated by buying the Canadian dollars in the forward market. As discussed in Chapter 2, the firm can contact its bank and enter into an agreement that will obligate both parties to exchange currencies at a rate of exchange specified today. The forward rates of exchange facing Interam are presented in Table 7-5. If Interam is willing to wait 90 days, the bank will be willing to sell Canadian dollars at a rate of $0.7433.

If Interam accepts the offered forward rate, it has eliminated transaction exposure. It knows with certainty how many dollars will be paid. The details of the dollar flow situation are presented in Table 7-6. The Canadian dollar exposure is converted to American dollars with certainty. Interam now knows that it is required to deliver $7,433,000 in 90 days. The bank is required to give Interam C$10,000,000 on the same date. Interam's first-quarter exposure in Canadian dollars is reduced to zero.

The situation with respect to the deutsche mark is the opposite. Clearly, Interam could sell DM40,000,000 in the forward market for

TABLE 7-5 Hypothetical Exchange Rates: Canadian Dollar, Deutsche Mark, and British Pound* (Direct Quotes: Price of One Unit of Foreign Currency in Dollars)

	Canadian Dollar	British Pound	Deutsche Mark
Spot rate	$0.7457	$1.5380	$0.5596
90-day forward	$0.7433	$1.5195	$0.5625
180-day forward	$0.7408	$1.5030	$0.5652
270-day forward	$0.7400	$1.5011	$0.5680

*We are ignoring the bid–ask differential at this time.

TABLE 7-6   Interam Corporation: 90-Day Forward Market Hedging

Exposure	Time	Forward Rate	Amount ($)
− C$10,000,000	90 days	C$1 = $0.7433	− $7,433,000
+ DM40,000,000	90 days	DM1 = $0.5625	+ $22,500,000

Note: For convenience, we have assumed that all cash flows take place at the end of the quarter.

delivery in 90 days. The equivalent dollar amounts are shown in Table 7-6. Interam could simply sell the DM40,000,000 forward 90 days in exchange for $22,500,000 (DM40,000,000 × 0.5625) and thus eliminate the foreign exchange rate risk. Interam's first-quarter exposure in deutsche marks is also reduced to zero.

Our illustration concentrated on Interam's transaction exposure during the first quarter. This was done in order to simplify the computations. For the first quarter, these hedging transactions have eliminated Interam's worry about the fluctuation in the exchange rate of the Canadian dollar, the deutsche mark, or the British pound. The firm has zero transaction exposure during this period. The total U.S. dollar cash flow to the firm will be equal to $125,067,000 ($110,000,000 + $22,500,000 − $7,433,000). Note that we assumed that the expected cash flows would take place at the end of each quarter. If the cash flows were received throughout the quarter, the firm would still have some transaction exposure. Firms do not necessarily try to eliminate foreign exchange rate risk on a day-by-day, week-by-week, month-by-month, or even quarter-by-quarter basis. Management generally accepts some transaction exposure for short periods of time. Hedging is normally used when the amounts involved are very large or when it is anticipated that long and/or short positions in foreign currencies will not be offset by future flows of the same currencies.[4]

Using the Money Market for Hedging Purposes

The *money-market hedge* involves borrowing one currency on a short-term basis and converting it to another currency immediately. This procedure eliminates the uncertainty associated with fluctuating exchange rates by accelerating the date at which the currency conversion is made. Perhaps the best way to explain how the money-market hedge works is to continue with the Interam Corporation example. The necessary interest

---

[4]If the firm wants to hedge its exposure for the second, third, and fourth quarters, it can follow the same methodology.

TABLE 7-7 Interest Rates for Different Currencies*

	American Dollar	British Pound	Canadian Dollar	German Mark
90-day rate	2.0000%	3.2418%	2.3293%	1.4741%
180-day rate	4.2000%	6.6264%	4.8892%	3.1675%
270-day rate	6.9000%	9.5278%	7.7234%	5.3190%

*These rates are not annualized. They reflect the actual interest due at the end of the period. For example, a borrower of $100 would be required to repay $102 if the loan is outstanding for 90 days.

rate information is presented in Table 7-7. In order to simplify the computations, we will assume that interest rates are the same whether the firm borrows or invests funds.

The Interam Corporation expects to be short C$10,000,000 in 90 days and presumably will have to convert U.S. dollars to Canadian dollars in order to meet its obligations. Since it is unsure about the future exchange rate, it can eliminate uncertainty by borrowing U.S. dollars now and converting them to Canadian dollars. The Canadian dollars can then be invested until they are needed to meet the short position requirements. For simplicity, we will assume that the funds are invested in a bank deposit. Of course, the firm will have to pay interest on the U.S. dollars borrowed, but it will also earn interest on the Canadian dollar deposit. The steps involved in the money-market hedge for the Interam Corporation are outlined in Table 7-8. Note that the uncertainty with respect to future exchange rates has been completely eliminated by the money-market hedge. Interam knows exactly how many Canadian dollars it will have and how many dollars it will be required to pay in 90 days. In 90 days, Interam will withdraw C$10,000,000 from the Canadian bank to meet its short position. On the same day, the firm will be required to repay $7,433,003 in principal and interest to the American bank.

A money-market hedge can also be used to hedge a long position in a foreign currency. If the firm is anticipating a foreign currency inflow in the future and plans to convert it to the home country currency, it can eliminate all exchange rate uncertainty by simply borrowing the foreign

TABLE 7-8 A Money-Market Hedge for Interam Corporation's 90-Day Short Position

1. Borrow $7,287,258 at an interest rate of 2.0% for 90 days from an American bank.
2. Immediately convert the U.S. dollars to Canadian dollars at the spot rate of $0.7457. The firm will now have C$9,772,372.
3. Immediately invest the C$9,772,372 at the 90-day rate of 2.3293%.
4. In 90 days, the firm's deposit of C$9,772,372 will have grown to C$10,000,000 ($9,772,372 × 1.023293), the amount needed to meet its short position.
5. In 90 days, $7,433,003 ($7,287,258 × 1.02) will have to be paid to the lending bank (the amount borrowed plus 2% interest).

TABLE 7-9   A Money-Market Hedge for Interam Corporations 90 Day Long Position

---

1. Borrow DM39,418,926 for 90 days at an interest rate of 1.4741% from a German bank.
2. Immediately, convert the deutsche marks to dollars at the spot rate of DM1 = 0.5596. The firm will receive $22,058,831 (DM39,418,926 × 0.5596).
3. Immediately invest the dollars at the 90 day dollar rate of 2%.
4. In 90 days, deliver DM40,000,000 to the German bank in order to repay the loan (DM39,418,926 × 1.014741). This is exactly the same "long" position that you have in the deutsche mark.
5. In 90 days, withdraw $22,500,007 from the bank. ($22,058,831 × 1.02). The firm is certain of receiving $22,500,007. There is no risk.

---

currency and immediately converting it to dollars at the spot rate. The dollars obtained in this manner will be invested in a bank deposit. The foreign currency loan will then be repaid with the future foreign currency inflows. Table 7-9 shows how Interam's 90-day long position in deutsche marks can be hedged.

The only real computational difficulties involved in these hedging transactions involve calculating the amount to be borrowed. The steps involved in computing the size of the loan for the "short" position are outlined below:

1. Determine how many foreign currency units are needed. In our example, the firm was short C$10,000,000.
2. Next determine how much of the foreign currency must be deposited now in order to provide the future cash flow. This can be accomplished by dividing the amount needed by one plus the interest rate at which the funds will be invested. [C$10,000,000/(1 + 0.023293) = C$9,772,372]
3. Calculate the number of dollars to be borrowed in order to acquire the necessary foreign currency by multiplying this amount by the spot rate for the currency.

$$(C\$9,772,372 \times 0.7457 = \$7,287,258)$$

The procedure for calculating the amount of foreign currency that must be borrowed in order to cover a long position is similar:

1. Determine how many foreign currency units will be available at the future date (DM40,000,000).
2. Determine the size of the borrowing that could be repaid with the amount available by dividing the amount available by 1 plus the

TABLE 7-10 Forward-Market Hedge Compared to Money-Market Hedge

90-day short position	*Forward-Market Hedge* Bought C$10,000,000 forward at a rate of C$1 = 0.7433. In 90 days, the firm pays a total of $7,433,000. *Money-Market Hedge** Borrowed $7,287,258 at an interest rate of 2%. In 90 days, the firm pays a total of $7,433,003.
90-day long position	*Forward-Market Hedge* Sold DM40,000,000 forward at a rate of DM1 = 0.5625. In 90 days, the firm receives $22,500,000. *Money-Market Hedge** Borrowed deutsche marks, converted them to dollars and invested $22,058,831 at 2.0%. In 90 days, the firm can withdraw a total of $22,500,007.

*The dollar amounts in the money-market hedge are not identical to the forward rate, since interest rates were rounded to four decimal points.

interest rate associated with the borrowing [DM40,000,000/ (1 + 0.14741) = DM39,418,926].

Hedging Cost Comparisons: No Transaction Costs

Either the forward market or the money market can be used to hedge transaction exposure. It is interesting to note that under the conditions for interest rate parity (see Chapter 2), the costs for both hedging techniques are the same. This proposition is illustrated in Table 7-10. On the 90-day short position, Interam delivers exactly the same number of dollars at exactly the same point in time. Hedging the long position results in the same dollar inflows at the same point in time. There is no difference between the money-market and the forward-market hedge in this regard.

There is no difference in cost between the two hedging techniques because interest rate parity is the rule rather than the exception. This means that the percentage loss or gain (discount or premium) associated with the forward transaction is exactly equal to the difference in interest rates between the two currencies. In the 90-day short position, the computation would be as follows:

$$\% \text{ discount on C\$ (90 days)} = \frac{\text{forward rate} - \text{spot rate}}{\text{spot rate}}$$

$$= \frac{0.7433 - 0.7457}{0.7457}$$

$$= -0.00322 = -0.322\%$$

$$\% \text{ difference in interest rates} = \frac{1 + i(h)}{1 + i(f)} - 1$$

$$= \frac{1 + 0.02}{1 + 0.023293} - 1$$

$$= -0.00322 = -0.322\%$$

In our example, Interam can buy Canadian dollars for 0.322 percent less than the spot rate if it agrees to postpone the exchange of currencies using a 90-day forward contract. In a sense, this represents a 0.322 percent gain for the firm. With a money-market hedge, Interam also gains 0.322 percent, since interest rates on the Canadian dollar are that much higher than interest rates on the U.S. dollar.[5] In general, the gain or loss associated with the discount or premium will be equal to the gain or loss associated with the differences in interest rates. Therefore, when interest rate parity exists, the forward-market hedge and the money-market hedge involve the same cash flows.

It can be shown that under the conditions assumed in this section (no transactions costs), the firm should always hedge. This can be demonstrated most clearly by looking at a forward market hedging situation—for example, the C$10,000,000 90-day short position of the Interam Corporation. The proof is based on the well-documented fact that the forward rate is an unbiased estimator of the future spot rate (see Chapter 5). Thus, on the average, the firm will obtain the same rate of exchange whether it enters into a forward contract or not.

1. As shown in Table 7-10, if Interam hedges the C$10,000,000 short position, it will have an exchange rate of C$1 = $0.7433 and the dollar outlay will be $7,433,000.

2. If the firm does not hedge (waits and converts at the spot rate), the expected exchange rate, as forecasted by the forward market, would be the same C$1 = $0.7433 and the expected dollar outlay will be the same $7,433,000.

---

[5]Note that the interest rate differential is not simply the U.S. rate minus the Canadian rate. See footnote 6 in Chapter 2 for the correct formula.

In other words, the firm gives up nothing to achieve the greater certainty associated with the forward contract.

What is true for a forward-market hedge on the short position is also true for a forward-market hedge on the long position. While it is more difficult to prove, the same principle applies to money-market hedges. In the absence of transactions costs, the firm can remove uncertainty and risk by hedging. The firm should always hedge.

Cost Comparisons with Transaction Costs

In the real world there are transaction costs, although sometimes these costs can be very low. With respect to the foreign exchange markets, the cost is inherent in the spread on the quotations. Remember (from Chapter 2) that there are actually two prices of a foreign currency. The bid price is the price at which the bank will buy the currency, and the ask price is the price at which the bank will sell the same currency. The bid price is always lower than the ask price, since the bank makes its profit by buying cheap and selling dear. There are no commissions or other costs. The sole cost is in the spread, and the higher the spread, the higher the cost.

The forward hedge has a cost to the firm because the spread on the forward contract is usually greater than the spread on spot transactions. The longer the period of time, the higher the spread and thus the higher the cost. For example, consider the information provided in Table 7-11. As the table shows, the percentage spread in the spot market is lower than that in the forward market. As a general rule, the longer the maturity of the forward contract, the higher the bid–ask spread. Thus, a firm that uses the forward market continuously will incur higher transaction costs than a firm that elects not to hedge. The difference in cost, as

TABLE 7-11 Typical Bid–Ask Spreads on the British Pound, 1988

	Bid	Ask	% Spread*
Spot rate	$1.7635	$1.7640	0.028%
30-day forward	$1.7605	$1.7611	0.034%
60-day forward	$1.7576	$1.7583	0.040%
1-year forward	$1.7285	$1.7300	0.087%

*See Equation 2-1. The spreads shown are for illustration purposes only.

Note: This information was given to the author over the phone by a major American bank in February 1988.

shown in Table 7-11, is very small. However, such small costs can be significant if you are hedging hundreds of transactions.

The cost of the money-market hedge is more difficult to identify. It is to be found in a more realistic look at how interest rates actually work. Looking back at Table 7-7, you will note that there appears to be a single 90-day interest rate on all four currencies. This is not realistic. In fact, there is a rate at which the bank is willing to lend (the borrowing rate) and a rate that the bank is willing to pay on deposits (the investment rate). Naturally, for any given bank, the deposit rates are almost always lower than the lending rates. Maintaining a spread on interest rates is the way the bank makes its profit.

When the analysis is confined to a single currency, clearly it is never profitable for a firm to borrow and then deposit the funds.[6] For example, the firm may pay 10 percent interest on the amount borrowed but receive only 8 percent on the amount deposited. The same idea applies to cross-currency transactions. Deposit rates are lower than borrowing rates after adjustments for expected changes in exchange rates. In other words, a firm borrowing in one currency, converting to another currency, and then depositing the funds would have an expected loss.[7] The magnitude of the cost associated with a money-market hedge will depend on the firms and the banks involved. The spread will be smaller for large firms and larger transactions. Borrowing rates, deposit rates, and the spread on interest rates will vary from bank to bank. While it is not possible to put a numerical value on the cost of the money-market hedge, you can be sure that it is there.

There is one set of circumstances that will lower the cost of the money-market hedge. Assume that a firm with a short position in a foreign currency has idle cash balances that are on deposit in the United States. These funds could be shifted immediately to the foreign currency at the cost of losing interest in the United States. Note that the firm loses interest at the deposit rate in the United States and earns interest at the deposit rate in the foreign country. There is no spread in the borrowing/investment rate of this type of transaction, and the cost of the hedge will depend solely on the difference in the deposit rates.

Similarly, a long position could be hedged if the firm has idle foreign currency balances. The foreign currency could be converted to dollars immediately and deposited. The firm loses interest on the foreign currency at the deposit rate and gains interest at the deposit rate for dollars. The cost associated with the spread between the lending and deposit

---

[6]We are assuming that the funds are deposited in a commercial bank. This would reduce transaction costs. The firm, however, may invest in money market securities—for example, Treasury bills. This may result in brokerage fees.

[7]With respect to interest rate parity, there will be a small difference between interest rate differentials and forward discounts/premiums. Covered interest arbitrage opportunities exist only to the extent that differences are large enough to cover the costs of forward contracts and interest rate spreads.

rates is absent. Of course, the attractiveness of these low-cost hedges depends on the availability of idle cash balances, and most firms try to keep their funds employed rather than leaving them idle.[8]

Other Hedging Techniques

There are a number of other alternatives that the firm may use in order to hedge transaction exposure. Management is always looking for strategies that will reduce exchange rate risk. Some of the things a firm can do are unique to a particular situation. For example, a firm may be able to get an agreement with a foreign government or its central bank that will eliminate all or part of the exchange rate risk associated with doing business in that country.

There are several other general techniques that are helpful in the management of transaction exposure. Appendix 7A discusses foreign exchange futures and options. Balance-sheet hedges are often employed. This technique is discussed together with capital structure in Chapter 10. In addition, parallel loans and currency swaps are presented in terms of managing the multinational firm's internal funds flows (Chapter 13). These techniques, while important hedging tools, are also important to the firm for other reasons.

Hedging Using a Proxy Currency

Considerations other than cost affect the choice of hedging technique. First, forward contracts are available for only a limited number of currencies. A glance at *The Wall Street Journal* reveals that only the currencies of those countries most heavily involved in international commerce have widely available forward contracts. Each country listed has a market-oriented financial system and a freely traded currency. With the exception of Switzerland, the countries with currencies heavily traded on a forward basis are the large Western industrial powers. While forward contracts may occasionally be available for the currencies of a few other countries, most currencies cannot be traded in the forward market.

The limited number of currencies available for forward trades appears to be more restrictive than it really is. Look back at Table 3-1. You will note that many currencies are pegged to one of the currencies for which there is a forward market. This means that the government of the country is committed to maintaining a fixed rate of exchange. For exam-

---

[8]If the parent or the subsidiary has to borrow in order to finance short-term operations, borrowing in the correct currency can also reduce the spread in the borrowing/deposit interest rate. This issue will be discussed in Chapters 9 and 10.

ple, a group of African countries use a common currency called the *CFA franc*. In 1987 the CFA franc was pegged to the French franc at a rate of approximately CFA(fr)1 = FF0.0231. Assuming that no official change in the value of the CFA franc relative to the French franc was anticipated, an American firm with a short position in any one of the CFA countries could have hedged its position by buying French francs forward (called the *proxy currency* in this example). At the execution date, dollars would be exchanged for French francs, which, in turn, could be converted to CFA francs. Of course, if the official pegged rate was changed during the open period, the firm could have suffered a loss. Since the pegged rates are relatively stable, this type of hedge offers partial protection against losses associated with transaction exposure.

Similarly, currencies pegged to the SDR could be hedged, although this would involve taking forward positions in several different currencies. It is also possible to hedge some of the transaction exposure associated with short and long positions in the currencies of smaller EMS countries for which no forward contracts are available. For example, since Denmark is a member of the EMS, it is pledged to maintain the rate of exchange between its currency (the Danish kroner) and the other EMS currencies. Thus, a short position in the Danish kroner could be hedged by buying deutsche marks forward. This would not be a perfect hedge, since some variation in the exchange rate is possible and even anticipated. In addition, the American hedger would be vulnerable to official EMS actions that could change the target exchange rates within the group.

Note that many countries peg their currencies to the American dollar (e.g., Venezuela's bolivar). Barring a change in the official rate established by the foreign government, an American firm has no exposure in these currencies. However, foreign firms do have exposure. For example, a French firm with a short position in Venezuelan bolivars is at risk. The French firm could reduce its risk by buying American dollars forward. Once again, such a transaction will not protect against official rate changes implemented by the Venezuelan government.

Managerial Implications

Should a firm hedge transaction exposure? If yes, which type of hedge should be employed? These are two questions for which there are no easy answers.

The major argument against hedging relates to its costs. This argument asserts that in the absence of transaction costs, the expected value of cash flows will be the same whether or not the firm hedges. Incurring costs in order to hedge reduces the expected value. Therefore, the argument continues, there is no justification for paying the fees associated with hedging. While there is no denying the logic inherent in this argument, there is another side to the story.

The equality of the expected values of cash flows is a long-term proposition. It is based on the idea that the forward rate is an unbiased estimator of the future spot rate. Thus, on the average, the firm has the same cash flow whether or not it hedges. However, firms do not always survive by making decisions based on expected average results. It is perfectly possible for a firm to have a long series of unexpected shortfalls on unhedged transaction exposure positions. We know that the forward rate may often misestimate the future spot rate for many periods in succession. A firm that maintains an unhedged position in such a situation will probably find little comfort in the knowledge that eventually things will average out. In fact, some firms may simply be unable to afford the long series of shortfalls. Thus, many firms choose to hedge transactions even though there is a cost associated with this alternative.

The appropriate strategy for a particular firm should reflect the extent to which the firm will be affected by an adverse exchange rate movement. Firms that have a relatively small portion of their total cash flows exposed to foreign exchange rate movements are in a better position to play the law of averages. Such firms are in a position to absorb shortfalls in anticipation of windfall gains at future points in time, thus saving the transaction costs associated with hedging. By contrast, firms that have a high proportion of their cash flows vulnerable to exchange rate movements may be willing to pay the costs associated with hedging. In return for paying the transaction costs, such firms achieve greater certainty with respect to future cash flows. This is a risk–return decision that must be made by management and for which there is no general solution.

Firms that have only occasional foreign currency cash flows may also find hedging an attractive alternative. For example, an occasional importer or exporter may simply have too few transactions for shortfalls to be eventually offset by windfall gains. This type of firm is deprived of the long-term certainty associated with the unbiased estimator concept. Such a firm should probably consider future spot rates unforecastable. In this situation, hedging may be an attractive alternative to the assumption of transaction exposure.

While some managers may find hedging costs to be money well spent, everyone should recognize that hedging techniques do not protect the long-term cash flows of the firm. For example, a firm that had a long-term commitment to purchase parts from a Japanese supplier was probably unable or unwilling to hedge such an exposure completely. Thus, as the dollar fell against the yen during the 1985–1988 period, the firm may have had some hedges in place. Most likely, however, these hedges covered the risk inherent in the yen purchases for the near future. At some point, the impact of the weaker dollar was felt by the importing firm and was translated into higher dollar prices paid for the imports. Hedging is not a means of permanently insulating the firm from long-term adjustments in currency values. The long-term problem is one of economic exposure rather than transaction exposure. Hedges do not solve the economic exposure problem.

How should the firm hedge if it chooses to do so? The answer to this question relates to the costs and availability of the alternative hedging techniques. While it is not possible to make absolute statements, it does appear that when both forward and money-market hedges are available, the forward market hedge tends to be less expensive. Remember, however, that forward market hedges are available in a very limited number of currencies. The money-market hedge is viable for a broader range of currencies, although costs can be very high in some cases as governments regulate lending and/or interest rates.[9]

Summary and Conclusions

This chapter has discussed the issues of transaction exposure. Before the firm can manage exposure, the exposure must be measured. With respect to transaction exposure, a consolidated cash budget (by currency) provides the necessary information. However, it is important to remember that the absolute numbers in the consolidated cash budget cannot be interpreted correctly without knowing more about the correlations among movements in the currencies.

The difficult concepts presented in this chapter are not related to the measurement of exposure. The problems lie in trying to manage transaction exposure. The benefits of using forward-market and money-market hedges were evaluated in terms of their costs. With respect to the hedging of transaction exposure, the decision is difficult. The managers of each firm must look carefully at the costs and benefits of hedging. Some firms should be fully hedged, while others may not need complete protection. The decision should be based on the magnitude of the impact of possible foreign exchange rate fluctuations on the financial position of the firm. There is no general rule that will apply to all firms.

Review Questions

1. Explain the meaning of transaction exposure and describe the transactions that give rise to such exposure.
2. Explain how each of the following transactions will affect a firm's net transaction exposure (assume that other factors are held constant):
   a. An American firm sells products to a foreign buyer and agrees to accept payment in Swiss francs in 30 days.

---

[9]Hedging with options and futures is also limited to a small number of currencies, all of which could also be hedged in the forward or money markets.

    b. An American firm enters into a forward contract that requires it to deliver Canadian dollars in return for American dollars in 90 days.

    c. An American firm enters into a contract with a foreign supplier under which the supplier agrees to deliver goods 1 year from the date of the contract. The American firm agrees to pay in British pounds on the delivery date.

    d. Over the next year, an American firm anticipates receiving a dividend of DM1,000,000 from its foreign subsidiary.

    e. An American firm has borrowed FF25,000,000 from a foreign bank and must make a payment of FF10,000,000 in 60 days.

    f. An American firm buys something from a foreign supplier and will pay $1,000,000 in 90 days.

3. "A firm should measure the amount of its transaction exposure over a 1-year period." True or false? Explain your answer.

4. "An American parent with many foreign subsidiaries does not have to worry about the transaction exposure of its subsidiaries." True or false? Explain your answer.

5. Explain how a firm can reduce transaction exposure through a diversification strategy, and discuss the limitations of this risk management approach.

6. Give a step-by-step description of how an American firm could use a forward contract to hedge a 90-day long position in a foreign currency.

7. Give a step-by-step description of how an American firm could use a forward contract to hedge a 30-day short position in a foreign currency.

8. Give a step-by-step description of how an American firm could use the money market to hedge a 90-day long position in a foreign currency.

9. Give a step-by-step description of how an American firm could use the money market to hedge a 30-day short position in a foreign currency.

10. "Since the forward rate is an unbiased estimator of the future spot rate, it makes no sense for a firm to hedge its transactions exposure." True or false? Explain your answer.

11. "Some transaction exposure simply cannot be hedged." True or false? Explain your answer.

12. "One of the conceptual problems associated with the cash budget (by currency) report is that this report looks at each currency individually and independently." True or false? Explain your answer.

Questions for Discussion

1. Assume that you are employed by an American firm that produces only in the United States (using domestic inputs) and regularly sells to customers in the United States (in U.S. dollars), France (in French francs), Italy (in Italian lire), and Mexico (in Mexican pesos). Top management is aware of the fact that the fluctuating value of the dollar places it at risk but does not understand the extent of the risk in each of the currencies. In order to achieve a better understanding, management asks you to construct a cash budget (by currency) covering the upcoming year.

    a. Explain how you would construct such a statement.

    b. Indicate whether you would attempt to project cash inflows on a daily, weekly, monthly, or annual basis.

    c. What would you recommend with respect to hedging?

2. Assume that you are employed by an American firm that is currently producing only in the United States (using domestic inputs) and selling in several foreign countries. Your firm is considering the acquisition of two competitors, one located in France and the other in Hong Kong. Top management wants to know how these acquisitions will affect transaction exposure and asks you to analyze the situation. Explain how you could use a cash budget (by currency) to perform this task. Discuss the problems associated with constructing such a statement. What would be the impact of these acquisitions on the total transaction exposure of the firm?

3. Assume that you are employed by an American exporter that is heavily and continuously involved in exporting to a number of foreign countries, including Canada, the United Kingdom, and Korea. The president of your firm recently overheard an executive with another firm suggest that hedging transaction exposure is unprofitable. This surprises him (since he thought that his firm has always hedged its net transaction exposure), and he wants to learn more about this issue. You are asked to gather information on the issue and report back to the president.

4. Assume that you are employed by an American firm that produces large turbines used by producers of electrical power. The firm makes only one to four foreign sales per year, but these sales are very large. For example, last year the firm made only one foreign sale (to the Canadian government), but it amounted to C$60,000,000 (Canadian dollars), which was equal to 18 percent of the firm's total sales for the year. Next year the firm expects to ship three turbines—one to the United Kingdom, one to Italy, and one to Mexico. Typically, sales are made in the local currency and on an open account basis, with full payment expected within 60 days of delivery of the turbine. You are asked to advise top management on the desirability of hedging the transaction exposure associated with these sales. If you recommend hedging, which particular hedging device would you consider best for the firm?

Research Activities

1. Your firm purchases £1,000,000 in British products on the first day of every month. Payments for the purchases are made on a 30-day basis in British pounds. Go back over the last year and determine the dollar cost of the purchases if the firm:
   a. Did not hedge its transaction exposure.
   b. Hedged its transaction exposure using the forward market.

2. Your firm sells DM3,000,000 in products to German firms on the first day of every month. Collections on the sales are made on a 30-day basis and in deutsche marks. Go back over the last year and determine the dollar revenues on the sales if the firm:
   a. Did not hedge its transaction exposure.
   b. Hedged its transaction exposure using the forward market.

Problems

1. Global Enterprises U.S. has prepared a cash budget (by currencies) for the next 3 months. Their expected receipts and disbursements are as follows (in millions):

(Assume that all cash flows take place at the end of the month)

	January	February	March
$ receipts	$100	$120	$200
DM receipts	DM140	DM60	DM80
FF receipts	FF200	FF100	FF90
$ disbursements	$70	$100	$160
DM disbursements	DM200	DM20	DM90
FF disbursements	FF100	FF120	FF60

Prepare a monthly cash budget (by currency) for the firm.

2. Global Germany, a subsidiary of Global Enterprises, has prepared a cash budget (by currencies) for the next 3 months. Their expected receipts and disbursements are as follows (in millions): (Assume that all cash flows take place at the end of the month)

	January	February	March
C$ receipts	C$80	C$20	C$20
DM receipts	DM100	DM50	DM20
FF receipts	FF20	FF10	FF30
C$ disbursements	C$70	C$10	C$60
DM disbursements	DM200	DM20	DM90
FF disbursements	FF80	FF20	FF60

Prepare a monthly cash budget (by currency) for Global Germany.

3. Using the information presented in Problems 1 and 2, prepare a consolidated monthly cash budget (by currency) for Global Enterprises.

4. Based on the transaction exposure shown in Problem 3 and the following information, compute the expected U.S. dollar cash flows to Global Enterprises if the firm uses the forward-market hedge. Assume that the firm desires to be fully hedged as of the end of January (30 days).

	Canadian $	Deutsche Mark	French Franc
Spot rate	$0.75	$0.40	$0.30
30-day forward	$0.752	$0.402	$0.29

5. Based on the transaction exposure shown in Problem 3, the foreign exchange information shown in Problem 4, and the following interest rate information, compute the expected U.S. dollar cash flow to Global Enterprises if the firm uses a money-market hedge. Assume that the firm desires to be fully hedged as of the end of January (30 days).

Interest	U.S.	Canada	Germany	France
30 days	1.2%	0.93%	0.7%	1.3%

6. Using the results from Problems 4 and 5, compare the forward to the money market as hedging alternatives. Do the results appear consistent with interest rate parity theory?

7. Based on the transaction exposure shown in Problem 3 and the following information, compute the expected U.S. dollar cash flows to Global Enterprises if the firm uses the forward-market hedge. Assume that the firm is fully hedged as of the end of January (30 days) and desires to be hedged as of the end of February (60 days).

	Canadian $	Deutsche Mark	French Franc
Spot rate	$0.75	$0.40	$0.30
60-day forward	$0.757	$0.404	$0.28

8. Based on the transaction exposure shown in Problem 3, the foreign exchange information shown in Problem 7, and the following interest rate information, compute the expected U.S. dollar cash flow to Global Enterprises if the firm uses a money-market hedge. Assume that the firm is fully hedged as of the end of January (30 days) and desires to be hedged as of the end of February (60 days).

Interest	U.S.	Canada	Germany	France
60 days	2.5%	1.55%	1.5%	2.7%

9. Using the results from Problems 7 and 8, compare the forward to the money market as hedging alternatives. Do the results appear consistent with interest rate parity theory?

10. Based on the transaction exposure shown in Problem 3 and the following information, compute the expected U.S. dollar cash flows to Global Enterprises if the firm uses the forward-market hedge. Assume that the firm is fully hedged as of the end of January (30 days) and February (60 days). The firm desires to be hedged as of the end of March (90 days).

	Canadian $	Deutsche Mark	French Franc
Spot rate	$0.75	$0.40	$0.30
90-day forward	$0.764	$0.407	$0.27

11. Based on the transaction exposure shown in Problem 3, the foreign exchange information shown in Problem 10, and the following interest rate information, compute the expected U.S. dollar cash flow to Global Enterprises if the firm uses a money-market hedge. Assume that the firm is fully hedged as of the end of January (30 days) and February (60 days). The firm desires to be hedged as of the

end of March (90 days).

Interest	U.S.	Canada	Germany	France
90 days	3.8%	1.9%	2.0%	4.1%

12. Using the results from Problems 10 and 11, compare the forward to the money market as hedging alternatives. Do the results appear consistent with interest rate parity theory?

13. The Christine Corporation is obligated to make a DM50 million payment in 90 days. The firm has obtained the following information:

		Bid	Ask
Forward market:	Spot	$0.300	$0.301
	90 days	$0.310	$0.315

Money Market (90-day Interest Rate)	Borrowing	Depositing
United States	3.0%	2.8%
Germany	2.7%	2.5%

a. Calculate the number of dollars that will be needed to obtain the DM50 million in 90 days if the firm uses the forward market.

b. Calculate the number of dollars that will be needed to obtain the DM50 million in 90 days if the firm uses the money market.

14. The Williams Corporation will receive FF50 million in 90 days. The firm has two hedging alternatives: (a) the money market and (b) the forward market. The following market information is available to the firm:

	Bid	Ask
French franc spot	$0.200	$0.203
90-day forward	$0.205	$0.210

90-Day Interest Rate	Borrowing	Investing
United States	3.2%	3.1%
France	2.9%	2.8%

In addition, it costs the firm $100 (FF500) per transfer of funds from the United States to France (and vice versa). Furthermore, if the firm invests in either country, it will incur brokerage fees of $800 in the United States or FF4,000 in France. Which hedging alternative would you recommend?

15. The Williams Corporation will have to pay FF50 million in 90 days. The firm has two hedging alternatives: (a) the money market and (b) the forward market. The

following market information is available to the firm:

	Bid	Ask
French Franc Spot	$0.200	$0.203
90-day forward	$0.205	$0.210

90-Day Interest Rate	Borrowing	Investing
United States	3.2%	3.1%
France	2.9%	2.8%

In addition, it costs the firm $100 (FF500) per transfer of funds from the United States to France (and vice versa). Furthermore, if the firm invests in either country, it will incur brokerage fees of $800 in the United States or FF4,000 in France. Which hedging alternative would you recommend?

16. The Christine Corporation buys and sells products from the United Kingdom. The firm is concerned with its transaction exposure. The expected receipts in 90 days are 50 million pounds. The expected disbursements in 90 days are 80 million pounds. Given the following information:

	Bid	Ask
Spot Value of the Pound	$1.500	$1.501
90-day forward rate	$1.520	$1.525

	90-Day Interest	
	Borrowing	Investing
United States	4.6%	4.4%
United Kingdom	3.0%	2.8%

a. Assuming that the firm has no excess funds at the present time, would you recommend the use of the forward or the money market in order to eliminate transaction exposure?

b. Assuming that the firm has $50 million in excess funds at the present time, would you recommend the use of the forward or the money market in order to eliminate transaction exposure?

Bibliography

Ankrom, Robert. "Among Their Hedges, Treasurers May Miss the Obvious." *Euromoney*, December 1977, pp. 99–100.

Biger, Nahum, and Hull, John. "The Valuation of Currency Options." *Financial Management*, Spring 1983, pp. 24–28.

Black, Fischer, and Scholes, Myron. "The Pricing of Options and Corporate Liabilities." *Journal of Political Economy*, May–June 1973, pp. 637–659.

Brigham, Eugene F. *Fundamentals of Financial Management*, 4th ed. Chicago: Dryden Press, 1986.

Calderon-Rossell, Jorge R. "Covering Foreign Exchange Risks of Single Transactions: A Framework for Analysis." *Financial Management*, Autumn 1979, pp. 28–85.

Chalupa, Karl V. "Foreign Currency Futures: Reducing Foreign Exchange Risk." *Federal Reserve Bank of Chicago Economic Perspectives*, Winter 1982, pp. 3–11.

Cornell, Bradford W., and Reinganum, Marc R. "Forward and Future Prices." *Journal of Finance*, December 1981, pp. 1035–1045.

Eaker, Mark R. "Denomination Decision for Multinational Transactions." *Financial Management*, Autumn 1980, pp. 23–29.

Evans, Thomas G., and Folks, William R., Jr. "Using Forward Contracts in Exposure Management." *Business International Money Report*, March 12, 1979, pp. 91–93.

Flood, Eugene, Jr., and Lessard, Donald R. "On the Measurement of Operating Exposure to Exchange Rates: A Conceptual Approach." *Financial Management*, Spring 1986, pp. 25–36.

Folks, William R., Jr. "Optimal Foreign Borrowing Strategies with Operations in the Forward Exchange Markets." *Journal of Financial and Quantitative Analysis*, June 1978, pp. 245–254.

Gadkari, Vilas. *Relative Pricing of Currency Options*. New York: Salomon Brothers, 1984.

Gendreau, Brian. "New Markets in Foreign Currency Options." *Business Review*, July–August 1984, pp. 3–12.

Giddy, Ian H. "Why It Doesn't Pay to Make a Habit for Forward Hedging." *Euromoney*, December 1976, pp. 96–100.

_____ "Foreign Exchange Options." *Journal of Futures Markets*, Summer 1983, pp. 143–166.

_____ "The Foreign Exchange Option as a Hedging Tool." *Midland Corporate Finance Journal*, Fall 1983, pp. 32–42.

Goldstein, Henry. "Foreign Currency Futures: Some Further Aspects." *Federal Reserve Bank of Chicago Economic Perspectives*. November–December 1983, pp. 3–13.

Goodman, Laurie S. "How to Trade in Currency Options." *Euromoney*, January 1983, pp. 73–74.

Heckman, Christine R. "Measuring Foreign Exchange Exposure: A Practical Theory and Its Application." *Financial Analysts Journal*, September–October 1983, pp. 59–65.

Jacque, Laurent L. "Management of Foreign Exchange Risk: A Review Article." *Journal of International Business Studies*, Spring–Summer 1981, pp. 81–99.

Kaufold, Howard, and Simirlock, Michael. "Managing Corporate Exchange and Interest Rate Exposures." *Financial Management*, Autumn 1986, pp. 64–72.

Kohlhagen, Steven W. "Evidence on the Cost of Forward Cover in a Floating System." *Euromoney*, September 1975, pp. 138–141.

Lessard, Donald R., and Lightstone, John B. "Volatile Exchange Rates Can Put Operations at Risk." *Harvard Business Review*, July–August 1986, pp. 107–114.

Madura, Jeff, and Nosari, E. Joe. "Utilizing Currency Portfolios to Mitigate Exchange Rate Risk." *Columbia Journal of World Business*, Spring 1984, pp. 96–99.

Maldonado, Rita, and Saunders, Anthony. "Foreign Exchange Futures and the Law of One Price." *Financial Management*, Spring 1983, pp. 19–23.

Mathur, Ike. "Managing Foreign Exchange Risks Profitably." *Columbia Journal of World Business*, Winter 1982, pp. 23–30.

Rodriguez, Rita M. *Foreign Exchange Management in U.S. Multinationals*. Lexington, MA: Lexington Books, 1980.

Serfass, William D., Jr. "You Can't Outguess the Foreign Exchange Market." *Harvard Business Review*, March–April 1976, pp. 134–137.

Shapiro, Alan C. "When to Hedge Against Devaluation." *Management Science*, August 1974, pp. 1514–1530.

Shepard, Sidney A. "Forwards, Futures, and Currency Options as Foreign Exchange Risk Protection." *Canadian Banker*, December 1983, pp. 22–25.

Swanson, Peggy E., and Caples, Stephen C. "Hedging Foreign Exchange Risk Using Forward Foreign Exchange Markets: An Extension." *Journal of International Business Studies*, Spring 1987, pp. 75–82.

Waters, Somerset R. "Exposure Management Is a Job for All Departments." *Euromoney*, December 1979, pp. 79–82.

Yang, Ho C. "The Value of a Forward Contract in Foreign Currencies." *Journal of Business, Finance, and Accounting*, Winter 1984, pp. 575–578.

Appendix 7A

Hedging with Foreign Currency Futures and Options

Foreign Currency Futures Contracts

Firms are able to hedge long or short positions in foreign currencies by buying and selling futures contracts. A foreign currency futures contract obligates a participant to either accept or deliver a specified amount of foreign currency at a specific future date. The futures market is organized by the International Monetary Market (IMM) of the Chicago Mercantile Exchange. At the present time, the IMM offers futures contracts on six currencies: the Australian dollar, the British pound, the Canadian dollar, the Japanese yen, the Swiss franc, and the West German mark. The reader should note that although these are today's most important international currencies, some major currencies are not traded. For example, the French franc and the Italian lire are not presently traded. Thus, hedging is possible only for transactions denominated in the aforementioned six currencies.

Table 7A-1 shows information published by *The Wall Street Journal* on the foreign exchange futures market. Note that the units of foreign currency included in each contract are specified. For example, the size of a British pound contract is set at £62,500, while that of a deutsche mark contract is set at DM125,000. If transaction exposure leaves a firm short in British pounds, it would buy one or more futures contract for that currency. If the transaction exposure leaves the firm long in British pounds, it would sell one or more futures contract. Note that contracts are available only in fixed sizes. Thus, if a firm is short £1,000,000, it

TABLE 7A-1 Quotations on Foreign Currency
Futures, October 19, 1988

FUTURES

	Open	High	Low	Settle	Change	Lifetime High	Low	Open Interest
JAPANESE YEN (IMM) 12.5 million yen; $ per yen (.00)								
Dec	.7912	.7923	.7897	.7898	− .0026	.8530	.7115	47,886
Mr89	.7982	.7996	.7970	.7969	− .0026	.8590	.7439	1,948
June	.8065	.8068	.8054	.8052	− .0026	.8400	.7500	784
Sept	.8140	.8140	.8135	.8126	− .0026	.8180	.7690	160
Est vol 26,724; vol Tues 31,483; open int 50,778, +1,604.								
W. GERMAN MARK (IMM) − 125,000 marks; $ per mark								
Dec	.5561	.5567	.5546	.5548	− .0015	.6610	.5252	47,287
Mr89	.5601	.5608	.5590	.5592	− .0015	.6240	.5304	999
June	....	....		.5639	− .0015	.5673	.5434	180
Est vol 15,552; vol Tues 20,380; open int 48,466, −545.								
CANADIAN DOLLAR (IMM) − 100,000 dlrs.; $ per Can $								
Dec	.8295	.8320	.8292	.8311	+ .0009	.8332	.7390	23,738
Mr89	.8270	.8294	.8265	.8283	+ .0009	.8300	.7570	1,220
June	.8270	.8270	.8260	.8254	+ .0009	.8270	.7670	526
Est vol 7,669; vol Tues 9,939; open int 25,545, +2,862.								
BRITISH POUND (IMM) − 62,500 pds.; $ per pound								
Dec	1.7404	1.7456	1.7388	1.7402	− .0004	1.9000	1.6394	19,880
Mr89	1.7332	1.7334	1.7270	1.7290	− .0004	1.7398	1.6320	525
Est vol 7,143; vol Tues 5,815; open int 20,459, −1,039.								
SWISS FRANC (IMM) − 125,000 francs-$ per franc								
Dec	.6598	.6604	.6574	.6579	− .0016	.8210	.6286	25,532
Mr89	.6672	.6675	.6644	.6647	− .0016	.7735	.6360	845
June	....	....		.6725	− .0016	.6670	.6450	107
Est vol 17,920; vol Tues 18,804; open int 26,486, −212.								
AUSTRALIAN DOLLAR (IMM) − 100,000 dlrs.; $ per A.$								
Dec	.8103	.8144	.8099	.8125	+ .0095	.8144	.7458	2,030
Est vol 323; vol Tues 250; open int 2,053, +144.								

─OTHER CURRENCY FUTURES─

Settlement prices of selected contracts. Volume and open interest of all contract months.

British Pound (MCE) 12,500 pounds; $ per pound
    Dec 1.7402 −.0004; Est. vol. 112; Open Int. 370
European Currency Unit (CTN) 100,000 ECU
    Dec 114.66 −.44; Est. vol. 0; Open Int. 998
Japanese Yen (MCE) 6.25 million yen; $ per yen (.00)
    Dec .7898 −.0026; Est. vol. 156; Open Int. 361
Swiss Franc (MCE) 62,500 francs; $ per franc
    Dec .6579 −.0016; Est. vol. 190; Open Int. 332
West German Mark (MCE) 62,500 marks; $ per mark
    Dec .5548 −.0015; Est. vol. 375; Open Int. 371
    IMM─International Monetary Market at the Chicago
Mercantile Exchange. MCE─MidAmerica Commodity Exchange. CTN─New York Cotton Exchange.

would buy 16 contracts. If the firm were short only £10,000, it would have to buy a single £62,500 contract or leave the position unhedged. The contract amount is not always evenly divisible into the exposure position.

The date on which contracts are *settled* is specified in advance. For example, contracts in Canadian dollars mature in September, December, March, and June of each year. The actual maturity date is usually the third Wednesday of the month specified. A firm that sold a single March Swiss franc futures contract would be (theoretically) required to deliver SF125,000 on the third Wednesday of March. In practice, firms may eliminate such an obligation by entering into the opposite transaction at an earlier date. Thus, a firm that sold a March Swiss franc contract could buy a March contract at any time prior to March. The buy contract would offset the sell contract, and the firm would no longer be at risk. The fact that the contracts are traded daily gives the firm substantial flexibility.

Let us illustrate the operations of the foreign exchange futures market with an example based on the information in Table 7A-1, which refers to the market as it existed on October 19, 1988. Assume that on that date a firm purchased two West German mark contracts with a settlement date of December 21, 1988 (third Wednesday in December). In effect, the firm purchased DM250,000 (2 × 125,000) for delivery in December. We will assume that it paid the settle price of December contracts, which is DM1 = $0.5548. This means that on December 21, the firm will have to deliver $138,700 (250,000 × 0.5548) in exchange for DM250,000, unless it offsets this transaction by selling a futures contract. The firm has locked in the cost of DM250,000 at $138,700, regardless of the fluctuation in the value of the deutsche mark between now and December 21. The futures contract allows the firm to shift the risk of foreign exchange fluctuations to another party.

Currency Futures Compared to the Forward Market

Note that both the futures and forward exchange markets allow the firm to accomplish the same objective: they lock in the price of foreign currencies. However, there are important differences between the two types of hedging transactions. First, forward contracts are executed by commercial banks, while futures contracts are executed by securities brokerage houses. The arrangement with the bank is more personal and, at least to some extent, the forward transaction can be tailored to meet the specific hedging needs of the individual firm. Thus, a forward contract is usually available in a greater variety of amounts, and the maturity dates can be set to coincide with expected foreign currency receipts or expenditures. The futures market also has its advantages. For one thing, the price paid for the futures contract is determined by market forces, not negotiated with the bank.[10] A participant simply orders his or her broker to purchase or sell the specified number of contracts. It is also argued that the futures market accommodates smaller transactions. Small firms may find the futures market more accommodating than the forward market. Another advantage of the futures market is that the participants are not required to be exceptionally strong financially. While forward market participants are generally of superior financial strength or have a solid relationship with a bank, this is not the case for the futures market. Another advantage of the futures market is that there is a good secondary market for the futures contracts. For example, if a firm's hedging needs change, it is relatively simple to buy an offsetting futures contract.

The most important disadvantage of the futures contract method of hedging is transaction costs. Transaction costs tend to be 10 times larger

---

[10]Banks do not establish the forward rate in a vacuum. Competition prevents banks from setting extreme prices. See Chapter 12 for a more complete discussion of the role of banks in this market.

than those for forward exchange contracts (for large amounts). In addition, the IMM requires a margin deposit of approximately 10 percent of the face value of the contract at the time of the purchase. In our previous illustration, the firm would have had to pay $13,870 at the time it purchased the two deutsche mark contracts.[11] By contrast, the forward market usually does not require any payment until the forward contract matures.

Should the firm hedge with futures contracts or in the forward market? While no definite answer that covers all circumstances is possible, a number of observations are in order. A large, financially strong firm with a good banking relationship and the need to hedge large transactions will usually be better off using the forward market. The primary advantage of this market is its lower transaction costs. On the other hand, small firms attempting to hedge small transactions may be excluded from the forward exchange market and may have to turn to the futures market.

Foreign Currency Options Contracts

Firms can also use currency options to hedge transaction exposure. Option contracts on several foreign currencies are traded on the Philadelphia Stock Exchange, and information on the options is published in *The Wall Street Journal* (Table 7A-2). There are two types of options: the *call* option and the *put* option. When a firm buys a call option, it purchases the right to buy the currency at the price specified in the options contract. The call option gives the firm the right (or option) to buy the currency specified, but it does not obligate the firm to do so. Thus, a firm can buy a call option allowing it to acquire currency at a future date and at a price specified now, but it may simply decide not to exercise the option. There is no penalty for failure to exercise. Call options may be useful in hedging transactions exposure when the firm has an expected short position in the foreign currency and is concerned about the exchange rate for that currency. In this case, the firm could purchase an option that guarantees the price of the foreign currency.

When a firm buys a put option, it purchases the right to deliver a foreign currency at the exchange rate specified in the contract. The other party to the option contract (the writer of the option) is obligated to buy the foreign currency. However, the firm that buys the put option is not obligated to sell. The option buyer has a right to sell, but not an obligation to sell. Put options may be used to hedge transaction exposure

---

[11]If the price of the futures contract drops significantly, the exchange would require the holders of such contracts to increase their deposit. This is done in order to reduce the risk of someone not honoring the contract upon maturity.

TABLE 7A-2   Quotations on Foreign Currency Options, October 19, 1988

OPTIONS

Option & Underlying	Strike Price	Calls—Last Oct	Nov	Dec	Puts—Last Oct	Nov	Dec
50,000 Australian Dollars-cents per unit.							
ADollr	...78	s	r	r	s	0.08	r
81.01	...79	s	r	r	s	0.20	r
81.01	...80	s	r	r	s	0.32	r
81.01	...81	s	r	1.47	s	r	1.64
81.01	...82	s	r	0.72	s	r	r
81.01	...84	s	r	0.31	s	r	r
81.01	...85	s	0.05	r	s	r	r
31,250 British Pounds-cents per unit.							
BPound	160	s	r	15.30	s	r	r
175.09	162½	s	r	12.60	s	r	r
175.09	.170	s	r	r	s	0.30	r
175.09	172½	s	r	4.00	s	r	r
175.09	.175	s	1.41	2.60	s	2.25	r
175.09	177½	s	0.62	r	s	r	r
50,000 Canadian Dollars-cents per unit.							
CDollr	...82	s	r	1.60	s	r	0.38
83.36	.82½	s	1.07	1.22	s	0.27	r
83.36	...83	s	0.69	0.90	s	0.40	0.73
83.36	.83½	s	r	r	s	0.62	r
83.36	...84	s	r	0.48	s	r	r
50,000 Canadian Dollars-European Style.							
CDollar	82½	s	1.07	r	s	r	r
83.36	...83	s	0.69	r	s	r	r
62,500 West German Marks-cents per unit.							
DMark	.. 53	s	r	r	s	0.03	0.17
55.17	...54	s	r	r	s	0.11	0.36
55.17	...55	s	0.67	r	s	0.36	0.68
55.17	...56	s	0.26	0.67	s	r	r
55.17	...57	s	0.13	0.36	s	r	r
55.17	...58	s	0.02	0.21	s	r	r
125,000 French Francs-10ths of a cent per unit.							
FFranc	..16	s	r	3.40	s	r	r
161.63	16¼	s	1.15	r	s	r	r
161.63	16½	s	r	1.30	s	r	r
6,250,000 Japanese Yen-100ths of a cent per unit.							
JYen	... 72	s	r	r	s	r	0.03
78.50	...73	s	r	r	s	r	0.04
78.50	...74	s	4.90	r	s	0.01	0.06
78.50	...75	s	3.90	r	s	0.01	0.14
78.50	...76	s	2.95	3.37	s	0.06	0.26
78.50	...77	s	r	2.47	s	0.18	0.45
78.50	...78	s	1.11	1.82	s	0.42	0.77
78.50	...79	s	0.60	1.18	s	0.86	r
78.50	...80	s	0.26	0.74	s	r	r
78.50	...81	s	s	0.53	s	r	r
78.50	...82	s	s	0.30	s	s	r
78.50	...83	s	s	0.15	s	s	r
62,500 Swiss Francs-cents per unit.							
SFranc	..61	s	r	r	s	r	0.06
65.26	...62	s	r	r	s	r	0.14
65.26	...63	s	r	r	s	0.07	0.20
65.26	...64	s	r	r	s	0.15	0.40
65.26	...65	s	r	1.65	s	0.40	0.71
65.26	...66	s	0.36	1.00	s	0.83	1.33
65.26	...67	s	0.19	0.63	s	r	1.87
65.26	...68	s	r	0.37	s	r	r
65.26	...69	s	r	0.20	s	r	r

Total call vol.	15,001	Call open int. 356,827
Total put vol.	21,160	Put open int. 316,807

r—Not traded.   s—No option offered.
Last is premium (purchase price).

Source: Reprinted by permission of *The Wall Street Journal,* © Dow Jones & Company, Inc., October 20, 1988. All Rights Reserved Worldwide.

situations in which the firm has an expected long position in the foreign currency.

Table 7A-2 shows the information presented by *The Wall Street Journal* on currency options. Note that options are available for only a limited number of currencies and that the option contracts have specified sizes—for example, A\$50,000, £31,250, or DM62,500. The options (the right to buy or sell) are for various lengths of time. For example, on

October 19, 1988, it is possible to purchase options on the West German mark that expire in either November or December. The options for some currencies are unavailable for some of these maturities. For example, no November British pound options were traded at a strike price of 170 on October 19, 1988. The options expire on a specific date in the maturity month, usually the third Wednesday.

The price information in Table 7A-2 is of two types and is a little difficult to follow. The second column indicates the *strike price*. This is the price at which the buyer of the option is entitled to buy or sell. Note that there are several strike prices for each currency. This means that there are actually several different types of options for each currency. For example, the buyer of a call option on the deutsche mark could have an option to buy marks at $0.53 per mark, $0.54 per mark, $0.55 per mark, and so on. The price that the buyer of the call option will have to pay depends on the specific option purchased.

The option to buy a foreign currency at a future point in time at a price specified now has value. In other words, a firm wishing to buy an option must pay for it. The price paid will depend on the strike price and the date on which the option matures. The price for each available option is listed to the right of the strike price. The price is given in American cents per foreign currency unit. Thus, a December option on $0.56 deutsche marks has a price of $0.0067 per mark. Since the size of the contract for the deutsche mark is 62,500 marks, the buyer of a single option must pay $418.75. This is the cost of the option; it is paid whether or not the option is exercised.

Let us illustrate the operations of the option market with an example. Assume that a firm will need (expects to be short) DM250,000 on December 21 (third Wednesday in December) and decides to hedge its transaction exposure through the purchase of a call option. First, the firm must decide which of the December deutsche mark options it wishes to purchase. In other words, it must decide on the strike price, or the price it desires to pay for the deutsche marks. As shown in Table 7A-2, the strike price varies from DM1 = $0.53 to DM1 = $0.58. If the firm chooses the call option with a strike price of DM1 = $0.57, it has the *right* to purchase DM62,500 at a price of DM1 = $0.57 at any time between the option's date of purchase and date of expiration. Let us assume that in order to cover its expected short position of DM250,000, the firm decides to purchase four December call options (DM62,500 × 4) at a strike price of DM1 = $0.57. Any time between now and December 21, the firm can turn in the contracts *plus* $142,500 (62,500 × 4 × 0.57) and receive DM250,000 (62,500 × 4). In order to obtain the four call options, the firm will have to pay $900.[12]

---

[12]The price of each call option will be $225 (DM62,500 × 36 cents). Note that the price is quoted in U.S. cents. Since the firm is purchasing four call options, the total cost will be $900 ($225 × 4).

In effect, the firm has paid $900 for the right to buy DM250,000 for $142,500. Is this a good investment? The answer to this question depends on the behavior of the foreign exchange rate over the period covered by the option. If we assume that on December 21 the spot exchange rate turns out to be DM1 = $0.60, the firm would have to pay $150,000 for DM250,000 (250,000 × 0.60) in the spot market for foreign exchange. If the firm had purchased the call options, its cost would be only $143,400 ($142,500 + $900 cost of the options).[13] Thus, by purchasing the options, the firm has reduced the cost of acquiring the DM250,000 by $6,600 ($150,000 − $143,400).[14]

Have we discovered the goose that lays the golden eggs? The answer is, of course not. If the value of the mark declines below the $0.57 strike price, the call options would be worthless on December 21. The firm would be better off throwing away the options and buying the DM250,000 at a price below $0.57. Note that if the actual exchange rate is equal to or below the strike price on the exercise date (December 21), the call option is worth *zero*. In other words, the $900 paid for the four call options will be lost.

Currency Options
Compared to the Forward Market

What are the advantages of call options compared to the forward exchange market? First, the option market allows the firm to hedge relatively small amounts. Second, it is impersonal and does not require a strong banking connection. Third, call options have a secondary market, which allows the firm to adjust its hedged position relatively easily. Finally, there is no obligation to buy or sell the currency should it move in an unexpected direction.

The disadvantages of the options contract approach to hedging relate to the costs. These costs include the purchase price of the option as well as transaction costs (commission) on the purchase. In addition, the maturity date of options is limited to perhaps 3 months. Thus it may be difficult to hedge for 180 days. Finally, as can be seen in Table 7A-2, the number of options available, as well as the number of trades in each option, is somewhat limited.

---

[13]The actual cost of hedging using either options or futures should also include the opportunity cost of the down payment at the time the contract was made.

[14]In practice, option contracts are traded. The trade value of a contract will depend on the difference between the strike price and the expected spot rate. When the strike price on a call option is below the expected spot price, the option can be sold at a premium. In practice, hedging firms frequently sell options at a premium and use the profit on the transaction to offset the decline in the foreign currency value.

In conclusion, options offer an alternative to the forward exchange market. For large firms dealing in large amounts, however, it may be more cost effective to use the forward market. Small firms, on the other hand, may not have access to the forward market and thus can use options in order to hedge against foreign currency fluctuations.

Review Questions

1. Assume that an American firm is short in British pounds at some point in the future. Explain how the firm can eliminate its transaction exposure using the foreign currency futures market.
2. Assume that an American firm is long in British pounds at some point in the future. Explain how the firm can eliminate its transaction exposure using the foreign currency futures market.
3. Discuss the advantages and disadvantages of using currency futures to manage transaction exposure.
4. Assume that an American firm is short in British pounds at some point in the future. Explain how the firm can eliminate its transaction exposure using the foreign currency options market.
5. Assume that an American firm is long in British pounds at some point in the future. Explain how the firm can eliminate its transaction exposure using the foreign currency options market.
6. Discuss the advantages and disadvantages of using currency options to manage transaction exposure.

Problems

1. The Donegal Corporation is obligated to pay £250,000 in March. The firm uses the futures market as a hedging alternative. Using the quotes in Table 7A-1, answer the following questions:
   a. How many futures contracts must be purchased?
   b. Assuming that a 10 percent deposit is required, how much would the firm have to pay today?
   c. What will happen in March upon maturity of the contracts?
2. The Williams Corporation is obligated to pay £250,000 in December. The firm uses the options market as a hedging alternative. Using the quotes in Table 7A-2, answer the following questions:
   a. How many call options must be purchased?
   b. How much would the firm have to pay today if it chooses a strike price of
      i. 160?
      ii. 175?
   c. What will happen in December upon maturity of the contracts?

8

Estimating and Managing Translation Exposure

The extent to which a firm is vulnerable (exposed) to exchange rate movements can be perceived from a number of different vantage points. Chapter 6 examined economic exposure and showed that the appropriate defensive strategies for its management are long-term (strategic) in nature. Chapter 7 reviewed transaction exposure and evaluated the available alternatives for hedging against it. This chapter examines translation exposure. It begins by explaining how the financial statements of a foreign subsidiary are translated into dollars and the problems created by such translation. The chapter then discusses the seriousness of the translation problem and management reactions to translation exposure. The final sections of the chapter evaluates the translation exposure minimization strategies available to the firm.

Definition of Translation Exposure

When a business is organized as several separate corporations, financial statements must be filed on a consolidated basis in order to give shareholders concise, complete information on the financial position and operating performance of the firm as a whole. For example, General Motors Corporation is organized into a number of separate subsidiaries. Among them are a corporation that produces cars in the United States, a separate corporation that finances sales of General Motors products (General Motors Acceptance Corporation), and a corporation that produces automobiles in the United Kingdom. Each of these corporations is a separate legal entity and generates its own financial statements. However, the parent corporation, General Motors Corporation, must take the statements of each of its subsidiaries, combine them, and publish them as the consolidated statements for the company as a whole. In practice, the financial statements of most large firms are consolidated statements. Even smaller firms are often organized into a number of separate corporations and must therefore prepare consolidated statements. The need for consolidation is so widespread that even beginning accounting students are introduced to the basic principles used in consolidating financial statements.

The general concepts that underlie the principles of consolidation are reasonably straightforward. Conceptually, consolidation of subsidiaries' financial statements with those of the parent involves nothing more than adding the subsidiaries' accounts to the parent accounts.[1] For example, subsidiary sales are added to parent sales, and subsidiary assets are added to parent assets. When the subsidiary and the parent are both domestic corporations (General Motors Corporation and General Motors Acceptance Corporation), the task of addition is relatively simple. All accounts are denominated in dollars, and thus no exchange rate conversion problem exists.

When the subsidiary operates in a foreign currency (e.g., the British subsidiary of General Motors), however, major complications affect the consolidation process. The difficulty stems initially from the fact that the financial statements of the foreign subsidiary are often in a currency that is different from that used by the parent corporation. The *functional* currency is defined as the currency of the primary economic environment in which the foreign entity operates.[2] Thus, foreign currency units must

---

[1]Such factors as intercompany accounts, less than 100 percent ownership, and the like create some implementation problems.

[2]In some cases, it may be permissible to maintain the financial statements of the subsidiary in dollars rather than the currency of the country in which the subsidiary is located. Subsidiaries operating in countries that have experienced hyperinflation (100 percent or higher) for more than 3 years are required to have dollar-denominated financial statements. There are other circumstances under which dollars may be used, and some firms may be able to choose between the local currency and the dollar. Generally, subsidiaries that conduct most of their activities in a foreign currency must maintain their financial statements in that currency. For example, the subsidiary of Ford Motor Company that is producing and selling in Germany has no choice but to maintain financial statements in deutsche marks. These statements must be translated into dollars when statements are consolidated.

be converted to the currency of the parent before accounts can be consolidated. The problem is made substantially more difficult by the fact that market exchange rates are constantly in flux, and there is always the question of which exchange rate gives the best picture about what is happening at the subsidiary level.

In the United States, the procedures used to consolidate the financial statements of foreign subsidiaries are detailed in the *Statement of Financial Accounting Standards No. 52 (FASB 52)*, which has been in effect since 1982.[3] To consolidate the financial statements of foreign subsidiaries with those of an American parent, FASB 52 establishes three different exchange rates that must be applied to different accounts in the financial statements of the firm. The standards require that the income statement of the foreign subsidiary be converted to dollars using the *weighted average exchange rate* for the period covered by the statement. With respect to the balance sheet, common stock equity accounts are translated to dollars using *historical exchange rates*. All other balance sheet items are converted to dollars at the *current exchange rate*. The next sections of the chapter define and illustrate the meaning of these three different exchange rates.

Translating Income Statements

Under the most common set of circumstances, annual income statements of foreign subsidiaries are translated to dollars using the weighted average exchange rate. This rate is relatively simple to compute when the exchange rate has changed evenly during the year and the sales of the subsidiary have been spread evenly throughout the year. Under these assumptions, the weighted average is equal to the simple average exchange rate (the beginning rate plus the ending rate divided by 2).

In some cases, it is not so easy to compute the exchange rate necessary for the proper translation of income statement accounts. For example, if most of the sales took place early in the year, when the value of the currency was higher, greater weight would be placed on these early exchange rates. That is, the weighted average exchange rate would be higher than the simple average exchange rate. Another complication arises when the exchange rate exhibits a short, rapid change rather than an even decline throughout the year. For example, assume that the exchange rate is relatively stable over the entire year but drops suddenly at the end of the year. In this case, it is necessary to construct a weighted exchange rate that reflects these circumstances, since the simple average

---

[3]FASB 8 was used before the introduction of FASB 52. The methodology used under FASB 8 is discussed in Appendix 8A.

TABLE 8-1 Computation of the Weighted Average Exchange Rate (Sales in Thousands)

Month	Sales	Weight*	×	Exchange Rate	=	Product
January	£300	0.0545		$2.00		0.109
February	£400	0.0727		$1.95		0.142
March	£200	0.0364		$1.96		0.071
April	£300	0.0545		$1.91		0.104
May	£500	0.0909		$1.90		0.173
June	£900	0.1636		$1.82		0.298
July	£400	0.0727		$1.92		0.140
August	£300	0.0545		$190		0.104
September	£500	0.0909		$1.85		0.168
October	£400	0.0727		$1.80		0.131
November	£500	0.0909		$1.75		0.159
December	£800	0.1455		$1.80		0.262
Annual	£5,500		Weighted average exchange rate =			$1.860

$$*\text{Weight} = \frac{\text{monthly sales}}{\text{annual sales}}.$$

rate will not give a true picture of what has happened during the year. Similar situations also arise when a currency that is pegged to the dollar is suddenly devalued by government action. When translating accounts under these conditions, it is necessary to use an exchange rate that is weighted by the proportion of sales that were booked during each of the two exchange rate periods.

Table 8-1 shows how the weighted average exchange rate is computed when sales and exchange rates change at an uneven rate during the year. In this illustration, the exchange rate was £1 = $2.00 at the beginning of the year and £1 = $1.80 at the end of the year. A simple average rate for this period would have been $1.90, but this rate would not accurately reflect what happened to the dollar value of sales. As noted in Table 8-1, the weighted average rate, however, is equal to $1.86, not $1.90. The rate is computed by weighting each month's exchange rate. The weight is the proportion of annual sales occurring in that month. The weighted average exchange rate differs from the simple average exchange rate for two reasons: (1) the exchange rate did not decline evenly throughout the year and (2) sales were not distributed evenly throughout the year. When sales and exchange rates do change at an even pace, the weighted average exchange rate (as computed in Table 8-1) will be exactly the same as the simple average exchange rate computed by adding the beginning and ending exchange rates and dividing by 2.

It should be noted that two multinational firms operating in the same foreign country may use different weighted average exchange rates for translation of their income statements. This reflects the fact that sales of their foreign operations may be distributed differently. For example,

TABLE 8-2 Sabicer U.K. Corporation:* Translated Annual
Income Statement, 1988 (000 Omitted)

	In Pounds	In Dollars	Rate Used[†]
Revenues	£500	$875	($1.75)
Costs	£400	$700	($1.75)
Income before taxes	£100	$175	($1.75)
Taxes (40%)	£40	$70	($1.75)
Income after taxes	£60	$105	($1.75)
Dividend	£0	$0	($1.75)
Retained earnings	£60	$105	($1.75)

*Assumes that costs and taxes are evenly distributed throughout the year.
[†]Weighted average exchange rate for 1988.

the sales of the subsidiary of one firm may be concentrated early in the year, while the sales of the other firm's subsidiary may be concentrated at the end of the year. The point to note is that the weighted average exchange rate is unique to the particular firm.

Table 8-2 illustrates how the income statement of a foreign subsidiary is translated in dollars. Let us assume that the value of the pound declined evenly throughout the year from a beginning value of $2.00 to an ending value of $1.50. In addition, assume that the sales of the Sabicer Corporation were evenly distributed throughout the year. In this case, the weighted average exchange rate is £1 = $1.75.[4] The translated income statement for Sabicer is presented in Table 8-2. Note that the exchange rate at the end of 1988 was £1 = $1.50, but that was not the rate used to translate the income statement. For income statement translation, it is necessary to develop an exchange rate that is representative of the entire year during which the income was earned.

It is important for the manager to recognize that translating the income statements of foreign subsidiaries is a relatively complicated process under our present fluctuating exchange rate system.[5] If sales and exchange rate movements even approximate the conditions assumed in Table 8-2, there is a tendency to use a simple average exchange rate. In other cases (Table 8-1), the pattern of revenue and exchange rate movement is so variable that more complicated procedures must be implemented.

---

[4](Beginning rate + ending rate)/2 = ($2.00 + $1.50)/2 = $1.75.

[5]The firm may have to compute more than one weighted average rate for a particular year. If, for example, the timing of cash expenses is not similar to that of sales, their weighted average rates may be different.

Impact of Exchange Rate Fluctuations on Translated Income Statements

The fact that the income statements of foreign subsidiaries are maintained in foreign currency units and must be translated into dollars for the publication of consolidated financial statements can cause reported consolidated income to fluctuate substantially. A strengthening foreign currency tends to inflate the reported dollar profits reported for the foreign operations. On the other hand, a weakening foreign currency makes it appear that foreign operations are less profitable than previously. These propositions are illustrated in Table 8-3, which assumes that the Sabicer U.K. Corporation's earnings after taxes are the same (£60,000) for each of the 3 years covered in the table. It is also assumed that Sabicer U.K. retains all of its income each year (pays no dividends to its parent). Thus, the parent gets the same amount of cash each year (zero), regardless of the exchange rate.

Note that the profits reported on the consolidated income statement fluctuate widely as the exchange rate fluctuates. As the price of the pound goes down to £1 = $1.75, the profits reported fall from $120,000 to $105,000. In other words, the subsidiary earns a lower dollar income even though it is earning just as many pounds as in the previous year. As the pound strengthens to £1 = $2.25 in 1989, the dollar value of the earnings increase dramatically. When considered from the point of view of dollars, subsidiary income appears to be fluctuating widely. When looked at from the point of view of pounds, subsidiary income is stable.

Of course, managers of multinational corporations are not usually pleased by the prospect of reporting reduced dollar profits due to exchange rate fluctuations. Reporting reduced profits is especially bothersome since flows to both the subsidiary and the parent are exactly the same, regardless of the exchange rate used to translate the accounts. The subsidiary still has its £60,000, and the parent receives no dividend in any case. A weakening of the pound may indicate less profitability when no

TABLE 8-3 Sabicer U.K. Corporation: Impact of Exchange Rate Movements on Translated Income and Retained Earnings (000 Omitted)

Year	Exchange Rate*	Income £	Income $	Dividends £	Dividends $	Retained Earnings £	Retained Earnings $
1987	$2.00	£60	$120	0	0	£60	$120
1988	$1.75	£60	$105	0	0	£60	$105
1989	$2.25	£60	$135	0	0	£60	$135

*The exchange rate used is the weighted average exchange rate for each year expressed as a direct quote of the pound.

one has less. This potential reduction in the reported dollar value of foreign subsidiary earnings is the essence of translation exposure.

Under the accounting rules in effect at the present time, translation exposure in the income statement may be labeled *exposure of profits*, since it arises from the fact that the decreased (or increased) dollar value of the profits of a foreign subsidiary must be reported even though these profits may be retained in the foreign country. Generally speaking, managers are quick to inform the public about the adverse effects of exchange rate movements on reported dollar profits associated with foreign subsidiary income. This may give management the opportunity to shift the blame for declining profits to events beyond their control. On the other hand, managers make much less noise when exchange rate movements drive up reported dollar profits. In a sense, managers tend to blame the exchange rate fluctuations for profit reductions but attribute reported dollar profit increases to their skill as managers. In reality, however, managers cannot do very much about either situation.

Note that dividend flows from the subsidiary to the parent have a different type of exposure than profits in general. Conceptually, the exposure of dividends is a type of transaction (not translation) exposure.[6] In this regard, an expected dividend is no different than an expected interest payment from a subsidiary. Thus, the profits of a foreign subsidiary are exposed in a transaction sense only if the subsidiary pays a dividend to the parent. In the context of Table 8-3, if the subsidiary had been paying out all of its earnings in dividends, the cash flow to the parent would indeed have been affected. Expected dividends are a component of transaction exposure. Profits are not included as part of transaction exposure if they are retained by the subsidiary. However, all profits (retained or not) are part of translation exposure.

Finally, note that the retained earnings in Table 8-3 come from the subsidiary income statement but will be transferred to accumulated retained earnings in the consolidated balance sheet of the parent firm. Naturally, a strengthening of the foreign currency will result in relatively large increases in the accumulated retained earnings account of the parent (and vice versa).

Translating Balance Sheets: The Equity Accounts

The local currency values of the equity accounts in the balance sheet of foreign subsidiaries of an American multinational firm are translated into dollars using historical exchange rates. Table 8-4 shows how the dollar

---

[6]Chapter 7 discussed the options open to the firm in hedging its transaction exposure.

TABLE 8-4   Donegal U.K. Corporation: Derivation of Balance Sheet Entries for
Common Stock (CS), December 31, 1986, (000 Omitted)

New CS sold (Pounds)	Total CS on Subsidiary Balance Sheet	Exchange Rate on Date of CS Sale	$ Value of New CS	Total CS on Parent Balance Sheet
£100 (1983)	£100	£1 = $1.75	$175	$175
£150 (1984)	£250	£1 = $2.00	$300	$475
£200 (1986)	£450	£1 = $2.25	$450	$925

value of common stock would be computed for the Donegal U.K. Corporation (a subsidiary of the Donegal U.S. Corporation). Note that in 1986
the value of the subsidiary's common stock is £450,000 and can be
translated to $925,000. The $925,000 value is computed by adding the
dollar value of all sales of common stock (in this case, there are three
sales). The dollar value of each sale is computed by multiplying the local
currency value of the sale by the exchange rate that prevailed on the date
of that sale. These dollar values for each sale never change even if the
exchange rate changes. The rate at which existing local currency common
stock accounts are translated into dollars is locked in and does not vary
as the exchange rate goes up and down. Exchange rate movements affect
the dollar value of common stock only to the extent that new common
stock is sold.

The accumulated retained earnings in the balance sheet of the
multinational firm are computed in a similar fashion. When a foreign
subsidiary earns income and retains it, that income is converted to dollars
at the weighted average exchange rate for the period (Table 8-1). The
dollar value of the new retained income is now added to the accumulated retained earnings on the balance sheet of the American parent. This
dollar value is isolated from future exchange rate movements. It does not
change as exchange rates go up and down. Looking back at Table 8-2,
$105,000 would be added to the parent's accumulated retained earnings.
Presumably, income retained by the subsidiary during 1988 would be
converted to dollars using a weighted average exchange rate reflecting
conditions in 1988. The dollar value of the 1988 retained earnings would
then be added to the parent's accumulated retained earnings. Note that
the weighted average 1988 exchange rate is applied only to 1988 retained
income, not to income retained in previous years. Once again, we see
that the dollar value of accumulated retained earnings is locked in and
does not vary as the exchange rate varies.

Translating Assets and Liabilities

The previous two sections have described the exchange rate that is used
to translate the income statement and the equity accounts in the balance

sheet. The computations required to determine the proper exchange rate are complex. FASB 52, however, requires a simple exchange rate for all assets and liabilities in the balance sheet: the *current rate*. The current rate is defined as the exchange rate existing at the instant the translation is made. Thus, the firm need only check *The Wall Street Journal* on the date the translation is made to determine the current rate.

The Cumulative Translation Adjustment

If exchange rates were fixed and never varied, the translation and consolidation of financial statements would be relatively simple. For example, consider the situation illustrated in Table 8-5: the 1987 balance sheet for the Sabicer U.K. Corporation, which is a subsidiary of the Sabicer Corporation. We will assume that the subsidiary was established in 1980 and that the exchange rate has remained constant (£1 = \$2.00) for the entire period of time. Since the exchange rate has been constant, the current, historical, and weighted average rates are all equal to £1 = \$2.00. This makes the translation process relatively simple. Note that when exchange rates are constant over the entire period, the balance sheet automatically balances.

Exchange rates, however, are not constant, and balance sheets are not so easily balanced. For example, Table 8-6 assumes that at the end of 1987, the value of the pound had a one-time drop to £1 = \$1.50. As discussed earlier, the common stock and retained earnings accounts are computed using historical rates, while the other balance sheet accounts use the spot exchange rate that existed on the statement date. Now comes the problem. When the current exchange rate departs from the

TABLE 8-5 Sabicer U.K. Corporation Balance Sheet as of December 1987 (000 Omitted)

	In Pounds	**In Dollars**	**Rate Used**
Current assets	£300	\$600	(\$2.00)
Fixed assets	£700	\$1,400	(\$2.00)
Total assets	£1,000	\$2,000	
Liabilities	£400	\$800	(\$2.00)
Common stock	£350	\$700	Historical*
Retained earnings	£250	\$500	Historical*
Total	£1,000	\$2,000	

*The historical rate used is equal to £1 = \$2.00, since there has been no change in the exchange rate.

TABLE 8-6 Sabicer U.K. Corporation: Translated 1987 Balance Sheet with Different Exchange Rates,* Ignoring the Cumulative Translation Account (000 Omitted)

	Current Rate = $2.00	Current Rate = $1.50	Difference
Current assets	$600*	$450*	$150
Fixed assets	$1,400*	$1,050*	$350
Total assets	$2,000	$1,500	$500
Liabilities	$800*	$600*	$200
Common stock	$700[†]	$700[†]	0
Retained earnings	$500[†]	$500[†]	0
Total claims	$2,000	$1,800	$200

*Translated using the current statement date exchange rate. The first column assumes that the current rate has held at its historical level of £1 = $2.00. The second column assumes that there has been a one-time drop in the exchange rate of £1 = $1.50.
[†]Translated using the historical rate of £1 = $2.00.

historical rate of £1 = $2.00, the balance sheet no longer balances. As shown in Table 8-6, when the current rate fell to £1 = $1.50, total assets equaled $1,500,000, while total claims equaled $1,800,000. That is, total assets declined by a larger amount than did total claims, and there is a $300,000 discrepancy between total assets and total claims. The reason for this is clear: while all of the assets were translated at the current exchange rate, those claims called *equities* were translated at the historical exchange rate. It is the unwillingness to translate the equity accounts at the current exchange rate that causes this problem.

TABLE 8-7 Sabicer U.K. Corporation: Translated 1987 Balance Sheet with Different Exchange Rates* and a Cumulative Translation Account (000 Omitted)

	Current Rate = $2.00	Current Rate = $1.50	Difference
Current assets	$600*	$450*	$150
Fixed assets	$1,400*	$1,050*	$350
Total assets	$2,000	$1,500	$500
Liabilities	$800*	$600*	$200
Common stock	$700[†]	$700[†]	0
Retained earnings	$500[†]	$500[†]	0
CTA	0	($300)	$300
Total claims	$2,000	$1,500	$500

*Translated using the current statement date exchange rate. The first column assumes that the current rate has held at its historical level of £1 = $2.00. The second column assumes that there has been a one-time drop in the exchange rate to £1 = $1.50.
[†]Translated using the historical rate of £1 = $2.00.

The most straightforward way of achieving balance would be to simply reduce the size of the retained earnings account. Using this solution, the $300,000 would first be reported as a loss on the income statement and would then be transferred to the balance sheet as a reduction in retained earnings. This solution is very unattractive to the multinational firm because income would fluctuate wildly as exchange rates go up and down.

FASB 52 solves the problem of fluctuating earnings by establishing an account that is called the *cumulative translation adjustment* (*CTA*). As shown in Table 8-7, a negative $300,000 would be recorded in the CTA account. Note that this account is considered part of equity, but the transactions that underlie the CTA account do not "pass through" the income statement. In effect, equity has been reduced by $300,000 even though no reduction appears on the income statement. Whenever the foreign currency used by the subsidiary changes in value, negative or positive amounts are added to the CTA account. At any point in time, this account may be positive or negative, depending on the cumulative effects of exchange rate changes. The CTA account can be viewed as the necessary entry that will force the statement into balance.

Translating Financial Statements: Foreign Currency Decreases in Value

In order to illustrate the procedures used to translate the financial statements of a foreign subsidiary into dollars, let us take another look at the Sabicer U.K. Corporation. Assume that during 1988 the subsidiary earns a profit of £60,000, all of which is retained and reinvested by the subsidiary in fixed assets. Once again, assume that the historical rate of exchange up to December 1987 was constant at £1 = $2.00, the current exchange rate (on December 1988) was £1 = $1.50, and the weighted average exchange rate for 1988 was £1 = $1.75. Table 8-8 shows the Sabicer U.K. financial statements in both British pounds and translated into dollars using FASB 52.

The only complicated part of the translation involves the equity accounts. Note the increase in the amount of retained earnings reported on the balance sheet. This reflects the fact that the subsidiary earned and retained £60,000. The £60,000 is translated into dollars using the weighted average exchange rate for 1988, which means that 1988 retained earnings are $105,000 higher than 1987 retained earnings (see Table 8-5). The total of liabilities, common stock, and retained earnings would be equal to $1,905,000. This figure would be $315,000 higher than total assets. The gap between total assets and total claims is balanced by the entry of ($315,000) in the cumulative translation adjustment. Note once again that

TABLE 8-8 Sabicer U.K. Corporation: Balance Sheet and Income Statement (000 Omitted)

| | Income Statement for 1988 | | |
	In Pounds	In Dollars	Rate Used*
Revenues	£500	$875	W ($1.75)
Costs	£400	$700	W ($1.75)
Income before taxes	£100	$175	W ($1.75)
Taxes (40%)	£40	$70	W ($1.75)
Income after taxes	£60	$105	W ($1.75)
Dividend	£0	$0	W ($1.75)
Retained earnings	£60	$105	W ($1.75)

| | Balance Sheet as of December 1988 | | | |
	1987 in Pounds	1988 in Pounds	1988 in Dollars	Rate Used*
Current assets	£300	£300	$450	C ($1.50)
Fixed assets	£700	£760	$1,140	C ($1.50)
Total assets	£1,000	£1,060	$1,590	
Liabilities	£400	£400	$600	C ($1.50)
Common stock	£350	£350	$700	Historical
Retained earnings	£250	£310	$605†	Historical
CTA	n/a	n/a	($315)‡	
Total Claims	£1,000	£1,060	$1,590	

*Exchange rate used in translation: W = weighted average rate, C = current rate, H = historical rate.

†Retained earnings, Dec. 1988 = R.E. Dec. 1987 + R.E. during 1988 = $500 (Table 8-7) + $105 = $605

‡CTA = assets (new − old) + liabilities(old − new) + profits
   (old − weighted average)
   = £1,060(1.50 − 2.00) + £400(2.00 − 1.50) + £60(2.00 − 1.75)
   = −$530 + $200 + $15 = ($315)

this adjustment is considered a reduction in equity, but it is not passed through the income statement.[7]

Translating Financial Statements: Foreign Currency Increases in Value

Table 8-9 illustrates the impact of an increase in the value of the pound on the financial statements of the Sabicer Corporation. We will assume that the current rate increased from £1 = $2.00 at the beginning of the

---

[7]The lower portions of Tables 8-8 and 8-9 show the computation of the CTA account.

TABLE 8-9   Sabicer U.K. Corporation: Balance Sheet and Income Statement
(000 Omitted)

| | Income Statement for 1988 | | |
	In Pounds	In Dollars	Rate Used
Revenues	£500	$1,100	W ($2.20)
Costs	£400	$880	W ($2.20)
Income before taxes	£100	$220	W ($2.20)
Taxes (40%)	£40	$88	W ($2.20)
Income after taxes	£60	$132	W ($2.20)
Dividend	£0	$0	W ($2.20)
Retained earnings	£60	$132	W ($2.20)

| | Balance Sheet as of December 1988 | | |
	In Pounds	in Dollars	Rate Used
Current assets	£300	$750	C ($2.50)
Fixed assets	£760	$1,900	C ($2.50)
Total assets	£1,060	$2,650	
Liabilities	£400	$1,000	C ($2.50)
Common stock	£350	$700	Historical
Retained earnings	£310	$632*	Historical
CTA	£0	+$318†	
Total	£1,060	$2,650	

*Retained earnings Dec. 1988 = R.E. Dec. 1987 + R.E. during 1988
$$= \$500 \text{ (Table 8-7)} + \$132 = \$632$$
†CTA = Assets(new − old) + liabilities(old − new) + profits
(old − weighted average)
$$= £1,060(2.50 − 2.00) + £400(2.00 − 2.50) + £60(2.00 − 2.20)$$
$$= +\$530 − \$200 − \$12 = +\$318$$

year to £1 = $2.50 on December 31, 1988. In this case, the value of the pound did not advance at a constant rate throughout the year, and the applicable weighted average exchange rate for the year is £1 = $2.20. The historical rate for common stock and retained earnings before 1988 remains at £1 = $2.00. The historical rate for the 1988 addition to retained earnings, however, is $2.20.

Under these assumptions, the translated financial statements of Sabicer U.K. look quite different.[8] The increase in the value of the assets caused by the increase in the value of the pound far exceeds the increase in the value of the liabilities. The total of liabilities, common stock, and retained earnings is equal to only $2,332,000. This figure is $318,000 lower than total assets. Thus, the CTA is a *positive* $318,000. Sabicer has experienced a gain due to the fluctuation in the value of the pound. Just

---

[8]Note that the British pound values in the balance sheet and the income statement are exactly the same as in Table 8-8.

TABLE 8-10 CTA Account for a Hypothetical Firm (in Millions)

Year	Foreign Exchange Profits/Losses during the Year	CTA
1980	+$50	+$50
1981	−$30	+$20
1982	−$40	−$20
1983	−$30	−$50
1984	+$40	−$10
1985	+$60	+$50
1986	−$20	−$30
1987	−$30	0

as in the previous case, FASB 52 excludes foreign exchange gains from the income statement and reported earnings of the firm. The gain is included in the CTA account.

CTA Account

As its name indicates, the cumulative translation adjustment (CTA) account measures the *cumulative* impact of foreign exchange fluctuations on the financial statements of the firm. In other words, the CTA shows all the changes caused by exchange rate fluctuations since the foreign subsidiary was established. As illustrated in Table 8-10, the fact that the CTA is negative at a given point in time does not mean that the firm incurred foreign exchange losses in the most recent year. A negative CTA should be interpreted as meaning that over its history, the firm's foreign exchange losses have been greater than its gains. In 1984, for example, Table 8-10 shows that the firm experienced a foreign exchange gain of $40,000,000. The CTA reported on the balance sheet, however, showed a negative $10,000,000. This negative amount reflects the cumulative effects of the firm's historical experience.

Hedging Translation Exposure: An Introduction

Translation exposure is the extent to which the multinational firm's consolidated financial statements are affected by the need to convert its foreign subsidiaries' financial statements into dollars. The translation exposure arises from the fact that the dollar values of the foreign subsidiaries' financial statements will fluctuate as the exchange rate fluctuates. When managers of the multinational firm worry about translation exposure, they tend to focus on two particular accounts: subsidiary profits and the CTA.

The amount of translation exposure associated with subsidary profits is determined by the relative size of expected subsidiary profits (or losses). For example, assume that the Sabicer U.K. Corporation expects next year's profits to be £60,000. As noted in Tables 8-8 and 8-9, the dollar value of this amount will be substantially different, depending on exchange rate developments. If the value of the pound declines to $1.50 (Table 8-8), the earnings will translate into $105,000. If the value of the pound increases to $2.50 (Table 8-9), the earnings will translate into $132,000.[9] If Sabicer U.K.'s operations are very small relative to the operations of the multinational corporation as a whole, exchange rate fluctuations will not present a major problem to the parent when it reports consolidated income. However, if the foreign subsidiary is a very large part of the multinational's total operations, the profits reported on the consolidated financial statements could be greatly affected by foreign exchange rate fluctuations. Thus, multinational firms that earn a substantial portion of their profits through foreign subsidiaries are most vulnerable to translation exposure.

The amount of translation exposure associated with the CTA is related to the relative size of the foreign subsidiary and the extent to which subsidiary assets are financed by equity. Even though the equity adjustments reflected in the CTA do not pass through the income statement, multinational managers are not very enthusiastic about having large negative entries in this account. Looking back once again at Tables 8-8 and 8-9, we see that the subsidiary had assets of £1,060,000 and the resulting CTAs were ($315,000) and +$318,000, respectively. If the assets were 10 times larger, the CTAs would have been 10 times larger (ceterus paribus) and the impact on the multinational firm would have been greater. It is also important to note that the multinational's CTA translation exposure will depend on the extent to which the subsidiary is financed by debt. If, taken to a ridiculous extreme, the subsidiary is financed 100 percent by debt (has no equity), there will be no CTA exposure because liabilities will be reduced and/or increased by the same amount as assets. Firms using higher proportions of equity are more vulnerable to CTA translation exposure.

Managers are concerned that foreign exchange rate–induced profit reductions and large negative CTAs will signal investors (the stock market) that there has been a change in the profitability of the firm when in fact the cash flows have not been affected in any way. Managers worry that the inability of the investment community to understand the nature

---

[9]Note that the weighted average exchange rate used in Table 8-8 was $1.75 and in Table 8-9 was $2.20.

of profit reductions due to exchange rate movements will cause undesirable fluctuations in stock price and lead to criticism of management policies. This concern over fluctuating profits, stock prices, and shareholder wealth has led managers to seek ways of reducing the impact of reduced foreign currency values on the reported financial statements of the multinational.

It should be noted that many economists and security market analysts disagree with the assertion that stock market prices will vary in response to translation changes attributable to exchange rate movements. These individuals maintain that security analysts are very proficient at identifying the source of income changes and recognizing that these exchange rate–related income changes may have no significant impact on the long-term profitability of the corporation as a whole. According to this view, stock prices will not go up and down just because exchange rates introduce artificial and perhaps purely cosmetic changes in income. Thus, many economists and security market analysts argue that the firm should ignore translation exposure and refrain from spending time and money in an attempt to manage it. Today this is still a controversial issue, but more and more managers are moving toward the "ignore" position.

The goal of financial management is to maximize stockholder wealth. Assuming that the market recognizes changes in financial statements caused by foreign exchange fluctuations, it leads to some interesting conclusions. Hedging transaction exposure to improve the appearance of financial statements may reduce stockholder wealth to the extent of the costs incurred in such actions.[10]

Hedging Translation Exposure of Profits

In the illustration that follows, we will show how a forward market hedge could be used to reduce translation exposure. Note that to hedge successfully the translation exposure associated with the profits of a foreign subsidiary, it is necessary to develop accurate forecasts of several values. First, it is necessary to develop a forecast of subsidiary profits in local currency. It is also necessary to forecast both the future spot rate and the expected weighted average exchange rate for the year covered by the income statement. Remember that it is particularly difficult to forecast exchange rates. This means, of course, that hedging strategies can backfire quite easily.

We will begin our illustration by assuming that the Sabicer U.K. Corporation forecasts 1988 earnings at £60,000. Sabicer believes that the value of the pound will deteriorate over 1988 and that the £60,000 will be

---

[10]Note that the same may not be said of either economic or transaction exposure. These issues were discussed in greater detail in the previous two chapters.

TABLE 8-11 Sabicer Corporation: Hypothetical Hedge for Translation Exposure of Profits

1. Sabicer sells £33,333 in the forward market at a rate of £1 = $1.95.
2. Expected dollar profit without the hedge:
   Pound profit × weighted average exchange rate = dollar profit
   £60,000 × $1.75 = $105,000
3. Expected profit on the hedge:
   Number of pounds sold forward × (forward rate − forecasted spot rate)
   £33,333 × ($1.95 − $1.50) = +$15,000
4. Expected total profits for 1988:
   Profits from subsidiary operations + profits from hedge
   $105,000 + $15,000 = $120,000.

worth fewer dollars than in previous years. If the firm desires to reduce the possible volatility in the dollar value of these earnings, it could sell the pounds forward. This would lock in an exchange rate and eliminate the uncertainty about the dollar value of the expected profit of £60,000. In order to implement the hedge, the firm must first develop precise forecasts of the number of pounds to be sold forward, the expected future spot rate, and the expected weighted average exchange rate for the year. Equation 8-1 shows the amount of foreign currency that must be hedged in the forward market.

Amount hedged = forecasted profits

$$\times \frac{(\text{forecasted weighted rate} - \text{current rate})}{(\text{forward rate} - \text{forecasted spot rate})} \quad (8\text{-}1)$$

Let us assume that the managers of the firm expect the spot rate on the pound to fall from a current level of £1 = $2.00 (current rate) to $1.50 (forecasted spot rate) in 1 year. In addition, the weighted average rate is expected to be $1.75. The managers know that if this happens, the translated value of subsidiary profits will be lower than if the exchange rate had not changed. In order to protect translated profits, the managers can sell pounds in the forward market at a rate of £1 = $1.95. The number of pounds that must be sold in the forward market would be equal to

$$\text{Amount hedged} = £60,000 \times \frac{(\$1.75 - \$2.00)}{(\$1.95 - \$1.50)} = -£33,333$$

Table 8-11 illustrates what happens if the forecasts made by Sabicer turn out to be completely accurate.[11] As shown in the table, Sabicer will make a profit on the forward transaction, which will offset the reduction

---

[11] The illustration is highly simplified and designed solely to show the difficulties of hedging translation exposure.

in the dollar value of subsidiary profits due to the reduction in the value of the pound. Subsidiary profits go down for one reason (a weaker pound) and go up for another (a gain on the forward transaction), and the dollar value of the subsidiary profits remain unchanged. The total profits of the subsidiary will be equal to $120,000, the same as they would have been if the exchange rate had remained at £1 = $2.00.[12]

Note that the amount of profit on the hedge depends on the difference between the forward rate and the expected future spot rate. Sabicer made a profit on the forward contract because it forecast the future spot exchange rate at $1.50, while the forward market had a $1.95 forecast. In other words, the profit really resulted from the firm's ability to outguess other forward market participants. As suggested in previous chapters, the evidence does not show that firms can consistently outguess the market. Generally, the forward rate is expected to be an unbiased estimator of the future spot rate. Therefore, the firm should expect to receive what the forward market promises.

The hedge could have backfired on the Sabicer Corporation. If, for example, the spot rate at the end of the year was £1 = $2.20, Sabicer made a mistake in selling £33,333 forward at a rate of £1 = $1.95. The firm would be required to deliver pounds in return for $1.95 rather than receive the $2.20 per pound it could have had if the position had remained unhedged.

While Table 8-11 shows the firm making a profit on its hedging transaction and thus stabilizing earnings, the story behind the table is more complicated. The real implication of Table 8-11 is that the translated profits of the subsidiary will generally be the same whether or not the firm hedges the profits. This type of hedge will eliminate translation exchange rate risk only if the firm is a superior forecaster. To stabilize reported dollar profits, the firm must accurately forecast the future spot rate. In addition, the firm must forecast the weighted average exchange rate for the period. This means that it must forecast both the sales pattern for the year and the pattern of change in the exchange rate. The ability of any firm to do this accurately and consistently is very doubtful. This is one of the reasons why many economists advise firms not to hedge the translation exposure of profits.

Hedging the CTA

Forward contract hedges cannot be used to eliminate the translation exposure associated with the CTA account, since the profits and losses on

---

[12]We will ignore any tax implications for gains or losses resulting from the forward contracts.

such transactions have very little impact on the CTA.[13] The major determinant of the size of the CTA is the difference between subsidiary assets and liabilities, not profits. Increasing profits, even if it were possible, would not solve the problem of negative CTAs.

There is one strategy that seems appropriate for managing the CTA translation exposure. This strategy involves financing the foreign subsidiary with debt rather than equity. By doing so, the firm increases the proportion of total claims that will be translated at the current rate and reduces the size of the CTA. Thus, an American parent may be able to reduce the CTA exposure associated with a foreign subsidiary by lending money to the subsidiary rather than taking a strong equity position in the subsidiary. The drawback of this strategy is that payments by the subsidiary to the parent can be deferred in the case of dividends but not in the case of interest payments. Thus, the parent may be exposing itself to American income taxes by using debt rather than equity financing for its subsidiaries. In addition, the profitability of the subsidiary may look artificially low due to the increased interest costs associated with high levels of debt financing. In addition, the strategy adopted by the multinational firm must reflect the tax laws as well as other regulations in the two countries.

Since the advisability of translation exposure hedging is questionable, this book contains no detailed discussion of the topic. Hedging activities should be aimed at reducing the riskiness of cash flows rather than dressing up financial statements. In fact, hedging for translation exposure may actually increase transaction exposure. In the context of Table 7-1, for example, an increase in forward contract commitments that is not related to transaction exposure may increase transaction exposure. That is, in its attempt to hedge translation exposure, the firm may wind up with a commitment to accept or deliver a foreign currency that may result in the creation of a long or short position in that currency.

Summary and Conclusions

Before the firm manages translation exposure, this exposure must be understood and measured. Under FASB 52, foreign subsidiary profits are less exposed to exchange rate movements than previously. This follows from the fact that balance sheet changes caused by foreign exchange fluctuations and reflected in the CTA do not directly affect the operating earnings of the firm. FASB 52 created a special account that reflects the cumulative impact of these profits or losses.

---

[13]Gains and losses on forward contracts may affect the amounts of retained earnings on the balance sheet and therefore the size of the CTA.

In addition to understanding the general rules for translating subsidiary financial statements into dollars, the manager must understand the limitations associated with attempts to hedge translation exposure. The risk reduction benefits of hedging transaction exposure (Chapter 7) are obvious. With respect to hedging translation exposure, the benefits are more difficult to calculate. Management may be able to reduce the volatility of translated subsidiary profits, but only if it can consistently outguess the forward market for foreign exchange. Reducing the volatility of the CTA through financial market hedging is not feasible and may result in an increase in the reported volatility of the operating earnings for the subsidiary. The managers of each firm must look carefully at the costs and benefits of translation exposure hedging.

Review Questions

1. Define translation exposure, indicate the type of firm that has such exposure, and discuss the relationship between translation exposure and shareholder wealth.
2. Explain how the income statements of a foreign subsidiary are translated. Why might two subsidiaries (located in the same country) of the same firm use different exchange rates when translating their income statements?
3. What is the purpose of the CTA account that has been mandated by FASB 52?
4. "The firm should use the forward market to fully hedge its total translation exposure (profits and CTA)." True or false? Explain your answer.
5. "Using the forward market to hedge the translation exposure associated with the CTA may result in an increase in the volatility of the reported operating earnings of the foreign subsidiary." True or false? Explain your answer.
6. Explain how attempts to hedge translation exposure using a forward market contract may increase transaction exposure.
7. Explain why a superior forecast of the future spot rate is needed if a forward market hedge of subsidiary profits is to be successful. Give a numerical example. What is the likelihood that a firm can make such a forecast?

Questions for Discussion

1. Assume that you are employed by a firm that is currently producing solely within the United States and selling in both the United States and the EEC. At the present time, your firm usually has a large long position in EEC currencies, and this results in substantial transaction exposure. The firm also believes that it has substantial economic exposure because a strengthening of the dollar will jeopardize both its foreign and domestic market shares. In order to control both its transaction and economic exposure, the firm is considering building a new production facility in the EEC (diversifying production) and establishing this facility as a separate, wholly owned subsidiary. However, top management is concerned about the impact of a foreign subsidiary on its consolidated financial statements. Specifically, it is worried that a foreign subsidiary would increase the volatility of its financial statements and affect stock prices. You are asked to evaluate and report on the situation.

2. Assume that you are employed by a moderate-sized American multinational firm with a subsidiary in France. The French subsidiary is expected to expand rapidly over the next decade and to have high, continuous French franc profits. If growth develops as expected, it is anticipated that the subsidiary's earnings will grow from 10 to 40 percent of total firm earnings. In order to finance the expected growth, the multinational parent anticipates that all of the French subsidiary's cash flows (profits plus depreciation) will be reinvested in France. Top management is worried that as the subsidiary's earnings grow, the translation exposure of the parent will increase. Management is particularly concerned that the consolidated profits of the firm as a whole will show increased variability, negatively affecting the value of the firm's common stock. You are asked to evaluate the desirability of using forward market hedging to reduce earnings volatility and thus increase the stock price.

Research Activities

1. "A typical German subsidiary of an American firm had negative entries in the CTA account during 1983." Based on published information, evaluate the validity of this statement.
2. "A typical Japanese subsidiary of an American firm had negative entries in the CTA account during 1986." Based on published information, evaluate the validity of this statement.

Problems

1. The Christine Corporation Germany has made the following sales of common stock:

Year	Stock Sold	Exchange Rate on That Date
1982	DM700,000,000	$0.40
1985	DM200,000,000	$0.30
1988	DM400,000,000	$0.20

a. What is the deutsche mark value of the firm's common stock account as of December 1988?
b. What is the translated dollar value of the firm's common stock account as of December 1988?

2. Estimate the current exchange rate for September and the weighted average exchange rate for the 3-month period, given the following information:

Month	Sales	Exchange Rate
July	DM30,000,000	$0.30
August	DM50,000,000	$0.28
September	DM20,000,000	$0.20

3. International Products Germany is a wholly owned subsidiary of International Products U.S. The 1988 income statement and balance sheet at the end of 1988 (in

millions) are as follows:

INCOME STATEMENT FOR 1988

Sales	DM300
Costs	DM200
Income before taxes	DM100
Taxes	DM20
Income after taxes	DM80

BALANCE SHEET

	Dec. 1987	Dec. 1988
Current assets	DM400	DM400
Fixed assets	DM600	DM680
Total assets	DM1,000	DM1,080
Liabilities	DM400	DM400
Common stock	DM400	DM400
Retained earnings	DM200	DM280
Total	DM1,000	DM1,080

a. Assuming that the rate of exchange has remained constant at DM1 = $0.40 throughout the entire history of the firm, prepare a translation to the dollar balance sheet and income statement for the subsidiary.

b. Assuming that the rate of exchange has remained constant at DM1 = $0.40 from the beginning of the subsidiary to December 1987 *and* that it has declined throughout 1988 to DM1 = $0.30, prepare a dollar balance sheet (December 1988) and an income statement (1988) for the subsidiary (assume that the weighted average exchange rate is $0.35).

4. Using the information provided in Problem 3, prepare a dollar balance sheet (December 1988) and an income statement (1988) for the subsidiary if the value of the deutsche mark has increased during 1988 to $0.50. In addition, assume that the weighted average exchange rate is $0.45.

5. International Manufacturing Britain is a wholly owned subsidiary of International Manufacturing U.S. The 1987 balance sheet of the subsidiary, in both dollars and pounds (in millions), and the 1988 income statement (in pounds) are as follows:

BALANCE SHEET (DECEMBER 1987)

	Pounds	Dollars
Current assets	£100	$150
Fixed assets	£300	$450
Total assets	£400	$600
Liabilities	£100	$150
Common stock	£100	$180
Retained earnings	£200	$290
CTA		($20)
Total	£400	$600

INCOME STATEMENT FOR 1988

Sales	£600
Costs	£500
Income before taxes	£100
Taxes	£20
Income after taxes	£80
Dividends	0
Addition to RE	£80

a. Prepare a balance sheet (denominated in pounds) as of the end of 1988. The subsidiary sold £50 million in new equity during March. The exchange rate at that time was £1 = $1.40. Assume that *all* increases in equity accounts are used to purchase fixed assets.

b. Prepare a dollar-denominated income statement for 1988, given the following assumptions:

	January–June	July–December
Sales	£240	£360
Exchange rate	£1 = $1.40	£1 = $1.35

c. Prepare a dollar-denominated balance sheet as of the end of 1988. Note that the exchange rate of the pound as of December 1988 is $1.35.

6. International Manufacturing Britain is a wholly owned subsidiary of International Manufacturing U.S. The 1987 balance sheet of the subsidiary, in both dollars and pounds (in millions), and the 1988 income statement (in pounds) are.

BALANCE SHEET (DECEMBER 1987)

	Pounds	Dollars
Current assets	£100	$150
Fixed assets	£300	$450
Total assets	£400	$600
Liabilities	£100	$150
Common stock	£100	$180
Retained earnings	£200	$290
CTA		($20)
Total	£400	$600

INCOME STATEMENT FOR 1988

Sales	£600
Costs	£500
Income before taxes	£100
Taxes	£20
Income after taxes	£80
Dividends	0
Addition to RE	£80

a. Prepare a balance sheet (denominated in pounds) as of the end of 1988. The subsidiary sold £50 million in new equity during March. The exchange rate at that time was £1 = $1.50. Assume that *all* increases in equity accounts are used to purchase fixed assets.

b. Prepare a dollar-denominated income statement for 1988, given the following assumptions:

	January–June	July–December
Sales	£200	£400
Exchange rate	£1 = $1.50	£1 = $1.65

c. Prepare a dollar-denominated balance sheet as of the end of 1988. Note that the exchange rate of the pound as of December 1988 is $1.65.

Bibliography

Adler, Michael, and Dumas, Bernard. "Should Exposure Management Depend on Translation Accounting Methods?" *Euromoney*, June 1981, pp. 132–138.

Aggarwal, Raj. "FASB No. 8 and Reported Results of Multinational Operations: Hazard for Managers and Investors." *Journal of Accounting, Auditing, and Finance*, Spring 1978, pp. 197–216.

Barrett, M. Edgar, and Spero, Leslie L. "Accounting Determinants of Foreign Exchange Gains and Losses." *Financial Analysts Journal*, March–April 1975, pp. 26–30.

Beaver, William, and Wolfson, Mark. "Foreign Currency Translation Gains and Losses: What Effect Do They Have and What Do They Mean?" *Financial Analysts Journal*, March–April 1984, pp. 28–36.

Choi, Frederick D. S., and Bavishi, Vinod. "Diversity in Multinational Accounting." *Financial Executive*, August 1982, pp. 45–49.

Donaldson, H., and Reinstein, A. "Implementing FASB No. 52: The Critical Issues." *Financial Executive*, June 1983, pp. 40–42.

Fantl, Irving L. "Problems with Currency Translation—A Report of FASB No. 8." *Financial Executive*, December 1979, pp. 33–36.

Financial Accounting Standards Board. *Accounting for the Translation of Foreign Currency Transactions and Foreign Currency Financial Statements*. Statement of Financial Accounting Standards No. 8. Stamford, CT: Financial Accounting Standards Board, 1975.

Financial Accounting Standards Board. *Foreign Currency Translation*. Statement of Financial Accounting Standards No. 52. Stamford, CT: Financial Accounting Standards Board, 1981.

Foreign Currency Translation: Understanding and Applying FAS 52. New York: Price Waterhouse and Company. 1981.

Garlicki, T. Dessa, Fabozzi, Frank J., and Fonfeder, Robert. "The Impact of Earnings Under FASB 52 on Equity Returns." *Financial Management*, Autumn 1987, pp. 36–44.

George, Abraham M. "Cash Flow versus Accounting Exposure to Currency Risk." *California Management Review*, Summer 1978, pp. 50–55.

Gernon, H. "The Effect of Translation on Multinational Corporations' Internal Performance Evaluation." *Journal of International Business Studies*, Spring–Summer 1983, pp. 103–112.

Giannotti, J. B. "FASB 52 Gives Treasurers the Scope FASB 8 Denied Them." *Euromoney*, April 1982, pp. 141–142.

Kemp, Donald. "The Attractiveness of Rule 52." *Euromoney*, November 1982, pp. 167–175.

Militello, Frederick C., Jr. "Statement No. 52: Changes in Financial Management Practices." *Financial Executive*, August 1983, pp. 48–51.

Reier, Sharon. "Life with FAS No. 52." *Institutional Investor*, November 1983, pp. 223–225.

Veazey, Richard F., and Kim, Suk H. "Translation of Foreign Currency Operations: SFAS No. 52." *Columbia Journal of World Business*, Winter 1982, pp. 17–22.

Wurst, Charles M., and Alleman, Raymond H. "Translation Adjustments for a Strong Dollar." *Financial Executive*, June 1984, pp. 38–41.

Appendix 8A

Other Methods of Translating Financial Statements

Since 1982, American multinational firms have been required to translate the financial statements of their foreign subsidiaries using the current rate method, which is defined in FASB 52.[14] The reader should be aware that this requirement is relatively new and could be changed in the future. It is also well to note that other countries have different requirements with respect to translating financial statements. For these reasons, it is useful to review two other widely used translation methodologies and compare them to the current rate method. In this appendix, we will look at the temporal method, which was required in the United States from 1976 to 1982 under FASB 8. We will also look at the current/noncurrent method, which is required in West Germany and several other important countries.

An Overview of Translation Methods

This appendix compares three translation methods: the *current rate method*, the *temporal method* (also called the *monetary/nonmonetary method*), and the *current/noncurrent method*. Each of these methods translates the

---

[14] The current rate method has been required for all financial statements with a fiscal year beginning December 15, 1982.

income statement in a similar manner: a weighted average exchange rate is used to convert the subsidiary's income statement into dollars. There is, however, one important exception related to the inclusion of balance sheet translation gains or losses on the income statement. Under the current rate method (FASB 52), a CTA is set up, thus bypassing the income statement. Under both the temporal method and the current/noncurrent method, the equivalent of a CTA is passed through the income statement. In other words, gains or losses caused by foreign exchange fluctuations are added to the annual income resulting from foreign operations. Thus, under the pre–FASB 52 arrangement, reported income tended to be much more variable.

The principles for translating the balance sheet are very different for each of the three translation methods. The differences lie in the particular exchange rate used to translate specific accounts. The principles underlying the translation methods are as follows:

1. *Current rate method* (FASB 52): All accounts (other than equity) are translated using the current rate.
2. *Temporal method* (FASB 8): Monetary accounts (other than equity) are translated using the current rate. Nonmonetary accounts (physical assets) and equity are translated using the rate that was in effect at the time the assets were acquired (historical rate).
3. *Current/noncurrent method*: Current assets and current liabilities are translated using the current rate. Long-term assets and liabilities are translated using the rate that was in effect at the time they were placed on the balance sheet (historical rate).

Each translation method requires that the equity accounts be translated using the rate in effect at the time they were entered in the balance sheet

TABLE 8A-1 Exchange Rate Used to Translate Selected Balance Sheet Accounts for Different Translation Methods

	Current Rate Method	Monetary/ Nonmonetary Method	Current/ Noncurrent Method
Cash	Current	Current	Current
Accounts receivable	Current	Current	Current
Inventory	Current	Historical	Current
Fixed assets	Current	Historical	Historical
Current liabilities	Current	Current	Current
Long-term debt	Current	Current	Historical
Common stock	Historical	Historical	Historical
Retained earnings	Historical*	Historical[†]	Historical[†]

*Includes the use of a CTA account. This account is separate from the retained earnings account.
[†]Translation gains (losses) are included in the retained earnings account.

(historical rate). The exchange rates used to translate the various accounts in the balance sheet for the three methods are outlined in Table 8A-1.

An Illustration:
Current Rate Method (FASB 52)

The Sabicer illustration presented in the chapter will be used in this appendix to illustrate the three different methods of translating balance sheets. The current rate method is the same as FASB 52, discussed in the chapter. Thus Table 8A-2 is essentially the same as Table 8-8 and differs only in that the accounts are given in slightly greater detail. Note that the dollar values of total assets and total claims are exactly the same as in the chapter.

An Illustration:
Temporal Method (FASB 8)

Table 8A-3 illustrates the temporal method. Note that inventory and fixed assets (physical assets) are translated using the historical rate. In the

TABLE 8A-2 Sabicer U.K. Corporation: Translated Balance Sheet—Current Rate Method (000 Omitted)

| | Balance Sheet as of December 31 | | | |
	1987 in Pounds	1988 in Pounds	1988 in Dollars	Rate Used*
Cash	£100	£100	$150	C ($1.50)
Accounts receivable	£100	£100	$150	C ($1.50)
Inventory	£100	£100	$150	C ($1.50)
Fixed assets	£700	£760	$1,140	C ($1.50)
Total assets	£1,100	£1,060	$1,590	
Current liabilities	£200	£200	$300	C ($1.50)
Long-term debt	£200	£200	$300	C ($1.50)
Common stock	£350	£350	$700	H ($2.00)
Retained earnings	£250	£310	$605[†]	H ($2.00)
CTA	n/a	n/a	($315)	
Total claims	£1,000	£1,060	$1,590	

*Exchange rate used in translation: W = weighted average rate, C = current rate, H = historical rate.

[†]Retained earnings Dec. 1988 = R.E. Dec. 1987 + R.E. during 1988
= $500 (Table 8-7) + $105 = $605.

TABLE 8A-3 Sabicer U.K. Corporation: Translated Balance Sheet—
Temporal Method (000 Omitted)

| | Balance Sheet as of December 31 | | | |
	1987 in Pounds	1988 in Pounds	1988 in Dollars	Rate Used
Cash	£100	£100	$150	C ($1.50)
Accounts receivable	£100	£100	$150	C ($1.50)
Inventory	£100	£100	$200	H ($2.00)
Fixed assets	£700	£760	$1,520	H ($2.00)
Total assets	£1,000	£1,060	$2,020	
Current liabilities	£200	£200	$300	C ($1.50)
Long-term debt	£200	£200	$300	C ($1.50)
Common stock	£350	£350	$700	H ($2.00)
Retained earnings				
Before trans. gain	£250	£310	$605*	
Trans. gain (loss)	n/a	n/a	+$115†	
Total R.E.	£250	£310	$720	
Total claims	£1,000	£1,060	$2,020	

*Retained earnings Dec. 1988 = R.E. Dec. 1987 + R.E. during 1988 + translation gains/losses
= $500 + $105 + $115 = $720.

†The amount necessary to bring total claims into equality with total assets. This is not the same as the CTA in FASB 52.

illustration, the historical rate is £1 = $2.00 in all cases.[15] Sometimes different historical rates are applied to the different accounts. This depends on the rate that was in effect at the time the asset was acquired. Note that the retained earnings amount that would actually appear on the balance sheet is the entry labeled "Total R.E." This would include the translation gain (loss). In this case, retained earnings as of December 1988 are equal to $720,000.

Perhaps the most interesting thing about Table 8A-3 is how different it is from Table 8A-2. Dollar-denominated total assets and total claims are very different, as are many of the accounts. In addition, retained earnings are treated differently. Under FASB 52, retained earnings are not affected by balance sheet gains and losses caused by foreign exchange fluctuations. Such gains or losses are included in the CTA. Under this methodology, however, balance sheet gains or losses are added to retained earnings. This is the case even though the pound-denominated assets and claims are *exactly* the same for both methodologies. The two methods

---

[15]We assume that the £60,000 in fixed assets, as well as the firm's inventories, were all acquired when the exchange rate was equal to $2.00.

give a completely different translated view of the subsidiary balance sheet. The reader is reminded, however, that in the real world nothing is different. The subsidiary has the same amount of pound assets and liabilities. The only difference between these two methodologies is the accounting system.

An Illustration: Current/Noncurent Method

The current/noncurrent method is illustrated in Table 8A-4. Note that the pound-denominated balance sheet of the foreign subsidiary is *exactly* the same as in the two previous illustrations. Current assets and liabilities are translated at the current rate, while long-term assets and liabilities are translated at historical rates. Once again, the historical rate for each account could be different and would reflect the exchange rate in effect on the date that the asset or liability was booked. In this example, we will assume that the historical rate is always equal to $2.00. Note that the

TABLE 8A-4   Sabicer U.K. Corporation: Translated Balance Sheet Using the Current/Noncurrent Method (000 Omitted)

	Balance Sheet as of December 31			
	1987 in Pounds	1988 in Pounds	1988 in Dollars	Rate Used
Cash	£100	£100	$150	C ($1.50)
Accounts receivable	£100	£100	$150	C ($1.50)
Inventory	£100	£100	$150	C ($1.50)
Fixed assets	£700	£760	$1,520	H ($2.00)
Total assets	£1,000	£1,060	$1,970	
Current liabilities	£200	£200	$300	C ($1.50)
Long-term debt	£200	£200	$400	H ($2.00)
Common stock	£350	£350	$700	H ($2.00)
Retained earnings				
Before trans. gain	£250	£310	$605*	
Trans. gain (loss)	n/a	n/a	−$35†	
Total R.E.	£250	£310	$570	
Total claims	£1,000	£1,060	$1,970	

*Retained earnings Dec. 1988 = R.E. Dec. 1987 + R.E. during 1988 + translation gains/losses
= $500 + $105 − $35 = $570.
†The amount necessary to bring total claims into equality with total assets.

dollar-denominated balance sheet looks different than under either of the other methods. With this method, there is no CTA. Gains or losses are added to the retained earnings of the firm. In this case, retained earnings as of December 1988 are equal to $570,000.

Balance Sheet Comparisons

Table 8A-5, compares some of the crucial accounts in the balance sheet of Sabicer U.K. Note that these differences can be traced solely to differences in accounting. In addition, the pound values of assets and claims were the same in each of the illustrations. Note that total assets and claims (denominated in dollars) are lowest under the current rate method. This reflects the fact that the current rate method translates more accounts (than the others) using the new lower exchange rate. Under the current rate method, total assets and total claims will show relatively wide fluctuations on a year-to-year basis as the exchange rate varies. This is the essence of the method. Note, however, that these wide fluctuations in asset and liability values do not show up on the income statement, since they are included in the CTA. Thus, the current rate method yields a balance sheet that fluctuates and an income statement that is relatively stable.

The impact of fluctuating exchange rates on the balance sheet if the temporal method is used is more complex. In our illustration, for example, the exchange rate declined from £1 = $2.00 in 1987 to £1 = $1.50 at the end of 1988, but total assets increased in value. This differs sharply from the picture presented by the current rate method. The reason is that, of Sabicer U.K.'s total assets of £1,060,000, only £200,000 were

TABLE 8A-5 Sabicer U.K. Corporation: Comparison of Translated Balance Sheets (000 Omitted)

	Total Assets and Total Claims	Retained Earnings	
		During 1988	Total
Current rate method	$1,590	$105[*]	$605[†]
Temporal method	$2,020	$220	$720
Current/noncurrent method	$1,970	$70	$570

[*]R.E. during 1988 = total in 1988 − total in 1987.
[†]Does not include the CTA of −$315,000. If the CTA had been included, retained earnings would have been only $290,000.

monetary and thus were translated at the current rate. The physical assets were not affected by the fall in the current rate. The reduction in the value of monetary assets was offset by the fact that the firm increased its investment in fixed assets by £60,000. The impact of an exchange rate movement on the claims side of the balance sheet will reflect the allocation of claims between liabilities and equities. The higher the proportion of liabilities, the greater the change in total claims. The size of the translation gain (loss) will depend on the distribution of both assets and claims. In our illustration, the translation gain is positive even though the current rate declined. We could have constructed the illustration to yield the opposite results by altering the relevant proportions in the assets of the firm. The impact of an exchange rate movement on the translated financial statements will depend upon how the firm is structured, as well as the direction of change in the exchange rate.

The impact of a change in exchange rate on a balance sheet translated using the current/noncurrent method will also depend on the distribution of assets and claims. A firm with a relatively low proportion of current assets will show relatively little variability of total assets in response to exchange rate movements. Similarly, firms with a low proportion of current liability claims will exhibit relatively small variability on the right-hand side of the balance sheet. This means that a decline in the value of a foreign currency may lead to either a translation gain or loss. Each situation must be evaluated separately.

The income statement, however, presents a different situation. Reported annual income will usually exhibit less volatility under the current rate method than under the temporal or current/noncurrent methods. This is due to the treatment of balance sheet gains or losses. The current method (FASB 52) isolates the annual income of the subsidiary from such gains or losses through the use of the CTA. This is not the case for either the temporal or the current/noncurrent methods.

Summary and Conclusions

This information has been presented for two reasons: (1) as a historical curiosity and (2) to show other methods that are currently in use in foreign countries. The student should concentrate on understanding the current method used in the United States: FASB 52. The information presented in this appendix could be used to gain a perspective on different views of translation accounting. In addition, the student should recognize that translation accounting has been changed in the past and may be changed in the future.

Problems

1. The balance sheet of American Enterprises in West Germany as of December 1988 is as follows (in millions):

Cash	DM300
Accounts receivable	DM500
Inventories	DM200
Current assets	DM1,000
Fixed assets	DM600
Total assets	DM1,600
Current liabilities	DM600
Long-term debt	DM300
Common stock	DM200
Retained earnings	DM500
Total claims	DM1,600

Assume that the exchange rate prevailing during the entire life of the subsidiary was DM1 = $0.40. On December 31, 1988, however, the exchange rate suddenly increased to DM1 = $0.50.

a. Prepare a translated balance sheet using the current method.
b. Prepare a translated balance sheet using the temporal method.
c. Prepare a translated balance sheet using the current/noncurrent method.

2. Based on the information in Problem 1, prepare a translated balance sheet using the current, temporal, and current/noncurrent methods. Assume that the exchange rate prevailing during the entire life of the subsidiary was DM1 = $0.40. On December 31, 1988, however, the exchange rate suddenly decreased to DM1 = $0.30.

PART **III**

International Sources of Funds

9

International Financial Markets

This is the first of three chapters that deal with the international consid-erations associated with raising capital for a firm.[1] The primary focus will be on the firm's ability to borrow in international markets. What kinds of loans are available? Can an American firm sell bonds in foreign countries? Is the cost of borrowing in foreign countries higher or lower than the cost of borrowing in the United States? These are the questions we will answer. In addition, this chapter will present an overview of interna-tional financial markets. In the next two chapters, we will look at how these factors can affect the firm's cost of capital and optimal capital structure.

---

[1]Throughout this book, we will use the term *capital markets* to refer to the markets for both short- and long-term capital. In addition, the student should review Eugene F. Brigham, *Fundamentals of Financial Management*, 4th ed., Chicago, Dryden Press, 1986, chapter 3, for a more detailed explanation of financial markets.

Domestic Financial Markets

Every modern economy is supported by a domestic financial market. The financial market facilitates the transfer of funds from savers to borrowers. A simplified view of domestic financial markets is presented in Figure 9-1. Let us examine this figure, using the United States as an example.

In the United States, there are some economic units (individuals, firms, other organizations) that can loosely be described as *savers*. This means that, for at least a short period of time, some units have funds for which they have no immediate use. In other words, their consumption is lower than their income. Perhaps an individual is saving for retirement. Perhaps a firm is accumulating funds in anticipation of a seasonal need. Whatever the motives, some units in the United States want to postpone using funds for purchases of goods and services. Of course, these savers would like to find someone to borrow the funds and pay interest. Fortunately for the savers, there are many economic units that can loosely be described as *borrowers*.[2] These are individuals, firms, and other organizations that would like to use the funds provided by the savers and are willing to pay interest in return. Financial intermediaries (banks, savings institutions, life insurance companies, and pension funds) assist in the orderly transfer of funds from one group, the savers, to another, the borrowers. Funds may be passed from savers to borrowers either directly or through these intermediaries.

At this point, it is necessary to highlight the crucial factor that differentiates domestic financial markets from the global financial markets that will be discussed later in this chapter. In the domestic financial market, all transactions are conducted in the currency of the country in which the market is located. For example, in the U.S. domestic financial market, savers save in dollars and expect repayment in dollars. Financial intermediaries accept deposits only in dollars and lend only in dollars. While the American domestic financial market has all transactions de-nominated in dollars, the domestic financial market in another country would use that country's currency. For example, in Britain, all transactions would be conducted in pounds. In France, the franc would be the unit of account. In a domestic financial market, it is not possible to deposit or lend a foreign currency.

It is also important to note that domestic markets have foreign participants. Foreign residents frequently maintain deposits in American banks. In fact, historically, the United States has attracted funds from abroad because of its political stability and the favorable outlook for its economy. For example, in the 1980s, vast amounts of money were

---

[2] In this discussion, it is convenient to view equity financing as a special type of borrowing.

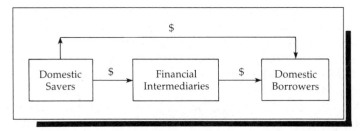

FIGURE 9-1   A Simplified View of Domestic Financial Markets.

invested in American banks and securities by Mexican residents. Foreigners also borrow in the United States. American banks lend to foreign firms and governments. Look in the *The Wall Street Journal* and you will see that foreign firms also sell stock in the United States. The principle to be noted is that there are many foreign participants in domestic financial markets. The key is that all transactions are conducted in the currency of the country in which the financial market is located.

The Role of Financial Intermediaries

Looking back at Figure 9-1, we can see that it is possible for funds to flow directly from savers to borrowers. The ease with which this flow takes place and the importance of this type of transaction vary from country to country. In the United States, stocks, bonds, and short-term debt instruments (commercial paper, Treasury bills) are sold, with relative ease, directly to the public by borrowing units.[3] Individual investors in the United States seem to be more willing than investors elsewhere to engage in direct lending. This partly reflects historical developments in the United States, as well as its institutional environment. The United States, for example, has good secondary markets for securities. A person who buys stock can usually sell it with little difficulty. In the United States there are also good secondary markets for bonds, commercial paper, and Treasury bills. While Japan and Britain are making great strides in the development of secondary financial markets, other nations lag considerably behind. As long as these secondary markets remain undeveloped, firms will find it difficult to sell securities directly to the public.

Most of the funds that flow from savers to borrowers pass through the financial intermediation process. In the United States, private firms

---

[3]Usually the saver will not deal directly with the firm. An individual buying bonds from General Motors in the new-issue market, for example, will obtain them through a broker. However, the broker merely facilitates the placement of the issue rather than changing the nature of the flows.

such as banks, pension funds, and insurance companies provide this crucial intermediation service. These financial intermediaries do a lot more than pass funds from savers to borrowers. They change the nature and size of the flows themselves. For example, banks accept deposits on a short-term basis, which allows savers to withdraw money with little or no notice. This is good for savers and encourages them to deposit money in banks. On the other hand, banks usually lend on a longer-term basis. This is good for borrowers, since they can plan to use funds for a definite period of time. Note what the bank has done in this case. It has, in effect, changed the short-term commitment of a saver into a longer-term commitment to a borrower. The bank has altered the maturity of the flow. Other financial intermediaries do more or less the same thing. In this sense, financial intermediaries provide an almost indispensable service to the economy.

Financial intermediaries provide another important service to the economy by accepting millions of small deposits, lumping them together, and making large loans to borrowers. Deposits are accepted in small amounts, and loans can be made in millions or even billions of dollars. This is good for both the savers and the borrowers. In addition, financial intermediaries are able, through diversification and in some instances government insurance, to reduce the risk borne by the saver.

While all countries have financial intermediaries, their nature varies from place to place. In the United States, private banks, savings institutions, and insurance companies, along with public and private pension funds, are the dominant types of financial intermediaries. Each type of institution specializes in one or more areas of intermediation. Banks accept short-term deposits and are the most important source of short- and intermediate-term loans to business. Savings associations specialize in home mortgages. Life insurance firms and pension funds advance money on a longer-term basis, often buying stocks, bonds, and mortgages, as well as lending directly to businesses. While the differences among American financial institutions are breaking down since the advent of deregulation in the early 1980s, each type of institution still has its own specialty.

Other countries have other social needs, which are reflected in different types of financial intermediaries. In Northern European countries, for example, the welfare state has reduced the need for life insurance and pension protection, which has retarded the development of insurance companies and pension funds. In other countries, France for example, the government owns and operates a substantial segment of the banking sector. Some countries have a variety of specialized institutions, while other have a few banks that handle almost all of the intermediation that takes place. The point is that each modern economy has a unique pattern of intermediation. Savers save in different ways. Borrowers raise funds from different types of institutions and on different terms. The American pattern of intermediation is just one variation on a common theme.

The Regulation of
Financial Intermediaries

In the United States, financial intermediaries, especially banks and savings institutions, are heavily regulated. The objective of the regulations is to ensure that savers have confidence in the intermediaries and continue to deposit funds with them. If savers stop depositing, funds will be unavailable to businesses and other borrowers, which would retard economic growth. For example, the Federal Reserve System and other regulatory agencies monitor bank activities in an attempt to reduce the probability of bank failure. In the United States, most deposits in banks and savings institutions are insured up to a maximum of $100,000. Today there is also federal regulation of pension funds. Note that in the United States the primary intent is to maintain confidence in the system. In general, American financial institutions have a broad array of options with respect to acquiring and using funds. Government regulation in the United States, however, does not mean that the government directs loans to particular places or organizations (although incentives are infrequently given).

It is important for the student of international business to recognize that not every foreign country has the same view of the financial regulation process as the United States. The regulatory objectives in the United Kingdom, for example, are similar to those in the United States, which means that financial institutions have substantial latitude in their activities. Other countries, especially developing ones, regulate financial intermediaries in such a way as to insure a flow of funds to *target* borrowers. For example, one country may decide that loans should go to manufacturers and not to importers. In some countries, the ability of intermediaries to lend to foreigners is limited by government regulations. From the international business perspective, this means that the source, availability, and characteristics of borrowing arrangement vary from country to country.

Foreign Bonds

Foreign borrowers have access not only to some domestic bank loans but also to domestic bond markets when such markets exist. The word *foreign*, when used in connection with the foreign bond market, refers to the origin of the borrower, not the location or the currency associated with the issue. For example, an American firm can sell deutsche mark–denominated bonds in Germany. This is a foreign bond because the issuer of the bonds (the American firm) is a foreigner in Germany. By definition, a foreign bond is always issued in the currency of the country

TABLE 9-1   Foreign Bond Issues (in Millions of Dollars)

	1984	1985	1986	1987
U.S. dollar	$5,487	$4,655	$6,064	$5,911
German mark	$2,243	$1,741	—	—
British pound	$1,292	$957	$322	—
Swiss franc	$12,626	$14,954	$23,401	$23,976
Japanese yen	$4,628	$6,379	$4,756	$3,068
Other	$1,677	$2,339	$3,898	$3,856
Total foreign bonds	$27,953	$31,025	$38,441	$36,811

Source: World Financial Market, Morgan Guaranty Trust Company of New York, September–October 1987, p. 18, and July 1988, p. 16. Used with permission of the copyright holder, Morgan Guaranty Trust Company of New York.

in which the bond is sold. For example, the American firm sells the bonds, receives deutsche marks, and is obligated to make future deutsche market payments to the owners of the bonds.

Table 9-1 gives some indication of the dimensions of the market for foreign bonds. While this market is relatively small compared to the domestic market in the United States or the Eurobond market (discussed later), it still accommodates billions of dollars. Note, first of all, that foreigners can and do issue bonds in the United States. For example, foreign borrowers raised almost $6 billion during 1987. The figure that will surprise most readers is that more than 65 percent of all foreign bonds sold are issued in Switzerland and, by definition, in Swiss francs. This unusual fact can be explained by the fact that the secrecy of Swiss bank accounts enables non-Swiss residents to avoid income taxes. A citizen of Italy, for example, could buy bonds in Switzerland through a Swiss bank and avoid taxes on the interest income.

As shown in Table 9-2 and discussed in Chapter 2, interest rates on bonds vary greatly from place to place. The differences in national interest rates can be attributed to several factors—most importantly,

TABLE 9-2   Bond Interest Rates in Domestic Markets* May 1988

	Currency	Interest Rate
United States	Dollar	10.38%
Canada	Canadian dollar	11.86%
Germany	Deutsche mark	6.80%
United Kingdom	Pound	10.69%
Switzerland	Swiss franc	4.36%
Japan	Yen	4.95%

*These interest rates are presented for illustration only. The bonds used in the comparison may not have the exact same maturity. Furthermore, there may be some variations in the credit risk of the borrowers.

Source: World Financial Markets, Morgan Guaranty Trust Company of New York, July 1988, p. 21. Used with permission of the copyright holder, Morgan Guaranty Trust Company of New York.

differences in expected inflation and foreign exchange rates. Note that the interest rate on a Swiss franc bond issue was relatively low in 1988, which reflects the relatively low Swiss inflation rate and the tax advantages associated with secret Swiss bank accounts. On the other hand, inflationary expectations in the United States, the United Kingdom, and Canada were higher. This resulted in higher interest rates in these countries.

The access of foreign borrowers to domestic bond markets, including the U.S. bond market, is sometimes restricted or prohibited. In some countries, government approval is required. In other cases, the private banking system is able to control the number of foreign bonds issued at any one time. This means that American firms, while perhaps wishing to borrow in foreign bond markets, may not be able to do so.

Global Financial Markets (Euromarkets)

In addition to domestic financial markets, there exists an important and growing global financial market. The two most notable features of the global market for financing are that (1) transactions are conducted in many different currencies and (2) the market is largely unregulated by governments. The physical location of the global market is impossible to define because it is electronic in nature. This means that market participants can be located anywhere in the world and still conduct transactions through modern communication systems. While the global market is dispersed throughout the world, London remains its spiritual center as well as its most important trading center.

The global financial market has developed rapidly since the end of World War II. Remember that in the immediate postwar period, the European and Japanese economies were rebuilding and experienced considerable stress. At that time, the dollar was viewed as the most secure currency in the world. Many savers who resided outside the United States wanted to save dollars because other currencies were viewed as unstable. However, these foreign-based savers did not want to deposit dollars in the United States for fear that the United States would freeze or confiscate them.

Ironically, it was the Soviet Union that provided the impetus for the early growth of the capitalistic global financial market. As the cold war heated up after World War II, the Soviet Union began to worry that the American government would act against its dollar deposits in New York. The Soviet Union needed to maintain dollar accounts for international trade and financing purposes, since the U.S. dollar was the only currency acceptable throughout the world. The possibility that the Soviet Union's dollar deposits would be frozen by the U.S. government was not paranoia. Even before the United States had entered World War II, European deposits were frozen. As recently as 1979, President Jimmy Carter froze Iranian deposits in response to the hostage crisis. Soviet fears were based on its perception of what the American government might do to its funds during a crisis. The Soviet Union responded to this problem by placing its dollar-denominated deposits in banks outside the jurisdiction of the U.S. government. British banks were the primary recipients of these deposits.

Up to this time, it was unusual for a bank to accept a deposit in a foreign currency, but the conditions that prevailed in the late 1940s and early 1950s were unusual. At that time, the British pound was not freely convertible into other currencies and the British economy was struggling. British importers needed dollars in order to purchase the foreign products required to rebuild their economy and sustain consumption. Thus, the demand for dollar loans by British firms was exceptionally high. British banks could accept dollar-denominated deposits from the Soviets and make dollar-denominated loans to British firms. It is important to note that at this point, the British government chose to confine its regulatory authority to pound deposits, since it was primarily interested in protecting the flow of pounds from British savers to British borrowers. As a consequence, the expansion of dollar-denominated deposits and loans proceeded in Britain on an unregulated basis.

Initially, this unregulated market was confined to dollars, since it was the only currency that was in great demand and was called the *eurodollar market*. A eurodollar is a dollar-denominated deposit placed in a bank that is domiciled outside the United States. As time went by, savers began to hold other currencies outside of their country of issue. Today a number of currencies are held outside the country of issue. The term *eurocurrency market* is used to reflect the fact that more than the dollar is involved in this global market (sometimes called the *euromarket*).

Not all currencies are eurocurrencies because there is no incentive to hold some currencies outside their country of issue. For example, in the 1980s, few individuals outside Mexico wanted to hold Mexican pesos. In order for a currency to achieve the status of eurocurrency, there must be savers (outside the country of issue) who choose to hold it. Eurocurrency status also implies that a financial institution is willing to accept deposits in that currency and that there are borrowers for that currency. The most important Eurocurrencies are the eurodollar, euro-Canadian dollar, euro-French franc, euromark, euro-Dutch guilder, euro-Swiss franc, eurosterling (the British pound), and the euroyen. Of course, this list is not fixed. As the economic prospects of a country diminish, it will loose favor as a eurocurrency. As other economies develop, their currencies may achieve eurocurrency status.

At this point, it is worthwhile to pause and reflect on the significance of this euro- or global market for American business. First, note that the euromarket allows the American firm to borrow (and deposit) dollars outside the United States. Second, firms are now able to borrow foreign currencies outside of domestic financial markets. This depositing and borrowing take place beyond the regulatory arm of the various governments. In a sense, the euromarket is a free market that operates on a supply-and-demand basis. It provides interesting alternatives for American businesses.

The Creation of Eurodeposits

Eurocurrency deposits are subject to the same multiple expansion as dollars deposited in U.S. banks. When funds are deposited in a bank, the bank lends them and, in effect, creates new deposits. Through this process, a small initial deposit can lead to large increases in total loans and deposits. In this sense, the euromarkets take on a life and size beyond those of the initial saving decision. The process of eurocurrency expansion is illustrated in the example that follows. While we will show that there is a multiple expansion of eurodollar deposits, the reader should keep in mind that the same principles apply to all eurocurrencies.

In the example, which is summarized in Table 9-3, a chain of events is set off when an American firm makes a purchase from a foreign supplier, pays in dollars, and the foreign supplier decides to hold the dollars outside of the United States. Eventually, the deposit leads to loans and additional deposits. When the process is completed, the volume of eurodollars far exceeds the initial purchase amount. Let us work through the example on a step-by-step basis, using T accounts to show what happens in the global banking system.[4]

First Step

Assume that General Motors purchases engines from Rolls Royce for $1,000,000 and gives Rolls a $1,000,000 check drawn on its Citibank account in New York. Rolls Royce then deposits the check in Lloyds Bank in London. At this point, a eurodollar deposit has been created, since Rolls Royce has a dollar-denominated account outside of the United States. Of course, Lloyds Bank now has a piece of paper (a check) drawn by General Motors on its bank in New York. Since most money center banks maintain accounts with each other, it is a simple matter for Lloyds to deposit the check at Citibank. As can be seen from Table 9-3, Citibank shows a change of ownership on a $1,000,000 deposit, from General

---

[4]This illustration has been highly simplified. Additional banks and transactions could be added to the example. Such changes, however, will not significantly affect the conclusions reached.

TABLE 9-3   The Eurodollar Market: An Illustration*

First Step		

CitiBank of New York	Lloyds Bank of London	
Deposits of G.M. −$1,000,000 Deposits of Lloyds +$1,000,000	Deposits at Citibank +$1,000,000	Deposits of Rolls Royce +$1,000,000

Second Step	

Lloyds Bank of London	
Loan to Renault +$980,000	Deposits of Renault +$980,000

Third Step		

CitiBank of New York	Lloyds Bank of London	
Deposits of Lloyds −$980,000 Deposits of Bank of France +$980,000	Deposits at Citibank −$980,000	Deposits of Renault −$980,000

	Bank of France	
	Deposits at Citibank +$980,000	Deposits of Paris, Inc. +$980,000

Fourth Step	

Bank of France	
Loan to Volkswagen +$950,000	Deposits of Volkswagen +$950,000

*The figures in this table constitute *changes* not the amounts outstanding.

Motors to Lloyds Bank. Total deposits in the United States are not changed. However, there is also a new eurodollar deposit in London.

Second Step

Now begins the expansion of eurodollar deposits. Since Lloyds Bank must pay interest to Rolls Royce, Lloyds will have to employ the funds by lending them to a worthy borrower at a higher rate of interest than is being paid to Rolls Royce. Let us assume that Renault of France wants to borrow $980,000, obtains a loan from Lloyds, and temporarily deposits the proceeds from the loan in an account with Lloyds Bank in London. At this point, a second eurodollar account has been created. A total of

$1,980,000 is now deposited in banks outside the United States. Rolls Royce owns $1,000,000 and Renault owns $980,000 of this amount. Note that nothing happens in the United States. The Lloyds Bank account at Citibank remains exactly as it was. The eurodollars are created outside the United States.

Third Step

Assume that Renault uses the proceeds from the loan to pay for purchases from a French automobile parts supplier called the Paris Company, and that the Paris Company is willing to accept payment in dollars. In our illustration, the Paris Company deposits the proceeds from its sale to Renault ($980,000) in the Bank of France. At this point, another eurodollar deposit has been created, but this deposit will be quickly offset by a reduction in Renault's dollar balance at Lloyds Bank. It is the act of lending rather than depositing that creates the eurodollar expansion.

The Bank of France now has a dollar-denominated check drawn on Lloyds Bank and is anxious to collect these funds. Essentially what happens is that $980,000 of Lloyds Bank dollar deposits at Citibank are transferred to the Bank of France. As can be seen in the T accounts, Lloyds experiences a decline in deposit liabilities to Renault of $980,000 and a similar decline in its deposits at Citibank. The Bank of France shows an increase in deposit liabilities to the Paris Company, as well as an increase in deposits at Citibank.

Fourth Step

Now the Bank of France has idle funds on which it must pay interest. In order to cover this cost, the bank now makes a $950,000 loan to Volkswagen and the borrowed funds are temporarily deposited at the Bank of France. At this point, the level of eurodollar deposits is

$ deposits of Rolls Royce at Lloyds	$1,000,000
$ deposits of Paris Co. at Bank of France	$980,000
$ deposits of Volkswagen at Bank of France	$950,000
Total increase in $ deposits	$2,930,000

The second and fourth steps are identical, except that different institutions and amounts are involved in the transactions. The expansion will continue as Volkswagen spends the proceeds from the loan and the recipient deposits the funds in a foreign bank. As long as the transactions are denominated in dollars, they are part of the eurodollar market. Note that the whole chain of events is the result of a single purchase by an American firm. It is also clear that in order for the eurodollar market to operate, foreign firms must be willing to sell and accept payments in dollars. In addition, foreign banks must be willing and able to accept deposits and make loans in dollars. The eurocurrency markets are complicated and require unusual behavior on the part of various participants.

Is there any limit on the number of eurodollars that can be created? In fact, the expansion of eurocurrency deposits is limited only by the fact that banks choose to hold a reserve for liquidity purposes. In our illustration, it was assumed that Lloyds Bank made a $980,000 loan upon receipt of a $1,000,000 deposit. Lloyds, in effect, maintained a $20,000 reserve in its Citibank account. Since eurodollar markets are unregulated and there are no legal reserve requirements, Lloyds could have actually made a $1,000,000 loan. Theoretically, the expansion would be limitless if all banks decided to keep zero reserves. In practice, however, banks maintain a small percentage of their deposits in the form of reserves. It is the size of the reserve that limits the expansion of eurodollar deposits. With larger reserves, less expansion can take place.

It should be noted that the conversion of a dollar loan to a foreign currency does not, by itself, end the eurocurrency creation process. Let us assume, for example, that the Paris Company wants French francs for the $980,000 check received from Renault and deposits the French francs in the Bank of France. The Bank of France will have the deposit liability in French francs, but its asset will still be $980,000 in deposits at Citibank. Presumably, the Bank of France would look for another customer who wishes to borrow dollars. Thus, individuals participating in the market can change their holdings to their local currency, but the eurocurrency market will continue to expand.

The expansion process will continue until the dollars are used to purchase products or financial instruments in the United States. Once again, we see that it is the willingness of foreigners to hold dollars and the willingness of foreign banks to accept dollar deposits that is the key to the eurodollar market. Only when the dollars are cashed in through a transaction in the United States does the eurodollar creation process come to a halt.

The Denomination
of Eurocurrency Deposits

In the initial post–World War II years, the dollar tended to be the only acceptable eurocurrency. As economic and political conditions moved toward postwar stabilization, the entire eurocurrency market expanded. Not only were more dollars available in the eurocurrency market, but other currencies also achieved eurocurrency status. Today the dollar is only one of several eurocurrencies, but it is still the dominant currency. Table 9-4 traces recent developments in the eurocurrency market. As of December 1987, this market had a size of approximately $4.5 trillion. The rapid growth of the market is reflected in the fact that over the 1982–1987

TABLE 9-4 Commercial Banks in the Eurocurrency Markets (in Billions of Dollars)

December	1982	1983	1984	1985	1986	1987
Eurocurrency loans	$2,146	$2,253	$2,359	$2,833	$3,560	$4,405
In dollars	$1,694	$1,797	$1,894	$2,101	$2,534	$2,891
In other currencies	$452	$456	$465	$732	$1,025	$1,515
Percentage in dollars	79%	80%	80%	74%	71%	66%
Eurocurrency deposits	$2,168	$2,278	$2,386	$2,846	$3,579	$4,461
In dollars	$1,741	$1,846	$1,950	$2,147	$2,553	$2,924
In other currencies	$427	$432	$436	$699	$1,026	$1,537
Percentage in dollars	80%	81%	82%	75%	71%	66%

Eurocurrency loans = eurocurrency claims or assets held by financial institutions
Eurocurrency deposits = eurocurrency liabilities of financial institutions

Source: World Financial Markets, Morgan Guaranty Trust Company of New York, September–October 1987, p. 17, and July 1988, p. 15. Used with permission of the copyright holder, Morgan Guaranty Bank of New York.

period, eurocurrency deposits increased at an annual rate of approximately 15 percent. Note that the dollar is still the most important eurocurrency. For the 1982–1984 period as a whole, approximately 80 percent of eurodeposits were in dollars. As the dollar weakened in foreign exchange markets, the attractiveness of holding assets in other currencies increased. By 1987, however, only 66 percent of eurodeposits were in dollars. It is unclear whether this downward trend in the use of the dollar as a eurocurrency will be reversed when the dollar once again begins to appreciate against other currencies.

For American businesses, there are two practical conclusions to be drawn from Table 9-4. First, the ability to borrow and deposit dollars outside the United States is growing even though the dominance of the dollar in percentage terms is declining. Second, it is increasingly possible to borrow other eurocurrencies outside their country of issue. Thus, if a French franc loan is unavailable in France, it may be obtainable in London. The market in which these eurocurrencies are traded is now global.

The Location of the Global Financial Market

London was and still is the most important center of the global financial market. Deposits in the United Kingdom (London) are greater than in any other country. Probably the most important reason is that London is where the market took off. Eurocurrency depositors were also reassured by the fact that the political environment of the United Kingdom was and still is stable. In addition, the British regulatory attitude toward eurocurrency deposits was permissive. By contrast, consider the situation in the United States. It was not until 1981 that American banks were permitted to hold eurodeposits in the United States. This late start, plus the fear of U.S. government action against depositors, has retarded the development of eurocurrency operations in the United States. London remains the center of eurocurrency operations for other reasons as well. Modern communication systems have made London accessible to almost anyone almost anywhere in the world. For a California firm, for example, it is just as easy to do business with a London bank as it is with a New York bank.

The fact that London is the center of the global financial market does not imply that British banks dominate this market. In fact, most of the world's large banks have facilities in London. For example, Bankamerica and Citibank have important eurocurrency operations in London. In fact, American banks conduct one-third of their eurocurrency operations in London (and another one-third in the Bahamas). The large Japanese, German, and Swiss banks (as well as large banks from other countries) also have an important presence in London. London is the center of the world market, and no large bank can afford to be absent from it.

In an attempt to lure the euromarket to the United States, the Federal Reserve now permits American banks to conduct some of their eurocurrency activities in the United States. The Federal Reserve allows banks to establish international banking facilities (IBF), which can be viewed as a department within existing bank operations. The creation of an IBF gives banks certain advantages. Unlike domestic deposits, IBF deposits are not subject to reserve requirements. In addition, IBF deposits are not subject to Federal Deposit Insurance Corporation (FDIC) insurance premiums. Thus, the IBFs are in almost the same position as eurobanks domiciled in London. The access by American business firms to the IBFs, however, is severely restricted. Basically, deposits can be accepted and loans made only from/to foreigners. A foreign corporate subsidiary of an American firm may be able to conduct some business with the IBF, but it must sign a written statement that the funds involved will be used only in international operations. Eurodeposits and loans associated with domestic operations of American firms must still be conducted outside the United States.

The outlook for the future is unclear. Some analysts believe that Japan and the United States will gain in relative importance. On the other hand, some argue that London will remain the hub of the market.

Eurocurrency Interest Rates

While the eurocurrency market initially developed in response to a political predicament, its vitality today reflects its interest rate advantage. As a general rule, deposit interest rates are higher, and lending rates lower, in the eurocurrency market. Believe it or not, an American firm can earn higher interest on dollar deposits in London than on dollar

TABLE 9-5 Differences in Dollar Deposit Interest Rates:
Eurocurrency versus U.S. Markets (December Rates, 3-Month Deposits)

Year	Interest Rate in Eurocurrency Market	Interest Rate in United States	Difference
1987	7.21%	7.10%	0.11%
1986	6.64%	6.26%	0.38%
1985	8.02%	7.72%	0.30%
1984	8.49%	8.34%	0.15%

Source: World Financial Markets, Morgan Guaranty Trust Company of New York, July 1988, pp. 17, 20.
Used with permission of the copyright holder, Morgan Guaranty Trust Company of New York.

deposits in the United States. In addition, it may be less expensive to borrow dollars from a London bank than from a bank domiciled in the United States. Foreigners can hold dollars outside the United States, isolate themselves from political actions of the American government, and, at the same time, receive higher interest rates. This is also true of other eurocurrencies. As a general rule, the eurocurrency market has an interest rate advantage in all currencies.

Table 9-5 provides some insight into the difference between eurocurrency and domestic market interest rates. The December deposit interest rate data for the years 1984 to 1987 reveal that an investor could have earned slightly more in the eurocurrency market than in the United States. The pattern displayed in Table 9-5 is typical. However, on relatively rare occasions, deposit interest rates in the United States are higher. The difference is relatively small in percentage terms but can amount to thousands of dollars when very large deposits are involved.

Not only are deposit rates higher in the eurocurrency markets, but lending rates are lower. The typical loan in the eurocurrency market has an interest rate that is approximately 1 percent higher than the deposit rate. In December 1985, for example, most eurodollar loans were priced at approximately 9 percent, although exceptionally strong borrowers may have done considerably better. The prime lending rate in the United States in December 1985 was 9.50 percent. As a general rule, the eurocurrency market has a lending interest rate advantage.[5]

One reason why eurocurrency markets tend to have an interest rate advantage over dollar (and other currency) deposit and lending rates is that government regulation of banks domiciled in the United States increases their costs relative to those of euromarket banks. A large money center bank in New York, for example, is required to maintain reserves that do not generate income. Currently, legal reserve requirements are 12 percent on checking accounts and 3 percent on savings accounts. These reserves must be maintained in vault cash or deposits at the Federal Reserve and do not earn interest income. Thus, the bank has an opportu-

---

[5]The reader is reminded that the prime rate is not necessarily the lowest cost of borrowing in the United States by a large, safe corporation. Large firms with low risk usually have access to the commercial paper market. The commercial paper rate is usually lower than the prime rate.

nity cost for these idle funds.[6] Banks holding eurodollar deposits are not required to hold these non-interest-earning assets and tend to lend a higher proportion of their deposits. The Federal Reserve cannot impose reserves on dollar deposits held by banks outside the United States. Nor are reserves required by the governments of the countries in which the eurobanks are located. Since eurobanks are not required to hold non-interest-earning reserves, they can afford to pay a little higher interest to the depositor and/or charge a little lower interest to the borrower. This does not necessarily mean that Eurobanks are riskier. The bank can decide to keep a certain percentage of deposits in reserves. These reserves, however, can be kept in low-risk money market investments earning a positive rate of return.

Domestic banks in the United States must also participate in a deposit insurance scheme, which increases the cost of doing business and the spread between deposit rates and lending rates in the United States. FDIC insurance premiums are approximately 1/12th of 1 percent of deposits. This increases the effective cost of funds to American banks. From time to time, American regulators have had other rules that have placed American banks at a cost disadvantage. In the past, for example, limits on interest payable on deposits (Regulation Q), taxes, and restrictions on foreign loans by American banks gave additional advantages to the eurodollar market. Today these rules are no longer in effect. The outlook for the future, however, is unclear.

It is difficult for governments to impose similar regulation and insurance costs in the eurocurrency market. For example, if the British government imposed legal reserve requirements on dollar-denominated deposits held by banks in Britain, the eurodollar market would simply move to other countries. Banks in the Bahamas, Singapore, or Japan are waiting with open arms for these eurodeposits. It would take a concerted action by all governments to bring the eurocurrency markets under a regulatory umbrella, and there are few incentives for governments to cooperate on this issue.

The size of euromarket participants and the size of average transactions also contribute to the cost advantage of the eurocurrency market. Participation in this market is limited to large business firms, large financial institutions, and governments. Borrowers must have the highest credit standing. These borrower characteristics tend to reduce default risk and permit eurobanks to reduce the amount of reserves that are maintained. Transactions in the eurocurrency market tend to be very large (millions of dollars). No small loans are made. Large transactions tend to reduce the administrative expenses of both the loans and deposits, and give the eurobanks a cost advantage.

---

[6]The opportunity cost is equal to the rate of return the bank could earn if the funds were invested in investments of comparable risk.

TABLE 9-6 Six-Month Eurocurrency Deposit Rates, May 1988

Currency	Annualized Rate
Eurodollar	7.81%
Euro-Canadian dollar	9.19%
Euro-French franc	7.63%
Euromark	3.81%
Euro-Dutch guilder	4.13%
Euro-Swiss franc	2.94%
Eurosterling	8.25%
Euroyen	4.25%
European currency unit	6.31%

Source: *World Financial Markets*, Morgan Guaranty Trust Company of New York, July 1988, p. 17. Used with permission of the copyright holder, Morgan Guaranty Trust Company of New York.

Characteristics of Eurodeposits

Deposits in the eurodollar market tend to be short-term and interest-bearing. The term of the deposit may vary from overnight to 1 year or longer. At the end of each term, the deposit may be renewed at the interest prevailing at that time. Under this system, a depositor may maintain deposits for a long period of time, but the interest rate will vary. The eurobanks realize that they must compete for funds and pay a rate high enough to attract deposits. Depositors receive an interest rate that reflects current market conditions. As shown in Table 9-6, there are different deposit interest rates for different currencies. As discussed in Chapter 2, the differences are attributed to differences in inflation rates and expected future exchange rates.

Euroloan Interest Rates

Loan interest rates in the eurocurrency market are tied to the London Interbank Offer Rate (LIBOR). This is the interest rate charged by one eurobank to another in the London eurocurrency market. The LIBOR is a market rate and can change daily. It represents the price at which transactions have actually taken place.[7] There is a different LIBOR for each eurocurrency. As shown in Table 9-7, there is considerable variation in the rates among currencies. Once again, these differences reflect

---

[7]It is misleading to compare the LIBOR rate to the prime rate in the United States. The prime rate is not a rate at which market transactions actually take place. It is an announced rate that serves as a guide for future transactions. The prime rate tends to stay constant over long periods of time. On the other hand, LIBOR is set by five major London banks every day, and transactions actually take place at this interest rate. LIBOR changes almost daily. For example, from July 25 to July 29, there were three changes in the LIBOR rate, as indicated in *The Wall Street Journal*.

TABLE 9-7   London Interbank Offer Rates, 1987 (3-Month Rates)

Currency	Annual Interest Rate
U.S. dollar	7.18%
French franc	8.64%
Deutsche mark	4.06%
Japanese yen	4.26%
Swiss franc	3.91%
Pound sterling	9.80%

Source: International Financial Statistics, International Monetary Fund, July 1988, p. 64.

differences in inflationary expectations and differences in expectations about future exchange rates.

The actual rate that the bank will charge a business borrower will be expressed as the LIBOR plus or minus a margin. For example, assume that an American firm wishes to borrow FF100,000 for 5 years and approaches a eurobank in London. Assume that the bank establishes the interest rate at LIBOR plus 1 percent with a 3-month rollover. As shown in Table 9-7, the French franc LIBOR is 8.64 percent. Thus, the firm will have to pay an annual interest rate of 9.64 percent for the use of the funds during the first 3 months of the 5-year loan. At the end of 3 months, the loan will be *rolled over*, which means, in effect, that the money will be loaned once again to the borrower, but at a new rate of interest. The new rate will be LIBOR plus 1 percent, as specified in the original agreement. Thus, if the LIBOR on the French franc falls to 6 percent, the firm will pay interest at an annual rate of 7 percent for the second 3-month period. The interest rate will be recomputed every 3 months, but always using the agreed-upon formula.

On occasion, a very strong borrower may be able to borrow at a rate lower than LIBOR. This will take place only when the borrower has a lower probability of default than the banks. Loans at rates below LIBOR usually are made to governments rather than businesses.

The actual LIBOR rate applied to a particular loan will depend on the length of the period for which the interest rate is fixed. Table 9-8 shows the dollar LIBORs that prevailed during 1987. The rate on a loan

TABLE 9-8   London Interbank Offer Rates 1987 (U.S. Dollars)

Term	Annual Interest Rate
Overnight	6.63%
1 month	6.99%
3 months	7.18%
6 months	7.30%
1 year	7.61%

Source: International Financial Statistics, International Monetary Fund, July 1988, p. 64.

that was issued with a 3-month rollover had 7.18 percent as the base LIBOR amount. On the other hand, if a 1-year rollover was used, 7.61 percent would have served as the basis for the interest rate computation. Remember that at the rollover date, a new set of rates similar to those in Table 9-8 would apply. It should also be noted that in some loan agreements the borrower can change the rollover period at each rollover date. For example, the borrowing firm may initially choose a 3-month rollover. After 3 months, when the new rate is established, another rollover period could be chosen (for example, 1 year). This choice is at the option of the borrower.

Other Features of Eurocurrency Loans

Eurocurrency loans frequently include *multicurrency clauses*. The multicurrency clause gives the borrower the option of choosing the currency in which the loan is denominated. In the typical situation, the currency of denomination can be changed at each rollover date. The borrower can select from among four or five currencies.

The reader may better understand how the multicurrency clause works if we use an example and restrict the number of permissible currencies to the American dollar and the German mark. Assume that a firm arranges a 5-year loan at a eurobank, decides on a 1-year rollover, and the loan agreement includes a multicurrency clause. Assume that the agreement specifies that if dollars are borrowed the interest rate will be LIBOR plus 1.25 percent, and if deutsche marks are borrowed the rate will be LIBOR plus 0.75 percent. If the LIBOR on dollars is 7 percent and the firm borrows $10,000,000, the interest rate will be 8.25 percent. If DM20,000,000 is borrowed (assume the DM1 = $0.50) and the LIBOR on deutsche marks is 5 percent, the interest rate will be 5.75 percent. That is, the interest rate that applies will depend on the currency selected by the borrower.

Let us assume that the firm chose to borrow deutsche marks. It is now 1 year later and time to roll over the loan. At this point, the firm would pay DM1,150,000, which is the interest due in marks (DM20,000,000 × 5.75 percent). The firm would also have the opportunity to change the loan to dollars. For example, if the exchange rate is DM1 = $0.40, the DM20,000,000 loan can be changed to an $8,000,000 loan. Note that it is the exchange rate at the rollover date that determines the number of dollars that are substituted for the mark balance. If the dollar had weakened over the period, the conversion to dollars would have resulted in a loan balance greater than the original $10,000,000 that could have been borrowed. No matter which currency is chosen by the firm, the appropriate LIBOR rate on the rollover date will be applied. It is also possible to denominate part of the loan in dollars and part in marks.

The appropriate LIBOR rates would be applied to the different parts of the loan. For the firm engaged in international commerce on a regular basis, this multicurrency feature of eurodollar loans may allow a reduction in transaction exposure caused by foreign exchange fluctuations.[8]

The euroloan market is characterized by large transactions (usually between $500,000 and $1 billion). This is not a market for small or even medium-sized firms. Very large loans are offered on a syndicated basis. This means that many different banks participate in the loan, with one bank serving as the leader (and receiving an extra commission). Loans are frequently issued on a *drawdown basis*, which operates much like a line of credit in the United States. Under this arrangement, the borrower is granted an amount against which withdrawals (drawdowns) can be made. Interest is paid only on the amount of the loan that has been drawn down. A commitment fee is paid on the unused portion of the loan.

The Eurobond Market

A eurobond is a bond that is denominated in a currency other than that of the country in which it is sold. For example, a dollar-denominated bond sold in France is a eurobond—more specifically, a eurodollar bond. A buyer of the eurodollar bond pays dollars for the bond and receives dollar interest payments. In order to be classified as a eurobond, the dollar-denominated bond must be sold outside the United States. Similarly, deutsche mark bonds sold outside Germany and British pound bonds sold outside the United Kingdom are eurobonds. The use of different currencies in the eurobond market is summarized in Table 9-9. Note that the dollar is the most important currency in the eurobond market. The preference for dollar-denominated bonds reflects several factors. First, the tendency of the United States to run trade deficits and the willingness of foreigners to invest in dollar-denominated securities means that there is a supply of dollars in this market. It also should be noted that American firms are large borrowers in the eurobond market and may prefer to borrow in dollars. International organizations, such as the World Bank, are also important borrowers in the eurobond market and tend to raise funds in dollars. Borrowers from other countries, both firms and governments, often issue dollar-denominated bonds in the eurobond market because of the availability and popularity of the dollar. It will be interesting to see how the slide in the dollar's value over the period from 1985 to 1987 will affect the denomination of issues in the

---

[8]This issue was introduced in Chapter 7. The impact of borrowing in foreign currencies on stockholder wealth will be discussed in the next two chapters.

TABLE 9-9 New Eurobond Issues (in Millions of Dollars)

	1984	1985	1986	1987
U.S. dollar	$63,593	$97,782	$118,220	$56,727
German mark	$4,604	$9,491	$16,870	$15,518
British pound	$3,997	$5,766	$10,510	$14,997
Japanese yen	$1,212	$6,539	$18,673	$23,116
ECU*	$3,032	$7,038	$6,965	$7,423
Other currencies	$3,020	$10,114	$16,713	$22,700
Total eurobonds	$79,458	$136,731	$187,952	$140,481
Dollar issues as a percentage of total issues	80%	72%	63%	40%

*ECU = European currency unit.

Source: *World Financial Markets*, Morgan Guaranty Trust Company of New York, September–October 1987, p. 18, and July 1988, p. 16. Used with permission of the copyright holder, Morgan Guaranty Trust Company of New York.

eurobond market. As shown in Table 9-9, the popularity of the dollar declined dramatically between 1984 and 1987.[9] This decline has been both absolute and as a percentage of new eurobonds. It is too early to tell if the decline is permanent or if the trend may be reversed in the future.

As shown in Table 9-9, the size of the eurobond market has been increasing rapidly, although a sharp decline took place in 1987. While precise measurements are difficult to make, it seems fairly clear that borrowing with eurobonds is now more important than euroloans. In addition, funds raised in the eurobond market far exceed funds raised in the foreign bond market. In 1987, for example, $37 billion in new foreign bonds were issued compared to over $140 billion in eurobonds. The eurobond market has emerged as the most important international financial market.

Factors Contributing to the Growth of the Eurobond Market

Just as with the eurocurrency loan market, the eurobond market's emergence has been encouraged by differences in the tax and regulatory actions of the various national governments. Government regulation of domestic bond markets makes domestic bond issues more time-consuming and expensive to market. An American firm can issue eurobonds in a

---

[9]The percentage decline in dollar-denominated issues can be attributed to a decline in the popularity of dollar issues and the decline of the value of the dollar. For example, if DM40 billion were issued when the exchange rate was DM1 = $0.40, it would mean $16 billion in deutsche mark issues. An increase in the value of the mark to DM1 = $0.50 will increase the dollar value of these issues to $20 billion, although the deutsche mark value remains unchanged.

matter of weeks, compared to the many months needed to issue bonds in the United States. It is also less expensive to issue eurobonds, since no prospectus need be printed and legal costs are much lower.

Eurobonds offer a tax advantage for both borrowers and lenders. Since eurobonds are issued on a bearer basis, many bond purchasers are able to avoid national income taxes; the reason is that no one has a record of their ownership of the bonds. Coupons are clipped from the bond and forwarded by a bank to the firm that issued the bond. Payment is made from the firm to the bank and then credited to the investor's account. For example, a French investor may be able to use a Swiss bank to purchase a French franc–denominated bond issued by an American corporation and sold in the United Kingdom. The French government has no record of the income, since the collection will be made by the Swiss bank from the American firm.[10] It may also be possible for American firms to avoid withholding taxes on eurobond interest if the borrowing is done through a tax haven subsidiary. Once again, we see that the tax law encourages borrowers and lenders to do strange things. To some extent, the euromarkets are the product of these tax laws.

Investors in fixed-interest-rate bonds have always borne interest rate risk; in the past, this retarded the development of bond markets. Eurobond investors are like other investors; they do not like to see the market value of their investment decline as interest rates rise. The eurobond market has attempted to allay investors' fears of interest rate increases by issuing floating rate notes and including sinking funds in fixed-rate bond issues. Floating rate notes are essentially variable-rate bonds issued with intermediate maturities. Most often the interest rate is adjusted periodically, based on a formula that is often tied to changes in the LIBOR. While in the past most eurobonds carried a fixed rate of interest, the floating rate note has now emerged as a very important type of bond issue. In fact, the existence of floating rate notes is one of the reasons that the eurobond market has surpassed the eurocurrency loan market in terms of dollar volume. Apparently, investors are more willing to commit funds if they are assured of getting a market interest rate.

Purchase and sinking fund arrangements are also used to minimize the risk borne by investors in eurobonds. A bond repurchase arrangement known as a *purchase fund* is often used to support bond prices. Under this arrangement, the issuing firm is required to repurchase a specified amount of bonds if, and only if, the bond price falls below its par value. Thus, if interest rates rise and bond prices fall, the firm must repurchase a specified amount. These purchases tend to support the price of the bonds and thus reduce the interest rate risk borne by bondholders. The traditional sinking fund arrangement is also used. Under this arrangement, the issuing firm is required periodically to repurchase bonds.

---

[10] Bearer bonds are no longer legal in the United States.

If the market price of the bonds is above the par value, the firm will pay the par value and the bonds will be picked by lottery. On the other hand, if the market price is below the par value, the firm simply purchases the bonds in the open market. Sinking funds reduce the default risk borne by bondholders. Note that in the sinking fund arrangement the issuer is obligated to repurchase at specified intervals. With the purchase fund, a repurchase takes place only if there is a fall in bond prices.

As noted earlier, the eurobond market is growing rapidly. This reflects the growing sophistication of the market and a desire on the part of investors to invest directly rather than through a eurobank. Note, however, that eurobanks are very important in the eurobond issuing process, since they participate in the eurobond market in much the same way as American investment bankers participate in the American bond market. In addition, banks are sometimes important borrowers in the eurobond market. Banks also play an important role in developing the secondary market for eurobonds (which has been traditionally weak). In general, the eurobond market is becoming more liquid, more flexible, and more efficient. The outlook is for continued expansion of this market.

International Lending Agencies

The post–World War II period witnessed an explosion in the number of international lending agencies whose primary purpose is to promote economic development, especially in developing countries. In order to achieve this objective, these agencies, in cooperation with governments, provide financing for specific projects or needs. Under normal circumstances, multinational firms are not the direct recipients of loans from these international organizations. For example, it is highly unlikely that General Motors would be able to obtain financing from any international lending organization in order to build a plant in Brazil. This does not mean, however, that the activities of international lending organizations will not affect General Motors. For example, if Brazil obtains project financing in order to develop its infrastructure (roads, power, etc.), foreign firms may benefit indirectly by this project. Some of the more important international lending agencies are the following:

The International Bank for Reconstruction and Development (World Bank). The World Bank makes "hard" loans to developing countries for specific projects. This means that the project must be one that is expected to generate enough future revenue to repay the loan. Borrowers of World Bank loans must meet strict requirements. A country (not a firm) submits a loan application to the World Bank. This application shows the costs and expected revenues of the project.

Officers of the World Bank analyze the application and extend the loan only if it meets high standards. From the borrowing country's point of view, World Bank loans are attractive because of their large size and favorable interest rates.

The International Development Association (IDA). The IDA is part of the World Bank. The IDA makes "soft" loans to developing countries. Its loans are more risky from the lenders' point of view and tend to go to projects that do not meet the high standards applied to regular World Bank loans. These loans, however, may improve the country's economy.

The International Finance Corporation (IFC). The IFC is another part of the World Bank group and is designed to provide loans to *private* firms operating in developing countries. Generally, the recipients of this financing are undertaking projects that will enhance the development of the country. This is a relatively small program.

The past 25 years have also seen an explosion of *regional development agencies*. The goals of these agencies are similar to those of the World Bank, except that their activities are restricted to a specific geographic area. For example, the African Development Bank (ADB) promotes the economic and social development of African nations.

A Global Equity Market?

The world is also moving toward greater integration in equity markets. This trend is demonstrated by the fact that the significant decline in American stock prices during October 1987 was mirrored in the stock markets of Japan, Hong Kong, London, Germany, and elsewhere. Stock markets are no longer isolated from each other. They are no longer purely domestic. Today it is possible to buy the common stock of American firms in London or Japan. It is also possible to buy the stock of Japanese or British firms in New York.

The purchase and sale of foreign stocks in a domestic market do not usually represent new issues. Rather, these are secondary market activities representing sales by an existing owner of the stock. A firm is not directly affected by the secondary market of its securities. For example, when shares of General Motors change hands in New York or London, General Motors does not receive or pay any funds. However, the importance of secondary markets to the firm cannot be minimized. The price and liquidity of securities affect the ability of the firm to issue new securities in the primary market. A worldwide interest in the common stock of a company reduces the liquidity risk borne by an investor and makes the investor more willing to hold the stock.

Can an American firm sell a new issue of stock in London or another foreign stock market? While such an event is possible, it is highly unlikely. The American financial market is still the place for American firms to sell new issues of common stock. However, some foreign firms, either directly or indirectly, sell new stock in the American common stock market. At this time equity markets are primarily domestic, but the future is unclear. There has been a movement toward the internationalization of equity markets in recent years. If this trend continues, it is possible that the market for new issues of common stock will develop along the same lines as the markets for bonds and loans.

Overview of the International Debt Market

The internationalization of financial markets is proceeding at a very rapid pace. As shown in Table 9-10, the size of this internationalized marketplace increased by more than 28 percent over the 1984–1987 period. Increasingly, firms are looking beyond national borders for financing. No firm of even moderate size can ignore this important development. The world of finance is no longer the same, and managers must begin to think differently than they have in the past. It is interesting to note that in 1987, Japan replaced the United States as the largest borrower of international bond issues and bank credits. This reflects the increasing importance of Japanese firms in international financial markets.

TABLE 9-10   International Bond Issues and Bank Credit* (in Millions of Dollars)

Borrower Is From:	1984	1985	1986	1987
United States	$65,054	$69,193	$56,774	$45,412
Japan	$17,526	$21,269	$35,508	$45,591
United Kingdom	$8,899	$25,424	$24,295	$33,225
Other industrial countries	$85,598	$110,825	$153,654	$124,530
Total industrial countries	$177,077	$226,711	$270,231	$248,758
Latin American countries	$17,464	$8,115	$3,192	$10,729
Asian countries	$15,893	$18,410	$15,291	$13,219
Middle Eastern and African	$6,368	$5,613	$5,834	$4,122
Eastern European	$3,244	$5,236	$4,091	$3,564
International organizations	$13,287	$20,635	$18,916	$20,013
Total issues and credits	$233,333	$284,720	$317,556	$300,405

*In addition to eurobonds and foreign bonds, these figures include new loans made by the international banking system.

Source: *World Financial Markets*, Morgan Guaranty Trust Company of New York, September–October 1987, p. 18, and July 1988, p. 16. Used with permission of the copyright holder, Morgan Guaranty Trust Company of New York.

Eurobonds Compared to Euroloans

The large size of the eurobond market should not obscure the fact that euroloans also have some advantages over eurobonds. From the borrower's point of view, the main advantage of the eurobond market is that it has longer maturities. In addition, some borrowers may feel that it is advantageous to borrow on a fixed rate basis, and such borrowing opportunities are available in the eurobond market. Today both the eurocurrency loan market and the eurobond market can undertake transactions in excess of $1 billion. Perhaps euroloans have a slight advantage in that a very large loan can be arranged more easily than a very large bond issue can be floated. The big advantages of eurocurrency loans are the multicurrency clause and the drawdown provision. These features give the borrower flexibility that is not available in the eurobond market. In addition, loans can be arranged more quickly (2–3 weeks) than eurobonds can be floated (6–7 weeks).

The Euromarket
Compared to the U.S. Market

The euromarket, which includes both the euroloan and eurobond markets, has real advantages for the borrower. Both interest rates and flotation costs are lower in the euromarkets. The multicurrency feature of euroloans has a real advantage for firms interested in managing foreign exchange rate risk exposure. It is much easier to issue eurobonds than it is to issue bonds in the United States. Further, the speed of issue associated with bank loans is believed to be greater in euromarkets than in the U.S. financial market. The major advantage of the American financial market is that it can accommodate both large and small firms, while the euromarket is the exclusive domain of the best-known and most sound borrowers.

The Euromarket
Compared to Foreign Markets

Just as the euromarket has advantages relative to the U.S. financial market, it has advantages over other domestic financial markets. From the American firm's perspective, it may be easier and less costly to borrow a foreign currency (e.g., deutsche marks) in the euromarket than in the foreign country (Germany). It is important to remember that foreign firms regularly engaged in business in a specific foreign country usually maintain a banking relationship in that country and frequently borrow from that bank. A close local banking relationship is essential for the conduct of business. In addition, most currencies are not traded on the euromarkets, and the only source of other foreign currency loans may be in the local financial market.

Foreign currency–denominated eurobonds may also be easier to sell than foreign bonds in the same currency, and the rate may be lower. Of course, foreign bonds are still used, although their volume is only 25 percent of the volume of eurobonds. However, the use of foreign bonds reflects the secrecy and tax advantages of floating foreign bonds in Switzerland and the great size and liquidity of the American financial market. If Switzerland and the United States are excluded from the list, less than $7 billion in foreign bonds were sold in 1987 (see Table 9-1). This compares to a eurobond market size of $140 billion in the same year. Today firms attempting to sell bonds in foreign countries are looking to the eurobond market, not the foreign bond market.

Summary and Conclusions

The post–World War II period has seen a significant change in financial institutions. This has been true in the domestic as well as the international environment. Large American firms now have the opportunity to borrow dollars both inside and outside the United States. This is true for bank loans as well as new bond issues.

In addition to borrowing dollars, American firms have the opportunity to borrow foreign currencies. Bank loans as well as bond issues can be denominated in a number of foreign currencies. This has important implications in the management of foreign exchange risk by American firms. This chapter has introduced the reader to international financial markets. The next two chapters will discuss how the existence of this global financial market can affect stockholder wealth.

Review Questions

1. Describe the role played by financial intermediaries in facilitating the flow of funds from savers to borrowers.
2. Define foreign bonds and explain how such a bond differs from a eurobond.
3. Explain the meaning of a eurocurrency deposit, and describe the factors that have contributed to the development of the eurocurrency market.
4. Explain how a single deposit can generate a multiple increase in eurodeposits.
5. Why are some American firms able to borrow dollars at a lower interest rate in London than in the United States?
6. What would happen if the government of the United Kingdom imposed reserve requirements on eurocurrency deposits in London?
7. In the second half of the 1980s, interest rates on euroyen and euromark deposits were well below the interest rate on eurodollar deposits. Why was this so?
8. What is LIBOR, and how is it used in the euroloan market?
9. Explain how a multicurrency clause included in a euroloan operates.
10. What is the eurobond market, and why has it grown so much in recent years?

11. Is it better for an American firm to raise funds in the euromarkets in the form of a euroloan or by selling eurobonds?
12. If interest rates are lower in euromarkets, why should an American firm ever borrow in the United States?

Questions for Discussion

1. Assume that you are employed by a large American multinational firm that produces and sells construction equipment. Your firm is increasing its penetration into world markets, and new funds are needed in order to expand production and distribution. Traditionally, your firm has raised all capital in the United States. The manager of the finance department has heard that it may be possible to save money by borrowing dollars in Europe rather than in the United States. You are asked to examine the feasibility of such dollar borrowing and to outline the advantages and disadvantages of this alternative.
2. (Continuation of Discussion Question 1). After you have completed your report on borrowing dollars in Europe, your supervisor learns that it may also be possible to borrow foreign currencies. Because of the low interest rates for deutsche mark, Swiss franc, and Japanese yen loans, your supervisor is particularly interested in these alternatives. You are asked to prepare another report, this time on foreign currency borrowing. You are asked to indicate the advantages and disadvantages of various strategies for borrowing these foreign currencies.

Research Activities

1. From published financial information, compare the cost of short-term (90-day) dollar borrowings for a large, low-risk American corporation using (a) the American financial markets or (b) the euromarkets.
2. From published financial information, compare the cost of long-term (20-year) dollar borrowings for a large, low-risk American corportion using (a) the American financial markets or (b) the euromarkets.
3. From published financial information, compare the cost of long-term (20-year) borrowings for a large, low-risk American corporation using (a) dollars or (b) foreign currencies.

Bibliography

Aubey, Robert T., and Cramer, Robert H. "The Use of International Currency Cocktails in the Reduction of Exchange Rate Risk." *Journal of Economics and Business*, Winter 1977, pp. 128–135.

Barrett, W. Brian, and Kolb, Robert W. "The Structure of International Bond Risk Differentials." *Journal of International Business Studies*, Spring 1986, pp. 107–118.

Brigham, Eugene F. *Fundamentals of Financial Management*, 4th ed. Chicago: Dryden Press, 1986.

Coats, Warren L., Jr. "The Weekend Eurodollar Game." *Journal of Finance*, June 1981, pp. 649–659.

Crabbe, Matthew. "All Change in the Eurobond Market." *Euromoney*, December 1987, pp. 42–48.

Dufey, Gunter, and Giddy, Ian H. *The International Money Market*. Englewood Cliffs, NJ: Prentice-Hall, Inc., 1978.

_____ "Innovation in the International Financial Markets." *Journal of International Business Studies*, Fall 1981, pp. 35–51.

Emery, Robert F. *The Japanese Money Market*. Lexington, MA: Lexington Books, 1984.

Finnerty, Joseph E., and Schneeweis, Thomas. "Time Series Analysis of International Dollar Denominated Interest Rates." *Journal of International Business Studies*, Spring–Summer 1979, pp. 39–52.

Finnerty, Joseph E., Schneeweis, Thomas, and Hegde, Shantaram P. "Interest Rates in the $Eurobond Market." *Journal of Financial and Quantitative Analysis*, September 1980, pp. 743–755.

Folks, William R., and Avanti, Ramesh. "Raising Funds with Foreign Currency." *Financial Executive*, February 1980, pp. 44–49.

Frankel, Jeffrey A. "The Diversifiability of Exchange Risk." *Journal of International Economics*, August 1979, pp. 379–393.

Friedman, Milton. "The Euro-Dollar Market: Some First Principles." *The Morgan Guaranty Survey*, October 1969, pp. 1–11.

Grabbe, J. Orlin. *International Financial Markets*. New York: Elsevier Science Publishing Co., 1986.

Johnson, R. Stafford, Hultman, Charles W., and Zuber, Richard A. "Currency Cocktails and Exchange Rate Stability." *Columbia Journal of World Business*, Winter 1979, pp. 117–126.

Johnson, R. Stafford, and Zuber, Richard A. "Model for Constructing Currency Cocktails." *Business Economics*, May 1979, pp. 9–14.

Kemp, Lynette J. *A Guide to World Money and Capital Markets*. New York: McGraw-Hill Book Company, 1982.

Kerr, Ian. *A History of the Eurobond Market: The First 21 Years*. London: Euromoney Publications, 1984.

Little, Jame S. *Euro-Dollars: The Money Market Gypsies*. New York: Harper and Row, 1975.

Lusztig, Peter, and Schab, Bernard. "Units of Account in the International Bond Market." *Columbia Journal of World Business*, Spring 1975, pp. 74–79.

Mahajan, Arvind, and Fraser, Donald R. "Dollar Eurobond and U.S. Bond Pricing," *Journal of International Business Studies*, Summer 1986, pp. 21–36.

Quinn, Brian S. "The International Bond Market for the U.S. Investor." *Columbia Journal of World Business*, Fall 1979, pp. 85–90.

Robichek, Alexander A., and Eaker, Mark R. "Debt Denomination and Exchange Risk in International Capital Markets." *Financial Management*, Autumn 1976, pp. 11–18.

Starr, Danforth W. "Opportunities for U.S. Corporate Borrowers in the International Bond Markets." *Financial Executive*, June 1979, pp. 50–59.

Yassukovich, Stanislas M. "Eurobonds and Debt Rescheduling." *Euromoney*, January 1982, pp. 60–62.

_____ "The Rise of International Equity." *Euromoney*, May 1984, pp. 63–68.

10

International Dimensions of Capital Structure

This is the second of three chapters dealing with international aspects of the firm's financing decisions. The focus now is on the right-hand side of the balance sheet and how the internationalization of the world of business has enlarged the range of financing opportunities available to the firm. In which financial market should the firm raise capital? Should the firm borrow dollars or foreign currency? These are the questions of interest in this chapter. Remember that the answers to these questions must be sought within the context of stockholder wealth maximization. In other words, the firm should choose the alternative that maximizes the wealth of its stockholders. Thus, the alternatives must always be evaluated in terms of both their risk and return implications.

The Cost of Capital Concept

When discussed in the introductory business finance course, the cost of capital is usually presented as a firmwide concept. That is, every firm is

TABLE 10-1 Computing the Cost of Capital: An Illustration

	Weight	Cost	Product
Debt	0.25	0.10 (1 − 0.34)	0.0165
Equity	0.75	0.16	0.12
	Weighted average cost of capital		0.1365 = 13.65%

assumed to have a cost of capital that reflects its unique risk profile. The steps involved in computing the firmwide cost of capital include the following:[1]

1. Estimate the optimal debt ratio for the firm.
2. Estimate the before- and after-tax cost of debt capital.
3. Estimate the cost of equity capital.
4. Estimate the weighted average cost of capital.

Mathematically, the weighted average cost of capital can be expressed as follows:

$$K_a = K_d(1 - T)\left(\frac{D}{A}\right) + K_s\left(1 - \frac{D}{A}\right) \qquad (10\text{-}1)$$

where K_a = weighted average cost of capital
K_d = before-tax cost of debt
K_s = required rate of return of stockholders
T = marginal tax rate of the firm
D/A = debt to total assets (debt ratio)

Note that the cost of debt is multiplied by 1 minus the tax rate in order to calculate the after-tax cost of debt. This is due to the fact that interest payments are tax deductible, while returns to stockholders are not.

Consider the situation in which a firm has $20,000,000 in assets (the left-hand side of the balance sheet) and $20,000,000 in capital (the right-hand side of the balance sheet). In addition, the firm determines that its optimal capital structure calls for a debt ratio of 25 percent.[2] Further assume that the before-tax cost of debt is 10 percent and the cost of equity is 16 percent. Finally, assume that the marginal tax rate of the firm is 34 percent. Using the methodology illustrated in Table 10-1, the cost of capital under these assumptions is equal to 13.65 percent.

The cost of capital is an important ingredient in any management strategy designed to increase stockholder wealth. Basically, the cost of

---

[1] For a more detailed discussion of the computation of the cost of capital see Eugene F. Brigham, *Fundamentals of Financial Management*, 4th ed., Chicago, Dryden Press, 1986, chapter 14.
[2] The concept of optimal capital structure is discussed in a later section of the chapter.

capital reflects the minimum amount that must be earned on assets and still return the amount required by capital (debt and equity) suppliers. For example, if a firm is making a $100,000 investment, it will need $100,000 in capital. If the cost of capital for the investment is 10 percent, the firm will need to earn $10,000 ($100,000 × 10 percent) simply to meet the required returns of the capital suppliers. If stockholder wealth is to be increased, the asset must earn more than 10 percent ($10,000). For example, if the firm earned $12,000 on the asset, $10,000 would go to meet the required returns of capital suppliers. The remaining $2,000 would belong to the stockholders and constitutes an increase in stockholder wealth. It is the present value of this excess return of $2,000 that would be reflected in a positive net present value for the investment. In other words, the stockholders will receive their required rate of return *plus* $2,000.

The Capital Structure Concept

The idea of *capital structure* can most easily be understood in the context of the balance sheet shown in Table 10-2. In order for the firm to function, it needs assets. It may need cash and other current assets. It may need fixed assets such as plant and equipment. In any event, the firm needs assets, and these assets must be financed in some manner. The firm finances the acquisition of assets by raising capital, and the types of capital raised by the firm are recorded on the right-hand side of the balance sheet. Capital is divided into two major categories: *liabilities* and *equity*. Total liabilities, which we will call *debt capital*, include current liabilities (maturing in less than 1 year) and long-term debt (maturing in more than 1 year). The most important equity accounts include the common stock and retained earnings accounts. The capital structure of the firm refers to the extent to which the firm's assets are financed by debt and is usually described using the *debt to total assets ratio* (the *debt ratio*). For example, a firm may be described as having a debt ratio of 60

TABLE 10-2 Hypothetical Balance Sheet

Assets	Liabilities and Equity
Current assets	Current liabilities
	Long-term debt
Fixed assets	Equity
Total assets	Total liabilities and equity

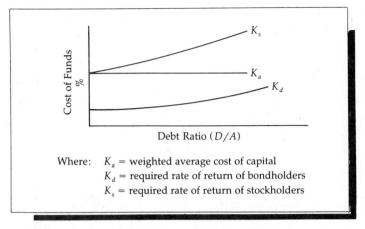

FIGURE 10-1 Optimal Capital Structure—CAPM

percent. This means that its capital structure is such that 60 percent of the total assets were financed by liabilities and the remainder by equity.

The concept of *optimal capital structure* has been extensively researched but still remains controversial.[3] The following discussion uses the capital asset pricing model (CAPM) to describe the optimal capital structure. We will first assume perfect markets. Specifically, we will assume no taxes and zero bankruptcy costs. As shown in Figure 10-1, under these unrealistic assumptions, the cost of capital (K_a) stays constant, regardless of the debt ratio of the firm. The advantage of substituting high-cost funds (equity) by lower-cost funds (debt) is entirely offset by the additional risk borne by the stockholders.[4]

The real world, however, is not as simple. Our conclusions may be significantly affected by relaxing the no-tax and zero bankruptcy cost assumptions in the following manner:

1. The U.S. tax laws create powerful incentives for the firm to use debt capital. In particular, the tax deductibility of interest payments makes the after-tax cost of debt capital, $K_d \times (1 - \text{tax rate})$, substantially less expensive than its before-tax cost (K_d). In effect the U.S. tax laws subsidize the use of debt. Equity, on the other hand, does not have such a subsidy. Dividends paid to stockholders are not deductible for tax purposes. Thus, stockholders may benefit if low-cost debt is substituted for higher-cost equity due to the reduction in taxes.

---

[3] The concepts of cost of capital and the optimal capital structure are discussed in Brigham, op. cit., chapters 14 and 15.

[4] The cost of capital remains constant due to interest arbitrage. A good illustration of this issue appears in James C. Van Horne, *Financial Management and Policy*, 7th ed., Englewood Cliffs, NJ: Prentice-Hall, Inc., 1986, pp. 280–282.

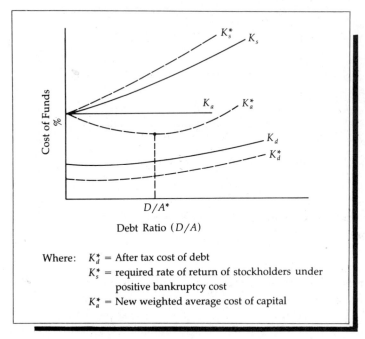

FIGURE 10-2 Optimal Capital Structure (Taxes and Bankruptcy Costs)

2. The existence of bankruptcy costs in the real world means that the heavy use of debt capital, which increases the firm's probability of bankruptcy, may result in losses to stockholders. The use of debt implies that the firm is contractually committed to make periodic payments to lenders, and failure to meet such payments may result in bankruptcy. This increase in the probability of bankruptcy would cause an increase in the expected bankruptcy cost (probability of bankruptcy ×bankruptcy costs). From the stockholders' point of view, an increase in the debt ratio increases the riskiness of the investment in the firm. This causes an increase in their required rate of return for the stock of the firm.

Using a high proportion of debt capital is beneficial to the stockholders in one way (lower cost due to the tax subsidy—higher dividends) and harmful in another (higher probability of bankruptcy—more risk). This relationship is illustrated in Figure 10-2. The deductibility of interest payments causes a decline in the after-tax cost of debt (dotted line). This reduces the cost of capital as the firm takes on additional debt. These benefits, however, are somewhat offset by the additional risks borne by stockholders. The increase in the probability of bankruptcy created by additional debt causes stockholders to demand a higher rate of return on their investment (dotted line). This increases the cost of capital as the firm takes on additional debt. The general conclusion is that the use of some debt capital reduces the cost of capital, because the tax benefits outweigh the additional expected costs of bankruptcy. At some level of debt, however, the tax benefits of additional debt are lower than the increase in expected bankruptcy costs. At this point, you have reached the minimum cost of capital that maximizes stockholder wealth. The controversy focuses on the issue of how much debt capital is too much.

Of course, firms have had to continue to do business while the controversy rages. In practice, well-run firms weigh the various factors involved and establish what might be called a *target capital structure*. This means that a target debt ratio is established, and the firm generally attempts to conduct its financing activities so that the target ratio is maintained. This does not mean, of course, that at every moment of every day the debt ratio is the same. For example, a firm may sell a very large bond issue in one year (which would drive up the debt ratio). Over the next few years, however, the firm may retain a substantial portion of earnings, which would drive down the debt ratio. The target debt ratio is just that, a target. It is not a straightjacket. While the target debt ratio for a particular firm is affected by many factors, most firms seem to have debt ratios in the 20–60 percent range.[5]

The Impact of International Capital Markets

Some American firms raise all their capital, both debt and equity, in dollars and in the United States. This chapter will discuss the impact of international financial markets on debt capital usage.[6] Firms that internationalize their financing strategy have a greater range of opportunities for raising debt capital. Specifically, an internationalized firm could borrow American dollars from a foreign source and/or could raise its debt capital by borrowing foreign currency (rather than American dollars). Remember that the firm has a target debt ratio and will always have a certain amount of debt capital.

The internationalization of the world's capital markets has two impacts on the way the firm raises capital. At the simplest level, access to world capital markets allows the firm to substitute money raised in foreign countries for money raised in the United States. There may be a

---

[5]The optimal capital structure is a function of many factors (e.g., stability of sales, costs). Different industries have different debt ratios. See Brigham, op. cit., pp. 520–521.

[6]Since the use of international equity markets by American firms has been almost nonexistent, it will not be discussed in this chapter. As noted in Chapter 9, however, future developments may lead to increased use of international equities by American firms.

number of motives for making such a substitution, the most important of which are likely to be the possibly lower cost of foreign borrowing and the relationship between foreign borrowing and lower foreign exchange rate risk. At a second level of analysis, access to the world's capital market may affect the capital structure of the firm. That is, international considerations may result in the firm's altering its target capital structure. For example, assume that before international borrowing opportunities became available, an American firm established a target debt ratio of 50 percent. This decision was reached only after management carefully weighed the benefits and risks associated with higher levels of debt. Now assume that the firm gains access to a foreign capital market, and that debt is much less expensive in that market compared to the U.S. debt markets (which is not usually the case). Given this new low-cost debt, the firm must reevaluate its target capital structure decision.

With the development of international capital markets, the capital structure decision has become more complicated. The firm must decide where to borrow (London, Tokyo, the United States, for example). It must decide on the currency in which to borrow (pounds, yen, or American dollars, for example). And it must decide on a target debt ratio. The difficulty in making these decisions stems from the fact that the decisions are interrelated. Proper decision-making procedure suggests that a simultaneous solution to all these problems be implemented. Once again, we find that the solution cannot be applied in a mechanical fashion. Management must use its skill and judgment. A conceptual framework for approaching the problem is presented in the sections that follow. The framework builds on the fact that different types of firms have different types of risk and therefore different borrowing opportunities.

Purely Domestic Firms: Borrowing Dollars Abroad

Let us begin by looking at firms that neither buy nor sell goods or services in foreign currencies. In the United States, for example, a public utility producing and selling electricity would fit into this category. While a public utility company can raise debt capital abroad if it is large enough, small firms are not likely to have access to global financial markets. The large firm, for example, could go to the London financial market and borrow dollars, pounds, deutsche marks, and a number of other currencies. All are available to a large, creditworthy customer, even if the firm operates solely within the United States and all the firm's revenues and expenses are denominated in dollars.

Should the domestic firm borrow dollars in the United States or abroad? The criterion for such a decision is primarily one of cost, since there is no exchange rate risk involved. And, as noted in Chapter 9, it is sometimes less expensive to borrow dollars abroad than in the United States. The eurodollar loans offered in London may be particularly attractive, since the rates there are often relatively low. It should be noted that while there are differences between the lending rates in the United States and London, these differences are usually very small. However, even annual interest savings of 0.10 percent can result in large dollar savings when the amounts borrowed are large.[7] In the ideal situation, the borrower gets exactly the same thing (dollars), but at a lower price. Of course, there are other considerations involved when deciding where the firm should borrow its dollars. An American bank may provide additional services and may have a more flexible relationship with its customers. An American firm looks at more than price when choosing a banking relationship. There is no reason, however, that an American firm cannot have both a foreign and an American bank.

The eurobond market also presents an opportunity for the domestic firm to borrow dollars in a foreign country. The interest rates on dollar-denominated eurobonds are usually lower than those on bonds sold in the United States. In addition, regulations on issuing the bonds are less burdensome than those in the United States. Again, the firm gets exactly the same thing (dollars) with a dollar eurobond issue, but at a lower cost, and gives up nothing in return. There seems to be no reason that eligible firms, even domestic ones, should avoid this market.

Purely Domestic Firm: Borrowing Foreign Currencies

The domestic firm could also borrow foreign currencies (e.g. deutsche marks, British pounds) in foreign markets. Presumably, the foreign currency would be converted to dollars and the funds employed in the United States. In order to make interest and principal payments, the domestic firm in the United States would periodically convert dollars to the foreign currency and remit the payment, in the foreign currency, to the lender. There is an obvious transaction exchange rate risk associated with this strategy. The firm that borrows in a foreign currency has contractually committed itself to make foreign currency payments. Since the domestic firm has no other foreign currency dealings, it will be in a permanent short position in that particular currency.

At this point, it is necessary to reintroduce one of the basic exchange rate relationships discussed in Chapter 2 and the ideas relating to the

---

[7]See Table 9-6 for the actual differences in deposit interest rates.

TABLE 10-3   Bobo Electrical Utility Corporation: Borrowing Alternatives

Basic Data
  a. Amount required = $1,000,000.
  b. Term of the loan is 1 year.
  c. Interest rate in the United States is 10%.
  d. Interest rate in Germany is 5%.
  e. Spot exchange rate is DM1 = $0.5000.
  f. The 1-year forward exchange rate is DM1 = $0.5238.

Alternative 1: Borrow $1,000,000 in the United States.
  a. Interest rate = 10%.
  b. Repay $1,100,000 in 1 year.

Alternative 2: Borrow DM2,000,000 in Germany.
  a. Convert to dollars at the spot rate of DM1 = $0.5000. This makes $1,000,000 available in the United States.
  b. Interest rate = 5%.
  c. Repay DM2,100,000 in 1 year.
  d. Cover exchange rate risk by buying DM2,100,000 forward at DM1 = $0.5238. At that forward rate, the firm will deliver (repay) $1,100,000 at the end of the year (slight rounding error). The amount repaid is exactly the same as if dollars had been borrowed in the United States.

hedging of transaction exposure discussed in Chapter 7. Consistent with the principle of interest rate parity, the difference in interest rates between two currencies will equal the forward discount or premium. In the absence of transaction costs, there would be no advantage or disadvantage in borrowing foreign currency at a lower interest rate and then covering the exchange rate risk with a forward contract. Consider the illustration presented in Table 10-3, in which the Bobo Electrical Utility Corporation, a domestic firm, needs to add $1,000,000 in debt and decides that a 1-year maturity is appropriate for its present financing requirements. The funds can be borrowed in the United States at an annual rate of 10 percent. As an alternative, the firm can borrow DM2,000,000 in Germany at an interest rate of 5 percent. The deutsche marks would be converted to dollars at the spot rate (DM1 = $0.5000), and the firm would have its $1,000,000.

If the firm borrows deutsche marks and does nothing else, it will be at risk, since it must repay the deutsche mark borrowings in the same currency. However, the firm could hedge this short position by buying deutsche marks forward. As shown in Alternative 2 of Table 10-3, DM2,100,000 will be needed to make the debt payment. These funds could be purchased at the forward rate of DM1 = $0.5238. Under these conditions (and in the absence of transaction costs), the firm winds up paying exactly the same number of dollars whether it borrows in the

United States or Germany. The lower German interest rate is offset by the higher forward exchange rate.

The preceding illustration worked out the way it did because the conditions of interest rate parity were present. Specifically, the difference in interest rates was equal to the forward premium on the mark. If transaction costs were incorporated into the example (in this case, the cost of converting marks to dollars at the time of borrowing and dollars to marks when principal and interest are repaid), borrowing deutsche marks would have been more expensive than borrowing in the United States. Once again, the reader must be reminded that the analysis represents a general tendency. In practice, one bank may offer a lower rate than another. This is true whether the banks are located in the same or different countries. However, a powerful conclusion must also be drawn: lower interest rates on foreign currency loans do not necessarily represent a good borrowing opportunity for the firm.

Of course, the firm does not have to cover its short position. It may decide to borrow at the lower foreign currency interest rate and hope that the foreign currency does not increase in value. This unhedged position is a gamble. Since, on the average, the future spot rate will be equal to the forward rate (the forward rate is an unbiased estimator of the future spot rate), the dollar consequences of both alternatives should be the same (ignoring transaction costs).[8] If transaction costs are included, the unhedged position should be slightly less expensive. However, the firm is at greater risk if it fails to hedge.

To summarize, only large domestic firms have access to international financial markets. Either dollars or foreign currencies can be borrowed in those markets. The attractiveness of foreign currency loans to the domestic firm should be minimal because such borrowing results in transaction exposure. Dollar-denominated loans contracted in foreign countries may be less expensive and, after considering service factors, may be attractive to the domestic firm. Note that the difference in interest rates is likely to be small. But even small differences in interest rates can amount to large dollar savings when the size of the borrowing is large.

Exporting Firms

For the large exporting firm, borrowing dollars in foreign markets has the same implications as for a domestic firm. No more or less risk is involved, and the cost savings associated with borrowing dollars abroad must be weighed against the differences in convenience and services. Firms that

---

[8]This issue was discussed in detail in Chapter 5.

regularly export, however, may have a greater incentive to borrow foreign currencies abroad. Such firms may be able to take advantage of possible lower foreign interest rates while at the same time reducing their transaction exposure to exchange rate risk. Some firms may be able to accomplish these very desirable objectives while simultaneously eliminating the transaction cost associated with converting foreign currency to dollars. Foreign borrowing by an exporting firm, if available, may be a very attractive alternative to domestic borrowing.

Whenever the exporting firm invoices sales in one or more foreign currencies, it will be long in those currencies. If the long-term strategy of the American firm is to sell abroad and accept payment in foreign currencies, it will be in a continuous long position. Since the firm does not know the level of future exchange rates, it is at risk. What is at risk for the firm is the current obligations to accept not only foreign currencies, but also future foreign currency revenues that have not yet been contracted. Such exposure is long-term and economic in nature. Continuous indebtedness in the foreign currencies to which the firm is exposed can be used to offset the risk of changes in foreign currency values. By using foreign currency–denominated debt on a continuous basis, the firm creates a foreign use for its projected foreign currency receipts. The firm no longer need worry about the dollar value of the foreign currency, since there is no reason to convert to dollars. This particular strategy is called a *balance sheet hedge*.

The Balance Sheet Hedge

The basic logic of the balance sheet hedge involves substituting foreign debt for American dollar-denominated debt (thus changing the balance sheet). The foreign debt is then repaid with revenues from foreign sales. The balance sheet hedging strategy may give the firm access to lower-cost foreign funds and simultaneously reduce exchange rate risk. An illustration of a balance sheet hedge is presented in Table 10-4.

The Denbo Corporation illustration provides two interesting insights into foreign borrowing and exchange rate risk minimization. Firms that have high levels of foreign sales may not be able to eliminate all exchange rate risk using the balance sheet hedge. For example, if the Denbo Corporation had Canadian dollar annual sales of C$25,000,000 it would have needed to borrow C$250,000,000 in order to eliminate exchange rate risk. This amount of Canadian borrowing would be equivalent to $175,000,000, which far exceeds the Denbo Corporation's target debt ratio. The general principle involved here is that it is frequently impossible to hedge all exchange rate risk using the balance sheet hedge.

But there is another important side to the story. A firm with a large volume of foreign currency sales may be able to borrow as much as it

TABLE 10-4   Denbo Corporation: Balance Sheet Hedge for Canadian Sales*

1. *Conditions*
   a. The Denbo Corporation is an American manufacturer of electronic test equipment.
   b. Denbo has long-term debt of $100,000,000. The entire debt is in the form of long-term loans. This amount is consistent with the firm's target debt ratio.
   c. The firm sells in Canada on a continuous basis, and sales of C$5,000,000 are anticipated every year for the next 5 years.
   d. Denbo is able to obtain long-term financing in Canada at an annual rate of 10%.
   e. The spot exchange rate is C$1 = $0.70.

2. *Balance Sheet Hedge*
   Borrow Canadian dollars and use the expected Canadian dollar inflows to repay the debt. Denbo then reduces its American dollar indebtedness.
   a. Obtain a long-term loan of C$50,000,000 at an annual interest rate of 10%. Annual interest payments will be C$5,000,000.
   b. Convert C$50,000,000 to American dollars at the spot rate of C$1 = $0.70. Denbo will now have $35,000,000.
   c. Use the proceeds of the currency conversion to reduce the dollar-denominated debt by $35,000,000. The firm will now owe $65,000,000 and C$50,000,000.
   d. Use Canadian dollar sales to meet interest payments on the Canadian dollar loan. No American dollars need be converted to meet this Canadian dollar obligation. Canadian dollar sales do not have to be converted to American dollars.

*We are assuming that the annual Canadian dollar cash flows are certain. In addition, we are ignoring the foreign exchange risk on the maturity of the C$50,000,000 loan.

wants in foreign markets without incurring additional exchange rate risk. In fact, exchange rate risk will be reduced. This is an entirely different situation than exists for the firm with no foreign currency revenues. For example, the number of Canadian dollars borrowed by the Denbo Corporation is a function of the difference between interest rates in Canada and the United States. If, for example, the interest rate on Canadian dollars is 10 percent, the interest rate on American dollars is 10 percent, and the exchange rates are not expected to change, the advantage would be toward the Canadian dollar, since borrowing that currency reduces exchange rate risk.

Some American firms sell continuously in many different countries and agree to accept payment in many different currencies. The international capital markets have responded to this situation by inserting multicurrency clauses in euroloan agreements. With a multicurrency clause, a single bank loan, for example, can include different currencies. For example, a loan may consist of 25 percent deutsche marks, 40 percent French francs, 20 percent Canadian dollars, and 15 percent British pounds. The rates on such loans are usually renegotiated periodically (every 3 months, for example), and at that time the proportions devoted to each currency can be altered at the discretion of the borrower. This vehicle is ideal for balance sheet hedging, since borrowing can be tailored to meet changing sales patterns. If the firm anticipates that sales in French francs will increase, an increased portion of the loan can be shifted to that currency.

For the exporting firm, there are powerful incentives to enter international capital markets. First, the cost of funds in these markets may be lower than in the United States. Second, the substitution of foreign currency borrowing for American dollar borrowing may reduce the riskiness of the firm due to the reduction in foreign exchange risk.

Importing Firms

American importing firms usually pay for purchases in dollars and thus have no foreign exchange rate risk. The advantages and disadvantages of such a firm's entry into the international capital markets are generally the same as those for a domestic firm. For qualifying firms, dollars borrowed abroad may be less expensive than dollars borrowed in the United States. The lower cost of foreign currency borrowing, however, must be weighed against the increase in foreign exchange risk. Generally, neither domestic nor importing firms find borrowing foreign currencies an attractive alternative.[9]

There is one special set of circumstances that may encourage importing firms to borrow abroad. A number of countries provide financing at below-market rates to foreign buyers of their goods. For example, assume that a West German manufacturer sells a machine to an American firm. If the item being sold and the buying firm are eligible, the German *export-import bank* may lend the money to the American buyer at a below-market interest rate. The intent of the program is to encourage exports from Germany by helping foreigners pay for the goods purchased. In the United States, the Export-Import Bank, an agency of the U.S. government, provides a similar service. While the eligibility rules for such subsidized financing are complicated and vary from country to country, the loans are usually reserved for expensive capital goods such as machinery and equipment.

An American importer may find an agency of a foreign government (the equivalent of the U.S. Export-Import Bank) that is willing to provide low-cost financing. Usually the loans offered by these government agencies will be in their own currency, although sometimes dollar loans may be available. For purposes of illustration, assume that an American firm purchases $10,000,000 in products from a German firm and the German

---

[9]If the American importer pays in foreign currency, it is continuously short in that currency. Therefore, borrowing foreign currencies would not reduce transaction exposure. In fact, transaction exposure would increase in such situations.

export financing bank agrees to finance the purchase for 1 year in deutsche marks at an annual interest rate of 4 percent. Also assume that the spot rate for the deutsche mark is DM1 = $0.50 and the 1-year forward rate is DM1 = $0.52. The firm will borrow DM20,000,000 ($10,000,000/0.50) and will be obligated to repay DM20,800,000 (DM20,000,000 × 1.04) in 1 year. This alternative, however, has the added risk of possible fluctuations in the value of the deutsche mark over the next year. The firm can, of course, hedge this risk in the forward market. It can enter into a forward contract to purchase DM20,800,000 for delivery in 1 year for $10,816,000 (DM20,800,000 × $0.52). If the firm chooses this option, it will have eliminated the risk of foreign exchange rate fluctuations. Note that the real cost of this loan is higher than is suggested by the 4 percent interest rate alone, since the deutsche mark is also expected to strengthen against the dollar over the next year. The attractiveness of the subsidized deutsche mark financing will depend on the cost of dollar-denominated loans. For example, if dollars can be borrowed at a rate of 10 percent per year, the firm would have to pay $11,000,000 at the end of the year. The firm would save $184,000 by accepting the deutsche mark financing package. As a general rule, the interest rates charged by government export financing organizations are low enough to make borrowing (and the goods being financed) attractive to foreign purchasers.

Multinational Firms

At the very least, the multinational firm has the same motivations for borrowing funds abroad as the exporting firm. That is, the firm may be enticed by lower interest rates into borrowing dollars in foreign markets. Like the exporting firm, the multinational may have continuous transaction exposure in foreign currencies and may find it attractive to borrow these currencies in order to create a balance sheet hedge.[10] However, two other factors complicate the multinational firm's financing strategy.

First, it may be easier for a multinational to borrow foreign currencies. While all firms of sufficient size have access to global capital markets (London, Switzerland, etc.), access to capital markets in less developed countries is often restricted to local firms. For example, an American firm exporting to or importing from Brazil will find it very difficult to borrow in Brazil. On the other hand, a multinational firm with a subsidiary in Brazil may have access to Brazilian currency loans. Since some foreign

---

[10]A multinational firm may also be diversified in a variety of countries and currencies. This issue was discussed in detail in Chapter 6. The reduction of economic exposure through diversification of sales, financing, and so on also applies to firms other than multinationals.

governments keep domestic interest rates artificially low, the multinational may have access to inexpensive foreign funds. However, one should not overemphasize the importance of the multinational's access to low-cost foreign borrowing, since governments often restrict the use of such funds by a foreign firms even when the firm is operating a subsidiary in the country. Many developing countries strive to get the multinational to finance operations with funds from abroad and attempt to minimize the availability of local debt capital to the firm.

Second, multinationals differ from other types of firms in terms of their risk profile. In addition to foreign exchange rate risk, the multinational firm may be exposed to political risks. By definition, the multinational firm makes an investment in a foreign country. To the extent that the parent corporation invests its own funds in the foreign operation, it becomes a hostage of the foreign government. The foreign government may so interfere with the operations of the subsidiary that it becomes unprofitable to the parent. In extreme cases, the government may take over the property of the multinational and refuse to pay fair compensation. Actions such as these are most likely to occur in the less developed countries, although even developed countries have sometimes responded in this fashion.[11]

One way a multinational firm can manage the political risks associated with foreign investments is by borrowing in foreign countries. By borrowing from local investors and banks, the multinational can reduce its investment and the potential losses due to political actions. In addition, governments may be less willing to take action against a multinational if local investors will also be affected. For these reasons, multinationals have often attempted to borrow from local investors. In some cases, the multinational may even be willing to pay a premium for the funds in order to reduce its political risk exposure. For the multinational, borrowing abroad is not only a question of cost and exchange rate risk management. Foreign borrowing may also be a method for managing political risk.

Once again, it is necessary to provide some "tone" to this picture of risk. Actions against multinational firms are not an everyday occurrence, and there are things (other than foreign borrowing) that the multinational firm can do to avoid losses due to political actions.[12] It is also important to note that while foreign borrowing may reduce the political risk, it may also lead to local investor interference with the management of the firm and reduce the profitability of the subsidiary. In addition, government regulation of underdeveloped capital market institutions

---

[11] Exporters also have some political risk, since governments may restrict foreign currency payments. Historically, this has been less of a problem than the nationalization of the assets of foreign firms. This issue will be discussed in Chapter 11.

[12] A more complete discussion of political risk is presented in Chapter 11.

may make it impossible to borrow from local investors. One should not leave this section with the idea that all multinationals that are threatened by political action will necessarily respond by borrowing in the host country. Foreign borrowing to avoid political risk is an alternative that is attractive only under some conditions.

Now back to the central questions: "Should the multinational firm borrow abroad?" "Should the multinational borrow in foreign currencies?" The answers to these questions will depend on how the management of the firm weighs various factors.

1. The attractiveness of potentially lower rates on dollar borrowings that are available in global capital markets must be weighed against the advantages of maintaining strong ties to financial institutions and markets in the United States.
2. The borrowing of foreign currency will depend on:
   a. The extent to which the firm has continuous transaction exposure in a foreign currency.
   b. The extent to which the firm has access to foreign currency borrowing.
   c. The level of political risk as perceived by management and the availability of alternative strategies for dealing with that risk.
   d. The extent to which management anticipates that foreign investors will interfere with the management of the foreign subsidiary.

It is impossible to develop guidelines that would be appropriate for every multinational in all circumstances. It seems reasonable, however, to conclude that there are so many incentives for a multinational to raise dollar and foreign currency capital abroad that most multinationals will do so. The policy implemented by a particular multinational firm will depend on its unique circumstances.

Target Capital Structure Reconsidered

In all of our discussions so far, we have assumed that the firm has a target capital structure and attempts to maintain it. In the absence of government-subsidized financing, differences in effective interest rates among currencies are not likely to be large enough to force the firm to reconsider its target capital structure. In rare cases, however, the availability of subsidized financing may alter the firm's target capital structure.

Remember, management arrives at a target capital structure by weighing the tax benefits of low-cost debt against the increased risk of bankruptcy associated with higher debt ratios. The final target capital structure reflects a balance between these to factors. Of course, if there is a sudden shift in the size of the benefit associated with using debt, the firm may have to reconsider its target debt ratio. Under some (albeit infrequent) circumstances, such situations are caused by export financing or other government subsidy programs. The cost savings generated by such programs may be great enough to encourage management to assume a debt position that is more likely to lead to bankruptcy. Consider the following illustration.

Assume that a firm is planning to develop a new mine in the United States and needs a wide variety of machinery and equipment, most of which could be purchased from American as well as foreign suppliers. Also assume that while foreign prices are competitive with those of American suppliers, the foreign sellers are able to offer subsidized financing as part of their package. Thus, the firm may end up buying trucks from a Swedish manufacturer and financing the purchase at subsidized rates through Svensk Export credit. It may buy crushing equipment from a German manufacturer and finance it through Ausfuhrkredit-Gesellschaft. It may buy French loading equipment, Italian steel, British ore-handling equipment, machinery from Japan, and so on. All of these purchases can be made with subsidized financing. The management of the firm may be willing to tolerate a very high target debt ratio in order to take advantage of all the subsidies involved.

Figure 10-3 illustrates how the availability of low-cost foreign debt will affect the capital structure of the firm. The lower cost of debt is reflected in the line K_d^*, which in turn leads to a lower firmwise cost of capital (K_a^*). Most importantly, the lowest point on the cost of capital curve is shifted to the right, which indicates that the firm's optimal capital structure now includes a higher proportion of debt.

Figure 10-3 shows another possible factor that will affect the target capital structure. In some cases, borrowing in international markets reduces the foreign exchange or political risk borne by the firm. When borrowing does reduce these risks, the stockholders' required rate of return (K_s^*) should be lowered. This change would also cause a decline in the cost of capital and move the optimal debt ratio to a higher level.

As shown in Figure 10-3, low-cost foreign debt will tend to raise the optimal debt ratio (from D/A to D/A^*) for the firm, which in turn lowers the firm's cost of capital from 16 percent to 14 percent. The firm, with its new, lower cost of capital, may be in a position to reevaluate its asset acquisition alternatives. This situation is illustrated in Figure 10-4. The investment opportunity schedule (IOS) represents all the investment opportunities available to the firm. Stockholder wealth will be maximized when the firm accepts all investment proposals with an internal rate of return (IRR) in excess of the cost of capital. Other things being equal, the net present value (NPV) of the individual projects will be higher, the greater the difference between the IRR and the cost of capital. Since NPV measures the change in stockholder wealth, a reduction in the cost of

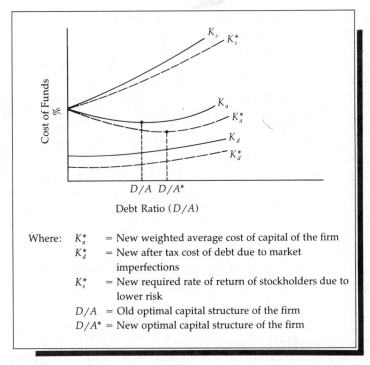

FIGURE 10-3 Optimal Capital Structure with International Borrowing

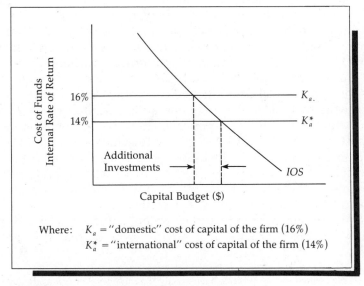

FIGURE 10-4 Capital Budget of the Firm

capital will increase stockholder wealth even if no new investment proposals are undertaken. Figure 10-4 also shows that some previously rejected projects would be acceptable at the new, lower cost of capital. For example, a project with an *IRR* of 15 percent would have been rejected when the cost of capital was 16 percent. The decline in the cost of capital to 14 percent, however, makes this an acceptable investment. These additional investments will also increase the wealth of the stockholders.[13]

The illustrations of the impact of low-cost foreign debt on the target capital structure and investment decisions of the firm were designed to dramatize economic principles. The financial manager cannot overlook the possibility of adjusting the firm's target capital structure to take advantage of international interest cost differentials. In practice, however, such differentials are likely to be relatively small (when adjusted for expected changes in exchange rates). Small differences in rates are not likely to result in a reevaluation of the capital structure decision. However, large interest rate differentials brought about by subsidized financing may force the firm to rethink its capital structure decision.

Subsidiary Capital Structure

Related to the issue of capital structure for the multinational firm as a whole is the issue of subsidiary capital structure. Basically, the multinational corporation can achieve its overall target capital structure in one of two ways. On the one hand, the top management of the multinational firm could insist that every subsidiary maintain the same target capital structure. On the other hand, the capital structures of individual subsidiaries could be varied while at the same time maintaining the target capital structure for the multinational firm as a whole. These alternatives are illustrated in Table 10-5. Note that in both cases the multinational firm has the same overall debt ratio (60 percent). What differs is the amount of borrowing by each of the three operating subsidiaries.

Before discussing the possible attractiveness of Alternative 2, it is important to understand the extent to which the multinational firm is responsible for the debt of its subsidiaries. The internationally recognized principles of commercial law suggest that each corporate subsidiary is a separate legal entity and that the liability of the owners of the subsidiary is distinct and separate from that of the subsidiary. One can imagine a situation in which a multinational parent could refuse to assume responsibility for a subsidiary's debt on the grounds that the subsidiary is a

---

[13]We assume that all projects have exactly the same level of risk as the firm as a whole. A more detailed discussion of this issue is presented in Brigham, op. cit., pp. 474–476.

TABLE 10-5 Hypothetical Capital Structure Alternatives for a Multinational Firm*

	Debt Ratio	
	Alternative 1	Alternative 2
U.S. operations	60%	20%
Subsidiary in Canada	60%	70%
Subsidiary in Brazil	60%	90%
Corporatewide debt ratio	60%	60%

*This multinational is organized into three operating subsidiaries, each of which is assumed to have the same amount of assets.

separate legal entity. In practice, the issue of separate legal entity as associated with subsidiary debt is less of a factor than one may imagine. Subsidiary loans are often unavailable unless the parent corporation specifically, and in writing, assumes responsibility for the debt in the event of default. This is especially true for bank loans, loans from other financial institutions, and bond issues. Even in cases where there is no written guarantee by the parent, it is unlikely that a multinational firm would allow its financial reputation to be tarnished by a default on a subsidiary's debt. As a general rule, most subsidiary debt is also the debt of the parent corporation, and multinational corporations cannot shield themselves from the liability associated with direct borrowing by the subsidiary. Avoiding responsibility is not a major motive for having different capital structures for various subsidiaries (Alternative 2 in Table 10-5).[14]

The decision to vary the capital structures of subsidiaries can be explained by other factors. Many multinational firms seek to profit from international capital market distortions that create opportunities for low-cost financing. That is, the multinational firm borrows through the subsidiary that has access to the least expensive funds. These funds may be used throughout the multinational firm but borrowed at the subsidiary level. In addition to cost-of-debt considerations, the heavy use of debt at the subsidiary level may result from the desire to reduce the political risk of the multinational firm. The belief that local investors will forestall arbitrary government actions against the subsidiary is widely held. Finally, the differences in subsidiary debt reflect restrictions placed on some subsidiaries. In some cases, subsidiaries are simply unable to borrow, and the borrowing must be done at another location.

Looking back at Table 10-5, it seems likely that Alternative 2 is a common scenario for many multinational firms. The exact pattern of borrowing will depend on the particular circumstances of the firm. In

---

[14]Loans from foreign governments may be made to the subsidiary without recourse. Trade credit may also be available to the subsidiary without a demand for guarantees by the parent corporation.

some cases, however, all borrowing will be done by the parent corporation, since no other alternatives are available. In other cases, the indebtedness will be spread over the subsidiaries.

Like other firms that have access to international capital markets, the multinational firm must consider the possibility of increasing its target debt ratio in response to the availability of low-cost debt in foreign markets. Since some multinationals operate subsidiaries in countries that maintain artificially low interest rates, the multinational firm has more incentive to substitute artificially low-cost debt for higher-priced equity raised in the United States. Such bargain rate financing is rarely available to the exporting firm. As noted previously, even the subsidiaries of multinationals are sometimes denied access to low-cost foreign financing. However, if financing at artificially low rates is available, stockholder wealth may be increased by employing this method. Under such circumstances, it may be desirable for the multinational to increase its target debt ratio.

Summary and Conclusions

This chapter focused on the involvement of American firms in international capital markets. American firms may be able to borrow dollars both in the United States and in euromarkets. In addition, firms can borrow a variety of foreign currencies and in many different countries. In fact, the modern firm has more financing alternatives than ever before.

The extent to which American firms involve themselves in international financial markets will depend on the characteristics of particular firms. All large firms (domestic, exporters, importers, and multinationals) should consider borrowing dollars in the form of eurodollar loans and bonds, since interest costs are likely to be lower and there is no increase in exchange rate risk. Firms may also be enticed to borrow foreign currencies, but this is a risky alternative. It is important for the manager to recognize that there is no real interest rate advantage associated with most lower foreign currency interest rates, since rate advantages are usually offset by expected changes in exchange rates. Borrowing foreign currencies (either loans or bonds) will increase exchange rate risk unless the firm has expected foreign currency revenues. In most cases, only exporters and multinational firms that have specific foreign currency revenues should consider borrowing foreign currency. For these firms, foreign currency borrowing may reduce exchange rate risk exposure, as well as the costs of converting foreign currency to dollars.

The American firm's borrowing decision must be viewed in the context of its target capital structure. It is important to recognize that firms attempt to maintain a capital structure that includes a substantial amount of debt. In this context, foreign borrowing can be used to reduce borrowing in the United States. It should also be noted that, under some circumstances, the availability of lower-cost foreign debt may cause the firm to reconsider its target capital structure and increase its use of debt.

We are well into a new era in corporate finance. During the post–World War II period, new financial markets developed and access to these markets improved. The outlook for the future is for continued development of these international markets. Financial managers of large firms can no longer ignore these developments. International borrowing is becoming a normal activity for American business firms.

Review Questions

1. Define the concept of optimal capital structure. Which factors determine the level of debt in this structure?
2. Explain how the concept of target capital structure is used by American firms.
3. Under which conditions would a purely domestic American firm find borrowing in international capital markets attractive?
4. Under which conditions would an American firm that sells primarily in the United States but is a large importer find borrowing in international capital markets attractive?
5. Under which conditions would an American firm that exports large amounts to foreign countries find borrowing in international capital markets attractive?
6. Under which conditions would an American multinational firm find borrowing in international capital markets attractive?
7. Is the availability of low-cost foreign borrowing likely to have an impact on the optimal capital structure of an American firm? Explain your answer.
8. Describe how a firm would construct a balance sheet hedge, and explain its usefulness to the firm.
9. Explain how the multicurrency clause in many eurocurrency loans may affect the firm's decision to borrow foreign currencies.

Questions for Discussion

1. Assume that you are employed by a large American manufacturer of glass bottles that has annual sales of $600,000,000 and assets of $75,000,000. The firm sells almost entirely to manufacturers of food products. Sales are nationwide, but the firm's most important customers are in the northeastern and western states. The top management of the firm is in the process of reevaluating its policy with respect to debt and has assigned you the task of evaluating several alternatives. Specifically, you are asked to evaluate the feasibility and desirability of borrowing in foreign capital markets. You are also asked to evaluate how the firm's target capital structure will be affected by access to foreign capital markets.
2. Assume that you are employed by a large American manufacturer of computer testing and related equipment. All production takes place in the United States, but sales are worldwide. Customers in Japan, Canada, the United Kingdom, and Germany are particularly important to the firm. Over 50 percent of the sales are made to customers in those countries. The top management of the firm is in the process of reevaluating its policy with respect to debt and has assigned you the task of evaluating several alternatives. Specifically, you are asked to evaluate the feasibility and desirability of borrowing in foreign capital markets. You are also

asked to evaluate how the firm's target capital structure will be affected by access to foreign capital markets.

3. Assume that you are employed by a large American multinational firm that has production facilities in several foreign countries and sales in more than 15 countries. In the past, your firm has raised most of its debt capital from American banks and by selling bonds in the United States. The top management of the firm is in the process of reevaluating its policy with respect to debt and has assigned you the task of evaluating several alternatives. Specifically, you are asked to evaluate the feasibility and desirability of borrowing in foreign capital markets. You are also asked to evaluate how the firm's target capital structure will be affected by access to foreign capital markets.

Research Activities

1. Locate five firms in a particular industry that are primarily domestic. Locate five firms in the same industry that have significant international operations. Are there any major differences in the capital structures of the two types of firms?

2. Obtain information about export financing provided by the governments of France, Germany, Japan, and Canada. Compare the costs of borrowing through such subsidized arrangements to the market interest rates in these currencies.

Problems

1. The optimal capital structure of the Denbo Corporation is 30 percent debt. The before-tax cost of debt of the firm is 12 percent. The required rate of return of the stockholders is 16 percent. The firm's marginal tax rate is 34 percent.
   a. Calculate the weighted average cost of capital for the Denbo Corporation.
   b. What is the minimum return that must be earned on investment proposals?

2. The Jartran Corporation is a large American multinational firm. At the present time, the firm uses only domestic capital markets. The costs of debt and equity at different levels of debt are as follows:

D/A	0%	20%	40%	60%	80%
$K_d(1-T)$	—	10%	11%	12%	15%
K_s	19%	20%	23%	28%	35%

What is the optimal capital structure of the firm?

3. The Jartran Corporation (Problem 2) wants to investigate the impact of using global markets on its optimal capital structure. The new costs of debt and equity at different levels of debt are as follows:

D/A	0%	20%	40%	60%	80%
$K_d(1-T)$	—	8%	9%	10%	13%
K_s	18%	19%	21%	26%	31%

a. What is the new optimal capital structure of the firm?

b. Explain the reasons for any difference in the results compared to those in Problem 2.

4. Southern California Electric is a large public utility operating solely in the United States. It needs to borrow $100,000,000 for 1 year. The firm has the following financing alternatives:

   a. Borrow dollars from an American bank at an annual interest rate of 12 percent.

   b. Borrow dollars from a British bank at an annual interest rate of 10 percent.

   c. Borrow pounds from a British bank at an annual interest rate of 14 percent. The spot rate of the British pound is £1 = $1.40. The 1-year forward rate is £1 = $1.35.

   What is the cost of borrowing (after hedging) British pounds? Where should Southern California Electric borrow if it does not want to change its risk profile?

5. The American Airline Company is planning to purchase a $40,000,000 plane from a British company. Financing is needed for 1 year. The firm has three financing alternatives:

   a. Borrow the dollars from an American bank for 1 year. The bank will charge 12 percent interest.

   b. Borrow the dollars from a subsidized British bank for 1 year. The bank will charge 10 percent interest.

   c. Borrow pounds from a subsidized British bank for 1 year. The bank will charge 8 percent interest on the pound-denominated loan. The spot rate on the pound is £1 = $1.50, and the 1-year forward rate is £1 = $1.52.

   What is the cost of borrowing (after hedging) British pounds? Which alternative would you recommend?

Bibliography

Adler, Michael. "The Cost of Capital and Valuation of a Two Country Firm." *Journal of Finance*, March 1974, pp. 119–132.

Aggarwal, Raj. "International Differences in Capital Structure Norms: An Empirical Study of Large European Companies." *Management International Review*, 1981/1, pp. 75–88.

Brigham, Eugene F. *Fundamentals of Financial Management*, 4th ed. Chicago: Dryden Press, 1986.

Collins, J. Markham, and Sekely, William S. "The Relationship of Headquarters Country and Industry Classification to Financial Structure." *Financial Management*, Autumn 1983, pp. 45–51.

Frankel, Jeffrey A. "The Diversifiability of Exchange Risk." *Journal of International Economics*, August 1979, pp. 379–393.

Lessard, Donald R., and Shapiro, Alan C. "Guidelines for Global Financing Choices." *Midland Corporate Finance Journal*, Winter 1984, pp. 68–80.

Levy, Haim, and Sarnat, Marshall. "International Diversification of Investment Portfolios." *American Economic Review*, September 1970, pp. 668–675.

Modigliani, Franco, and Miller, Merton H. "The Cost of Capital, Corporation Finance, and the Theory of Investment." *American Economic Review*, June 1958, pp. 261–297.

Rugman, Alan M. "Risk Reduction by International Diversification." *Journal of International Business Studies*, Fall 1976, pp. 75–80.

_____ *International Diversification and the Multinational Enterprise.* Lexington, MA: Lexington Books, 1979.

Sekely, Williams S., and Collins, J. Markham. "Cultural Influences on International Capital Structure." *Journal of International Business Studies*, Spring 1980, pp. 87–100.

Senbet, Lemma W. "International Capital Market Equilibrium and the Multinational Firm Financing and Investment Policies." *Journal of Financial and Quantitative Analysis*, September 1979, pp. 455–480.

Shapiro, Alan C. "Financial Structure and Cost of Capital in the Multinational Corporation." *Journal of Financial and Quantitative Analysis*, June 1978, pp. 211–226.

Stanley, Marjorie T. "Capital Structure and Cost of Capital for the Multinational Firm." *Journal of International Business Studies*, Spring–Summer 1981, pp. 103–120.

Stonehill, Arthur I., and Stitzel, Thomas. "Financial Structure and Multinational Corporations." *California Management Review*, Fall 1969, pp. 91–96.

Strebel, Paul. "Managing the Information Cost of Financing." *Columbia Journal of World Business*, Summer 1986, pp. 39–46.

Van Horne, James C. *Financial Management and Policy*, 7th ed. Englewood Cliffs, NJ: Prentice-Hall, Inc., 1986.

International Risks
and the Cost of Capital

This chapter focuses on the cost of capital, one of the most important topics in financial management. We will begin by explaining why a reasonable estimate of the cost of capital is important if stockholder wealth is to be maximized. In addition, we will show why it is necessary to use a risk-adjusted cost of capital when making international investment decisions. We then discuss the special factors that affect the cost of capital for international projects. Specifically, we will consider how the cost of capital is affected by international financial risk, exchange rate risk, and political risk. We will also examine some of the strategies used to reduce these risks and their impact on the cost of capital.

The Risk-Adjusted Cost of Capital

The concept of the *risk-adjusted cost of capital* is particularly important when considering the acquisition of foreign assets, because such assets are likely to have higher risks than domestic assets. Higher risks result in

285

TABLE 11-1 Leigh Chemical Manufacturing Corporation: Firmwide and Risk-Adjusted Costs of Capital

	Proposed Domestic Operations	Proposed Foreign Investment	Firmwide*
Cost of debt	0.10	0.15	0.1214
Cost of equity	0.16	0.20	0.1815
Target debt ratio	0.40	0.30	0.35
Marginal tax rate	0.34	0.34	
Cost of capital†	0.1224	0.1697	0.14605‡

*Weighted averages of debt and equity.
†Using Equation 10-1:

K_a (domestic) $= 0.1(1 - 0.34)(0.4) + 0.16(1 - 0.4) = 0.1224$

K_a (foreign) $= 0.15(1 - 0.34)(0.3) + 0.2(1 - 0.3) = 0.1697$

K_a (combined) $= 0.1214(1 - 0.34)(0.35) + 0.1815(1 - 0.35) = 0.14602$

‡K_a (combined) $= \dfrac{(0.1224 + 0.1697)}{2} = 0.14605$

higher required rates of return by investors and thus higher costs of capital for the foreign assets. When acquiring a foreign asset, it is generally inappropriate to use the firmwide cost of capital. A cost of capital that reflects the risk profile for each foreign asset is needed.

Consider the illustration in Table 11-1, which is based on an analysis being conducted by the Leigh Chemical Manufacturing Corporation (an American firm) in connection with the proposed construction of two chemical production facilities, one in the United States and the other in a foreign country. For convenience, we will assume that the Leigh Corporation is a completely new firm with no assets or capital. The proposed investments will each involve an outlay of $10,000,000 and will have the same expected dollar cash inflows. If the Leigh Corporation builds the U.S. facility only, it can borrow debt capital at an interest rate of 10 percent and can sell stock to yield 16 percent. For domestic operations alone, the firm has a target debt ratio of 40 percent and a marginal tax rate of 34 percent. As shown in Table 11-1, the cost of capital of domestic operations is 12.24 percent.

Constructing the foreign facility only would require a higher cost of capital, which reflects the fact that the foreign facility will expose the firm to greater exchange rate and political risks. If the Leigh Corporation raised capital for the foreign facility alone, the before-tax cost of debt would be 15 percent and the cost of equity would be 20 percent. Furthermore, the optimal capital structure of the foreign project may be different (30 percent). The foreign investment must be able to earn a return greater than the 16.97 percent cost of capital if stockholder wealth is to be increased.

It would be a mistake to confuse the cost of capital of the foreign investment (16.97 percent) with the cost of capital for domestic opera-

TABLE 11-2 Leigh Chemical Corporation: Required Dollar Returns for Different Alternatives

Alternative	$Outlay	Cost of Capital	Required Annual $Return
Build U.S. only	$10,000,000	0.1224	$1,224,000
Build foreign only	$10,000,000	0.1697	$1,697,000
Build both*	$20,000,000	0.14605	$2,921,000

*Note that the required return for the build-both alternative can be computed either by multiplying the outlay ($20,000,000) by the weighted average cost of capital (0.14605) or by adding the required returns for the individual alternatives. This illustration ignores the repayment of the original investment.

tions (12.24 percent) or the firmwide cost of capital (14.605 percent). In the ideal situation, the cost of capital for the foreign operation should be computed as if it had nothing to do with domestic operations. This proposition can be studied by examining Table 11-2. We can see that if only the American facility is constructed, the investment must earn at least $1,224,000 in order to meet the requirements of investors. Any earnings beyond that amount would increase stockholder wealth. Note that if the firm builds both facilities, it will have to raise $20,000,000 in capital at a weighted average cost of 14.605 percent. This means that more than $2,921,000 must be earned if stockholder wealth is to be increased. Thus the foreign investment must earn at least $1,697,000, which is exactly the same as the risk-adjusted cost of capital for the foreign project times the outlay for the project. The important conclusion that flows from this example is that when investments are considered on a project-by-project basis (as they usually are), it is necessary to evaluate each project using a cost of capital that reflects the unique riskiness of that investment. Since the risk of foreign investments obviously differs from that of domestic projects, managers must understand the nature of these risks, how they can be managed, and how they affect the cost of capital. Failure to do this will lead to poor foreign investment decisions.

Financial Risk and the Cost of Capital

Financial risk refers to the risk associated with using debt capital to finance the activities of the firm. As a firm substitutes debt for equity, it increases its required interest and principal payments. Failure to meet debt payments can result in bankruptcy or other legal actions against the firm. In the ideal situation, the firm weighs this negative aspect of debt financing against the cost advantage associated with the use of debt and arrives at a target or optimal capital structure. In the absence of international financial market imperfections and special risks associated with foreign investments, the target capital structure would be the same for both domestic and foreign investments. Of course, international capital markets do have imperfections, foreign investments do have different target capital structures, and therefore the costs of capital are different for foreign and domestic investments.[1] In addition, the desire to minimize exchange rate and political risks may encourage a firm to use a relatively high proportion of debt in the capital structure of the foreign subsidiary.

Impact of Subsidized Financing on the Cost of Capital

The availability of subsidized, low-cost foreign debt financing could either reduce or increase the cost of capital for a potential asset acquisition.[2] For example, if the firm used the same amount of debt (maintained the same capital structure) after the cost of debt was reduced, the cost of capital would go down. However, the availability of subsidized, low-cost foreign debt for a foreign investment may dramatically increase the debt ratio and raise the riskiness of equity to the point where the cost of capital actually goes up. Increasing the use of debt in this way may reduce the net present value of investments being considered for acquisition.

The impact of subsidized financing on the cost of capital for an investment and the net present value of that investment is best explained with an example. Assume that the Stevo Corporation is considering a foreign investment proposal under various financing alternatives. The firm will need $6,600,000 at time zero in order to undertake the investment and anticipates annual cash inflows of $1,140,000 for years 1 through 10. In addition, the project will be sold to the foreign government for $1,000,000 in year 10. The firm has to finance the project with debt and equity. Its marginal tax rate is 34 percent. The firm has the following financing alternatives:

1. The firm could use unsubsidized debt at a cost of 8 percent. If this alternative is chosen, the firm plans to have a debt ratio of 25 percent and expects that the required rate of return of the stockholders will be 13 percent. Using Equation 10-1, the cost of capital of the project is 11.07 percent.
2. The firm could use subsidized debt at a cost of 7 percent. The firm plans to maintain the same capital structure (25 percent debt), and the

---

[1]Chapters 9 and 10 discussed international financial markets, including their imperfections.

[2]See Chapter 10 for a more complete discussion of the issues involved in the use of subsidized financing.

TABLE 11-3   Stevo Corporation: Evaluation of Foreign
Investment Proposal Alternative Capital Structure Assumptions*

	Alternative 1 No Debt Subsidy Debt Ratio = 25%	Alternative 2 Debt Subsidy Debt Ratio = 25%	Alternative 3 Debt Subsidy Debt Ratio = 45%
K_d	8%	7%	7%
K_s	13%	13%	20%
K_a	11.07%	10.905%	13.079%
NPV†	+$444,035	+$495,766	($141,028)

*It is assumed that the choice of capital structure will not affect the size of the cash flows to the parent.
†Calculated using a computer program. You may obtain slightly different results using present value tables.

required rate of return of the stockholders is expected to remain the same (13 percent). Using Equation 10-1, the cost of capital of the project is 10.905 percent.

3. The firm could use subsidized debt at a cost of 7 percent. If this alternative is chosen, the firm plans to increase its debt ratio to 45 percent in order to gain as much of the subsidy as possible. This rise in the debt ratio is expected to cause an increase in the risk borne by stockholders, which in turn, is expected to cause an increase in the cost of equity capital to 20 percent. Using Equation 10-1, the cost of capital of the project is 13.079 percent.[3]

As illustrated in Table 11-3, under Alternative 1 the project has a net present value of +$444,035. Under Alternative 2 the net present value increases to +$495,766. The increase in net present value is attributable to the reduction in the cost of capital of the project that results from the subsidized financing. As shown in Alternative 3, however, the subsidized financing may backfire if it encourages the firm to use too much debt. Under Alternative 3, the net present value of the project declines to a negative $141,028.

The results presented in Table 11-3 are hypothetical. Different numbers could have been used, and the net present value could have been increased with the use of more debt. The illustration is designed solely to point out that debt can be misused. Attempts to capture the benefits of subsidized, low-cost debt may backfire by increasing the financial risk

[3]We are assuming that the increased use of foreign debt is not offset by a reduction in the use of home country debt.

borne by equity investors. The point is that the firm must look very closely at the debt ratio used for each foreign asset, because the debt ratio will affect the cost of capital, which, in turn, will affect the net present value of the asset.

Exchange Rate Risk and the Cost of Capital

The nature of foreign exchange rate risk and strategies for managing that risk were discussed in Chapters 6 through 8 and will not be viewed here. The discussion that follows relates exchange rate risk concepts to the cost of capital.

When firm is considering an investment in a foreign country, and that investment is expected to generate revenues and expenses in foreign currencies, the firm must consider the exchange rate risk implications of the investment. Consider, once again, the proposals being considered by the Leigh Chemical Corporation (Tables 11-1 and 11-2). Presumably, the Leigh Corporation would have to invest dollars in the foreign operation should it be undertaken. Since the foreign operation will generate cash flows in a currency other than the dollar, there is an exchange rate risk associated with the investment. Because of possible fluctuations in exchange rates, the Leigh Corporation is less sure about the dollar values of the expected cash flows from the subsidiary than it would be about the expected dollar cash flows from the American facility. From the corporation's point of view, other things being equal, the foreign investment would have a higher risk and thus a higher cost of capital.

Generally speaking, a firm can do little about the exchange rate risk associated with a long-term asset acquisition. Other things being equal, costs of capital will be higher and the net present values lower. This result is, more or less, the by-product of the fluctuating exchange rate system that characterizes the international economy at the present time. Fluctuating exchange rates increase the risk to the foreign investor and may discourage foreign investments. A solution to the problem, if one exists, is outside the grasp of individual firms. However, government action and cooperation could stabilize exchange rates, reduce costs of capital, increase net present values, and encourage international investing. At the present time, however, governments are unwilling to coordinate their efforts for long periods of time to achieve this end.[4]

---

[4]See chapter 3 for a detailed discussion of the present foreign exchange system.

Impact of Hedging
on the Cost of Capital

At this point, it is worthwhile to review a few other concepts presented earlier in this book. First, forward market hedging techniques are not likely to be useful in reducing the exchange rate risk associated with a long-term foreign asset acquisition. First of all, traditional forward market contracts are available in only a limited number of currencies, and contracts with maturities greater than 1 year are highly unusual. Even more important, forward discounts or premiums reflect the level of uncertainty with respect to future exchange rates. Forward market hedges do not provide a significant benefit to a firm that is continuously converting currencies. Almost by definition, a firm that invests in a long-term asset falls into this category.

The term *money-market hedge* usually refers to a short-term hedging situation. A longer-term money market hedge is usually called a *balance sheet hedge*.[5] Such a hedge involves long-term borrowings in a foreign currency. These borrowings are then repaid with foreign currency cash inflows, and there is no need to convert the foreign currency to dollars. However, the uncertainty about the future value of a foreign currency will be reflected in the interest rates charged on foreign currency loans. Thus, a currency that is expected to decline in value should have a relatively high interest rate. The balance sheet hedge reduces risk, but possibly at the cost of higher interest charges. With respect to balance sheet hedges, it is also important to recognize that only a portion of the firm's investment could be protected in this fashion unless 100 percent of all capital was borrowed in the foreign country. Balance sheet hedges can reduce but not eliminate foreign exchange risk.

Political Risk and the Cost of Capital

The political risk associated with particular investment will also affect the cost of capital. The amount of political risk will depend on the investor's perception of the possibility of hostile government action. Since not all governments act in the same manner, political risk varies from country to country. When the political risk associated with investing in a particular country is high, there is less certainty about the ability of the investment to provide future cash flows to the foreign investor. High political risk

---

[5] The balance sheet hedge is discussed in Chapter 10.

implies a high cost of capital for investments and a low net present value. Other things held constant, high political risk discourages investment by foreigners in a particular country.

The remainder of this chapter is devoted to a discussion of political risk and its impact on the cost of capital and net present value. The discussion is organized into the following three parts:

1. First, we will consider the nature of political risk and show that it appears in various forms and has various consequences.
2. Next, we will discuss which countries are riskiest and which industries, as well as which types of firms, are most vulnerable to hostile political actions taken by host governments.
3. Finally, we focus on the steps that a foreign investor can take to manage political risk.

The Spectrum of Political Risks

Ordinarily when we talk and hear about the political risks associated with investing in foreign countries, the most drastic situations come to mind. We think of the nationalization of American businesses after the fall of the shah in Iran. We think of Castro's takeover of American businesses in Cuba. These are the "glamourous" cases: highly visible and very dramatic. But there are many other actions taken by host governments that can have significant impacts on foreign investors. These actions do not make headlines, but their consequences can be even more severe than those of nationalization. Table 11-4 is designed to help organize our thoughts about political risk. Risks have been categorized in terms of their general visibility to the business manager and the public. The items listed in each category illustrate the basic nature of the risk. Many other examples could be included.

The first thing to keep in mind about Table 11-4 is that *least visible* does not necessarily mean *least important*. Even though regulations (Category 1) may not be aimed specifically at foreign businesses, their results can be devastating. For example, the post–World II policies imposed in the United Kingdom seriously affected returns on investment earned by foreigners, as well as domestic investors, for many decades (at least until 1980). The uncertainty about the future actions of the British government not only discouraged foreign investment in Britain but also encouraged British investors to seek investments in foreign countries. In effect, the actions of a well-meaning government created an uncertain and unprofitable investment climate. Of course, the uncertainty about the nature and severity of government regulation results in relatively high costs of capital for investments in that country. On the other hand, investments in countries with an atmosphere of stability and predictability have relatively low costs of capital.

TABLE 11-4   The Spectrum of Political Risks Associated with Foreign Investments

1. *Regulation* (least visible)
   Actions by host governments that affect all firms, not just foreign investors. Even though the regulations may not be directed against the foreign investor, their impact can be significant. The actions in this category include the following:
   a. Radical changes in the tax burden.
   b. Changes in labor force regulations such as minimum wages, the right to discharge, and hiring requirements.
   c. The imposition of price controls.

2. *Discrimination Against Foreign Firms* (somewhat visible)
   Host governments sometimes take actions (short of expropriation) that are aimed directly at foreign firms. The actions in this category include the following:
   a. Restrictions on repatriation of funds. Sometimes firms are required to invest blocked funds in government securities that quickly lose their value.
   b. Special labor conditions, including rules relating to wages, hiring, and discharge. Foreign firms can lose all control over labor costs. In addition, governments may encourage strikes against the foreign investor.
   c. Special royalties, taxes, higher fees for utilities, and so on, applied to foreign investments. These extra payments can sometimes reach a level that makes the foreign operation unprofitable.
   d. Requiring excessive documentation and harassing the firm in other ways, which can make management of the investment very difficult.

3. *Expropriation* (highly visible)
   Host countries sometimes take over (expropriate) the property of foreign businesses with the intention of operating the businesses in the "public interest." There are two types of expropriation:
   a. Expropriation with fair compensation: International law recognizes the right of governments to seize and operate businesses as long as fair compensation is paid, and is paid promptly and in a convertible currency. In the ideal case, this is similar to a forced sale of the business at a fair price.
   b. Expropriation with inadequate or no compensation: Frequently foreign businesses are expropriated, and compensation is neither fair nor timely. This results in losses to foreign investors.

4. *War and Civil Disorders* (most visible)
   The property of foreign investors is sometimes destroyed in wars and other disturbances.

Discrimination Against Foreign Investors

It may be that the second category of political risks, discrimination, creates the greatest problem for business. Clearly, governments have the right to pursue most of the actions in this category as long as they act in moderation. For example, a country may have a legitimate obligation to insist on a minimum wage and substantial benefits for workers employed in a new, underground mine being developed by a foreign investor. The problem is that all of the actions included in Category 2 of Table 11-4 can be taken too far. In effect, governments can disguise their hostile intent behind the appearance of concern for workers or other citizens. Their real purpose may be to cripple the business without a formal expropriation. Since the discriminatory actions are directed only at foreign investors, it is less likely that local residents will object to such government actions. In fact, some local businesses may benefit from the crippling of a foreign competitor.

In a sense, these discriminatory actions pose the greatest threat to foreign investors. Discrimination can usually be implemented a little at a time, thus reducing its visibility and muting opposition to such actions. Host governments usually try to justify the discriminatory actions by asserting that they are consistent with the welfare of the nation. The impact of discriminatory actions, however, could be severe. For example, a country may insist that a portion of the inputs used by a firm be purchased from local suppliers. Gradually, the price of the inputs could be increased or their quality could decline. The government may gradually increase the purchase requirement imposed on the foreign firm. Eventually, the foreign firm may be unable to operate at a profit. Note that the government has not expropriated the firm; it has simply diverted profits to itself or local suppliers. Even the possibility of such actions by foreign governments makes investments in the country very risky, drives up the cost of capital, and reduces net present values on prospective foreign investments.

Expropriation of Investments

Expropriation is one of the most visible political risks. It also occurs less frequently than the other situations. While usually associated with actions by the governments of less developed countries, it is not uncommon to find expropriation or its threat in Western industrial nations. For example, the 1981 election of a socialist government in France raised fears of expropriation. Canada's economic independence policy of the 1970s was associated with government takeovers of foreign businesses. The differences between these cases and the expropriations in less developed countries focus on the issue of compensation. The Canadian and French governments advocated fair and prompt compensation. In many cases, expropriation of businesses in less developed countries have involved less than fair compensation.

Of course, it is difficult to say what constitutes fair compensation. The owners of the foreign investment usually focus on market value, which should reflect the value of the asset if sold to an uncoerced, independent purchaser. Governments often have a different view of the fair value of a foreign investment. For example, governments may claim that the fair value of the foreign investment is equal to the amount of the initial investment or the depreciated book value. Foreign governments may also use the *tax assessed value* as the fair value of the investment. The point is that the parties involved in the dispute frequently have different views about the fair value of a particular investment.

Firms do not acquire assets in foreign countries if they expect them to be expropriated before an adequate return can be earned. Of course, the political environment in many countries is unknown, and there is usually some chance that foreign assets will be expropriated. Businesses that are exposed to expropriation with "fair" compensation are risky, have high costs of capital, and have lower net present values. Businesses that are exposed to expropriation with inadequate compensation are riskier and have even lower not present values.

Finally, wars and civil disturbances may change the political system of a country. In many cases, these changes may result in losses to foreign investors. The new political leadership may believe that foreigners were allied with the previous regime. Thus, foreign investors may be considered to be opposed to the new government, and expropriations may result. In addition, wars and/or large civil disturbances may result in the physical destruction of the foreign investment. For example, during the 1980s, many investments in Beirut were destroyed by the Lebanese civil war.

Political Risk in Historical Perspective

There are no comprehensive data that measure the extent to which firms have suffered (or benefited) from political actions by host governments. There are some data relating to expropriations since World War II. With respect to expropriations alone, the following observations can be made:

1. Expropriations of American businesses tended to be associated with the ascent of a new leftist government in the host country.
2. American businesses located in Latin America were most likely to be expropriated.
3. The type of business most likely to be expropriated was one in an extractive industry (petroleum, agriculture, etc.).
4. The tendency to expropriate seems to have lessened in recent years.

These observations, while pertaining directly to expropriation only, have implications for all types of political risk.

The total political risk (war, expropriation, discrimination, and regulation) associated with a particular foreign investment tends to be related to both the industry in which the investment is made and the size of the investment. Small investments are less likely to be subjected to drastic political actions. A small manufacturer, for example, may be highly regulated but is less likely to face discrimination and/or expropriation. Investments made in industries that call for international integration and/or special technical skills by the owners are less likely to be subjected to arbitrary actions. Electronics and automobile manufacturers fall into this category. The point is that not all investments face the same amount of political risk, even in the same country. The investments most vulnerable to government action are those that produce a standardized product (e.g., oil), employ a technology that can be mastered by the residents of the host country (e.g., mining and agriculture), and are both large in size and owned by foreign firms.

The amount of political risk facing foreign investors has gone through a cycle since the end of World War II. For the 25 years after the war, actions by governments against foreign businesses were relatively frequent and severe. Over the past 15 years, however, the incidence of discrimination and expropriation has declined. These developments must be interpreted in the context of postwar historical developments. Remember that World War II followed a great worldwide depression. When the war came to an end, the peoples of the world realized that they had to develop an economic and social system that minimized the likelihood of a repeat performance of past catastrophes. Since the root causes of the war were perceived by many to be imperialism and capitalism, these two institutions were "reformed." The great British and French empires eventually collapsed, with the emergence of many new nations, almost all of which had a government that attempted to implement policies that would improve the living standards and quality of life in the new nation. Other nations that had been politically independent (e.g., the Latin American countries) sought economic independence. Some of the industrial nations (e.g., the United Kingdom and the Scandinavian countries) prepared to embark on a new economic course as a result of the dislocations caused by depression and war. The governments of many of these countries believed that the best way to solve their basic problems was to regulate closely and/or operate the businesses in their political jurisdictions. This led to a great wave of new controls on foreign business and an increase in expropriations. The tendency to expropriate was not confined to the less developed countries. Foreign investments located in communist Eastern Europe were completely nationalized. Many investments in Western Europe were also nationalized. The point is that in the early postwar period, nationalization was recognized as a legitimate alternative to private business operation.

During the 1970s, some nations began to realize that events were not unfolding as expected. National independence did not necessarily lead to political freedom and a better quality of life. Even more importantly, there was a growing perception that socialism had failed to provide expected economic benefits. The perception that socialism may have failed is a worldwide phenomenon. Today some of the Western industrial powers are privatizing industries that had been previously nationalized. In Britain, for example, oil, gas, airlines, shipbuilding, coal, and automobiles have all been privatized or are scheduled for privatization. France has similar but less ambitious plans. Even the Soviet bloc countries have adopted some market-oriented economic principles. Chairman Mikhail Gorbachev is at the leading edge of a movement away from long held socialist central planning principles. Today less developed countries, instead of expropriating foreign businesses, are actively pursuing foreign investors. There is a growing recognition that the economic problems of many of these nations cannot be solved with domestic economic resources alone. Even the Peoples Republic of China is attempting to attract foreign investment.

For managers of American firms that are considering investments in foreign countries, understanding these recent developments is critically important. Certainly, hostile discrimination and expropriation are still possible. But the trend is in the opposite direction. It does not make much sense to look at what has happened over the past 50 years without recognizing that the political environment has definitely changed. In terms of political risk, the climate right now is relatively stable. Of course, conditions could change. Countries may once again become disenchanted with free enterprise and foreign investments. It is up to foreign investors to show that they can succeed in meeting legitimate social and economic aspirations more effectively than had been previously done by planned economies. If private investors fail in this regard, they are inviting future hostile political actions.

Despite the development of less hostile attitudes toward foreign investors, there are still political risks associated with investments in foreign countries. The risks are likely to be highest when revolutions take place. The developments in Iran, for example, represent a search for a religious rather than a socialist–Marxist solution to social and economic problems. The result of the Iranian revolution, however, has been the same as those of the earlier left-leaning revolutions. Foreign investments have been expropriated. The possibility of similar developments in other Islamic countries is present. Remember also that we do not know what new political movements will develop in other parts of the world. In addition, many groups are still fully committed to a socialist solution to the problems facing less developed countries. The point is that political risks have not disappeared, but they do appear to be in a period of remission.

Forecasting Political Risk

While the likelihood of political action against an investment in a particular country depends on many different factors, it is especially affected by the attitude and stability of the government of the host country. When committing large sums of money to an investment in such a country, management must make a careful evaluation of the political conditions. This is not an easy thing to do from a distance. Expert assistance is needed and is available to perform this function.[6]

There are publicly available surveys of the political risk associated with investing in different countries. For example, Business International surveys executives regularly and records their perceptions of the risks involved in investing in selected foreign countries. Other organizations employ similar techniques, and the results are widely available. For example, *Business Week* regularly publishes such surveys. However, the reliability of these surveys has not been established. It is not clear that the executives who are asked to respond are in a position to make judgments about the political risks involved in particular countries. Some analysts view the surveys as popularity contests rather than serious attempts to assess political risk.

Many studies have attempted to provide a more objective estimate of the political risk associated with a particular country. These studies have incorporated social and political data into a quantitative framework and attempted to provide a numerical measure of political risk. These quantitative methods involve looking very closely at each country and attempting to identify the underlying causes of political risk. The data used in making the computation include income, unemployment, number of political prisoners, size of the military, number of changes in governments, and so on. Unfortunately for the business decision maker, the usefulness of such studies is limited by the reliability, availability, and comparability of data. In many cases, the data needed to make decisions about investments in particular countries are not available on a timely basis. For example, it may take some time before information on unemployment or the number of political prisoners becomes available. For these reasons, such studies are interesting but not very useful in many foreign investment situations.

Most large firms making investments in foreign countries rely on the advice of consultants who specialize in evaluating the political risks associated with particular countries. These consultants are often former foreign service officers of the United States or other countries who have, over the years, developed a substantial amount of expertise and information with respect to one or more countries. These consultants maintain contacts with foreign government officials, foreign businesspeople, and diplomats located in the foreign country. The information gathered from such sources is often invaluable to the business decision maker.

From the business manager's point of view, it is not a question of using one source or another. If the investment is large, all sources are

---

[6]See David K. Eiteman and Arthur I. Stonehill, *Multinational Business Finance*, 3rd ed., Reading, MA, Addison-Wesley Publishing Company, 1982, pp. 297–309.

likely to be evaluated. Even when all the information is studied, however, a poor decision could still be made. A bad decision can take either of two forms. On the one hand, the firm may underestimate the amount of political risk and make an investment when it would have been wiser not to do so. On the other hand, the firm may overreact to current political events, overestimate the political risk, and fail to make a foreign investment that would have been very profitable. Fear of unfavorable political developments could paralyze an American firm and place it at a worldwide competitive disadvantage. It is no longer acceptable to avoid all situations in which there is some political risk. It is often possible for a firm to invest in countries with considerable political risk and still earn a good return.

Using Insurance
to Manage Political Risk

From the perspective of an American multinational firm, the risk of investing in developed countries is smaller than the risk of investing in less developed countries. Thus, investments in countries like Canada, the United Kingdom, or Japan are perceived as having less political risk than investments in India, Turkey, or Argentina. This belief reflects the differences in the political environment of the two types of countries but also reflects economic reality. For example, since Japanese investors have huge investments in the United States, it is unlikely that Japan will act arbitrarily against American investors in Japan. Japan may have more to lose than to gain by such actions, since the American government may retaliate. On the other hand, Indian investments in the United States are quite small, which means that any retaliation by the United States for actions taken by the Indian government would have a limited impact. Thus, as a group, investments in less developed countries are relatively risky, and, other things being equal, American investors tend to shy away from them.

The reluctance of American investors to commit funds to projects in less developed countries runs counter to official U.S. policy. The U.S. government encourages less developed countries to seek private capital from abroad and urges these countries to choose the capitalist alternative to socialism. The government also actively encourages American firms to invest in less developed countries by providing an insurance program for investors. The insurance covers political risks and is provided by the Overseas Private Investment Corporation (OPIC), which is wholly owned by the U.S. government. When OPIC was established, the government provided the initial capital. However, OPIC was designed to operate on a self-sustaining basis. This means that it must charge premiums at a level that reflects the true riskiness of the insured projects. The government subsidy for the insurance program is relatively small.[7]

Features of OPIC Insurance

OPIC's major program involves insuring the equity contributions made by American investors in projects located in qualified, less-developed countries. In order to qualify for the program, the host country must be both less developed and willing to enter into an agreement with the United States. The agreement specifies the types of restrictions permitted by the host government. Should a host government fail to comply with the agreement, OPIC will refuse the insure future investments in that country. This equity insurance program is very popular with American investors, and more than two-thirds of all nonpetroleum investments in eligible countries are covered. In 1984, the insurance in effect amounted to $5.5 billion.[8]

In order to be eligible for OPIC insurance, the investor must be American. An American corporation is eligible for the insurance only if 50 percent or more of the corporation is owned by U.S. citizens. A foreign corporation may also be eligible for the program if it is at least 95 percent owned by U.S. citizens. The OPIC insurance programs covers losses due to inconvertibility, expropriation, and war/revolution/insurrection/civil strife. The maximum insurance coverage is set at 90 percent of the amount invested. In order to be eligible for insurance, the investment must be in a new project or constitute an expansion of an existing project. Thus, a purchase of a foreign business by an American firm would not be eligible for coverage under the usual OPIC rules. Investments may be insured for periods of up to 20 years, although shorter periods may apply to more sensitive situations. The American firm seeking insurance would negotiate with OPIC over the particular amount and maturity of the coverage.[9]

Inconvertibility refers to situations in which political actions result in the inability of the American investor to convert the foreign currency to dollars. The inability to convert dividend payments, fees, or funds associated with the repatriation of the original investment would be covered by this aspect of the insurance program. Political actions covered by the inconvertibility insurance include direct actions by the government block-

---

[7]OPIC also has a very small direct lending program. In 1984, OPIC was authorized to make up to $50 million in direct loans. However, only $26.5 million were outstanding at that time.

[8]Eiteman and Stonehill, op. cit., p. 313.

[9]OPIC also has a relatively small loan guarantee program. This program guarantees loans made to American businesses that invest in eligible countries. In 1984, $156 million in loans were guaranteed. OPIC charges an annual fee ranging from 1.75 percent to 2.5 percent of the outstanding loan.

ing conversion. A simple refusal by the host government to convert currency would also be covered, even if no formal government action has been taken. In addition, losses that result from the imposition of discriminatory exchange rates on foreign investors are covered. In other words, almost any action or inaction by a host government that retards the conversion of the foreign currency to dollars would be covered by the policy.[10] The fee for inconvertibility is 0.3 percent per year. Thus, if the amount of insurance purchased is $1,000,000, a premium of $3,000 would be paid every year for the inconvertibility insurance.

Insurance against expropriation provides protection against political actions by host governments that result in the effective loss of control over an investment located in the foreign country. Nationalization and confiscation are covered under this provision. Coverage is even more comprehensive than that, since any action that denies ownership rights for more than a year is covered. Thus, if a business was "temporarily" taken over by the host government and the period of takeover lasted for more than 1 year, OPIC would pay the claim. It should be noted that the adverse effects of regulatory actions not specifically directed against the American investor are not covered by the OPIC insurance policy. For example, a firm that was forced to cease activity because a host government imposed price controls on all businesses in the country would not be covered by the expropriation insurance. The premium for expropriation insurance alone is 0.6 percent per year. Thus, if the amount insured is equal to $1,000,000, the annual insurance premium for expropriation only would be $6,000.

Insurance against losses attributed to war, revolution, insurrection, or civil strife is also available. It is clear that war does not have to be officially declared in order for losses to be covered by the insurance program. While losses due to riots are not covered, losses due to civil strife are. The difference between these two categories, however, has not been clearly defined. The annual rate applied to this type of coverage is 0.75 percent, which means that an annual premium of $7,500 would be paid on an insured amount of $1,000,000.

Note that the different coverages offered by OPIC are priced separately, and a firm can select one or all of them. If all are selected, the total premium per year would be 1.65 percent of the amount insured. On a total insured amount of $1,000,000, the total annual premium would be $16,500. If the insurance is maintained for the 20-year maximum insurance period, total premiums would amount to $330,000 on a $1,000,000 investment. OPIC insurance is not inexpensive. With respect to costs, it should also be noted that rates may be increased or decreased slightly,

---

[10] It should be noted that the decline in the value of a currency is related to foreign exchange, not political risk. OPIC insurance does not provide protection against losses caused by foreign exchange fluctuations.

TABLE 11-5 Christine Corporation's OPIC Insurance Decision

Years	No Insurance	OPIC Insurance $K_a = 10\%$	OPIC Insurance $K_a = 11\%$
0	−$100,000,000	−$100,000,000	−$100,000,000
1–10	+$18,000,000	+$16,911,000	+$16,911,000
K_a	12%	10%	11%
NPV	+$1,704,015	+$3,910,774	($407,197)

depending on the risk factors associated with each investment. In addition to the aforementioned premiums, special rates apply to natural resource investments.

Impact of OPIC
Insurance on the Cost of Capital

The availability of OPIC political risk insurance has a profound effect on the cost of capital for a project located in a developing country. For a fee, a firm can eliminate much of the political risk associated with such investments. This reduces the risk borne by investors and decreases the required rate of return on the investment. This, in turn, reduces the cost of capital for the project. The impact of the insurance on the net present value of a project will depend on the relative impacts of the reduction in the cost of capital and the increased cash outflow associated with the insurance premium.

Consider the situation depicted in Table 11-5. The Christine Corporation is considering a $100,000,000 investment in Costa Libre. The project has annual expected cash inflows of $18,000,000 every year for 10 years. The cost of capital, which reflects the risk of the investment, is 12 percent. Thus, net present value is equal to +$1,704,015. The Christine Corporation, however, can insure the investment with OPIC, and the annual fee would be $1,650,000. This would result in a reduction in annual after-tax cash inflows of $1,089,000.[11] Thus, the annual inflows would be only $16,911,000. OPIC insurance, however, reduces the political risk, thus reducing the cost of capital of the project to only 10 percent. In this illustration, the benefit outweighs the cost, and net present value increases to +$3,910,774. The firm should use OPIC insurance in this case. Note that if the cost of capital had declined to only 11 percent, for

---

[11]We are assuming that the firm has a marginal tax rate of 34 percent. In addition, insurance premiums are a deductible expense. Thus, the after-tax cost of the premium would be equal to $1,650,000 × (1 − 0.34), or $1,089,000.

example, net present value would be a negative $407,197. Thus, in order to maximize stockholder wealth, the firm must weigh the risk reduction benefit against the insurance premium.

Since about two-thirds of all eligible projects (nonpetroleum related) are insured, it is safe to say that the insurance program has widespread appeal. As suggested in the sections that follow, it may be possible to reduce the political risk in other, less expensive ways, thus making the political risk insurance offered by OPIC unnecessary.

Reducing Political Risk
Through Investment Agreements

The multinational firm may be able to reduce the political risk by negotiating an agreement with the host government prior to making an investment. Such an investment agreement is usually formal and written, and details the rights and obligations of both the investing firm and the host government. A formal written agreement may provide the basis for legal action against either party should its terms be violated. Thus, if the investing firm violates the agreement, the host government has a basis for legal action. If the host government violates the agreement, the firm also has a right to a legal remedy. It is often difficult, however, to enforce such remedies when applied against sovereign nations.

Investment agreements have another, perhaps more valuable, function: they enhance communication between the investor and the host government. When needs and expectations are formally detailed, better understanding is likely to develop. By addressing contentious issues, the agreement can set a pattern for the resolution of other future conflicts. The general idea is to identify areas of potential conflict and attempt to work out an agreement beforehand. Typically, investment agreements cover a variety of sensitive topics, such as the following:

1. Employment and wage clauses are often included. Will management and/or skilled workers be local or foreign? What benefits and wages will be paid to local workers?
2. It is not unusual to find a clause relating to the sources of funds used by the firm. Will the firm have access to local capital markets and, if so, on what terms?
3. The agreement may also specify the conditions under which funds can be repatriated to the parent. Understandings relating to dividends, royalties, management fees, interest payments, and transfer prices could be included.

4. Conditions relating to the operation of the investment may also be included. In which country will raw materials be purchased? Where will the output be sold? How will prices be determined?

5. The investment agreement may also include a *divestiture clause*. This clause specifies that at some point in the future, the investment will shift to local ownership. The terms of such a transfer will also be specified. The investing firm usually hopes that this feature will deter the host government from expropriating the investment.

The purpose of these negotiated agreements is to identify all issues that might cause a problem in the future and reduce the political risks inherent in foreign investments. This should reduce the cost of capital associated with the foreign investment and, other things held constant, increase the net present value of that investment. This should benefit both the firm and the host country.

But, of course, other things are not held constant, and prior investment agreements do not necessarily increase the net present value of investments. The firm may be asked to pay high wages, employ less qualified personnel, sell output at low prices, and buy inputs at high prices. The host government may insist on restrictions on repatriation of funds to the parent or limit the use of blocked funds. The divestiture clause may be unrealistic from the investor's point of view. All of these factors tend to reduce the expected cash flows associated with the foreign investment and may lead to a reduction in net present value, even when a lower cost of capital is used to discount the cash flows. In order to serve a constructive purpose, investment agreements must be written in such a way that each party gets something out of the investment. Each party must recognize the needs of the other, and the goal should be mutual benefit rather than exploitation by one party.

Investment Agreements: Historical Record and Outlook

Investment agreements must also be viewed and evaluated in a historical context. This is not a new idea. The British and the French, for example, tended to operate their great trading companies (e.g., the Hudson's Bay Company) under *concessionary* agreements similar to the investment agreements just discussed. American mining and agriculture companies (e.g., the United Fruit Company) have also used investment agreements. These agreements ultimately failed to protect the foreign investment.

One reason for the failure of many of the older investment agreements can be found in the context in which they were drafted. The investors were frequently economically powerful and were supported by their national governments. Both the United States and the United Kingdom used military force to support the claims of their early multinationals. By contrast, the host governments were weak both economically and militarily. They were not in a strong bargaining position and frequently entered into concessionary agreements that benefited the investor more than the host country. In the post–World War II period, less developed countries achieved greater political power (e.g., participation in the United Nations) and colonialism began to decline. Independence also brought new governments to power, some of which were left-leaning. Most governments, regardless of their position in the political spectrum, worked to repudiate the earlier investment agreements on the grounds that they were entered into under duress. Many governments also took a hard line on new investment agreements, wishing to win popular support by demonstrating that they were able to stand up to the world's economic giants.

At the present time, however, we seem to have entered a new era. Many host governments recognize the need to attract foreign capital and understand that foreigners will be unwilling to invest unless a favorable investment climate exists. At the same time that host governments have become sensitized to the needs of investors, foreign investors have become more aware of the rights, obligations, and aspirations of host governments. Today most investors consider less developed countries as something more than a source of inexpensive labor and raw materials. They recognize that these countries can develop into important markets in their own right. More than ever, multinational firms are conducting themselves in a fashion that is conducive to political stability and economic growth in the less developed countries. This new awareness on both sides means that negotiated investment agreements may create opportunities for political risk reduction without crippling effects on cash flows. It is possible that investment agreements can be used both to reduce the cost of capital and to increase net present values.

It is clear that investment agreements are not a cureall for the political risk problem associated with investing in less developed countries. Some governments still insist on terms that make investments unattractive to foreigners. As governments change in the host country, government policies also tend to change. This means that host governments may unilaterally alter the terms of investment agreements. The more radical the change in government, the more likely it is that radical changes in the investment agreement will be made. However, even today's revolutionary governments are taking more moderate positions than previously. It is more likely than ever that fair agreements will not be repudiated. The outlook for the future of investment agreements is favorable. While many governments (e.g., that of Mexico) insist on investment agreements, it is becoming increasingly common for investors to seek such agreements and negotiate them on terms favorable to both themselves and the host government.

Operational Strategies
for Reducing Political Risk

It is sometimes possible for a multinational firm to reduce the political risk associated with investing in a foreign country by operating the foreign investment in such a way that it becomes a less attractive target for hostile host government action. Specifically, the multinational may be able to structure its production and marketing power in such a way that the investment cannot be successfully operated without the participation of the parent.

Production facilities that are completely integrated are relatively vulnerable to hostile political actions. By contrast, production facilities that depend on inputs from other countries have great difficulty operating alone. For example, a multinational farm machinery manufacturer in Latin America could produce tires in one country, engines in another, transmissions in a third, electrical systems in a fourth, and so on. A single country acting alone would gain little value from a hostile action against the multinational, since it would probably have difficulty operating the investment without the inputs from the other countries. In the ideal situation, the availability of the inputs is controlled by the multinational owner. The practicality of this particular strategy is strongly related to the product produced. Mining operations, oil production, and similar investments are, almost by definition, integrated at the production level, and it is not generally possible to scatter the production process.

The multinational firm must also consider the impact of the diversification strategy on the cash flows from the investment. By spreading production into different countries, the multinational investor may be forced to forgo economies of scale and incur increased costs. Thus, diversification may reduce the political risk and the cost of capital for a particular investment, but the net present value may be lowered by the increased costs.

The multinational may also be able to reduce the political risk associated with investing in foreign countries by controlling the marketing and transportation of the product. For example, during the 1950s, the ability of nations to nationalize oil companies without fair compensation was limited by the fact that the marketing of oil was controlled by the major oil companies. Iran and Saudi Arabia, for example, did not have the ability to market their petroleum products in Europe or America without the cooperation of the oil companies. This marketing dependence on the oil companies ensured relatively fair treatment on the part of host governments. The oil companies also exercised substantial control over the transportation of oil, which gave them another type of protection against arbitrary political action. The relative strengths of the oil companies and the producing countries shifted in favor of the producing countries during the 1970s. The marketing power of the big oil companies declined, allowing the governments of the oil-producing nations to demand and receive a larger share of revenues. Thus, the ability of a firm to reduce political risks by such means can change over time.

Some multinational firms separate the locations of production from the sources of raw materials in order to reduce political risk. For example, oil refineries, aluminum refineries, and steel mills may be shielded from political risk by the fact that the producer controls the sources of raw materials necessary for the production process.

Other firms protect themselves by maintaining control over the processes and patents needed for production. The electronics industry employs a dynamic technology that is often protected by patents and secret processes. A government would have difficulty operating such a business without those important ingredients. This fact reduces the likelihood of political action against such a firm.

Each of the preceding strategies is, of course, limited by the circumstances of the firm, the industry in which it is located, and the attitude of the government involved. There are no guarantees that any of these strategies will work. Some firms and industries are vulnerable to political action regardless of the operational strategies employed. For example, a low-technology manufacturer of clothing that uses local inputs and local labor cannot do much to protect against discrimination and expropriation. In other situations, governments are determined to discriminate or expropriate the foreign enterprise regardless of the economic consequences. For example, automobile production facilities and mines have been expropriated even though the facilities could not be managed at the local level. When governments change, it is very difficult to predict what will happen in this area.

It is best to consider operational strategies to reduce political risk as a partial hedge against arbitrary political action. Generally, such actions should reduce the political risks associated with foreign investments. Other things held constant, the cost of capital for foreign investments should go down and the net present value of the investment should go up. Once again, the reader is reminded that these operational strategies may have an impact on cash flows, and this factor must be considered when implementing them.

Financial Strategies for Reducing Political Risk

It is also possible to reduce potential losses on foreign investments by reducing the amount of funds committed to the investment. This could be accomplished by increasing the amount of debt financing used for a particular project. In the ideal situation, the parent firm would provide less equity and the borrowing would be done directly by the subsidiary, with the lenders having no recourse against the parent firm. Note that this strategy does not reduce the riskiness of the investment; it simply shifts the risk to the lenders. In fact, this policy would increase the debt ratio and the financial risk of the foreign operation.

If borrowing at the subsidiary level is organized in a specific fashion, it may also reduce political risk. Some firms, for example, have attempted to use local debt (e.g., bank borrowing). Thus, if the subsidiary fails, local residents (e.g., banks) may suffer losses. For example, assume that an American multinational invests in Brazil and receives loans from a Brazilian bank. Arbitrary political actions by the Brazilian government against the American multinational may result in substantial losses to the local bank. By borrowing in the host country, foreign investors may gain a local political ally and thus reduce the probability of hostile government actions. Note that this strategy is not dependent on increasing the debt ratio of the foreign operation, since local debt may be a substitute for U.S. debt. Keep in mind that this option may not be available in all situations, since the ability of foreign firms to borrow in local financial markets is often restricted.

Another financing strategy used to reduce political risk involves borrowing from third-country banks. For example, an American multinational's copper mining operation in Indonesia may be partly financed by loans from German and Japanese banks. Thus, actions by the Indonesian government against the American firm will have consequences in countries that are important trading partners of Indonesia. In effect, the American multinational diversifies the financing over a number of countries in order to gain political allies. Once again, this strategy does not necessarily imply an increase in the foreign facilities' debt ratio, since foreign debt may simply substitute for American debt. This should reduce the cost of capital and thus increase the net present value of foreign investments.

Organizational Strategies for Reducing Political Risk

In some cases, firms may be able to reduce the political risks associated with investing in foreign countries by reducing the size of the investment while still retaining many of the benefits associated with investing. For example, an American firm may be able to produce in a foreign country by granting a license to a local firm. These license agreements may be reinforced by an agreement that employs the American firm as the manager for the project. Fiat automobiles, for example, are often produced under different names by local firms in less developed and Eastern Europe countries. Fiat provides the license to use the technology and assists the local firm in many other activities. Fiat neither owns the local firm nor receives any of the profits. Fiat receives its compensation by charging licensing and management fees to each local firm. This strategy minimizes political risk, since invested capital is minimized. Whether or not this alternative is better than direct investments depends on the specific situation.

Joint ventures may be used to reduce the equity contribution of the American multinational and decrease the possibility of hostile political action. A joint venture for this purpose usually involves taking a local firm as a partner. The local partner provides some capital, participates in the management of the firm, and may serve as a political buffer between the American investor and the host government. The disadvantage of this strategy is related to management efficiency, since the local partner and the American multinational may often disagree on appropriate business strategies. In fact, tax considerations and currency restrictions often result in situations that affect the local investor in the joint venture differently than they affect the parent. American firms usually prefer to avoid joint ventures due to the loss of managerial control.

Summary and Conclusions

This chapter focused on the cost of capital and its impact on the decision to invest in a foreign country. It is clear that the firm must estimate the cost of capital that reflects the true riskiness of the foreign investment. Otherwise, net present value would be a meaningless concept. It is also clear that an American firm should not use its firmwide cost of capital when evaluating foreign investment projects. It is highly unlikely that the risk of the American firm would be identical to the risk of the foreign investment.

While the very nature of foreign investments usually implies a relatively high risk, a high cost of capital, and a lower net present value (other things held constant), there are some things that a firm can do in order to reduce the risk. In some situations, it may be possible to reduce the cost of capital by taking actions to reduce exchange rate risk. In other cases, the firm can organize its financial activities so that financial risk is controlled. Finally, there are a number of things that a firm can do to control political risk. International investing is not hopelessly risky. However, the risk reduction effort must be approached in a creative and aggressive fashion.

In the final analysis, the goal of the firm should be to maximize stockholder wealth. The strategies discussed in this chapter may increase costs, thus reducing expected cash flows. However, they may also reduce the risks of the foreign investment, thus decreasing the applicable cost of capital. The firm, using net present value, can determine whether the benefits of lower risk outweigh the additional costs.

Review Questions

1. "The firm should always use its firmwide cost of capital to evaluate foreign investment proposals." True or false? Explain your answer.
2. Explain how the subsidized financing that is sometimes associated with foreign investments will affect the firm's cost of capital and the net present value of the foreign investment.
3. Describe some of the important discriminatory political actions that could be taken against foreign investors. Explain the nature of the threat posed by each of these actions.
4. Describe the two types of expropriation faced by foreign investors and evaluate their probable impact on stockholder wealth.
5. Discuss how the risk of war and civil disorder affects the cost of capital of the firm and the net present value of investments (ignore insurance).
6. Which types of investments are most risky? Which countries are characterized by high political risk?
7. Describe the equity insurance provided by OPIC. Which countries are covered, and what is the cost of the insurance?
8. "The use of OPIC insurance always benefits an American firm investing in eligible countries because it reduces political risk." True or false? Explain your answer.
9. Describe investment agreements with host governments and evaluate their usefulness in reducing the political risks associated with investing in a foreign country.
10. Evaluate local borrowing, licensing agreements, and joint ventures as methods for reducing political risk.
11. Explain how a worldwide operations diversification strategy may reduce the political risks borne by an American multinational firm. In addition, evaluate the probable success of such a policy.

Questions for Discussion

1. Assume that you are employed by an American manufacturer of bicycles and exercise equipment. Your firm has been increasing its involvement in the world economy. In recent years, it has opened a production facility in Taiwan and a distribution center in France. The firm is considering a number of other proposals, including the development of production facilities in Australia, Argentina, and Turkey. Top management believes that these investments will increase sales and profits, but it is also concerned about the growing political risk profile of the firm and its impact on stockholder wealth. You are assigned the task of reviewing the

situation and making recommendations concerning methods for controlling the risks and the desirability of continuing the international expansion program.

2. Assume that you are employed by an American manufacturer of electronic testing equipment, and your firm is considering building a production facility in India. You are asked to evaluate the desirability of using OPIC insurance for the investment. You must make recommendations with respect to the particular types of coverage that should be considered, the probable cost of such coverage, and its impact on stockholder wealth.

3. Assume that you are employed by an American firm that manufactures office equipment in the United States and exports it to many countries. In the past, the firm sold to wholesalers in these countries and allowed them to market the products. The firm is now considering a new strategy that would involve establishing its own marketing operations in 16 countries with high sales potential (including some in Western Europe, Latin America, and Asia). In order to do this, the firm will have to make substantial investments in warehouses and equipment at each location. At the present time, the firm's overall cost of capital is 14 percent. You are asked to study the expansion plan in terms of its impact on the cost of capital to the firm. In addition, you are asked to make recommendation with respect to reducing the cost of capital, if possible.

Research Activities

1. Try to evaluate the extent to which American firms have suffered losses on foreign investments due to war and civil disturbances. Look at magazines, newspapers, history books, and so on, and try to identify countries in which losses (ignoring insurance) took place and the American firms that were affected by war or civil disorders. For the political hot spots that you have identified, what is the outlook for the future?

2. Look at the current economic and political environments in the United States and try to identify possible regulatory changes and the risk posed by these changes for American firms. Choose one foreign country and examine its regulatory/discriminatory environment. Compare the political risk in the United States to that in the foreign country.

Problems

1. The Williams Corporation is a new American firm considering an investment in the United States and an investment in Parana. The firm has prepared the following estimates:

	United States	Parana
K_d	10%	14%
K_s	15%	20%
D/A	20%	40%
Tax rate	34%	34%

a. Calculate the cost of capital applicable to the U.S. investment.
b. Calculate the cost of capital applicable to the Parana investment.

c. Calculate the cost of capital applicable if both investments are undertaken (investments of equal size).

d. Assuming that the cost of each investment is $20 million, how much would the firm have to earn annually in order to accept each investment?

2. The firmwide cost of capital of the Donegal Corporation is 13 percent. The firm is planning to make an investment in Costa Libre. It estimates that for this investment, the before-tax cost of debt is 12 percent, the required rate of return of the stockholders is 20 percent, and the optimal capital structure calls for 20 percent debt. In addition, the marginal tax rate of the firm is 34 percent. Should the investment be accepted if it has an annual internal rate of return of 16 percent?

3. The AnnCa Corporation is contemplating an investment proposal in South Sierra. The project will cost $10 million. The firm anticipates annual cash inflows of $2 million for 8 years. AnnCa's firmwide cost of capital is 10 percent. The cost of capital that reflects the riskiness of the South Sierra investment is 12 percent. Should the project be undertaken?

4. American Manufacturing is considering an investment in farm machinery in a foreign country. The host government promotes such investments by offering subsidized financing. The cash outflows of the project are $50 million at time zero. The firm anticipates annual after-tax cash inflows of $15 million for 5 years. The firm's debt ratio is 40 percent, and its marginal tax rate is 34 percent. American Manufacturing has the following options:

(*Note*: Round off K_a to the nearest percent if you are using present value tables.)

	No Subsidy	Foreign Subsidy
K_d	10%	8%
K_s	20%	20%

a. Calculate the net present value of the project if American Manufacturing cannot use the subsidy.

b. Calculate the net present value of the project if American Manufacturing can use the subsidy and maintains the same capital structure.

c. Calculate the net present value of the project if American Manufacturing can use the subsidy. The firm, however, increases its debt ratio to 60 percent. This action causes an increase in the required rate of return of the stockholders to 30 percent.

5. The Denbo Corporation is evaluating a foreign investment proposal. The project has a cost of $28.5 million at time zero. Expected annual after-tax cash inflows are $5 million for 10 years. The cost of capital applicable to the project is 12 percent. The firm is concerned with the political risk of the country. It can obtain OPIC insurance for the project at an annual premium of 1.65 percent. The firm's marginal tax rate is 34 percent (insurance premiums are deductible). If the firm takes OPIC insurance, the cost of capital for the project will decline to 10 percent.

a. Calculate the net present value of the project if the firm does not take OPIC insurance.

b. Calculate the net present value of the project if the firm does take OPIC insurance.

6. Using the information provided in Problem 5, calculate the net present value of the project if the firm does not take OPIC insurance. The firm, however, enters into an agreement with the host government that reduces the political risk of the

investment. The cost of capital of the project declines to 11 percent. This agreement will reduce the annual after-tax cash inflows of the project by $300,000.

7. Using the information in Problems 5 and 6, what is the optimal policy for the firm in regard to this investment?

8. The Donegal Corporation is evaluating a foreign investment in Sierra Libre. The investment will require an original cash outflow at time zero of $80 million. The project will generate annual after tax cash inflows of $10 million each year for 20 years. The cost of capital that reflects the riskiness of the cash flows is 10%.

   a. Should the project be undertaken?

   b. Should the firm obtain OPIC insurance? The annual premium will be 1.65%. The use of OPIC insurance will reduce the risks of the project, thus the cost of capital that reflects the risk of the project will decline to 9%. The marginal tax rate of the firm is 34%.

Bibliography

Adler, Michael. "The Cost of Capital and Valuation of a Two Country Firm." *Journal of Finance*, March 1974, pp. 119–132.

Bhalla, Bharat. "How Corporations Should Weigh Up Country Risk." *Euromoney*, June 1983, pp. 66–72.

Brigham, Eugene F. *Fundamentals of Financial Management*, 4th ed. Chicago: Dryden Press, 1986.

Burton, F. N., and Inoue, Hisashi. "Country Risk Evaluation Methods: A Survey of Systems in Use." *The Banker*, January 1983, pp. 41–43.

Chaudhuri, Adhip. "Multinational Corporations in LDCs: What Is in Store?" *Columbia Journal of World Business*, Spring 1988, pp. 57–64.

Cohn, Richard A., and Pringle, John J. "Imperfections in International Financial Markets: Implications for Risk Premia and the Cost of Capital to Firms." *Journal of Finance*, March 1973, pp. 59–66.

Davidow, Joel. "Multinationals, Host Governments and Regulation of Restrictive Business Practices." *Columbia Journal of World Business*, Summer 1980, pp. 14–19.

Denison, Daniel. "A Pragmatic Model for Country Risk Analysis." *Journal of Commercial Bank Lending*, March 1984, pp. 29–37.

Eiteman, David K., and Stonehill, Arthur I. *Multinational Business Finance*, 3rd ed. Reading, MA: Addison-Wesley Publishing Company, 1982.

Haal, Duane R. *The International Joint Venture*, New York: Praeger Publishers, 1984.

Harrigan, Kathryn R. "Joint Ventures and Global Strategies." *Columbia Journal of World Business*, Summer 1984, pp. 7–13.

Jacquillat, Bertrand, and Solnik, Bruno H. "Multinationals Are Poor Tools for Diversification." *Journal of Portfolio Management*, Winter 1978, pp. 8–12.

Killing, J. Peter. "How to Make a Global Joint Venture Work." *Harvard Business Review*, May–June 1982, pp. 120–127.

Kobrin, Stephen J. "Political Risks: A Review and Reconsideration." *Journal of International Business Studies*, Spring–Summer 1979, pp. 67–80.

Kraar, Louis. "The Multinationals Get Smarter About Political Risks." *Fortune*, March 24, 1980, pp. 86–100.

Mehra, Rajnish. "On the Financing and Investment Decisions of Multinational Firms in the Presence of Exchange Rate Risk." *Journal of Financial and Quantitative Analysis*, June 1978, pp. 227–244.

Modigliani, Franco, and Miller, Merton H. "The Cost of Capital, Corporation Finance, and the Theory of Investment." *American Economic Review*, June 1958, pp. 261–297.

Poynter, Thomas A. "Managing Government Intervention: A Strategy for Defending the Subsidiary." *Columbia Journal of World Business*, Winter 1986, pp. 55–66.

Rugman, Alan M. "Risk Reduction by International Diversification." *Journal of International Business Studies*, Fall 1976, pp. 75–80.

Shaked, Israel. "Are Multinational Corporations Safer?" *Journal of International Business Studies*, Spring 1986, pp. 83–106.

Shapiro, Alan C. "Financial Structure and Cost of Capital in the Multinational Corporation." *Journal of Financial and Quantitative Analysis*, June 1978, pp. 211–226.

Stanley, Marjorie T. "Capital Structure and Cost of Capital for the Multinational Firm." *Journal of International Business Studies*, Spring–Summer 1981, pp. 103–120.

Van Horne, James C. *Financial Management and Policy*, 7th ed. Englewood Cliffs, NJ: Prentice-Hall, Inc., 1986.

PART IV

International Working Capital Management

12

International Dimensions of American Banking

The international dimensions of American banking are of interest to the student of international business and finance for at least two reasons. First, some American banks are important international businesses whose size and importance rival those of other American multinational firms. However, the management of an international bank is very different from that of the multinational production-oriented firm. In this chapter, we will look at some of the unique risk and return aspects associated with the management of international bank operations. Second, it is important that managers of all firms engaged in international commerce understand the nature of international banks and the services they provide. The most obvious and perhaps the most important function of the bank is to make loans to businesses. However, banks also provide a number of other services that are essential for the conduct of international business. Banks play a central role in currency exchange, the management of liquid funds for international businesses, and the letter of credit process.

American banks are relatively new to international banking. While they have always endeavored to provide full financial services to American business firms, it was unnecessary for them to internationalize as long as American businesses operated primarily in the U.S. domestic market. The internationalization of banking has followed the internationalization of American business in general. This change took place after World War II. In the future, as American firms become more and more involved in international business, both the range and volume of services provided by banks should continue to increase.

It is conceivable, but not likely, that American banks could provide all international services from existing banking facilities in the United States. Banks, however, conduct many of their international activities through branches located in foreign countries. For example, letter of credit services can be provided in the United States as well as through foreign branches. Other services—for example, accepting deposits and making international loans—may best be provided through foreign branches. The way the bank is organized has important implications for the range, cost, and efficiency of the services provided.

International Banking Services Provided by Small Banks

Even very small American banks are capable of providing some international banking services. The fact that small banks tend to deal only with small firms means that in many cases the small bank can fulfill all of the international banking needs of its customers. Small banks are able to provide service to their customers by maintaining a correspondent relationship with a larger American bank.[1] The large bank provides services for the small bank, and the small bank passes the services on to its customers. For example, assume that a small store in California imports some products from Japan and needs a letter of credit to pay for them.[2] The importing firm turns to its local bank, the Last National Bank of Yorba Linda. Since, in this case, the local bank is small and not heavily involved in financing international transactions, it would immediately (or perhaps after a little confusion) turn to its correspondent bank, in this illustration the Bank of America. The Bank of America would guarantee payment for the purchase (issue or confirm a letter of credit), and the Last National Bank of Yorba Linda would guarantee payment to the Bank of America. The importing firm would be responsible for payment to the Last National Bank of Yorba Linda. Clearly, this is a cumbersome,

---

[1]Banks frequently enter into long-term agreements under which one bank agrees to perform certain services for another. This is called a *correspondent* relationship. The bank receiving services usually maintains deposits in the correspondent bank as payment for such services.

[2]Letters of credit will be discussed in a later section and more fully in Chapter 14.

costly, and relatively inefficient method of conducting international business. It is acceptable to the importing firm only if its international transactions are infrequent. Firms that are more active in international commerce seek larger banks that have an ongoing capacity to provide directly international services such as letters of credit and currency exchanges.

International Banking Services Provided by Medium-Sized Banks

Medium-sized banks often have international departments with the expertise and information required to provide directly some international services and advice about international transactions. The bank's international department could provide its American customers with immediate information about such things as forward contracts, letters of credit, and funds transfers. However, even medium-sized banks may be unable to provide directly more complex services, such as letters of credit. The reason is that medium-sized banks are usually not well enough known internationally to serve as a guarantor of payment. Thus, these banks must maintain a correspondent relationship with one or more large American money center banks. By using a correspondent banking relationship, a medium-sized bank may be able to provide a full range of services and at the same time have no physical presence abroad. It should be noted that not all medium-sized banks provide international services, but this reflects on the bank's choice, not the technical feasibility of providing such services.

If a bank is heavily involved in providing international services for its customers, it is likely to develop more sophisticated international arrangements. At the simplest level, an American bank could establish correspondent relationships with foreign banks. Under a correspondent relationship, a foreign bank acts as an agent for an American bank in the foreign country. If the American bank needs some services in England, for example, it would simply contact its British correspondent and request that the services be provided. Of course, the American bank would have to compensate the British bank for providing the services. American banks frequently have correspondents in many different countries and effectively provide worldwide service.[3]

---

[3]Even large banks use correspondents in countries that prohibit foreign ownership of banks.

The Organization
of Large International Banks

Large banks have found it attractive to go beyond the correspondent banking arrangement and establish offices in foreign countries. This allows American banks to provide international services without sharing the business with other banks. The simplest foreign banking facility for an American bank is called a *representative office*. The representative office helps generate loan and deposit business for the American parent bank, assists in the documentation process associated with letters of credit, and monitors the outstanding loans of the American bank that are located in the foreign country. The representative office is usually staffed by a few employees of the American bank, some or all of whom are likely to be citizens of the country in which the representative office is located. The most important characteristic of the representative office is that it neither directly accepts deposits nor directly makes loans. Customers dealing with the representative office are actually doing business with a bank located in the home country of the office.[4] For example, a representative office of an American bank located in Spain may actually be conducting business for the bank located in the United States or for a subsidiary of the American bank located outside of Spain. The representative office may help a customer arrange for a loan from the bank, or it may help generate deposits for the American bank. However, it does neither of these things on its own behalf.

From an American bank's perspective, representative offices permit an international presence at a relatively low cost. In some cases, representative offices may be the only presence allowed by the foreign government. In addition, government regulations pertaining to representative offices are usually less burdensome than those placed on full-service banks. At the same time, the representative office system allows the American bank to provide worldwide service without depending on correspondent banks, which are often viewed as competitors and/or also represent competing American banks. The representative office arrangement is a relatively inexpensive way of maintaining a worldwide international banking capability that directly and exclusively represents the interest of the American bank and its customers.

The activities of an American bank in a particular foreign country may be so great and/or the profit potential so large that the representative office system may be deemed inadequate. In such cases, the American bank may decide to establish a more complete physical presence in a foreign country. A true international banking presence can be imple-

---

[4]Representative offices are not unique to international banking. For example, large New York banks have had representative offices in major U.S. cities for many years.

mented either through the acquisition of a foreign bank, which is then operated as a separate subsidiary, or through the establishment of a foreign branch of the American bank. Both branches and subsidiaries are able to conduct all of the activities associated with a representative office; they are also able to accept deposits and make loans. American banks seem to prefer conducting foreign banking activities through branches. This arrangement permits the full economic resources of the bank to be used throughout the world. For example, a small foreign subsidiary bank may be unable to make large loans, while the branch of a large bank may be able to do so. In addition, depositors may feel safer if funds are placed within the larger branch system than if they are deposited in the smaller subsidiary.

In order for an American bank to operate a foreign branch, it must obtain permission from the Federal Reserve System and the government of the country in which the branch will be located. A foreign branch is an integral part of the American bank. If the foreign branch is closed, the American bank is legally responsible for all obligations. It should be noted, however, that some countries do not permit foreign branches. In these countries, American banks have no alternative but to operate through wholly owned subsidiaries.[5]

Foreign branches of American banks have a number of regulatory advantages over representative offices, which accept deposits in the American-domiciled bank. Foreign branches do not need to maintain reserves against their deposits with the Federal Reserve, nor are they required to pay insurance premiums on foreign deposits to the FDIC. In addition, they are not subject to the interest rate limitations that characterized American bank regulation up to the recent past. While foreign branches of American banks may be subject to regulations by the governments of the countries in which they operate, often these regulations are less onerous than those in the United States. In addition, foreign branches may escape regulation entirely by limiting themselves to euromarket activities.[6] The international strategy of American multinational banks has been to focus on large borrowers and depositors and to avoid small deposit taking and lending functions. Thus, one branch in any particular country is usually sufficient to meet the objectives of the American bank. In fact, American banks usually operate in foreign countries as *wholesale* banks, similar to those existing in the United States in the middle to late nineteenth century.

The regulatory advantages associated with operating branches outside the United States, especially for banks that confine their operations to euromarket activities, are very important for American banks. Lower operating costs resulting from the lower regulatory costs of foreign

---

[5]For convenience, we will refer to foreign branches and subsidiaries as *branches*. This reflects usual usage.

[6]See Chapter 9 for a more detailed discussion of the euromarket.

TABLE 12-1   Assets of Foreign Branches of U.S. Banks (in Millions)

Year	Total Assets	Year	Total Assets
1975	$176,493	1982	$469,712
1976	$219,420	1983	$477,090
1977	$258,897	1984	$453,656
1978	$306,795	1985	$458,012
1979	$364,166	1986	$456,627
1980	$401,135	1987	$519,095
1981	$462,790	1988	$505,037

Source: Federal Reserve Bulletin, Board of Governors of the Federal Reserve System, various issues.

branches allow American banks to compete with other eurobanks. In particular, the more favorable regulatory environment gives American banks that have foreign branches a big advantage over American banks that have no such operations. Banks with international operations can (1) lend at lower rates, (2) pay higher rates on deposits, (3) provide better service for customers with international financial transactions, and (4) have the opportunity to earn higher profits. Thus, American banks have powerful incentives to establish banking facilities outside the United States.

As shown in Table 12-1, the assets of foreign branches of U.S. banks grew rapidly from 1975 to 1981 but slowed down after that time. While the data in Table 12-1, viewed in isolation, suggest that there has been a slowdown in the expansion of American banks into the international banking business, this conclusion is incorrect. What has happened is that since 1981, American banks have been permitted to operate international banking facilities (IBFs) in the United States. Since an IBF has many of the advantages of a foreign branch, many American banks have substituted domestic IBFs for foreign branch operations. In effect, international banking facilities have "stolen" the asset growth of foreign branches. Total assets held by IBFs were $198 billion as of December 1986. If IBFs had not been established, a significant percentage of these assets may have ended up in foreign branches of American banks.

International Banking Facilities

Since December 1981, American banks have been allowed to create IBFs. These facilities operate under almost the same regulations as foreign branches. The most important differences are the following: (1) customers are limited to nonresidents of the United States, and (2) the minimum size of any transaction is $100,000. These limits effectively restrict the clientele of the IBFs to wealthy foreign individuals and large foreign business firms. In effect, American banks can now service foreign customers on the same terms as foreign bank competitors, and this service can be provided from within the United States. Note, however, that American banks cannot service their American customers with these IBFs. For example, a large American firm wishing to arrange for a euroloan cannot do so through the IBF of an American bank. An American bank wishing to attract this type of business must still have eurobank operations located outside the United States. Thus, American banks are not likely to abandon their euromarket branches because doing so would limit their ability to provide a full range of services to American customers.

In addition to IBFs, the Edge Act, enacted in 1919, permits American banks to conduct certain international banking activities through wholly owned Edge Act corporations. An Edge Act bank is a domestic bank owned by an American bank and chartered within the United States. Its activities are limited to international operations. Customers can be either foreigners or Americans. Edge Act bank deposits and loans, however, can only be internationally related; they cannot be used for domestic purposes. Generally speaking, Edge Act banks are subjected to the same regulations as other American banks, which places them in a less favorable position than eurobanks and IBFs. Today, Edge Act banks play a relatively minor role in the international operations of American banks. However, Edge Act banks have one important feature that may encourage their use under certain circumstances. While American banks are generally prohibited from taking an equity position in a firm, Edge Acts are permitted limited equity positions in firms operating outside the United States. Thus, an American bank may be able to use an Edge Act bank to accomplish something (equity ownership) that could not be done through domestic operations.

Services Provided by American Banks

At this point, we will take a closer look at the international banking services provided by American banks. The emphasis will be on the range of services provided to business firms. For each service, we will examine the cost to the customer, as well as the profitability and risks to the bank. These services have been divided into four major categories: (1) transfer of funds, (2) foreign exchange, (3) letters of credit, and (4) loans.

Services Designed to Transfer Funds

American business firms engaged in international commerce regularly accept payments from and make payments to foreign firms. The payout and receiving process is referred to as *transferring funds*, and such transfers are the normal course of business. Conceptually, there is no difference between domestic and international transfers. The international environment, however, may be complicated by differences in law, language, and distance. It is important to differentiate between the transfer of funds and the conversion of one currency to another. These are two distinct services provided by banks, each of which has its own costs, risks, and profitability. This section discusses only the transfer of funds. It may be helpful for the reader to imagine that all transfers are taking place in dollars, which makes it unnecessary to consider currency conversion costs (which will be discussed in the next section).

Firms transferring funds from one country to another can use several different procedures. The alternative chosen by the firm must reflect three cost considerations. First, there is the direct cost associated with the transfer. In other words, banks charge a fee for transferring funds, and the size of the fee reflects the type of transfer employed. Second, there is an opportunity cost to the recipient of the funds that is directly related to the time elapsed before funds are available. Slower transfer methods result in a delay before the funds are available, and this delay translates into a cost for the receiving firm. Third, there may be an opportunity "gain" (a negative cost) for the paying firm when the transfer process takes a long time. The funds may still be available to the paying firm for some time after the payment is made. This situation is usually called the *float*. The selection of the proper procedure to transfer funds must reflect these three considerations. Of course, the method of transferring funds is usually associated with a commercial transaction, and the details of the funds transfer are generally specified. Since the method of transfer is negotiated, neither the paying nor the receiving firm has complete discretion about how the transfer is made.

For domestic transactions within the United States, the *check* is still the most popular method of transferring funds. The paying firm issues a check that authorizes a transfer of funds to the receiving firm. The check is deposited by the receiving firm and then makes its way through an elaborate check-clearing process. In the United States, checks can usually be cleared in 5 days or less. The relative speed of the clearing process reflects the efficiency of the elaborate network established by the Federal Reserve System.[7] The efficiency of the system also keeps the cost of the clearing process within acceptable bounds. The use of checks for international transfer of funds is considerably less popular, and for good reasons. This method is often unacceptable to the receiving firm because it

---

[7]Nonbankers view the time it takes a check to clear as still too long. Cash management procedures designed to speed up the process of gaining access to funds is an important aspect of financial management, and some of these techniques may be applied to international transactions. See Eugene F. Brigham, *Fundamentals of Financial Management*, 4th ed., Chicago: Dryden Press, 1986, chapter 18. In addition, recent legislation (September 1988) mandated maximum hold periods for different types of checks deposited in domestic transactions.

takes too long for the check to work its way through the international check-clearing process. A firm that receives a check drawn on a foreign bank and deposits it may have to wait 4 to 6 weeks before the funds are available. Since this is usually unacceptable to receiving firms, checks are either not used as a means of payment or special arrangements to shorten the clearing period are made.

One method used to shorten the check-clearing time for international transactions involves using foreign banks and bank accounts. Firms that regularly do business in a foreign country and accept payment in that country may simply establish a banking relationship with a local bank. For example, a foreign firm doing business in the United States may have an account with an American bank. Checks received from American firms can be deposited in the American bank and cleared through the normal U.S. check-clearing process. Of course, the foreign firm still does not have the funds available in its home country. But it is relatively simple to have the funds transferred from a large money center bank in the United States to one of its foreign branches or foreign correspondents. This second transfer can take place within hours. The use of foreign bank accounts is appropriate only for larger firms. Smaller firms and firms only occasionally involved in international commerce may not find it profitable to maintain foreign bank accounts. To summarize the use of checks for the international transfer of funds: The direct cost associated with the transfer is negligible. The opportunity cost to the receiving firm, however, could be very high due to the length of the clearing process. The opportunity gain to the paying firm is very high due to the long period that elapses between the time the check is written and the time the funds are deducted from the firm's checking account.

The use of checks to transfer funds internationally has another important drawback. Since there is a possibility that a check may not be honored by the bank on which it is drawn, the firm that receives the check is at risk. Banks may refuse to honor a check if the issuer has insufficient funds on deposit, or the issuing firm may simply decide to stop payment on the check. In any case, the receiving firm does not know if the funds will be available until the check has actually cleared. Since the international check-clearing process takes so long, the probability of difficulties in this regard may be higher than for domestic transactions.

Even for domestic transactions within the United States, there is a trend away from using checks to make payments.[8] Today everyone talks about *electronic transfers*. A domestic electronic transfer begins with an instruction from the paying firm. The instruction may be in writing but is often transmitted to the paying firm's bank over the telephone or by computer. The bank is instructed to transfer funds directly to the account

---

[8]For a more detailed discussion of electronic transfers, see Timothy W. Koch, *Bank Management*, Chicago: Dryden Press, 1988, pp. 318–332.

of the receiving firm. Note that the payment goes directly to the receiving firm's designated bank account, not to the firm. Note also that the process is fast and that there is no check-clearing process with which to contend. Payment can be effected within hours and at a relatively low cost. Most experts agree that at some point in the future, this will become the dominant method for transferring funds in the United States. The banking systems of some industrialized foreign countries (Germany, for example) have used direct transfers of funds for years. Foreign firms often view the use of checks as inconvenient and anachronistic.

Electronic transfers rather than checks dominate the international funds transfer process. Large commercial banks can make electronic transfers in almost any amount, in almost any currency, to almost any place in the world. These transfers are called *wire transfers*. They are fast, of modest cost, and eliminate the risk of nonpayment often associated with checks. The funds are quickly available to the receiving firm, which means that there is almost no opportunity cost associated with waiting for access to the funds. For example, a transfer of $20 million from a New York bank to a London bank will be available to the receiving firm within hours. The cost of wire transfers is a function of the amount transferred. For large transfers, the costs are negligible when viewed as a percentage of the amount transferred. This may not be the case when smaller amounts are involved. For example a $1,000 wire transfer from California to Spain may cost $30, which is 3 percent of the amount transferred. Firms that make many small payments to foreigners may find the wire transfer procedure too expensive. The speed of wire transfers has made this method the preferred alternative for large international transfers.

Currency Conversion Services

As discussed in Chapter 2, commercial banks are the key players in the currency conversion process. If an American firm needs Italian lire in order to meet a financial obligation, it converts dollars to lire through its bank. If an American firm receives a payment in Spanish pesetas, it converts the pesetas to dollars through its bank. Almost all conversions of one currency to another involve the use of banks. If banks discontinued this service, international commerce would come to a halt.

At this point, we are interested in the incentives for banks to participate in the currency conversion process. Obviously, the motive for entering the foreign exchange market and providing the currency conversion service is the profit associated with this service. Bank profits have two sources: (1) the bid–ask spread and (2) possible changes in the value of foreign currencies. The profit associated with the bid–ask spread is relatively straightforward. Assume, for example, that a bank buys £100 million in the spot market at a bid price of £1 = $1.6000 and at the same time sells the pounds at its ask price of £1 = $1.6010. This means that the bank simultaneously pays out $160 million and receives $160.1 million, thus earning a profit of $100,000. The same profit potential can be found in forward market transactions. If a bank buys £100 million for delivery in 90 days at a bid price of £1 = $1.5970 and simultaneously sells the entire amount at its ask price of £1 = $1.5990, it will earn a profit of $200,000. In both the spot and forward transactions, the bank earned a guaranteed profit and took absolutely no risk. There were no risks in either case because the bank simultaneously bought and sold exactly the same amount of foreign currency. The bank was not required to hold any foreign currency today or in the future and would have been unaffected by any fluctuations in the value of the foreign currency.

The real world is not so simple. Banks do incur risk because rarely do they simultaneously sell every unit of foreign currency purchased. Thus, a bank may buy more foreign currency than it immediately sells and, in so doing, develops an inventory of that currency.[9] If the value of the foreign currency increases, the bank will make a profit on its inventory. Of course, a decline in the foreign currency value will result in an inventory loss to the bank. The bank is at risk, since it does not know whether it will make a gain or a loss on its foreign currency inventories.

The word *inventory* is being used here in an unorthodox way. In spot transactions there is a true inventory, but in forward market transactions the inventory is a bookkeeping entry rather than an actual inventory of a foreign currency. Assume, for example, that a bank purchases DM50 million in the spot market and sells only DM30 million. The bank's physical inventory of deutsche marks increases by DM20 million and will thus be affected by changes in the value of the deutsche mark. Compare this spot market situation to a forward market situation in which the bank buys FF100 billion and sells FF60 million, with both transactions to be completed in 90 days.[10] Since in 90 days the bank is committed to accept more French francs than it has thus far sold, the bank has, in a sense, an unsold inventory of 90-day French francs. Any changes in the value of the franc will affect the profits of the bank. Note that the forward market situation differs from the spot market situation in the sense that there is no physical inventory of French francs. The inventory is only a bookkeeping entry. However, the risk implications of both types of inventory are exactly the same for the bank. The bank will make a profit if the value of the foreign currency increases and suffer a loss if it declines.

---

[9]Banks can also have negative inventories of foreign currencies. This is the result of borrowing foreign currencies. A bank with negative inventories will experience losses if the value of the foreign currency increases.

[10]This situation is called a *long exposure*. The bank will make a profit if the value of the foreign currency increases. A *short exposure* (purchasing less than what will be sold in the future), however, will result in losses if the value of the foreign currency increases.

There are good reasons why banks hold inventories of foreign currencies. Banks must compete for customers, and providing service is part of this competition. Thus, if a regular customer wants to sell British pounds to its bank, the bank is likely to accept them, even if there are no immediate buyers. Large banks with many foreign currency conversion transactions may sometimes have large inventories of foreign currencies. The institutional arrangements that allow a bank to maintain a zero risk exposure are in place. Under usual circumstances, banks maintain small inventories of actively traded currencies, and sell and buy through foreign currency dealers and/or other banks as the need dictates. Sometimes banks will make gains on the inventories and at other times they will suffer losses. Over time, hopefully, the losses and gains will cancel each other out. The bank's profit should be earned on the spread between the bid and ask prices, not on changing inventory values and not in a way that exposes the bank to undue risk.

As discussed in Chapter 5, the ability to forecast foreign exchange rate movements has not been demonstrated. However, despite impressive evidence of the failure to predict foreign exchange rate movements consistently, banks occasionally speculate on such movements by taking a long or short position in foreign currencies. The temptation to speculate with forward market inventories is particularly great since no dollars have to be expended to acquire such inventories. For example, a bank that believes the Japanese yen will rise in value by more than the amount reflected in the current forward rate will buy yen forward (resulting in a bookkeeping inventory). Hopefully, the yen will be sold at a later date at the expected higher spot rate. Note that no initial expenditure of dollars is needed to accumulate this bookkeeping inventory, since transactions will not be executed until the agreed-upon forward date, at which time the bank will immediately sell the currency, hopefully at a profit. Theoretically, a bank could acquire as much of a particular currency as it wanted in the forward market because no immediate outlays are required. The ability to acquire inventories of currencies in the spot market, however, is limited by the number of dollars available for immediate purchase. Thus, when banks speculate, they prefer to use the forward market. Banks do speculate in this way. Sometimes spectacular profits are earned. Sometimes the losses are so great that it is hard to understand why banks ever engage in these speculative endeavors. It is the spectacular losses that find their way to the headlines.[11]

It is possible, although unlikely, that banks will sometimes make consistent speculative profits in the market for foreign exchange, since they may, on occasion, have inside information. Banks may have a better understanding of how and when central banks will intervene in the foreign exchange markets. Banks may have better information about

---

[11]According to some analysts, a significant factor in the failure of the Franklin National Bank in 1974 was losses due to foreign exchange speculation.

economic, financial, and political conditions in particular countries. Nevertheless, speculating in the market for foreign exchange is still highly risky for banks. The principle that the forward rate is an unbiased estimator of the future spot rate is just as true for banks as it is for other speculators. As long as banks are unable to forecast the random events that affect exchange rates, they will be susceptible to large foreign exchange losses.

Letters of Credit

American banks facilitate international commerce by issuing letters of credit. A firm engaged in a specific importing transaction would apply to its bank for a letter of credit. The letter of credit substitutes the bank's promise of payment for that of the importer. In effect, the bank agrees to pay the exporter and the importer agrees to pay the bank. The existence of letters of credit eliminates most of the default risk associated with the transaction. Banks profit from issuing letters by charging a fee to the firms that request them. A representative fee is $130 *plus* one-quarter of 1 percent of the face value of the letter of credit. Note that under the typical letter of credit arrangement, the bank does not lend any funds. The bank simply guarantees the payment.

While letters of credit are highly profitable, there is a risk to the bank. The bank guarantees payment and is thus obligated to pay as specified in the letter of credit. The risk is that the firm that requested the letter of credit may not pay the bank. The bank tries to protect itself against such risk by extending letters of credit only to customers with the best credit rating. If a customer with a substandard credit rating applies for a letter of credit, the bank could still agree to this arrangement but would probably require that the customer provide some type of security. The bank may require a partial or full deposit of the funds before granting the letter of credit. As another alternative, the bank could have the goods involved in the transaction shipped to the bank and not released to the importer until the importer renders the payment.

Even though writing letters of credit is highly profitable for American banks, not all banks provide this service. Only large, well-known, financially stable banks have reputations of sufficient quality that their guarantee of payment will be accepted by foreign sellers. A British company, for example, may be willing to accept a promise of payment from the Bank of America but unwilling to accept a letter of credit from the Podunk State Bank. Smaller banks that wish to issue letters of credit must usually have them *confirmed* by larger, better-known banks. The confirmation process means that the larger bank is guaranteeing the payment of the smaller bank. A confirmation or guarantee makes letters of credit issued by small banks acceptable in international commerce.

Lending to American Firms

Foreign branches of American banks are important lenders to American business. These euroloans may be used in the United States or abroad. Through this mechanism, American banks are able to provide customers with the advantages of dealing with a eurobank while eliminating the need for customers to establish a relationship with a foreign bank. The use of euroloans by American business was discussed in Chapters 9 and 10.

International Lending

American banks are important lenders to foreign customers. They lend through their eurobank branches, through international banking facilities located in the United States, and directly from American bank operations. Since World War II, lending to foreigners has been one of the growth areas in American banking. Recently, however, the international lending operations of American banks have encountered major problems that may permanently change the extent of American banks' involvement in international lending. In addition, such lending may be impairing the safety of some sectors of the American banking system itself.

American banks rushed into international lending because high profits were anticipated. Due to differences in the regulatory environments, banks could generally earn a higher rate of return on loans to foreigners than could be earned on domestic loans. The higher margin on loans would result in higher profits and increases in shareholder wealth for the bank as long as the risks associated with international loans were no greater than those associated with domestic loans. Banks attempted to structure their operations in such a way as to minimize the risks associated with lending to foreigners and for many years believed that they were successful. Recent developments, however, suggest otherwise. A closer look at the risk management strategy of American banks is in order.

From the American banks' perspective, there are four distinct risks involved in lending to foreigners: (1) interest rate risk, (2) foreign exchange rate risk, (3) political risk, and (4) default risk. *Interest rate risk*, in the context of banking, refers to the risk that the bank will lend funds at a fixed rate on the assumption that the cost of funds will not rise. For example, the cost of funds to the bank may be 7 percent, and the bank may lend at a fixed rate of 9 percent for 5 years. If the cost of funds rises to 10 percent, the bank will simply lose money.[12] Banks engaged in

---

[12]Note that if interest rates decline, the borrower can always repay the loan. Thus, banks will not necessarily earn high profits by making fixed-rate loans under this scenario.

international lending have reduced their interest rate risk by issuing loans on a *variable rate* basis. Specifically, loan interest rates are adjusted periodically to reflect changes in the LIBOR.[13] This procedure has worked well, and interest rate risk has not been a major problem for international lenders.

Banks' Foreign Exchange Rate Risk

Foreign exchange rate risk, in the context of banking, refers to the risk that the value of loans outstanding will be affected by changes in exchange rates. For example, if an American bank has a FF100,000,000 loan outstanding and the value of the franc declines, the dollar value of the asset (the loan) is lower. Banks manage this risk by matching the currency in which loans are made to the currency in which deposits are accepted. If, for example, the preceding bank also has deposits (liabilities) of FF100,000,000, their dollar value will fall as the french franc declines in value. The loss in asset value is exactly offset by a reduction in liability value, and the overall financial position of the firm is unaffected.

By managing the denomination of loans in such a way that they reflect the denomination of deposits, international lenders are able to keep foreign exchange rate risk within acceptable bounds. Table 12-2 shows the assets and liabilities of foreign branches of American banks. Foreign branches denominate 71 percent of their assets and 73 percent of their liabilities in dollars. Assets and liabilities denominated in German, Swiss, British, and Japanese currencies are less important. Note that there is a gap of approximately $9 billion between foreign currency–denominated assets and liabilities. This may introduce a certain amount of foreign exchange risk to the foreign branch operations of American banks. If the value of foreign currencies declines, the dollar value of both the assets and liabilities of foreign branches will drop. The decline in the value of the assets, however, will be greater than the decline in liabilities. Therefore, foreign branch operations will experience a loss as a result of a decline in foreign currency values. The opposite, of course, will occur if the value of the foreign currencies increases. The total foreign exchange rate risk of the bank may not be accurately reflected in Table 12-2, since the exposure of foreign exchange operations in the United States is not included. In general, banks manage their assets and liabilities in such a way as to avoid major losses due to exchange rate movements.[14]

---

[13]See Chapter 9 for a more detailed discussion of LIBOR.

[14]As noted earlier, banks have been adversely affected by exchange rate movements. However, the large losses have usually resulted from speculative positions, not from the asset/liability structure.

TABLE 12-2   Assets and Liabilities of Foreign Branches of American Banks as of December 1988 (in Millions)

Dollar-denominated assets	$357,461	Dollar-denominated liabilities	$366,506
Dollar value of foreign currency– denominated assets	$147,576	Dollar value of foreign currency– denominated liab.	$138,531
Total assets	$505,037	Total liabilities	$505,037

Source: *Federal Reserve Bulletin*, Board of Governors of the Federal Reserve System, May 1989.

Banks' Political Risk

Political risk refers to the possibility that foreign governments will take actions that restrict the repayment of loans. Many countries have repudiated loans after a change in government. Banks that had loans outstanding in Cuba (1959) or China (1948) are still waiting for repayment. Governments in other countries occasionally decide unilaterally to reduce the size of debt repayments. For example, Peru recently limited debt service to 10 percent of its annual exports. The imposition of government restrictions on loan repayment usually reflects domestic economic difficulties and/or political changes and can create a major problem for banks that have loaned money in that country. Banks attempt to minimize the political risks associated with international lending by extending loans only to borrowers located in countries that are believed to have a low probability of imposing repayment restrictions. As we will see, banks have made serious mistakes in this regard.

The Default Risk
Associated with International Lending

The *default risk* associated with bank loans refers to the likelihood that borrowers will be unable or unwilling to repay. International banks have always recognized this potential risk and have attempted to deal with it by restricting loans to the most creditworthy customers. By and large, American banks make loans only to the largest, most creditworthy firms and to stable governments with good financial reputations. It is this last group of customers, stable governments with good financial reputations, that has created the current crises in American banking and international lending.

In the typical commercial loan made to a firm rather than to a government, the bank considers two factors when evaluating the default risk. First, the bank looks at the borrower's ability to repay the loan. Then the bank examines the assets of the firm to evaluate their adequacy as collateral should the borrower default on the loan. In case of a default, the bank seizes the assets, sells them, and compensates itself for the loan repayment not received. The system works when loans are made to commercial customers in the United States and other industrial countries. In these cases, there is a clear legal remedy that can be applied to loan defaults.

The most glaring default problem involves loans to governments. What legal remedies are available when a government is unable or unwilling to pay? This is an internal U.S. problem as well as an international problem. During the 1970s both New York City and Cleveland were unable to meet their debt obligations. How does a lender foreclose on a city? In the United States, the federal government tends to bail out local governments that encounter this difficulty. But who bails out a sovereign government such as that of Brazil when it is unable to repay its debts? This is the crisis facing international banking in the 1990s. Banks lent money to foreign governments, and these governments are unable (unwilling?) to repay. The amounts involved are enormous. The legal remedy in cases of default is not clear. The economic consequences of default are likely to be tremendous to the banks involved, the U.S. economy, and the debtor countries. At the time of this writing, the final chapter in the story has yet to be written.

The international debt crisis has been on the horizon for many years and is focused on loans to less developed countries.[15] As early as 1969, some of these countries were in danger of default, but favorable economic developments postponed the impending crisis. The current crisis is partly the result of the phenomenal rise in oil prices that took place during the 1970s. The options available to the governments of the countries facing rising oil prices were not attractive. Basically, in order to meet the new, higher oil bills, these governments could either cut back on current consumption and investment or increase foreign borrowing. Most countries chose to borrow rather than reduce living standards that were already relatively low. Note that the borrowing was not being used for productive investments that would increase the future ability of the countries to repay the loans. The proceeds were often used to maintain current levels of consumption. In other words, some countries incurred debts almost beyond their ability to repay in order to maintain the same (relatively low) standard of living.

The initial catastrophe associated with the rise in oil prices was compounded by other developments. No doubt, as in almost all situations in which large amounts of money are involved, there was some mismanagement and corruption associated with the loans to less developed countries. In addition, these countries were affected by the reduc-

---

[15] Included in this category are most of the Latin American, African, and Asian countries.

tion in the demand for and price of their exports due to the worldwide slowdown in the economies of the developed countries. When oil prices did fall, most countries were already so heavily in debt that it made little difference to their ability to repay. In fact, the fall in oil prices made their loan problem worse in some instances because several oil-exporting less developed countries, most notably Mexico and Venezuela, borrowed heavily and planned to repay with oil revenues. But revenues were lower than anticipated because oil prices retreated from the high levels reached during the early days of the Organization of Petroleum Exporting Countries (OPEC), and repayment problems followed. It should also be remembered that the U.S. government and the World Bank continued to encourage banks to lend to the less developed countries throughout the period.

The success of the OPEC cartel in raising prices shifted significant wealth to the oil-producing countries, especially those in the Middle East. The governments of these countries were unwilling to make long-term loans to the importing countries. Instead, they deposited the funds in banks on a short-term basis, and the banks made longer-term loans to the less developed countries. Apparently, banks saw a profit opportunity in recycling these so-called petrodollars, but the situation has backfired on

TABLE 12-3 Claims on Foreign Countries Held by U.S. Offices and Foreign Branches of U.S. Banks (in Billions)

Country	1975	1979	1984	1987
Argentina	$1.7	$5.0	$8.7	$9.4
Brazil	$8.0	$15.2	$26.3	$24.1
Chile	$0.5	$2.5	$7.0	$6.9
Mexico	$9.0	$12.0	$25.7	$23.6
Other Latin American countries*	$5.2	$7.4	$9.0	$5.9
Total Latin America	$24.4	$42.1	$76.7	$69.9
Other developing countries	$9.8	$20.9	$35.1	$26.8
Venezuela	$2.3	$8.7	$9.3	$8.2
Other OPEC countries	$4.6	$14.2	$15.6	$9.1
Total OPEC	$6.9	$22.9	$24.9	$17.3
Developed countries	$98.7	$158.3	$181.7	$186.7
Eastern Europe	$3.7	$7.3	$4.4	$3.0
Offshore banking†	$19.4	$40.4	$65.6	$53.1
Miscellaneous	$4.1	$11.7	$17.3	$24.4
Total debt	$167.0	$303.6	$405.7	$381.2

*Excludes Venezuela and Ecuador, since they are members of OPEC. Also excluded is Panama, since its borrowings are included in offshore banking.

†The principal offshore banking centers are located in the Bahamas, Cayman Islands, Panama, Hong Kong, and Singapore.

Source: Federal Reserve Bulletin, Board of Governors of the Federal Reserve System, various issues.

them. Some less developed countries are simply unable to pay. The banks made a serious miscalculation in this regard. While precise information is unavailable, the amounts involved in this debacle are enormous. Table 12-3 shows the amounts owed to American banks by some foreign borrowers.

Magnitude and Riskiness of Loans to Less Developed Countries

The data in Table 12-3 reveal some interesting information. First, the debt is not as high as indicated in newspaper reports. While Mexico may have a total foreign debt of close to $100 billion, the debt owed to American banks is only $24 billion. Second, the foreign debt of less developed countries increased at a fast pace from 1975 to 1984, but there has been a decline in the last 3 years as banks have attempted to reduce their default risk exposure in these debts. Third, most of the foreign debt held by American commercial banks has been issued to developed countries. These countries currently have no significant difficulties in debt repayment. Finally, the magnitude of the debt must be placed in perspective. The $24 billion Mexican debt sounds large, but not when compared to the $180 billion in capital of the American banking system. It is clear that widespread defaults would hurt the American banking system and may cause the failure of individual banks. It is not clear, however, that the American banking system would collapse under such circumstances.

What is the probability of default on the loans to less developed countries? The answer to this question depends on how the word *default* is defined. In its most straightforward meaning, default implies that a borrower indicates that no debt payment will occur, now or ever. Thus far, no major borrowing country has taken this position. Since it is in the interest of neither the borrowing country nor the lending bank to have a default, the two parties frequently enter into agreements that make it appear that there has been no default when in fact there has been one. For example, a bank can make loans to the borrowing country, and the proceeds of the loans are then used to make payments to the bank. Thus, the bank makes interest and principal payments to itself, and the borrowing country incurs more and more debt. The Mexican and Argentinian debts have been handled in this fashion. Another technique that is being employed is the rescheduling of debt. Under this arrangement, the parties agree to a moratorium or slowdown in repayment. An interesting development took place at the end of 1987. Mexico paid $2 billion for $10 billion (face value) in zero coupon U.S. government bonds maturing in 20 years. The Mexican government is negotiating with American banks to buy back some of its debt. Mexico would like to replace $14 billion of its existing debt with $10 billion in 20-year loans. Mexico will continue to

TABLE 12-4 Merchandise Trade Balances of Selected Countries from 1980 to 1986
(Billions of U.S. Dollars)

Year	Argentina	Brazil	Mexico
1980	($1.4)	($ 2.8)	($ 2.3)
1981	$0.7	$ 1.2	($ 4.1)
1982	$2.7	$ 0.8	$ 6.8
1983	$3.7	$ 6.5	$13.8
1984	$4.0	$13.1	$12.9
1985	$4.9	$12.5	$ 8.5
1986	$2.4	$ 8.3	$ 4.6

*The merchandise balance is computed by subtracting merchandise imports from merchandise exports. A negative entry indicates that imports are greater than exports. A positive entry indicates that exports exceed imports.

Source: *International Financial Statistics*, International Monetary Fund, various issues.

pay interest for 20 years and, upon maturity, the U.S. government bonds will be used to repay the principal. This is but the most recent example of "creative" refinancing.[16]

Most economists question whether most of the loans will ever be repaid. This question reflects the assumption that most governments of less developed countries will be unwilling to pay the domestic political price that would be required. Basically, in order to service foreign debt, a less developed country must export more goods and services than it imports on a continuing basis. The positive trade balance that results from such a policy will yield the hard currencies required for the repayment of debt. Of course, this policy will result in a lower standard of living in the less developed country, since goods are being produced but not consumed in that country. From the perspective of the less developed countries, the poor are being made even poorer by the international debt situation. This is a politically explosive situation.

It should be noted that many of the less developed countries have the positive trade balances needed to service foreign debt. As shown in Table 12-4, there was a transfer of wealth from debtor to creditor nations during the 1980s. However, the amounts involved were inadequate to cover interest payments. There is certainly no realistic possibility that these trade surpluses would be large enough to retire the debt. If banks are ever to be repaid, trade surpluses must be significantly higher and, in all likelihood, living standards in the less developed countries significantly lower. The likelihood of this happening does not appear to be great.

---

[16]For a more detailed discussion of this recent development, see "Loan Plan May Help Mexico, Some Banks; But It's No Panacea," *The Wall Street Journal*, December 30, 1987, pp. 1, 9. Other creative solutions have included a trade of debt for equity, a change of dollar-denominated debt for local currency–denominated debt, and other plans. The common denominator of all these alternatives is the inability of the foreign country to make payments on the original debt.

American banks have a serious problem and there is not much that they can do about it. At first, the banks simply tried to ignore the problem in the hope that it might disappear. But it is impossible to ignore nonpayment of outstanding debt for very long. Banks have also attempted to get the governments of the industrialized countries to help solve the problem. In effect, they hoped for a bailout similar to that provided New York City. In 1987, banks began facing reality and started to recognize publicly that some loans to less developed countries may never be repaid. Citicorp of New York announced a $3 billion allocation to bad debt loss reserves. Bank of America, Manufacturers Hanover, and other large American banks quickly followed suit.[17]

The Decline in the Relative Size of American Banks

The recognition of bad debt losses has important implications for American banking. First, it reduces the profitability and capitalization of banks. Both of these factors will eventually be reflected in a reduction in the level of services provided to both American and foreign customers. This is already being demonstrated by the fact that American banks are losing ground to foreign banks. Clearly, the foreign debt problem of American banks is one of the reasons that the Japanese banks have replaced them as the largest in the world.[18] Table 12-5 shows the largest 10 banks in the world in 1975 and 1985. Note that in 1975 three American banks made the top 10, while no Japanese bank was included. The situation in 1985 was entirely different. Only one American bank made it in the top 10, compared to 7 Japanese banks. The potential difficulties for American banking, however, are even greater than the obvious problems. Conceivably, there could be a massive loss of confidence in certain American banks, which could result in a run on deposits and bank panic. While the Federal Reserve and the U.S. government are not likely to let the problem get out of hand, there could still be substantial damage to the banking system.

---

[17]There is a secondary market for the debt of less developed countries. Prices paid in this market reflect the risk perceived on this debt. At the present time, the debt sells at prices below par value. See "For Investors Who Are Strong of Heart, Third-World Debt Holds Some Allure," *The Wall Street Journal*, May 17, 1988, p. 33.

[18]The decline in the relative size of American banks has also been affected by other factors. For example, the decline in the value of the dollar versus the yen caused an increase in the dollar value of the yen deposits held by Japanese banks. American banks may have also decided to reduce their loan portfolio in order to meet stricter capital requirements. The loan crisis of the less developed countries, however, has played a role in the relative decline of American banks.

TABLE 12-5   Change in Bank Rankings from 1975 to 1985*

	Ten Largest Banks in 1975			
Rank	Bank	Country	Deposits (Billions)	Rank in 1985
1	Bank of America	United States	$57	12
2	Citibank	United States	$45	8
3	Credit Agricole	France	$38	14
4	Banque Nationale	France	$38	5
5	Chase Manhatten	United States	$34	28
6	Societe Generale	France	$32	15
7	Deutsche Bank	West Germany	$32	13
8	Credit Lyonnais	France	$32	7
9	Barclays Bank	Britain	$29	16
10	National Westminster	Britain	$27	11

	Ten Largest Banks in 1985			
Rank	Bank	Country	Deposits (Billions)	Rank in 1975
1	Dai-Ichi Kangyo	Japan	$125	13
2	Fuji	Japan	$110	17
3	Sumitomo	Japan	$109	16
4	Mitsubishi	Japan	$103	22
5	Banque Nationale	France	$103	4
6	Sanwa	Japan	$ 99	25
7	Credit Lyonnais	France	$ 96	8
8	Citibank	United States	$ 94	2
9	Norinchukin	Japan	$ 93	n.a.
10	Industrial Bank	Japan	$ 90	26

*The end of 1985 was chosen because it was the last year that an American bank was one of the largest 10 banks in the world. As of the end of 1986, Citibank was 17th in the world.

Source: *Moody's Bank and Finance Manual*, Vol. 1, Moody's Investor Services, 1977 and 1987, p. 2a.

Government actions make the risks associated with foreign lending very high. As the governments of the less developed countries move to renegotiate their debt with American banks and limit the ability of private borrowers to repay foreign debt, banks are being forced to reevaluate all foreign loans. In this environment, lending of any type to less developed countries or to firms operating in these countries has already been and will continue to be cut back. This has implications for American businesses operating in those countries. It also has important worldwide economic and political implications.

Summary and Conclusions

American banks provide important international services to American business firms. It is hard to imagine how international business could continue without the assistance of banks in transferring funds from one country to another, converting currencies, and issuing letters of credit. In addition, the eurobank posture of the larger American banks gives American firms easy access to euroloans, with resulting favorable interest rates. Thus, American banks constitute an essential service link in the international business operations of American firms.

But some American banks are important multinational firms in their own right. Facilities located throughout the world make it possible for large banks to accept deposits and make loans in many currencies to customers throughout the world. The international lending operations of banks, however, have fallen on bad times as less developed countries have been unable to repay their large outstanding loans. This threatens the viability of several American banks and may cause a serious disruption in the international activities of these banks. It is safe to say that the future international role of American banks is uncertain. The resolution of the loan crisis of the less developed countries will be worked out over the next few years, and after the dust has settled, the role of American banks in international lending may look quite different than it has in the past.

Review Questions

1. "It is possible for a large American firm with substantial international involvement to receive all necessary services from even the smallest commercial bank in the United States." True or false? Explain your answer.
2. Evaluate the use of foreign correspondents by American banks as a method for providing international services.
3. How do foreign representative offices of American banks help banks provide international services? What are the advantages and disadvantages (from the American bank's point of view) of providing services in this fashion?
4. Explain how a foreign branch of an American bank differs from a representative office and a correspondent bank. How do American banks organize and operate foreign branches? What are the advantages and disadvantages (from the American bank's point of view) of providing services through the branch system?
5. What is an international banking facility? How is it organized? What are its allowed and disallowed activities? How can American firms use it?
6. Describe the alternative methods of transferring funds from one country to another. What factors must be considered by the firm when choosing a transfer method?
7. How does a bank make a profit on its foreign exchange operations? What are the risks to banks in dealing in foreign exchange?
8. What are the risks to a bank when it issues a letter of credit? How does a bank make a profit on a letter of credit?
9. What are the risks associated with international lending by banks? How do these risks compare to the risks associated with lending dollars to domestic borrowers?
10. How can American banks reduce the interest rate risk and foreign exchange rate risk associated with international lending?
11. How can an American bank reduce the default risk associated with international loans?

12. What are the origins of the debt crisis of less developed countries? How great a crisis is this? What is the outlook for the future?

Questions for Discussion

1. Assume that you are employed by a moderate-sized ($3 billion in assets) regional bank in the United States. Traditionally, most of the bank's business has been with customers who are involved solely in the U.S. economy. In recent years, however, an ever-increasing percentage of the bank's customers are asking for international services as they begin to buy more from and sell more to foreigners. The firms in your area seem to be developing particularly close relationships with firms in Mexico, Taiwan, Korea, and Japan. At the present time, your bank is servicing its customers by maintaining a correspondent relationship with a large New York City bank. Top management asks you to prepare a report on alternative strategies for meeting the international needs of its customers. You are directed to study both the profit and risk implications of the alternatives you may recommend.

2. Assume that you are employed by a large American bank with no loans to less developed countries. Recently, however, your bank has been pressured by the American government and other large banks to participate in loans made to these countries. While the board of directors of your bank knows that many existing loans are in virtual default, they believe (and have been so advised) that it may be possible to design new loans so that they will be paid before other loans. You have been assigned the task of evaluating the situation. You must evaluate both the risks and the profit potential of such loans.

3. Assume that you are employed by an American firm with a large volume of exports and imports. At the present time, your firm is conducting business with firms located in 14 countries, but it expects this number to increase. You are asked to evaluate the different services provided by banks with respect to the transfer of funds and to recommend the services that your firm should request from your bank.

4. Assume that you are employed by a large American bank that has been doing business in the southeastern United States. The bank has been conducting its foreign exchange business through a large New York City bank. Presently, a customer's request for foreign currency service is simply passed along to the correspondent in New York, and the customer rarely knows this. The New York bank has been able to provide any amount of currency requested by the southeastern bank's customers (both spot and forward), and there have been no complaints about the service. The board of directors of the southeastern bank is considering direct entry into the foreign exchange market. This means that the bank would actively buy and sell foreign currencies for itself and its customers. You have been asked to evaluate this strategy and make a recommendation. You have been directed to pay close attention to both the risks and the profits associated with this proposal.

Research Activities

1. Look at recent data on the size of U.S. banks relative to the banks of other countries. Try to explain why these relative sizes have changed. Pay particular attention to exchange rate fluctuations and the way they affect the international ranking (as to size) of banks.

2. Update the situation regarding loans to less developed countries. Has a solution been found in the last few years? Have any new solutions emerged? What is the outlook for the future? How is the loan situation likely to affect the U.S. banking system in the future?

3. Study one of the very large (over $25 billion in assets) U.S. banks. Has this bank been expanding or contracting its international network? What are the implications for the bank's strategy to meet the service needs of its American customers?

Bibliography

Abrams, Richard K. "The Role of Regional Banks in International Banking." *Columbia Journal of World Business*, Summer 1981, pp. 62–71.

Aliber, Robert Z. "International Banking: Growth and Regulation." *Columbia Journal of World Business*, Winter 1975, pp. 9–15.

_____ "The Integration of Offshore and Domestic Banking Systems." *Journal of Monetary Economies*, October 1980, pp. 509–526.

Ball, Clifford A., and Tschoegl, Adrian E. "The Decision to Establish a Foreign Bank Branch or Subsidiary: An Application of Binary Classification Procedures." *Journal of Financial and Quantitative Analysis*, September 1982, pp. 411–424.

Blasi, Andrew B. "International Banking Facilities." *North Carolina Journal of International Law and Commercial Regulation*, Summer 1983, pp. 61–76.

Boatler, Robert W. "Bank Evaluation of LDC Country Risk." *Inter-American Economic Affairs*, Autumn 1984, pp. 71–76.

Cholst, Anthony W. "Building Flexibility and Performance Into Developing Country Loans." *Columbia Journal of World Business*, Spring 1985, pp. 23–28.

Crane, Dwight B., and Hayes, Samuel L. III. "The New Competition in World Banking." *Harvard Business Review*, July–August 1982, pp. 88–94.

Dale, Richard S., and Mattione, Richard P. *Managing Global Debt*. Washington, DC: The Brookings Institution, 1983.

Damanpour, Faramarz. "A Survey of Market Structure and Activities of Foreign Banking in the U.S." *Columbia Journal of World Business*, Winter 1986, pp. 35–46.

Decoodt, Patrick. "The Debt Crisis of the Third World: Some Aspects of Causes and Solutions." *Columbia Journal of World Business*, Fall 1986, pp. 11–18.

Edwards, Franklin R. "The New 'International Banking Facility': A Study in Regulatory Frustration." *Columbia Journal of World Business*, Winter 1981, pp. 6–18.

Fieleke, Norman S. "International Lending in Historical Perspective." *New England Economic Review*, November–December 1982, pp. 5–12.

_____ "International Lending on Trial." *New England Economic Review*, May–June 1983, pp. 5–13.

"For Investors Who Are Strong of Heart, Third-World Debt Holds Some Allure." *The Wall Street Journal*, May 17, 1988, p. 33.

Garg, Ramesh C. "Loans to LDCs and Massive Defaults." *Intereconomics*, January–February 1981, pp. 19–25.

_____ "Will Argentina Default?" *The Bankers Magazine*, January–February 1983, pp. 13–17.

Jain, Arvind K. "International Lending Patterns of U.S. Commercial Banks." *Journal of International Business Studies*, Fall 1986, pp. 89–100.

Key, Sidney J. "International Banking Facilities." *Federal Reserve Bulletin*, October 1982, pp. 565–577.

Koch, Timothy W. *Bank Management*. Chicago: Dryden Press, 1988.

Korth, Christopher M. "The Evolving Role of U.S. Banks in International Finance." *Bankers Magazine*, July–August 1980, pp. 68–73.

Leatherberry, James D. "Foreign Lending: Regulation Risk." *Bankers' Monthly Magazine*, February 15, 1983, pp. 12–18.

"Loan Plan May Help Mexico, Some Banks; But It's No Panacea." *The Wall Street Journal*, December 30, 1987, pp. 1, 9.

Mascarenhas, Briance, and Sand, Ole C. "Country-Risk Assessment Systems in Banks: Patterns and Performance." *Journal of International Business Studies*, Spring 1985, pp. 19–36.

Naidu, G. N. "How to Reduce Transaction Exposure in International Lending." *Journal of Commercial Bank Lending*, June 1981, pp. 39–45.

Park, Yoon S., and Zwick, Jack. *International Banking in Theory and Practice*. Reading, MA: Addison-Wesley Publishing Company, 1985.

Pringle, Andreas R. *Japanese Finance: A Guide to Banking in Japan*. New York: John Wiley & Sons, Inc., 1981.

Puz, Richard. "Lending to Multinational Corporations." *Journal of Commercial Bank Lending*, October 1977, pp. 18–24.

Rhoades, Stephen A. "Concentration of World Banking and the Role of U.S. Banks Among the 100 Largest, 1956–1980." *Journal of Banking and Finance*, September 1983, pp. 427–437.

Sachs, Jeffrey D. "A New Approach for Managing the Debt Crisis." *Columbia Journal of World Business*, Fall 1986, pp. 41–50.

Shapiro, Alan C. "Currency Risk and Country Risk in International Banking." *Journal of Finance*, July 1985, pp. 881–891.

Tygier, Claude. *Basic Handbook of Foreign Exchange*. London: Euromoney Publications, 1983.

Walter, Ingo. "Country Risk, Portfolio Decisions and Regulation in International Bank Lending." *Journal of Banking and Finance*, May 1981, pp. 77–92.

Young, John. "Supervision of Bank Foreign Lending." *Economic Review*, May 1985, pp. 31–39.

Zwick, Charles J. "Miami—The New International Banking Center." *Bankers Magazine*, January–February 1982, pp. 19–22.

13

Managing the Multinational's Internal Funds Flow

The movement of funds within a corporation presents special problems to the multinational firm, since the firm often operates under several different tax laws and various government restrictions. The inconsistency of government policies throughout the world has encouraged managers to adopt complicated procedures for transferring funds from one part of the corporation to another. Of particular interest to us in this chapter will be the ways in which the parent corporation makes loans to subsidiaries and the way in which payment is made for intracorporate purchases of goods and services. The discussion that follows has the following five major sections:

1. "Intracorporate Cash Flows in the Absence of Taxes And Currency Blockages" shows how the multinational firm would move funds from one subsidiary to another if there were no taxes and no government blockages on the movement of funds.
2. "The Impact of Income Taxes" examines the alternatives open to multinational firms to reduce corporate income taxes in various countries.

3. "The Impact of Currency Blockages" examines what the multinational firms try to do in order to circumvent government restrictions on the movement of currencies from one country to another.
4. "Government Reactions to the Evasive Actions of Multinational Corporations" discusses how governments have responded to attempts by multinational firms to circumvent taxes and currency blockages.
5. "Special Issues Relating to Funds Transfers within the Multinational Firms" examines several other arrangements for funds transfers that are not necessarily related to tax and currency blockage problems.

Intracorporate Cash Flows in the Absence of Taxes and Currency Blockages

Large corporations, both domestic and multinational, tend to be organized as a parent corporation with one or more subsidiaries. A large American automobile manufacturer, for example, may be composed of a parent corporation and a number of domestic and foreign subsidiaries. Since the parent corporation owns each subsidiary, it has the power to determine the nature and amount of cash that flows from one part of the

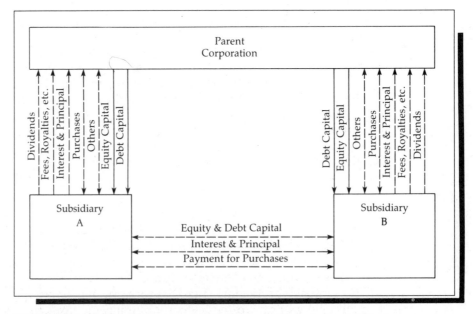

FIGURE 13-1   Selected Patterns of Cash Flows (Parents & Subsidiaries)

company to the other. A simplified picture of the cash flow possibilities is presented in Figure 13-1. The first thing that should strike you about this figure is that there are many more types of intracompany cash flows than one realizes.

While it may be possible for the purely domestic corporation to reduce taxes by managing subsidiary income, most domestic corporations have chosen not to do so. This decision reflects the predominant American management philosophy, which prescribes that each subsidiary or division should be evaluated as if it were a separate firm. Subsidiaries are expected to be profitable; if a subsidiary's management fails to achieve profit goals, it is held responsible. Stated another way, subsidiary profitability is a vital component of the evaluation and management control procedure. If the parent interferes with the subsidiary's profit, how will the management of the subsidiary be evaluated? How will dangerous situations be identified? In order to encourage efficiency, purely domestic American corporations tend to decentralize decision making and avoid overmanaging domestic subsidiaries.

A Fee-for-Service Approach

A *fee-for-service approach* provides a framework for evaluating the true effectiveness of corporate subsidiaries. In order to understand the rationale for the use of various fees imposed by the multinational firm, it is best to view the parent corporation as providing a bundle of services to its foreign subsidiaries. Associated with each service is a charge, which should reflect the value of the service provided. Table 13-1 provides a partial list of possible services and charges.

Note that in Table 13-1, the provision of capital, both equity and debt, is considered a service provided by the multinational to the sub-

TABLE 13-1   Selected Services Provided by a Multinational Parent

Service	Charge
Provision of equity capital	Dividends
Provision of debt capital	Interest
Provision of technology	Royalty
Use of patents	Royalty
Use of copyrights	Royalty
Use of trade names	Royalty
Direct provision of management services	Fee
Direct provision of technical services	Fee
Access to corporatewide activities*	Overhead charge
Intracorporate purchases	Transfer price

*Includes such centralized services as research and development, advertising, cash management, accounting, and legal services.

sidiary, and the parent expects to receive compensation for this service.[1] Corporate parents also provide a service to foreign subsidiaries by allowing them to use technology, patents, copyrights, and trade names. In many cases, the parent corporation has expended large sums in developing these items, which may have a well-defined fair market value. For example, IBM would have little difficulty in finding foreign buyers for the rights to its technology, patents, copyrights, and trade names, and could receive royalties from foreign producers without directly investing a single penny in a foreign country. The point is that any flows from a foreign subsidiary to a parent corporation should be viewed partly as a royalty for the use of valuable intangible assets owned and controlled by the parent corporation.

A parent corporation may also receive specific fees from its foreign subsidiaries. These direct fees reflect the fact that the parent corporation frequently provides direct services to a foreign subsidiary. For example, an executive from the parent corporation may be assigned to help the subsidiary arrange a bond issue. In another case, the subsidiary may encounter a technical problem that is addressed by parent corporation engineers. Note that the parent corporation incurs costs in providing these services. It is reasonable to expect that such costs will be allocated to the subsidiary and that part of the cash flow from the subsidiary to the parent will be viewed as a fee that compensates for these services.

In addition to the direct, clearly identifiable services provided by the multinational parent to its subsidiaries, there is also the provision of many general services, and an overhead charge can be made for these services. For example, the parent corporation may be spending a considerable amount of money on research and development (R & D), the benefits of which will also accrue to the subsidiary. In principle, each unit of the multinational that will benefit from the R & D effort should be charged for part of the cost. Parallel logic suggests that the foreign subsidiary should bear part of the cost of worldwide public relations or advertising efforts. Foreign subsidiaries may also be expected to shoulder part of the expense associated with such centralized corporate activities as cash management. Once again, it is clear that part of the cash flow from the subsidiary to the parent represents a payment for services received.[2] For convenience, and to facilitate analysis, we also view pay-

---

[1] In the absence of taxation and/or restrictions on the movement of currency, there is no major incentive for the multinational to provide investment funds in the form of debt instead of equity. On the one hand, it may be attractive for the parent to provide capital to the subsidiary in the form of debt (rather than equity), since the parent would be viewed as a creditor should the subsidiary go bankrupt. This advantage is balanced by the fact that parent lending to a subsidiary increases the subsidiary debt ratio and may inhibit the subsidiary's ability to borrow independently.

[2] While this discussion has focused on payments between a parent corporation and a subsidiary, the analysis can be extended to include cash flows between two or more subsidiaries of the same corporation.

ments for intracorporate purchases as if they were fees. Thus, if a parent sells materials to a subsidiary, the sale is viewed as a service and the payment received is a fee, which is called a *transfer price*. Corporate parents also buy from foreign subsidiaries and pay a fee for these goods. This fee is also called a *transfer price*.

While the logic involved in the fee-for-service approach is quite clear, implementation of such a policy in the multinational environment is fraught with difficulties.[3] In a perfect world, each fee would reflect the true economic value of the good or service involved in the exchange. For example, transfer prices would truly reflect the value of goods bought and sold, and a charge for overhead would truly reflect the amount of services provided to the foreign subsidiary. When the fees charged the subsidiary represent true economic values, the profits of the subsidiary are a meaningful indicator of how well it is performing. Of course, if the fees do not reflect economic values, the profit of the subsidiary is difficult to interpret. While it is clear that the parent corporation has the ability to alter the appearance of profitability of any corporate subsidiary, there is little incentive to do so unless there are currency blockages and/or differences in national taxes.

The Impact of Income Taxes

The fact that different nations tax business income in different ways and at different rates has a major impact on the methods used by multinational corporations to shift income from one location to another. Differences in national income tax rates create interesting tax planning possibilities. Generally, the overall tax payment of the multinational will be minimized by shifting reported income to low-income tax locations. In the example that follows, it is assumed that the United States is the low-tax location (34 percent) and that the foreign tax rate is 50 percent.[4]

An American multinational parent firm can receive revenues from the subsidiary in two general forms: (1) dividends and (2) other payments. Under the conditions of this example, corporatewide income taxes will be minimized by adjusting intracorporate cash flows in such a way that subsidiary income is very low (because tax rates are high) and parent income is very high (because tax rates are low). In this tax minimization context, the parent attempts to substitute other payments for dividends. This reflects the fact that dividend payments by a foreign subsidiary to a parent do not usually reduce the tax liability of the subsidiary. Other

---

[3]Hereafter, we will refer to all such payments, with the exception of dividends and interest, as *fees*.

[4]In situations in which the U.S. tax rate is higher than the foreign tax rate, policies would be more or less opposite those discussed in this illustration.

payments by the subsidiary to the parent are usually tax deductible, thus reducing taxes to the foreign government. The multinational firm could pursue one or a combination of the following policies for tax reduction:

1. The parent could make the original investment in the foreign subsidiary in the form of debt rather than equity. The parent will then receive interest rather than dividend payments. Interest payments made by the subsidiary are tax deductible and reduce foreign income taxes. Since the parent pays the same tax on either dividend or interest income, total taxes (subsidiary plus parent) are reduced.[5]
2. The royalty charge made by the parent to the subsidiary for the use of technology, patents, copyrights, and trade names can be higher than it would be if true market prices were used. This results in a higher income for the parent corporation and a lower income for the subsidiary. Since the parent is taxed at a lower rate than the subsidiary, overall taxes will be reduced.
3. The fees levied by the parent on the subsidiary for managerial and technical services rendered can be set at levels higher than justified by market considerations. Once again, the expenses of the subsidiary are increased and corporatewide tax burdens are reduced.
4. The parent corporation can allocate a disproportionate share of corporatewide overhead to the foreign subsidiary, thus shifting income away from the subsidiary to the parent.
5. The parent can set transfer prices at levels that are disadvantageous to the subsidiary. The price of products sold by the parent to the subsidiary can be set artificially high. Artificially low prices can be attached to products sold by the subsidiary to the parent. In both cases, subsidiary income taxes are reduced by more than parent income taxes are increased.

Shifting Income from High-Tax Countries

The technique for shifting income from a foreign subsidiary located in a high tax country to the parent is illustrated in Tables 13-2 and 13-3. Table 13-2 shows the income statements for the parent and the subsidiary under the assumptions that a fee-for-service approach is being utilized. In other words, the intracorporate payments represent true economic values. Under these conditions, the parent has a tax bill of $34 million and the subsidiary pays $57 million in taxes. This means that the total corporatewide tax bill is $91 million.

---

[5] Dividends received from a foreign subsidiary are not eligible for the dividend exclusion rules that may apply to domestic dividends.

TABLE 13-2   Income Statements When a Fee-for-Service Approach Is Used (in Millions)

Parent (Unconsolidated)		Subsidiary	
Revenues		Revenues	
From other parties	$300	From other parties	$180
Sales to sub.	$ 30	Sales to parent	$ 40
Interest from sub.	$ 0	Total revenues	$220
Royalties from sub.	$ 20		
Fees from sub.	$ 8		
Overhead from sub.	$ 2	Expenses	
Total revenues	$360	Purchases from others	$ 40
		Purchases from parent	$ 30
		Interest to parent	$ 0
Expenses		Royalties to parent	$ 20
Purchases from others	$200	Fees to parent	$ 8
Purchases from sub.	$ 40	Overhead to parent	$ 2
Other expenses	$ 20	Other expenses	$ 6
Total expenses	$260	Total expenses	$106
Taxable income	$100	Taxable income	$114
Taxes (34%)	$ 34	Taxes (50%)	$ 57
Income after taxes	$ 66	Income after taxes	$ 57

TABLE 13-3   Income Statements After Tax Minimization Strategies (in Millions)

Parent (Unconsolidated)		Subsidiary	
Revenues		Revenues	
From other parties	$300	From other parties	$180
Sales to sub.	$ 60	Sales to parent	$ 20
Interest from sub.	$ 26	Total revenues	$200
Royalties from sub.	$ 30		
Fees from sub.	$ 18		
Overhead from sub.	$ 6	Expenses	
Total revenues	$440	Purchases from others	$ 40
		Purchases from parent	$ 60
		Interest to parent	$ 26
Expenses		Royalties to parent	$ 30
Purchases from others	$200	Fees to parent	$ 18
Purchases from sub.	$ 20	Overhead to parent	$ 6
Other expenses	$ 20	Other expenses	$ 6
Total expenses	$240	Total expenses	$186
Taxable income	$200	Taxable income	$ 14
Taxes (34%)	$ 68	Taxes (50%)	$ 7
Income after taxes	$132	Income after taxes	$ 7

Of course, the parent corporation could abandon the fee-for-service approach and attempt to minimize corporatewide taxes. The consequences of a possible tax minimization policy are reflected in Table 13-3. The illustration assumes that the parent corporation has instituted a number of departures from the fee-for-service approach.

1. The parent lends money to the subsidiary, and the subsidiary uses this money to redeem stock from the parent corporation. This reduces the parent's equity in the subsidiary and increases its loans to the subsidiary. This action increases the interest payments of the subsidiary to the parent from $0 to $26 million.
2. While the physical volume of sales by the parent to the subsidiary remains unchanged, the charge made by the parent to the subsidiary is increased from $30 to $60 million. In other words, the subsidiary pays more for the same amount of products.
3. While the physical volume of sales by the subsidiary to the parent remains constant, the parent reduces the charge made by the subsidiary from $40 to $20 million. In other words, the subsidiary sells the same amount to the parent but receives less.
4. The parent increases its royalties charge to the subsidiary from $20 to $30 million.
5. The parent increases managerial service fees paid by the subsidiary from $8 to $18 million.
6. The parent increases the overhead charge to the subsidiary from $2 to $6 million.

Comparing Tables 13-2 with 13-3 we find that the taxable income of the parent has increased by $100 million, with a corresponding decline in the subsidiary's taxable income. Note, however, that the corporatewide taxable income of the organization ($214) has not changed. All that has happened is that taxable income has been shifted from the high-tax subsidiary to the low-tax parent, and this has a major impact on the total taxes paid. Before the tax reduction policies were implemented (Table 13-2), the multinational paid $34 million to the United States and $57 million to the foreign government, and corporatewide taxes were $91 million. Under tax minimization (Table 13-3), taxes paid in the United States are $68 million and foreign taxes are $7 million. The corporatewide tax bill is $75 million, which is $16 million less than would have been paid under the fee-for-service approach. Corporatewide income after taxes is increased from $123 million to $139 million. These figures suggest that there are important incentives that encourage the multinational firm to abandon the fee-for-services approach for transferring funds.

Strategies that distort transfer prices in order to reduce income taxes are complicated by the existence of tariffs. Most countries, including the

United States, levy tariffs on some imports.[6] Most of these tariffs are *ad valorem* tariffs, which means that the amount of the tariff is based on the value of the imported goods. In order to minimize income taxes in our illustration, the price paid by the subsidiary on imports from the parent increased from $30 to $60 million. If the foreign government imposes a 10 percent tariff, taxes payable by the subsidiary would have increased. The optimal strategy for the multinational will depend on (1) the differences in tax rates between the two countries, (2) the size of the import tariff, and (3) the ability of the importer to use tariffs as a tax deduction. While a full discussion of this topic is beyond the scope of this book, it is possible for the multinational to work through this problem and arrive at an optimal tax/tariff policy.

The Impact of Currency Blockages

Governments, especially those of less developed countries, commonly impose restrictions on the movement of currencies across national boundaries. Dividend payments by a subsidiary to its foreign parent are particularly vulnerable to government restriction and blockage. On the other hand, interest payments, even if they are made to the corporate parent, tend to be viewed as having greater urgency and are less likely to be subject to government restrictions. Interest payments are also less likely to be subject to withholding taxes than are dividend payments to a corporate parent. The situation is complicated by the fact that a withholding tax is sometimes applied to the interest payments associated with a direct intracompany loan but not to interest payments to independent third parties. For example, an interest payment made by a subsidiary to its parent may be subject to withholding taxes, but interest payments to banks may not. These actions by host country governments have stimulated the development of specialized loan arrangements designed to circumvent the intentions of the host government. In addition, the use of artificially high fees, discussed in the previous section, would result in the repatriation of blocked currencies. In the sections that follow, we will review three types of specialized intracompany loan arrangements: back-to-back loans, parallel loans, and currency swaps. In addition, we will show how, under certain conditions, compensating balances can be manipulated, with results that are similar to those of the back-to-back loan arrangement.

---

[6]Tariffs on exports are relatively uncommon, since most governments are anxious to stimulate exports. The United States, for example, does not levy export tariffs.

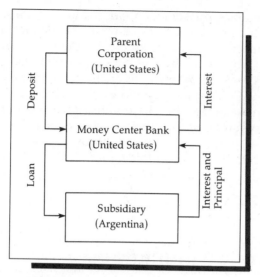

FIGURE 13-2   Back-to-Back Loans

Back-to-Back Loans

Back-to-back loans involve the use of a large, well-established commercial bank as a middleperson or front.[7] The simplest form of back-to-back loan has the multinational parent firm depositing money in a home country bank. The bank then makes a loan to a foreign subsidiary of the multinational, using the home country deposit as collateral. The essence of the transaction is that the parent company is lending money to its foreign subsidiary. In appearance, however, a bank is making an independent loan to a foreign company. Interest payments are made by the foreign subsidiary to the bank. The bank, in turn, makes interest payments on the deposits to the parent. Figure 13-2 illustrates a hypothetical back-to-back loan. An American multinational parent deposits funds in one of the large New York banks. The bank then makes a loan to the Argentine subsidiary of the multinational. The Argentine subsidiary makes interest and principal payments to the New York bank. The bank, in turn, pays interest to the multinational parent. Upon repayment of the loan by the Argentine subsidiary, the parent is permitted to withdraw its deposit in the bank.

The reason that firms use such convoluted arrangements can be found in the vagaries of politics. Specifically, host country governments

---

[7]Back-to-back loans are sometimes referred to as *fronting loans*.

tend to treat interest payments to banks differently than interest payments to the multinational parent. Governments fear that failure to pay interest on a bank loan will discourage all banks from making loans to businesses in the host country. Eventually, governments recognize that back-to-back loans circumvent their currency restrictions. This results in changes to applicable regulations. In addition, some host countries may levy a withholding tax on interest payments to the multinational parent, while no such tax is levied on interest payments to a bank. Thus, interest payments to banks are less vulnerable to restrictions and less likely to be subject to withholding taxes. In effect, back-to-back loans may enable a multinational corporation to reduce its risk while simultaneously increasing its return.

Back-to-back loans can also be used to transfer accumulated blocked funds. For example, assume that Subsidiary A (located in Brazil) has funds that cannot be remitted to the multinational parent (located in the United States). At the same time, Subsidiary B (located in Venezuela) needs funds. The multinational parent may be able to find a bank with branches in both Brazil and Venezuela. If the needs of the multinational bank coincide with the needs of the other parties involved, the bank may agree to accept deposits in Brazil and make the loan in Venezuela. In effect, the multinational has been able to execute a back-to-back loan without depositing hard currency.

Just as with any loan agreement, the terms of back-to-back loans can be tailored to meet the needs of the parties involved. The currency in which the deposit and loan are denominated is open to negotiation. For example, a multinational may be able to deposit dollars in the bank, with the loan being repaid in soft currency by the subsidiary. Maturities and other features are also open to negotiation.

Of course, the more services the bank is asked to provide and the more risk the bank is asked to assume, the higher the cost of the back-to-back loan. The major portion of the bank's compensation comes from the spread between the rate paid on the deposit made by the multinational parent and the rate charged on the loan made to the subsidiary. For example, a parent may deposit funds in an account yielding 7 percent, while the bank lends funds to the subsidiary at a rate of 9 percent. Note that if both the deposit and the loan are denominated in the same currency, the risk to the bank is minimal. If the subsidiary is unable to pay, the bank will be compensated by the parent's deposit.

When the bank lends in a currency other than the currency of deposit, it is exposing itself to greater risk, since a shift in exchange rates may result in a loss. If the agreement calls for repayment in a foreign currency, either the bank will have to be compensated for taking exchange rate risk or the parent must agree to provide contingency payments should exchange rates fluctuate. One way or another, the bank will expect to be compensated for assuming risk and providing service.

Parallel Loans

Parallel loans involves lending by one corporation directly to another. These loans do not utilize the lending facilities of commercial banks. For example, assume that the Ford Motor Company has wholly owned subsidiaries in Egypt (Ford Egypt) and Brazil (Ford Brazil). Also assume that Ford Egypt has $20 million in blocked Egyptian pounds that cannot be employed effectively in Egypt and that Ford Brazil needs $20 million in Brazilian cruzados to finance a planned expansion. Under ordinary conditions, Ford Brazil would have to convert dollars to cruzados in order to finance its expanded operations. However, the parent corporation may be reluctant to convert dollars to cruzados, since there is a significant probability that Brazil will block future dividend payments to the parent.

A parallel loan arrangement may offer a solution to this problem. In some cases, there may be other multinationals whose position is the exact opposite of Ford's. Imagine, for example, that the Xerox Corporation has two subsidiaries, Xerox Egypt and Xerox Brazil. Xerox Egypt needs $20 million in Egyptian pounds but is unwilling to convert dollars to pounds because Egypt has a record of blocking repatriation of hard currency. Xerox Brazil has $20 million in excess cruzados that cannot be repatriated. In this situation (shown in Figure 13-3), Ford Egypt lends $20 million in Egyptian pounds to Xerox Egypt and Xerox Brazil lends $20 million in Brazilian cruzados to Ford Brazil. Note that the entire deal is engineered by the parent corporations. In effect, each parent corporation has found a method to utilize previously unusable funds. In practice, a parallel loan transaction could be more complex. It is possible that more than two multinational firms and their subsidiaries could be involved. In addition, loans between the two subsidiaries are sometimes offset by a loan between operating units in the United States.

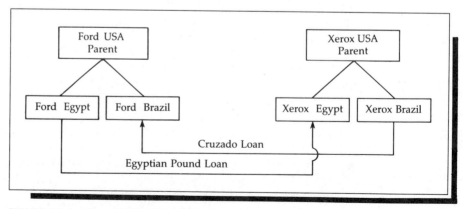

FIGURE 13-3 Hypothetical Parallel Loan

The terms of a parallel loan contract are negotiable. The parties involved must agree on the relative interest rates on the loans. The differential in rates will depend on the extent to which one currency is expected to depreciate against the other. In some cases, potential losses due to unexpected devaluation can be shared by the two firms. The details associated with parallel loans are usually worked out by money center banks. Bankers in London and New York search out opportunities for parallel loans and assist in the negotiating process. In return, the bankers receive a fee of up to 0.5 percent of the transaction. Note that banks serve as middlepersons but are not directly involved in the lending.

Currency Swaps

Currency swaps are similar to parallel loans, except that under a currency swap arrangement, corporations simultaneously sell currencies to each other and enter into a contract to reverse the transaction at a specified future date. For example, assume that the Ford Motor Company sells 1 million Egyptian pounds to the Xerox Corporation for 100 million Brazilian cruzados. At the same time, the parties agree that at a specified future date, the transaction will be reversed (Xerox will sell Egyptian pounds to Ford in return for Brazilian cruzados). As you can see, the net effect is almost identical to that achieved by the use of parallel loans. Ford now has cruzados and Xerox has Egyptian pounds.

The terms of a currency swap are negotiable, and the actual contracts vary. In general, however, protection against changing currency values is built into the agreement. This ensures that a multinational firm lending 1 million Egyptian pounds will receive 1 million pounds in purchasing power when the transactions are reversed. Currency swaps of up to $50 million have been arranged. Some of these transactions are arranged directly by corporate treasurers. In other cases, money center banks arrange the transaction, charging a fee of approximately 0.5 percent.

Currency swaps can have advantages over parallel loans. Depending on the tax situation of the parties involved, there may be tax savings, since there is no interest income or expense. In addition, since no loans are involved, currency swaps are not directly shown in the respective balance sheets. This is more realistic than the accounting treatment of parallel loans, since parallel loans increase the debt ratios of both of the multinationals involved in the transaction. Under a currency swap arrangement, one asset, for example Egyptian pound balances, is replaced by another asset, Brazilian cruzado balances. All that happens in either case (swaps or parallel loans) is that currencies are temporarily exchanged. There is no intention to borrow in the sense that the word *borrow* is commonly used, and there is no real increase in the indebtedness of either firm. The intent of a currency swap is to find a legal method of gaining access to funds already owned.

Shifting Compensating Balances

In some cases, it may be possible to gain access to blocked funds by shifting compensating balances. For example, assume that an American multinational corporation borrows $50 million from an American bank, and the proceeds from the loan are used to finance operations in the United States. The loan agreement with the bank may require that 10 percent of the outstanding balance ($5 million) be maintained on deposit in the bank. This is the *compensating balance* frequently required by American banks (but not usually by European banks). Ordinarily, it would be expected that the compensating balance would be maintained in dollars and that the deposit would be physically located in the United States. However, if the borrowing firm has blocked currency abroad and the bank has a branch in the country blocking the currency, it may be possible to negotiate an agreement that allows the blocked currency to serve as all or part of the compensating balance. For example, if the borrowing firm has $5 million in blocked Brazilian cruzados and the bank has a branch in Brazil, the bank may agree to accept the cruzado deposit in lieu of a dollar deposit in the United States. In effect, the firm has been able to "exchange" cruzados for dollars. The American firm has found a way to utilize the blocked currency temporarily, since its dollar borrowing requirements have declined by $5 million.

The use of compensating balances as a means of repatriating blocked currencies has limited applicability. The amount involved depends on the size of bank loans requiring compensating balances. If the compensating balance requirement or the size of the bank loan is reduced, the blocked currency deposits are no longer required and the firm must find some other way of dealing with the blocked currency problem.

Government Reactions to the Evasive Actions of Multinational Firms

In a perfect world, all countries would tax on the same basis, there would be no currency blockages, and multinational firms would use a fee-for-service approach for transferring funds. But, in fact, these perfect conditions do not exist. As a result, governments and multinationals often clash over the funds transfer procedures employed by multinational firms.[8] There is, in effect, a battle between governments and multinational firms. Governments are neither passive nor powerless in this struggle. As a result, the multinational's ability to manipulate the funds-transfer process is severely circumscribed. For example, in the United States, Section 482 of the U.S. Internal Revenue code instructs the Secretary of the Treasury accordingly:

> In any case of two or more organizations, trades or businesses (whether or not incorporated, whether or not organized in the United States, and whether or not affiliated) owned or controlled directly or indirectly by the same interests, the Secretary may distribute, apportion, or allocate gross income, deductions, credits, or allowances between or among such organizations, trades or businesses, if he determines that such distribution, apportionment, or allocation is necessary in order to prevent evasion of taxes or clearly to reflect the income of any such organizations, trades or businesses.

In effect, the American government says that if it does not approve of the way a multinational firm allocates costs and/or income, the Internal Revenue Service can simply recompute the taxable income and levy taxes accordingly. In some cases, additional penalties could be assessed.

The intent of the U.S. government is to ensure that multinational firms do not transfer income outside the United States in order to avoid paying U.S. income taxes. Other countries have similar concerns, and in almost every country, one or more government agencies have the same powers as those granted to the Secretary of the Treasury by the U.S. Internal Revenue Code. It should be noted that this can cause a real problem for a multinational firm. Assume, for example, that an American multinational uses transfer prices to shift income away from a foreign subsidiary and that the shift results in a reduction in foreign taxable income of $1,000,000. Also assume that the income is shifted to the American parent and results in an additional American tax of $340,000. The tax enforcement authorities of the foreign government may review the situation, recompute the income of the multinational, and levy additional taxes on the $1,000,000 income of the subsidiary. The total tax paid to the foreign government is now exactly what it would have been before transfer prices were managed. The only problem is that the multinational has now paid an additional $340,000 tax to the U.S. government. The Internal Revenue Service is likely to maintain that the original transfer prices were realistic and will not be very receptive to a recomputation of American income taxes. In this simplified example, the multinational's attempt to manipulate transfer prices backfired because the taxing authorities in different nations disagreed over the appropriate transfer price. The point is that other nations will not necessarily agree with the

---

[8]This section emphasizes how governments limit the ability of multinationals to use transfer prices in order to evade taxes and/or currency restrictions.

rulings of the U.S. Internal Revenue Service. Nor is the Internal Revenue Service obligated to accept the rulings of foreign tax authorities.

Considerations such as those presented in the previous paragraph have discouraged firms from manipulating the funds transfer process too aggressively in order to minimize taxes. Today's multinational firms generally attempt to provide an economic or legal rationale for all funds transfers. The intention is to justify the transfer procedure employed and to minimize conflicts with the various governments affected by the transfers. As tax enforcement has become more sophisticated, large multinationals have tended to use objective, arm's-length pricing policies that can be defended if a controversy arises. If, for example, the goods being traded among the units of the multinational are also traded among independent parties at uncontrolled prices, these comparable prices could be used to support the transfer prices employed by the multinational. Most governments accept such an approach. In many cases, however, comparable uncontrolled prices are not available. For example, no real comparisons are available for semifinished products (a partially finished garment) or unique items (a particular brand of automobile). For these types of products, large corporations tend to use some form of cost-plus transfer pricing. This involves estimating the cost of production, adding a defensible profit margin, and using the resulting figure as a transfer price.

While the principles for setting transfer prices seem to be emerging with some clarity, the computations are more difficult than they appear at first glance. The use of comparable uncontrolled prices is complicated by differences in quality, quantity, the date at which goods are shipped, and many other factors.[9] Cost-plus techniques are complicated by differences in accounting policies and the related problems associated with allocating shared costs. In fact, multinationals interested in using reasonable transfer pricing policies may still become involved in disagreements with the affected governments. On the other hand, ambiguity even in the preferred methods for establishing transfer prices does allow the multinational some room to manipulate taxable income.

Multinational firms also attempt to provide an economic or legal rationale for dividends and interest payments, royalties, fees, and overhead allocations. Often the rate at which such payments are made is negotiated with a government before the multinational establishes its foreign subsidiary. In some cases, the policies of other multinational firms and other governments are used as a guide. Both governments and multinational firms are now dealing with these issues on a more sophisticated level. Clearly, governments have asserted themselves, and multinational firms are now expected to defend funds transfer procedures.

Before leaving our discussion of funds transfer strategy, two other observations are in order. First, large multinationals are subject to much

---

[9]In addition, there are real cost differences on identical products. For example, selling expenses or bad debt losses are lower for intracompany sales than for sales to unrelated parties.

more scrutiny than smaller firms. On the other hand, large multinationals may have considerable economic impact and influence. Second, devious funds transfer procedures are often used for purposes other than tax minimization. Specifically, blocked funds can sometimes be repatriated by adjusting the method used to repatriate funds. In such cases, the multinational may be unconcerned about the tax implications but very concerned about the blockage of funds. The entire funds transfer issue is complicated by the differences in motives, the number of firms involved, and the number of governments involved. There are no easy solutions or guidelines for this problem. Management still has substantial control over its own fortunes. However, governments are becoming increasingly vigilant.

Special Issues Relating to Funds Transfers within the Multinational Firm

Multinational corporations have developed many specialized procedures for transferring funds that are not necessarily related to either tax or currency blockage issues. In the sections that follow, three techniques for managing the multinational firm's internal funds flow will be analyzed: (1) the use of reinvoicing centers, (2) the use of credit terms for intracompany sales, and (3) netting of intracompany payments. Keep in mind that these techniques have value even in situations with no tax or currency blockage considerations. Each technique can be justified in terms of its contribution to managerial efficiency in the multinational environment. We will also see, however, that these same techniques may also be used in the multinational's conflict with foreign governments over tax and currency blockage issues.

Reinvoicing Centers

Multinational firms may use reinvoicing centers to manage international purchases and sales. A *reinvoicing center* is a separate subsidiary of the multinational, usually organized in a tax haven nation. All foreign sales and purchases made by subsidiaries are passed through the reinvoicing center. Assume, for example, that a subsidiary in France wants to sell something to a customer in Denmark. Legally, the sale is made to a reinvoicing center owned by the multinational (which we will assume is located in Luxembourg), and the reinvoicing center then sells the product to the Danish purchaser. The goods are shipped directly from France to Denmark, never finding their way to Luxembourg. Basically, only the paperwork takes place at the reinvoicing center.

Reinvoicing centers may be useful in managing foreign exchange risk. By centralizing the system of payments, the multinational has a better idea of which currencies will be needed and when. If the need for a particular currency is forecasted for a particular point in time, the reinvoicing center can invoice in the needed currency. For example, the shipment from France to Denmark could be invoiced in British pounds if there is a perceived need for this currency. In the absence of reinvoicing, Danish kroner would probably have been converted to French francs, and then the francs would have been converted to British pounds. Reinvoicing permits kroner to be converted directly to pounds, thus eliminating one step in the currency conversion process. This, of course, reduces the cost of converting currencies. In effect, the reinvoicing center can serve as a central office from which foreign currency receipts and disbursements can be managed. Cash budgets by currency can be constructed by the reinvoicing center, and both transaction costs and foreign exchange rate risk can be managed.[10] Note that these advantages of a reinvoicing center are unrelated to the desire to avoid taxes or currency blockages.

Multinational firms may gain additional benefit by using a reinvoicing center to minimize taxes. The general strategy would involve adjusting intracorporate fees so that income is shifted to the reinvoicing center, which, as previously noted, is located in a tax haven country. However, the tax advantages of locating the income in the reinvoicing center are limited. Since 1962, reinvoicing center income has been considered Subpart F income and is taxable in the United States even if it is not repatriated to the parent.[11] A multinational wishing to keep income outside the United States in order to avoid American taxes should leave the money with operating companies. In general, it is advantageous (in a tax sense) to shift income to a tax haven reinvoicing center only when the income tax rate in the country of an operating subsidiary is higher than that of the United States. For example, assume that a multinational has a subsidiary in a nation with a 55 percent corporate tax rate. In this situation, the multinational parent firm will have excess U.S. foreign tax credits. Shifting income to the tax haven reinvoicing center reduces the taxes payable in the high-tax nation without increasing taxes in the United States so long as excess foreign tax credits exist.[12]

Just as host governments monitor transfer pricing, they also play close attention to reinvoicing centers. Multinationals do not have complete freedom in this area. In addition, the multinational must evaluate the impact of reinvoicing centers on the management of the subsidiaries

---

[10]See Chapter 7 for a discussion of cash budgets by currencies as well as transaction exposure.

[11]See Chapter 15 for a more detailed discussion of this issue.

[12]The reader is reminded that foreign governments may have laws similar to those of the United States.

involved. Shifting too much income to the reinvoicing center makes subsidiary profits meaningless. The usual problems of management effectiveness and evaluation arise.

Leads and Lags in Payments

Multinational business is not only expanding rapidly, it is also becoming more integrated. One part of a product may be manufactured in one country and other parts in other countries. The various units of the multinational corporation then buy and sell to each other. The intracorporate sales are made on an open account basis, which means that accounts receivable and payable are created. Usually a sale by one subsidiary to another requires payment in 30, 60, or 90 days. One interesting aspect of this worldwide integration of production is that the subsidiaries of a multinational firm frequently owe money to each other. For example, the Canadian subsidiary may have an account payable in favor of the United Kingdom subsidiary at the same time that the United Kingdom subsidiary has an account payable in favor of the Canadian subsidiary. Everyone within the multinational owes everyone else money.

Funds can be transferred within the multinational by adjusting the credit terms associated with intracompany sales. In effect, *the multinational parent can speed up or slow down intracompany payments*, which effectively alters the relative liquidity positions of the various units. The extension of trade credit allows one subsidiary to delay payment to another and can be viewed as informal loans from one unit of the multinational to another. The nature of the lending is highlighted in Table 13-4. Under the initial conditions of this example, there is a single subsidiary of a multinational parent. The multinational parent sells $1,000,000 per month to the subsidiary, using an open account arrangement that calls for payment at the end of 90 days. At any given time, then, the subsidiary has accounts payable to the parent totaling $3,000,000. Note that these accounts payable play an important role in financing the subsidiary. Had open account financing been unavailable to the subsidiary, additional external financing would have been required.

The multinational parent can further reduce the subsidiary's need for external financing by extending even more generous terms. The second part of the example shows the subsidiary's balance sheet under the assumption that the parent requires payment after 180 days (rather than 90). Assuming that sales by the parent to the subsidiary remain at $1,000,000 per month, the new accounts payable balance is now $6,000,000. In the example, it is assumed that the additional financing provided by the parent permits the subsidiary to reduce bank loans by $3,000,000.

Note that by lagging payments from the subsidiary, the multinational has reduced subsidiary bank borrowing. The situation could have been reversed by leading (speeding up) the subsidiary payments to the

TABLE 13-4 Impact of Lagging Subsidiary Payments on the Subsidiary Balance Sheet

A. Initial Conditions (90 Days)			
Assets		**Liabilities and Equities**	
Current assets	$ 7,000,000	Accounts payable	$ 3,000,000
Fixed assets	$10,000,000	Bank loans	$10,000,000
Total Assets	$17,000,000	Equity	$ 4,000,000
		Total	$17,000,000
B. New Conditions (180 Days)			
Assets		**Liabilities and Equities**	
Current assets	$ 7,000,000	Accounts payable	$ 6,000,000
Fixed assets	$10,000,000	Bank loans	$ 7,000,000
Total Assets	$17,000,000	Equity	$4,000,000
		Total	$17,000,000

parent. If, for example, the parent firm required payment at the end of 30 days, the accounts receivable of the subsidiary would be only $1,000,000. Thus, $2,000,000 in additional bank borrowing would have been required.

A similar scenario could be constructed for a situation in which the parent is buying from the subsidiary. By speeding up (leading) payment to the subsidiary, the parent can reduce the subsidiary's need to borrow. By delaying (lagging) payment to the subsidiary, the parent can increase the need for subsidiary borrowing. As you can see, in cases where the subsidiary is either selling to or buying from the multinational parent, the parent can, to some extent, control the external financing needs of the subsidiary.

The ability to lead or lag payments can be of value to the multinational firm under several circumstances. In some cases, the ability to lead or lag payments may allow the multinational to borrow at favorable rates (or avoid borrowing at unfavorable rates). Assume, for example, that due to government intervention in capital markets, the conditions of interest rate parity do not exist and interest rates in the country of the parent are artificially high. The parent can reduce the need for expensive home country borrowing by adjusting payments to/from the foreign subsidiary. In this case, the subsidiary can then borrow at more reasonable rates in the foreign country. As a second example, assume that the foreign country has artificially high interest rates. In this case, the parent can borrow at home and allow the foreign subsidiary to lag payments. In both of these examples, the multinational is able to take advantage of capital markets imperfections and borrow at favorable rates. The funds borrowed at these favorable rates can be shifted to the needed location merely by altering the terms of open account purchases.

The use of leads and lags can also assist the firm in circumventing exchange controls. If, for example, a host country blocks dividend and interest payments to a multinational parent, the parent may be able to get limited relief by speeding up payments made by the subsidiary. In order for such a solution to work, however, the host government must continue to allow the subsidiary to pay for purchases made from foreign suppliers. Assume, for example, that a parent sells $1,000,000 a month to a foreign subsidiary and extends open account terms of 90 days. Under these assumptions, the subsidiary's accounts payable to the parent will equal $3,000,000. If the host country limits other payments to the parent, the parent could retaliate by gradually making the open account terms less favorable to the subsidiary. If, for example, payment terms were gradually reduced to 30 days, the parent would retrieve an additional $2,000,000 from the subsidiary. It should be noted that this is a one-shot gain. Continued host country blockages will have to be dealt with in some other fashion.

As in the other situations we have discussed, there are major problems associated with implementing a comprehensive lead/lag strategy. While the benefits of access to lower-cost borrowing and the possibility of circumventing exchange controls are clear, the costs of operating such a liquidity management program can be quite high. A parent company with many different subsidiaries would require information on local borrowing rates, local tax laws, exchange control regulations, and subsidiary liquidity positions. While such a strategy is possible, it is expensive and requires considerable expertise.

In addition to direct cost considerations, managerial effectiveness must be considered. A subsidiary is usually an operating firm with the usual production, marketing, and financing problems. When management is asked to speed up payments and then slow them down, managing the subsidiary becomes even more difficult. When subsidiary management is asked to increase local borrowing for reasons unrelated to conditions at the subsidiary, things become even more confusing. The multinational parent that continuously interferes with the operations of the subsidiary runs the risk of destroying the subsidiary's managerial effectiveness.

Government regulations can also be a factor. Many governments limit the use of leads and lags. Restrictions are of two general types. First, most governments insist that the terms of the original sale be honored. For example, assume that a subsidiary sells to a parent on 30-day terms and that after the sale has been made, the parent decides to postpone payment for an additional 60 days. Most governments would require that the payment be made as scheduled (except in very unusual conditions). While new sales could have other terms, the terms established on past sales must be adhered to by both parties. The ability of the subsidiary to speed up payments is similarly restricted.

In addition to requiring firms to adhere to the original terms of a sale, some countries place specific limits on the ability of firms to lead or lag. Exports from Canada, for example, must be paid for within 30 days. Leads and lags associated with imports are similarly regulated. Some countries, the United States included, have no such restrictions. The point is that governments are aware of potential abuses and monitor the situation. Since it is quite easy for countries to change policies on a moment's notice, the ability of the multinational to formulate a long-term strategy with respect to leads and lags is limited.

Netting of Intracorporate Payments

At one time, multinational corporations were content simply to have their subsidiaries pay each other when accounts payable or accounts receivable came due. Today there is a growing recognition that substantial savings can be associated with netting intracorporate payments. *Netting* means that rather than having each subsidiary pay the full amount of its payable, only the difference in payables is remitted. Assume, for example, that the Canadian facility has an account payable of $150,000 in favor of the British subsidiary and that the British subsidiary has an account payable of $100,000 in favor of the Canadian subsidiary. Netting payments would imply that only one payment of $50,000 would be made by the Canadian subsidiary to the British subsidiary. Under netting, only the differences in accounts payable are remitted.

There are big cost savings associated with netting intracorporate payments, since the cost of converting currencies and transferring funds from one country to another can amount to 0.01 percent to 1.00 percent of the amount remitted. In addition, multinationals can often avoid the opportunity costs associated with the fact that while the funds are in transit, neither subsidiary has access to them.[13] In our simple example described in the previous paragraph, the multinational would have had $250,000 in currency transfers in the absence of netting. With netting only $50,000 was transferred, which amounted to an 80 percent reduction in transaction costs. For a large multinational corporation, reductions of this magnitude can result in savings of millions of dollars.

Multilateral Netting

Netting arrangements are usually classified as bilateral or multilateral. As illustrated in the previous example, *bilateral netting* involves just two units of the multinational corporation. The accounts payable of one are used to offset the accounts payable of the other, and the balance is paid directly to the subsidiary with the smaller account payable. *Multilateral netting* is more complicated, since it attempts to net simultaneously the accounts payable of all of the multinational's subsidiaries. A multilateral

---

[13]See chapter 12 for a more detailed discussion of the cost of transferring funds.

TABLE 13-5 Multilateral Netting (Thousands of Dollars)

A. Intracorporate Receivables and Payables				
Receiving Subsidiary	Paying Subsidiary			Total Receivables
	United States	Germany	Canada	France	

Receiving Subsidiary	United States	Germany	Canada	France	Total Receivables
United States	—	$10	$ 8	$12	$30
Germany	$15	—	$ 5	$ 5	$25
Canada	$ 0	$ 5	—	$10	$15
France	$ 0	$ 5	$ 5	—	$10
Total payable	$15	$20	$18	$27	$80

B. Net Receivables				
	United States	Germany	Canada	France	Total
Receivables	$30	$25	$15	$10	$80
Payables	−$15	−$20	−$18	−$27	−$80
Net receivable	+ $15	+ $ 5	− $ 3	− $17	$ 0

netting example is presented in Table 13-5. In the example, the multinational firm has four subsidiaries, and each has some economic relationship with the others. For example, the U.S. subsidiary does not have any accounts payable to the Canadian subsidiary, but the Canadian subsidiary has a payable in favor of the U.S. subsidiary. Thus, there can be no bilateral netting between these two subsidiaries. However, multilateral netting is possible. As indicated in Part B, multilateral netting will result in the U.S. subsidiary receiving $15,000 and the German subsidiary receiving $5,000. Payments will be made by the Canadian subsidiary ($3,000) and the French subsidiary ($17,000). Note that total payments will be only $20,000, which is $140,000 lower than would have been the case if no netting had been used. Once again, the percentage reduction in the volume of transactions (and costs) is very high. Multinational netting can be very profitable for large multinational corporations.

Implementing a netting program is not easy. First, there is the problem of government regulation. Netting is prohibited in some countries. Some nations permit bilateral but not multilateral netting, while others allow both types. Some nations require that the multinational firm receive permission before netting can be conducted. There are no restrictions on netting in the United States and its most important trading partner, Canada. However, Japan does not permit multilateral netting. Thus, the multinational firm may not be permitted to implement a program that has substantial cost-saving possibilities. Of course, these regulations change over time, and one would think that netting will become more acceptable as the integration of the world economy increases.

There are also conceptual and managerial difficulties associated with multilateral netting schemes. When many subsidiaries are involved, it becomes difficult to determine who should pay whom. In recent years, managers have been successful in developing mathematical models to answer this question. Large multinational firms have developed centralized payment centers that coordinate the netting effort. Sometimes payments are funneled through the center, and sometimes they are made from one subsidiary directly to another. There is also the problems of the date at which netting takes place and the exchange rate employed. Despite these substantial problems, however, netting programs have been successfully implemented and are likely to be used with increasing frequency in the future.

Summary and Conclusions

The process of transferring funds within the multinational firm is complicated by the fact that many host governments block certain types of payments (most often dividends and interest) by a subsidiary to the parent. Multinationals often attempt to circumvent such restrictions by collecting fees that are set at artificially high levels and by devising specialized lending arrangements. Intracorporate funds flows are also affected by differences in national income and withholding tax rates. These taxes encourage the multinational to shift income away from the high-tax jurisdiction and through withholding-tax-free avenues. Such policies distort the fee-for-service approach and disguise the true profitability picture of both the parent and the subsidiary. Thus, evaluation of performance becomes more difficult. There are two consequences of funds transfer policies designed to reduce taxes and evade currency blockages. First, the governments of the host countries respond to devious methods of transferring funds by intensifying regulation. Evasion of regulations brings more regulations. Today the multinational is severely restricted as to the use of fees. The multinational firm has some flexibility, but it is limited. Second, such methods distort the true profitability picture of the subsidiary.

Flexibility in the way funds are transferred within the multinational firm, and the resulting control over the appearance of the subsidiary's profitability, can benefit the multinational in a number of other situations. In some cases, political conditions in the host country may be such that the appearance of a profitable foreign-owned firm may cause local indignation and increase the probability of nationalization or other restrictions on the firm. In such an environment, it may be desirable for the multinational to make the subsidiary appear less profitable than it really is. This can be accomplished through the manipulation of fees. In other cases, it may be desirable to make the subsidiary appear more profitable than it really is. Assume, for example, that the subsidiary is operating in a country with artificially low interest rates. It may be in the interest of the multinational to attempt to borrow in that country through the subsidiary. In such situations, the multinational parent can bolster the subsidiary's ability to borrow by increasing its profitability through the manipulation of fees.

Restrictions on the multinational firm's ability to manipulate internal funds flows are not necessarily bad, since a true fee-for-service approach makes managerial sense. Charges to the subsidiary that are justified by costs enable both the management of the multinational and the management of the subsidiary to make some sense out of what is really happening at the subsidiary level. The fee-for-service approach is also politically attractive from the host country government's point of view. Whether we like it or not, *profit* is regarded by many people as a dirty word. Host country governments are not anxious to have it appear that they are inviting foreign businesses into the country and permitting them to make huge profits. One way to head off dissatisfaction is to be sure that the profit figure reported to the public represents only a return on capital. Keeping other charges and fees separate makes both political and economic sense.

Review Questions

1. What is a fee-for-service approach for transferring funds among the subsidiaries of a multinational firm? What are the advantages and disadvantages of such a strategy? What are the factors that discourage a multinational firm from using a fee-for-service approach?

2. How can a multinational firm reduce its total tax burden through the manipulation of fees paid for services (among subsidiaries)? Use a numerical example in your answer.

3. How can a multinational firm manipulate fees for services in order to reduce the negative impact of host government blockages on the movement of currency? Use a numerical example in your answer.

4. How have host governments responded to attempts by multinational firms to avoid income taxes and circumvent currency controls? What risks are taken by the multinational firm when it attempts to circumvent host country tax and currency regulations?

5. What are the features of back-to-back loans, and which conditions favor their use? How do back-to-back loans affect the riskiness of the multinational firm? How does the firm pay for a back-to-back loan?

6. What are the features of parallel loans, and which conditions favor their use? What role is played by banks in the parallel lending process? How do parallel loans affect the riskiness of the multinational firm? How does the firm pay for a parallel loan?

7. What are the features of currency swaps, and which conditions favor their use? What role is played by banks in the currency swap process? How do currency swaps affect the riskiness of the multinational firm? How does the firm pay for a currency swap?

8. Assume that a multinational firm is operating in a country that is blocking subsidiary payments to the parent. How can compensating bank balance requirements be used to circumvent such restrictions? What are the limitations of such a strategy?

9. What is a reinvoicing center? How can it be used to minimize foreign exchange rate risk? What are the cash management advantages of reinvoicing centers? How can a reinvoicing center be used to minimize corporatewide taxes?

10. How can funds be transferred within a multinational corporation by adjusting the credit terms associated with intracompany sales? Under which conditions would the leading and lagging of payments be of value to the multinational firm? What factors limit the use of leads and lags?

11. What is multilateral netting of intracorporate payments? How can netting result in savings to the multinational firm? What factors limit the use of netting?

Questions for Discussion

1. Assume that you are employed by an American firm that has a single production facility in the United States. The firm is now considering building new production facilities in both Canada and Mexico and organizing them as wholly owned foreign subsidiaries. Building these facilities will involve a large outlay in American dollars. In addition, the parent corporation will provide technical and managerial services for a number of years. The subsidiaries will also use the parent's existing and future technology, trademarks, patents, licenses, and other valuable assets owned by the parent. Each of the subsidiaries will buy from and sell to the American parent, as well as among each other. The top management of the firm wants you to design a system for transferring funds between the two subsidiaries and between each subsidiary and the parent corporation in the United States. Management wants the transfer of funds system to both reduce the uncertainty associated with receiving payments from subsidiaries and permit an accurate assessment of the performance of each subsidiary. You are expected to recommend and defend a system for transferring funds.

2. Assume that you are employed by an American multinational firm with operations in many countries, including Brazil and Argentina. At the present time, the Brazilian and Argentinian operations are very profitable, but the foreign exchange situation is such that the subsidiaries are temporarily prohibited from making payments to the corporate parent. Since the firm has no desire to increase investments in either country, the funds are underemployed. At the same time, your firm is considering an expansion into India. This will require a considerable outlay. Top management is worried that at some future point in time the Indian government will also restrict payments to foreign corporate parents. You are assigned the task of making recommendations about structuring the Indian investment. The aim is to structure it in such a way that the risk of not receiving future payments is minimized. You are specifically asked to make recommendations about (a) the advantage of debt versus equity investments, (b) the use of back-to-back loans, parallel loans, and currency swaps, and (c) the use of fees as a way of retrieving funds from the subsidiary.

3. Assume that you are employed by a large American multinational firm with production and sales subsidiaries in 10 countries. In addition to buying from and selling to hundreds of outside firms, the subsidiaries have substantial transactions with each other. At the present time, sales by one subsidiary to another are made

on the same terms as sales to outside firms (net 30 days). You are assigned the task of reevaluating this situation. Specifically, you are asked to make recommendations about (a) establishing a reinvoicing center and (b) establishing a multilateral netting system. Your recommendations must include an analysis of the feasibility of each of these alternatives, as well as the possible risks and returns associated with both of them.

Research Activities

1. Investigate the restrictions on the flow of funds from a foreign subsidiary located in Mexico and from its parent located in the United States. Can the techniques discussed in this chapter be used to circumvent such restrictions (if any)?
2. Investigate the restrictions on the flow of funds from a foreign subsidiary located in Brazil and from its parent located in the United States. Can the techniques discussed in this chapter be used to circumvent such restrictions (if any)?
3. Investigate the restrictions on the flow of funds from a foreign subsidiary located in Canada and from its parent located in the United States. Can the techniques discussed in this chapter be used to circumvent such restrictions (if any)?

Problems

1. The income statements of the Altman Corporation, located in the United States, and its foreign subsidiary are as follows (millions omitted):

Revenues of the Parent

From other parties	$300
Sales to sub.	$ 70
Interest from sub.	$ 0
Royalties from sub.	$ 6
Fees from sub.	$ 10
Overhead from sub.	$ 14
Total revenues	$400

Expenses of the Parent

Purchases from others	$200
Purchases from sub.	$100
Other expenses	$ 20
Total expenses	$320

Revenues of the Subsidiary

From other parties	$200
Sales to parent	$100
Total revenues	$300

Expenses of the Subsidiary

Purchases from others	$ 60
Purchases from parent	$ 70
Interest to parent	$ 0
Royalties to parent	$ 6
Fees to parent	$ 10
Overhead to parent	$ 14
Other expenses	$ 10
Total expenses	$170

The U.S. tax rate is 34 percent. The tax rate applicable to the foreign subsidiary is 60 percent.

a. Given this information, compute the net income of the parent and the subsidiary.

b. Assume that the parent corporation increases all payments from the subsidiary (purchases, royalties, fees, and overhead) by 50 percent. In addition, the parent reduces the price on its purchases from the subsidiary by 25 percent. Given this additional information, compute the net income of the parent and the subsidiary.

c. What is the benefit of using transfer prices to minimize tax liabilities?

2. The income statements of the Janaca Corporation, located in the United States, and its foreign subsidiary are as follows (millions omitted):

Revenues of the Parent		Revenues of the Subsidiary	
From other parties	$800	From other parties	$200
Sales to sub.	$ 80	Sales to parent	$200
Interest from sub.	$ 0	Total revenues	$400
Royalties from sub.	$ 20		
Fees from sub.	$ 30		
Overhead from sub.	$ 50		
		Expenses of the Subsidiary	
Total revenues	$980		
		Purchases from others	$ 60
		Purchases from parent	$ 80
		Interest to parent	$ 0
Expenses of the Parent		Royalties to parent	$ 20
		Fees to parent	$ 30
Purchases from others	$300	Overhead to parent	$ 50
Purchases from sub.	$200	Other expenses	$ 10
Other expenses	$100		
Total expenses	$600	Total expenses	$250

The U.S. tax rate is 34 percent. The tax rate applicable to the foreign subsidiary is 10 percent.

a. Given this information, compute the net income of the parent and the subsidiary.

b. Assume that the parent corporation reduces all payments from the subsidiary (purchases, royalties, fees, and overhead) by 50 percent. In addition, the parent increases the price on its purchases from the subsidiary by 30 percent. Given this additional information, compute the net income of the parent and the subsidiary.

c. What is the benefit of using transfer prices to minimize tax liabilities?

3. Williams Manufacturing operates in the United States. In addition, the firm has foreign subsidiaries in Canada and Germany. The intracompany payables and receivables are as follows (millions omitted):

WILLIAMS MANUFACTURING (U.S.)

Accounts Receivable		Accounts Payable	
From Canadian sub.	$100	To Canadian sub.	$ 40
From German sub.	$ 60	To German sub.	$100

CANADIAN SUBSIDIARY

Accounts Receivable		Accounts Payable	
From U.S. parent	$ 40	To U.S. parent	$100
From German sister	$ 30	To German sister	$ 50

GERMAN SUBSIDIARY

Accounts Receivable		Accounts Payable	
From U.S. parent	$100	To U.S. parent	$ 60
From Canadian sister	$ 50	To Canadian sister	$ 30

Prepare a table, similar to Table 13-5, showing how netting would be undertaken under these circumstances.

Bibliography

Barrett, M. Edgar. "Case of the Tangled Transfer Price." *Harvard Business Review*, May–June 1977, pp. 20–36, 176–178.

Bokos, William J., and Clinkard, Anne P. "Multilateral Netting." *Journal of Cash Management*, June–July 1983, pp. 24–34.

Burns, Jane O. "How IRS Applies the Intercompany Pricing Rules of Section 482: A Corporate Survey." *Journal of Taxation*, May 1980, pp. 308–314.

_____ "Transfer Pricing Decisions in U.S. Multinational Corporations." *Journal of International Business Studies*, Fall 1980, pp. 23–39.

Goeltz, Richard K. "Managing Liquid Funds Internationally." *Columbia Journal of World Business*, July–August 1972, pp. 59–65.

Griffiths, Susan H. "Strategies to Upgrade Cash Management at Overseas Subsidiaries." *Cashflow*, March 1983, pp. 41–43.

Keegan, Warren J. "Multinational Pricing: How Far Is Arm's Length?" *Columbia Journal of World Business*, May–June 1969, pp. 57–66.

Kopits, George F. "Intra-Firm Royalties Crossing Frontiers and Transfer-Pricing Behaviour." *Economic Journal*, December 1976, pp. 791–805.

Kuhlmann, A. R. "Computers: The Answer for Global Cash Management." *Cashflow*, November–December 1980, pp. 48–50.

Madura, Jeff, and Nosari, E. Joe. "Global Money Management: One Approach." *Financial Executive*, June 1984, pp. 42–46.

_____ "Operational Approach to International Cash Management." *Financial Executive*, June 1984, pp. 42–47.

Meierjohann, Friedrich W. "A Multinational's Currency Management Philosophy." *Euromoney*, September 1981, pp. 129–137.

Obersteiner, Erich. "Should the Foreign Affiliate Remit Dividends or Reinvest?" *Financial Management*, Spring 1973, pp. 88–93.

Parkinson, Kenneth L. "Dealing with the Problems of International Cash Management." *Journal of Cash Management*, February–March 1983, pp. 16–25.

Pugel, Thomas, and Ugelow, Judith L. "Transfer Pricing and Profit Maximization in Multinational Enterprise Operations." *Journal of International Business Studies*, Spring–Summer 1982, pp. 115–119.

Sangster, Bruce. "International Funds Management." *Financial Executive*, December 1977, pp. 46–52.

Shapiro, Alan C. "International Cash Management: The Determination of Multicurrency Cash Balances." *Journal of Financial and Quantitative Analysis*, December 1976, pp. 893–900.

_____ "Payments Netting in International Cash Management." *Journal of International Business Studies*, Fall 1978, pp. 51–58.

Shoch, James R., III. "Management of U.S. Cash Flows for a Foreign-Based Multinational." *Journal of Cash Management*, May–June 1984, pp. 40–44.

Srinivasan, Venkat, and Kim, Yong H. "Payments Netting in International Cash Management: A Network Optimization Approach." *Journal of International Business Studies*, Summer 1986, pp. 1–20.

Stone, Bernell K. "International versus Domestic Cash Management: The Sophistication Lag Fallacy." *Journal of Cash Management*, June–July 1983, pp. 6, 58.

Waldner, Stanley C. "How to Invest in a Foreign Currency." *Euromoney*, July 1980, pp. 154–165.

14

Managing International Accounts Receivable

This chapter examines the impact of the international environment on the accounts receivable policies of the firm.[1] The first part of the chapter reviews the issues involved in establishing a receivables policy. The second part of the chapter discusses the various ways in which the firm can reduce the default risk associated with accounts receivable. The final section of the chapter examines the ways in which international accounts receivable can be used to help the firm raise capital.

Domestic Accounts Receivable

Before beginning our discussion of the management of international accounts receivable, it is helpful to review the options open to the

---

[1]Under usual circumstances, accounts receivable are short-term in nature (less than 1 year). However, firms selling capital goods often assist buyers in arranging medium- or long-term financing. Such arrangements are discussed in Appendix 14A.

American firm selling to a buyer located in the United States.[2] Generally, the selling firm must decide upon both credit terms and credit standards. *Credit terms* refer to the period of time during which credit is extended to customers. *Credit standards* refer to the types of customers that will receive credit. Both decisions should be made in a manner consistent with the primary goal of stockholder wealth maximization. In addition, the ability to obtain short-term financing using accounts receivable as collateral should be viewed as an integral part of the decision process.

Domestic sales are usually made on open account. In a typical situation, for example, the seller will ship goods to the buyer and receive payment at a specified later date. Typical terms for an open account sale may be *net 30*. Under these terms, the buyer is required to pay the entire amount shown in the invoice within 30 days.[3] In the typical open account transaction, there is no formal document of indebtedness, and the credit extended by the seller is known as *trade credit*. Although sellers may prefer to receive cash before delivery or cash on delivery (COD) rather than to extend trade credit, competitive pressures prevent the widespread use of these payment procedures. Generally, only financially weak buyers are required to pay cash. Most customers are extended some form of credit.

Granting credit for a certain period of time increases the financing costs of the seller. The financing cost problem results from the fact that open account sales increase accounts receivable. Somehow the selling firm must raise capital in order to finance this asset increase. In effect, the seller on an open account disposes of goods but receives no immediate cash. Labor, raw materials, and other costs remain to be paid, and funds must be raised in some other fashion. If the selling firm borrows in order to raise the needed cash, interest must be paid. In one sense, this interest payment is the financing cost associated with providing the open account financing.[4] The firm is willing to incur this financing cost because it anticipates that extending open account financing will increase sales and profits. The firm must weigh the benefits of extending credit (increased profits due to increased sales) against the opportunity costs (interest payments) of carrying receivables. If the benefits outweigh the costs, trade credit should be extended.

---

[2] The reader should review Eugene F. Brigham, *Fundamentals of Financial Management*, 4th ed., Chicago, Dryden Press, 1986, chapter 19, for a more detailed discussion of receivables management.

[3] A more typical form of credit terms would be 2/10, n/30. This indicates that the buyer has two options: (1) take a 2 percent discount from the face value of the invoice if payment is made within 10 days or (2) pay the full face value of the invoice by day 30. The decision to offer a discount for early payment is similar for both the domestic and the international environment.

[4] More correctly, receivables should be viewed as being financed by the risk-adjusted cost of capital.

The second problem associated with the use of open account financing relates to the risk taken by the seller. In effect, the seller releases goods, turns them over to a buyer, and receives nothing more than a general promise from the buyer to pay at a future date. The risk is that the buyer will not pay on the due date. For example, the buyer may encounter financial hardship and be unable to pay its bills. Or the buyer may be unwilling to pay, perhaps disputing the quality of the product. In either case, the selling firm has a problem. It has not received its cash and no longer has the product. Most firms have found it profitable to extend a certain amount of trade credit and to accept a certain amount of bad debt losses. The optimal level of accounts receivable is that level at which the marginal costs (financing costs plus bad debt costs) associated with additional accounts receivable begins to exceed the marginal income (profits from increased sales) of any new accounts receivable.[5]

Domestic firms sometimes *pledge* accounts receivable associated with domestic sales. When a firm uses *pledging*, it is essentially using the accounts receivable as collateral for a loan from a financial institution. The availability of this option, as well as the amount that can be borrowed, depend on the financial standing of the firm and its customers. Only firms that sell to customers with good credit reputations can use the accounts receivable so generated as the basis for secured bank loans. Firms that sell to customers with poor credit reputations will have difficulty using the accounts receivable as collateral for loans from financial institutions.

Borrowing by pledging accounts receivable reduces (at a cost) the financial burden associated with selling on open account. However, pledging does not solve the problem of bad debt losses, since the seller is still responsible for making the payment to the financial institution should the buyer fail to pay.

Factoring arrangements are used by domestic firms both to provide cash for operations and to shift the risk of non-payment of the accounts receivable. A factoring arrangement requires that, before making a sale, the seller must obtain prior approval of the customer from the *factor* (a financial service firm). Once approval is granted and the sale is made, the account receivable is turned over to the factor. In turn, the factor assumes the risk of nonpayment. One major disadvantage of factoring, from the seller's point of view, is that it is expensive. Perhaps more importantly, firms tend to avoid factoring because it results in the loss of control over marketing decisions. When a firm factors, it is the factor (not the seller) who decides whether or not credit can be extended to particular customers.

---

[5]There are many computational techniques to determine both the desirability of the firm's credit terms and credit standards. See Brigham, op. cit.

Despite the availability of alternatives, most sales in the United States are made on open account. This is because both buyers and sellers benefit from open account sales. It is simply more convenient and less costly to separate the movement of goods from the movement of money. While sellers would undoubtedly prefer to receive cash before or on delivery, they recognize that buyers would often be unwilling to go along with such demands. Insistence on immediate cash payment may reduce sales and result in lost profits. Factoring is usually viewed as too expensive and/or too restrictive. For domestic sales, sellers have found it profitable to make sales on open account and to monitor the system closely in order to protect against excessive financing costs and bad debt losses. In the competitive U.S. market, it is clear that a well-managed open account system can increase both sales and profits to the firm. In this manner, stockholder wealth is maximized.

In order for an open account system to work well, several institutional conditions must be in place. Perhaps most importantly, sellers need access to a very good information system covering the creditworthiness of potential buyers. The existence of such a system in the United States allows sellers to eliminate the most risky buyers from open account sales programs. The second necessary condition is the ability to take swift legal action (at a reasonable cost and with a reasonable chance of success) should a buyer default on a promise to pay. The existence of the Uniform Commercial Code in the United States provides this crucial element of support for the open account domestic sales programs of American firms.

International Accounts Receivable

Conceptually, international accounts receivable policy is the same as domestic accounts receivable policy. In both situations, the firm must weigh the costs of accounts receivable (financing and bad debt costs) against the potential profits from credit extension. The computation of the costs and profits is different for international accounts receivable, but the conceptual approach is the same.[6]

Foreign buyers of American products would like to purchase on open account.[7] While open account international sales are made with

---

[6]The chapter assumes that all sales made by American firms to foreign buyers are invoiced in dollars. Invoicing sales in a foreign currency may expose the firm to exchange rate risk. See Chapter 7 for a discussion of exchange rate risk management.

[7]The discussion throughout the chapter will concentrate on the American firm selling abroad. Of course, if an American firm buys from foreign firms, it may have to follow similar procedures.

some regularity, sellers are clearly more reluctant to do for foreign buyers what they are willing to do for domestic buyers. This hesitation can be attributed to (1) differences in available information about foreign buyers, (2) differences in legal systems, and (3) the fact that a sale on an open account to a foreign buyer can increase political risk. These factors are not present when open account credit is given to domestic buyers. Thus, while foreign buyers would like to purchase on open account, sellers are often unwilling to accommodate such transactions.

The absence of a well-developed open-account system to accommodate international trade transactions has led to the use of specialized international trade credit procedures. These procedures are primarily designed to minimize the risk borne by the seller. In the usual international trade credit situation, both parties get what they want because independent third parties (banks, other financial institutions, government agencies, etc.) are involved in the transaction. While it is sometimes not obvious, there are often substantial costs associated with the use of these third parties. The three most commonly used techniques for reducing the risk of nonpayment of international accounts receivable are as follows:

1. *Letters of credit*: Utilization of this technique shifts the risk of nonpayment of an international account receivable to one or more commercial banks. This technique involves a bank's guarantee of payment by the purchaser. Financing becomes available because the exporter can easily use this bank guarantee of payment as the basis for raising funds.
2. *International factoring*: This technique is basically the same as domestic factoring.
3. *Insurance approach*: In some cases, insurance companies assume the risk of nonpayment on international trade credit. Financing becomes available because insured accounts receivable serve as excellent collateral for loans.

Each of these techniques is exceedingly complicated. This can be attributed to the fact that the parties providing funds and/or bearing risk are anxious to develop legally binding contracts as a means of protecting themselves against losses. The fact that each transaction can be modified in many different ways also contributes to the complexity of the situation. By and large, each technique can be tailored to meet the special needs of the importer and the exporter. Thus, there are many variations on the general techniques. The presentation in this book simplifies the discussion by concentrating on the general concepts associated with each technique. You will find that this presentation is complicated enough. No attempt has been made to provide a comprehensive guide to the actual administration of the various techniques.

Letters of Credit

Letters of credit are one of the most common and oldest financial instruments used in international trade. The letter of credit allows the seller of the product to shift the risk of nonpayment to a commercial bank. With the use of this instrument, the creditworthiness of the buyer is immaterial to the seller. The seller's only interest is the credit standing of the bank issuing the letter of credit.

A typical transaction involving a letter of credit is outlined in Figure 14-1. This situation assumes that the Arso Instruments Corporation, an American manufacturer of high-technology testing equipment, has the possibility of receiving an order for $250,000 from the Bekko Manufacturing Corporation, a German manufacturing firm. It is also assumed that Arso is unwilling to assume the risk of nonpayment and that a letter of credit will be used. Note that in this idealized version of the letter of credit transaction there are four parties involved. In addition to the importer and exporter, there is a bank located in the importer's country (German bank) and a bank located in the exporter's country (American bank).

Step 1: The process is set in motion when the German firm, Bekko Manufacturing, places an order for specific equipment at a specified price. At this time, Arso Instruments indicates that it wants a letter of

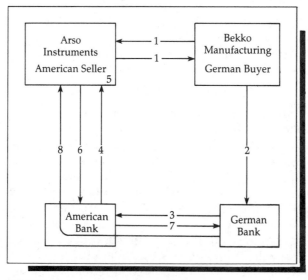

FIGURE 14-1 Letter of Credit

TABLE 14-1   Hypothetical Letter of Credit

DATE: January 1, 19XX
NAME OF BANK: German Bank
LETTER OF CREDIT #: 12345
ISSUED IN FAVOR OF: Arso Instruments Corporation
CORRESPONDENT BANK: American Bank
MADE BY REQUEST OF: Bekko Manufacturing
AMOUNT OF LETTER OF CREDIT: $250,000
REQUIREMENTS:
  1. Invoice
  2. Bill of lading. Destination: Hamburg, dated on board no later than April 10, 19XX.
  3. Insurance policy/certificate for 120% of invoice value, covering all risks.
PAYMENT: Draft drawn on German bank at 60 days' sight.

credit to be used for payment. Arso and Bekko agree on the use of a letter of credit as a means of paying for the merchandise. In addition, they agree upon all conditions pertinent to the sale. Arso prepares an invoice indicating all the conditions and forwards it to Bekko Manufacturing.

Step 2: Bekko Manufacturing, the importer, goes to the German bank and requests that a letter of credit be sent to Arso in the United States. If issued by the German bank, the letter of credit will say that if Arso Instruments fulfills the conditions specified in the letter of credit, the German bank (not Bekko Manufacturing) will pay $250,000 in favor of Arso Instruments. In effect, the letter of credit substitutes the promise of payment by the German bank for the promise of Bekko Manufacturing. As shown in Table 14-1, the usual minimum requirements for a letter of credit include (1) an invoice, (2) a bill of lading, and (3) insurance.

Step 3: Once the German bank issues the letter of credit, it is sent to the American bank in the exporter's country. The American bank is selected by the German bank to act as an intermediary between itself and the exporter. It is absolutely essential that the German bank have great confidence in the American bank, since it will have an important role in determining whether or not Arso Instruments has fulfilled the conditions specified in the letter of credit. Sometimes the American bank is a branch or subsidiary of the German bank, in which case trust and competence are not an issue. In other cases, the American bank has earned the trust and confidence of the German bank through a long-standing correspondent relationship.

Step 4: The American bank notifies the exporter, Arso Instruments, that a letter of credit has been issued in its favor. A copy of the letter of credit is provided to the exporter. Note (Table 14-1) how the letter of credit specifies the amount to be paid, the time at which the funds will be paid, and the conditions that must be fulfilled in order for the German bank to make the payment.

Step 5: Arso Instruments, the exporter, is now able to complete the transaction. At this point, extreme caution must be exercised in order to ensure that all of the conditions of the letter of credit are fulfilled. For example, the goods must be shipped on or before the date specified in the letter of credit: April 10, 19XX. If the shipment is even 1 day late, the letter of credit transaction will be voided and the entire deal may be canceled. It is also very important that Arso accumulate all the required proof that the conditions of the letter of credit have been fulfilled. A bill of lading and proof of insurance must be obtained by Arso; if they are improperly drawn, the deal will be voided. It should be noted that this documentation process is very technical and requires the attention of trained, experienced personnel. Also note that the entire letter of credit process depends on this documentation. Without the protection provided by these documents, the German bank would be unwilling to issue a promise to pay. The documents confirm the facts that the goods have been shipped, are insured, and so on.

Step 6: At this point, Arso takes the properly drawn documents (invoice, bill of lading, and insurance certificate) and a draft to the American bank. This begins the process that, in a short time, will result in the receipt of funds by the exporting firm in accordance with the terms specified in the letter of credit. The draft instructs the German bank to pay $250,000 into Arso's account in the United States. The payment is to be made on the date indicated in the letter of credit. In our illustration, payment will be 60 days after the documentation has been approved by the German bank.

Step 7: At this point, the American bank, serving the interests of the German bank, closely examines all documents in order to ensure that they are properly drawn and that the German bank is protected. The draft and the documents are then sent to the German bank. The German bank also examines the documents to ensure that they are in order. If Arso has met all the requirements specified in the letter of credit, the German bank is obligated to pay the draft on the date specified. That is, the German bank accepts the draft, thus making it a bankers' acceptance.

Step 8: The German bank now sends the accepted draft to the American bank, which, in turn, contacts the exporter. At this point, several things could happen. The exporter, Arso Instruments, is entitled to payment in accordance with the terms specified in the letter of credit. There are two basic types of payment: (1) sight or (2) sight plus a certain number of days. If the letter of credit specifies sight, the German bank is obligated to pay Arso on the date the documents are accepted. In our illustration, however, the letter of credit specified sight plus 60 days. Thus, the German bank is obligated to pay Arso 60 days after the documents are accepted.

The previous discussion presented a summary of a very simple letter of credit. We have not addressed the motivation of the various parties, nor have we discussed the financing issue. Before turning to these topics, a more detailed explanation of the required documentation is in order.

Required Documentation on a Letter of Credit

In order to make the letter of credit transaction viable, extensive documentation is required. The documents are prepared by or for the exporter and are designed to ensure that the bank issuing the letter of credit is protected to the maximum extent possible. In the previous illustration, only three documents were required: the invoice, a bill of lading, and insurance coverage. Specific situations or particular banks, however, may require other types of documents. Some of the documents involved and their function are as follows:

Bill of lading: The bill of lading is issued by a shipper (often a shipping line but increasingly an air freight company) and is required in almost every letter of credit transaction. It shows that the goods involved in the transaction have been transferred to the custody of the shipper and obligates the shipper to transport the goods to the destination specified in the bill of lading. The bill of lading also serves as a document of title to the goods in transit, since it specifies that the exporter is still the owner. In effect, the exporter will permit ownership to be transferred to the importer only after the payment process has begun. Note that the bank insists on this clear statement of ownership so that it can transfer clear title for the goods to the importer. This protects the bank in any potential disputes with its customer (the importer).

Commercial invoice: In some letter of credit transactions, a commercial invoice is required. While the bill of lading provides a general description of the goods being shipped (e.g., 100 cartons of machinery), the commercial invoice provides a detailed description of the merchandise included in the shipment (12 engines, 3 pumps, etc.). The commercial invoice is useful in avoiding later conflicts between the importer and its bank.

Packing list: While the commercial invoice provides a detailed listing of the merchandise included in the shipment, the packing list describes the contents of each container.

Insurance documents: Banks issuing letters of credit often require that the goods in transit be insured. The risk insured against can vary, but it is possible and usual for the exporter to acquire *all-risk* coverage. This covers all losses or damage from any external causes except war, strikes, riots, and civil disturbances. The insurance protects the importer and the bank issuing the letter of credit.

Other documents: In addition to the preceding documents, other documentation may be required in specific situations. For example, some transactions require government approval for the importation of the goods. In such situations, the exporter may have to receive permission from the consulate of the importing country (consular invoice); may have to provide proof of the origin of the goods (certificate of origin); and, when food and drugs are involved, may have to provide proof that certain requirements, such as weight and purity, have been met (certificate of analysis).

Note that the documentation used to support the letter of credit process is primarily designed to make the transaction as uncontroversial as possible. Other transactions may need additional documentation. This allows the bank issuing the letter of credit to give its unqualified promise to pay on the date specified in the letter of credit.

The Letter of Credit: An Evaluation

The seller clearly benefits from the letter of credit process because the risk of nonpayment is transferred to a large, financially sound bank. Generally, the creditworthiness of the foreign bank is superior to that of most importers. In addition, the seller may benefit from the fact that it is provided with a clear and unambiguous listing of the requirements that must be met before payment will be made. This feature alone may eliminate many misunderstandings. The seller, however, has one major disadvantage. Letters of credit increase the costs associated with the sale when compared to an open account.[8] Although the buyer may actually pay for the letter of credit, the sale price may reflect this added cost to the buyer. In a competitive environment, the seller may have to reduce the selling price in order to make the purchase more attractive to the buyer.

At first glance, the buyer does not appear to benefit from the use of a letter of credit. The buyer has the additional cost of obtaining the letter of credit. There is, however, a silver lining. As previously discussed, the letter of credit is very specific in stating the obligations of the seller. There

---

[8]In addition, processing all the required documentation imposes additional costs on the exporter.

could be a significant reduction in commercial disputes arising out of the use of these instruments.

The bank issuing the letter of credit benefits in two ways. First, it charges a fee of approximately $130 + one-fourth of 1 percent of the amount of the letter of credit. In the Bekko Manufacturing illustration, for example, the fee for the $250,000 letter of credit would have been approximately $755. Note that the bank is not lending any funds, and the fee received is not an interest payment. A second benefit to the bank is that the letter of credit promotes a good customer relationship with the importer. The primary disadvantage to the bank issuing the letter of credit is that it has assumed the risk of payment. In our illustration, for example, the German bank would have to pay the accepted draft even if Bekko Manufacturing is unable or unwilling to make the payment to the bank. The bank issuing the letter of credit can protect itself by granting letters of credit only to creditworthy customers. For example, if the credit standing of Bekko is in doubt, the German bank could request a partial or full deposit of the $250,000 before the leter of credit is written.[9]

In our illustration, the American bank is the party least affected by the transaction. It does not bear any risk. Its compensation for the minor expenses incurred comes either from fees charged to the German bank or from the fact that the German bank maintains correspondent deposits. On occasion, the bank in the exporting country gets more involved in the issuing process by confirming the letter of credit.

Confirmed Letters of Credit

Letters of credit may be either confirmed or unconfirmed. A letter of credit is confirmed when another bank, usually a bank in the exporter's country, guarantees the letter of credit issued by the importer's bank. In the Bekko Manufacturing illustration, for example, the American bank confirming the letter of credit would be obligated to pay should the German bank be unwilling or unable to do so. Such a confirmation gives the exporter more confidence that the letter of credit will be honored. Most exporters are not familiar with the financial integrity of foreign banks and may be unwilling to accept a foreign bank's promise to pay. On the other hand, home country banks are quite familiar with foreign banks, often having long-term working arrangements with them. When large, well-known foreign banks are involved, confirmation may be unnecessary and the letter of credit may remain unconfirmed.

---

[9]The advantages and disadvantages of letters of credit to commercial banks are more fully discussed in Chapter 12.

Irrevocable Letters of Credit

Letters of credit may be revocable or irrevocable. As the word implies, the *revocable* letter of credit can be withdrawn by the importer's bank at any time.[10] For example, the exporter may receive an order accompanied by a revocable letter of credit and begin work on meeting the specified terms. At this point, the importer may have a change of mind; the order can then be canceled and the letter of credit revoked. The revocable letter of credit does not protect the exporter should cancellation take place before the shipment is made. However, once the exporter has fulfilled all of the conditions specified in the letter of credit and forwarded the documentary evidence, the bank cannot refute its obligation to pay.

With an *irrevocable* letter of credit, the bank is obligated to meet the terms of its commitment regardless of what happens after the letter of credit is issued (assuming that the exporter meets the terms of the letter of credit). The cancellation of an order by the buyer does not release the bank from meeting the terms specified in an irrevocable letter of credit. The exporter can safely begin work on meeting the order and be assured that payment will be forthcoming. Most letters of credit are irrevocable. An irrevocable letter of credit can be changed only with agreement by all parties to the transaction.

The letter of credit has become an important part of the process of international trade. Its primary usefulness is for situations in which an exporter sells to an unrelated importer. In such situations, the pattern of cash flows and risks is altered by third-party banks. The utilization of banks in the selling process increases the direct costs associated with international transactions. In addition, the selling firm may lose some control over its marketing strategy (resulting in lost sales) if it insists on letters of credit for all sales, since some potential customers may not be able to obtain a letter of credit. These costs must be compared to the obvious risk reduction benefits to the exporter.

International Factoring

International factoring is similar to domestic factoring, except that there are some firms that specialize in factoring international accounts receivable. The largest and most important international factoring organization is the International Factors Group. This group of factoring firms has offices in more than 20 countries. In each country, it maintains extensive

---

[10]It may also indicate specific circumstances that will allow the bank to revoke the letter of credit.

credit files on potential buyers. An American firm wishing to sell to foreign buyers can contact the local member of the International Factors Group. The American factoring company would then contact a member firm in the country of the purchaser, and the foreign factoring firm would evaluate the creditworthiness of the foreign buyer. On that basis, the factoring firm can decide whether or not the potential account receivable will be accepted. If the buyer is acceptable to the factoring firm, the sale can be made. The factors have thus assumed the risk of nonpayment by the buyer of the products, and the seller has no default risk.[11]

The relationship between the selling firm and the factoring firm is usually an ongoing one. The selling firm enters into a factoring arrangement that covers virtually all its international sales. The selling firm and the factor agree on the parameters of the relationship. For example, the factoring agreement may require prior approval by the factor of any new customer. In some cases, the factoring firm may require approval only if the credit extended to a particular customer exceeds a certain amount. The whole relationship is open to negotiation.

International factoring is most appropriate for American firms that export only occasionally or have sales throughout the world. It may also be appropriate in cases where the buyer is a relatively small firm and may not meet the size requirements associated with letter of credit arrangements. Factoring (as opposed to letters of credit) may also be appropriate when the size of the sale is relatively modest. In such situations, it would be very expensive for the firm itself to evaluate and manage credit or to require a letter of credit. Factoring firms are in a better position to assess the risk and to handle defaults when they do take place.

The cost of international factoring is a significant issue in deciding whether to use it. The nature of factoring, the flexibility of its arrangements, and the fact that the services of factoring firms often result in less direct costs by firms make it difficult to provide a precise estimate of factoring costs.[12] Generally, factoring costs vary between 1 percent and 3 percent of sales. The actual costs depend on the type of customer, the country to which sales are made, and the size of each transaction. For example, if the firm sells to Canadian firms with the best credit ratings and the amount of each sale is $1 million, the factoring commission should be very low. On the other hand, if sales are to small Nicaraguan grocery stores and the amount of each sale is only $100, the factoring commission should be extremely high (if factoring is available). The loss of control over marketing policy can also be considered a cost, since

---

[11]Usually the factor will establish a reserve to cover potential commercial disputes between the buyer and the seller.

[12]The use of factors may reduce the selling firm's direct costs, since the firm may no longer need to maintain credit checking and collection departments.

failure of the factor to approve sales to certain customers may result in forgone profits to the exporter. In effect, the factor often determines the customers to which the firm can sell.

Accounts Receivable Insurance

As an alternative to letters of credit and factoring, it is possible for a firm to manage the risks associated with international accounts receivable through the purchase of insurance. In the United States, accounts receivable insurance is available from the Foreign Credit Insurance Association (FCIA), a consortium of 50 private insurance companies that operates in cooperation with the Export-Import Bank (an agency of the U.S. government). The risk covered by accounts receivable insurance is of two kinds: commercial risk (insured by the consortium) and political risk (insured by the Export-Import Bank). Commercial risks include the usual business reasons for nonpayment, including bankruptcy. The Export-Import Bank insures against political risks, including (1) losses due to a cancellation of an export license, (2) losses due to government restrictions on either the right to export or the right to import, (3) losses due to war, civil war, and similar events, and (4) losses due to expropriation or confiscation. Note that neither the insurance companies nor the Export-Import Bank insure against changes in the value of a currency. The exchange rate risk associated with transactions must be assumed by the seller and/or the buyer.[13]

The FCIA has a number of different policies, but the *short-term policy* is most relevant for accounts receivable management. This policy covers accounts that have maturities of up to 180 days. The availability of the short-term policy enables the seller to offer open account terms with a minimum of risk. Short-term policies provide 100 percent coverage for political risk and up to 90 percent coverage for commercial risk. In order to be eligible for the FCIA short-term insurance, the merchandise involved in the international transaction must be at least of 50 percent U.S. origin.

Short-term policies are usually written to cover almost all accounts, which means that even the most creditworthy accounts are covered. Only prepaid sales, sales covered by irrevocable letters of credit, and sales to Canadian buyers can be excluded from the insurance arrangement. Sales by a multinational to its subsidiaries may be excluded from the commercial insurance portion of the program, but participation in the political insurance program is required. These requirements are designed

---

[13]This issue is discussed in greater detail in Chapter 7.

to minimize the phenomenon of *adverse selection* and are what make the insurance plan work. If firms were allowed to select only the most risky accounts, either premiums would be very high or the insurance companies would lose money.

The rates for accounts receivable insurance are established by looking at a variety of factors. The loss experience of the exporter and the countries to which exports are made, the types of customers, the maturity of the receivables, and other factors are among those considered. The insurance premium can range from as low as 0.1 percent to as high as 2 percent. These percentage figures, however, do not indicate the true cost of the insurance. Assume, for example, that an American firm is making 10 sales of $100,000 each (for a total of $1 million) to firms located in countries for which an insurance rate of 0.5 percent has been established. Also assume that eight of these accounts are with old, reliable customers and are perceived as having little or no chance of default. The unknown reliability of the other two accounts is the real reason for the firm's use of insurance. Note, however, that the real cost of insuring these two accounts is $5,000 ($1 million × 0.5 percent), which is 2.5 percent ($5,000/$200,000) of the more risky accounts.

It should also be noted that the FCIA insurance program has a *coinsurance* feature. The commercial portion of the coverage requires that the exporter assume 10 percent of the loss. This feature is designed to encourage the exporter to seek economically sound buyers. High insurance charges plus the coinsurance feature add up to higher costs for using the FCIA accounts receivable insurance.

A Comparison of the Three Alternatives

Table 14-2 summarizes some of the crucial factors that must be considered when choosing a technique for managing international accounts

TABLE 14-2   Comparison of Letters of Credit, Factoring, and FCIA Insurance

Instrument	$ Cost Sale = $250,000	$ Cost Sale = $10,000	Other Credit Costs	Default Risk	Covered Sales
Letter of credit	$750	$155	None	None	Selected
Factoring	$5,000*	$200*	None	None	Almost all
FCIA insurance	$2,500†	$100*	Some	10%	Almost all

*Factoring commissions range from 1% to 3%. We will assume a 2% commission.
†Premiums range from 0.1% to 2%. We will assume a 1% premium.

receivable. Note, first of all, that the costs of the various alternatives depend on the size of the average transaction. When individual sales have a large dollar value, the letter of credit has a clear cost advantage. However, when the size of a sale is smaller, the letter of credit loses its cost advantage. As shown in Table 14-2, the dollar cost figure does not tell the whole story, because there may be other costs. A firm using letters of credit can choose the customers from whom it will request a letter of credit. For example, if the firm is selling to Volkswagen in Germany, a letter of credit may not be necessary, since the default risk is so low. Factoring and FCIA insurance, however, usually require that all sales be included in the agreement. Thus, the firm will have to pay premiums or commissions on very-low-risk receivables. In addition, the amount of coverage of FCIA insurance is only 90 percent of the receivable and, should a loss occur, the firm must assume 10 percent of the total loss. Finally, factoring arrangements allow the firm to reduce the costs associated with credit evaluation and collection. All these factors should be taken into consideration in order to arrive at the best alternative for the international receivables of the firm.

Short-Term Financing Using International Accounts Receivable

Many domestic American business firms use accounts receivable to obtain short-term financing. There are basically two methods: (1) using receivables as collateral (pledging) and (2) selling receivables outright (usually in factoring). There is no reason why international receivables cannot be used in the same fashion. However, it is extremely difficult to do so unless one of the three techniques outlined in this chapter has been implemented. Lenders will not usually allow unsecured international receivables to be used as collateral for short-term loans.

Letters of credit can be used as the basis for raising funds. This process can best be understood by looking back at the Arso Instruments illustration presented earlier. Our discussion ended at Step 8, at which time Arso Instruments was entitled to be paid in the manner specified in the letter of credit. In the illustration, the bank accepted the draft and took on the obligation to make a payment in 60 days (sight plus 60 days). The draft is now called a *bankers' acceptance*. Arso now has two choices: (1) receive $250,000 in 60 days or (2) sell the bankers' acceptance today. If Arso desires to receive the money immediately, it will instruct the American bank to discount the acceptance at current market values. There is a strong, efficient financial market in which bankers' acceptances of large, well-established banks are bought and sold. Note also that since the bankers' acceptance is discounted, the exporter receives less than the $250,000 price stated in the original order. In a conceptual sense, the discount is similar to the discount frequently offered when open account receivables are used to finance domestic trade transactions. For example, when a firm offers credit terms of 2/10, net/60, it is offering a discount for early payment. The discount of the bankers' acceptance has a similar function. Given that the market rate of interest that applies to the German bank is 7.3 percent per year, Arso would realize approximately $247,000. Arso gives up $3,000 in order to receive its money 60 days sooner.

In 60 days, the German bank redeems its bankers' acceptance by paying the outside investor. It is important to recognize that the bank will pay the investor whether or not it has received the funds from the importer. The bankers' acceptance is an unconditional promise to pay on a specified date, and, as such, is not dependent on the importer's payment to the bank. The unconditional nature of the bankers' acceptance is exactly what makes it a viable money market instrument. The risk of the bankers' acceptance is equal to the risk of the German bank.

The United States has an extremely active secondary market for bankers' acceptances. Since bankers' acceptances are typically of low default risk, they are usually held by investors as an alternative to cash and are often an important component of the marketable securities portfolio of large firms. Other important investors in bankers' acceptances include money market funds and investors seeking a short-term outlet for investment funds. The exporting firm wishing to sell its high-quality bankers' acceptances will have no problem finding a market for them.

If the American firm uses an international factor, obtaining financing before the due date of the receivables is a simpler proposition. The exporting firm would receive the funds directly from the factoring firm, and the factoring firm would subtract an *anticipation charge*. The anticipation charge is, in essence, prepaid interest, which means that the selling firm receives less than the face value of the sale. Once again, the exporter pays a price in order to receive the funds at an earlier date.

If the receivables of the American firm are insured by the FCIA, lenders will be more than willing to extend short-term financing using the receivables as collateral. The interest rate will reflect the cost of money for securities with similar maturities and risk. Since the risk of the receivables is almost nonexistent (ignoring the coinsurance feature), there will be no measurable risk premium on the loan. The firm with insured international accounts receivable can receive its money sooner but must pay interest.

Summary and Conclusions

The international environment complicates the optimal accounts receivable policy of the firm. This is especially true with respect to the default risk of international sales. Due to this problem, three major alternatives have been developed to reduce the default risk of international accounts receivable. These alternatives are letters of credit, factoring, and accounts receivable insurance. The primary advantage of these devices is that they reduce the default risk associated with international accounts receivable. There are, of course, additional costs associated with each of the three alternatives. The firm must, as always, weigh the benefits of risk reduction against the cost. Another advantage of letters of credit, factoring, and accounts receivable insurance is that they may be used as the basis for raising funds.

Review Questions

1. Which factors tend to make international open account trade credit more risky than domestic open account trade credit?
2. Describe (in detail) the eight steps in the letter of credit process.
3. Describe the documents usually associated with a letter of credit and explain why each is important to the process.
4. Explain how a letter of credit reduces the risks borne by the exporting firm. Who assumes the risks? Who pays, and how much is paid for the letter of credit?
5. What are the advantages to the exporter of the use of letters of credit?
6. What are the advantages to the importer of the use of letters of credit?
7. How does a revocable letter of credit differ from an irrevocable letter of credit?
8. What are the circumstances that favor confirming a letter of credit? Why does a confirmed letter of credit tend to have less risk than an unconfirmed letter of credit?
9. How does the letter of credit process make it easier for the firm to raise short-term financing?
10. What is international factoring? How does it reduce the risks of the exporting firm? Which conditions favor its use?
11. What are the costs and other possible disadvantages of using international factoring to reduce the risk associated with international accounts receivable?
12. Describe the different risks covered by the accounts receivable insurance provided by the FCIA.
13. Describe the features of the typical FCIA short-term policy. How much does it cost? How is the insurance premium determined? What are the implications of the coinsurance feature of the policy?
14. How does the use of FCIA insurance make it easier for the exporting firm to obtain short-term financing?
15. How does international factoring make it possible for the exporting firm to obtain short-term financing?

Questions for Discussion

1. Assume that you are employed by a moderate-sized American firm that produces specialized farm equipment in the United States. Traditionally, sales have been made almost exclusively to American retailers of farm equipment. In recent years,

however, the firm has expanded its sales effort and is now receiving 1,000 orders per year from domestic customers and 100 orders per year from foreign customers. The typical sale is between $50,000 and $100,000. The number of foreign orders, however, is increasing rapidly. By this firm's standards, each of these sales is very large, and a default on any particular account would present a real problem. Initially, sales to foreign buyers were made on the same credit terms as sales to American buyers (net 30 days). Unfortunately, the firm has had difficulty collecting on a number of foreign sales. A British customer has encountered financial difficulties and is unable to pay. A customer in Latin America would like to pay, but its government is limiting foreign currency payments. A number of other problem situations have developed, and your firm sees a growing problem of nonpayment of foreign sales. You are assigned the task of studying the situation and developing policy recommendations. Specifically, top management wants you to (a) identify the various alternatives for reducing risk, (b) evaluate the extent to which the alternatives will reduce the risk of nonpayment, (c) evaluate the cost of using each alternative, and (d) evaluate their impact on the growth of foreign sales.

2. Assume that you are employed by an American wholesaler of pharmaceutical products. Your firm has recently discovered a low-cost foreign supplier and has placed an order for $500,000 with this firm. You have received word from the supplier that they would be delighted to sell to you but that they would like your firm to provide a letter of credit. Since your firm is new to the importing business, it does not know what to do. You are assigned the task of explaining to top management exactly what will have to be done in order to comply with the request. You are also asked to indicate the costs associated with the letter of credit and any difficulties you may foresee.

3. Assume that you are employed by an American chemical manufacturer that has recently expanded into international sales. The policy of your firm has been to require that foreign buyers provide a letter of credit. This has worked well in the sense that your firm has suffered no losses due to default. In recent weeks, however, two strange things have happened.

   a. An order was received from a customer in the country of Parana. While there are several well-known banks in Parana, this letter of credit was issued by a small bank that is unknown to both your finance department and your local bank.

   b. An order was received from a customer in Italy, and the letter of credit was issued by a large, well-known bank. The letter of credit, however, was revocable. Since the letters of credit used in the past have been irrevocable, management is wondering what to do about this situation.

   You are assigned the task of analyzing these situations and making recommendations. Specifically, you are asked to explain any difficulties that you envision and to make suggestions for solving these problems. Your company is concerned about developing its market and controlling costs, as well as reducing risk.

Research Activities

1. Contact three major banks in your area. Ask each bank to provide you with cost information concerning letters of credit. Compare the cost of the letters of credit issued by the three banks.

2. Using information available in most newspapers (e.g., *The Wall Street Journal*), compare the prime rate to the bankers' acceptances rate over the last 3 years. In order to simplify the search for information, use the first day of each month for comparison purposes.

Problems

1. American Equipment (AE) is a large manufacturer of earth haulers. The firm makes 10 annual sales in foreign countries. Each sale is invoiced for $100,000. AE is concerned about the risk of nonpayment of receivables and has the following three alternatives to eliminate this risk:
   a. Request *letters of credit* from customers. The customers would have to pay $100 plus one-fourth of 1 percent for each letter of credit. In order to remain competitive, AE would reduce the sale price by the cost of the letter of credit.
   b. Use a *factor*. The factor will charge a 1.5 percent factoring commission.
   c. *Insure* the receivables through the FCIA. The insurance premium will be 1 percent of sales.
      i. Given this information, what alternative would you recommend to the firm?
      ii. What additional factors should be considered by AE in making the decision?

2. The American Appliances Corporation (AAC) is a medium-sized manufacturer of toasters. The firm makes 500 annual sales in foreign countries. Each sale is invoiced for $2,000. AAC is concerned about the risk of nonpayment of receivables and has the following three alternatives to eliminate this risk:
   a. Request *letters of credit* from customers. The customers would have to pay $100 plus one-fourth of 1 percent for each letter of credit. In order to remain competitive, AAC would reduce the sale price by the cost of the letter of credit.
   b. Use a *factor*. The factor will charge a 1.5 percent factoring commission.
   c. *Insure* the receivables through the FCIA. The insurance premium will be 1 percent of sales.
      i. Given this information, what alternative would you recommend to the firm?

Bibliography

Barovick, Richard L. "Export Credit Insurance: An Important Marketing Tool." *Business America*, August 23, 1982, pp. 6–7.

Bayalic, Arthur E. "The Documentation Dilemma in International Trade." *Columbia Journal of World Business*, Spring 1976, pp. 15–22.

Bowen, David. "Learning to Be Safe, Not Sorry." *Euromoney*, January 1985, pp. 133–139.

Brady, Donald L., and Bearden, William O. "The Effect of Managerial Attitudes on Alternative Export Methods." *Journal of International Business Studies*, Winter 1979, pp. 79–84.

Brigham, Eugene F. *Fundamentals of Financial Management*, 4th ed. Chicago: Dryden Press, 1986.

Bueso, Albert T., and Fredman, Albert J. "Export Credit Insurance for Bankers and Their Customers." *The Journal of Commercial Bank Lending*, October 1978, pp. 42–49.

_____ "The Export Options: Letter of Credit, FCIA Insurance or Factoring." *Credit and Financial Management*, January 1979, pp. 28–29, 34–35.

Celi, Louis J., and Czechowicz, I. James. *Export Financing, A Handbook of Sources and Techniques*. Morristown, NJ: Financial Executives Research Foundation, 1985.

Curtin, Donald. "The Uncharted $4 Billion World of Forfaiting." *Fortune*, August 1980, pp. 62–70.

Dufey, Gunter, and Giddy, Ian H. "Innovation in the International Financial Markets." *Journal of International Business Studies*, Fall 1981, pp. 33–51.

Export-Import Bank: Financing for American Exports—Support for American Jobs. Washington, DC: Export-Import Bank of the United States, 1980.

Melton, William C., and Mahr, Jean M. "Bankers Acceptances." *Federal Reserve Bank of New York Quarterly Review*, Summer 1981, pp. 39–52.

Ryder, Frank R. "Challenges to the Use of Documentary Credit in International Trade Transactions." *Columbia Journal of World Business*, Winter 1981, pp. 36–47.

Stolz, Richard. "Eximbank: What It Does for American World Traders." *Cashflow*, November–December 1980, pp. 34–39.

Weigand, Robert E. "International Trade without Money." *Harvard Business Review*, November–December 1977, pp. 28–30, 34, 38, 42, 166.

Appendix 14A: Sales of Capital Goods

Firms selling capital goods such as airplanes, expensive machinery, and factories frequently assist buyers in arranging financing for the purchases. Some manufacturers, for example General Motors, have their own finance subsidiaries that lend directly to buyers. Such arrangements involve a direct, formal obligation on the part of the buyer to the financial subsidiary of the selling corporation. Other manufacturer maintain contacts with financial institutions that are willing to make loans to potential customers. This appendix discusses the specialized institutions that facilitate the financing of international sales of capital goods. We will consider four such institutions: (1) the Export-Import Bank (EXIMBANK), (2) the Private Export Funding Corporation (PEFCO), (3) the Foreign Credit Insurance Association (FCIA), and (4) forfaiting. The common denominator of these specialized institutional arrangements is that they facilitate medium- and long-term financing of American capital goods.

The Export-Import Bank

The Export-Import Bank (EXIMBANK) is a U.S. government agency that facilitates the financing of American capital goods exports. EXIMBANK achieves this objective by either guaranteeing the payment of foreign buyers or providing loans to buyers. Its program was designed to supplement rather than replace private financial institutions in the United States.

An American manufacturer of machine tools, for example, may sell to a foreign buyer. Payment is spread over 4 years. Generally, the American seller is unwilling to provide trade credit for that long a period of time, and other sources of financing are needed. In many cases, the foreign buyer personally raises the needed funds. In other cases, the buyer may seek the help of the seller. EXIMBANK was established in order to help American firms compete in the international marketplace. It does this by assisting foreign buyers to acquire the funds needed to purchase from American manufacturers. EXIMBANK assists in the financing process by guaranteeing loans made by banks to the foreign buyer. In the event of default by the foreign buyer, EXIMBANK will honor its obligation and pay the firm or the American financial institution that has made the loan.

In certain cases, EXIMBANK may provide direct financing. When private lenders are unwilling or unable to provide the entire financing package, EXIMBANK participates with private lenders in providing loans to foreign buyers.

Generally, EXIMBANK financing and/or guarantees range from 6 months to as long as 10 years. The usual procedures require a specified down payment by the foreign buyer and regular payments (installments). In order to be eligible for EXIMBANK programs, goods must have a minimum U.S. content.

The goal of EXIMBANK is to encourage exports of American capital goods by diminishing the credit risk involved in such sales. EXIMBANK may also encourage American sales to foreign buyers by charging below-market interest rates on loans. Since almost all developed countries have similar financial institutions, EXIMBANK allows American firms to compete in this market. EXIMBANK should be viewed as an institution that assists American firms in marketing their products. The financial assistance is provided to the foreign firm, not the American firm.

Private Export Funding Corporation

The Private Export Funding Corporation (PEFCO) is a private American corporation whose stockholders include American commercial banks, investment banks, and manufacturing firms. PEFCO's main function is to facilitate the export of American capital goods to foreign buyers. It accomplishes this objective by purchasing the medium-term obligations of foreign buyers of American goods. PEFCO obtains the funds for these purchases through the sale of securities in American financial markets. In other words, PEFCO sells securities of its own in the United States and lends the money to foreign buyers of American capital goods.

This description of PEFCO as a private corporation, while technically correct, is somewhat misleading. In fact, PEFCO is the creation of EXIMBANK and cannot operate without its assistance. What EXIMBANK does is to guarantee the securities sold by PEFCO to the public. Since EXIMBANK is an agency of the U.S. government, the guaranteed PEFCO securities have no default risk and can be sold at attractive interest rates in American capital markets. This allows PEFCO to provide financing to foreign buyers of American capital goods at relatively low rates. Note that the financing is provided to foreign firms, not American firms. The PEFCO program represents another way in which the American government assists the international marketing efforts of American firms.

Foreign Credit Insurance Association

The chapter discussed the use of the Foreign Credit Insurance Association (FCIA) to reduce the risk of international accounts receivable. There we concentrated on the risk associated with short-term accounts receivable. The short-term policy offered by FCIA has become an important ingredient of the financial management strategy of many American firms. FCIA has other, longer-term policies that are designed to accomplish the same objectives as other EXIMBANK-related programs (i.e., encourage the export of capital goods by American manufacturers). These longer-term FCIA programs should be viewed as assisting foreign firms with their financing problem and thus facilitating the marketing efforts of American firms.

For example, FCIA offers a very popular medium-term policy that covers receivables between 181 days and 5 years. Note that the receivables in question are not those usually covered by open account financing and, as such, should not be viewed as an alternative to that method of financing. Instead, this policy should be seen as a method of providing medium-term financing to foreign buyers. Presumably, the exporter will either sell the insured medium-term receivables or use them as collateral for loans.

Forfaiting

Forfaiting is primarily a European technique used to facilitate the export of capital goods. Under this system, the payment for a purchase by a foreign firm is guaranteed by a bank. Since the guarantors have a good credit rating, the financial obligations can easily be sold in secondary markets.

Let us assume that a German manufacturer has the opportunity to sell machine tools to a government firm in Hungary and that payment is expected to be spread over 5 years.[14] As the first step in the forfaiting process, the Hungarian firm would obtain a guarantee of payment from the Hungarian central bank or some other financial institution. This guarantee is forwarded to the forfaiter, which is usually a strong financial institution (most frequently located in Switzerland). The forfaiter (e.g., the Swiss bank) then issues its own guarantee of payment. Because of these guarantees, the credit risk of the debt is not that of the Hungarian firm but that of both the Hungarian central bank and the Swiss forfaiter. Financial markets view this debt obligation as having a low credit risk. Forfaiting allows the German firm to discount (sell) the debt obligation issued by the Hungarian buyers. Forfaited discount rates are generally 1.25 percent above the LIBOR rate for the currency used in the transaction.

The key issue in forfaiting is that the German firm has significantly diminished the credit risk of the transaction. Forfaited obligations are sold in secondary markets without recourse. In other words, if the Hungarian firm defaults on its obligation, the Hungarian central bank and the Swiss forfaiter are obligated to make the payments. The German firm has no obligation in the event of default. The reader should note that this is very similar to factoring, discussed earlier in this chapter.

---

[14]Although forfaiting is now primarily a European alternative, some American financial institutions are evaluating this market.

PART V

International
Capital Budgeting

15

International Dimensions of Business Taxation

This chapter highlights some of the important tax issues facing American businesses involved in international commerce. Its initial focus is on the nature, scope, and importance of taxation in an international context. This is followed by a closer look at some of the international aspects of U.S. tax law. It is almost impossible to make decisions about international commerce without first considering their tax implications. The fact that the United States taxes international business somewhat differently than it taxes domestic business may have important consequences for business decision making.

Some Taxation Concepts

It is a fact of life that all national governments tax and spend. While each nation taxes in order to foster the common good of its people, the definition of *common good* varies from country to country. Different governments use different types of taxes in order to raise revenues. Each nation has its own spending priorities, and these priorities reflect the basic problems facing the society. The spending of some nations stresses social welfare programs, others stress economic development, others stress defense, and some simply reflect a desire to survive. We must accept the fact that each nation has a right to decide for itself what is and what is not important. Americans, especially businesspeople, must realize that the United States does not have a monopoly on either wisdom or stupidity when it comes to government spending and taxation. Foreigners doing business in the United States often view our tax and spending policies with the same disbelief that we view those of foreign nations.

In principle, a nation levies taxes on its residents. That is, the people who are expected to benefit from the programs supported by government expenditures are expected to provide the necessary tax revenues. Sometimes tax laws attempt to achieve social justice by reallocating tax burdens among residents in accordance with some ability-to-pay or fairness principle. In many countries, including the United States, some groups pay more in taxes than they receive in benefits. Whether or not this is fair depends on one's own perspective. The controversy over fairness and the ability to pay taxes are not absent from the area of taxation of international commerce. Many firms feel that they are penalized by foreign governments. Many firms feel that foreign taxation is unfair. But remember that American businesses often feel that they are taxed unfairly in the United States. It should not be surprising that they have even more intense feelings about some aspects of foreign taxation. Whether foreign tax policies are fair or unfair, American firms have little choice but to live with them. To do otherwise would imply withdrawal from the international marketplace.

Businesses, in the United States and elsewhere, are subject to a variety of taxes. Some taxes are levied on all business transactions, whether they involve international commerce or not. The income tax, the value-added tax, the sales tax, the turnover tax, and the property tax fall into this category. In addition, there are taxes designed specifically to raise tax revenue from international transactions. Withholding taxes on dividends to foreigners, royalties on minerals extracted, export taxes, and tariffs fall into this category. Let us take a closer look at some of these taxes, leaving the important income tax for last.

Sales-Related Taxes

Sales-related taxes are important sources of revenue to many governments, especially those in Western Europe. There are three basic types of sales-related taxes: (1) regular sales taxes, (2) turnover taxes, and (3) value-added taxes. The *sales tax* is relatively easy to understand. The government imposes a rate that is applied to the *final* purchase price of a product. No sales taxes are paid on items that are being used for production. Thus, for example, a retailer who buys shirts for later sale does not pay a sales tax to the wholesaler. The only time the sales tax is paid is when the final consumer purchases the shirt from the retailer. The *turnover tax* differs from the sales tax in that a tax is paid on every transaction. For example, our retailer in the preceding example paid a tax on the purchase from the wholesaler, and the consumer pays a tax to the retailer. There is a tax at every level of sale.

Conceptually, the sales tax and the turnover tax could be designed to yield the same amount of tax and the same final price to the consumer. In order to accomplish this, the turnover tax rate would have to be lower than the sales tax rate, since tax is being paid on previously taxed items. For example, the retailer buys the shirt for $20 and pays a 5 percent turnover tax, which results in a total cost of $21. If the retailer marks up the shirt by $10, the cost to the consumer will be $31 plus $1.55 turnover tax. The final consumer winds up paying tax on the amount of tax already paid by the retailer. In our example, the consumer pays a tax on the $1 tax paid by the retailer, since the $1 is included in the purchase price. The impact of this double taxation can be minimized by reducing the size of the turnover tax rate at each level.

The problem with the turnover tax, and the reason it has fallen into disfavor, is that it affects the ways goods are produced. Under the turnover tax system, goods produced by firms that have integrated production and sales operations have a lower total cost. This reflects the fact that the turnover tax is applied every time goods change ownership. If a producer can eliminate sales during the production process, it can eliminate the double taxation aspect of the turnover tax. It should be noted that the turnover tax is advantageous to large, integrated firms and disadvantageous to smaller firms.

The *value-added tax* is similar to the turnover tax, except that double taxation is eliminated. This is accomplished by redefining the amount on which the tax is paid to be equal to the value added by the firm. This is illustrated in Table 15-1. The example assumes that the farmer purchases no inputs and sells his output for $100. The farmer pays a 10 percent tax

TABLE 15-1 An Illustration of a 10% Value-Added Tax

Stage of Production	Cost	Sale Price	Value Added	Tax	Net Revenue
Farmer sells cotton	$ 0	$100	$100	$10	$ 90
Manufacture of cloth	$100	$150	$ 50	$ 5	$145
Manufacture of shirts	$150	$250	$100	$10	$240
Retailer sells shirts	$250	$300	$ 50	$ 5	$295
			Total tax	$30	

on the $100, which is the amount of his value added to the product. Note that the value-added tax is paid by the farmer, and his net revenue is less than the sale price. The manufacturer of cloth purchases inputs for $100 (from the farmer) and sells the cloth to a shirt manufacturer for $150. The cloth manufacturer pays tax only on the amount of value that has been added, which is the sale price minus the cost of purchases. There is no tax on previous taxes paid, since the taxes paid at the lower stages are included in the cost of purchases, and this cost is subtracted from the sale price in order to calculate the value added. The taxation process continues through the other stages of production, with taxes being paid only on the value added at each level. Note that the total tax paid at all levels is equal to the tax rate times the total value added.

While the sale, turnover, and value-added taxes accomplish more or less the same objective, they have different implications for consumers and businesses. Sales taxes are collected at the retail level. They are paid by consumers to retailers and then forwarded to the government. Sales taxes are highly visible, and consumers do not like them. Turnover and value-added taxes, on the other hand, are paid directly by businesses, and the collection is spread over the entire production process. These taxes are less visible to the final consumer, since no additional tax is paid at the time of purchase. The value-added tax gives the illusion that the tax is being paid by business firms and not the consumer. It is easy to overlook the fact that the tax paid by business is passed along to the consumer and is thus reflected in the price of the final product. One of the realities of doing business in some Western European countries is that all firms are in the business of collecting this value-added tax for various governments.[1] There is no similar circumstance in the United States.

Taxes Aimed at International Business

Firms involved in international commerce are often subjected to special forms of taxation. Sometimes the objective of these taxes is to affect business behavior rather than to raise revenues for the government. Tariffs are one such tax. A *tariff* is a tax placed on imports into a country, with the amount of the tariff usually being stated in terms of a specific percentage of value.[2] In 1987, for example, the United States imposed a 100 percent tariff on certain electronic items imported from Japan. Under this tariff, which has since been repealed, the importer of a Japanese

---

[1]European countries tend to rebate all or part of the value-added taxes for exported goods. This is done in order to encourage exports.

[2]On rare occasions, tariffs are also levied on exports.

compact disk player with a value of $200 would have paid an additional $200 tariff. The intent of the tariff was not to raise revenues for the United States but to make the disk players so expensive to American buyers that they would not be imported at all. This tariff was punitive in nature. Other countries pursue similar policies. The EEC has a common tariff wall designed to restrict the flow of goods into the Common Market. Many developing countries that are short of foreign exchange impose heavy tariffs on the importation of consumer goods.

Since 1960, tariffs have generally been reduced. The official policy of most governments of industrial or industrializing countries is to eventually eliminate all tariffs. However, while their rhetoric implies that tariffs are a temporary phenomenon that will be eliminated, the reality is different. Interest groups in every country fight very hard to maintain tariffs. In the EEC and Japan there are very high tariffs on farm products, which reflects the strong political position of farmers. Governments of developing countries often place tariffs on imported manufactured goods in order to protect their infant industries. For example, in 1988 Brazil was involved in a bitter controversy over the very high tariffs placed on computers imported into that country. Thus, despite declarations to the contrary, it appears that tariffs will exist for some time, and firms engaged in international business must incorporate this sometimes important tax into their business plans.

Governments also levy a variety of taxes that can be grouped together under the heading of *withholding taxes*. Withholding taxes are basically taxes on international financial flows, with the tax being related to the size of the flow. For example, Belgium levies a 15 percent withholding tax on dividends paid by a subsidary to its foreign parent corporation.[3] Thus, if a dividend payment of $500,000 is made, the Belgian government withholds $75,000 and the parent corporation receives only $425,000. Interest payments to foreigners may also be subject to a withholding tax. During the 1970s, for example, the United States imposed an *interest equalization tax*, which was a withholding tax on all interest paid to foreign residents. Today Australia imposes a 10 percent withholding tax on interest paid to foreigners. When a foreign subsidiary of an American corporation pays a management fee, royalty, copyright fee, or many other types of fees, it may also be subjecting the flow to a withholding tax. For example, France imposes a 5 percent tax on royalties paid to foreigners. The exact intrafirm cash flows subject to the withholding tax and the size of the tax depend on the country in which the foreign subsidiary is located.

Withholding taxes are used for two reasons. In one sense, withholding taxes are taxes on income designed to raise revenue. Since withhold-

---

[3]The withholding taxes mentioned in this section were obtained from *1988 Foreign and U.S. Corporate Income and Withholding Tax Rates*, New York: Ernst & Whinney, 1988.

ing taxes raise revenue from foreign taxpayers, they are popular from a domestic political point of view. But sometimes withholding taxes are designed to alter business behavior by discouraging the flow of funds out of a country. It is hoped that high withholding taxes will encourage firms to reinvest in the foreign country, which, in turn, will encourage economic growth. Mexico's 55 percent withholding tax on dividends falls into this category. Whatever the reason for their existence, withholding taxes can have an important impact on firms engaged in international commerce, especially multinational firms.

The last tax that will be reviewed in this section is the *royalty* on minerals. Countries that are rich in natural resources prefer to tax extracted minerals on a per unit basis. Thus, there may be a fixed tax on each barrel of oil, each ton of copper, or each shipload of bauxite. Companies paying the royalty tax usually do not have to pay any income tax, at least on the portion of their operations devoted to the extraction of the natural resource. From the taxing government's point of view, the big advantage of the royalty tax is that it eliminates the need to collect income taxes and the auditing associated with income tax systems. The royalty tax approach also reflects the belief that corporations are frequently able to avoid income taxes by shifting income from one subsidiary to another. The royalty approach is relatively straightforward and is more difficult for foreign firms to avoid. For firms engaged in extracting natural resources, the royalty tax is likely to be the most important of all the taxes discussed.

Income Taxes

Both the United States and its major trading partners tax business income. Income related to international commerce is taxed under two general taxation concepts. The first concept asserts that all income earned in a particular country should be subject to taxation by that country, even if the earner is a foreigner. Thus, if an American business earns income in Italy, it must pay Italian income tax. The fact that the firm is American owned does not eliminate its tax liability. The second taxation concept asserts that residents of a country must pay taxes on their worldwide income, wherever that income is earned. Thus, income earned by an American business in Italy is subject to American income tax. As a general rule, U.S. businesses that earn income in a foreign country may have an income tax liability in both that country and the United States. Not all countries, however, impose taxes on foreign income earned by their residents. This phenomenon of multicountry income taxation has important implications for business strategy and tax planning.

TABLE 15-2 A Simplified Format for Corporate Income Taxation

Revenue
− Deductible expenses
= Taxable income
× Tax rate
= Tentative tax liability
− Tax credits
= Income tax payable

While the general concept of business income taxation is relatively easy to understand, there are a number of complex problems in implementing and coordinating tax laws. These problems are especially severe when the income being taxed is international. The nature of the problems can best be understood in the simplified income taxation format presented in Table 15-2. The problems begin right at the top line. Specifically, firms engaged in international commerce and the taxing governments frequently disagree about the amount of revenue earned in a particular country. For example, an American manufacturer with a facility in Germany may produce part of a product in the United States and another part in Germany; the product may then be shipped to a sales subsidiary in Greece. It is not easy to determine which portion of the income finally derived from the sale is taxable in each country. Disputes can arise not only between the firm and particular governments, but among the governments themselves.

The issue of expense recognition is also complicated. Different countries have different accounting standards, and these standards affect the amount and timing of expense recognition. First, there are differences of opinion about where international expenses should be recognized. Should an American multinational corporation with a substantial research and development effort in the United States make a charge to a wholly owned subsidiary located in France? Will the French government permit such a cost allocation? The answers to these questions will affect the taxable income of the French subsidiary and the income tax paid in France. A second accounting-related factor that introduces controversy into the taxation of international operations relates to the tax laws themselves. The United States, for example, uses a depreciation procedure called *ACRS*, (Accelerated Cost Recovery System) which provides for substantial acceleration of depreciation recognition. Other countries may use other procedures for recognizing depreciation expense. The same problem is associated with many other expenses. The fact is that the "taxable income" line in the income statement reflects generally accepted accounting procedures, and these procedures are often controversial and vary from country to country. When all is said and done, differences in revenue and expense recognition procedures result in substantial differ-

TABLE 15-3 Selected Maximum Corporate
Income Tax Rates (1989)

Country	Maximum Rate
Belgium	43%
Canada	44%
France	42%
Germany	56%
Italy	36%
Japan	42%
Sweden	52%
United Kingdom	35%
United States	34%

Source: Corporate Taxation: A Worldwide Guide. 1989 Edition. New York: Ernst & Whinney International Operations, 1989.

ences in the amount of income subject to taxation. Even though operations may be identical in each country, the earnings before taxes could be much higher in one country than in another.

Table 15-3 provides a general idea of the corporate income tax level in various countries. The rates are for illustration purposes only, since actual rates are frequently changed. Also note that some countries have progressive corporate income tax systems, which involve taxing some income at lower rates. The amount of income subject to lower rates of taxation varies among countries. Some countries also have different rates for branches and corporate subsidiaries. In addition, some countries tax income distributed to shareholders differently than income retained by the firm. The rates reported in Table 15-3 are those that would apply under the worst set of circumstances.

The fact that emerges from the discussion thus far is that the actual rate applicable in a particular country does not necessarily indicate whether corporate income taxes are high or low in that country. The tax rate is only one of several factors that must be considered when evaluating the taxation level. Regulations relating to income and expense recognition are equally important. In addition, the availability of tax credits may be significant. Some nations give tax credits to firms making certain types of investments or conducting certain activities deemed to be advantageous to the nation. The United States, for example, had an investment tax credit until its repeal in 1986. In addition, firms are sometimes able to negotiate special *tax holidays* in connection with activities in some countries. Comparisons with U.S. tax rates are also made more difficult by the fact that corporations in the United States may also be subject to state taxation.

Leaving the tax rate and accounting procedure issues aside, it is safe to say that, historically, the corporate income tax burden in the United

States has been relatively heavy.[4] Since most foreign countries tended to rely less on the corporate income tax and more on other form of tax, American firms earning income abroad tended to pay less income tax to the foreign government than they would have paid if the income had been earned in the United States. Relative tax burdens have and continue to undergo significant changes. As shown in Table 15-3, the U.S. corporate tax rate is now lower than those of many countries. This reflects the fact that foreign countries have tended to increase corporate tax rates over the past two decades, while American rates have been reduced from a high of 52 percent to the current 34 percent.[5] Today it is possible to pay more income taxes abroad than on a similar amount of income earned in the United States. As we shall observe later in the chapter, this may mean that no additional taxes are due in the United States. However, the outlook for the future is unclear, because other nations are now reevaluating corporate income tax policy and foreign income tax rates may also decline. At the time of this writing, however, it is safe to say that the U.S. corporate income tax rate is not among the highest in the world.

U.S. Taxation of Foreign
Operations of American Firms

American firms are taxed on their worldwide income. American tax laws are designed so that income earned in a foreign country is taxed at a rate that is no lower than if the income had been earned in the United States. As a general rule, if foreign income taxes are equal to or higher than taxes in the United States, no additional tax is paid in the United States. On the other hand, if foreign taxes are lower, additional taxes may have to be paid in the United States. The general procedure involved in computing the U.S. tax payable on foreign income involves two basic steps: (1) compute the U.S. tax on the foreign income as if the income had been earned in the United States and (2) use foreign taxes as a *foreign tax credit* against the tentative tax liability. For example, if $500,000 is the tentative

---

[4]The word *heavy* in this context refers to corporate income taxes in the United States relative to those in other countries. In terms of total taxes paid in the united states, personal income and payroll taxes are a much more important source of tax revenues for the U.S. government.

[5]As of 1988, the U.S. corporate income tax rates were as follows:

Taxable Income	Marginal Tax Rate
Up to $50,000	15%
$50,000–$75,000	25%
$75,000–$100,000	34%
$100,000–$335,000	39%
Over $335,000	34%

tax liability in the United States and the American corporate taxpayer has paid $300,000 in income taxes to the foreign government, only an additional $200,000 would be paid in American taxes. That is, the firm used a foreign tax credit of $300,000 to partially offset its tentative liability of $500,000. Under this system, the total tax paid is the same as if the income had been earned in the United States.

In order for a foreign tax to be eligible for inclusion in the U.S. foreign tax credit, the foreign tax must be imposed on the income of the firm. A foreign corporate income tax would, of course, be eligible. The Internal Revenue Service also considers withholding tax on dividends and interest to be a tax on income and permits it to be included in the foreign tax credit. Thus, if a foreign subsidiary pays a dividend to its American parent corporation and a withholding tax is imposed by the foreign government, the amount withheld can be taken as a foreign tax credit in the United States. On the other hand, foreign sales taxes, value-added taxes, royalty taxes, turnover taxes, property taxes, and other non-income-related taxes cannot be included as part of the foreign tax credit.[6]

Taxes Paid by the Subsidiary

The principles of taxation for income earned in a foreign country can best be explained by the use of an extended example. To begin, we will assume that the Donegal Corporation is an American multinational corporation with a wholly owned foreign subsidiary. Note that, by definition, the subsidiary is a separate corporation and has a legal life of its own. We will assume that Donegal has $90 million in taxable income derived from purely domestic sources.[7] Donegal's foreign subsidiary also has income, and the subsidiary's income statement is presented in Table 15-4. Note particularly that the subsidiary pays foreign income taxes at a rate of 20 percent and has a net income of $8 million.

Up to this point in the taxation process, the Donegal Corporation still has no tax liability in the United States. This reflects the fact that the foreign subsidiary is a legal entity that is separate and distinct from its owner. The income of the foreign subsidiary is taxable in the United States only when the income is sent to the parent.[8] If the subsidiary retains all the income abroad, no income taxes in the United States need

---

[6]Firms have attempted to treat royalty taxes as an income tax. In fact, some foreign countries have designed their royalty taxes in such a way that they can be construed as an income tax. In addition, income taxes paid to some foreign governments (e.g., South Africa, Libya, and North Korea) cannot be used as a foreign tax credit.

[7]The assumption that the firm has $90 million in taxable income is made in order to have a marginal corporate tax rate of 34 percent of all foreign income.

[8]Exceptions to this rule will be discussed later in the chapter.

TABLE 15-4 Donegal Corporation: Income Statement
of the Foreign Subsidiary in Country X

Revenue	$100,000,000
− Labor costs	$ 35,000,000
− Raw materials	$ 32,000,000
− Property taxes	$ 11,000,000
− Royalty taxes	$ 1,000,000
= Gross profit	$ 21,000,000
− Advertising expense	$ 8,000,000
− Advertising taxes	$ 3,000,000
= Taxable income	$ 10,000,000
− Foreign income tax*	$ 2,000,000
= Net income	$ 8,000,000

*The foreign corporate income tax rate is 20 percent of taxable income. The subsidiary has no tax credits.

be paid. Of course, retaining income abroad may not always be in the interest of the owners of the American firm. Donegal has made an investment in the foreign subsidiary and is interested in receiving a return on that investment. While Donegal could postpone U.S. tax liabilities by investing the funds abroad, eventually funds will flow back to the parent corporation. When this occurs, U.S. income taxes may be due.

Subsidiary U.S. Taxable Income

For simplicity, the first part of this illustration assumes that all (100 percent) of the subsidiary's net income is paid in dividends to the parent corporation in the year in which it is earned. We will also assume that the foreign government imposes a 10 percent withholding tax on dividends. As shown in Part A of Table 15-5, the Donegal Corporation receives a net amount of $7,200,000 from the $8,000,000 dividend paid by the foreign subsidiary.

Now comes the tricky aspect of computing the U.S. corporate income tax on foreign income. The confusion is related to the fact that while U.S. taxes are due only when dividends are paid to the parent, the taxable income is not equal to the dividend received. A special computation is needed to derive the foreign income taxable in the United States. The procedure used in this computation is called *grossing up*. It involves adding foreign income taxes and withholding taxes to dividends received in order to arrive at the taxable income. The process is illustrated in Part B of Table 15-5. Once again, the important thing to note is that the taxable income is not equal to the dividend received by the parent in the United States.

TABLE 15-5   Donegal Corporation: U.S. Tax on Foreign
Subsidiary Income—Country X [All Income (100%) Sent to Parent]

A. Subsidiary Income Statement	
Foreign taxable income	$10,000,000
− Foreign income taxes (20%)	$ 2,000,000
= Net income of subsidiary	$ 8,000,000
= Gross dividend (100%)	$ 8,000,000
− Dividend withholding tax (10%)	$ 800,000
= Net dividend received by the parent	$ 7,200,000
Income retained by subsidiary	-0-
B. Foreign Income (Country X)—Taxable in U.S.	
Net dividend received by the parent	$ 7,200,000
+ Foreign corporate income taxes	$ 2,000,000
+ Foreign dividend withholding tax paid	$ 800,000
= Foreign income taxable in U.S.	$10,000,000
C. U.S. Tax Payable on Subsidiary Income—Country X	
Foreign income taxable in U.S.	$10,000,000
× U.S. tax rate (34%)	
= Tentative U.S. tax	$ 3,400,000
− Foreign tax credit*	$ 2,800,000
= U.S. taxes payable	$ 600,000
D. Net Benefit to the Parent	
Net dividend received by the parent	$ 7,200,000
− U.S. taxes payable	$ 600,000
= Net benefit to the parent	$ 6,600,000

*Since all (100 percent) earnings are sent to the parent, all foreign income taxes and withholding taxes can be taken as a foreign tax credit in the United States.

Computation of the U.S. Tax

We are now in a position to compute the U.S. taxes payable by Donegal on the income received from its foreign subsidiary. As shown in Part C of Table 15-5, the Donegal Corporation's tentative tax is $3,400,000 (34 percent of taxable income). The firm, however, can claim as a credit all foreign income taxes paid in the foreign country. In this case, it is $2,800,000. The foreign tax credit is simply the sum of foreign income taxes and withholding taxes. Note that property, royalty, and advertising taxes (Table 15-4) are not considered income taxes. Thus, the firm must pay an additional tax of $600,000 in the United States. The net benefit to Donegal is computed by subtracting the U.S. tax payable from the dividend received. In this case, it is equal to $6,600,000.

This illustration provides a useful insight into one of the major features of U.S. tax law as it relates to foreign income. Specifically, if foreign taxes are lower than taxes in the United States, additional taxes will be paid in the United States on repatriation of dividends. The total tax paid on the foreign income will be exactly the same as if the income were earned in the United States. If the Donegal Corporation had earned $10,000,000 in the United States, it would have paid tax at a rate of 34 percent, for a total U.S. tax of $3,400,000. The firm paid exactly the same amount of tax on the $10,000,000 in foreign income. It paid $2,800,000 to the foreign government and $600,000 to the U.S. government, for a total of $3,400,000. It is clear that American firms are not able to reduce total income-related taxes by shifting operations and income to low-tax foreign locations.[9]

Foreign Tax Rates Higher Than U.S. Rates

What happens if foreign income tax rates are higher than those in the United States? This scenario is illustrated in Table 15-6, which assumes that Donegal has a subsidiary in Country Y rather than in Country X. In every way, the subsidiary in Country Y is the same as the subsidiary in Country X, except that the tax rate in Country Y is 40 percent (rather than 20 percent, as in the Country X example). As shown in the Country Y illustration, the higher tax rate means that this subsidiary has higher taxes and lower net income. This, of course, translates into a lower dividend paid to the Donegal Corporation. Note, however, that the foreign taxable income in the United States is exactly the same ($10,000,000) as before.

The most interesting part of Table 15-6 is Part C, the computation of the tax payable in the United States. While the subsidiary has paid $4,600,000 in foreign income and withholding taxes, only $3,400,000 can be used as a foreign tax credit. This reflects the fact that the U.S. tax law does not permit taking a foreign tax credit in excess of the tentative tax liability. In a sense, the subsidiary has $1,200,000 in potential tax credit that cannot be used (given the assumptions of our illustration). Specifically, the $1,200,000 cannot be used to offset Donegal's U.S. taxes on domestic income.[10] Taxes on domestic income are kept separate from taxes on foreign income.

We can now see how the United States coordinates its corporate income tax with those of other nations. If the foreign tax is lower than the U.S. tax (Country X), additional taxes will be paid in the United States. This eliminates the tax reduction incentive to locate operations in foreign countries with very low tax rates. On the other hand, if taxes in foreign countries are higher than those in the United States, the firm pays the higher foreign tax. In such a case, a firm would, in effect, be paying a

---

[9]American firms are, however, able to postpone the U.S. tax, and this may have significant financial advantages.

[10]The excess foreign tax credits can be carried forward.

TABLE 15-6 Donegal Corporation: U.S. Tax on Foreign
Subsidiary Income—Country Y [All Income (100%) Sent to parent]

A. Subsidiary Income Statement	
Foreign taxable income	$10,000,000
− Foreign income taxes (40%)	$ 4,000,000
= Gross dividend paid by the sub.	$ 6,000,000
− Dividend withholding tax (10%)	$ 600,000
= Net dividend received by the parent	$ 5,400,000
Income retained by the subsidiary	-0-
B. Foreign Taxable Income—Country Y	
Net dividend received by the parent	$ 5,400,000
+ Foreign corporate income taxes paid	$ 4,000,000
+ Foreign dividend withholding tax paid	$ 600,000
= Foreign taxable income	$10,000,000
C. U.S. Tax Payable on Subsidiary Income—Country Y	
Foreign income taxable in the U.S.	$10,000,000
× U.S. tax rate (34%)	
= Tentative U.S. tax	$ 3,400,000
− Foreign tax credit*	$ 3,400,000
= U.S. taxes payable	-0-
D. Net Benefit to the Parent	
Net dividend received by the parent	$ 5,400,000
− U.S. taxes payable	-0-
= Net benefit to the parent	$ 5,400,000

*The foreign tax credit cannot exceed the amount of the tentative U.S. tax liability. Even though the subsidiary in Country Y paid $4,600,000 in income and withholding taxes, the maximum foreign tax credit allowed in the preceding situation is $3,400,000.

tax penalty for operating in a foreign country rather than the United States. Thus, foreign subsidiaries of American corporations are taxed no less, and possibly more, than operations located in the United States.

Combining Income from Foreign Operations

American corporations with more than one foreign subsidiary are required to combine the income and tax credits of their subsidiaries. This situation is illustrated in Table 15-7, which assumes that the Donegal Corporation operates subsidiaries in both Country X and Country Y (Tables 15-5 and 15-6). The combined foreign taxable income is simply the sum of the taxable incomes of the two subsidiaries. The U.S. tax is then computed just as if a single subsidiary is involved. Note that by combining the incomes of the two subsidiaries, the Donegal Corporation pays less income tax than if the subsidiaries were taxed separately. This reflects the fact that, if taxed separately, the subsidiary in Country X would have

TABLE 15-7 Donegal Corporation: U.S. Tax on Combined Income of Subsidiaries

A. Subsidiary Income Statements

	Country X	Country Y	Combined
Taxable income	$10,000,000	$10,000,000	$20,000,000
Income taxes	$ 2,000,000	$ 4,000,000	$ 6,000,000
Gross dividend	$ 8,000,000	$ 6,000,000	$14,000,000
Withholding tax	$ 800,000	$ 600,000	$ 1,400,000
Net dividend	$ 7,200,000	$ 5,400,000	$12,600,000
Income retained	-0-	-0-	-0-

B. Combined Foreign Taxable Income

Net dividends received by the parent	$12,600,000
+ Foreign corporate income taxes paid	$ 6,000,000
+ Foreign dividend withholding tax paid	$ 1,400,000
= Foreign income taxable in U.S.	$20,000,000

C. U.S. Tax on Combined Income of Subsidiaries

Foreign income taxable in U.S.	$20,000,000
× U.S. tax rate (34%)	
= Tentative U.S. tax	$ 6,800,000
− Foreign tax credit*	$ 6,800,000
= U.S. taxes payable	-0-

D. Net Benefit to the Parent

Net dividends received by the parent	$12,600,000
− U.S. taxes payable	-0-
= Net benefit to the parent	$12,600,000

*Combined, the subsidiaries paid $6,000,000 in income taxes and $1,400,000 in withholding taxes, for a total of $7,400,000. Only $6,800,000 can be used, since the size of the foreign tax credit cannot exceed the tentative U.S. tax.

had to pay $600,000 in taxes, while the Country Y subsidiary would have had an excess foreign tax credit of $1,200,000. Combining the two subsidiaries has the effect of using the excess tax credit of the Country Y subsidiary to offset the tax due on income from the subsidiary in Country X. Table 15-7 shows that while excess foreign tax credits cannot be used to offset taxes due on domestic income, they can be used to offset taxes due on other foreign income.

When combining income to compute the combined foreign tax credit, certain types of income cannot be included. This income, which is usually called *Subpart F income*, includes financial services income, shipping income, and other forms of passive income. This income may be fully taxable in the United States, and taxes paid in other countries cannot be used to offset the U.S. tax liability on passive income. This provision of the U.S. tax law is designed to prevent firms from artificially transferring income to tax havens and then using excess foreign tax credits to offset taxes that would have to be paid on the transferred amounts. In effect, only foreign income from an active and productive operation can be used in computing the combined foreign income tax credit.

Partial Repatriation of Earnings

Thus far, our discussion of the Donegal Corporation has assumed that 100 percent or all earnings are repatriated to the parent.[11] Of course, not all foreign subsidiaries send back all of their earnings. Often funds are retained by and reinvested in the subsidiary. Remember that the subsidiary is controlled by the parent (100 percent ownership), and if earnings are retained abroad, it is the decision of the parent. The retention of earnings at the subsidiary level indicates that the parent corporation is increasing its equity investment in the foreign operation. The decision to retain earnings at the foreign subsidiary level has tax implications in the United States, since income retained abroad is not subject to American income taxation. If the entire income of subsidiaries is retained abroad, the parent has no U.S. income tax liability. If only part of the income of the subsidiary is repatriated to the American parent, only the repatriated portion of such income is subject to U.S. taxation.

The procedures for computing the tax paid by and the benefit to the parent are a little more complicated and are illustrated in Table 15-8. The illustration focuses on Donegal's subsidiary in Country X, but this time we assume that only 40 percent of the subsidiary's earnings are paid as a dividend to the parent. Note that the subsidiary income statement looks just as it did before, since there has been no change in the subsidiary's revenues or expenses. However, the foreign income taxable in the United States is very different than under the earlier assumptions. Now the parent is obligated to pay American income taxes on only $4,000,000. Notice that the grossing-up procedure used to arrive at taxable income in the United States includes only a portion of the subsidiary's income (40 percent) and a portion of the subsidiary's foreign income taxes (40 percent). All of the withholding taxes are included in the foreign income that is taxable in the United States. When computing the foreign tax credit needed to arrive at the U.S. tax payable, the same proportions of income and taxes are used. The actual percentage that applies reflects the percentage of income repatriated to the parent. Withholding taxes (100 percent) are always used both in grossing up and in computing the foreign tax credit.

---

[11] The word *repatriated* as used in this book refers to sending funds back to the home country. When a foreign subsidiary makes a payment to its American parent, it is repatriating funds.

TABLE 15-8 Donegal Corporation: U.S. Tax on Foreign Subsidiary
Income—Country X (40% of subsidiary Income Repatriated)

A. Subsidiary Income Statement	
Foreign taxable income	$10,000,000
− Foreign income taxes (20%)	$ 2,000,000
= Net income of subsidiary	$ 8,000,000
Gross dividend (40%)	$ 3,200,000
− Dividend withholding tax (10%)	$ 320,000
= Net dividend received by the parent	$ 2,880,000
Income retained by subsidiary	$ 4,800,000
B. Foreign Income (Country X)—Taxable in U.S.	
Net dividend received by the parent	$ 2,880,000
+ Foreign corporate income taxes	$ 800,000
+ Foreign dividend withholding tax paid	$ 320,000
= Foreign income taxable in U.S.	$ 4,000,000
C. U.S. Tax Payable on Subsidiary Income—Country X	
Foreign income taxable in U.S.	$ 4,000,000
× U.S. tax rate (34%)	
= Tentative U.S. tax	$ 1,360,000
− Foreign tax credit*	$ 1,120,000
= U.S. taxes payable	$ 240,000
D. Net Benefit to the Parent	
Net dividend received by the parent	$ 2,880,000
− U.S. taxes payable	$ 240,000
= Net benefit to the parent	$ 2,640,000

*Since only 40% of the subsidiary's income is repatriated, only 40% of the foreign taxes are used
when grossing up to determine the foreign income taxable in the United States. One hundred percent
of withholding taxes are included. These same amounts are used to compute the foreign tax credit.

Conditions Favoring the Retention of Earnings by Foreign Subsidiaries

The design of the U.S. corporate income tax allows multinational corporations to escape American taxation on the income earned by a foreign
subsidiary, but only so long as that income is not repatriated to the
parent. This tax provision may be useful to the American multinational as
long as both of the following characteristics are present: (1) the foreign
corporate tax rate is lower than the U.S. corporate tax rate, and (2) there
are stockholder wealth-enhancing opportunities available outside the
United States. While in the past U.S. corporate tax rates were very high
by world standards, this is no longer the case. As American corporate tax
rates decline, the incentive to allow subsidiaries to retain income may be
lessened. If American tax rates are below those of other countries,
American multinationals pay no tax penalty for bringing funds back to

the United States, even if the funds are eventually reinvested abroad. Since most foreign governments would like to encourage American investment (and the employment and income that follow it), it will be interesting to see if they lower their own corporate tax rates in order to attract the reinvestment of earnings.

But more than low foreign tax rates are needed to encourage American firms to reinvest the earnings of foreign subsidiaries. The objective of the firm is to maximize stockholder wealth (not to minimize taxes), and poor prospects for economic growth, strong competition, unfavorable government policies, and many other factors could more than offset any advantageous tax rate. The management of the American multinational must weigh all of these factors before deciding to retain earnings in foreign countries. It is perfectly possible that stockholder wealth could be increased by bringing funds back to the United States, even if additional taxes may have to be paid to the U.S. government.

Repatriation of Retained Earnings

Firms sometimes retain income at the subsidiary level for a number of years and then repatriate the funds. At the time of repatriation, U.S. income tax is payable at the prevailing income tax rate. Assume, for example, that our subsidiary in Table 15-8 has been operating in Country X for 5 years, and each year the situation was exactly the same as described in the illustration.

1. Each year the foreign subsidiary would have retained $4,800,000. At the end of 5 years, total retained earnings would be equal to $24,000,000 (5 × $4,800,000). If these earnings are sent to the parent, they are fully taxable. The parent would receive a dividend of $21,600,000 (reduced by the $2,400,000 withholding tax).
2. Each year the foreign subsidiary paid $2,000,000 in foreign income tax. But only $800,000 per year was claimed as a credit in the United States. In effect, the subsidiary had an unused foreign tax credit of $1,200,000 for each year. At the end of 5 years, this would amount to $6,000,000. If the firm repatriates all of its retained earnings, it would also be allowed to use all of this unused foreign tax credit.

The actual procedures used to compute the U.S. tax payable are the same as those described in Table 15-8. Total foreign income taxable in the United States would be equal to $30,000,000 ($21,600,000 dividend + $2,400,000 withholding + $6,000,000 foreign income tax). The tentative U.S. income tax liability would be $10,200,000. The firm, however, would only have to pay $1,800,000 in U.S. taxes, since it could claim $8,400,000 in foreign tax credits. Thus, its benefit would be equal to $19,800,000 ($21,600,000 received − $1,800,000 taxes).

One final point about repatriating funds from foreign operations is in order. Presumably, the multinational corporation made an initial monetary investment in the foreign subsidiary. If the subsidiary is sold, the parent corporation recaptures its initial investment. This recapture is not income and is not subject to income tax in either the United States or the foreign country.[12] Assume, for example, that the Donegal Corporation invested $20,000,000 in its Country X subsidiary. If the subsidiary is sold, the first $20,000,000 is not taxable.[13] Only income is subject to the income tax.

Controlled Foreign Corporation

The possibility of deferring U.S. taxes on corporate income by taking advantage of the tax provisions relating to foreign subsidiaries has not escaped the notice of corporate tax planners. If tax planners were left to their own devices, they would shift as much income as possible to a foreign subsidiary located in a country that has very low tax rates and then retain the income in that subsidiary. Why not create a foreign subsidiary in a tax haven country, with a very low tax rate, and use it to conduct all foreign operations? The tax haven subsidiary would be owned 100 percent by the American parent and would, in turn, own 100 percent of all operating and productive foreign subsidiaries. Using this device, dividends from the real foreign subsidiaries could be paid to the tax haven subsidiary, thus avoiding payment of U.S. taxes. In addition, some of the profits of the real foreign subsidiaries, and in some instances of the American parent, could be transferred to the tax haven subsidiary through intracorporate transfer price manipulation and the use of fees.

Of course, multinational firms do not have an unrestricted ability to shift profits from one country to another. Most countries have tax enforcement agencies that vigorously monitor corporations to ensure that reported profits give a fair representation of economic activity.[14] In order to eliminate some of these abuses and ensure that foreign tax haven subsidiaries are not used to defer American income taxes on foreign income, Congress created the *controlled foreign corporation (CFC) rules*. A controlled foreign corporation is defined as a foreign corporation in

---

[12]An analogy from personal finance makes this point quite clear. Assume that you deposit $10,000 in a savings account and withdraw it at a later date. Naturally, you would be expected to pay income taxes on the interest earned. You would not be expected, however, to pay taxes on the original $10,000 deposit.

[13]We are ignoring the issue of depreciation. This will be discussed in Chapter 16.

[14]Section 482 allows the Internal Revenue Service to ensure that the transfer price between related corporations is not used to evade taxes. This issue was discussed in Chapter 13.

which 50 percent or more of the voting power is owned by fewer than 10 U.S. citizens. Almost all foreign subsidiaries owned by American firms are CFCs. If a foreign corporation is classified as a CFC, the Internal Revenue Service has the power to *deem* that a dividend has been paid to the American parent, even though no actual dividend has been paid, and the American parent would then be required to pay U.S. income tax on the deemed income. In other words, if the Internal Revenue Service believes that income is being shifted to the tax haven subsidiary solely to defer U.S. taxes, it will require that taxes be paid even though the income has not been paid to the parents in the form of a dividend. The Internal Revenue Service scrutinizes each CFC to see how its income is earned. Special attention is paid to subsidiaries located in tax haven countries and to foreign subsidiaries of American corporations that do not produce anything and receive their income from such things as dividends, sales, services and shipping income, and other passive or non-production-related income.

Taxation of Foreign Branches

Thus far, it has been assumed that the foreign operations of our hypothetical American multinational firm have been organized as foreign subsidiaries. The Donegal Corporation has a subsidiary in Country X and another in Country Y, each of which has its own legal identity. But it is also possible for a multinational firm to organize foreign operations as branches of the parent corporation. When a branch is utilized, there is no separate foreign corporation. The foreign operations are an integral part of the American parent.

Perhaps a domestic analogy will make the difference between a foreign branch and a foreign subsidiary a little clearer. Assume that you own a successful restaurant in San Francisco and desire to open another in Los Angeles. You could set up the Los Angeles restaurant as a subsidiary of the parent.[15] This means that the new restaurant is a separate legal entity. If it fails and goes bankrupt, the parent is not responsible. On the other hand, the Los Angeles restaurant could be organized as branch, in which case it is not a separate legal entity. It is part of the firm in the same way that an arm is part of the human body. The parent is completely responsible for the branch.

In the United States, income from foreign branches is taxed differently than income from foreign subsidiaries. The general principle is that all of the income (and losses) of a foreign branch must be recognized

---

[15]Alternatively, a holding company could be established and each of the restaurants could be organized as a separate subsidiary.

TABLE 15-9 Donegal Corporation: U.S. Tax on Foreign Branch Income—Country X (40% of Branch Income Repatriated)

A. Branch Income Statement

Foreign taxable income	$10,000,000
− Foreign income taxes (20%)	$ 2,000,000
= Net income of branch	$ 8,000,000
Payment to parent (40%)	$ 3,200,000
− Withholding tax on payment (10%)	$ 320,000
= Amount received by the parent	$ 2,880,000
Income retained by the branch	$ 4,800,000

B. Foreign Income (Country X)—Taxable in U.S.

Foreign income taxable in U.S.	$10,000,000

C. U.S. Tax Payable on Branch Income—Country X

Foreign income taxable in U.S.	$10,000,000
×U.S. tax rate (34%)	
= Tentative U.S. tax	$ 3,400,000
− Foreign tax credit*	$ 2,320,000
= U.S. taxes payable	$ 1,080,000

D. Net Benefit to the Parent

Amount received by the parent	$ 2,880,000
− U.S. tax payable	$ 1,080,000
= Net benefit to the parent	$ 1,800,000

*When foreign operations are organized as a branch, all foreign income taxes and all foreign withholding taxes are taken as a tax credit in the United States.

immediately by the parent. As we have seen, this differs from the tax treatment afforded foreign subsidiary income, which is taxed only when it is received by the parent. Table 15-9 shows how foreign branch income is taxed differently than foreign subsidiary income. The scenario for Table 15-9 is the same as for Table 15-8, except that the foreign operation is assumed to be a branch. The foreign operation still has the same taxable income, still pays the same foreign income tax (20 percent), and still pays 40 percent of its net income to its American parent. All that differs is the form of organization.

The first part of the two tables is identical, reflecting the fact that the form of organization has nothing to do with the foreign operations themselves. We are interested in what happens in the United States.[16] The difference in tax treatment shows up dramatically in Part B of Table 15-9. All (100 percent) of the taxable income of the foreign subsidiary is taxed in the United States.[17] It does not matter that the foreign branch

---

[16]Some foreign governments do tax subsidiaries differently than they do foreign branches.

[17]We assume that the foreign government has not imposed any restrictions on the outflow of its currency.

forwarded only $3,200,000 to its American owner; $10,000,000 is taxed. While the American parent must report all of the taxable income of its foreign branch as income in the United States, it is permitted to include all foreign income and withholding taxes in the computation of the foreign tax credit. Nevertheless, in the scenarios depicted in Tables 15-8 and 15-9, the branch form of organization clearly results in higher U.S. taxes. It is interesting to note that if the foreign subsidiary remitted all (100 percent) of its income to the parent (rather than only 40 percent), the U.S. tax would be identical to that paid by the foreign branch. Thus, the taxes paid in Table 15-5 (a subsidiary repatriating 100 percent of income) and Table 15-9 are exactly the same (ignoring withholding taxes). It is the ability of the foreign subsidiary to retain and shield foreign income from U.S. taxes that sometimes gives it an advantage.

Form of Organization and American Taxes

Foreign subsidiaries do not always have a tax advantage over foreign branches. Possible organizational scenarios can be grouped into three categories.

Category 1: From a U.S. taxation perspective, it is attractive for an American parent to organize foreign operations in the form of a foreign subsidiary whenever (a) the foreign subsidiary is earning a profit *and* (b) U.S. taxes are higher than foreign taxes, *and* (c) favorable investment opportunities are available outside the United States.

Category 2: From a U.S. taxation perspective, the American parent can gain a tax advantage by organizing foreign operations as a branch whenever the foreign operation is generating losses.

Category 3: American tax law does not favor either type of organization (even if the foreign operation is earning a profit) whenever (a) foreign taxes are higher than U.S. taxes *or* (b) there are no stockholder wealth-enhancing investments available outside the United States.

The illustration presented in Table 15-9 shows two of the conditions that favor the use of a foreign subsidiary (Category 1), since the foreign operations are earning a profit and foreign taxes are lower than U.S. taxes. However, retaining earnings abroad will enhance stockholder wealth if, and only if, the firm can invest the funds profitably. In other words, if a firm can earn a much higher rate of return on the funds in the United States, it may be beneficial to bring all of the funds back to the United States, pay the additional American taxes, and then invest the funds in the United States. The fact that foreign taxes are lower than

American taxes does not always mean that funds will be retained abroad. However, Category 1 represents the classical case for American business. In the past, American taxes were higher than foreign taxes, and many American firms were optimistic about the profitability of foreign investments. Thus, the general tendency for American multinationals to organize foreign operations as subsidiaries has been at least partly attributed to tax-saving considerations.

Category 3 conditions are such that U.S. taxes will not be affected one way or another by the form of business organization chosen for foreign operations. American taxes will be the same whether the operations are organized as a branch or a subsidiary. If foreign tax rates are higher than U.S. tax rates, the subsidiary will generate more foreign tax credits than can be used. The parent corporation will not pay any additional U.S. tax on the foreign income whether that income is retained abroad or sent back to the parent in the United States. This implies that if American tax rates continue to fall relative to foreign tax rates, the tax incentive for organizing foreign operations as subsidiaries will decrease.

Expected losses associated with foreign operations encourage the American parent to organize the operations as a branch. Of course, a firm does not make an investment either at home or abroad, if losses are expected to persist for a long period of time. But many business operations are characterized by losses in the early years, hopefully followed by many profitable years. In such a case, the American parent may be better off, from a tax point of view, if the losses accrue to a branch rather than a subsidiary. This follows from the fact that the branch is a part of its parent. Just as all income of the branch must be recognized by the parent, all losses can also be recognized. Thus, if a new foreign branch shows a $1,000,000 loss in its first year, the loss will immediately reduce taxable income and taxes in the United States. A loss for a foreign subsidiary is treated very differently. It is not immediately recognized by the parent and does not result in an immediate reduction in U.S. taxes. Instead, it is carried forward and applied against future income. Thus, if the foreign subsidiary had a $1,000,000 loss in its first year and taxable income of $1,000,000 in its second year, the loss in the first year would be applied against the income in the second year and no taxes would be paid in the second year.[18] If subsidiary losses persisted and continued to accumulate, they could not be recognized by the American parent until the foreign subsidiary was liquidated. This tax treatment of foreign subsidiaries is less advantageous than that of branches.

If American firms were concerned solely with minimization of taxes, new foreign ventures would tend to be organized initially as branches. The branch form of organization would be maintained until foreign

---

[18]This assumes that foreign taxes are lower than U.S. taxes and that all earnings are repatriated.

operations began to show a profit, at which point they would be reorganized as a subsidiary (assuming that Category 1 conditions exist). Of course, factors other than taxes enter into the decision about the organization of foreign operations. The subsidiary form is favored in cases where the American parent is concerned about limiting its liability or would like to have a joint venture with another investor. The branch form may be more appropriate when the parent wants to lend its full resources to the foreign operation. For example, American banks have followed the branch strategy. Taxes are important, but they are not the sole factor that is considered when deciding on the organizational form that is most desirable for foreign operations.

U.S. Taxation of Exports by American Firms

Thus far, our discussion of American taxation has focused on the multinational firm that has a physical presence in a foreign country. What about taxation of the revenue that a domestic American firm generates when it sells to foreign buyers? If the domestic firm simply sells to a foreign buyer, the revenue derived from the sale is treated exactly the same way as the revenue from a domestic sale. Thus, no special tax considerations are involved when an American clothing manufacturer sells garments to a British department store.

The U.S. government, however, does try to stimulate exports and has created a tax incentive for exporters. In order to get this advantage, however, the exporter must conform to certain rules. American firms are permitted to establish foreign sales corporations in order to reduce American income taxes on income from exports.[19] A foreign sales corporation is a corporation that is owned by an American firm and is established to facilitate sales to foreigners. The corporation must have a permanent foreign office and be managed outside the United States. The foreign sales corporation is a separate legal entity that solicits and negotiates sales to foreigners outside the United States.

Some of the profits of the foreign sales corporation are exempt from U.S. taxation even if the income on such sales is repatriated to the United States. In other words, the parent will have to pay U.S. taxes on only some of the dividends received from the foreign sales corporation. The computation of the amount of income from the foreign sales corporation

---

[19] The foreign sales corporation is the latest vehicle designed to provide tax incentives to exporters. In the past, domestic international sales corporations and Western Hemisphere trade corporations accomplished similar objectives.

that is exempt from taxation is complex and thus is not explained in this book. However, it is clear that an American firm with significant export sales should consider establishing a foreign sales corporation in order to reduce taxes.

Summary and Conclusions

This chapter provided an introduction to some of the important tax considerations affecting the international operations of American firms. It began by explaining that firms operating in foreign countries are subject to a number of different taxes. The value-added tax is a significant business tax in Western Europe, and the royalty tax is often the largest tax levied against mining and oil companies. Significant income taxes are also levied against foreign operations of American corporations.

The U.S. tax law is structured in such a way that foreign income taxes are coordinated with U.S. taxes through the foreign tax credit. The foreign tax credit is designed so that American firms with operating units located in foreign countries with lower taxes than those in the United States will have to pay additional U.S. taxes. The additional taxes will be just large enough to bring the total tax bill on the foreign income up to the amount that would have been paid had the income been earned in the United States. When foreign taxes are higher than American taxes, the firm pays more taxes than would have been paid if the income had been earned in the United States. In other words, foreign income is taxed at either the U.S. or the foreign tax rate, whichever is higher. On the surface, at least, there is no income tax advantage associated with shifting operations to a foreign country.

However, the ability of an American multinational corporation to organize foreign operations in the form of a corporate subsidiary and retain earnings in the subsidiary does permit a postponement of corporate income taxes in the United States, and this may be valuable to the multinational parent. In order for the postponement feature of the tax law to have value to the American firm, the foreign subsidiary must be operating at a profit in a country that has lower taxes than the United States. Whether the foreign operations of an American multinational should be organized as a branch or a subsidiary depends on a number of factors. A new foreign operation that expects to operate at a loss in its early years may best be organized as a branch and later converted to a subsidiary. Subsidiaries are most attractive when foreign tax rates are lower than those in the United States.

The reader should keep several things in mind. First, international taxation is a complicated topic, and this chapter has done no more than provide a basic introduction. Firms engaged in international commerce need expert tax advice, and this is available from the large accounting firms. Second, tax laws, both in the United States and in foreign countries, are revised regularly, and such changes may alter the optimal business strategy. Third, business decisions are not based solely on tax considerations. The business executive must have a broad view of the decision-making process.

Review Questions

1. What are the differences between sales, turnover, and value-added taxes? Give numerical examples.
2. What are tariffs, and how do they affect the firm engaged in international commerce?
3. What are withholding taxes on international payments, and how do they affect the firm engaged in international commerce?
4. Why is it often difficult for the multinational firm to determine the country in which income is earned and the country in which expenses are incurred? What are the implications of these difficulties for tax preparation by the multinational firm?
5. Which foreign taxes can and cannot be included in the U.S. foreign tax credit? If you were managing an American multinational firm, how would you prefer to be taxed by foreign governments?
6. Under which conditions would organizing foreign operations as a branch (rather than as a subsidiary) reduce the worldwide income taxes paid by an American multinational firm? Which conditions would encourage the use of the subsidiary form of organization?
7. "When the foreign tax credit available to the U.S. multinational firm exceeds its tentative tax liability on foreign income, the excess foreign tax credit is lost forever." True or false? Explain your answer.
8. How and when is income retained by a foreign subsidiary taxed in the United States?
9. "It is possible to pay higher income taxes in a country with a lower income tax rate." True or false? Explain your answer.
10. Is it possible (for U.S. tax purposes) to combine income and foreign tax credits from foreign subsidiaries located in different countries?
11. Under which conditions is it likely that the Internal Revenue Service will deem that a subsidiary has paid a dividend to its American parent when in fact no dividend has been recorded? What are the implications of the fact that the Service has the power to deem the payment of dividends?
12. How could an American exporter use a foreign sales corporation to reduce American taxes on income associated with exports?

Questions for Discussion

1. Assume that you are employed by an American manufacturer of high-quality molded plastic products used in the manufacture of machines and electronic equipment. Your firm currently produces in the United States and sells to machinery and equipment manufacturers throughout the world. Since a large percentage of its foreign sales are made to European firms, your firm is considering building a production facility within the boundaries of the EEC. You are asked to study this

possible course of action from a tax perspective. Specifically, you are asked to consider the following issues:

a. Will building a facility in Europe increase or decrease the tax bill of the corporation as a whole?

b. Is it better to organize this operation as a foreign subsidiary or as a foreign branch?

You have completed a tentative review of these issues and find that you do not have the information needed to make a final recommendation. Your manager asks you to draw up a list of the information that you need.

2. Assume that you are employed by a domestic American firm that is considering building a production facility in a foreign country and organizing it as a foreign subsidiary. The income tax rate in the foreign country is only 10 percent. The top management of your firm believes that this will be of no value to them, since additional taxes will be levied in the United States. You have been assigned the task of analyzing the situation and developing strategies that would allow the firm to capitalize on the lower foreign income tax rate.

3. Assume that you are employed by a domestic American corporation that is considering building a production facility in a foreign country and organizing it as a foreign subsidiary. The income tax rate in the foreign country is a very high 60 percent. This means that taxes on foreign income will be higher than taxes on domestic income. You are asked to study the situation and develop strategies for reducing the total tax bill of the firm.

Research Activities

1. Determine the maximum corporate tax rate in the following countries: the United States, Canada, France, Great Britain, Italy, Japan, West Germany.
2. Determine the dividend, interest and royalty withholding tax rate in the following countries: the United States, Canada, France, Great Britain, Italy, Japan, West Germany.

Problems

1. Prepare a schedule of value-added taxes payable, using a format similar to that presented in Table 15-1. Base your table on the following information:

> Farmers sell wheat to millers for $300
> Millers sell flour to bakeries fr $500
> Bakeries sell bread to the public for $800

Assume that these are the only inputs and that the value-added tax is 12 percent.

2. The AnnCa Corporation has a foreign subsidiary in Country *A*. The subsidiary has the following financial information:

> | | |
> |---|---|
> | Revenues | $50 million |
> | Labor and raw materials | $25 million |
> | Property taxes | $ 5 million |
> | Royalties on minerals | $ 4 million |
> | Selling expenses | $ 8 million |

The foreign country has a 15 percent corporate income tax rate. In addition, the foreign government imposes a 10 percent withholding tax on any repatriated dividends. The subsidiary repatriates all income after taxes. The U.S. corporate tax rate is 34 percent. Calculate the net benefit received by the parent.

3. The AnnCa Corporation has a foreign subsidiary in Country B. The subsidiary has the following financial information (ignore Problem 2):

Revenues	$130 million
Labor and raw materials	$ 70 million
Property taxes	$ 20 million
Advertising expenses	$ 20 million

The foreign country has a 50 percent corporate income tax rate. The foreign government, however, does not impose a withholding tax on any repatriated dividends. The subsidiary repatriates all income after taxes. The U.S. corporate tax rate is 34 percent. Calculate the net benefit received by the parent.

4. Using the information provided in Problems 2 and 3, prepare a consolidated estimate of the net benefits received by the parent.

5. Using the information provided in Problem 2, and assuming that the subsidiary repatriates only 30 percent of its earnings, calculate the following:
   a. Annual net benefit to the parent.
   b. After 10 years (each year is exactly the same), the subsidiary repatriates all its retained earnings. Calculate the net benefit of this distribution to the parent.

6. The Donegal Corporation has foreign operations in Country A. These operations are organized as a branch. The branch has the following financial information:

Revenues	$500 million
Labor and raw materials	$200 million
Property taxes	$ 50 million
Royalty taxes	$ 40 million
Selling expenses	$ 10 million

The foreign country has a 20 percent business income tax rate. In addition, the foreign government imposes a 10 percent withholding tax on any repatriated income. The U.S. corporate tax rate is 34 percent.
   a. Calculate the net benefit received by the parent if the branch repatriates all income after taxes.
   b. Calculate the net benefit received by the parent if the branch repatriates 40 percent of income after taxes.

Bibliography

Bavishi, Vinod B., and Wyman, Harold E. "Foreign Operations Disclosures by U.S. Based Multinational Corporations: Are They Adequate?" *International Journal of Accounting*, Fall 1980, pp. 153–168.

Burns, Jane O. "Transfer Pricing Decisions in U.S. Multinational Corporations." *Journal of International Business Studies*, Fall 1980, pp. 23–39.

Ernst & Whinney. *1988 Foreign and U.S. Corporate and Withholding Tax Rates*. New York: Ernst & Whinney, 1988.

Hartman, David G. "Tax Policy and Foreign Direct Investment in the United States." *National Tax Journal*, December 1984, pp. 475–487.

Heyde, Robert D. "Interplay of Capital Gains and Foreign Tax Credit." *Tax Executive*, July 1980, pp. 257–267.

Horst, Thomas. "American Taxation of Multinational Firms." *American Economic Review*, June 1977, pp. 376–389.

Howard, Fred. "Overview of International Taxation." *Columbia Journal of World Business*, Summer 1975, pp. 5–11.

Kaplan, Wayne S. "Foreign Sales Corporations: Politics and Pragmatics." *Tax Executive*, April 1985, pp. 203–220.

Kopits, George F. "Taxation and Multinational Firm Behavior: A Critical Survey." *IMF Staff Papers*, November 1976, pp. 624–673.

Madison, Roland L. "Responsibility Accounting and Transfer Pricing: Approach with Caution." *Management Accounting*, January 1979, pp. 25–29.

Paules, Edward P. "A Guide Through the Tax Maze." *Euromoney*, October 1980, pp. 252–260.

Price Waterhouse. *U.S. Corporations Doing Business Abroad*. New York: Price Waterhouse, 1982.

Sale, Timothy J. "Tax Planning Tools for the Multinational Corporation." *Management Accounting*, June 1979, pp. 37–41.

Williams, Thomas J. "The Credibility of Foreign Income Taxes: An Overview." *Taxes*, October 1980, pp. 699–709.

16

International Dimensions of Long-Term Asset Acquisitions

American firms often consider the option of investing in foreign countries. An American company may have the opportunity to build a factory in England, buy a department store chain in Italy, develop an oil field in Indonesia, or establish a banking facility in Japan. This type of investment typically involves a very large outlay by the American owner, and the returns are expected to be spread over a long period of time. Figure 16-1 provides a picture of this process. Typically, the investment is made in the early years (in this illustration, the first 2 years), and returns extend into the distant future. Since the typical long-term asset acquisition involves very large outlays, decisions relating to such acquisitions are closely analyzed by the firm. It is not easy to estimate the size of the investment, the estimated future cash inflows, the timing of those cash inflows, and the certainty attached to the estimates of both cash outflows and inflows. Thus, analyzing long-term asset acquisitions is usually a time-consuming (months, even years) and expensive process.

The basic logic used to evaluate foreign long-term asset acquisitions is the same as that applied to domestic acquisitions. In both cases, it is necessary to estimate the cash flows, estimate an appropriate cost of

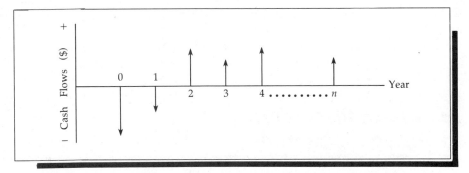

FIGURE 16-1 Typical pattern of cash flows long-term asset acquisitions

capital, and then evaluate the cash flows. In the international environment, however, the situation is more complex. There are special factors that are crucial for evaluating the cash flows of a foreign long-term investment. This chapter will examine those special factors that must be incorporated into long-term asset acquisition decisions when the asset is located in a foreign country. Remember, however, that the conceptual framework for the international decision is the same as that used in regard to the acquisition of domestic long-term assets.[1]

The presentation that follows will be organized into eight sections.

1. We will first examine the volume as well as the reasons for American foreign direct investment.
2. We will then examine the procedure used by a foreigner to evaluate an investment project in his or her own country. This is effectively a domestic investment. We will also consider how this same investment project looks from an American investor's point of view. We will assume that there are no restrictions on the movement of currency from one country to another, that taxes are the same in both countries, and that there are no exchange rate or political risks associated with the foreign investment.
3. Next, we will show how differences in national taxes affect the desirability of the project to the American investor.
4. We will then show how the investment decision can be affected by government restrictions on the movement of currencies from one country to another.
5. Following this, we will evaluate the impact of foreign exchange fluctuations on the decision to invest in the project.
6. The impact of risk on the project's cost of capital and its net present value will be discussed next.

---

[1]See Eugene F. Brigham, *Fundamentals of Financial Management*, 4th ed., Chicago, Dryden Press, 1986, chapters 9 and 10, for a more detailed discussion of capital budgeting.

7. Several special issues relating to the acquisition of assets in foreign countries will then be considered.
8. Finally, we will outline the procedure employed when the firm has more than one foreign investment opportunity.

American Investments in Foreign Countries

Since the end of World War II, American firms have invested very heavily in foreign countries. It may surprise some students to learn that they continue to do so. Table 16-1 shows that by 1987, the accumulated amount of foreign direct investments of Americans totaled approximately $309 million. Most of this investment (76 percent) has been concentrated in developed countries, with Canada and the United Kingdom accounting for almost one-third of the total. As shown in Table 16-1, only 23 percent of American direct foreign investment abroad is located in developing countries, primarily in Latin America.

The single most important direct foreign investment made by American business is in the petroleum industry. However, American manufacturers as a group are also very important holders of foreign direct investments. As shown in Table 16-2, there are substantial investments in all major manufacturing industry categories. In effect, firms in all manufacturing industries are now involved in foreign investing.

TABLE 16-1   Accumulated U.S. Direct Foreign Investment by 1987 (in Millions)

Country	Amount	Percentage
Canada	$ 56,879	18%
United Kingdom	$ 44,673	14%
Germany	$ 24,450	8%
Netherlands	$ 14,164	5%
Other Europe	$ 65,667	21%
Other developed countries	$ 27,482	9%
Total developed countries	$233,315	76%
Latin America	$ 42,337	14%
Africa	$ 5,085	2%
Middle East	$ 4,762	2%
Other Asia	$ 18,991	6%
Total developing countries	$ 71,174	23%
Other investments	$ 4,304	1%
Total direct investment	$308,793	100%

Source: *Survey of Current Business*, U.S. Department of Commerce, August 1988, p. 65.

TABLE 16-2   Accumulated U.S. Direct Foreign Investment by 1987 (by Industry) (in Millions)

Industry	Amount	Percentage
Food	$ 12,643	4%
Chemicals	$ 26,914	9%
Metals	$ 5,662	2%
Machinery	$ 27,344	9%
Electrical	$ 9,784	3%
Transportation	$ 17,708	6%
Other manufacturing	$ 26,584	9%
Total manufacturing	$126,640	41%
Petroleum	$ 66,381	21%
Wholesale trade	$ 31,330	10%
Banking	$ 15,354	5%
Other financial*	$ 49,097	16%
Services	$ 6,812	2%
Other industries	$ 13,179	4%
Total	$308,793	99%†

*Includes nonbank finance, insurance, and real estate.
†Does not add up to 100% due to rounding.

Source: Survey of Current Business, U.S. Department of Commerce, August 1988, p. 67.

Why American Firms Invest in Foreign Countries

The reasons that American firms invest in foreign countries are many and varied. Some of the more frequently heard arguments in favor of foreign investments are as follows:

1. Firms invest in foreign countries in order to increase total sales. In this manner, they are able to spread overhead costs (research, technology, etc.) over a much larger sales level. Firms that do not grow usually fall by the wayside. As penetration of domestic American markets reaches a saturation point, firms frequently look to foreign markets. Budweiser, for example, is trying very hard to penetrate the United Kingdom's beer market as its potential for expanding its dominant position in the U.S. beer market diminishes.

2. Firms invest in foreign countries in order to protect their worldwide market share from trade restrictions imposed by foreign governments. By having production facilities in foreign countries, firms are not affected by the tariffs and quotas imposed on imports by a foreign

government. This motive explains the large investments by American firms in EEC (Common Market) countries. In the 1980s, Japanese firms invested in the United States for the same reason.

3. Firms invest in foreign countries in order to reduce costs. This so-called cheap labor argument is not restricted to labor costs. It can also apply to transportation, raw materials, and other costs. An obvious example is the *maquiladoras* in the special border zone on the United States–Mexican border. While these investments are located in Mexico, their output can be shipped to the United States almost as if they were produced in the United States.

4. Firms invest in foreign countries in order to ensure their supplies of raw materials. Steel and aluminum companies, for example, have invested heavily in developing mineral deposits located in foreign countries to ensure a supply of raw materials that were not available in adequate quantities in the United States.

5. Firms invest in foreign countries in order to diversify. Diversification of production facilities may reduce the risk of the firm, thus providing a benefit to the stockholders. For example, American manufacturers of farm implements and construction equipment lost a major slice of their world market share as the dollar strengthened during the early 1980s. Their response was to diversify production on a worldwide basis.

6. Firms also move into foreign markets in order to compete with foreign firms that have entered the U.S. market. In 1987, for example, American automobile manufacturers attempted to penetrate the Japanese automobile market. The hope was that this action would weaken the Japanese producers by threatening their home market and make them weaker competitors in the American market.

Of course, ultimately, these (and other) reasons for investing in foreign countries must translate into profit and stockholder wealth maximization. For example, firms should not be anxious to expand their world market share if the final result is a reduction in stockholder wealth due to increased costs and/or increased risk. In other words, the initial motives for investing must be evaluated in terms of the final impact of the decision on the firm's profits and the stockholders. The international investment decision should be made using the same techniques that are used in evaluating domestic investment alternatives. The firm must analyze the impact of the potential asset acquisition on both the amount and the riskiness of expected cash flows. Both cash inflows and outflows must be considered. The firm should undertake only those projects that lead to an increase in stockholder wealth, rejecting those that reduce stockholder wealth. Whatever the initial stated motive for investing in a foreign country, the actual investment must be subjected to the test of stockholder wealth maximization.

TABLE 16-3   Cash Flows for Pengoland Investment: A Pengoland Investor's Perspective (in Millions of Pengos)

Cash outflows in year 0	Pg100
Annual cash inflows in years 1–5	
Sales	Pg 70
− Cash expenses	− Pg 30
− Depreciation*	− Pg 20
= Earnings before taxes	Pg 20
− Foreign income taxes (20%)	− Pg 4
= Earnings after taxes	Pg 16
+ Depreciation	+ Pg 20
= Annual cash inflows	Pg 36

*The straight-line method of depreciation, with an assumed terminal value of $0, is used in this illustration.

Domestic Investments

Let us begin our discussion by looking at the building of a new factory in the nation of Pengoland from the point of view of a resident of Pengoland. This is a domestic investment, since the firm is making the investment in its home country. We will assume that the firm has spent a considerable amount of time and effort estimating the cash flows that would be generated by the investment. Estimates of these cash flows are presented in Table 16-3. Note that the cash flows are expressed in pengos (Pg), which is the currency of Pengoland. Building the factory will require an initial outlay of Pg100 million, and cash inflows of Pg36 million are expected in each of the next 5 years. The illustration assumes that the income tax rate in Pengoland is 20 percent and that the factory will have a zero salvage value at the end of the fifth year.

In order to determine whether building the factory is consistent with stockholder wealth maximization, it is necessary to compute its net present value.[2] The net present value is equal to the present value of the cash flows of the project discounted at a cost of capital that reflects the risk of the investment. Net present value measures the change in stockholder wealth resulting from the acceptance of a project. Mathematically,

---

[2] The internal rate of return can also be used to accept or reject a project. This method is also consistent with the goal of stockholder wealth maximization. In this chapter, however, we will use only net present value to determine the acceptability of a project.

net present value can be expressed as follows:

$$NPV = \sum_{t=0}^{n} \frac{CF(t)}{(1 + k_a)^t} \qquad (16\text{-}1)$$

where

$$CF(t) = \text{cash flows at time } t$$

$$ka = \text{required rate of return (cost of capital)}$$

Assuming that because of the risk of the project the cost of capital is 14 percent, net present value will be equal to Pg23,590,915.[3]

Evaluating an Investment in a Foreign Country

A long-term investment in a foreign country may look quite different to the American investor (compared to the local investor). Assume, for example, that an American investor is considering establishing a subsidiary that will build and operate the Pengoland factory on the same basis and with the same success as the local Pengoland investor. As indicated in Figure 16-2, the parent corporation (a foreign investor) is interested in different cash flows than the local investor. The management of the American parent, in its quest for stockholder wealth maximization, invests dollars and anticipates dollar returns that can be passed on to stockholders and other suppliers of dollar capital. Generally speaking, the net present value to the American parent corporation will be the same as the net present value to the Pengoland investor (adjusted for exchange rates) only if the following conditions exist:

1. The subsidiary is free to repatriate all cash flows to the parent at the time that they are received.
2. Taxes in Pengoland (20 percent) are exactly the same as in the United States (20 percent). In addition, income taxes paid in Pengoland can be used as a tax credit in the United States.
3. Funds are free to move from one country to another. In other words, there are no blockages or restrictions on funds movement.

---

[3]Throughout the chapter, we will use a personal computer to calculate net present values. Present value tables can also be used to calculate net present value and are included at the end of the book. However, you will obtain slightly different answers due to rounding in the tables. In this case, the use of a present value of an annuity table would provide the following result:

$$NPV = \text{Pg36,000,000 (3.433)} - \text{Pg100,000,000} = \text{Pg23,588,000}$$

Note that this is not exactly the same as the Pg23,590,915 shown in the text. If you use present value tables for the rest of the problems, you will get slightly different results.

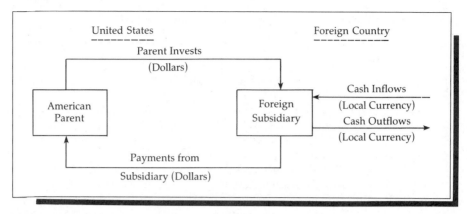

FIGURE 16-2   Cash flows from an international investment

4. Exchange rates are fixed at Pg1 = $0.25, and there is no chance that they will change over the period of the investment.
5. There are no special political risks attached to the fact that the investment is owned by a foreign investor. In other words, the probability of arbitrary actions by the government (e.g., nationalization of the investment) is the same for local and foreign investors. Thus, the cost of capital in pengos (14 percent) is exactly the same as the cost of capital in dollars (14 percent).

The impact of these perfect conditions can best be understood by comparing Table 16-3 with Table 16-4. Note that the cash flows to the parent corporation are computed quite differently than the cash flows to the subsidiary. While the subsidiary is concerned with revenues, costs, and taxes, the parent looks at cash flows from the subsidiary to the parent. The subsidiary cash flows are important only in that they provide the capacity to make payments to the parent. Under the previous assumptions, the net present value to the American investor in the Pengoland factory is proportionally the same as the net present value to the local investor. The net present value for the local investor was Pg23,590,915. If we multiply this figure by 0.25 (the exchange rate between the pengo and the dollar), the net present value will be equal to $5,897,729. This is exactly the same figure shown in Table 16-4. The investment in the foreign country looks the same from both the American and the local investor's perspective because all funds are moving to the parent. Of course, the perfect conditions described previously rarely exist in the real world; therefore, net present values will often be different for local and foreign investors. In the sections that follow, we will examine how differences in taxes and other factors affect the net present value to the American parent firm.

TABLE 16-4   Cash Flows for the Pengoland Investment:
An American Investor's Perspective (in Millions of Currency Units: Pgl = $0.25)

Cash outflows in year 0	Pg100	$25
Annual cash inflows in years 1–5		
Gross dividend from subsidiary	Pg 16	$4
− Withholding taxes	Pg 0	$0
= Net dividend	Pg 16	$4
+ Withholding taxes	Pg 0	$0
+ Pengoland income taxes	Pg 4	$1
= U.S. taxable income	Pg 20	$5
Tentative U.S. tax (20%)	Pg 4	$1
− Foreign tax credit in U.S.	Pg 4	$1
= U.S. tax due	Pg 0	$0
Earnings after taxes*	Pg 16	$4
+ Depreciation	Pg 20	$5
= Annual cash flow	Pg 36	$9
NPV (14%) = Pg23,590,915		
NPV (14%) = $5,897,729		
Note that the dollar NPV is exactly equal		
to the pengo NPV times the exchange rate (0.25)		

*Earnings after taxes are equal to the net dividend received less the U.S. tax due.

Impact of Differences in Taxes

When U.S. corporate income taxes are greater than foreign taxes, foreign investments become less attractive to the American investor than for the local investor. High U.S. taxes may discourage investments in foreign countries. Consider the situation presented in Table 16-5 (called the *basic case*), in which the tax rate in Pengoland is exactly the same as in the previous example (20 percent) but the U.S. rate is now increased to 34 percent. From the local investor's point of view, the higher U.S. tax rates have absolutely no impact on annual cash flows. Thus, the pengo cash flows will be exactly the same as shown in Table 16-3. This follows from the fact that the local investor has no involvement with the United States and is not subject to the higher tax rate. From the American investor's perspective, things are quite different. The new, higher tax rate means that the firm's annual American tax bill is increased from zero (when the U.S. tax rate was 20 percent) to $0.7 million.[4] This reduces annual cash flows to the parent to only $8.3 million. In other words, the American

---

[4]Review Chapter 15 for a longer discussion on the computation of the foreign tax credit, as well as other tax issues.

TABLE 16-5   The Basic Case: Cash Flows for the Pengoland Investment:
An American Investor's Perspective
(Tax Rates—Pengoland, 20%; U.S., 34%) (in Millions)

Cash outflows in year 0	$25.0
Annual cash inflows in years 1–5	
Gross dividend from subsidiary	$ 4.0
−Withholding taxes	$ 0
= Net dividend	$ 4.0
+Withholding taxes	$ 0
+Pengoland income taxes	$ 1.0
= U.S. taxable income	$ 5.0
Tentative U.S. tax (34%)	$ 1.7
−Foreign tax credit in U.S.	$ 1.0
= U.S. tax due	$ 0.7
Earnings after taxes*	$ 3.3
+Depreciation[†]	$ 5.0
= Annual cash flow	$ 8.3
NPV (14%) = Pg23,590,915	
NPV (14%) = $3,494,572	

*Earnings after taxes is equal to the net dividend received less the United States tax due.
[†]In millions of currency units/Pg1 = $0.25.

firm pays higher total taxes than does the Pengoland investor, and this reduces the American firm's cash flows from the investment.

The higher taxes paid by the American firm may or may not make the investment unattractive. Remember, management should select only those investments with positive net present values, and a reduction in annual cash flows will reduce net present value. Sometimes the reduction will be so small that net present value is lower but not negative. That is, the increase in stockholder wealth for the American firm is lower than the increase for the local firm, but both still have a positive net present value. The Pengoland factory investment described in Table 16-5 falls into this category. While the net present value to the local investor (in pengos) is unchanged by the higher American tax rate, the net present value to the American investor is reduced from $5,897,729 to $3,494,572. Stockholder wealth would still be increased if the American firm invested in the Pengoland factory, but by a lesser amount than would have been the case if the U.S. tax rate were 20 percent rather than 34 percent.

In other cases, the increased tax burden may result in a situation in which the investment is attractive to the local investor (a positive net present value) and unattractive to the American investor (a negative net present value). The particular situation that develops will depend on the magnitude of the tax differential.

It is now possible to make several general observations about the impact of income taxes on the decision to acquire a long-term asset in a foreign country. First, it is clear that the American firm should not use the net present value of its foreign subsidiary as a guide in evaluating the impact of a foreign investment on stockholder wealth. It is quite possible that the subsidiary (a domestic investor) could have a positive net present value while the parent has a negative net present value. The focus should always be on the cash flows from the subsidiary to the parent. In the Pengoland illustration presented in Table 16-5, we have seen how differences in tax rates can result in substantial differences in net present value. In the sections that follow, we will show how restrictions on the flow of currency, foreign exchange fluctuations, and differences in risk can have a similar effect. Whatever the imperfection, it must be evaluated in terms of its impact on the cash flows to the American investor.

It is also worth noting that changes in American tax laws may have a substantial impact on the decision to invest abroad. Whenever U.S. taxes are higher than in a foreign country, investments in that country will be discouraged by the U.S. tax law. However, the recent reduction in the maximum U.S. corporate tax rate to 34 percent means that it is now less likely that American firms investing in foreign countries will have to pay an additional tax to the U.S. government. It is more likely that American firms will be able to compete on the same basis with local firms operating in the same market. If the trend in American corporate tax rates is reversed and they begin to rise, American firms will be more likely to find themselves at a tax disadvantage when competing with local firms. In the context of this discussion, it should also be recognized that if foreign taxes are higher than American taxes, all firms (including American firms) pay the higher foreign tax and no additional tax is payable in the United States. While such a tax law would not discriminate against foreign investors, it does reduce the net present value of investments made in the foreign country.

Impact of Currency Blockages

It should be no surprise to the student of finance that restrictions on the movement of cash flows from an investment in a foreign country to its American owner will reduce the net present value of the investment. Such restrictions are likely to reduce the total size of the cash flows and/or delay the payment to the parent. Since net present value is affected by both the size and the timing of cash flows, it should be reduced by currency blockages. Blockages may result in a situation in which a particular investment is attractive to a local investor but unattractive to a foreign investor.

Let us illustrate this issue by making some changes in the assumptions made in Table 16-5 (the basic case). The foreign income tax rate of

20 percent and the American tax rate of 34 percent remain unchanged. Since the riskiness of the pengo and dollar cash flows are assumed to be equal, the cost of capital is the same for both investors (14 percent). The major difference between this example and the basic case is that we are now assuming that the host government restricts the repatriation of cash flows to the American parent in the following ways:

1. The host government permits only 60 percent of the earnings after taxes of the subsidiary to be repatriated to the American parent.
2. The host government also restricts the repatriation of depreciation funds until the end of the investment's life. Thus, the parent receives its initial investment of $25 million after 5 years rather than receiving the depreciation funds at a rate of $5 million per year (as in Table 16-5).
3. Finally, all blocked cash flows must be deposited in a government bank earning no return. The purpose of this assumption is to simplify the computations.[5]

The impact of these assumptions on the cash flows of the investment are presented in Table 16-6. The reader should note that pengo cash flows have not been affected. Thus, pengo cash flows are identical to those presented in Table 16-3. The cash flows to the parent, however, have been significantly affected. As shown in the table, the annual cash flows to the parent have declined to only $1,980,000. In addition, the parent will receive a net benefit of $25,000,000 (depreciation) and $6,600,000 (liquidating dividend) at the end of year 5. Thus, the parent's cash flows have been significantly affected by the foreign government's restrictions on currency movements.

Note that the net present value to a local investor is exactly the same as before, Pg23,590,915. However the net present value to the American investor is a negative $1,790,450. Thus, a previously acceptable investment would be rejected by the American investor. This rejection can be attributed entirely to the fact that the host government restricted the cash flows from the subsidiary to the foreign owner.

The exact assumptions used in the preceding illustration are unlikely to be found in the real world. However, many governments do have restrictions on payments to foreigners, and these restrictions are often related to the distribution of profits and the withdrawal of investment funds. While such restrictions are often more complicated than those used in the preceding illustration, their impact is the same. They could make it unattractive for foreigners to invest in a particular country.

---

[5] Throughout the chapter, we will assume that blocked funds (depreciation or retained earnings) will not earn any return. Removal of this assumption will have no major impact on the implications of the illustrations. It would, however, increase the complexity of the computations.

TABLE 16-6   Cash Flows for the Pengoland Investment:
An American Investor's Perspective
(Currency Restrictions) (in Millions)

Cash outflows in year 0	$25.0	
	Annual cash inflows (Year 1–5)	**Cash inflow (Year 5)**
Gross dividend from subsidiary	$2.4	$8.0*
− Withholding taxes	$0	$0
= Net dividend	$2.4	$8.0
+ Withholding taxes	$0	$0
+ Pengoland income taxes	$0.6	$2.0†
= U.S. taxable income	$3.0	$10.0
Tentative U.S. tax (34%)	$1.02	$3.4
− Foreign tax credit in U.S.	$0.6	$2.0
= U.S. tax due	$0.42	$1.4
Earnings after taxes	$1.98	$6.6
+ Depreciation	$0	$25.0‡
= Annual cash flow	$1.98	$31.6
NPV (14%) = Pg23,590,915		
NPV (14%) = ($1,790,450)		

*Gross dividend = accumulated retained earnings = (Pg16 − Pg9.6) × 5 years × $0.25 = $8
†Pengoland taxes = unclaimed foreign taxes = (Pg4 − Pg2.4) × 5 years × $0.25 = $2
‡Depreciation = Pg20 × 5 years × $0.25 = $25

Of course, a variety of situations can actually exist. In some cases, foreigners invest in countries that are blocking funds because they view the blockages as temporary and believe that the long-term outlook for repatriation of funds is favorable. For example, an American firm may invest in Brazil, despite current restrictions on converting cruzados to dollars, because of a forecast that such restrictions may eventually be lifted. The problem facing a firm in such a situation involves putting the blocked funds to productive use. This may be possible in a dynamic environment such as that of Brazil. Thus, the funds stay in Brazil, but they are expected to grow at a rapid rate. Eventually, the blocked funds are expected to yield dollar returns to the American investor. It should be noted, however, that if Brazil has excellent investment opportunities, it would have no need to force foreign firms to undertake them. The situation may be different in less dynamic countries. An American firm considering an investment in a bauxite mine in Ghana, for example, may find little opportunity to reinvest blocked funds at reasonable rates of return.

Several conclusions can be drawn. Other things being equal, host government restrictions on the movement of currencies will reduce the net present value of an investment to a foreign investor. Net present value may still be positive, but it will be lower than if no restrictions existed. In some cases, restrictions may create negative net present values for foreign investors and thus discourage investments in the host country. The impact of currency movement restrictions may be reduced or even reversed in cases where reinvestment opportunities are very favorable and/or when it is anticipated that the restrictions will be lifted in the near future.

Impact of Expected Changes in Exchange Rates

Expected changes in exchange rates can also be included in the analysis of a foreign investment. It is possible that an investment that is attractive to a local investor is unattractive to a foreign investor who wishes to exchange the local currency for another currency. This situation is illustrated in Table 16-7. Here we are once again looking at the Pengoland investment (the basic case in Table 16-5), but the focus is now on the individual annual cash flows. In this illustration, the Pengoland tax rate is 20 percent and the U.S. tax rate is 34 percent. In addition, the cost of

TABLE 16-7　Cash Flows for the Pengoland Investment from an American Investor's Perspective (Exchange Rate Expected to Change) (in Thousands)

	Year 1	Year 2	Year 3	Year 4	Year 5
Foreign tax	Pg 4,000	Pg 4,000	Pg 4,000	Pg 4,000	Pg 4,000
Net income	Pg16,000	Pg16,000	Pg16,000	Pg16,000	Pg16,000
Depreciation	Pg20,000	Pg20,000	Pg20,000	Pg20,000	Pg20,000
Cash flows	Pg36,000	Pg36,000	Pg36,000	Pg36,000	Pg36,000
Exchange rate					
Pengol =	$0.25	$0.23	$0.21	$0.19	$0.17
Gross dividend	$4,000	$3,680	$3,360	$3,040	$2,720
Withholding	$0	$0	$0	$0	$0
Net dividend	$4,000	$3,680	$3,360	$3,040	$2,720
Withholding	$0	$0	$0	$0	$0
Foreign tax	$1,000	$920	$840	$760	$680
U.S. income	$5,000	$4,600	$4,200	$3,800	$3,400
Tentative tax	$1,700	$1,564	$1,428	$1,292	$1,156
Tax credit	$1,000	$920	$840	$760	$680
U.S. tax due	$700	$644	$588	$532	$476
Net	$3,300	$3,036	$2,772	$2,508	$2,244
Depreciation	$5,000	$4,600	$4,200	$3,800	$3,400
Cash flows	$8,300	$7,636	$6,972	$6,308	$5,644

$$NPV\ (14\%) = Pg23,590,915$$
$$NPV\ (14\%) = (\$471,584)$$

capital is the same in each country (14 percent). Finally, there are no restrictions on the movement of currency from one country to another. This illustration differs from the others in that it is no longer assumed that the exchange rate is constant on a year-by-year basis. Now the pengo is expected to decrease in value from $0.25 in the first year to $0.17 in year 5. As shown in Table 16-7, the domestic investor has no change in net present value (Pg23,590,915). For the foreign investor, however, the net present value of the investment declines to a negative $471,584. Of course, we could have constructed an illustration in which the pengo increased in value, thus improving the net present value to the parent. The point of the discussion is that expected exchange rate movements could have an important impact on the decision to invest in a foreign country.

The major difficulty associated with incorporating expected exchange rates into the analysis of foreign long-term asset acquisition alternatives is that our ability to forecast (expect) is not very good.[6] The exchange rates included in Table 16-7 are forecasted rates that may not materialize. Granted, there are some situations in which exchange rate movements are inevitable. For example, if Pengoland has a 150 percent inflation rate and the United States has a 5 percent inflation rate, the pengo is bound to devalue (purchasing power parity theory). However, Table 16-7 requires an estimate about the timing and the amount of the decline in the value of the pengo on a year-by-year basis. This is a very difficult, if not impossible, task.

The relationship between exchange rate movements and inflation must also be considered in the context of Table 16-7. Ordinarily, a country whose currency is declining in value is also experiencing inflation (purchasing power parity theory). Inflation will increase reported sales, expenses, and probably profit in the local currency. While different firms will be affected differently by inflation, the general expectation is that inflation will increase the local currency value of profits. The increased local currency profits may offset the fact that each local currency unit is now worth less in terms of foreign currencies. While we have not included such cash flow considerations in Table 16-7, firms making actual decisions cannot ignore this phenomenon.

Impact of Risk Differentials

In order to evaluate the attractiveness of long-term asset acquisitions, the investor must first estimate the cash inflows and outflows associated with the investment. However, this is a difficult task, and the investor is never

---

[6] It is very difficult, if not impossible, to forecast foreign exchange rates accurately. See Chapter 5 for a more detailed discussion of this issue.

sure about the accuracy of the cash flow forecasts. Generally, the more certain the investor is about the cash flows, the less risky the project is. For example, long-term U.S. government bonds are considered to carry a low default risk, because the payment by (cash flow from) the government is virtually guaranteed. In some cases, however, the investor has so many variables to consider that it is impossible to feel confident about the cash flow estimates. The possibility of strikes, shortages of supplies, war, boycotts, actions of competitors, and so on all contribute to the uncertainty. When uncertainty about future cash flows is high, the investment is defined as being risky. For example, if an American investor invests in an American firm that has a new product that must be produced and sold in a very competitive environment, there is a reasonable probability that the expected returns to the investor will not materialize. When investing in long-term assets, this is a risky proposition.

The risk associated with a particular investment may be different for different investors. More specifically, American firms acquiring assets in a foreign country may be exposed to different degrees of risk than local investors. For example, if a local investor builds the Pengoland factory, cash flows may be more certain than if an American firm builds exactly the same factory. The risk disadvantage that is borne by the American investor can be evaluated in terms of differences in business risk, exchange rate risk, and political risk.

Business risk refers to the risks that are associated with running all businesses. While some business risks are borne equally by all investors, others fall more heavily on foreigners. The possibility of a competitor developing a new and superior product or the possibility of an accident destroying a valuable asset of the firm are business risks that are generally borne in the same manner by local and foreign investors. By contrast, foreign ownership may result in poorer decisions with respect to marketing, labor relations, sourcing of materials, and so forth. The local investor may have better information and may be in a better position to make good decisions with respect to these important aspects of management.

It is not impossible for a firm to operate efficiently in a foreign country, just more difficult. Look at the foreign firms operating in the United States, and you will realize that it is possible for such firms to be managed successfully. For example, when Japanese manufacturers began building automobiles in the United States and implemented the quality circle approach, they were taking a risk. They could have been very successful or they could have failed badly. Success in foreign countries is not, however, guaranteed. American manufacturers have entered many foreign markets and tried to do some things in the same way they were done in the United States. On occasion, the projects failed badly.

The foreign ownership of an asset also implies relatively great economic, translation, and transaction exposure to exchange rate risk. Since future exchange rates are unknown and difficult to forecast, the American investor in a foreign country does know how many dollars will be received for the local currency cash flows generated by a foreign

TABLE 16-8 Risk-Adjusted Cost of Capital and the Net Present Value of the Pengoland Factory (a Modification of the Basic Case)

Cost of Capital	Net Present Value
14%	$3,494,572
16%	$2,176,637
20%	($177,919)

subsidiary. This creates an element of uncertainty for the foreign investor that does not affect the local investor. It suggests that the riskiness of an investment to a foreigner is greater than the riskiness of the same investment to a local investor.

Foreign owners may also face greater political risks.[7] Host governments may restrict payments from a subsidiary to a foreign parent. On occasion, foreign firms are taxed more heavily than local firms and are subjected to other discriminatory actions. On rare occasions, foreign firms may even be nationalized. These are not everyday occurrences, but they do happen. The possibility of such actions creates a risk for the foreign firm that is greater than the risk to the local investor.

While it is certainly not true in every situation, it is at least possible that foreign investors have higher risks than local investors, and these differences must be incorporated into the procedure used to evaluate investments. This can be accomplished by adjusting the cost of capital for the various investors. The higher the risk to an investor, the higher the required rate of return demanded by that investor and the higher the cost of capital applied to the present value of the cash flows for that investment. Other things being equal, the higher cost of capital will result in a lower net present value for the investment and discourage firms from undertaking the project.[8]

The impact of differences in risk on net present value can be illustrated by modifying Table 16-5 (the basic case). Assuming that no special risks were borne by the foreign investor, the cost of capital would be the same for both the local and the foreign investor (14 percent in Table 16-5). Under these conditions, the net present value to the investor is a positive $3,494,572. Table 16-8 shows how different costs of capital (discount rates) will affect the net present value of the cash flows described in Table 16-5. Note that when the cost of capital is 16 percent, the net present value is positive, but lower than it would have been if no

---

[7] Political risks were discussed in more detail in Chapter 11.

[8] See James C. Van Horne, *Financial Management and Policy*, 7th ed., Englewood Cliffs, NJ, Prentice-Hall, Inc., 1986, chapter 7, for a more detailed discussion of risk adjustment in capital budgeting.

special risks were present. At a cost of capital of 20 percent, however, the net present value is negative. As is obvious, the increase in the level of risk, as reflected in the higher cost of capital, makes it unattractive for the firm to invest in the Pengoland factory.

An Integrated Example

Now it is time to examine a more complicated asset acquisition situation in which many different factors must be simultaneously considered. Let us assume that the Janaca Corporation, an American manufacturing firm, is contemplating an investment in the nation of Costa Libre. Costa Libre's currency is the corona (C), and the current exchange rate is C1 = $0.50. An investment of C80 million in a foreign subsidiary is being contemplated; the project has an expected life of 4 years and no expected salvage value at the end of its life. The foreign subsidiary uses the straight-line method of depreciation. The project will result in sales of C60 million and cash expenses of C30 million every year for 4 years. Costa Libre's corporate tax rate is 15 percent and, in addition, Costa Libre imposes a foreign dividend withholding tax of 10 percent. The government of Costa Libre imposes two restrictions on repatriation. Only 75 percent of earnings after taxes and no depreciation cash flows can be repatriated to foreign parent corporations until the project is over (year 4). The blocked funds will earn no return and can be repatriated at the end of year 4. The corporate tax rate in the United States is 34 percent. Janaca has made the following forecast of the value of the corona:[9]

Years 0 and 1	C1 = $0.50
Year 2	C1 = $0.52
Year 3	C1 = $0.54
Year 4	C1 = $0.56

Finally, Janaca has estimated that the risk-adjusted cost of capital for corona cash flows is 10 percent. Due to additional risks borne by the foreign investor, the discount rate applicable to dollar cash flows is 12 percent. The task confronting us at this point is to determine the potential impact of the Costa Libre investment on the wealth of Janaca's stockholders.

The decision-making process has three steps: (1) estimate the corona cash flows of the foreign subsidiary, (2) estimate the dollar cash flows to Janaca, and (3) evaluate the impact of the project on the wealth of Janaca's stockholders. The first step is summarized in Table 16-9, which

---

[9]We are assuming that corona cash flows will not be affected by changes in the exchange rate. This assumption is made solely to reduce the complexity of the computations.

TABLE 16-9 Janaca's Foreign Subsidiary Cash
Flows (in Millions of Coronas)

Cash outflows in year 0	C80
Annual cash inflows in years 1–4	
Sales	C60
− Cash expenses	− C30
− Depreciation	− C20
= Earnings before taxes	C10
− Foreign income tax (15%)	− C1.5
= Earnings after taxes	C8.5
+ Depreciation	+ C20
= Annual cash inflows	C28.5
NPV (10%) = C10,341,165	

shows the expected corona cash flows to the subsidiary. The project requires an outflow of C80 million in year 0 and has an annual cash inflow of C28.5 million every year for 4 years. Using a discount rate of 10 percent, the net present value is equal to C10,341,165. Thus, from the point of view of a Costa Libre resident, this is an acceptable investment.

The second step involves estimating the dollar cash flows to the Janaca Corporation (the parent) and is shown in Table 16-10. Estimating dollar cash flows is complicated by the fact that we have differences in tax rates, currency restrictions, and changes in the value of the corona. Let us first concentrate on the annual dividends. The subsidiary has a net income of C8,500,000. Dividends to the parent, however, are limited to 75 percent of net income, or C6,375,000. Thus, this amount must be converted to dollars at the prevailing exchange rate in order to determine the gross dividend paid to the parent. For year 1, the dollar value of the gross dividend is $3,187,500 (C6,375,000 × 0.50), but it increases over the next 3 years because of the strengthening of the corona. Note that in this example there is a withholding tax, which means that the gross dividend paid to the parent is not equal to the net dividend received.

The liquidating cash flows include all of those funds that have been blocked by the host country government and are repatriated at the end of the investment's life. Since the firm has been forced to retain 25 percent of its earnings each year (C2,125,000), it will have retained C8,500,000 over the 4-year life of the investment. The accumulated retained earnings can be changed into $4,760,000 at the prevailing exchange rate of C1 = $0.56. The receipt of $4,760,000 by Janaca is income and is thus taxable in the United States. Of course, Janaca has already paid income taxes on this income in Costa Libre, and these foreign income taxes can be used as a tax credit in the United States. Janaca must calculate the amount of income taxes paid to the Costa Libre government that have not been claimed as a foreign tax credit in previous years. In this case, the foreign tax credit would reflect the fact that only 75 percent

TABLE 16-10   Cash Flows for the Costa Libre Investment
from an American Investor's Perspective
(Rounded to the Nearest Thousand)

	Year 1	Year 2	Year 3	Year 4
Foreign tax	C1,500	C1,500	C1,500	C1,500
Net income	C8,500	C8,500	C8,500	C8,500
Depreciation	C20,000	C20,000	C20,000	C20,000
Cash flows	C28,500	C28,500	C28,500	C28,500
Exchange rate Corona 1 =	$0.50	$0.52	$0.54	$0.56

	Annual Dividend	Annual Dividend	Annual Dividend	Annual Dividend	Liquidating Cash Flow
Gross dividend	$3,188	$3,315	$3,443	$3,570	$4,760*
Withholding	−$319	−$332	−$344	−$357	−$476
Net dividend	$2,869	$2,984	$3,098	$3,213	$4,284
Withholding	$319	$332	$344	$357	$476
Foreign tax	$563	$585	$608	$630	$840[†]
U.S. income	$3,750	$3,900	$4,050	$4,200	$5,600
Tentative tax	$1,275	$1,326	$1,377	$1,428	$1,904
Tax credit	−$881	−$917	−$952	−$987	−$1,316
U.S. tax due	$394	$410	$425	$441	$588
Net	$2,475	$2,574	$2,673	$2,772	$3,696
Depreciation	$0	$0	$0	$0	$44,800[‡]
Cash flows	$2,475	$2,574	$2,673	$51,268[§]	

$$NPV\ (10\%) = C10,341,165$$
$$NPV\ (12\%) = (\$1,253,872)$$

*Liquidating cash flows = accumulated retained earnings = (C8,500 − 0.75 × C8,500) × 4 years
× 0.56 = $4,760
[†]Foreign tax = unclaimed foreign income taxes = (C1,500 − 0.75 × C1,500) × 4 years × 0.56 =
$840
[‡]Accumulated depreciation = C20,000 × 4 years × $0.56 = $44,800
[§]Cash flows in year 4 = annual dividend + liquidating + dep. = $2,772 + $3,696 + $44,800 =
$51,268

of each year's foreign taxes have been used for tax credit purposes in the
United States. Since the retained earnings are now being repatriated, the
remaining 25 percent of foreign income taxes can be used as a tax credit.
Finally, the accumulated depreciation (C20,000,000 × 4) is also converted
at the prevailing exchange rate. Since this cash flow received by Janaca is
not taxable, the dollar inflow will be $44,800,000.[10]

The final step in the long-term asset acquisition evaluation process is
to determine the change in Janaca's stockholders' wealth in the event
that the Costa Libre investment is undertaken. This is accomplished by

---

[10]We are ignoring any possible tax consequences as the result of capital gains on the
investment. The firm invested $40,000,000. However, it received $44,800,000 in year 4.

computing the net present value of the project. The reader should note that Janaca has decided to use a 12 percent cost of capital, which is higher than that used by a local investor. This reflects the fact that dollar cash flows are perceived as being less certain than corona cash flows. Thus, the risk-adjusted net present value to Janaca is a negative $1,253,872.

The illustration presented in Table 16-10 deserves a little thought. Note, for example, that the expected strengthening of the corona would ordinarily make the net present value to the parent more positive than the net present value to the subsidiary. In this case, however, this favorable development is more than offset by the negative features of the situation. Specifically, the higher cost of capital to the parent corporation and the fact that funds are blocked by the host government result in a negative net present value for the parent. The point of the illustration is to show that all of the factors affecting the long-term investment decision must be evaluated simultaneously in order to determine their cumulative effect on net present value.

Other Cash Flows

Thus far, the illustrations of long-term asset acquisition situations have included only selected cash flows. Cash flowed from the parent to the foreign subsidiary when the investment was undertaken. Repayment was received in the form of dividends and depreciation cash flows from the subsidiary. In fact, the cash flows between a parent corporation and its foreign subsidiary are usually much more complicated.[11] The following are just a few of the many questions that must be answered by the parent corporation.

1. Would the acceptance of an investment opportunity in a foreign country reduce or increase exports of the parent corporation to that country?
2. Would the acceptance of the foreign project result in sales from the parent to the subsidiary?
3. Would the acceptance of the foreign project result in royalties or fees paid by the subsidiary to the parent?

Let us illustrate this issue with a numerical example that is an extension of the Janaca Corporation case summarized in Table 16-10. Now we will consider a number of new complicating factors. Specifically,

---

[11]See Chapter 13 for a review of this issue. In this chapter, we will assume that the parent's transactions with the subsidiary are not motivated by either tax minimization or the wish to bypass currency restrictions.

we will assume the following:

1. The parent corporation currently sells $3 million every year in the foreign country. These sales will be lost, since the subsidiary will now serve this market. Janaca's earnings before taxes are equal to 20 percent of the sales.
2. Every year, Janaca will sell raw materials with a value of C2 million to the subsidiary. Janaca's earnings before taxes are 20 percent on the sales of raw materials.
3. The subsidiary will pay the parent a fee of C5 million per year for the use of Janaca's corporate goodwill. Janaca does not incur any expenses on this item.
4. Janaca's earnings before taxes of 20 percent of sales will not be affected by the fluctuation in the value of the corona.

The impact of these new complications is summarized in Table 16-11. On an after-tax basis, the reduction of direct sales by Janaca to the foreign country results in a reduction of after-tax cash flows by $396,000 every year for 4 years. This decline in cash flows is partly offset by the fact that Janaca will receive an after-tax cash flow of $132,000 in year 1 as a result of raw material sales to its subsidiary. Also in year 1, the imposition of fees on the subsidiary will result in a $1,650,000 after-tax cash inflow to the parent corporation. Note that both of these cash flows increase over time, since they are in the form of coronas and the corona is expected to

TABLE 16-11 Janaca Corporation's Total Cash Flows
(Rounded Off to the Nearest Thousand)

	Year 1	Year 2	Year 3	Year 4
Before-tax cash flows				
Lost sales	$-$3,000	$-$3,000	$-$3,000	$-$3,000
New sales	$+$C2,000	$+$C2,000	$+$C2,000	$+$C2,000
Royalties	$+$C5,000	$+$C5,000	$+$C5,000	$+$C5,000
Exchange Rate	$0.50	$0.52	$0.54	$0.56
After-tax cash flows				
Lost sales*	$-$396	$-$396	$-$396	$-$396
New sales[†]	$+$132	$+$137	$+$143	$+$148
Royalties[‡]	$1,650	$1,716	$1,782	$1,848
Project (Table 16-10)	$2,475	$2,574	$2,673	$51,268
Total cash flows	$3,861	$4,031	$4,202	$52,868
NPV (12%) = $3,250,089				

*Lost sales $= -\$3,000\ (0.20)\ (1-0.34) = -\$396$
[†]New sales $= C2,000\ (0.20)\ (1-0.34) \times$ prevailing exchange rate
[‡]Royalties $= C5,000\ (1-0.34) \times$ prevailing exchange rate

increase in value over the period under analysis. These additional cash flows are combined with the operating cash flows from the investment (Table 16-10), and the total cash flows applicable to the investment are shown at the bottom of Table 16-11. Because of these additional cash flows, the net present value of the project becomes a positive $3,250,089.

While the Janaca Corporation would have rejected the Costa Libre investment proposal as presented in Table 16-10, the project now has a positive net present value and should be accepted. This suggests that the firm must be very careful in estimating the impact of a foreign investment on the total cash flows of the parent corporation. Every factor that will have any impact on the parent's cash flows must be considered.

Capital Budgeting

Thus far, our discussion has focused on the procedures used to evaluate a single foreign investment proposal. In practice, firms must evaluate several different alternatives simultaneously. For example, the firm may be looking simultaneously at projects in Canada, Korea, and Germany. In addition, the firm may be evaluating a number of different projects in the United States. The well-managed firm analyzes the various alternatives and then constructs a plan with respect to action on such alternatives. This plan is called the *capital budget*.

The procedures used to construct a capital budget that includes foreign investments are the same as those used when only domestic investment alternatives are under consideration. These procedures are illustrated in Table 16-12, which shows a series of investment proposals available to the American Manufacturing Corporation. Included are the cash outflows and inflows for six different projects, as well as the risk-adjusted discount rate for each project. In order to simplify the discussion, we will assume that the cash flows of the projects are independent. In other words, the acceptance or rejection of Project *A* will not affect the cash flows of Project *B*. Net present values are computed in the same manner as before.

If the firm has no limit on the amount of funds available for investment purposes, the decision is very simple. All projects with positive net present values (or with an internal rate of return in excess of the risk-adjusted cost of capital) should be accepted. In our illustration, the firm should reject Project *F* and accept Projects *A* through *E*. The reader should note that the cash flows of Project *F* are identical to those of Project *A*. The risk-adjusted net present value of Project *F*, however, is negative. The acceptance of the five projects with positive net present values will increase stockholder wealth by $12,953, which is the summation of the net present values of the accepted proposals. The firm should invest $175,000, and stockholder wealth will increase by $12,953.

TABLE 16-12 Capital Budget for the American
Manufacturing Corporation*

	Project					
	A	**B**	**C**	**D**	**E**	**F**
Cash outflow	$50,000	$50,000	$25,000	$25,000	$25,000	$50,000
Cash inflows, Years 1–10	$9,000	$11,000	$5,000	$5,000	$6,000	$9,000
Risk-adjusted discount rate	10%	16%	12%	14%	20%	14%
NPV	$5,301	$3,166	$3,251	$1,080	$155	($3,055)
Internal rate of return	12.4%	17.6%	15%	15%	20.1%	12.4%

*The investment alternatives are:
Project *A*: trucks in the United States
Project *B*: machinery in the United States
Project *C*: office equipment in the United States
Project *D*: trucks in Parana (foreign country)
Project *E*: machinery in Costa Libre (foreign country)
Project *F*: computers in Costa Libre (foreign country)

TABLE 16-13 Capital Budget of the American Manufacturing Corporation

	Projects	Investment	Change in Stockholder Wealth
Package I	A + B	$100,000	$8,467
Package II	A + C + D	$100,000	$9,632
Package III	A + C + E	$100,000	$8,707
Package IV	A + D + E	$100,000	$6,536
Package V	B + C + D	$100,000	$7,497
Package VI	B + C + E	$100,000	$6,572
Package VII	B + D + E	$100,000	$4,401

In the real world, however, the firm may not have access to the $175,000 needed to undertake all acceptable projects. This situation is generally called a *capital rationing constraint*.[12] For purposes of illustration, we will assume that the firm has access to only $100,000. In this situation, the decision is not simple: accept the combination of projects that will maximize stockholder wealth. The first step is to prepare "packages" of projects that meet the capital rationing constraint ($100,000). Table 16-13 shows all possible packages that meet this constraint. The best possible combination includes Projects *A*, *C*, and *D*. This package of projects results in the highest increase in stockholder wealth, $9,632. Note that the

[12]See J. Van Horne, op. cit., pp. 144–146, for a more detailed discussion of capital rationing and stockholder wealth maximization.

machinery investment in Costa Libre is rejected even though it has a positive net present value. This highlights the fact that not all foreign investments with positive net present values are necessarily accepted when capital rationing conditions exist.

Note that under conditions of capital rationing, the net present value of the investments accepted by the firm is lower than it would have been if unlimited funds were available. Specifically, the net present value is $3,321 lower, which is exactly the same as the net present value of Projects *B* and *E*, which were not included in the final budget. In this case, capital rationing has reduced stockholder wealth.

Summary and Conclusions

This chapter focused on the procedures used to evaluate foreign long-term asset acquisition alternatives. As we have shown, the conceptual framework for making such decisions is basically the same as that used for domestic assets. In both situations, the decision must be based on the asset's impact on stockholder wealth. Foreign assets are more difficult to analyze not because the general framework for decision making is different, but because there are many more factors that affect the cash flows and appropriate discount rate of the foreign investment.

The expected cash flows of a foreign investment must be adjusted due to various factors. First, tax implications must be considered. Second, the analyst must include the impact of foreign government restrictions on repatriation of cash flows to the parent. Third, the fact that many exchange rates fluctuate against the dollar may have a significant impact on cash flows to the parent. And finally, it is necessary to consider how the acquisition will affect the other cash flows of the parent corporation. A sound strategy would require all of these things to be considered simultaneously.

The required rate of return of investors can also be affected by the international environment. Uncertainty about future foreign exchange rates, restrictions on currency movements, and other possible political actions by host governments expose the foreign investor to risks not borne by the local investor. This suggests that, in many cases, the required rate of return of an individual project should be higher for a foreigner. This implies a higher cost of capital and a lower net present value for the foreign investor.

Once cash flows have been estimated and the cost of capital determined, the decision process for the foreign investment is identical to the domestic decision. In the absence of a capital rationing constraint, the firm will accept all projects with positive net present values. A capital rationing constraint, however, will force the firm to evaluate all projects together at the same point in time and choose the package of assets that has the highest net present value, thus maximizing stockholder wealth, and falls within the capital rationing constraint.

Review Questions

1. Which cash flows should be used by the foreign subsidiary when computing the net present value of an investment in the foreign country? Which cash flows should be used by the American parent when computing its net present value for the same project? Why are different cash flows used at the different levels of analysis?

2. How can the net present value of a foreign investment be positive for a foreign subsidiary but negative for the American parent?

3. Assuming that there are no expected changes in local currency cash flows to a foreign subsidiary, how would an American multinational firm's net present value for a foreign investment be affected by an expected decline in the value of the foreign currency? By an expected increase in the value of the foreign currency? Is it reasonable to expect that local currency cash flows to the foreign subsidiary would be constant in light of expected increases or decreases in the value of the currency? Explain your answers.

4. How would host government restrictions on subsidiary payments to foreign parents affect the net present value of foreign investments (from the perspective of the American multinational firm)?

5. Why may a foreign investor have a higher cost of capital for an investment than a local investor?

6. "A multinational firm that includes only dividends and depreciation cash flows in its net present value computations is likely to misestimate seriously the net present value of a foreign investment." True or false? Explain your answer.

7. How would a multinational firm choose among foreign investment alternatives when there are more investments with positive net present values than can be undertaken with the firm's available investment funds?

8. In which countries have American firms invested (direct investment) most heavily? How would you explain American preferences for the various countries?

9. In which industries have American firms invested (foreign direct investment) most heavily? How would you explain American preferences for the various industries?

10. Why do American firms invest in foreign countries? Why not just stay at home and avoid the risks associated with foreign investments?

11. What is the meaning of a positive net present value for a foreign investment? What conditions must be present for net present value to be an accurate measure of the impact of an investment on stockholder wealth?

Questions for Discussion

1. Assume that you are employed by an American multinational manufacturer of tires for automobiles, buses, trucks, and motorcycles. The multinational parent has recently received an analysis of an investment project that is being considered by its subsidiary in Turkey. The investment will enable the subsidiary to double its

production. The tires would be produced in Turkey and sold to Turkish customers for Turkish lire. The project would require an outlay of $10 million to be provided by the parent, which would be converted to turkish lire and then invested in the project. The analysis provided by the Turkish subsidiary is denominated in Turkish lire and shows a very high net present value for the project. On this basis, the manager of the Turkish subsidiary makes a strong positive recommendation. You are assigned the task of analyzing the project from the point of view of the multinational parent rather than that of the subsidiary. What questions would you ask? What information would you need?

2. Assume that you are employed by a large American multinational firm that is simultaneously considering seven investment proposals located in each of the following countries: Canada, Mexico, Singapore, Taiwan, France, Denmark, and India. Thus far, these proposals have been presented only in general and preliminary terms. You have been assigned the task of accumulating the needed information and making recommendations. Before you begin, top management has requested that you provide a detailed report on the procedure you will employ for evaluating each investment.

Research Activities

1. Choose a less developed country. Obtain information from the consulate of that country with regard to investment opportunities for American firms. You should pay particular attention to (a) tax laws, (b) limits on the repatriation of dividends, and (c) other limitations on the transfer of funds from the subsidiary and the American parent.

2. Choose a developed country. Obtain information from the consulate of that country with regard to investment opportunities for American firms. You should pay particular attention to (a) tax laws, (b) limits on the repatriation of dividends, and (c) other limitations on the transfer of funds from the subsidiary and the American parent.

Problems

1. An American corporation is planning to make an investment in a wholly owned foreign subsidiary located in Parana. The investment required at time zero is 100 million soles. The investment has a useful life of 10 years and no expected salvage value in year 10. The subsidiary uses the straight-line method of depreciation. It anticipates revenues of 60 million soles every year for 10 years. In addition, annual cash expenses are expected to be 30 million soles for the 10-year period. The current exchange rate is soles1 = $0.20. The corporate tax rate in Parana is 30 percent. The tax rate in the United States is 34 percent. The government of Parana has no restrictions on the repatriation of funds, and the foreign subsidiary plans to repatriate all funds to the parent. The required rate of return that reflects the risk of the project is 12 percent. Calculate the net present value of the project.

2. Using the information in Problem 1, calculate the net present value of the project if the government of Parana imposes a 5 percent withholding tax on dividends repatriated to other countries.

3. Using the information in Problem 1, calculate the net present value of the project if the corporate income tax rate in Parana is 50 percent.

4. Using the information in Problem 1, calculate the net present value of the project if the government of Parana does not allow the repatriation of depreciation cash flows until year 10. Depreciation cash flows must be deposited in a checking account earning no return.

5. Using the information in Problem 1, calculate the net present value of the project if the government of Parana does not allow the repatriation of depreciation cash flows and limits dividends to 30 percent of net income. These funds must be deposited in a checking account earning no return and can be repatriated at the end of year 10.

6. Using the information in Problem 1, calculate the net present value of the project if the foreign exchange rate is expected to be as follows (assume no changes in soles cash flows and ignore the U.S. tax implications of the decrease in exchange rates):

Years 1–5	Years 6–10
Soles1 = $0.18	Soles1 = $0.16

7. Using the information in Problem 1, calculate the net present value of the project if the foreign exchange rate is expected to be as follows (assume no changes in soles cash flows and ignore the U.S. tax implications of the increase in exchange rates):

Years 1–5	Years 6–10
Soles1 = $0.22	Soles1 = $0.25

8. Using the information from Problem 1, calculate the net present value of the project if the parent has these additional transactions:
   a. The parent currently sells $5 million annually in Parana. The parent's earnings before taxes are 25 percent of sales. These sales will be lost, since the subsidiary will now serve this market.
   b. The parent corporation will sell raw materials with a value of 20 million soles to the subsidiary every year. The parent's earnings before taxes are 25 percent of sales.

9. The Donegal Corporation has the following foreign investment proposals (in millions):

$$\text{Project } A\text{: Cash outflows at time zero} = \$100$$
$$\text{Annual inflows (years 1–10)} = \$20$$
$$\text{Project } B\text{: Cash outflows at time zero} = \$100$$
$$\text{Annual inflows (years 1–10)} = \$22$$

   a. Calculate the net present value of Projects A and B if you use a required rate of return of 12 percent for both proposals. If you had to choose between the two, which project would you recommend?
   b. Calculate the net present value of Projects A and B if you use a risk-adjusted required rate of return of 12 percent for Project A and 16 percent for Project B. If you had to choose between the two, which project would you recommend?

10. American Enterprises is evaluating its capital budget. The cash flows from the projects, as well as the risk-adjusted discount rates, are as follows:

Project	Cash Outflow Year 0	Cash Inflows Years 1–10	Risk-Adjusted Discount Rate
A	$20,000	$4,000	10%
B	$20,000	$4,500	14%
C	$10,000	$2,000	10%
D	$10,000	$3,000	12%
E	$10,000	$3,000	16%

  a. Which projects should be accepted in the absence of a capital rationing constraint? Show the change in stockholder wealth.
  b. Which projects should be accepted if American Enterprises has only $40,000 available for investments? Show the change in stockholder wealth.

11. An American corporation is planning to make an investment in a wholly owned foreign subsidiary located in Sierra Madre. The investment required at time zero is 400 million pesos. The investment has a useful life of 4 years and no expected salvage value in year 4. The subsidiary uses the straight-line method of depreciation. It anticipates revenues of 300 million pesos every year for 4 years. In addition, annual cash expenses are expected to be 80 million pesos for the 4-year period. The corporate tax rate in Sierra Madre is 20 percent. The tax rate in the United States is 34 percent. The government of Sierra Madre has no restrictions on the repatriation of funds, and the foreign subsidiary plans to repatriate all funds to the parent. The required rate of return that reflects the risk of the project is 10 percent. The exchange rate today is pesos1 = $0.10. It is not expected to remain constant. The firm anticipates the following rates to prevail in the future:

Year 1	Peso1 = $0.09
Year 2	Peso1 = $0.08
Year 3	Peso1 = $0.07
Year 4	Peso1 = $0.06

Given the previous information (ignore the impact of exchange rate gains or losses on U.S. taxes), calculate the net present value of the project.

12. Using the information in Problem 11, calculate the net present value of the project, given the following changes:
  a. The government of Sierra Madre limits repatriation in two ways: (1) no depreciation cash flows can be sent back to the parent, and (2) only 60 percent of net income can be sent back to the parent in the form of dividends. All blocked funds must be deposited in a government checking account earning no return and can be repatriated at the end of year 4.
  b. Sales and cash expenses (in millions of pesos) are expected to be as follows:

	Year 1	2	3	4
Sales	300	340	380	420
Cash expenses	80	90	100	120

Bibliography

Adler, Michael, and Dumas, Bernard. "Optimal International Acquisitions." *Journal of Finance*, March 1975, pp. 1–19.

Amsden, Alice H. "Private Enterprise: The Issue of Business-Government Control." *Columbia Journal of World Business*, Spring 1988, pp. 37–42.

Austin, James E., Wortzel, Lawrence H., and Coburn, John F. "Privatizing State-Owned Enterprises: Hopes and Realities." *Columbia Journal of World Business*, Fall 1986, pp. 51–60.

Baker, James C., and Beardsley, Laurence J. "Multinational Companies' Use of Risk Evaluation and Profit Measurement for Capital Budgeting Decisions." *Journal of Business Finance*, Spring 1973, pp. 38–43.

Barrone, Robert N. "Risk and International Diversification: Another Look." *Financial Review*, Spring 1983, pp. 184–194.

Bavishi, Vinod B. "Capital Budgeting Practices of Multinationals." *Management Accounting*, August 1981, pp. 32–35.

Beamish, Paul W. "The Characteristics of Joint Ventures in Developed and Developing Countries." *Columbia Journal of World Business*, Fall 1985, pp. 13–20.

Boddewyn, Jean J. "Foreign and Domestic Divestment and Investment Decisions: Like or Unlike? *Journal of International Business Studies*, Winter 1983, pp. 23–35.

Booth, Laurence D. "Capital Budgeting Frameworks for the Multinational Corporation." *Journal of International Business Studies*, Fall 1982, pp. 114–123.

Brigham, Eugene F. *Fundamentals of Financial Management*, 4th ed. Chicago: Dryden Press, 1986.

Calvet, A. Louis. "A Synthesis of Foreign Direct Investment Theories and Theories of the Multinational Firm." *Journal of International Business Studies*, Spring–Summer 1981, pp. 43–59.

Errunza, Vihang R., and Senbet, L. "The Effects of International Operations on the Market Value of the Firm: Theory and Evidence." *Journal of Finance*, May 1981, pp. 401–417.

Ghertman, Michel. "Foreign Subsidiary and Parents' Roles During Strategic Investment and Divestment." *Journal of International Business Studies*, Spring 1988, pp. 47–68.

Gordon, Sara L., and Lees, Francis L. "Multinational Capital Budgeting: Foreign Investment Under Subsidy." *California Management Review*, Fall 1982, pp. 22–32.

Hisey, Karen B., and Caves, Richard E. "Diversification Strategy and Choice of Country: Diversifying Acquisitions Abroad by U.S. Multinationals, 1978–1980." *Journal of International Business Studies*, Summer 1985, pp. 51–64.

Jacquillat, Bertrand, and Solnik, Bruno. "Multinationals Are Poor Tools for Diversification." *Journal of Portfolio Management*, Winter 1978, pp. 8–12.

Lessard, Donald R. "Evaluating International Projects: An Adjusted Present Value Approach." In *International Financial Management: Theory and Application*. Edited by Donald R. Lessard. New York: John Wiley & Sons, Inc., 1985, pp. 570–584.

Mathur, Ike, and Hanagan, Kyran. "Are Multinational Corporations Superior Investment Vehicles for Achieving International Diversification?" *Journal of International Business Studies*, Winter 1983, pp. 135–146.

Oblak, David J., and Helm, Roy J., Jr. "Survey and Analysis of Capital Budgeting Methods Used by Multinationals." *Financial Management*, Winter 1981, pp. 37–41.

Shapiro, Alan C. "Capital Budgeting for the Multinational Corporation." *Financial Management*, Spring 1978, pp. 7–16.

_____ "International Capital Budgeting." *Midland Corporate Finance Journal*, Spring 1983, pp. 26–45.

Stanley, Marjorie T., and Block, Stanley B. "A Survey of Multinational Capital Budgeting." *Financial Review*, March 1984, pp. 36–54.

Stonehill, Arthur, and Nathanson, Leonard. "Capital Budgeting and the Multinational Corporation." *California Management Review*, Summer 1968, pp. 39–54.

Stulz, Rene M. "On the Determinants of Net Foreign Investment." *Journal of Finance*, May 1983, pp. 459–468.

Taggart, Robert A. "Capital Budgeting and the Financial Decision." *Financial Management*, Summer 1977, pp. 59–64.

Van Horne, James C. *Financial Management and Policy*, 7th ed. Englewood Cliffs, NJ: Prentice-Hall, Inc., 1986.

Appendix A

Selected Statistics of Various Countries

United States
Argentina
Australia
Brazil
Canada
Egypt
France
Germany
India
Italy
Japan
Korea
Mexico
Nigeria
South Africa
United Kingdom

Selected Statistics
Country: UNITED STATES
Currency: DOLLAR ($)

	1960	1970	1980	1985	1986	1987
Exports (billions)	$21	$43	$221	$213	$227	$250
Imports (billions)	$16	$43	$257	$362	$387	$424
Current account balance (billions)	$3	$2	$2	−$116	−$139	−$154
Private capital formation (billions)	$75	$146	$445	$632	$655	$672
Private consumption (billions)	$331	$640	$1,733	$2,629	$2,800	$2,968
Gross domestic product (billions)	$512	$1,008	$2,684	$3,971	$4,195	$4,461
Gross national product (billions)	$515	$1,016	$2,732	$4,010	$4,235	$4,489
GNP per capita (dollars)	$2,845	$4,956	$11,982	$16,778	$17,500	$18,398
Government deficit or surplus (billions)	0	−$11	−$76	−$212	−$213	−$156
Population (millions)	181	205	228	239	242	244
Treasury bill interest rate (%)	2.94%	6.44%	11.62%	7.49%	5.97%	5.83%
Government bond long-term rate (%)	4.12%	7.35%	11.46%	10.62%	7.68%	8.38%
Gold (millions of fine troy ounces)	509	316	264	263	262	262

Source: International Monetary Fund, *International Financial Statistics Yearbook, 1988*, pp. 716–721.

Selected Statistics*
Country: ARGENTINA
Currency: AUSTRAL (A̶)

	1960	1970	1980	1985	1986	1987
Exports (millions)	$1,079	$1,773	$8,021	$8,396	$6,852	$6,360
Imports (millions)	$1,249	$1,694	$10,541	$3,814	$4,724	$6,119
Current account balance (millions)	−$60	−$163	−$4,774	−$952	−$2,859	−$4,285
Private capital formation (millions)	†	†	†	†	†	†
Private consumption (millions)	†	†	†	†	†	†
Gross domestic product (millions)	†	†	†	$49,452	$59,150	†
Gross national product (millions)	†	†	†	†	†	†
GNP per capita (dollars)	†	†	†	†	†	†
Government deficit or surplus (millions)	†	†	−$5,000	−$3,652	†	†
Population (millions)	20	24	28	31	31	32
Deposit interest rate (%)	†	†	88%	520%	61%	†
Government bond long-term rate (%)	†	†	†	†	†	†
Exchange rate 1 austral =	†	†	$5,000	$1.249	$0.796	$0.267
Gold (millions of troy ounces)	3	4	4	4	4	4

*Unless otherwise stated, all figures are in U.S. dollars.
†Not available.

Source: International Monetary Fund, *International Financial Statistics Yearbook, 1988*, pp. 200–203.

Selected Statistics*
Country: AUSTRALIA
Currency: DOLLAR ($A)

	1960	1970	1980	1985	1986	1987
Exports (billions)	$2	$5	$22	$22	$22	$26
Imports (billions)	$2	$4	$20	$24	$24	$27
Current account balance (billions)	−$1	−$1	−$4	−$9	−$10	−$9
Private capital formation (billions)	$4	$10	$37	$38	$40	$47
Private consumption (billions)	$11	$22	$91	$92	$98	$116
Gross domestic product (billions)	$17	$37	$154	$154	$164	$200
Gross national product (billions)	$17	$37	$152	$149	$158	$193
GNP per capita (dollars)	$1,616	$2,921	$10,311	$9,443	$9,904	$11,882
Government deficit or surplus (billions)	0	0	$2	$5	$4	†
Population (millions)	10	13	15	16	16	16
Treasury bill interest rate (%)	†	5.38%	10.67%	15.34%	15.39%	12.80%
Government bond long-term rate (%)	4.99%	6.72%	11.65%	14.10%	13.56%	13.47%
Exchange rate 1 A$ =	$1.1190	$1.1150	$1.1807	$0.6809	$0.6648	$0.7225
Gold (millions of troy ounces)	4	7	8	8	8	8

*Unless otherwise stated, all figures are in U.S. dollars.
†Not available.

Source: International Monetary Fund, *International Financial Statistics Yearbook, 1988,* pp. 206–209.

Selected Statistics*
Country: BRAZIL
Currency: CRUZADO (Cz$)

	1960	1970	1980	1985	1986	1987
Exports (billions)	$1	$3	$20	$26	$22	$26
Imports (billions)	$1	$3	$25	$14	$16	$17
Current account balance (billions)	−$1	−$1	−$13	0	−$4	†
Private capital formation (billions)	†	†	$40	$24	$51	†
Private consumption (billions)	†	†	$128	$63	†	†
Gross domestic product (billions)	†	†	$181	$134	$247	†
Gross national product (billions)	†	†	$182	†	†	†
GNP per capita (dollars)	†	†	$1,507	†	†	†
Government deficit or surplus (billions)	†	†	0	$1	†	†
Population (millions)	70	93	121	136	138	141
Bank rate (%)	8.0%	20.0%	38.0%	219.4%	50.7%	391.5%
Government bond long-term rate (%)	†	†	†	†	†	†
Exchange rate 1 cruzado =	†	†	$14.29	$0.0953	$0.0671	$0.01384
Gold (millions of troy ounces)	8	1	2	3	2	2

*Unless otherwise stated, all figures are in U.S. dollars.
†Not available.

Source: International Monetary Fund, International Financial Statistics Yearbook, 1988, pp. 250–255.

Selected Statistics*
Country: CANADA
Currency: DOLLAR (Can$)

	1960	1970	1980	1985	1986	1987
Exports (billions)	$6	$17	$67	$90	$89	$98
Imports (billions)	$6	$14	$59	$77	$81	$89
Current account balance (billions)	−$1	$1	−$1	$1	$8	$8
Private capital formation (billions)	$9	$19	$61	$66	$72	$87
Private consumption (billions)	$26	$51	$144	$197	$216	$251
Gross domestic product (billions)	$39	$88	$259	$343	$369	$426
Gross national product (billions)	$38	$87	$253	$333	$357	$413
GNP per capita (dollars)	$2,120	$4,144	$10,533	$13,309	$13,735	$15,890
Government deficit or surplus (billions)	0	$1	−$1	−$21	†	†
Population (millions)	18	21	24	25	26	26
Treasury bill interest rate (%)	3.20%	5.99%	12.80%	9.43%	8.97%	8.14%
Government bond long-term rate (%)	5.19%	7.91%	12.48%	11.04%	9.52%	9.95%
Exchange rate 1 Can$ =	$1.004	$0.988	$0.837	$0.716	$0.724	$0.769
Gold (millions of troy ounces)	25	23	21	20	20	19

*Unless otherwise stated, all figures are in U.S. dollars.
†Not available.

Source: International Monetary Fund, *International Financial Statistics Yearbook, 1988*, pp. 272–277.

Selected Statistics*
Country: EGYPT
Currency: POUND (£E)

	1960	1970	1980	1985	1986	1987
Exports (billions)	$0	$1	$4	$4	$3	†
Imports (billions)	$1	$1	$7	$8	$7	†
Current account balance (billions)	0	0	0	−$2	−$2	†
Private capital formation (billions)	0	$1	$6	$10	$11	$11
Private consumption (billions)	$3	$5	$16	$35	$39	$49
Gross domestic product (billions)	$4	$7	$22	$49	$55	$63
Gross national product (billions)	$4	$7	$24	$51	$56	$66
GNP per capita (dollars)	$154	$204	$567	$1,046	$1,125	$1,291
Government deficit or surplus (billions)	†	†	†	−$5	−$7	†
Population (millions)	26	33	42	49	50	51
Treasury bill interest rate (%)	†	†	†	†	†	†
Government bond long-term rate (%)	†	†	†	†	†	†
Exchange rate 1 pound =	$2.8500	$2.3000	$1.4286	$1.4286	$1.4286	$1.4286
Gold (millions of troy ounces)	5	2	2	2	2	2

*Unless otherwise stated, all figures are in U.S. dollars.
†Not available.

Source: International Monetary Fund, *International Financial Statistics Yearbook, 1988*, pp. 334–337.

Selected Statistics*
Country: FRANCE
Currency: FRANC (FF)

	1960	1970	1980	1985	1986	1987
Exports (billions)	†	$18	$108	$96	$118	†
Imports (billions)	†	$18	$121	$101	$120	†
Current account balance (billions)	†	0	−$4	0	$3	†
Private capital formation (billions)	$8	$35	$143	$119	$149	$192
Private consumption (billions)	$37	$83	$364	$378	$470	$601
Gross domestic product (billions)	$61	$144	$622	$621	$780	$990
Gross national product (billions)	$61	$145	$628	$619	$779	$992
GNP per capita (dollars)	$1,326	$2,891	$11,588	$11,263	$14,165	$17,707
Government deficit or surplus (billions)	−$1	$1	0	†	†	†
Population (millions)	46	50	54	55	55	56
Money market interest rate (%)	4.08%	8.68%	11.85%	9.93%	7.74%	7.98%
Government bond long-term rate (%)	5.15%	8.06%	13.03%	10.94%	8.44%	9.43%
Exchange rate 1 franc =	$0.2040	$0.1811	$0.2214	$0.1323	$0.1549	$0.1873
Gold (millions of troy ounces)	47	101	82	82	82	82

*Unless otherwise stated, all figures are in U.S. dollars.
†Not available.

Source: International Monetary Fund, International Financial Statistics Yearbook, 1988, pp. 356–359.

Selected Statistics*
Country: GERMANY
Currency: DEUTSCHE MARK (DM)

	1960	1970	1980	1985	1986	1987
Exports (billions)	$11	$34	$183	$174	$231	$279
Imports (billions)	$9	$29	$174	$145	$175	$209
Current account balance (billions)	$1	$1	−$14	$17	$40	$45
Private capital formation (billions)	$18	$47	$171	$147	$194	$245
Private consumption (billions)	$41	$101	$429	$423	$556	$708
Gross domestic product (billions)	$73	$185	$755	$744	$998	$1,273
Gross national product (billions)	$73	$185	$758	$750	$1,004	$1,279
GNP per capita (dollars)	$1,321	$3,033	$12,226	$12,295	$16,463	$20,970
Government deficit or surplus (billions)	0	$2	−$14	−$8	−$8	†
Population (millions)	55	61	62	61	61	61
Treasury bill interest rate (%)	†	†	7.79%	4.96%	3.85%	3.28%
Mortgage long-term rate (%)	6.3%	8.2%	8.7%	7.0%	6.1%	5.9%
Exchange rate 1 deutsche mark =	$0.2400	$0.2741	$0.5105	$0.4063	$0.5153	$0.6323
Gold (millions of troy ounces)	85	114	95	95	95	95

*Unless otherwise stated, all figures are in U.S. dollars.
†Not available.

Source: International Monetary Fund, *International Financial Statistics Yearbook, 1988*, pp. 368–371.

Selected Statistics*
Country: INDIA
Currency: RUPEE (Rs.)

	1960	1970	1980	1985	1986	1987
Exports (billions)	$1	$2	$8	$9	$10	†
Imports (billions)	$2	$2	$14	$15	$16	†
Current account balance (billions)	−$1	0	−$2	−$4	−$5	†
Private capital formation (billions)	$5	$8	$33	$45	$48	†
Private consumption (billions)	$25	$39	$125	$143	$150	†
Gross domestic product (billions)	$31	$53	$171	$215	$223	†
Gross national product (billions)	$31	$53	$172	$214	$222	†
GNP per capita (dollars)	$72	$98	$255	$285	$290	†
Government deficit or surplus (billions)	−$1	−$2	−$12	−$17	†	†
Population (millions)	429	539	675	751	766	781
Money market interest rate (%)	3.67%	5.68%	7.24%	10.00%	9.97%	9.91%
Government bond long-term rate (%)	4.07%	5.00%	6.71%	8.99%	†	†
Exchange rate 1 rupee =	$0.210	$0.132	$0.126	$0.082	$0.076	$0.078
Gold (millions of troy ounces)	7	7	9	9	10	10

*Unless otherwise stated, all figures are in U.S. dollars.
†Not available.

Source: International Monetary Fund, *International Financial Statistics Yearbook, 1988*, pp. 410–413.

Selected Statistics*
Country: ITALY
Currency: LIRA (Lit)

	1960	1970	1980	1985	1986	1987
Exports (billions)	$4	$13	$77	$76	$97	$116
Imports (billions)	$4	$13	$94	$82	$92	$116
Current account balance (billions)	0	$1	−$10	−$4	$3	−$1
Private capital formation (billions)	$8	$22	$102	$102	$134	$167
Private consumption (billions)	$24	$64	$262	$304	$412	$523
Gross domestic product (billions)	$37	$101	$419	$486	$664	$841
Gross national product (billions)	$37	$101	$364	$404	†	†
GNP per capita (dollars)	$749	$1,876	$6,507	$7,094	†	†
Government deficit or surplus (billions)	−$1	−$8	−$40	−$72	−$81	−$97
Population (millions)	50	54	56	57	57	57
Money market interest rate (%)	†	7.38%	17.17%	15.25%	13.41%	11.51%
Government bond long-term rate (%)	5.01%	9.01%	16.11%	13.00%	10.52%	9.65%
Exchange rate 1 lira =	$0.0016	$0.0016	$0.0011	$0.0006	$0.0007	$0.0009
Gold (millions of troy ounces)	63	82	67	67	67	67

*Unless otherwise stated, all figures are in U.S. dollars.
†Not available.

Source: International Monetary Fund, *International Financial Statistics Yearbook, 1988*, pp. 434–437.

Selected Statistics*
Country: JAPAN
Currency: YEN (¥)

	1960	1970	1980	1985	1986	1987
Exports (billions)	$4	$19	$127	$174	$206	$225
Imports (billions)	$4	$15	$125	$118	$113	$128
Current account balance (billions)	0	$2	−$11	$49	$86	$87
Private capital formation (billions)	$13	$73	$293	$398	$469	$568
Private consumption (billions)	$25	$107	$546	$838	$984	$1,136
Gross domestic product (billions)	$43	$205	$927	$1,437	$1,693	†
Gross national product (billions)	$44	$204	$927	$1,442	$1,699	$1,971
GNP per capita (dollars)	$468	$1,962	$7,923	$11,917	$14,041	$16,156
Government deficit or surplus (billions)	0	−$1	−$45	†	†	†
Population (millions)	94	104	117	121	121	122
Money market interest rate (%)	8.40%	8.28%	10.93%	6.46%	7.49%	3.51%
Government bond long-term rate (%)	†	7.19%	9.22%	6.34%	4.94%	4.21%
Exchange rate 1 yen =	$0.0028	$0.0028	$0.0039	$0.0045	$0.0051	$0.0057
Gold (millions of troy ounces)	7	15	24	24	24	24

*Unless otherwise stated, all figures are in U.S. dollars.
†Not available.

Source: International Monetary Fund, International Financial Statistics Yearbook, 1988, pp. 441–445.

Selected Statistics*
Country: KOREA
Currency: WON (W)

	1960	1970	1980	1985	1986	1987
Exports (billions)	0	$1	$17	$26	$34	$46
Imports (billions)	0	$2	$22	$26	$30	$39
Current account balance (billions)	0	−$1	−$5	−$1	$5	$10
Private capital formation (billions)	0	$2	$18	$25	$30	$39
Private consumption (billions)	$3	$6	$38	$50	$55	$66
Gross domestic product (billions)	$3	$9	$57	$85	$101	$126
Gross national product (billions)	$4	$9	$56	$82	$98	$123
GNP per capita (dollars)	$151	$270	$1,462	$1,996	$2,322	$2,932
Government deficit or surplus (billions)	0	0	−$1	−$1	0	−$2
Population (millions)	25	32	38	41	42	42
Money market interest rate (%)	†	†	22.9%	9.4%	9.7%	8.9%
Government bond long-term rate (%)	†	†	28.8%	13.6%	11.6%	12.4%
Exchange rate 1 won =	$0.0154	$0.0032	$0.0015	$0.0011	$0.0012	$0.0013
Gold (millions of troy ounces)	0	0	0	0	0	0

*Unless otherwise stated, all figures are in U.S. dollars.
†Not available.

Source: International Monetary Fund, *International Financial Statistics Yearbook, 1988*, pp. 456–459.

Selected Statistics*
Country: MEXICO
Currency: PESO (Ps)

	1960	1970	1980	1985	1986	1987
Exports (billions)	$1	$1	$16	$22	$16	$21
Imports (billions)	$1	$2	$19	$13	$11	$12
Current account balance (billions)	0	−$1	−$8	$1	−$2	$4
Private capital formation (billions)	$2	$7	$44	†	†	†
Private consumption (billions)	$10	$26	$114	†	†	†
Gross domestic product (billions)	†	†	$184	$122	$86	†
Gross national product (billions)	$12	$35	$179	†	†	†
GNP per capita (dollars)	$346	$689	$2,592	†	†	†
Government deficit or surplus (billions)	†	0	$4	$11	†	†
Population (millions)	36	51	69	79	80	81
Treasury bill interest rate (%)	†	†	22.46%	63.36%	88.57%	103.07%
Government bond long-term rate (%)	†	†	†	†	†	†
Exchange rate 1 peso =	$0.08	$0.08	$0.043	$0.00267	$0.0011	$0.00045
Gold (millions of troy ounces)	4	5	2	2	3	3

*Unless otherwise stated, all figures are in U.S. dollars.
†Not available.

Source: International Monetary Fund, *International Financial Statistics Yearbook, 1988*, pp. 512–515.

Selected Statistics*
Country: NIGERIA
Currency: NAIRA (₦)

	1960	1970	1980	1985	1986	1987
Exports (billions)	0	$1	$26	$13	$7	†
Imports (billions)	0	$1	$15	$8	$4	†
Current account balance (billions)	0	0	$5	$1	0	†
Private capital formation (billions)	0	$1	$20	$6	†	†
Private consumption (billions)	$3	$6	$58	$50	†	†
Gross domestic product (billions)	$3	$8	$91	$65	†	†
Gross national product (billions)	$3	$7	$91	$65	†	†
GNP per capita (dollars)	$78	$128	$1,128	$687	†	†
Government deficit or surplus (billions)	†	0	$17	−$2	−$1	−$2
Population (millions)	43	56	81	95	98	101
Deposit interest rate (%)	†	3.00%	5.27%	9.12%	†	†
Government bond long-term rate (%)	†	†	†	†	†	†
Exchange rate 1 naira =	$1.4000	$1.4000	$1.8367	$1.0004	$0.3015	$0.2415
Gold (millions of troy ounces)	0	1	1	1	1	1

*Unless otherwise stated, all figures are in U.S. dollars.
†Not available.

Source: International Monetary Fund, *International Financial Statistics Yearbook, 1988*, pp. 544–547.

Selected Statistics*
Country: SOUTH AFRICA
Currency: RAND (R)

	1960	1970	1980	1985	1986	1987
Exports (billions)	$2	$3	$26	$16	$18	$21
Imports (billions)	$2	$4	$18	$10	$11	$14
Current account balance (billions)	0	−$1	$4	$3	$3	$3
Private capital formation (billions)	$1	$4	$22	$11	$13	$17
Private consumption (billions)	$5	$11	$41	$26	$35	$22
Gross domestic product (billions)	$7	$18	$83	$47	$64	$85
Gross national product (billions)	$7	$17	$80	$44	$60	$81
GNP per capita (dollars)	$417	$789	$2,742	$1,388	$1,830	†
Government deficit or surplus (billions)	0	0	−$2	−$2	$3	$5
Population (millions)	17	22	29	32	33	†
Treasury bill interest rate (%)	3.60%	4.39%	4.65%	17.56%	10.43%	8.71%
Government bond long-term rate (%)	4.40%	7.15%	10.09%	16.79%	16.37%	15.30%
Exchange rate 1 rand =	$1.4000	$1.3943	$1.3416	$0.3910	$0.4580	$0.5182
Gold (millions of troy ounces)	5	19	12	5	5	6

*Unless otherwise stated, all figures are in U.S. dollars.
†Not available.

Source: International Monetary Fund, International Financial Statistics Yearbook, 1988, pp. 638–641.

Selected Statistics*
Country: UNITED KINGDOM
Currency: POUND STERLING (£)

	1960	1970	1980	1985	1986	1987
Exports (billions)	$10	$20	$110	$101	$107	$131
Imports (billions)	$12	$20	$106	$103	$119	$146
Current account balance (billions)	−$1	$2	$7	$5	0	−$3
Private capital formation (billions)	$11	$24	$100	$87	$94	$129
Private consumption (billions)	$48	$77	$327	$311	$349	$481
Gross domestic product (billions)	$73	$124	$551	$512	$556	$765
Gross national product (billions)	$73	$124	$551	$516	$565	$775
GNP per capita (dollars)	$1,402	$2,263	$9,838	$9,050	$9,908	$13,593
Government deficit or surplus (billions)	−$1	$2	−$26	−$17	†	†
Population (millions)	52	55	56	57	57	57
Treasury bill interest rate (%)	4.88%	7.01%	15.11%	11.56%	10.37%	9.25%
Government bond long-term rate (%)	5.77%	9.22%	13.79%	10.62%	9.87%	9.48%
Exchange rate 1 pound =	$2.8038	$2.3937	$2.3850	$1.4450	$1.4745	$1.8715
Gold (millions of troy ounces)	80	39	19	19	19	19

*Unless otherwise stated, all figures are in U.S. dollars.
†Not available.

Source: International Monetary Fund, International Financial Statistics Yearbook, 1988, pp. 712–715.

Glossary

Accommodating Transaction A balance of payments transaction that is undertaken by governments in order to finance a trade imbalance.

Accurate Exchange Rate Forecast A forecast that predicts the future value of a foreign currency accurately every time.

Arbitrage A technique that enables an investor to obtain a riskless profit through the simultaneous purchase and sale of an asset in two different markets.

Arbitrageur Investor who practices arbitrage.

Ask Price The price at which a dealer is willing to sell a product (e.g., foreign currency).

Autonomous Transaction A balance of payments transaction that is undertaken by private parties for valid business purposes, not to finance a trade imbalance.

Back-to-Back Loan Loan from a bank to a foreign subsidiary of an American firm, in return for which the parent maintains an equivalent deposit in the bank.

Balance on Current Account An entry in the balance of payments that measures the difference between exports and imports of goods and services (e.g., merchandise, travel, unilateral transfers, dividends, and interest payments).

Balance of Trade The difference between the exports and imports of goods.

Bankers' Acceptance Promissory note, the payment for which has been guaranteed by a commercial bank.

Basic Balance A balance of payments amount that is computed by adding the balance of current account to any long-term investments (portfolio and direct).

Bid – Ask Spread Percentage difference between the bid and ask prices of a currency.

Bid Price The price a dealer is willing to pay for a product (e.g., foreign currency).

Bretton Woods Conference Conference that established the international monetary system used from 1945 to 1971.

Convertible Currency Currency that can be freely converted to another currency without any government restrictions.

Correspondent Bank A bank that provides services to another bank in return for deposits and fees.

Cost of Capital (K_a) The weighted average cost to the firm of raising funds (debt and equity).

Covered Interest Arbitrage The ability to obtain a riskless profit by exploiting differences between the forward premium/discount on a foreign currency and international differences in interest rates.

Cumulative Translation Adjustment An entry that appears in financial statements that have been translated from a foreign currency. The account includes any balance sheet gains and/or losses resulting from the fluctuation of foreign exchange.

Currency Blockage Restrictions imposed by a foreign government on the movement of its currency. In the usual case, the conversion of the local currency to a foreign currency is restricted.

Default Risk The risk assumed by a lender that the borrower will not repay the loan.

Direct Quote of a Foreign Currency Number of dollars required to purchase one unit of a foreign currency.

Econometric Model Forecasting methodology that uses the statistical relationship among economic variables in order to forecast the future value of a currency.

Economic Exposure The extent to which foreign exchange rate fluctuations will affect the value of the firm (as distinct from the firm's financial statements).

Efficient Market A market in which all the relevant information is reflected in the market price. The markets in which major foreign currencies are sold are reputed to be efficient.

Eurobond Bond issue denominated in a currency different from the official currency used in the country in which the bonds are sold (e.g., a dollar-denominated bond sold in the United Kingdom).

Eurodeposits Deposits denominated in a currency different from the official currency used in the country in which the deposit is made (e.g., a French franc deposit in Germany).

Eurodollar Bond Bond issue denominated in U.S. dollars and sold outside the United States.

Eurodollar Deposits Dollar-denominated deposits placed in a bank located outside the United States.

Euroloans Loans denominated in a currency different from the official currency used in the country in which the loan is made (e.g., a loan made in British pounds by a Singapore bank).

European Currency Unit Artificial currency equal to the weighted average of the currencies of the European Monetary System members.

European Economic Community (Common Market) Group of nations in Western Europe that have agreed to maintain common economic policies (e.g., tariffs, movement of goods). Their eventual goal is complete economic integration.

European Monetary System Monetary system established by certain European nations to reduce the exchange fluctuations between their currencies.

Export-Import Bank (EXIMBANK) U.S. government agency that encourages U.S. exports by guaranteeing payment by foreign buyers.

Factoring A procedure used to reduce the risk associated with the nonpayment of accounts receivable and to speed up the cash flows on credit sales. A specialized financial firm (called a *factor*) is employed and paid for these services.

Financial Hedge Involves entering into a financial contract that will exactly offset expected future cash flows (e.g., selling foreign currency in the forward market in order to offset the risk of receiving the same amount of foreign currency on the same date).

Fixed Exchange Rate System A system that attempts to maintain a target exchange rate between currencies. Under this system, currency values change infrequently.

Fluctuating Exchange Rate System A system that allows exchange rates to be determined by supply and demand forces. Under this system, exchange rates change frequently and by small amounts.

Foreign Bond Bond issued by an American firm in a foreign country. The bond is denominated in the currency of that foreign country (e.g., a Swiss franc-denominated bond sold by an American firm in Switzerland).

Foreign Credit Insurance Association (FCIA) A consortium of American insurance companies that allows American exporters to insure against the nonpayment of receivables by foreign buyers.

Foreign Currency Futures A contract that requires the holder to purchase/sell a specified amount of foreign currency on a specified data at a specified price. The contract compels the holder (rather than giving an option) to complete the agreement.

Foreign Currency Options: Call A contract that gives the holder the option to purchase a specified amount of foreign currency at a specified price before a specified date.

Foreign Currency Options: Put A contract that gives the holder the option to sell a specified amount of foreign currency at a specified price before a specified date.

Foreign Direct Investments Investments located in a foreign country and over which the investor has control (e.g., building and operating a factory in a foreign country).

Foreign Tax Credit Provision of the Internal Revenue Code that allows American firms to take as a tax credit the foreign income taxes paid. This credit can be used to reduce or eliminate U.S. taxes due on foreign income.

Forfaiting The use of a third party, commonly a financial institution, as a guarantor for the medium-term debt of a firm. Used primarily by Eastern European enterprises.

Forward Discount The difference between the forward and spot prices expressed as an annual percentage rate. In the case of a discount, the forward price is below the spot price.

Forward Exchange Forecast The use of the forward market to forecast the future value of a currency. Such forecasts tend to be unbiased but not very accurate.

Forward Exchange Rate The price of a foreign currency that applies to a transaction that will be completed at a future point in time (e.g., the price of deutsche marks that will apply if the exchange takes place 30 days from today).

Forward Market Hedge The use of the forward market to reduce the transaction exposure of the firm (e.g., the sale of French francs 30 days forward in order to offset an expected inflow of French francs on the same date).

Forward Premium The difference between the forward and spot prices expressed as an annual percentage rate. In the case of a premium, the forward price is above the spot price.

Fronting Loan See *Back-to-back loan*.

Functional Currency A primary currency that is used in the economic environment in which a foreign subsidiary of an American firm operates (e.g., a subsidiary of an American firm located in Italy and making purchases and sales in Italian lire would have the Italian lire as its functional currency).

Gold Standard An international payments system that uses gold to settle trade imbalances.

Gross National Product (GNP) The market value of all the final goods and services produced by the economy during 1 year.

Historical Rate As used in translation accounting, the rate of exchange existing at the time an entry was made in financial statements.

Imperfect Market A market that has certain imperfections, such as transaction costs, government intervention, and so on.

Indirect Quote of a Foreign Currency Number of foreign currency units needed to purchase one dollar.

Interest Rate Risk Risk taken by the holder of a financial instrument. When interest rates increase, the value of fixed interest rate instruments will decline.

International Bank for Reconstruction and Development (World Bank) International financial organization that makes hard loans to the governments of less developed nations.

International Banking Facilities (IBFs) Departments of American banks, located in the United States, that are allowed to accept deposits and make loans to foreigners in foreign currency.

International Fisher Effect Theory that states that interest rate differentials between two countries will be reflected in the future spot exchange rate between their currencies (e.g., the value of the currency of a country with relatively high interest rates should decline).

International Monetary Fund (IMF) An international financial organization that makes loans to member nations for the purpose of financing deficits in balance of payments. In addition, the IMF encourages and promotes trade between nations.

Investment Agreements Agreements made between a firm and a foreign government specifying the rights and obligations of both the foreign investor and the host government.

Joint Venture A form of ownership of a foreign investment that uses a local investor as a partner in the enterprise.

Law of Comparative Advantage A theory that asserts that world output will be increased if each country specializes in the production of those goods and services in which it is *relatively* efficient.

Leads and Lags in Payables and Receivables   Adjusting the timing of international payments and disbursements in order to optimize the flow of funds within a multinational corporation.

Letter of Credit   Financial document issued by a bank that guarantees the payment of a specified transaction on behalf of an importer, provided that all specified conditions are met.

LIBOR   London Interbank Offer Rate, the interest rate charged on transactions between banks in the London money market. It is used as a benchmark interest rate in international financial transactions.

Locational Arbitrage   Taking advantage of price differentials between two markets in order to make a riskless profit.

Long Exposure   A measurement of risk that indicates that the firm will have a net inflow of a foreign currency over a specified period of time.

Money Market Hedge   Borrowing or investing in foreign currencies in order to reduce the transaction exposure of the firm.

Multinational Corporation   Firm that conducts business operations in many different countries.

Net Present Value   Present value of all the cash flows of an investment discounted at a cost of capital that reflects the risk of the investment. It measures the change in stockholder wealth caused by undertaking the investment.

Netting   A system used to manage intersubsidiary payments within the multinational firm. Subsidiaries pay or receive only the difference (net) between intersubsidiaries' accounts payable and receivable.

Optimal Capital Structure   The optimal combination of debt and equity that will minimize the cost of capital of the firm and thus maximize stockholder wealth.

Overseas Private Investment Corporation (OPIC)   U.S. government-supported agency that insures approved investments made by American firms in qualified less developed countries.

Parallel Loan   A loan that involves two transactions. First, a loan is made by the foreign subsidiary of one multinational (Firm *A*) to the foreign subsidiary of another multinational (Firm *B*), usually in the currency of the country in which both subsidiaries are located. Second, Firm *B* makes an offsetting loan to Firm *A* in a different country.

Performance Balance   A balance of payments amount that is computed by adding short-term autonomous flows to the basic balance.

Pledging of Accounts Receivable   Using the receivables of the firm as collateral for loans.

Portfolio Foreign Investment   A balance of payments category that includes investments made in foreign countries. Portfolio investments are financial (e.g., stocks, bonds, bank accounts) and, by definition, cannot result in ownership control of the foreign investment.

Private Export Funding Corporation (PEFCO)   A private organization that provides medium- and long-term financing for the purchase of US. goods. PEFCO is sponsored by the Export-Import Bank.

Purchasing Power Parity Theory   A theory that asserts that the percentage change in the spot exchange rate for two countries will be equal to the difference in inflation rates between these countries. Relatively high inflation should lead to a decline in the value of a country's currency.

Reinvoicing Centers Centralized invoicing centers used by multinational firms in order to improve their cash management techniques.

Required Rate of Return of the Bondholders (K_d) Rate of return that bondholders want to earn in order to be compensated for the risk undertaken.

Required Rate of Return of the Stockholders (K_s) Rate of return that stockholders want to earn in order to be compensated for the risk undertaken.

Short Exposure A measurement of risk that indicates that the firm will have a net outflow of foreign currency over a specified period of time.

Special Drawing Right (SDR) Artificial currency created by the International Monetary Fund that is used for certain transactions among governments. The value of an SDR is equal to a weighted average of the world's most important currencies.

Spot Exchange Rate The price of one currency in terms of another for transactions that are to be completed immediately (on the spot).

Stockholder Wealth Maximization The goal of financial management, achieved by maximizing the market price of the firm's common stock.

Technical Forecast Forecasting methodology that uses historical price patterns as the sole determinant of forecasting future prices (exchange rates).

Transaction Exposure The extent to which foreign exchange rate fluctuations will affect the future contractual cash flows of the firm.

Translation Exposure The extent to which foreign exchange rate fluctuations will affect the financial statements of the firm, especially profits.

Unbiased Forecast A forecast that has random errors. In other words, underestimates of the future value are offset by overestimates.

Value-Added Tax Tax that is imposed on the increase in value at each stage of the production cycle.

Weighted Average Exchange Rate A concept used to translate foreign subsidiary income statements to dollars. The parent firm uses a weighted average of the exchange rates that existed over time as a series of transactions took place.

Withholding Tax Tax imposed by foreign countries on the cash flows from a foreign subsidiary to a parent corporation. This tax is often imposed on dividend and interest payments.

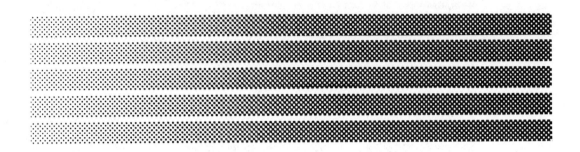

Selected Answers to Numerical Problems*

Chapter 2
1. 0.32 percent, 0.62 percent, 3.85 percent
2. £0.67, C$1.25, Ps1,000
3. (a) $1,500,000, (b) $3,010,000, (c) $4,560,000, (d) $3,850,000, (e) £3,322,259, (f) £1,962,067
4. $500,000
6. (a) $6,000,000, (b) $5,843,750
7. DM2.5
8. +$115,000
10. (a) Germany: $5,171,200, (b) Germany: $5,170,793
11. (a) Germany: DM20,480,000

Chapter 4 **Appendix 4A: 1.** −$9,000, −$5,000, −$3,000

Chapter 7
4. −$15,200,000
5. −$14,809,558
7. +$47,450,000
8. +$46,863,551
10. −$23,120,000
11. −$23,124,076

---

*You may get slightly different answers if you use present value tables in your computations.

13. (a) $15,750,000, (b) $15,123,415
14. $10,250,000 & $10,018,508
15. $10,500,000 & $10,190,436
16. (a) $45,750,000 & $45,818,463, (b) $45,730,856
Appendix 7A: 1. (a) 4, (b) $43,225
           2. (a) 8, (b) $38,250 and $6,500

Chapter 8
2. (a) $0.20, (b) $0.27
3. Total assets: (a) $432,000,000, (b) $324,000,000
4. Total assets: $540,000,000
5. (c) Total assets: $715,500,000
6. (c) Total assets: $874,500,000
Appendix 8A: 1. Total assets: (a) $800,000,000, (b) $720,000,000, (c) $740,000,000
Appendix 8A: 2. Total assets: (a) $480,000,000, (b) $560,000,000, (c) $540,000,000

Chapter 10
1. 13.576 percent
2. 20 percent
3. 40 percent
4. $112,000,000, $110,000,000, and $109,928,571
5. $44,800,000, $44,000,000, and $43,776,000

Chapter 11
1. (a) 13.32 percent, (b) 15.7 percent, (c) 14.508 percent
2. 17.584 percent
3. −$64,720
4. (a) +$713,909, (b) +$1,357,899, (c) +$82,966
5. (a) −$248,885, (b) +$315,777
6. −$820,610
8. (a) +$5,135,637, (b) +$3,332,667

Chapter 13
1. (a) $52,800,000 and $52,000,000, (b) $102,300,000 and $22,000,000, (c) +$19,500,000
2. (a) $250,800,000 and $135,000,000, (b) $151,800,000 and $270,000,000, (c) $36,000,000

Chapter 14
1. $3,500
2. $10,000

Chapter 15
2. $5,280,000
3. $10,000,000
4. $16,120,000
5. (a) $1,584,000, (b) $36,960,000
6. (a) $132,000,000

Chapter 16
1. +$6,217,035
2. +$6,217,035
3. +$2,600,892
4. +$1,356,054
5. −$3,135,493
6. +$2,646,244
7. +$10,262,369
8. +$5,284,748
10. (a) +$21,791, (b) +$16,029
11. +$3,278,006
12. −$1,765,658

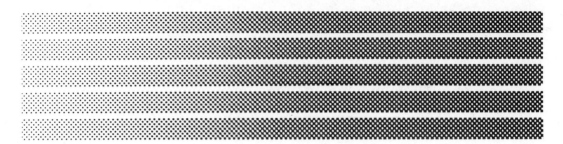

Present Value of $1

$$PV = \frac{1}{(1 + i)^t}$$

Received at the end of:

Discount Rate

Period	1%	2%	3%	4%	5%	6%	7%	8%	9%	10%	11%	12%	13%
1	0.990	0.980	0.971	0.962	0.952	0.943	0.935	0.926	0.917	0.909	0.901	0.893	0.885
2	0.980	0.961	0.943	0.925	0.907	0.890	0.873	0.857	0.842	0.826	0.812	0.797	0.783
3	0.971	0.942	0.915	0.889	0.864	0.840	0.816	0.794	0.772	0.751	0.731	0.712	0.693
4	0.961	0.924	0.888	0.855	0.823	0.792	0.763	0.735	0.708	0.683	0.659	0.636	0.613
5	0.951	0.906	0.863	0.822	0.784	0.747	0.713	0.681	0.650	0.621	0.593	0.567	0.543
6	0.942	0.888	0.837	0.790	0.746	0.705	0.666	0.630	0.596	0.564	0.535	0.507	0.480
7	0.933	0.871	0.813	0.760	0.711	0.665	0.623	0.583	0.547	0.513	0.482	0.452	0.425
8	0.923	0.853	0.789	0.731	0.677	0.627	0.582	0.540	0.502	0.467	0.434	0.404	0.376
9	0.914	0.837	0.766	0.703	0.645	0.592	0.544	0.500	0.460	0.424	0.391	0.361	0.333
10	0.905	0.820	0.744	0.676	0.614	0.558	0.508	0.463	0.422	0.386	0.352	0.322	0.295
11	0.896	0.804	0.722	0.650	0.585	0.527	0.475	0.429	0.388	0.350	0.317	0.287	0.261
12	0.887	0.789	0.701	0.625	0.557	0.497	0.444	0.397	0.356	0.319	0.286	0.257	0.231
13	0.879	0.773	0.681	0.601	0.530	0.469	0.415	0.368	0.326	0.290	0.258	0.229	0.204
14	0.870	0.758	0.661	0.577	0.505	0.442	0.388	0.340	0.299	0.263	0.232	0.205	0.181
15	0.861	0.743	0.642	0.555	0.481	0.417	0.362	0.315	0.275	0.239	0.209	0.183	0.160
16	0.853	0.728	0.623	0.534	0.458	0.394	0.339	0.292	0.252	0.218	0.188	0.163	0.141
17	0.844	0.714	0.605	0.513	0.436	0.371	0.317	0.270	0.231	0.198	0.170	0.146	0.125
18	0.836	0.700	0.587	0.494	0.416	0.350	0.296	0.250	0.212	0.180	0.153	0.130	0.111
19	0.828	0.686	0.570	0.475	0.396	0.331	0.277	0.232	0.194	0.164	0.138	0.116	0.098
20	0.820	0.673	0.554	0.456	0.377	0.312	0.258	0.215	0.178	0.149	0.124	0.104	0.087
25	0.780	0.610	0.478	0.375	0.295	0.233	0.184	0.146	0.116	0.092	0.074	0.059	0.047
30	0.742	0.552	0.412	0.308	0.231	0.174	0.131	0.099	0.075	0.057	0.044	0.033	0.026
35	0.706	0.500	0.355	0.253	0.181	0.130	0.094	0.068	0.049	0.036	0.026	0.019	0.014
40	0.672	0.453	0.307	0.208	0.142	0.097	0.067	0.046	0.032	0.022	0.015	0.011	0.008
50	0.608	0.372	0.228	0.141	0.087	0.054	0.034	0.021	0.013	0.009	0.005	0.003	0.002

Period	14%	15%	16%	17%	18%	19%	20%	22%	24%	26%	28%	30%	40%
1	0.877	0.870	0.862	0.855	0.847	0.840	0.833	0.820	0.806	0.794	0.781	0.769	0.714
2	0.769	0.756	0.743	0.731	0.718	0.706	0.694	0.672	0.650	0.630	0.610	0.592	0.510
3	0.675	0.658	0.641	0.624	0.609	0.593	0.579	0.551	0.524	0.500	0.477	0.455	0.364
4	0.592	0.572	0.552	0.534	0.516	0.499	0.482	0.451	0.423	0.397	0.373	0.350	0.260
5	0.519	0.497	0.476	0.456	0.437	0.419	0.402	0.370	0.341	0.315	0.291	0.269	0.186
6	0.456	0.432	0.410	0.390	0.370	0.352	0.335	0.303	0.275	0.250	0.227	0.207	0.133
7	0.400	0.376	0.354	0.333	0.314	0.296	0.279	0.249	0.222	0.198	0.178	0.159	0.095
8	0.351	0.327	0.305	0.285	0.266	0.249	0.233	0.204	0.179	0.157	0.139	0.123	0.068
9	0.308	0.284	0.263	0.243	0.225	0.209	0.194	0.167	0.144	0.125	0.108	0.094	0.048
10	0.270	0.247	0.227	0.208	0.191	0.176	0.162	0.137	0.116	0.099	0.085	0.073	0.035
11	0.237	0.215	0.195	0.178	0.162	0.148	0.135	0.112	0.094	0.079	0.066	0.056	0.025
12	0.208	0.187	0.168	0.152	0.137	0.124	0.112	0.092	0.076	0.062	0.052	0.043	0.018
13	0.182	0.163	0.145	0.130	0.116	0.104	0.093	0.075	0.061	0.050	0.040	0.033	0.013
14	0.160	0.141	0.125	0.111	0.099	0.088	0.078	0.062	0.049	0.039	0.032	0.025	0.009
15	0.140	0.123	0.108	0.095	0.084	0.074	0.065	0.051	0.040	0.031	0.025	0.020	0.006
16	0.123	0.107	0.093	0.081	0.071	0.062	0.054	0.042	0.032	0.025	0.019	0.015	0.005
17	0.108	0.093	0.080	0.069	0.060	0.052	0.045	0.034	0.026	0.020	0.015	0.012	0.003
18	0.095	0.081	0.069	0.059	0.051	0.044	0.038	0.028	0.021	0.016	0.012	0.009	0.002
19	0.083	0.070	0.060	0.051	0.043	0.037	0.031	0.023	0.017	0.012	0.009	0.007	0.002
20	0.073	0.061	0.051	0.043	0.037	0.031	0.026	0.019	0.014	0.010	0.007	0.005	0.001
25	0.038	0.030	0.024	0.020	0.016	0.013	0.010	0.007	0.005	0.003	0.002	0.001	·
30	0.020	0.015	0.012	0.009	0.007	0.005	0.004	0.003	0.002	0.001	0.001	·	·
35	0.010	0.008	0.006	0.004	0.003	0.002	0.002	0.001	0.001	·	·	·	·
40	0.005	0.004	0.003	0.002	0.001	0.001	0.001	·	·	·	·	·	·
50	0.001	0.001	0.001	·	·	·	·	·	·	·	·	·	·

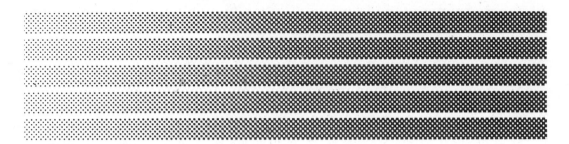

Present Value of a $1 Annuity

Received at the
end of each
period for:

$$PV = \sum_{t=1}^{n} \frac{1}{(1 + i)^t}$$

Discount Rate

Period	1%	2%	3%	4%	5%	6%	7%	8%	9%	10%	11%	12%	13%
1	0.990	0.980	0.971	0.962	0.952	0.943	0.935	0.926	0.917	0.909	0.901	0.893	0.885
2	1.970	1.942	1.913	1.886	1.859	1.833	1.808	1.783	1.759	1.736	1.713	1.690	1.668
3	2.941	2.884	2.829	2.775	2.723	2.673	2.624	2.577	2.531	2.487	2.444	2.402	2.361
4	3.902	3.808	3.717	3.630	3.546	3.465	3.387	3.312	3.240	3.170	3.102	3.037	2.974
5	4.853	4.713	4.580	4.452	4.329	4.212	4.100	3.993	3.890	3.791	3.696	3.605	3.517
6	5.795	5.601	5.417	5.242	5.076	4.917	4.766	4.623	4.486	4.355	4.231	4.111	3.998
7	6.728	6.472	6.230	6.002	5.786	5.582	5.389	5.206	5.033	4.868	4.712	4.564	4.423
8	7.652	7.326	7.020	6.733	6.463	6.210	5.971	5.747	5.535	5.335	5.146	4.968	4.799
9	8.566	8.162	7.786	7.435	7.108	6.802	6.515	6.247	5.995	5.759	5.537	5.328	5.132
10	9.471	8.983	8.530	8.111	7.722	7.360	7.024	6.710	6.418	6.145	5.889	5.650	5.426
11	10.368	9.787	9.253	8.760	8.306	7.887	7.499	7.139	6.805	6.495	6.207	5.938	5.687
12	11.255	10.575	9.954	9.385	8.863	8.384	7.943	7.536	7.161	6.314	6.492	6.194	5.918
13	12.134	11.348	10.635	9.986	9.394	8.853	8.358	7.904	7.487	7.003	6.750	6.424	6.122
14	13.004	12.106	11.296	10.563	9.899	9.295	8.745	8.244	7.786	7.367	6.982	6.628	6.302
15	13.865	12.849	11.938	11.118	10.380	9.712	9.108	8.560	8.060	7.606	7.191	6.811	6.462
16	14.718	13.578	12.561	11.652	10.838	10.106	9.447	8.851	8.313	7.824	7.379	6.974	6.604
17	15.562	14.292	13.166	12.166	11.274	10.477	9.763	9.122	8.544	8.022	7.549	7.120	6.729
18	16.398	14.992	13.754	12.659	11.690	10.828	10.059	9.372	8.756	8.201	7.702	7.250	6.840
19	17.226	15.679	14.324	13.134	12.085	11.158	10.336	9.604	8.950	8.365	7.839	7.266	6.938
20	18.046	16.352	14.878	13.590	12.462	11.470	10.594	9.818	9.128	8.514	7.963	7.469	7.025
25	22.023	19.524	17.413	15.622	14.094	12.783	11.654	10.675	9.823	9.077	8.422	7.843	7.330
30	25.808	22.396	19.600	17.292	15.373	13.765	12.409	11.258	10.274	9.427	8.694	8.055	7.496
35	29.409	24.999	21.487	18.665	16.374	14.498	12.948	11.655	10.567	9.644	8.855	8.176	7.586
40	32.835	27.356	23.115	19.793	17.159	15.046	13.332	11.925	10.757	9.779	8.951	8.244	7.634
50	39.196	31.424	25.730	21.482	18.256	15.762	13.801	12.333	10.962	9.915	9.042	8.304	7.675

Period	14%	15%	16%	17%	18%	19%	20%	22%	24%	26%	28%	30%	36%
1	0.877	0.870	0.862	0.855	0.847	0.840	0.833	0.820	0.806	0.794	0.781	0.769	0.735
2	1.647	1.626	1.605	1.585	1.566	1.547	1.528	1.492	1.457	1.424	1.392	1.361	1.276
3	2.322	2.283	2.246	2.210	2.174	2.140	2.106	2.042	1.981	1.923	1.868	1.816	1.674
4	2.914	2.855	2.798	2.743	2.690	2.639	2.589	2.494	2.404	2.320	2.241	2.166	1.966
5	3.433	3.352	3.274	3.199	3.127	3.058	2.991	2.864	2.745	2.635	2.532	2.436	2.181
6	3.889	3.784	3.685	3.589	3.498	3.410	3.326	3.167	3.020	2.885	2.759	2.643	2.339
7	4.288	4.160	4.039	3.922	3.812	3.706	3.605	3.416	3.242	3.083	2.937	2.802	2.455
8	4.639	4.487	4.344	4.207	4.078	3.954	3.837	3.619	3.421	3.241	3.076	2.925	2.540
9	4.946	4.772	4.607	4.451	4.303	4.163	4.031	3.786	3.566	3.366	3.184	3.019	2.603
10	5.216	5.019	4.833	4.659	4.494	4.339	4.192	3.923	3.682	3.465	3.269	3.092	2.650
11	5.453	5.234	5.029	4.836	4.656	4.486	4.327	4.035	3.776	3.544	3.335	3.147	2.683
12	5.660	5.421	5.197	4.988	4.793	4.611	4.439	4.127	3.851	3.606	3.387	3.190	2.708
13	5.842	5.583	5.342	5.118	4.910	4.715	4.533	4.203	3.912	3.656	3.427	3.223	2.727
14	6.002	5.724	5.468	5.229	5.008	4.802	4.611	4.265	3.962	3.695	3.459	3.249	2.740
15	6.142	5.847	5.575	5.324	5.092	4.876	4.675	4.315	4.001	3.726	3.483	3.268	2.750
16	6.265	5.954	5.668	5.405	5.162	4.938	4.730	4.357	4.033	3.751	3.503	3.283	2.758
17	6.373	6.047	5.749	5.475	5.222	4.990	4.775	4.391	4.059	3.771	3.518	3.295	2.763
18	6.467	6.128	5.818	5.534	5.273	5.033	4.812	4.419	4.080	3.786	3.529	3.304	2.767
19	6.550	6.198	5.877	5.584	5.316	5.070	4.843	4.442	4.097	3.799	3.539	3.311	2.770
20	6.623	6.259	5.929	5.628	5.353	5.101	4.870	4.460	4.110	3.808	3.546	3.316	2.772
25	6.873	6.464	6.097	5.766	5.467	5.195	4.948	4.514	4.147	3.834	3.564	3.329	2.776
30	7.003	6.566	6.177	5.829	5.517	5.235	4.979	4.534	4.160	3.842	3.569	3.332	2.778
35	7.070	6.617	6.215	5.858	5.539	5.251	4.992	4.541	4.164	3.845	3.571	3.333	2.779
40	7.105	6.642	6.233	5.871	5.548	5.258	4.997	4.544	4.166	3.846	3.571	3.333	2.779
50	7.133	6.661	6.246	5.880	5.554	5.262	4.999	4.545	4.167	3.846	3.571	3.333	2.779

Author Index

Subject Index